The Routledge Research Companion to Popular Music Education

Popular music is a growing presence in education, formal and otherwise, from primary school to postgraduate study. Programmes, courses and modules in popular music studies, popular music performance, songwriting and areas of music technology are becoming commonplace across higher education. Additionally, specialist pop/rock/jazz graded exam syllabi, such as RockSchool and Trinity Rock and Pop, have emerged in recent years, meaning that it is now possible for school leavers in some countries to meet university entry requirements having studied only popular music. In the context of teacher education, classroom teachers and music-specialists alike are becoming increasingly empowered to introduce popular music into their classrooms. At present, research in Popular Music Education lies at the fringes of the fields of music education, ethnomusicology, community music, cultural studies and popular music studies. *The Routledge Research Companion to Popular Music Education* is the first book-length publication that brings together a diverse range of scholarship in this emerging field. Perspectives include the historical, sociological, pedagogical, musicological, axiological, reflexive, critical, philosophical and ideological.

Gareth Dylan Smith is Research Fellow at the Institute of Contemporary Music Performance in London, UK.

Zack Moir is a Lecturer in Popular Music at Edinburgh Napier University and the University of the Highlands and Islands, UK.

Matt Brennan is a Chancellor's Fellow of Music at the University of Edinburgh and has served as Chair of the UK and Ireland branch of the International Association for the Study of Popular Music (IASPM).

Shara Rambarran is Assistant Professor of Music at the Bader International Study Centre, Queen's University, Canada.

Phil Kirkman is Principal Lecturer at Anglia Ruskin University, UK.

The Routledge Research Companion to Popular Music Education

*Edited by Gareth Dylan Smith,
Zack Moir, Matt Brennan,
Shara Rambarran and Phil Kirkman*

LONDON AND NEW YORK

First published 2017
by Routledge
2 Park Square, Milton Park, Abingdon, Oxon OX14 4RN

and by Routledge
711 Third Avenue, New York, NY 10017

Routledge is an imprint of the Taylor & Francis Group, an informa business

© 2017 Gareth Dylan Smith

The right of Gareth Dylan Smith to be identified as author of this work has been asserted by him in accordance with sections 77 and 78 of the Copyright, Designs and Patents Act 1988.

All rights reserved. No part of this book may be reprinted or reproduced or utilised in any form or by any electronic, mechanical or other means, now known or hereafter invented, including photocopying and recording, or in any information storage or retrieval system, without permission in writing from the publishers.

Trademark notice: Product or corporate names may be trademarks or registered trademarks, and are used only for identification and explanation without intent to infringe.

British Library Cataloguing-in-Publication Data
A catalogue record for this book is available from the British Library

Library of Congress Cataloging in Publication Data
A catalog record for this book has been requested

ISBN: 978-1-4724-6498-9 (hbk)
ISBN: 978-1-315-61344-4 (ebk)

Typeset in Bembo
by Apex CoVantage, LLC

Contents

List of contributors   x

PART I
Introduction   1

1 Foreword   3
   Lucy Green

2 Popular music education (r)evolution   5
   Gareth Dylan Smith, Zack Moir, Matt Brennan,
   Shara Rambarran and Phil Kirkman

3 Popular music education: a step into the light   14
   Rupert Till

PART II
Past, present and future   31

4 The historical foundations of popular music education in
   the United States   33
   Andrew Krikun

5 Navigating the space between spaces: curricular change in
   music teacher education in the United States   46
   David A. Williams and Clint Randles

6 Developing learning through producing: secondary
   school students' experiences of a technologically aided
   pedagogical intervention   60
   Aleksi Ojala

Contents

7 A historical review of the social dynamics of school music education in Mainland China: a study of the political power of popular songs 74
Wai-Chung Ho

8 Towards 21st-century music teaching-learning: reflections on student-centric pedagogic practices involving popular music in Singapore 87
Siew Ling Chua and Hui-Ping Ho

9 Popular music education in Hong Kong: a case study of the Baron School of Music 100
Hei Ting Wong

10 Mediations, institutions and post-compulsory popular music education 114
Seán McLaughlin

11 Where to now? The current condition and future trajectory of popular music studies in British universities 127
Simon Warner

12 Parallel, series and integrated: models of tertiary popular music education 139
Gavin Carfoot, Brad Millard, Samantha Bennett and Christopher Allan

PART III
Curricula in popular music 151

13 Do the stars know why they shine? An argument for including cultural theory in popular music programmes 153
Emma Hooper

14 'I've heard there was a secret chord': do we need to teach music notation in UK popular music studies? 166
Paul Fleet

15 'Art' to artistry: a contemporary approach to vocal pedagogy 177
Diane Hughes

16 Defeating the muse: advanced songwriting pedagogy and
creative block 190
Jo Collinson Scott

17 Missing a beat: exploring experiences, perceptions and
reflections of popular electronic musicians in UK higher
education institutions 203
Paul Thompson and Alex Stevenson

18 Artists to teachers – teachers to artists: providing a space
for aesthetic experience at secondary schools through
popular music 217
Axel Schwarz and David-Emil Wickström

19 Musical listening: teaching studio production in an
academic institution 231
Eirik Askerøi and André Viervoll

20 Popular music and Modern Band principles 243
Bryan Powell and Scott Burstein

PART IV
Careers, entrepreneurship and marketing 255

21 Professional songwriting: creativity, the creative process
and tensions between higher education songwriting and
industry practice in the UK 257
Matt Gooderson and Jennie Henley

22 Popular music pedagogy: dual perspectives on DIY musicianship 272
Don Lebler and Naomi Hodges

23 Towards a framework for creativity in popular music degrees 285
Joe Bennett

24 Re-Mixing Popular Music Marketing Education 298
Ray Sylvester and Daragh O'Reilly

25 University music education in Colombia: the
multidimensionality of teaching and training 313
Luz Dalila Rivas Caicedo

Contents

26 Popular music entrepreneurship in higher education: facilitating group creativity and spin-off formation through internship programmes 328
Guy Morrow, Emily Gilfillan, Iqbal Barkat and Phyllis Sakinofsky

27 Teaching music industry in challenging times: addressing the neoliberal employability agenda in higher education at a time of music-industrial turbulence 341
Michael Jones

PART V
Social and critical issues **355**

28 Popular music meta-pedagogy in music teacher education 357
Ian Axtell, Martin Fautley and Kelly Davey Nicklin

29 A place in the band: negotiating barriers to inclusion in a rock band setting 369
Jesse Rathgeber

30 Teaching the devil's music: some intersections of popular music, education and morality in a faith-school setting 382
Tom Parkinson

31 Social justice and popular music education: building a generation of artists impacting social change 395
Sheila C. Woodward

32 Popular music and (r)evolution of the classroom space: Occupy Wall Street in the music school 412
Nasim Niknafs and Liz Przybylski

33 Popular music education, participation and democracy: some Nordic perspectives 425
Catharina Christophersen and Anna-Karin Gullberg

34 Feral Pop: the participatory power of improvised popular music 438
Charlie Bramley and Gareth Dylan Smith

35 Epistemological and sociological issues in popular music
   education 451
   David G. Hebert, Joseph Abramo and Gareth Dylan Smith

Index 479

Contributors

Joseph Abramo is Assistant Professor of Music Education in the Neag School of Education, University of Connecticut, in Storrs, USA. His areas of research include popular music, music teacher education, gender, cultural studies and poststructuralism. He has more than 20 journal articles and book chapters, serves on editorial committees of several music education journals and is the Immediate Past Chair of the Philosophy Special Research Interest Group of the National Association for Music Education.

Christopher Allan is Senior Lecturer in Voice at University of Newcastle, NSW, Australia. Christopher is currently Deputy Head of School for the School of Creative Arts and has presented a number of papers on the synergies of classical and contemporary singing in a collaborative environment. He is particularly interested in healthy voice use across genres.

Eirik Askerøi works at Hedmark University of Applied Sciences in Hamar, Norway. His teaching and research interests include music production, identity and popular musicians such as Morrissey, Johnny Cash and Joy Division. In 2013 he defended his PhD thesis entitled *Reading Pop Production: Sonic Markers and Musical Identity*, and in 2016 he published 'Who Is Beck?: Sonic Markers as a Compositional Tool in Popular Music' in *Popular Music* (35/3). His article 'Spectres of Masculinity: Manly Markers of Vulnerability and Nostalgia in Johnny Cash' is currently in press in *The Routledge Research Companion to Popular Music and Gender*.

Ian Axtell is Subject Leader for Music Education in the School of Education at Birmingham City University. Ian spent 20 years teaching in schools before moving into higher education. He focuses on music education as part of compulsory education. Music for all is a particular passion, prioritizing the critical pedagogy that lies behind creative music-making. Ian's research interests include signature pedagogy in music teacher education and the universe of discourse in a rich and varied cultural environment.

Iqbal Barkat is Lecturer in Screen Production at Macquarie University, Sydney, Australia, and his co-written book *Screen Media Arts* won an Australian Educational Publishing award in 2009. He is a director, writer and producer of short and feature-length films, with research interests that include community filmmaking, independent cinema, early Soviet cinema, novelty in cinema, the cinematic practice of Dziga Vertov and the philosophy of Alain Badiou.

Joe Bennett is Vice President for Academic Affairs at the Boston Conservatory at Berklee. His research focuses on the creative practice and psychology of songwriters. In his previous role as Professor of Popular Music at Bath Spa University, he launched the world's first master's degree in Songwriting. As an expert witness forensic musicologist, Joe advises music lawyers, publishers, artists and songwriters on matters of plagiarism and musical similarity. www.joebennett.net.

Samantha Bennett is Associate Professor in music at the Australian National University. She is the author of *Modern Records, Maverick Methods: Technology and Process in Contemporary Record Production* and is widely published in phonomusicology, popular music analysis and music technology. Samantha has worked in further and higher education for 15 years, won multiple teaching awards and grants and is a Senior Fellow of the Higher Education Academy.

Charlie Bramley is an active researcher in the fields of popular music studies, popular music education and improvisation studies. He earned his PhD in 2015 from Newcastle University. His research explores the role of improvisation within popular music-making and addresses the extent to which improvised models of music-making can widen access to and participation in music. This is explored through participatory action research projects and workshops in a variety of community settings.

Matt Brennan is a Chancellor's Fellow of Music at the University of Edinburgh and has served as Chair of the UK and Ireland branch of the International Association for the Study of Popular Music (IASPM). His current research interests are the drum kit, live music and music and sustainability. He is the co-author of *The History of Live Music in Britain* (2013) and is currently writing a social history of the drum kit.

Scott Burstein is the National Director of Training for the non-profit organization, Little Kids Rock. His duties include managing training, professional development and higher education. He received his Doctorate in Music Education from the Thornton School of Music at the University of Southern California after studying Music Theory at the University of California, Santa Barbara and the Eastman School of Music. He previously taught public high school in Los Angeles for 12 years, with subjects including marching band, jazz band and guitar ensemble.

Luz Dalila Rivas Caicedo teaches at the Javeriana University of Colombia. She is a member of the research group Agora Latinoamericana. Recent publications include 'Educación superior en música y formación docente', *Revista A Contratiempo, 25* (territoriosonoro.org/CDM/acontratiempo/) and 'Nuevos retos para la educación musical: El docente de música como investigador', in la *Revista de la Asociación Brasilera de Educación Musical*, 20(29).

Gavin Carfoot is Lecturer in Music at the Queensland University of Technology. He has worked extensively in popular music education and community engagement at undergraduate and postgraduate levels, winning a Griffith Award for Excellence in Teaching in 2012. He has recent publications in the *Oxford Handbook in Artistic Citizenship*, *Popular Music* and *Popular Communication*. Gavin has worked across many musical styles, including collaborations with pop artists from *Australian Idol* and *X Factor*.

Catharina Christophersen is Professor of Music Education at Bergen University College, Faculty of Education, Norway. She has worked with popular music pedagogy since the late 1990s and wrote her PhD dissertation on the aesthetic and cultural practices of a popular music conservatory. Current research involves interdisciplinary studies of arts education in schools, musician-teacher collaborations and game-based popular music learning in higher education.

Siew Ling Chua is Master Teacher (Music) at the Singapore Teachers' Academy for the aRts, Ministry of Education. She co-authored the book *Teaching Living Legends: Professional Development and Lessons for the 21st Century Music Educator* in 2016, and she has contributed to publications such as *Enhancing 21st Century Competencies in Physical Education, Art and Music* (2016); *Connecting the Stars: Essays on Student-Centric Music Education* (2013); and *Contextualized Practices in Arts Education* (2013).

Jo Collinson Scott is Lecturer in Commercial Music at the University of West of Scotland, where she helped develop the MA Music: Songwriting programme. She is a practising songwriter and performer who has worked with artists such as David Byrne, Vashti Bunyan and Teenage Fanclub. Her recent AHRC-funded songwriting research explores environmental sustainability. Her broader research interests include popular music pedagogy in a range of contexts, such as criminal justice, community and higher education.

Martin Fautley is Professor of Education at Birmingham City University. He was a school music teacher for many years before undertaking doctoral study into composing and assessment. He spends much of his time researching these areas still. He is the author of eight books and more than 50 journal papers and book chapters on aspects of music education, creativity and assessment.

Paul Fleet is Director of Excellence in Learning and Teaching and Senior Lecturer at Newcastle University, UK. He is head of music theory provision across classical, contemporary and popular, and folk degree music programmes. His research interests include analysis, theory, phenomenology, pedagogy, teaching and learning strategies and cross-disciplinary collaboration. Paul is an academic advisor to awarding bodies and a Fellow of the RSA and Senior Fellow of the HEA.

Emily Gilfillan is a PhD candidate at Macquarie University. Her research aims to bridge the gaps between understandings of group creative practices and experiences and knowledge informing current practices in the creative industries. Her work thus examines collaborative creative practices, with a particular focus on micro-collaborations in dance-making. With a background in creativity research, she has also examined the impacts of funding conditions on artists practising in Australia's cultural sectors.

Matt Gooderson is a composer/producer with a successful international career. As a founder member of electro-punk band Infadels, he played more than 500 live shows in 20 countries and released a chart-topping album with total sales of more than 40,000. Matt's solo compositions have been used for computer games (Grand Turismo, FIFA), television (CSI Miami) and advertising (3 Mobile, Mazda). He is also Senior Lecturer in Popular Music Performance at the University of Westminster. mattgooderson.com

Lucy Green is Professor of Music Education at the UCL Institute of Education. Her research is in the sociology of music education, specializing in meaning, ideology, gender, informal learning and new pedagogies. Lucy led the 'Informal Learning' part of the 'Musical Futures' movement, which is now being implemented in many countries. She has written five, and edited two, books on music education. Her forthcoming book, co-authored with David Baker, is *Insights in Sound: The Lives and Learning of Visually Impaired Musicians*.

Anna-Karin Gullberg holds a PhD in Music Education, an MA in Experimental Psychology and postgraduate certificates in music, dance and science of ideas. In her work as senior lecturer at Luleå University of Technology's School of Music in Sweden, she supervises students and staff in research strategies and coordinating trans-disciplinary projects in music and consciousness. Her work focuses on knowledge, empowerment and sustainability within music education. Anna-Karin founded BoomTown Music Education (BTME).

David G. Hebert is Professor of Music at Bergen University College and leads the Grieg Academy Music Education (GAME) research group. He has taught for universities on every inhabited continent. His authored and edited books include the following: *Patriotism and Nationalism in Music Education*, *Theory and Method in Historical Ethnomusicology* and *Wind Bands and Cultural Identity in Japanese Schools* and the forthcoming *Translation, Education and Innovation in Japanese and Korean Societies* and *Music Glocalization: Heritage and Innovation in a Digital Age*. sociomusicology.blogspot.com.

Jennie Henley is Area Leader for Music Education at the Royal College of Music, London. She is an experienced music educator, having worked as an instrumental tutor and ensemble director across primary and secondary schools and in community settings. Jennie has been working in higher music education since 2011. Her research interests surround developing musicianship in adulthood, with a particular interest in music in criminal justice and the musical development of primary generalist teachers.

Hui-Ping Ho works at the Singapore Teachers' Academy for the aRts, Ministry of Education. She co-edited its 2013 publication *Connecting the Stars: Essays on Student-Centric Music Education* and contributed articles in relation to the contextualization of non-formal and informal learning pedagogies in Singapore music classrooms. Her latest publication (2016) is a contribution to the chapter on music pedagogies in *Enhancing 21st Century Competencies in Physical Education, Art and Music: PAM Research Report*.

Wai-Chung Ho received her PhD in music education from the UCL Institute of Education at the University of London and is now a professor in the Department of Music at Hong Kong Baptist University. Her substantive research interests include the sociology of music, sociology of education, China's music education and the comparative study of East Asian music education. Her book *Popular Music, Cultural Politics and Music Education in China* was published by Routledge in 2016.

Naomi Hodges graduated from the Queensland Conservatorium of Music with a Bachelor of Popular Music (1st Class Honours) in 2013. Her honours thesis illustrated the rise of do-it-yourself (DIY) musicians and new pedagogical structures that prepare students for diverse outcomes. As a DIY musician, Naomi forms half of Brisbane's indie/pop duo *Phoncurves*, who have supported notable Australian and international artists. Their self-titled debut EP was released in 2012, followed by the *Heartstrings* EP in 2014.

Emma Hooper is a musician, author and academic. She teaches Commercial Music at Bath Spa University, researches gender and pop, plays solo and with others and has one novel out with another forthcoming (Penguin Books, 2018). emmahooper.co.uk.

Diane Hughes is Associate Professor in Vocal Studies and Music at Macquarie University, Sydney, Australia. Her research areas include the singing voice, pedagogy, film and sound, recording practices, songwriting, the music industries and popular music and song. She is co-author of *The New Music Industries: Disruption and Discovery* (Hughes, Evans, Morrow and Keith, 2016, Palgrave Macmillan) and is currently the National President of the Australian National Association of Teachers of Singing.

Michael Jones is a member of the Institute of Popular Music in the Department of Music at the University of Liverpool. He is Programme Director for the MA in Music Industry Studies and has authored *The Music Industries: From Conception to*

Consumption (2012, Palgrave). He is currently working on the sequel, *Music Industry and Digitization*.

Phil Kirkman is Principal Lecturer at Anglia Ruskin University. He was previously Course Director for Music and for Professional Studies (PGCE) at the University of Cambridge. Before this, Phil worked for over a decade as a teacher, pastoral manager and department leader in UK secondary schools. He regularly consults and provides training for education professionals in the UK and internationally. Phil's current research interests include educational technologies, innovative pedagogy, dialogic education and practitioner research.

Andrew Krikun is Professor of Music at Bergen Community College, where he teaches courses in songwriting and music business. He received his MA in Ethnomusicology from UCLA and his PhD in Music Education from NYU. His research on popular music education and community music has appeared in journals and book chapters. Still active as a performing musician, Krikun was the founder of the Los Angeles new wave band Andy and the Rattlesnakes.

Don Lebler is Professor of Popular and Contemporary Music at the Queensland Conservatorium Griffith University. His work in the Bachelor of Popular Music programme led to an interest in research, completing a Doctor of Education in 2007. He was an ISME CEPROM Commissioner and led the OLT Assessment in Music project. Recent publications have focused on popular music education and assessment in music.

Seán McLaughlin completed his PhD in Music at University of Edinburgh in 2012. His thesis dealt with ideas of authenticity in professional Scottish folk music. His research interests include teaching and assessment of popular music's creative practices and identities in contemporary Scottish music. He has previously taught at Edinburgh Napier University and University of Edinburgh and holds a lectureship in Popular Music at University of the Highlands and Islands. Seán is an active musician and songwriter.

Brad Millard is Lecturer in Music at the Queensland University of Technology, where he coordinates core practical units in the Bachelor of Music program. He has taught clarinet and saxophone, directed and toured with university ensembles and lectured extensively in jazz and popular musicianship, orchestration, arranging and multi-instrumental music. As a musician Brad has performed across a wide range of genres and has composed works for big band, concert band and chamber ensembles.

Zack Moir is Lecturer in Popular Music at Edinburgh Napier University and the University of the Highlands and Islands, UK. His research interests are in popular music in higher education, popular music composition pedagogy and the teaching and learning of improvisation. He is an active composer and performer and has published on the topics of popular music pedagogy, popular music-making and leisure and popular music songwriting/composition.

Guy Morrow is Lecturer in Creative Industries at Macquarie University, Sydney, Australia. Creativity lies at the core of Guy's research. His work focuses on understanding how artists are managed, in terms of both direct artist management and cultural policies. By examining the relationship between artists and their managers, as well as the practices of self-management and artist entrepreneurship, Guy generates insights relating to the super-creative core of the creative industries.

Kelly Davey Nicklin is Senior Lecturer in Music Education in the School of Education at Birmingham City University. Kelly taught music in secondary schools in the West Midlands and was Head of Faculty for Performing Arts for 10 years before moving into teacher education. Kelly lectures and tutors on the PGCE Secondary and PGCE Post-Compulsory Education and Training courses at Birmingham City University. Her research interests focus on digital learning pedagogies in initial teacher education.

Nasim Niknafs, the recipient of the Connaught New Researcher Award and Faculty Mobility Grant, is Assistant Professor of Music Education at the Faculty of Music, University of Toronto. Born and raised in Iran, Nasim's publications have appeared in *IASPM@Journal*, *Visions of Research in Music Education*, *The Recorder* and *General Music Today*. Her research interests include improvisation in general music education, equity and politics of music education with special focus on Iran, and community music.

Aleksi Ojala is a music teacher working at the Tapiola General Upper Secondary School in Espoo, Finland. He is currently finishing his doctoral studies in the department of Music Education Jazz and Folk Music at Sibelius Academy, University of the Arts Helsinki. He is also a musician, songwriter and music producer who has released two solo albums through Universal Music Finland and written songs for various Finnish mainstream artists.

Daragh O'Reilly is Senior Lecturer in Creative and Cultural Industries at the University of Sheffield. His research deals with the relationship between arts and the market, with a particular emphasis on culture. He is a co-author of *Music, Markets and Consumption* (Goodfellows Publishers, 2013).

Tom Parkinson is Lecturer in Higher Education at the University of Kent. He has previously taught music at undergraduate, postgraduate and secondary levels and as a guitar teacher in private practice. His research focuses on the value frameworks of arts education and how these relate to different cultural and policy contexts. He is an active musician and performs regularly in the UK and abroad with various groups and ensembles.

Contributors

Bryan Powell is Director of Programs for Amp Up NYC, an initiative to expand Modern Band. Bryan is the founding co-editor of *Journal of Popular Music Education*, a peer-reviewed academic journal and also serves as the Executive Director of the Association for Popular Music Education. Dr Powell has recently been published in the *International Journal of Music Education* and the *IASPM@Journal* special edition on Popular Music Education.

Liz Przybylski is an interdisciplinary popular music scholar who specializes in hip-hop practices in the United States and Canada. Recent and forthcoming publications in academic journals and edited volumes focus on her on- and offline hybrid ethnographic research in Indigenous hip-hop as well as popular music pedagogy. An Assistant Professor of Ethnomusicology at the University of California, Riverside, she teaches courses on ethnographic methods, popular music, Indigenous music and gender and sexuality studies.

Shara Rambarran is Assistant Professor of Music at the Bader International Study Centre, Queen's University, Canada. She received her PhD in Music from the University of Salford, UK. Her research interests include popular musicology, post-production, digital technology, remixology, music industry, events management, education and law (Intellectual Property Rights). She is an editor of the *Journal on the Art of Record Production* and co-editor of *The Oxford Handbook of Music and Virtuality* (2016).

Clint Randles is Associate Professor of Music Education at the University of South Florida, where he teaches Progressive Music Education Methods and Graduate Philosophy of Music. He has published more than 20 peer-reviewed journal articles and has helped found three edited book series in music education research and applied practice. Dr Randles performs as a guitarist in two Tampa Bay area bands and runs a custom guitar shop out of his garage.

Jesse Rathgeber is Assistant Professor of Music Education at James Madison University. Jesse's research examines and troubles conceptions of disability and inclusion in music-making and music learning. He is working on his dissertation as part of his PhD study at Arizona State University and has earned degrees from the University of Illinois (BME) and Northwestern University (MM).

Phyllis Sakinofsky is Communications & Media Manager for Fundraising and Communications at the St Vincent de Paul Society. Her career in public relations has spanned three continents and the areas of retail, health and local and state government. Her principal research interest is around the media skills of Indigenous organizations and communities and their engagement with governments and corporations. In her research and teaching she also focuses on social inclusion and capacity-building among disadvantaged and marginalized communities.

Axel Schwarz is an accomplished studio and live keyboarder, composer, lyricist, arranger and producer with many years of professional experience within the field of popular music. In addition to his creative work, he is also an experienced coach and workshop leader. Since 2003 he has worked at the Popakademie Baden-Württemberg, Germany, teaching various courses, some with an emphasis on the educational field of popular music. In 2015 he was appointed professor.

Gareth Dylan Smith is Research Fellow at the Institute of Contemporary Music Performance in London. He is founding co-editor of *Journal of Popular Music Education*, lead editor of the forthcoming *Punk Pedagogies in Practice* and co-author, with Hildegard Froehlich, of *Sociology for Music Teachers: Practical Applications* (second edition). Gareth's research interests include identity, music and leisure, eudaimonism, autoethnographic research methods and embodiment in performance. He plays drums with V1, Oh Standfast and Stephen Wheel.

Alex Stevenson is Senior Lecturer at Leeds Beckett University, where he teaches Studio Recording, Production Analysis and Mixing modules on the BSc (Hons) Music Technology and BA (Hons) Music Production programmes. Alex continues to works as a freelance musician and engineer and is a Fellow of the Higher Education Academy and member of The Association for the Study of the Art of Record Production. His main area of research is hip-hop production practice.

Ray Sylvester is Associate Professor of Marketing at Anderson University, IN, USA. He co-wrote Europe's first music business degree in 1996 and manages chart-topping artists/musicians. Ray presents globally on music marketing and branding and has published in academic books. His doctoral research is related to music artist brand management. His most recent publication is 'Beyoncé – how brand licensing influences popular music acts', in C. Fill and S. Turnbill's *Marketing Communications: Discovery, creation and conversations* (Pearson, 2016).

Paul Thompson is a professional recording engineer and Senior Lecturer in Music technology. His work has been played on BBC6 Music, BBC Radio 2, BBC Radio 4 and on independent radio stations across Europe and the USA. His doctoral research investigated creativity and collaboration inside the recording studio, and his ongoing research interests include popular music and audio education, informal music learning practices and creativity and cultural production in popular music.

Rupert Till is Reader in Music at the University of Huddersfield and Chair of the International Association for the Study of Popular Music's UK and Ireland branch. He is on the editorial board of *IASPM@Journal* and co-edited a special issue on Popular Music in Education in 2015. He also co-organized a conference on Research in Popular Music Education at the University of Huddersfield in 2015.

André Viervoll is a producer and performer based in Oslo, Norway. His collaborations include Noora Noor, Sidiki Camara, Lars Andreas Haug and Monica

Ifejilika. He has been working as a lecturer teaching studio production, both at the University of Oslo and Hedmark University of Applied Sciences.

Simon Warner is Visiting Research Fellow in Popular Music Studies at the School of Music, University of Leeds. He takes an interest in the relationship between literature and popular music, particularly the impact of Beat Generation writers on generations of rock musicians. His most recent book is *Text and Drugs and Rock 'n' Roll: The Beats and Rock Culture* (Bloomsbury, 2013). As a journalist he has worked for *The Guardian* and the BBC.

David-Emil Wickström, Professor of Popular Music History at the Popakademie Baden-Württemberg, has conducted research on the revival of Norwegian traditional vocal music, as well as on post-Soviet popular music. He is the author of *Rocking St. Petersburg: Transcultural Flows and Identity Politics in Post-Soviet Popular Music* (ibidem, 2014) and a founding member of the German-language branch of the International Association for the Study of Popular Music (IASPM D-A-CH), where he served on the association's board until 2016.

David A. Williams is Associate Professor of Music Education and Associate Director of the School of Music at the University of South Florida in Tampa, Florida, USA. He joined the faculty at USF in the fall of 1998. He holds a PhD in music education from Northwestern University. His research interests involve the use of student-centred and informal learning pedagogies and how these impact teaching and learning in music education.

Hei Ting Wong is a PhD student in Ethnomusicology at the University of Pittsburgh. She received bachelor's degrees in Sociology and Applied Mathematics from the Chinese University of Hong Kong and the University of Oregon, respectively, and an MA in Ethnomusicology from the University of Pittsburgh. Her research interests include Chinese popular music in relation to identity construction, media and new media development; political influences in postcolonial Hong Kong; and music-related educational issues.

Sheila C. Woodward is Chair of Music and Associate Professor of Music Education at Eastern Washington University. President of the International Society for Music Education, Dr Woodward also serves on the Editorial Board of the *International Journal of Music Education*. A native of South Africa, her research focuses on Music and Well-being. Publications include a chapter in Benedict, Schmidt, Spruce and Woodford's *The Oxford Handbook on Social Justice in Music Education* (Oxford, 2015).

Part I
Introduction

1
Foreword

Lucy Green

Popular music education has come of age. This volume stands as one of the first major testaments to that maturation process. Its 60 contributing authors together represent research from a wide and varied range of localities, nations and cultures, adopting an equally diverse set of research methods and theoretical perspectives. There has always been and will always be music – whether it is labelled popular or anything else – outside of schools, universities, instrumental teaching studios and other educational institutions. There will, therefore, always be ways of passing on music which occur relatively or completely independently of such institutions. Thank goodness. But what these authors have shown, collectively, is just how much can be gained by bringing all kinds of popular music into the educational field. They've also shown what a complicated, challenging and controversial operation that is.

In their Introduction the editors suggest the entrance of popular music into education represents something of a paradigm shift, and I agree. The primary stage in the shift involved a slow change of curriculum content from around the 1960s on. Soon after the turn of the millennium, this was followed by an increasing interest in and willingness to adapt pedagogies so as to accommodate the new content through teaching and learning practices which reflect the qualities of the music involved as closely as feasible. What we have now is a meta-field: one that researches what else happens when popular music's presence in education causes changes to both curriculum and pedagogy; and, more importantly perhaps, what could happen and what should happen. Furthermore, the answers to those questions are – as is abundantly clear from this Research Companion – very different depending on the social, cultural and musical contexts.

The authors would probably all agree that, despite regional differences, the majority of children and adults, at least in those geographical localities represented between these pages, have for too long been alienated from music-making. Whilst opportunities to listen to a vast range of music have soared exponentially for the majority of people in the last few decades, opportunities to make music, alone or with others, seem to have narrowed, especially perhaps during the second half of the 20th century. Now those opportunities are burgeoning, and part of the reason for that is of course because the music which is most popular to most listeners is being made available to them in other ways: available so that they can play, sing, compose, improvise, record and produce it, as well as listen to it with more open ears.

I suggested above that there has been and will always be music outside educational institutions. But that goes along with the fact that the musical production and transmission processes involved in such music have been limited to small numbers within any society: members of musical families, for example, or of specialist or subcultural musical groups, not the vast majority of people. Now there is the chance to change that situation. The authors in this Research Companion represent that chance, which is also reflected in the practices and scholarship of many others throughout the world. Congratulations PME – good luck; and congratulations too to the editors, authors and publishers of this step forward in the field of music education.

2

Popular music education (r)evolution

Gareth Dylan Smith, Zack Moir, Matt Brennan, Shara Rambarran and Phil Kirkman

In the last several decades (and to greater and lesser extents in different countries), the presence of popular music has grown in schools, universities and conservatoires. Perhaps this amounts to a paradigm shift. When describing the structure of scientific revolutions, Thomas S. Kuhn wrote the following:

> At the start a candidate for paradigm may have few supporters, and on occasion the supporters' motives may be suspect. Nevertheless, if they are competent, they will improve it, explore its possibilities, and show what it would be like to belong to the community guided by it. And as that goes on, if the paradigm is one destined to win its fight, the number and strength of the persuasive arguments in its favor will increase. More scientists will then be converted, and the exploration of the new paradigm will go on. Gradually the number of experiments, instruments, articles, and books based upon the paradigm will multiply.
>
> *(Kuhn, 1962/2012, pp. 157–158)*

It is possible to see to the evolution of scholarship and practice in popular music education as somewhat analogous to what Kuhn describes here. Without wishing to claim the burgeoning scholarship around popular music education (PME) to amount to an entirely fresh paradigm, it has reached a point where it deserves recognition as its own field. PME sits within music education and often falls under popular music studies (PMS); PME and PMS share, for instance, much of the terrain surrounding *The Ashgate Research Companion to Popular Musicology* (Scott, 2009). Mantie (2013) discusses the lack of a coherent conversation around "popular music pedagogy" in (principally US) writing, and in Jørgensen's (2009) comprehensive study of higher music education, the reference to PME is minimal, with a majority of higher popular music education provision taking place in institutions not recognized by his typology of "institutions for higher music education" (Parkinson & Smith, 2015). PME is a discrete area of scholarly focus; to quote an album title by drummer Bill Bruford (1999), it often finds itself to be both "a part, and yet apart".

Contributing authors to this book work mostly, although not exclusively, in higher education settings of one kind or another, teaching and with experience and expertise in a wide range of intersecting, overlapping subjects and sectors pertinent and party to PME. These include early years, primary, secondary, further and higher education, adult education, musicology, music teacher education, sociology of music, sociology of music education, music business, music marketing and promotion, popular music studies, community music, songwriting, music production, composition, technology, performance, improvisation and special educational needs. This diversity speaks to the breadth and depth of the community forming in and around PME. The purpose of this book, then, is to take stock of PME – to see some of *who, what, why, where* and *how* popular music education is in the present, and to suggest some considerations that might help with (to use a colleague's phrase) "navigating the future" (Randles, 2014).

2010 saw the birth of the Association for Popular Music Education (APME), and in 2015 there were at least three international conferences on popular music education – the Research in Popular Music Education one-day symposium at the University of Huddersfield in the UK, the APME conference at the University of Miami in the US and the Ann Arbor Symposium at the University of Michigan in the US. The July 2016 launch of the Popular Music Education Special Interest Group at the 32nd World Conference of the International Society for Music Education followed three biennial PME conferences (in 2010, 2012 and 2014) at the Institute of Contemporary Music Performance in the UK, and conferences hosted by the International Association for the Study of Popular Music (UK and Ireland branch) with the UK's Higher Education Academy (2014) and the Suncoast Music Education Research Symposium VIII (2011) in the US.

Academics have written elsewhere about epistemological issues surrounding what the scholarly and education communities might mean by 'popular music education' (Abramo, 2011a, 2011b; Allsup, 2008; Ballantyne & Lebler, 2013; Cloonan, 2005; Cloonan & Hulstedt, 2012; Feichas, 2010; Hebert, 2011a, 2011b; Humphreys, 2004; Karlsen, 2010; Kratus, 2007; Lebler et al., 2009; Mantie, 2013; Parkinson & Smith, 2015; Smith, 2013, 2014, 2015a, 2015b; Snell & Söderman, 2014; Väkevä, 2006, 2010; Wang & Humphreys, 2009; Westerlund, 2006). The present volume is thus not intended to provide a definitive account or description of PME. Rather, we aim to highlight something of the breadth of the field, including some of its interests, salience, shortcomings and challenges. One issue faced by popular music education as an emerging area of scholarship is that many popular music educators, institutions and communities exist 'beneath the radar' of publications such as this. We are also sensitive to perennial issues around language and access to scholarly discourse, meaning that many perspectives and practices would necessarily be excluded from these pages. Nonetheless we invite readers to engage with this volume, and to critique its approach, its contents and its assumptions. Following collections such as those by Rodriguez (2004), Oehler and Hanley (2009) and Audubert et al (2015), and a special issue of *IASPM Journal* (2015), we view this volume very much "as part of an ongoing process of the development of PME" (Green et al., 2015). We hope this book serves to help our field avoid becoming one in which "we seem to be more prone to acting our way into implicit thinking than we are able to think our way explicitly into acting" (Bruner, 1996, p. 79). *Viva la (r)evolución!*

Overview of the book

Part I: Introduction

Lucy Green and the book's editors have provided what we hope is a helpful introduction to this volume, and Rupert Till concludes the opening part with an overview of perspectives and practices in popular music education internationally, focusing primarily on higher education. Contextualizing these perspectives with accounts of his own approaches to teaching, learning and assessment, Till takes the view that, given the breadth of popular music(s) in the world and the learning that takes place, publications such as the present volume are timely and necessary in an expanding field.

Part II: Past, present and future

This part contains a range of chapters that provide descriptive and analytical accounts of PME, taking stock of historical contexts, discussing contemporary practices and approaches, and suggesting frameworks relevant to reflexive work in the field for the future. It opens with Andrew Krikun's exploration of historical precedents for contemporary PME in the US. He describes the emergence of commercially motivated PME in private schools, and the vocational rationale for the inclusion of popular music training in technical colleges in a new era of mass culture. This chapter is complemented by David A. Williams and Clint Randles' discussion of the complexity and complications inherent in trying to incorporate popular music learning into the curricula of mainstream schools and the programmes training teachers who work in compulsory public education in the US today; since, and perhaps despite, the development of popular music in North America, it appears difficult to weave this music into school experiences. Aleksi Ojala then describes the development of a new pedagogical approach called 'learning through producing' in Finland, a country where PME is normative and highly developed. Based on studies with secondary-school students, the method uses online and other technologies to connect in-school music-making with the 'real-life' experiences of technology-conversant students in the 21st century.

In the first of three papers presenting perspectives and practices from the Asian continent, Wai-Chung Ho discusses the power and cultural politics of popular song in the People's Republic of China, and the role of the education system in perpetuating and (re)producing meanings of artefacts and attitudes, emphasizing national connectivity and collectivity. Siew Ling Chua and Hui-Ping Ho discuss incorporation of informal and non-formal learning approaches in popular music pedagogy in schools in Singapore. They focus on the roles and approaches taken by teachers in a student-centric learning paradigm, and ask how emphases on technology and cognitive autonomy could inform developments for the future. Hei Ting Wong then presents a case study of a for-profit popular music college in postcolonial Hong Kong, in the context of a national and historical Eurocentric classical music tradition. She compares ideology and curriculum at the school – which focuses on local 'Cantopop' culture and music industry – with similar institutions in the US and the UK.

The next three chapters explore models, contexts and implications of higher popular music education (HPME) from perspectives giving particular consideration to the position of HPME in preparing students for life beyond the education system. Seán McLaughlin looks at the ways in which UK institutions construct popular music through perpetuating ideologies and the pervasive emphasis on vocationalism in higher education, in the context of the music-industrial landscape in which graduates seek employment. Simon Warner then presents empirical data interrogating the purpose and epistemological locus of popular music studies in a UK context, finding tensions between axes of practical/critical, traditional/popular and private/public provision. Gavin Carfoot, Brad Millard, Samantha Bennett and Christopher Allan follow with a typology of undergraduate PME in Australia, proposing parallel, series and integrated modes as a potentially helpful means of differentiating, studying, reflecting upon and developing PME provision internationally.

This part explores the context and broad content of PME on four continents, across public, private, compulsory and higher education, leading into the following part, where the focus narrows to discuss more specific 'delivery' of PME in a wide range of studies.

Part III: Curricula in popular music

Chapters in this part discuss and critique aspects of curricula – past, present and potential – raising various issues salient to popular music education in a range of higher and mainstream education contexts. In the first of four chapters centring on provision in higher education, Emma Hooper presents a case for inclusion of cultural theory in popular music programmes, arguing that the music must be understood in terms of its context, and raising the question of the responsibility of musicians *vis-à-vis* social-political activism. Paul Fleet gets to grips with another perennial issue in teaching in HPME, discussing – via an overview of UK provision – the role of musical (stave) notation in an arena that frequently elides this traditional Western representation of musical intentions. Diane Hughes then gives a detailed explanation of and rationale for an approach to pedagogy in contemporary popular singing – an increasingly taught, but under-theorized, mode of voice application warranting its own approach separate from reified pedagogical methods in other musical traditions. Jo Collinson Scott follows, deconstructing myths around inspiration and 'creative block' in the context of songwriting pedagogy and assessment. Focusing on teaching at the master's-degree level in the UK, she analyzes empirical data from songwriting pedagogues, and argues that the key to successful songwriting education may lie in abandoning the notion of the muse.

Two chapters span higher education and compulsory mainstream education: Paul Thompson and Alex Stevenson present interview data from an empirical study into the dearth of UK HPME and broader PME provision that focuses on electronic music. The authors contend that in order to meet artistic needs of contemporary popular musicians, further scholarly and practitioner attention in this area is required. Axel Schwarz and David-Emil Wickström describe a music intervention project in Germany in which HPME students visit local schools to engage children and adolescents in music-making workshops. This programme seeks to develop musicking in school pupils as well as to broaden the career horizons of college students studying popular music.

The final two chapters in this part focus on complementary elements of music education. Eirik Askerøi and André Viervoll discuss learning the requisite skill set for producer-engineers, and highlight the range of practices and abilities necessary to operate effectively in that (producer) domain. They urge for students to "listen musically" to one another in a recording environment so as to receive the best from people with whom they may one day work as producer-engineers. Bryan Powell and Scott Burstein, meanwhile, describe the curricular approach of non-profit music education organization, Little Kids Rock, providing popular music in mainstream public schools in the United States. They present a rationale for the pedagogical approach of Modern Band, modelled on understandings of language acquisition and aimed at providing teacher training and relevant experiences of popular music learning to children.

This part draws together a range of PME curricula with the shared goal of creating and curating relevant, applicable experiences for music students at all levels of education, some aimed more explicitly than others at engaging learners in practices and approaches that may last into (later) adulthood and even careers – a theme pursued further in the following part.

Part IV: Careers, entrepreneurship and marketing

This part brings together chapters that explore overlapping areas of creativity in careers and career preparation, and in business- and entrepreneurship-orientated elements of PME. The writing in these chapters is thus more focused on undergraduate 'training' programmes and the points of intersection between these and people's lives in music and society – in what Toby Bennett (2015, p. 67) has termed the "skills ecosystem". Matt Gooderson and Jennie Henley follow the discussion from the previous part around curricula, linking songwriting education with employment as songwriters. They compare approaches to songwriting taken by students and professionals, exploring differences through models of creativity. Their findings suggest that the mandated national assessment framework for undergraduate programmes in the UK may hinder development of attributes central to creative work. By contrast, Don Lebler and Naomi Hodges describe – in respective roles as professor and alumna – how aspects of an undergraduate popular music degree programme in an Australian university specifically prepare students for creative, entrepreneurial careers in a 21st-century music employment marketplace. In a similar vein to these authors, Joe Bennett takes a historical view of music training, suggesting that an effective HPME for present conditions is one that works backwards from the commercial imperatives of finished products and that fully takes into account working practices of contemporary musicians.

The next two chapters look at differing areas of higher music education, critiquing current practices and proposing changes to align pedagogical approaches more effectively with realities for employed music graduates. Ray Sylvester and Daragh O'Reilly present a case and model for making popular music marketing education more attuned to the nuances of the new and shifting commercial music environment that has emerged since the turn of the millennium, focusing on popular music as a commercially orientated medium. Luz Dalila Rivas Caicedo explains a range of issues facing higher music education in Colombia, locating the discussion in a national context and sociological, pedagogical frameworks. The chapter works towards proposing a new shape for music teacher education, one which takes into account a diversity of musicking outside of schools and the breadth of understandings relevant to working as a musician/teacher.

The final two chapters in this part offer ideologically divergent interpretations of imperatives facing institutions of higher music education. Guy Morrow, Emily Gilfillan, Iqbal Barkat and Phyllis Sakinofsky describe an entrepreneurial internship programme at an Australian university, and discuss the ways in which, conceptually and pedagogically, this approach helps to prepare students for careers in a changing music-industrial environment. Michael Jones presents an alternative argument, contending that to walk in step with the unstoppable march of neo-liberalization is to mis-serve students. At the core of his chapter is the conviction that misconceived notions of the music industry as a place or destination may be helpfully usurped by construing music-industrial systems and practices as networks of relationships through which industry occurs as activity.

This part of the book examines issues at the core of a key juncture of popular music and education – music-making beyond formal education systems. From creativity and curriculum to power relationships in music and related industries, it explores how creativity and curricula play out in pedagogical approaches across continents. The next part continues to contextualize and critique PME from a variety of sites and situations.

Part V: Social and critical issues

This final part of the book contains a selection of chapters that offer critique of and perspectives on PME, and that seek to locate discussion of the field in a social realm. Music education happens in societal contexts, but is not always considered in this broader frame. The first four chapters describe diverse PME scenarios that share the common desire to ensure and curate meaningful engagement with music in education for individuals and groups in particular communities.

Ian Axtell, Martin Fautley and Kelly Davey Nicklin present a compelling case for popular music meta-pedagogy in secondary-school music teacher training in England. They argue that school music experiences ought not to be guided exclusively by narrow conceptions of musical expertise developed in higher music education, and explain how pedagogical approaches can be conceptualized and developed. Jesse Rathgeber's chapter follows with a detailed exploration of teaching and learning in a music therapy rock band. Describing music learning facilitators and music learning spaces, the author demonstrates how the case of this ensemble is indicative of a need in PME literature for language that is more adaptable, fluid and inclusive. Related to the theme of inclusion, Tom Parkinson discusses in his chapter the complex matrix of relationships, agendas and expectations at play in the context of PME in a faith school setting in England. He traces historical discourses around music, religion and education, connecting these to practical considerations around ethical conduct in the music classroom and issues of power and agency.

The following four chapters explore aspects of democracy in a range of contexts, including Nordic public education, improvised music in the UK and music classes for 'non-musicians' in US higher education. Sheila C. Woodward opens this debate by discussing PME as a platform for raising awareness of social justice issues in and through music in schools. In an age of unprecedented global, regional and local strife, this chapter asks tough questions of music educators, and demands that we 'step up to the plate' as empowered and socially responsible adults. Nasim Niknafs and Liz Przybylski explore the potential of democratized learning spaces in higher education, discussing the empowering potential of incorporating pedagogies and practices inspired by Occupy Wall Street into a course ideologically interwoven with the politics and people of that movement. Catharina Christophersen and Anna-Karin Gullberg consider the ways in and extent to which conceptions and constructions of democracy are understood and, for instance, taken for granted in understandings and practices of PME in Nordic countries. They leave open the questions of how the increased use of technologies in PME may in time prove to be democratizing. Charlie Bramley and Gareth Dylan Smith discuss a developing practice of improvised popular music performance in the UK, one which focuses on participation, collaboration and groove as its primary features and aims. This non-commercial form deliberately works counter to neoliberal imperatives in contemporary societal encounters with music, focusing instead on music-making for its own sake.

In the final chapter, David G. Hebert, Joseph Abramo and Gareth Dylan Smith conclude the book with a discussion of epistemological and sociological considerations drawn from matters raised in this volume and salient to the field. Taking into account 'success', neoliberalism, Bourdieu's models of habitus and masculine domination, and theories of performativity and institutionalization, these authors conclude with recommendations for the future of popular music education, inviting readers to be active participants on an exciting journey.

References

Abramo, J.M. (2011a). Gender differences of popular music production in secondary schools. *Journal of Research in Music Education, 59*(1), 21–43.

Abramo, J.M. (2011b). Queering informal pedagogy: Sexuality and popular music in school. *Music Education Research, 13*(4), 465–477.

Allsup, R.E. (2008). Creating an educational framework for popular music in public schools: Anticipating the second-wave. *Visions of Research in Music Education, 12*(1), 1–12.

Audubert, P., Bizien, G., Chrétiennot, L., Dupouy, B., Duval, T., Krzewina, T., Parent, H., Rivac, F. & Touché, M. (2015). *Learning and teaching popular music: Sharing experiences from France* (P. Moseley, Trans.). Paris: RPM Editions.

Ballantyne, J. & Lebler, D. (2013). Learning instruments informally: A collaborative process across disciplines in popular music and education. In H. Gaunt & H. Westerlund (Eds.), *Collaborative learning in higher music education* (pp. 213–218). Farnham: Ashgate.

Bennett, T. (2015). *Learning the Music Business: Evaluating the "vocational turn" in music industry education*. London: UK Music.

Bruford, B. (1999). *A Part, and Yet Apart* [CD].

Bruner, J. S. (1996). *The culture of education*. Cambridge, MA: Harvard University Press.

Cloonan, M. (2005). What is popular music studies? Some observations. *British Journal of Music Education, 22*(1), 1–17.

Cloonan, M. & Hulstedt, L. (2012). Taking notes: A mapping of HE popular music and an investigation into the teaching of theory and analysis. A report for the Higher Education Academy. Retrieved from Higher Education Academy website: https://www.heacademy.ac.uk/sites/default/files/cloonan_2012.pdf [Accessed 10 October 2015].

Feichas, H. (2010). Bridging the gap: Informal learning practices as a pedagogy of integration. *British Journal of Music Education, 27*(1), 47–58.

Green, L., Leber, D. & Till, R. (2015). Editors' introduction: Popular music in education [special issue]. *IASPM Journal, 5*(1), 1–3.

Hebert, D.G. (2011a). Originality and institutionalization: Factors engendering resistance to popular music pedagogy in the U.S.A. *Music Education Research International, 5*, 12–21.

Hebert, D.G. (2011b). Jazz and rock music. In W.M. Anderson & P.S. Campbell (Eds.), *Multicultural perspectives in music education*, vol. 1, third ed (pp. 112–127). Lanham, MD: Rowman and Littlefield.

Humphreys, J.T. (2004). Popular music in the American schools: What history tells us about the present and the future. In C.X. Rodriguez (Ed.), *Bridging the gap: Popular music and music education* (pp. 91–106). Reston, VA: Music Educators National Conference.

Jørgensen, H. (2009). *Research into higher music education: An overview from a quality improvement perspective*. Oslo: Novus Press.

Karlsen, S. (2010). BoomTown music education and the need for authenticity: Informal learning put into practice in Swedish post-compulsory music education. *British Journal of Music Education, 27*(1), 35–46.

Kratus, J. (2007). Music education at the tipping point. *Music Educators Journal, 94*(2), 42–48.

Kuhn, T.S. (1962/2012). *The structure of scientific revolutions* (50th anniversary edition). London: University of Chicago Press.

Lebler, D., Ballantyne, J., Harrison, S. & Carey, G. (2009). Challenging the learning of teaching: Perspectives on the influence of popular music pedagogy in tertiary music education. In *Reflective conservatoire conference 2009: Building connections*. London: Guildhall School of Music and Drama.

Mantie, R. (2013). A comparison of "popular music pedagogy" discourses. *Journal of Research in Music Education, 61*(3), 334–352.

Oehler, S. & Hanley, J. (2009). Perspectives of popular music pedagogy in practice: An introduction. *Journal of Popular Music Studies, 21*(1), 2–19.

Parkinson, T. & Smith, G.D. (2015). Towards an epistemology of authenticity in higher popular music education. *Action, Criticism, and Theory for Music Education, 14*(1), 93–127.

Randles, C. (2014). *Music Education: Navigating the Future*. New York, NY: Routledge.

Rodriguez, C.X. (Ed.) (2004). *Bridging the gap: Popular music and music education*. Reston, VA: MENC, The National Association for Music Education.

Scott, D.B. (2009). *The Ashgate research companion to popular musicology*. Farnham: Ashgate.

Smith, G.D. (2013). Seeking "success" in popular music. *Music Education Research International, 6*, 26–37.

Smith, G.D. (2014). Popular music in higher education. In G. Welch & I. Papageorgi (Eds.), *Advanced musical performance: Investigations in higher education learning* (pp. 33–48). Farnham: Ashgate.

Smith, G.D. (2015a). Neoliberalism and symbolic violence in higher music education. In L. DeLorenzo (Ed.), *Giving voice to democracy: Diversity and social justice in the music classroom*. New York, NY: Routledge.

Smith, G.D. (2015b). Masculine domination and intersecting fields in private-sector popular music performance education in the UK. In P. Burnard, Y. Hofstander & J. Söderman (Eds.), *Bourdieu and the sociology of music and music education*. Farnham: Ashgate.

Snell, K. & Söderman, J. (2014). *Hip-hop within and without the academy*. Lanham, MD: Lexington Books.

Väkevä, L. (2006). Teaching popular music in Finland: What's up, what's ahead? *International Journal of Music Education, 24*(2), 126–131.

Väkevä, L. (2010). Garage band or GarageBand®? Remixing musical futures. *British Journal of Music Education, 27*(01), 59–70.

Wang, J.C. & Humphreys, J.T. (2009). Multicultural and popular music content in an American music teacher education program. *International Journal of Music Education, 27*(1), 19–36.

Westerlund, H. (2006). Garage rock bands: A future model for developing musical expertise? *International Journal of Music Education, 24*(2), 119–125.

3

Popular music education

A step into the light

Rupert Till

Introduction

Popular music education (PME) is a fast-developing field of study in terms of educational programmes and activities, but relatively few relevant publications are available featuring, for example, case studies of best practice, or relevant theoretical considerations; this volume attempts to provide both, building on such pioneering publications as the special issue of the *Journal of Popular Music Studies* on popular music education (Oehler & Hanley, 2009), *Bridging the Gap: Popular Music and Music Education* (Rodriguez, 2004) (both of which focus largely on the US) and the special issue of *IASPM Journal* on popular music in education (Green et al., 2015). In 2015, the *Journal of Music Technology and Education* also published a special issue (Smith & Powell, 2015), on technology and performance in popular music education. The volume you are reading complements and further develops this and other existing PME scholarship as it relates to both critical and musical theories and practices.

At the 2011 International Association for the Study of Popular Music (IASPM) international conference in South Africa, IASPM founder member Philip Tagg gave a keynote speech discussing how popular music studies (PMS) has progressed over the 30 years since the organization was founded. He concluded that musicologists working in popular music have failed to make such inroads into conventional musicology that popular music and art music are treated equally. He "also questions why researchers from non-musical backgrounds still struggle to address the music of popular music studies, and offers solutions" (Tagg, 2012, p. 3). PMS has featured comparatively little focus on either music-making or pedagogy. Educational programmes that explore popular music practice in particular have proliferated recently around the world. From schools to higher education institutions (HEIs), numerous institutions have begun to explore PME further, changing music education provision, which was in many cases dominated by Western European Art Music (WEAM).

The study of popular music has made greater inroads where it explores sociological or cultural studies approaches to the subject, but in many countries (with notable exceptions, such as Scandinavia) institutions focused on music performance and composition have frequently shown epistemic inertia, sidelining popular music as a fringe activity (Williams & Randles, chapter 5, this volume). This is despite popular music making up the majority of musical activity, perhaps 90% of recorded music and 74% or more of live music, whereas the genre of classical music makes up only 3.5% of recorded music and between 1% and 16% of live music, depending on whose data you use (Till, 2013, pp. 6–8).[1] PMS has focused primarily on the study of popular music *culture*, rather than popular music itself; as a result the poietic processes (Nattiez, 1990, p. 92) of music-making as they relate to popular music, and how to teach and learn them, have lacked substantial attention. Music curricula in community settings, schools, colleges, conservatoires and universities only slowly began to integrate popular music over the last 30 years. Initial exclusion from music departments in the UK, for instance, led to PMS developing a focus on critical, sociological or media studies approaches. As a result there has existed a separation between PMS and the more poietic-focused PME. These are somewhat separate fields currently – PMS is somewhat excluded from musicology, and PME somewhat excluded from PMS. Historic divisions between PME, other popular music research and PMS, are unhelpful. PME should have been an important part of PMS from its beginning (and *vice versa* – see Hooper, chapter 13, this volume), and this book goes some way to rebalance the relationship between the two. This chapter presents an overview of the current state of PME internationally, focusing largely on HE provision and discussing a selection of key relevant publications. It is not possible to cover every relevant publication in a book chapter, and so this focuses on recent material. It then moves on to an emic discussion of some of my own PME activities before presenting conclusions that reflect on the discussion above.

PME around the world

PME is beginning to flourish in an increasing number of countries, and in recent years developments indicate that a tipping point has been reached (Kratus, 2007), with more rapid expansion occurring and cascading outwards. This situation is highly inconsistent internationally. In a number of cases something specific has afforded PME the opportunity to thrive (Clarke, 2005). For example, Bendrups (2013) describes the situation in Australia and New Zealand, where prominent

---

1 This relates to UK recordings. Of the 3.5% of recordings that are labelled as within the classical genre, 1% is accounted for by André Rieu, and popular material sung by the likes of Katherine Jenkins, Russell Watson, Lesley Garrett, Rolando Villazon, The Priests, and Hans Zimmer is strongly represented.

streams of ethnomusicological study have focused on Aboriginal and Maori musical cultures, and ethnomusicology has become a significant part of music education culture, tying into national debates addressing issues of culture and identity. This focus on ethnomusicology has afforded opportunities to PMS and PME, which have become firmly established within curriculum in all sectors. Appropriate pedagogical approaches have also been explored for this curriculum. An ethnographically inspired approach has allowed educators to explore modes of teaching and learning inspired by popular music culture. One way of understanding PMS is to view it as being like an ethnomusicology of industrial, commercial or contemporary cultures. Indeed, it is possible to cast PMS as a subset of ethnomusicology; with such a perspective in mind, the links between ethnomusicology, PMS and PME seem not only healthy but also a possible model approach. Certainly some of the most highly developed PME practices are in Australia and New Zealand.

Lebler and Weston (2015) describe the undergraduate Bachelor of Popular Music programme at Griffith University's Queensland Conservatorium in Australia, and how approaches to the programme are drawn from popular music industry practices. A student-run record label is an important part of the learning experience, as are self-directed and collaborative learning and participatory assessment. The programme uses educational methods that echo how popular musicians learn outside of institutional contexts (Green, 2001, 2008, 2014). This contrasts with adopting pedagogical principles from existing music education, which may be based on WEAM traditions and culture (Parkinson & Smith, 2015; Williams & Randles, chapter 5, this volume).

As Bennett (chapter 23, this volume) discusses, WEAM involves a tiered hierarchy of highly trained, specialized and elite professionals, with a stratified system of performers, conductors and composers who focus upon a canon of 'great masters' such as Bach, Beethoven, Wagner and Stockhausen. WEAM education schools musicians in adopting the aesthetic values and musical parameters espoused by such dominant figures, in order to perpetuate a highly specific codification of correct musical behaviour. It thus adopts a master/pupil approach in which students have to learn the system precisely and accurately from those further up this musical stratification than themselves, from an elite of gatekeepers. Pedagogy based on such practices is sometimes appropriate in PME, but not always. Although it arguably still has canon (Smith, 2014) and elite figures, popular music is somewhat differently structured, depending to a greater extent on the opinions of audiences – of the many, rather than the few – and with a history of appreciating divergence from accepted behaviour (Jones, 2008; Kassabian, 2010). A system such as that described by Lebler and Weston, with a range of participatory and democratized approaches to teaching and learning, is fitting for such a popular cultural musical form. As we will see, this approach emerges from a number of sources as suggested good practice.

A key characteristic of the Griffith programme is that, although the students nominally want to pursue careers as popular music performers, popular music is addressed as a recorded medium, as one in which the text lies in the recording, a defining characteristic of much contemporary popular music (Attali, 1985, 2001;

Cutler, 1984, p. 9; Frith, 1996, p. 15). As a result, study related to recording and music technology is integrated as a standard core skill (Lebler & Hodges, chapter 22, this volume). This is a feature of many other existing PME programmes, such as the first undergraduate popular music programme, the BA (hons) in Popular Music and Recording at the University of Salford in the UK (University of Salford, 2015), and the BA in Professional Music at the International College of Music in Kuala Lumpur (International College of Music, 2016).

Another characteristic evident at Griffith (and elsewhere) is that in order to stay relevant to technological and industry developments, staff maintain relationships with external music industry partners, and regularly update the curriculum to remain current (Morrow et al., chapter 26, this volume). The inclusion of masterclasses and workshops taught by music industry professionals is an important element of provision. A balance is struck between industrial training and educational development, between encouraging knowledge and understanding, and acquisition of skills and abilities (Jones, chapter 27, this volume; Lebler & Hodges, chapter 22, this volume).

Anthony (2015) addresses the use of music technology on the same programme as Lebler and Weston, discussing the detail of approaches to performance and recording. He describes these two elements as mutually dependent and informative fields, reflecting other publications by Lebler (2006, 2007), emphasizing the necessity of embedding the use of technology within pedagogy (Moir & Medbøe, 2015). Blom and Poole (2015) also describe student-led educational cultures in Australia, focusing specifically on composition/songwriting classes. Their study explores 'presage', the knowledge and skills students bring with them to the classroom. It discusses three separate institutions, exploring how students bring a range of experiences of songwriting into the classroom. Some students have a great deal of in-depth knowledge of the subject, and many have implicit levels of understanding as well as a deeply embedded level of associated context, upon which they are able to draw when exploring songwriting. Teaching staff draw upon this body of student knowledge to enrich class activities, democratizing the pedagogical approach, allowing students to contribute to and own the educational experience (see also Niknafs & Przybylski, chapter 32, this volume).

The situation is somewhat different in the UK. Cloonan and Hulstedt (2013) examined UK PME provision, reporting on research commissioned by the Higher Education Academy (HEA). They found PME in 47 UK HEIs, around one in three. They found PME to be "doubly new" (p. 5): to be a new subject that is less than 30 years old, and to be taught predominantly in new institutions that are often less than 20 years old, many with little or no research culture. They identify a number of needs within the sector, calling for more support for educators working in the field, more opportunities for networking and the sharing of good practice, as well as more links with the music industry. Programmes are found to be highly varied, with no consensus about entry requirements, graduate qualities, benchmarking or programme content (see also Fleet, chapter 14, this volume).

In the UK, there is a divide between older research-intensive universities and 'new' institutions that were granted permission to use the term 'university' after

1992 and which are principally focused upon and funded by teaching. PME is focused in the latter (hence the lack of research focus identified above), featuring strong vocational content (Parkinson & Smith, 2015). Although the UK featured the first PME degree programmes, its lack of consensus or debate about best practice in PME pedagogy is perhaps due to a theoretical vacuum in new institutions, where practitioners may be afforded little opportunity for research-led reflection on practice, and may have no research training or postgraduate qualifications. Indeed, many staff have music industry rather than academic backgrounds. Programmes and teaching tend to be based on the individual experiences of tutors, with strong content in terms of *what* is taught, but less rigour in *how* that content is taught and learned. Popular music staff in teaching-intensive Higher Popular Music Education (HPME) institutions often have to deal with large groups sizes, high staff-student ratios and heavy teaching loads, providing little time for research into teaching methodologies.[2]

UK music education in universities is changing, partly due to market forces (Jones, chapter 27, this volume; Smith, 2015). Increasingly, older universities are addressing popular music in order to recruit more students, as application numbers in WEAM-focused music departments have decreased due to demographic and funding changes, as well as an increased focus on popular music in schools (Winterson & Russ, 2009). Cloonan and Hulstedt (2013, pp. 76–77) ask highly pertinent questions about the nature of PMS, about whether critical, vocational or musical studies should be at the centre of PME. Their research supports the conclusion that best practice features interaction between a research-focused critical approach and a practically orientated musical, vocational or technological approach – that these areas should be synthesized and integrated.

UK school education is closely regulated, and is enriched by up-to-date educational theory. Increasingly school curricula have included 'world music', popular music, jazz and film music alongside WEAM (Winterson & Russ, 2009), and integrate performance, composition and analysis. For example, UK examination board Edexcel's level 3 (GCE A level aimed at 16–18 year olds) qualification is arranged to

> allow students the opportunities to perform as soloists and/or as part of an ensemble. Teachers and students can choose music in any style. Any instrument(s) and/or voice(s) are acceptable as part of a five-six minute assessed performance. Notated and/or improvised performances may be submitted.
>
> *(Edexcel, 2004)*

---

2 My own experience has involved regularly teaching PMS to classes in sizes of 60 to 120 students. Teaching in a College of Further and Higher Education I regularly had 24 hours of student teaching contact per week, compared to 14 hours in a research-active university. According to the Complete University Guide, none of the 30 UK universities with the best staff-student ratios are new universities, and none of the 30 UK universities with the worst staff-student ratios are old (pre-1992) universities (http://www.thecompleteuniversityguide.co.uk).

Any piece of popular (or other) music can be performed, and this accounts for 15% of the assessment. Historical and analytical study is based on the *Edexcel Anthology of Music* (Winterson, 2008), which includes works by Bach, Beethoven, Cage, Bernstein, Jerry Goldsmith, Barrington Pheloung, Miles Davis, Ram Narayan, Howlin' Wolf, The Kinks and Oasis. An essay question in the Developing Musical Understanding section of an Edexcel sample examination paper is "Describe the stylistic features of 'You can get it if you really want' by Jimmy Cliff that show that this is an example of Jamaican popular music" (Edexcel, 2007, p. 21). Clearly, PME is part of UK schools' music education. In addition, music teaching in the UK school and further education sector now integrates practical and theoretical considerations within project-based activities, which can include reading, analysis, composition, performance and recording. Teachers can choose to select classical options within such curriculum. As one can see, PME in the UK is somewhat inconsistent, with little discussion or alignment of best practice.

John Collins (2011) has discussed the development of PME in universities in Ghana. As with provision in Australia and New Zealand, Collins describes Ghanaian PME as being afforded by ethnomusicological developments. PME programmes in Ghana emerged from a focus on African popular music and performance. These programmes spread and developed from the late 1980s on. They were encouraged and developed by a growing sense of postcolonial national identity, in which environment it was increasingly possible to focus upon music from Ghana rather than the WEAM that dominated previously. This was further enabled by popular music and ethnomusicology sharing many common goals, interests, methodological approaches and fields of study.

In Germany and some neighbouring countries, it was jazz that afforded the development of PME. Martin Pfleiderer (2011, p. 45) writes:

> [By] winter 2010/11 almost 200 courses concerning popular music were offered by university programs in Germany, Austria and Switzerland, mostly provided by musicology and music pedagogy departments . . . almost every university and music high school (*Musikhochschule*) offers courses filed under *populäre Musik*.

He explains that such programmes are typically taught by postgraduates or recently qualified staff, with more senior and prestigious posts held by WEAM scholars. The existence of these programmes was made possible by the development of jazz education in Germany in the 1970s. Linked to experimental music, jazz was absorbed into mainstream curricula, subsequently affording similar opportunities for other forms of popular music.

Michael Ahlers (2015) provides an evaluation of five years of teaching in German HE, drawing upon the hermeneutical helix (exploring understanding, knowledge and meaning, and the influence of study upon the studied), and the concept of style copies. He suggests that the use of formal and informal learning together is good practice within PME. Ahlers refers to Green (2001) exploring how popular musicians learn by copying others. Indeed, this is something that happens (and happened) frequently in popular music culture, artists such as the Beatles, the Rolling Stones, the Beach Boys, Oasis and others learning to write songs by copying or even plagiarizing the work of others (Till, 2007). Style copies (also known as covers), have often been the equivalent of scales and exercises in WEAM for popular musicians, helping them learn the language of the music. Writing songs based on the music of others is certainly a useful compositional exercise, but there is little evidence of an understanding of this as a form of practice-based research (Smith & Shafighian, 2013). Ahlers suggests that despite a proliferation of programmes in popular music in Germany, there is a lack of research that explores how such programmes should be taught. He describes a course element in which students create a style copy and subsequently analyze the result, mixing practice and theory so that they enhance one another, adopting a trans-disciplinary methodology.

Like Ahlers, Jost (2015) explores a binary relationship in German PME, discussing critical and post-critical approaches to popular music. He addresses the legacy of Adorno, as well as recent developments synthesizing didactic and action-based explorations of popular music. He suggests musicological analysis as a bridge between the two, as a way of bringing together theory and practice. Such an approach requires popular music educationalists to become well acquainted with musicological analysis, methodology and language. This is a far from simple issue for popular music researchers from a cultural studies background, but, as mentioned above, is something Tagg has been calling for over the last 30 years (Tagg, 2012).

PME is less well-established in the US than in many countries, although US PMS has a long history (Krikun, chapter 4, this volume). As mentioned above, one collection of chapters on popular music education (Rodriguez, 2004) focused largely on policy development in US schools, and most of the papers in a special issue of *Journal of Popular Music Studies* on popular music education (Oehler & Hanley, 2009) were also focused on the US. A proliferation of new programmes is described by Powell et al. (2015), including Music Makes Us in Nashville; Little Kids Rock/Amp Up in New York City and beyond; Music For Everyone; Girls Rock Alliance in Oregon; The Travelling Guitar Foundation; Rock and Roll: An American Story (a rock music history curriculum developed by Steven Van Zandt); and School of Rock, which exists in 31 states. Furthermore, Powell et al. (2015) describe the US-based Association for Popular Music Education (APME), which provides a forum for representatives of different PME organizations to collaborate and share practice. There is certainly scope for this to become a more widely internationalized association, perhaps through collaboration with the International Society for Music Education and the research-focused IASPM. There has for too long been a gulf between Popular Music Research and Popular Music Education, both of which are core to Popular Music Studies.

Przybylski and Niknafs (2015) also discuss PME in the US, addressing DIY (do-it-yourself) and DIWO (do-it-with-others) approaches, and the differences between PME in, for example, the US, the UK and Australia. They explore formal and informal approaches, drawing on music education and ethnomusicological theories, focusing on improvisation and composition, as well as autonomy, play, peer learning and peer teaching.

Barreto and Modirzadeh (2015) describe new developments in Brazil, where programmes in popular music are proliferating rapidly. Unlike in the US, Brazilian educators are struggling to find resources and pedagogical models to use in order to establish the content of curriculum. They address issues of balancing sensitivity to culture, context and existing musical frameworks with music-making that is original and maintains a sense of authenticity. Much as in the work of Ahlers (2015), they discuss the difficulty inherent in understanding which rules to follow and which to break in order to achieve success. The lack of a connection to external musical communities within educational institutions such as universities is cited as a key problem for PME in Brazil. Although the focus here is on jazz education, Barreto and Modirzadeh's study has wider relevance. The authors suggest including experiences within and outside the institution, as well as the integration of theoretical and practical approaches. They emphasize the importance of space for experimentation, by educators as well as students (see also Niknafs & Przybylski, chapter 32, this volume). Again two conflicting needs pull against one other – the need for freedom to experiment with new approaches, and the need for a rigorous, theoretically mature pedagogical approach.

Although PME programmes are proliferating in both North and South America, development processes are problematic. O'Brien (2015) illustrates this through a study of the politics surrounding a state-run school of *música popular* in Buenos Aires, Argentina. As is the case for many popular music programmes, this illustrates how the most prestigious facilities and opportunities remain unavailable to PME, forcing it to be an edge-dweller, navigating the peripheries of educational spaces, struggling for recognition and funding. It is clear that there is a long way to go before PME is afforded equal status in all educational contexts.

Dairianathan and Francis (2015) discuss similar issues. They explore PME developments in Singapore, addressing the importance of understanding a local perspective, and not, for example, ascribing US- or UK-based musical qualities to another culture. They explore consolidating performance technique in a way that embraces global practices, addresses global and local soundscapes, and encourages learning that reaches out across the world. This research points out the dangers of teaching a clichéd cultural package when addressing subjects such as locality, gender, sexuality or religion/philosophy (Parkinson, chapter 30, this volume). Dairianathan and Francis also suggest that PME is particularly powerful when it addresses the whole person, as well as values that reach beyond mere instrumentality. They focus on allowing learners to engage bodily with music, engaging their whole selves as a means both of forming and informing the individual, and of self-actualization and self-transcendence. Again this research references Green (2001), and the idea of connecting PME with the world outside the classroom in order to engage with local popular music communities of practice (Lave & Wenger, 1991) beyond the institution. Guitar tuition is the focus of Dairianathan and Francis' research, and the work of Casas-Mas and Ignacio Montero (2015), who explore a case study related to jazz guitar tuition in Spain. They address issues of learner autonomy, as well as dichotomies related to the competing requirements of ear-led training and traditional educational approaches drawn from WEAM culture.

An emic perspective

My own initial pedagogical approaches (from 1993) developed from insider music industry experience rather than hermeneutical or other theories, in the context of a lack of established models of teaching and learning in PME (Mantie, 2013). Despite this, a number of pedagogical approaches are evident in my teaching practice. I am typical of the new context of PME discussed by Cloonan and Hulstedt (2013) – my music degree was from a 'new' university (a polytechnic programme that focused on practice rather than research); I have a music-industry background as a sound engineer, producer, composer and performer, and have adopted similar approaches to those discussed by Lebler and Weston (2015); my students have released their compositions/productions on iTunes, Spotify and Amazon; performance students have performed public concerts, and provided their own backstage services such as ticket sales, marketing and technical production; students have created music-based business plans; an optional year in industry has been available; and students experience a range of concerts, talks and master classes from visiting music industry representatives. Part IV of this book contains several chapters that discuss the richness and complexity of relationships between higher education and the music industry.

Most of the assignments I set are project-based, usually involving a mixture of practical music-making, written work and self-directed learning. For example, a final-year project is to compose and produce an EP of music, with an accompanying report that includes critical self-reflection as well as discussion of aesthetics and the research sources involved. I have used participatory assessment, including peer assessment and self-assessment, especially in self-directed group work, such as recording or performance projects. Most assignments are submitted online, with online and sometimes audio-file feedback, grading provided following a timetable provided in advance. Such approaches are similar to those discussed by Lebler (2007) and Kleiman (2007). I have always conceived of popular music as principally a recorded medium, routinely mixing music technology, recording and production, much like Lebler and Weston (2015) at Griffith University – a blended learning approach (Chew et al., 2008). I use flipped classroom (Strayer, 2012) and rhizomatic learning (Sanford et al., 2011) approaches, such as online tutorials to teach the use of music software tools like Apple's Logic Pro. I allow students to choose their own groups, musical genres, musical content and assessment criteria, a student-focused approach similar to that of Green (2008) or Lebler (2007) (see also Sharples et al., 2012).

In teaching poietic subjects such as performance and composition, I have minimized requirements to use scores or traditional music theory, instead emphasizing technological, oral and aural approaches (see also Fleet, chapter 14, this volume). I have run gospel choirs with up to 100 participants, teaching songs orally: a non-formal learning approach, as discussed by Mok (2010), Smith (2013) and Powell and Burstein (chapter 20, this volume). I have found such approaches particularly valuable when teaching outside of HEIs, in, for example, community choirs; DJ skills workshops in housing estates in deprived areas; and rap production projects with children excluded from conventional schooling due to behavioural problems. Such projects begin with the needs and interests of the participants and take place in informal/non-formal settings (Howell, 2011; Veblen, 2007).

I value presage – the existing knowledge of students, as discussed by Blom and Poole, 2015. I have integrated constructivist approaches, rather than focusing uniquely on a developmental, master/disciple approach (Fosnot, 2005; Morford, 2007; Rinaldo, 2004). Presentations and participation in blogs, discussion boards and Facebook groups feature in my classes, students posting examples of the subject we are studying online or offering them in seminars. This helps to keep curriculum up to date, and gives students a sense of ownership in the learning activities (Partti & Westerlund, 2012).

Style copies such as those discussed by Ahlers (2015) have always featured in my teaching, included within composition, performance, music production and recording. One assignment requires students to add a new melody and lyrics to an existing hit song; group performance begins with style copies, before moving on to writing new material collaboratively in the same genre; in music technology classes, students accurately reproduce short sections of electronic dance music (EDM) as exercises; and recording classes have required students to research and put into practice the methods of specific producers. I routinely encourage students to work collaboratively, introducing, for example, collaborative composition projects (Gaunt & Westerlund, 2013).

Such projects used a range of pedagogical methodologies, but not consciously or responding to specific written texts. Mantie (2013, p. 344) notes that it is typical for those teaching popular music in the UK to "focus more on what students do rather than what teachers do" – on content and on popular music, rather than on pedagogy. He finds that UK PME prioritizes "matters of utility and efficacy" (p. 334), and observes:

> The fundamental difference I detected in the corpus is that non-American discourses appear to focus on student experiences and how teachers can better bring about "quality learning" on the part of students. That is, quality is a function of the educational encounter, not an immutable property of repertoire or teachers.
>
> *(p. 344)*

Various approaches discussed in this book (my own among them) emerged over the last 30 or more years within PME practice, but have been used in the past somewhat uncritically, lacking the context of rigorous study or grounding in educational research. This volume takes steps towards addressing this, and will make it easier in the future to make informed decisions about pedagogical approaches, and to develop PME programmes with increasingly sophisticated methods in teaching, learning and assessment.

Conclusions

I have tried to provide an overview of recent PME developments in a number of countries, primarily focused on higher education contexts, presenting case studies of educational activities and relevant theoretical perspectives, and relating some of my own PME experiences. In doing so, a number of key issues emerge. One in particular is that of basing pedagogical approaches on specifically tailored methods evolved from popular music, rather than uncritically adopting methodologies from WEAM or other existing educational models. Popular music is highly diverse, and differs hugely in national, regional and local contexts, and such methods allow teaching and learning to be adapted to the specific popular music cultures of the student body concerned.

The research of Lucy Green (2001, 2008) is clearly a key influence, and was one of the first – and most influential – in-depth PME studies. Green describes how informal learning is used in PME and can be effectively adapted for application in schools, but has not suggested in her publications that this should be the principal approach in all situations. Indeed, I specifically asked her about this, and she made it clear that she thought there was certainly a place for formal learning methodologies, especially in HPME and other formal institutional contexts where learners have already undertaken a range of tuition or other learning. There is much for PME to learn from existing musical pedagogy, including that of WEAM and other formal musical traditions from around the world. As the level of study advances, a mix of formal and informal learning methodologies is required, chosen to fit the circumstances, akin to what Smith (2013, p. 26) has termed "hybridized learning".

Popular music is defined by the opinions of the many, rather than the few, and pedagogical approaches grounded in a democratized perspective fit PME particularly well (Christophersen & Gullberg, chapter 33, this volume). Examples of relevant contemporary pedagogical methodologies include blended learning (Chew et al., 2008), seamless learning, rhizomatic learning and personal enquiry learning (Sharples et al., 2012). These approaches include methods such as flipped classroom, student-directed learning, collaborative learning and participatory assessment. Using these pedagogical techniques, coursework, group projects, wikis, blogs, online video lectures, virtual classrooms or software educational tools might be expected to replace lectures and exams as dominant PME forms and formats.

Such methodologies are quite common in PME, but are not always used knowingly. In school-age learning in the UK, teaching methods are more regulated and inspected than in HEIs, and this sector has consciously adopted new pedagogical approaches. Universities may need to look to how music is taught in schools for examples of transferable best practices in PME. In terms of PMHE, Australian institutions are perhaps the most pedagogically sophisticated, the publications of Lebler being particularly influential (2006, 2007; Lebler and Weston, 2015). In terms of school-age learning, Nordic countries lead the way, as evidenced by, for example, Folkestad (2006), Karlsen (2010, 2011), Partti and Westerlund (2012), Stålhammar (2006), Väkevä (2013), and Westerlund (2003).

PME programmes cover a number of areas, which are discrete but interrelated. Cloonan (2005, p. 83) categorizes these as musical (including composition and performance, revised to "practical" in Cloonan and Hulsteadt, 2013), vocational (including music business) and critical (including cultural studies and analysis). I would recommend adding a fourth category to the model: 'technical'. Technical work includes recording, production, live sound, digital and computer music-making, programming and web applications. This final category could be described as vocational, or, within musical studies, as production; however, the activities do not fit adequately within either category, and involve such a significant range of activities they necessitate separation.

The use of technology in PME is a core focus or set of skills. All music is technological; scales, notation, pianos and scores are all technologies. Popular music today makes extensive use of the latest digital technologies, from the computer technology used by DJs and producers, to the social media, smartphones and tablets used for dissemination and reception of music. Although scores, notation, music theory and knowledge of canonical works are all useful within PME, they are of no more (and perhaps less) significance than elements that are centred on popular culture, such as web design, social media etiquette or digital recording techniques.

Engagement with the music industry is a feature of many of the most successful and well-developed PME programmes. Inter-professionalism, alongside inter/multi/cross-disciplinarity, is important for PME as a whole. Where it has been practised, interaction between a research-focused critical approach and a practically orientated musical, vocational or indeed technological approach, has been successful, suggesting that these areas should be synthesized rather than separated.

There is no single pedagogical approach that is appropriate to all cultural and educational contexts. PME requires neither greater uniformity nor diversity, but can only benefit from further discussion of pedagogical theory. PME has not always been well-researched or theorized, nor has it involved a great deal of international or even national co-operation. Alongside other recent publications, this book will hopefully assist educators to explore a range of relevant approaches to teaching and learning popular music by presenting PME case studies supported by theoretical frameworks and conceptualization. Current developments mark a coming of age of PME, and will hopefully lead not just to a proliferation of activities, but also to a maturing of the field so that it includes increasingly considered programmes and curricula that reflect a range of pedagogical approaches.

There is a political dimension to the development of PME, especially as such development will inevitably be at the expense of high art forms of music to some extent, as only so many educational resources are available. Both education and music are increasingly available to the many, rather than the few, both democratized and changed irrevocably by digital mediation and distribution. The music industry is undergoing huge changes at present, and these wider developments underscore the significance of this volume.

The appearance of publications focused on PME is not merely timely but long overdue. There is clearly a need for further qualitative, quantitative and philosophical research in PME, but this book provides an important contribution and a useful starting point. Popular music (and indeed society and culture more generally) can only benefit from PME and relevant scholarship becoming more widespread and better developed. The research I have discussed, and that in the rest of this volume, will be beneficial both in countries that have long histories of PME, and in those where its development is new. It is intended that this volume will be the beginning of a larger, longer conversation, a step in the development of a community of practice, which will immensely benefit both popular music educators and popular music education.

References

Ahlers, M. (2015). Opening minds – style copies as didactical initiators. *IASPM Journal*, 5(2), 181–194.

Anthony, B. (2015). Creative conceptualisation: Nurturing creative practice through the popular music pedagogy of live recording production. *IASPM Journal*, 5(2), 139–156.

Attali, J. (1985). *Noise: The political economy of music*. Minneapolis: University of Minnesota Press.

Attali, J. (2001). *Bruits: Essai sur l' économie politique de la musique*. Paris: Presses Universitaires de France.

Barreto, A.C. & Modirzadeh, H. (2015). A discourse on Brazilian popular music and U.S. Jazz education. *IASPM Journal*, 5(2), 23–35.

Bendrups, D. (2013). Popular music studies and ethnomusicology in Australasia. *IASPM Journal*, 3(2), 48–62. Doi: 10.5429/2079–3871(2013)v3i2.4en

Blom, D. & Poole, K. (2015). Presage: What knowledge and experience higher education songwriting students bring to the classroom. *IASPM Journal*, 5(2), 157–180.

Casas-Mas, A. & Ignacio Montero, J.I.P. (2015). Discourse on practice of a semi-professional jazz guitarist: A case study of constructive musical learning (El discurso sobre la práctica de un guitarrista de jazz semi-profesional: estudio de caso de aprendizaje musical constructivo). *IASPM Journal*, 5(2), 54–80.

Chew, E., Jones, N. & Taylor, D. (2008). Critical review of the blended learning models based on Maglow's and Vygotsky's educational theory. *Hybrid Learning and Education: Lecture Notes in Computer Science*, 5169, 40–53.

Clarke, E. (2005). *Ways of listening: An ecological approach to the perception of musical meaning*. Oxford: Oxford University Press.

Cloonan, M. (2005). What is popular music studies? *British Journal of Music Education*, 22(1), 77–93.

Cloonan, M. & Hulstedt, L. (2013). Looking for something new: The provision of popular music studies degrees in the UK. *IASPM Journal*, 3(2), 63–77. Doi: 10.5429/620.

Collins, J. (2011). The introduction of popular music courses to Ghanaian universities. *IASPM Journal*, 2(1–2), 34–44. Doi: 10.5429/2079–3871(2011)v2i1–2.4en

Cutler, C. (1984). *File under popular: Theoretical and critical writings on music*. London: November Books.

Dairianathan, E. & Francis, L.H. (2015). Learning to perform on the electric guitar; some observations of teaching and learning of popular music-making among music education trainee teachers in higher education in Singapore. *IASPM Journal*, 5(2), 81–99.

Edexcel. (2004). *Specification: GCE music*. Retrieved from: http://qualifications.pearson.com/content/dam/pdf/A%20Level/Music/2013/Specification%20and%20sample%20assessments/UA035245_GCE_Lin_Music_Issue_5.pdf

Edexcel. (2007). *Sample assessment materials*. Retrieved from: http://qualifications.pearson.com/content/dam/pdf/A%20Level/Music/2013/Specification%20and%20sample%20assessments/sam-gce2008-Music.pdf

Folkestad, G. (2006). Formal and informal learning situations or practices vs formal and informal ways of learning. *British Journal of Music Education, 23*(2), 135–145.

Fosnot, C.T. (2005). Preface. In C.T. Fosnot (Ed.), *Constructivism: Theory, perspectives, and practice*, second ed (pp. ix–xii). New York: Columbia University Teachers College.

Frith, S. (1996). *Performing rites: On the value of popular music*. Cambridge, MA: Harvard University Press.

Gaunt, H. & Westerlund, H. (Eds.) (2013). *Collaborative learning in higher music education*. Surrey: Ashgate.

Green, L. (2001). *How popular musicians learn: A way ahead for music education*. Vermont: Ashgate.

Green, L. (2008). *Music, informal learning and the school: A new classroom pedagogy*. Vermont: Ashgate.

Green, L. (2014). *Music education as critical theory and practice*. Vermont: Ashgate.

Green, L., Lebler, D. & Till, R. (2015). Popular music in education [special issue]. *IASPM Journal, 5*(1).

Howell, G. (2011). "Do they know they're composing?": Music making and understanding among newly arrived refugee and immigrant children. *International Journal of Community Music, 4*(1), 47–58. Doi: 10.1386/ijcm.4.1.47_1.

International College of Music. (2016). Welcome to ICOM. Retrieved from: http://icom.edu.my [Accessed 1 July 2016].

Jones, C.W. (2008). *The rock canon: Canonical values in the reception of rock albums*. Vermont: Ashgate.

Jost, C. (2015). Beyond Adorno: Post-critical teaching of popular music in the German educational system and its theoretical and practical challenges. *IASPM Journal*, 5(2), 195–212.

Karlsen, S. (2010). Revealing musical learning in the informal field. In R. Wright (Ed.), *Sociology and music education* (pp. 193–206). Farnham: Ashgate.

Karlsen, S. (2011). Using musical agency as a lens: Researching music education from the angle of experience. *Research Studies in Music Education, 33*(2), 107–121.

Kassabian, A. (2010). Have canons outlived their usefulness? *Journal of Popular Music Studies, 22*(1), 74–78.

Kleiman, P. (2007). Towards transformation: Conceptions of creativity in higher education. *Creativity Special Edition: Innovations in Education and Teaching International, 45*(3), 209–217.

Kratus, J. (2007). Music education at the tipping point. *Music Educators Journal, 92*(2), 42–48.

Lave, J. & Wenger, E. (1991). *Situated learning: Legitimate peripheral participation*. Cambridge: Cambridge University Press.

Lebler, D. (2006). The master-less studio: An autonomous education community. *Journal of Learning Design, 1*(3), 41–50.

Lebler, D. (2007). Student-as-master? Reflection on a learning innovation in popular music pedagogy. *International Journal of Music Education, 25*(3), 205–221.

Lebler, D. & Weston, D. (2015). Staying in sync: Keeping popular music pedagogy relevant to an evolving music industry. IASPM Journal, 5(2), 124–138.

Mantie, R. (2013). A comparison of "popular music pedagogy" discourses. *Journal of Research in Music Education, 61*(3), 334–352. Doi: 10.1177/0022429413497235

Moir, Z. & Medbøe, H. (2015). Reframing popular music composition as performance-centred practice. *Journal of Music, Technology and Education, 8*(1), 147–161.

Mok, A.O.N. (2010). Musical enculturation, learning and the values of four Hong Kong socio-musical groups (unpublished doctoral thesis). Institute of Education, London, UK.

Morford, J.B. (2007). Constructivism: Implications for postsecondary music education and beyond. *Journal of Music Teacher Education, 16*(75). Doi: 10.1177/10570837070160020108

Nattiez, J. (1990). *Music and discourse: Toward a semiology of music.* (C. Abbate, Trans.). Princeton: Princeton University Press. (Original work published 1987).
O'Brien, M. (2015). Activism, authority, and aesthetics: Finding the popular in academies of música popular. *IASPM Journal, 5*(2), 36–53.
Oehler, S. & Hanley, J. (2009). Perspectives of popular music pedagogy in practice: An introduction. *Journal of Popular Music Studies, 21*(1). 2–19.
Parkinson, T. & Smith, G.D. (2015). Towards an epistemology of authenticity in higher popular music education. *Action, Criticism, and Theory for Music Education, 15*(1), 93–127.
Partti, H. & Westerlund, H. (2012). Democratic musical learning: How the participatory revolution in new media challenges the culture of music education. In A. R. Brown (Ed.), *Sound musicianship: Understanding the crafts of music* (pp. 300–312). Newcastle upon Tyne: Cambridge Scholars Publishing.
Pfleiderer, M. (2011). German-language popular music studies in Germany, Austria and Switzerland. *IASPM Journal, 2*(1–2), 45–50. Doi: 10.5429/2079–3871(2011)v2i1–2.5en
Powell, B., Krikun, A. & Pignato, J.M. (2015). "Something's happening here!": Popular music education in the United States. *IASPM Journal, 5*(2), 4–22.
Przybylski, L. & Niknafs, N. (2015). Teaching and learning popular music in higher education through interdisciplinary collaboration: Practice what you preach. *IASPM Journal, 5*(2), 100–123.
Rinaldo, V. (2004). Subject matter is the vehicle and not the focus of learning: A constructivist perspective of music education. *Canadian Music Educator, 45*(34), 31–34.
Rodriguez, C.X. (Ed.) (2004). *Bridging the gap: Popular music and music education.* Reston, VA: MENC, The National Association for Music Education.
Sanford, K., Merkel, L. & Madill, L. (2011). "There's no fixed course": Rhizomatic learning communities in adolescent videogaming. *Loading . . ., 5*(8). Retrieved from: http://journals.sfu.ca/loading/index.php/loading/ article/view/93
Sharples, M., McAndrew, P., Weller, M., Ferguson, R., FitzGerald, E., Hirst, T., Mor, Y., Gaved, M. & Whitelock, D. (2012). *Innovating pedagogy 2012: Open University innovation report 1.* Milton Keynes: The Open University.
Smith, G.D. (2013). *I drum, therefore I am: Being and becoming a drummer.* Farmham: Ashgate.
Smith, G.D. (2014). Popular music in higher education. In G. Welch & I. Papageorgi (Eds.), *Advanced musical performance: Investigations in higher education learning* (pp. 33–48). Farnham: Ashgate.
Smith, G.D. (2015). Neoliberalism and symbolic violence in higher music education. In L. DeLorenzo (Ed.), *Giving voice to democracy: Diversity and social justice in the music classroom* (pp. 65–84). New York: Routledge.
Smith, G.D. & Powell, B. (Eds.) (2015). Technology and performance in popular music education [special issue]. *Journal of Music, Technology and Education, 8*(2).
Smith, G.D. & Shafighian, A. (2013). Creative space and the "silent power of traditions" in popular music performance education. In P. Burnard (Ed.), *Developing creativities in higher music education: International perspectives and practices* (pp. 256–276). London: Routledge.
Stålhammar, B. (2006). *Musical identities and music education.* Aachen: Shaker Verlag.
Strayer, J.F. (2012). How learning in an inverted classroom influences cooperation, innovation and task orientation. *Learning Environments Research, 15*(2), 171–193. Doi: 10.1007/s10984–012–9108–4
Tagg, P. (2012). Caught on the back foot: Epistemic inertia and visible music. *IASPM Journal, 2*(1–2), 3–18. Doi: 10.5429/2079–3871(2011)v2i1–2.2en
Till, R. (2007). The blues blueprint: The blues in the music of the Beatles, the Rolling Stones, and Led Zeppelin. In N. Wynn (Ed.), *Cross the water blues: African American music in Europe* (pp. 183–202). Jackson, MS: University Press of Mississippi.

Till, R. (2013). Twenty first century popular music studies. *IASPM Journal, 3*(2), 1–14. Doi: 10.5429/664

University of Salford. (2015). *Popular music and recording*. Retrieved from: http://www.salford.ac.uk/ug-courses/music-popular-music-and-recording [Accessed 1 August, 2015].

Väkevä, L. (2013). Digital musicianship in the late modern culture of mediation: Theorizing a new praxis for music education from a pragmatist viewpoint. *Journal of Pedagogy and Psychology "Signum Temporis", 6*(1), 38–47.

Veblen, K. (2007). The many ways of community music. *International Journal of Community Music, 1*(1), 5–21. Doi: 10.1386/ijcm.1.1.5_1.

Westerlund, H. (2003). Reconsidering aesthetic experience in praxial music education. *Philosophy of Music Education Review, 11*(1), 45–62.

Winterson, J. (2008). *The Edexcel anthology of music*. London: Peters.

Winterson, J. & Russ, M. (2009). Understanding the transition from school to university in music and music technology. *Arts and Humanities in Higher Education, 8*(3), 339–354.

Part II
Past, present and future

4
The historical foundations of popular music education in the United States

Andrew Krikun

Introduction

American music education historian Jere Humphreys (2004) has argued that

> popular music has been taught continuously in American schools from the beginning, arguably more so than in other countries. However, the American music education establishment did not formally acknowledge popular music as worthy of being taught until the "Tanglewood Declaration" of 1968.
>
> (p. 92)

Given Humphreys' assertion, why is there no existing historiography of American popular music education inside and outside of American schools? Even though popular music education has made great strides in the United States during the first two decades of the 21st century (Powell, Krikun & Pignato, 2015), the history of popular music education during the previous two centuries remains largely unwritten. Contributing to this historical lacuna is the appropriation of popular music education by jazz educators, constructing a history of jazz education while ignoring the greater historical context of jazz as popular music (Prouty, 2012, pp. 46–77). While two entries exist under "jazz education" in *Grove Music Online* (Kennedy, n.d.; Worthy, 2011), no such entry exists for "popular music education". This chapter presents a brief overview of the development of popular music education within formal educational institutions in the United States, while also highlighting trends in popular music education outside of these institutions.

Andrew Krikun

Learning popular music 'by the book': Popular music education and music publishing in the 19th century

Facilitated by the forces of industrialization and urbanization, the expansion of the middle class in the United States during the 19th century provided a paying audience for professional live entertainment as well as for the sale of sheet music and instructional books to amateur musicians. Although popular musicians continued to learn music by oral tradition in the manner of the folk musicians of the past (McLucas, 2010, pp. 81–99), the availability of printed material and the services of professional music educators contributed to their education. American music historian Richard Crawford (2003) described the growth of home music-making in the 19th century, which created a market for both music publishing and music education:

> By the mid-nineteenth century, a substantial music business existed in this country to meet the desires of women and men, playing and singing at home, for recreation and entertainment as well as edification. The publishers who fashioned that business did so by coordinating three separate forces: the artistic production of composers, the social aspiration of amateur singers and players, and their own commercial ambition.
>
> *(p. 221)*

In his autobiography, American songwriter Charles K. Harris (1926), author of the 1892 hit song "After the Ball", recalled his youth as an aspiring banjoist in Saginaw, Michigan, during the 1870s. Harris befriended an itinerant actor and banjoist staying at a local hotel, Bill Carter, who gave him an old banjo along with a few lessons:

> He taught me several chords, just enough to accompany myself when I sang a song … "Now, kid," said he, "when you save up enough money buy a George C. Dobson Banjo Book, that contains a chart showing where the notes belong upon the neck of the banjo and the position of your fingers on the instrument. When I come back here next season I hope you will be a first-class banjo player."
>
> *(p. 3)*

The events in Harris's tale were shared by numerous amateur and professional musicians in the 19th century, as the music publishing industry began to supply resources targeted to musicians learning popular music. The White Smith Music Publishing Company, with offices in Boston, New York and Chicago, published a later edition of *Geo. C. Dobson's World's Banjo Guide* in 1890. The book's introduction demonstrated the emerging cultural hierarchy and racism endemic in the United States during the late 19th century, stating that,

> There is far more extensive disparity between the old box and strings, or the primeval gourd of the plantation negro of a half century ago and the present

perfected banjo, than there is between the crude spinet of the old masters of music and the massive concert grand piano of today.

(Dobson, 1890)

The widening gulf between popular culture and elite culture that emerged in the United States during the second half of the 19th century has been detailed by American cultural historian Lawrence Levine in his book *Highbrow/Lowbrow* (1988):

> The new meanings that became attached to such words as "art," "aesthetics," and "culture" in the second half of the nineteenth century symbolized the consciousness that conceived of the fine, the worthy, and the beautiful as existing apart from ordinary society.
>
> *(p. 225)*

In the final decades of the 19th century, this cultural milieu was manifested in the division between 'art music', represented by the Western European classical music tradition, and 'popular music', encompassing all other musical styles. Majestic concert halls in major cities became sanctuaries for the patrons of the European classical music tradition. Music conservatories and university music departments were established to educate students in European art music and to help facilitate appreciation of the great works of the classical music tradition (Hays, 1999). The creation of this popular/art music dichotomy served to set the stage for the advancement of art music in formal music education in the United States during the 20th century, divorced from popular musical practices such as minstrelsy, ragtime, jazz and dance band music.

'After the ball': American popular music education from Tin Pan Alley to the swing era

One of the turning points in the history of American popular music was the development of Tin Pan Alley, beginning in the late 19th century, when American music publishers became centralized in offices located on 28th Street, between 5th and 6th Avenues, in New York City. Popular music during this time became truly 'popular', measured by the commercial success of sheet music sales. Charles K. Harris's "After the Ball" sold over two million copies over several years after its release in 1892 and eventually sold over five million copies (Hamm, 1983, p. 285). After his initial success in the 1890s, Harris self-published an instructional guide to songwriting in 1906, in which he provided the following definition of popular music:

> The word "popular," as used in this treatise in reference to songs, has been employed to expressly designate the various classes of songs which are written, published and sung, whistled and hummed by the great American "unmusical" public, as distinguished from the more highly cultivated musical class which often decries and scoffs at the tantalizing and ear-haunting melodies that are heard from ocean to ocean in every shape and form.
>
> *(p. 10)*

This revealing statement by a hit songwriter demonstrates the degree to which the highbrow/lowbrow dichotomy was established in the United States, even in the popular discourse of the time.

South African musicologist Peter van der Merwe (1989) points to the year 1896, with the successful performances of pianist Ben Harney in New York City, as the start of the "ragtime craze" in the US (pp. 279–284). Soon after, Harney published an instructional book, *Rag Time Instructor* (Harney & Northrup, 1897), aimed at the growing amateur audience hoping to learn the intricacies of ragtime piano. In 1908, acclaimed ragtime composer Scott Joplin self-published a book of piano exercises titled *School of Ragtime*. In Joplin's introduction, he defended the artistic value of ragtime:

> That real ragtime of the higher class is rather difficult to play is a painful truth which most pianists have discovered. Syncopations are no indication of light or trashy music, and to shy bricks at "hateful ragtime" no longer passes for musical culture. To assist amateur players in giving the "Joplin Rags" that weird and intoxicating effect intended by the composer is the object of this work.
>
> (p. 1)

One of the most successful entrepreneurs to take advantage of the popularity of ragtime was pianist, composer and music teacher Axel Christensen (1881–1955). He established the Christensen School of Popular Music to teach ragtime piano in Chicago in 1903. Adopting the nickname the 'Czar of Ragtime' (distinguished from Scott Joplin's title of 'King of Ragtime'), he self-published an instructional guide, including exercises and original arrangements of popular tunes, which he began selling by mail order. Christensen authorized music schools in other cities to teach the "Original Christensen System" and by the mid-1920s, there were almost 100 branch schools across the United States. The economic downturn that paralyzed the United States during the Great Depression (1929–39) had a negative impact on Christensen's franchise, and most of the schools were closed by the early 1940s (Jasen & Jones, 2000, pp. 123–131).

Popular music education was first introduced into formal educational institutions in the US during the 1920s and 1930s (Krikun, 2014). The rationale for introducing popular music into the American music curriculum was to equip music students with adequate vocational training. The aim of vocational or technical education was to prepare students for specific careers, rather than to provide them with the foundation to pursue further education (Kleibard, 1999). Following the Smith-Hughes Act of 1917, which first authorized federal funding for vocational education in public schools, several vocational high school and junior college music programs began to offer popular music performance and composition classes in order to prepare students for music careers (Krikun, 2014).[1]

---

1 This recalls current educational policy and ideology in, for example, the UK, Hong Kong and Australia – see Jones (chapter 27, this volume), Wong (chapter 9, this volume) and Morrow et al. (chapter 26, this volume).

The largest professional organization in the United States currently representing K–12[2] public school music teachers is the National Association for Music Education (NAfME), which was founded in 1907 as the Music Supervisors National Conference and renamed the Music Educators National Conference (MENC) in 1934 before assuming its current name in 2011 (National Association for Music Education, 2015). At the annual meeting of the Music Supervisors National Conference in Detroit in April 1926, Clarence Byrn, head of the music department at Cass Technical High School in Detroit, told the music educators present that "we must train our music students to live in 1926 not 1620" (Byrn, 1926, p. 240). Byrn argued that music students must be given skills that would serve them well in pursuing music professionally, observing that only a small minority of music students would receive employment in the Detroit Symphony Orchestra. In the Cass High School music program, students were taught to perform on musical instruments such as banjos, drums and saxophones, which were shunned by classical musicians but embraced by the popular dance orchestras of the time. Byrn believed that this practical music education would offer his students the ability to make a living as musicians:

> These boys would have been compelled to drop their education entirely at the age of 16 and go into the factories, foundries, shops or laboratories to make their own way, had we not taught them how to make a living in Detroit. If they had spent all their school time studying sonatas, quartets, and symphonys [sic], there would have been no position that they could hold down open to them. But we have taught them how to teach instrumental classes and to conduct school orchestras and bands. We have also taught them how to play good dance music and the result is that some thirty young men have been added to the musical life of our city and they are filling a very definite sphere in the musical evolution of the age. They are being well paid and are happy in their work. The dance work our boys are doing has no evil effect whatever upon their musical training. It broadens and humanizes them instead.
>
> *(pp. 241–242)*

Another important high school popular music program was developed by music educator Samuel Browne at Jefferson High School in Los Angeles, located in close proximity to the Central Avenue district, with its thriving African-American music community. Browne, a Jefferson High alumnus with a graduate degree in music from the University of Southern California, was the first black instructor to be hired at a high school in the Los Angeles school district. Soon after assuming his position as a music teacher at Jefferson in 1936, Browne created a Jazz Band class that included composing, arranging and performing current swing music (Isoardi, 2006, pp. 20–22). Looking back at the formation of the program, Browne remembered, "I didn't bring jazz in; it was already there" (quoted in Isoardi, 2006, p. 20). Alumni from the Jefferson program included

---

2 The term "K–12" refers to the public education system in the US, from Kindergarten (K) to the final year of secondary school or high school (12).

some of the foremost jazz musicians of the time, such as Ernie Andrews, Sonny Criss, Eric Dolphy, Art Farmer, Dexter Gordon, Chico Hamilton and Vi Redd (Snowden, 1987).

Recent historical research has examined the introduction of popular music in the junior colleges of Los Angeles County, beginning in 1924. Junior colleges (now known as community colleges) were public two-year colleges that provided vocational education in a variety of fields, including music. Junior colleges located in the Los Angeles metropolitan area were well-positioned to offer vocational training for musicians interested in pursuing professional careers in the burgeoning film, recording and radio studios of Hollywood. Pasadena Junior College was the first American post-secondary institution to offer a course in popular music – Practical Music Arranging – in 1933, and Long Beach Junior College was the first institution to offer a popular music degree – a two-year vocational Associate's Degree in Modern Music – in 1937 (Krikun, 2014). By 1938, Fred Beidelman, a music professor at San Diego State University, found in a survey of junior colleges in California that "in seven of the colleges giving theory courses, we find several courses in popular music – arranging popular music for ensembles, theater, and dance orchestra, occurring in the bulletins under those names" (Curtis, 1938, p. 147). Junior college music educators continued to discuss the role of popular music at meetings of the Music Educators National Conference in 1938 and 1940 (Krikun, 2008).

Following the United States' entry into World War II in 1941, music educators were hard-pressed to offer rationales for the study of music during wartime. Max Kaplan (1943), the sole faculty member of the music department at Pueblo Junior College in southern Colorado, noted "the dramatic intensity of the war and the crying need it has brought for scientifically and technically trained youth has crowded from the popular mind the abiding necessity for training our young people through the social sciences and the arts" (p. 373). In response to the reversal of priorities engendered by the war, Kaplan challenged music educators to devise a student-centred curriculum inclusive of popular music:

> Somehow, we have refused to pollute our Divine Mission by beginning from the assumption that music is something that permeates every nook and cranny of most of our lives . . . If Johnny came into a harmony class with the object of learning how to arrange for his jazz band or to write popular music, we pulled out our old harmony texts with all their junk-heap of rules and more rules.
> *(1943, p. 375)*

Modern Jazz and the emergence of the dance band curriculum

During the post-war period, as jazz was gradually embraced as a highbrow art form by American critics and institutions, jazz education began to flourish in post-secondary institutions, which eschewed contemporaneous popular musical styles such as pop, folk, country and R&B (Ake, 2002, pp. 112–145; Brennan, 2013, pp. 570–573). The American post-secondary institutions credited by jazz historians for introducing jazz education are the Schillinger House in Boston (now the Berklee College of Music) and the Westlake College of Music in Los Angeles, both established in 1945. The dance band curriculum at North Texas State College and the Commercial Music programme at Los Angeles City College, followed soon after in 1946. Although these programmes can be viewed as early instances of what came to be known as jazz education, I argue that these seminal programmes are better understood as popular music programmes; they were vocational in nature and aimed to prepare post-war American musicians for opportunities as studio and dance band musicians – playing the popular music of the time.

During the 1950s, as jazz education expanded into a number of other institutions, such as Indiana University, and the stage band movement proliferated in K–12 public schools, popular music performance programs grew nationally in public community colleges. Community colleges were at the forefront of programs in music business, music technology and popular music performance and composition during the 1950s and 1960s and influenced the adoption of these subjects in other American higher education institutions (Hays, 1999, pp. 135–138). The place of popular music in American higher education in the early 1960s can be better understood by reviewing John Parker's doctoral dissertation at the University of Kentucky: "American Popular Music: An Emerging Field of Academic Study" (1962). Parker concluded that four popular music styles deserved greater attention by academics: ragtime, jazz, swing and be-bop, as opposed to the "morass of confusion" posed by other popular music styles. Of particular interest in Parker's dissertation is the absence of any discussion of rock 'n' roll. In his estimation, contemporary popular music was banal and, unlike the jazz styles he was promoting as 'popular music', unworthy of academic study:

> At present we are in a slough of despond, only hoping that a new style may be born out of our present degradation. The form of jazz, however, remains, even though in retirement. The question of what happens to it in the future depends upon the motivations of the individual.
>
> *(p. 189)*

"Roll Over Beethoven": American music educators learn to rock

As a result of the social unrest in the US during the 1960s,[3] many American music educators saw the need to reassess the relevancy of music curricula and address the role of previously marginalized groups, such as youth, ethnic minorities and women. According to US music education historians Michael Mark and Charles

---

3 See historian Todd Gitlin's book *The Sixties: Years of Hope, Days of Rage* (1987) for an engaging description of the turbulent social and political movements dividing the United States during the 1960s, including the civil rights movement, the anti-Vietnam War movement and the development of the youth counter-culture.

Gary (2007), the Tanglewood Symposium was "arguably the most important event in recent music education history in regard to professional planning and implementation" (p. 460). Sponsored by the Music Educators National Conference (MENC), a committee made up of representatives from the arts, education, government and business met to discuss the theme of "Music in American Society" in Tanglewood, Massachusetts, from July 23 to August 2, 1967. In the *Tanglewood Declaration*, published in 1968, the committee concluded that

> educators must accept the responsibility for developing opportunities which meet man's individual needs and the needs of a society plagued by the consequences of changing values, alienation, hostility between generations, racial and international tensions and the challenges of a new leisure.
> *(Choate, 1968, p. 139)*

Openly embracing the teaching of popular music, the attendees agreed that

> Music of all periods, styles, forms, and cultures belongs in the curriculum. The musical repertory should be expanded to involve music of our time in its rich variety, including currently popular teenage music and avant-garde music, American folk music, and the music of other cultures.
> *(Choate, 1968, p. 139)*

It is difficult to gauge the impact of the *Tanglewood Declaration* in the years following this affirmation of the role of popular music in school music education. In a recent literature review of popular music in the American public school music curriculum, Dan Isbell (2007) concluded, "There are no existing status reports showing the extent to which or in what capacity popular music is currently being used by public school music teachers" (p. 61). Nevertheless, there are several individual reports of public school popular music programmes, such as the Miami Beach High School Rock Ensemble, founded by music teacher Doug Burris in 1972 (Rock Ensemble, n.d.), and the junior high school popular music programme led by music teacher Dick Thompson (1979) in Ridgewood, New Jersey. Thompson described a multifaceted popular music programmes that included rock music history, popular music production and choral performance. Even though research and documentation of existing popular music programmes have been scarce, American music educators continued to debate the place of popular music in the K–12 music curriculum. David Hebert and Patricia Shehan Campbell (2000) traced the discourse on the role of rock in music education, noting six arguments made by music educators opposed to the inclusion of rock music in the curriculum in the second half of the 20th century:

1   Rock is aesthetically inferior music, if it is music at all;
2   Rock is damaging to youth, both physically and morally;
3   School time should not be expended teaching what is easily acquired in the vernacular;

4   Traditional teacher education has not provided substantial training in rock music;
5   Rock music is rebellious and anti-educational, characteristics that problematize its appropriation by teachers;
6   Effective instructional curriculum for rock music is relatively difficult to acquire in the United States (p. 16).

In the 1970s, several community colleges in the southern and southwestern United States introduced country and bluegrass music into their curricula, including the Hank Thompson School of Country Music at Claremore Junior College (now Rogers State University) in Oklahoma and the Commercial Music program at South Plains College in Levelland, Texas. Established in 1975, the Country and Bluegrass Music Program at South Plains College offered a two-year degree in Commercial Music. By 1997, the programme grew to include twenty-five faculty members, over 700 students and a dedicated building with recording and broadcasting facilities. In an interview with the *New York Times*, the founder of the program, bluegrass musician John Hartin, observed that "We specialize in the forms of American music that most educational institutions haven't been interested in: bluegrass, Southern gospel, blues, old-time country, Western swing" (Jennings, 1997, p. 26). In addition to country and bluegrass, students at South Plains studied other popular music genres, including rhythm and blues, Tejano, gospel, rock and jazz (Jennings, 1997, p. 26).

With Los Angeles City College serving as a model, many community colleges in California developed vocational programmes in recording technology, music business, musical instrument repair, songwriting and music performance, including popular music courses in the curriculum. Although each programme differs in course offerings and requirements, they are grouped statewide under the umbrella of "Commercial Music". Presently, at least 17 community colleges in California offer commercial music performance degrees and certificates (California Community Colleges, 2015).

For-profit popular music colleges, such as the Guitar Institute of Technology (now known as Musicians Institute) in Los Angeles, were founded in the late 1970s and continue their expansion globally. According to its website, the Guitar Institute of Technology "was the only school of its kind at the time to offer a practical, experience-based education in contemporary music" (Musicians Institute, 2015). Another for-profit college, the McNally Smith College of Music in St. Paul, Minnesota, was founded in 1985 as Musictech College and offers undergraduate and graduate degrees in popular music performance and composition, including a diploma in Hip-Hop Studies (McNally Smith College, 2015).

"Something's happening here!": Popular music education in the United States in the 21st century

The 21st century has seen unprecedented growth in the field of popular music education in the US, expanding in every teaching context from internet delivery to community music schools and private music studios, to all levels of public and private education (Powell, Krikun & Pignato, 2015; Rodriguez, 2012). Since its founding in 1998, the for-profit after-school music program School of Rock has grown to include over 150 franchised schools across the US, and has opened branches in Chile, Mexico, Brazil, Canada and the Philippines (School of Rock, n.d.). A number of non-profit organizations have collaborated with school districts and higher education institutions to promote popular music in K–12 schools. The largest of these organizations, Little Kids Rock, was founded by elementary school music teacher David Wish in 2002. Offering its Modern Band Curriculum to public schools, Little Kids Rock has donated musical instruments, trained music teachers in popular music pedagogy and served over 400,000 students across the US (Little Kids Rock, 2015).

Recent years have seen a growing number of American colleges and universities include popular music in their music curricula. In 2009, the Thornton School of Music at the University of Southern California became the first university school of music in the US to offer a Bachelor of Music degree in Popular Music Performance. In an interview with the *Los Angeles Times*, Robert Cutietta, dean of the USC Thornton School of Music, explained: "I've been in higher education for 20-some years, and it's been talked about, but everyone has been afraid to do it. No one wanted to be first" (Lewis, 2008). In 2010, the founding director of the USC popular music program, Chris Sampson, became the chair for a new organization devoted to popular music education, the Association for Popular Music Education (APME), consisting of a group of 10 American higher education institutions with popular music performance programs: Belmont University, Berklee College of Music, Catawba College, Greenville College, McNally Smith College of Music, New York University Tisch School of the Arts, the Contemporary Music Center, the University of Colorado at Denver, the University of Southern California Thornton School of Music and the University of Miami Frost School of Music. APME sponsors annual national conferences for popular music education practitioners and researchers, and inaugurated regional events in Los Angeles and New York in 2015. The conferences and events have been attended by international practitioners and researchers from all levels of music education, including higher education, K–12 and community music schools (Association for Popular Music Education, 2015).

Although music educators in the United States continue to debate the place of popular music in formal music education (Hebert, 2011; Humphreys, 2004, 2013; Krikun, 2009; Mantie, 2013), significant developments in popular music education research have been spurred by two landmark publications: British music education researcher Lucy Green's *How Popular Musicians Learn* (2002) and the collection of essays included in *Bridging the Gap*, edited by Carlos Xavier Rodriguez (2004), which included chapters by leading scholars in popular music education from the United States, Canada, Great Britain and Australia sharing philosophical, historical and practical perspectives on popular music education. Subsequently, a number of music education research conferences in the US have been dedicated to popular music education, such as the Suncoast Music Education Research Symposium on

Popular Music Pedagogy held at the University of South Florida in February 2011, and the Ann Arbor Symposium IV: Teaching and Learning Popular Music, held at the University of Michigan in November 2015. In addition, popular music museums, such as the Rock and Roll Hall of Fame in Cleveland, the Experience Music Project in Seattle, the Stax Museum of American Soul Music in Memphis and the Grammy Museum in Los Angeles, have all established education departments and offer programmes for teachers and students. Susan Oehler and Jason Hanley (2008) of the Rock and Roll Hall of Fame Department of Education edited a special issue of the *Journal of Popular Music Studies* on popular music pedagogy, including contributions from a diversity of popular music scholars and from teachers in the fields of music education, ethnomusicology and popular music studies.

Further research

In this chapter, I have endeavoured to present an overview of the history of educational programmes dedicated to the performance and composition of popular music in the US. Still, there remains a huge gap in the literature regarding the history of popular music education practices as well as the history and proliferation of popular music programmes across the US. Due to the brevity of my overview, I have had to leave out important ancillary areas of interest to popular music education, including programs in music business, music technology, ethnomusicology, musicology, music theory and popular music studies – subdisciplines that may or may not include popular music performance and composition as parts of their program requirements. Nevertheless, my hope is that this brief survey will lead to a stronger emphasis on historical research in popular music education, providing a glimpse into a storied past that will help pave the way to an exciting future.

References

Ake, D. (2002). *Jazz cultures*. Berkeley, CA: University of California Press.
Association for Popular Music Education. (2015). About. Retrieved from: http://popular musiceducation.org [Accessed 1 June 2015].
Brennan, M. (2013). "Nobody likes rock and roll but the public": Down Beat, genre boundaries and the dismissal of rock and roll by jazz critics. *Popular Music and Society*, *36*(5), 559–577.
Byrn, C. (1926). A vocational music course in the high schools. *Journal of Proceedings of the Nineteenth Annual Meeting of the Music Supervisors National Conference*, 238–247.
California Community Colleges. (2015). CCC curriculum inventory [Data Set]. Retrieved from: http://curriculum.cccco.edu [Accessed 4 May 2015].
Choate, R.A. (1968). *Music in American society: Documentary report of the Tanglewood Symposium*. Washington: Music Educators National Conference.
Crawford, R. (2003). *America's musical life: A history*. New York: W.W. Norton.
Curtis, L.W. (1938). Junior college music for general and special students. *M.E.N.C. Yearbook 1938*, 142–153.
Dobson, G.C. (1890). *Geo. C. Dobson's world's banjo guide*. Boston: White Smith Music.
Gitlin, T. (1987). *The sixties: Years of hope, days of rage*. New York: Bantam.

Green, L. (2002). *How popular musicians learn: A way ahead for music education.* Burlington, VT: Ashgate.
Hamm, C. (1983). *Yesterdays: Popular song in America.* New York: W. W. Norton.
Harney, B. & Northrup, T.H. (1897). *Ben Harney's rag time instructor.* Chicago: S. Bloom.
Harris, C.K. (1906). *How to write a popular song.* New York: Self-published.
Harris, C.K. (1926). *After the ball: Forty years of melody.* New York: Frank-Maurice.
Hays, T.O. (1999). The music department in higher education: History, connections, and conflicts, 1865–1998 (Unpublished doctoral dissertation). Loyola University, Chicago.
Hebert, D.G. (2011). Originality and institutionalization: Factors engendering resistance to popular music pedagogy in the U.S.A. *Music Education Research International, 5,* 12–21.
Hebert, D.G. & Campbell, P.S. (2000). Rock music in American schools: Positions and practices since the 1960s. *International Journal of Music Education, 36,* 14–22.
Humphreys, J.T. (2004). Popular music in the American schools: What history tells us about the present and the future. In C.X. Rodriguez (Ed.), *Bridging the gap: Popular music and music education* (pp. 91–105). Reston, VA: MENC.
Humphreys, J.T. (2013). Relationships between popular music and democracy: Implications for popular music pedagogy. *Music Education Research International, 6,* 1–14.
Isbell, D. (2007). Popular music and the public school music curriculum. *UPDATE Fall-Winter 2007,* 53–63.
Isoardi, S.L. (2006). *The dark tree: Jazz and community arts in Los Angeles.* Berkeley: University of California Press.
Jasen, D.A. & Jones, G. (2000). *That American rag: The story of ragtime from coast to coast.* New York: Schirmer.
Jennings, D.A. (1997, January 5). The Julliard of bluegrass music. *New York Times,* EL25–28.
Joplin, S. (1908). *School of ragtime: Six exercises for piano.* New York: Self-published.
Kaplan, M. (1943). "Beethoven or a bottle of beer?" *Junior College Journal, 13,* 373–375.
Kennedy, G.W. (n.d.). Jazz education. In B. Kernfeld (Ed.), *The New Grove Dictionary of Jazz,* 2nd ed. Retrieved from: *Grove Music Online*: http://www.oxfordmusiconline.com/subscriber/article/grove/music/J602300.
Kleibard, H.M. (1999). *Schooled to work: Vocationalism and the American curriculum, 1876–1946.* New York: Teachers College Press.
Krikun, A. (2008). Popular music and jazz in the American junior college music curriculum during the Swing Era (1935–1945). *Journal of Historical Research in Music Education, 30*(1), 39–49.
Krikun, A. (2009). Mixing Memphis soul into the community college curriculum stew. *Journal of Popular Music Studies, 21*(1), 76–89.
Krikun, A. (2014). Teaching the "people's music" at the "people's college": A historical study of American popular music in the junior/community college curriculum, 1924–1955 (Doctoral dissertation). Retrieved from: ProQuest Digital Dissertations database. (Publication No. 3624557).
Levine, L.W. (1988). *Highbrow/Lowbrow: The emergence of cultural hierarchy in America.* Cambridge, MA: Harvard University Press.
Lewis, R. (2008, October 22). USC acts by popular demand. *Los Angeles Times,* E1.
Little Kids Rock. (2015). What we do | Little Kids Rock. Retrieved from: http://www.littlekidsrock.org/about/what-we-do/ [Accessed 1 May 2015].
Mantie, R. (2013). A comparison of "popular music pedagogy" discourses. *Journal of Research in Music Education, 61*(3), 334–352.
Mark, M.L. & Gary, C.L. (2007). *A history of American music education* (3rd ed.). Lanham, MD: Rowman & Littlefield.

McLucas, A.D. (2010). *The musical ear: Oral tradition in the USA*. Burlington, VT: Ashgate.

McNally Smith College of Music. (2015). Hip hop music school and studies | McNally Smith College of Music. Retrieved from: http://www.mcnallysmith.edu/diplomas/hip-hop-studies [Accessed 4 May 2015].

Musicians Institute. (2015). History of MI. Retrieved from: http://mi.edu/about-mi/history/ [Accessed 3 April 2015].

National Association for Music Education. (2015). About us. Retrieved from: http://www.nafme.org/about/ [Accessed 4 April 2015].

Oehler, S. & Hanley, J. (2008). Perspectives of popular music pedagogy in practice. *Journal of Popular Music Studies*, 21(1), 2–19.

Parker, J.W. (1962). American popular music: An emerging field of academic study (Doctoral dissertation). Retrieved from: ProQuest Digital Dissertations database. (Publication No. 6920429).

Powell, B., Krikun, A., & Pignato, J. (2015). "Something's happening here!": Popular music education in the United States. *IASPM@Journal*, 5(1). 4–22.

Prouty, K. (2012). *Knowing jazz: Community, pedagogy, and canon in the information age*. Jackson: University Press of Mississippi.

Rock Ensemble. (n.d.). About. Retrieved from: http://www.rockensemble.com/about/ [Accessed 2 March 2015].

Rodriguez, C.X. (2004). Popular music in music education: Toward a new conception of musicality. In C.X. Rodriguez (Ed.), *Bridging the gap: Popular music and music education* (pp. 13–27). Reston, VA: MENC.

Rodriguez, C.X. (2012). Popular music ensembles. In G.E. McPherson & G.F. Welch (Eds.), *The Oxford handbook of music education, Volume 1* (pp. 783–906). New York: Oxford University Press.

School of Rock. (n.d.). FAQ| School of Rock Franchising. Retrieved from: http://franchising.schoolofrock.com/faqs [Accessed 4 March 2015].

Snowden, D. (1987, September 17). Fringe festival: Tribute to a swinging teacher. *Los Angeles Times*, 4.

Thompson, D. (1979). Plugging into pop at the junior high level. *Music Educators Journal*, 66(4), 54–59.

Van der Merwe, P. (1989). *The origins of the popular style: The antecedents of twentieth-century popular music*. Oxford: Clarendon.

Worthy, M.D. (2011). Jazz education. Retrieved from: *Grove Music Online*: http://www.oxfordmusiconline.com/subscriber/article/grove/music/A2093226 [Accessed 4 May 2015].

5

Navigating the space between spaces

Curricular change in music teacher education in the United States

David A. Williams and Clint Randles

Introduction

Music was introduced into the secondary, and later the primary, schools of the United States beginning in the late 1800s, and by 1920 had become well-established in many areas of the country. By the 1960s the vast majority of schools covering grades kindergarten through twelfth grades included music in their curricula. Most elementary level schools (roughly grades kindergarten through fifth or sixth grade) had mandated 'general' music where students would sing, play on simple instruments and learn music notation. Many lessons included movement activities and dance. Music was commonly a required subject for students at the elementary grades, but often students would only have music instruction once or twice per week. Some elementary schools also included lessons on orchestral instruments and voice and would provide opportunities for students to participate in ensemble classes. Music offerings in secondary schools (generally grades six and above) primarily consisted of teacher-centred performing ensembles of concert bands, choirs and orchestras, which rehearsed and performed music based on the Western European classical music tradition. Modeling the classical orchestra, the school music teacher would select music, schedule concerts and make most, if not all, the musical decisions for the students. The students' role was to develop performing techniques, practice music and bring the music teacher's musical ideas to fruition. Music education at the secondary level was predominately offered in electives – not compulsory, as at the elementary level – in which students could choose, or not choose, to participate (Mark & Gary, 2007).

By the middle of the 20th century, music teacher training was established in colleges and universities across the country. Entire degree programmes devoted to educating music teachers ('pre-service teachers' while training) were developed and implemented. With very few exceptions, these degree programmes looked very similar to one another and broke down into four specific areas:

1. a core of music classes including music history, written music theory, aural skills, private instruction on a principal instrument and music ensembles (concert bands, choirs and orchestras);
2. music education courses, including methods of teaching instrumental and vocal music, and various techniques courses so that pre-service teachers could gain experience with a wide range of orchestral instruments, piano and voice. The music education sequence normally concluded with a semester-long experience assigned to in-service music teachers in schools so they could practice teaching under direct supervision;
3. general education courses that often included child and adolescent psychology and sociology courses as well as specific courses required by state legislators;
4. general requirements required by individual colleges and universities for all students.

By the middle of the 20th century, a self-perpetuating structure was in place to sustain this system of music-making in schools.

Little has changed, even as we move further into the 21st century. School music programmes in the US look very much today as they have for the past 100 years. Certainly some changes have occurred. Marching bands were slowly established, and jazz music classes became accepted by the profession. Some creative activities, such as composition and improvisation, made their way into music classrooms, especially after the National Music Content Standards were established in 1994,[1] and more recently there have been aspects of digital music technology added to some school music programmes. Yet, at its core, especially in secondary school music classrooms, making music in large, teacher-centred ensembles and in the classical orchestra tradition still dominates. (For discussion of the 20th-century trajectory of popular music education in the United States, see Krikun, chapter 4, this volume.)

While music-making in schools in the early 1900s looked, and sounded, very much like the music-making of the surrounding prevalent mainstream US culture at the time, the way music is practised in schools today has very little to do with music practices outside schools, especially in youth culture. This chapter provides an example of the first wave of curricular changes in the undergraduate music education programme at the University of South Florida, in Tampa, Florida. Curricular expansion was undertaken in this undergraduate programme, in part to provide pre-service teachers with experiences of making popular music as a part of their pre-service music teacher education; these changes were made to help prepare pre-service music teachers to offer and teach classes that do not yet exist

---

1. See http://www.musicstandfoundation.org/images/National_Standards_-_Music_Education.pdf for the 1994 National Music Content Standards. Note that these were recently (2014) replaced by the National Core Music Standards (http://www.nationalartsstandards.org).

widely in K–12 schools in the United States – classes that could go a long way in helping the music education profession become more germane to the society around it, classes that might help music education discover an audience among the vast majority of school-age students that currently find little relevance in school music offerings (Wright, 2008) and classes that could help students develop lifelong music-making skills.

Curricular change in the United States

Calls for change in music education practice in the United States had certainly begun by the mid-1960s, as exemplified by the Yale Seminar[2] and the Tanglewood Symposium.[3] One interest, as recognized by attendees from both these meetings, was the need to broaden school music repertory to include popular musical styles. However, little movement towards the incorporation of serious popular music study has occurred in the United States.

Over the last several years, however, we have witnessed an increase of interest in popular music education, both from within and outside the music teaching profession. The non-profit organization Little Kids Rock was founded in 2002 and has since trained music teachers in almost 2000 schools across the country (see Powell & Burstein, chapter 20, this volume). Also in 2002, the Music Educators National Conference (now the National Association for Music Education) published *The Guide to Teaching with Popular Music* and followed this up with *Bridging the Gap: Popular Music and Music Education* (Rodriguez, 2004).[4] The Association for Popular Music Education was formed in 2010.[5] Guided by the leadership of the Center for Music Education Research at the University of South Florida, the 2011 Suncoast Music Education Research Symposium's (SMERS) theme was 'Popular Music Pedagogy'. Attendees at this symposium presented on topics related to how popular music was being included in primary and secondary music programmes and in what ways music education students in colleges were being exposed to popular music practices and pedagogies.[6]

---

2 The Yale Seminar on Music Education was held at Yale University in 1963. Participants included 31 musicians, scholars and teachers who gathered to consider the problems facing music education and to propose possible solutions.
3 Not long after the Yale Seminar, the Tanglewood Symposium was held in an effort to improve music education and to make school music study more useful to the general society. This two-week symposium was held at the Tanglewood Music Center in Tanglewood, Massachusetts.
4 *The Guide to Teaching with Popular Music* is a collection of six lesson plans to help students be able to meet the (then) nine National Standards for Music Education through studying popular music. Each lesson cites objectives, lists materials needed and gives step-by-step procedures for classroom implementation.
5 To learn more about The Association for Popular Music Education, see http://www.popularmusiceducation.org
6 To see current work from the Center for Music Education Research at USF, go to http://cmer.arts.usf.edu/content/templates/?a=901&z=137

Setting the stage for change: USF music education

Leading up to the 2011 SMERS, the music education faculty (those who specifically prepare music education students for music teaching careers in schools) at the University of South Florida (USF) embarked on some significant changes to the undergraduate music education programme. Beginning in 2007, the music education faculty at USF spent the better part of two years discussing, considering and planning curricular change. There were two realities that guided our decision-making and influenced every decision made. First was the fact that no additional credit hours could be added to the music education degree programme without the elimination of the same number of credit hours from current offerings. Music education degree programmes in the United States are often completely full with required coursework, with very few, if any, elective hours. Increasingly, these programs are capped as to the total number of credits that can be required so that it is not possible simply to add new courses.

The second issue was that any changes to the music education degree programme would have to be approved by a vote of all School of Music faculty, which, as Greher (2008) suggests, is a daunting task:

> And perhaps the biggest hurdle for us may be that we may also need to push the envelope and encourage our music colleagues at our institutions of higher learning to accept that non-traditional music and musicians have a place in our programs lest we all be participants in our own extinction.
>
> (p. 3)

The majority of these faculty are in traditional performance fields that tend to be quite conservative and resistant to change, especially any change that may be perceived as threatening to aspects of traditional (Western classical) performance. The real issue here had to do with definitions of musicianship. As normally practised by music teachers in educational institutions in the United States, musicianship is seen as having a solitary definition (Bartel, 2004; Randles, 2013b; Tobias, 2013; Williams, 2007). To be considered 'musical' one must be an expert performer on an orchestral instrument, piano or voice and perform the significant works composed by masters on one's instrument. In support of this, a musician is one who reads and writes musical notation, interprets 18th- and 19th-century counterpoint and understands the classical music lineage from plainsong to neo-classicism and polystylism. Other involvements with music are not considered as honourable and do not lead to the same or equivalent lofty level of musical understanding or musicianship.

As we considered possibilities of curricular change, we began to understand that we were really interested in more than just curriculum. We recognized that the most important issue for our students would be understanding and practising different pedagogical models – pedagogies that could be used with various curricula. So our work took on two parts: (1) to develop a new curriculum that would allow students to become competent and confident working within an expanded definition of musicianship; and (2) to situate a good deal of this curriculum in pedagogical models that were significantly different from the traditional US large ensemble model mentioned above.

Much of our thinking about pedagogy was guided by three sources. First was the work of Lucy Green (2008) concerning informal learning processes in music. Second was material on constructivist learning theories and cognitive psychology, especially from Jerome Bruner (1977), John Dewey (1998) and Jean Piaget (1970); most important here was the concept of learner-centred pedagogical techniques and the idea that students learn best when they do the work they really are interested in doing. Third, we looked to previous research involving established practices in other countries. For example, Byrne and Sheridan (2000) report on three decades of change in Scottish school music practice, where the inclusion of a wider range of instruments and musical styles with alternative teaching methods has resulted in a marked upturn in the numbers of students studying music. Folkestad (2006) studied different aspects of learning (including the situation, learning style, ownership and intentionality) in societies outside Western cultures, and Price (2005, 2006) details the Musical Futures project in the United Kingdom which, beginning in 2003, set out to devise new and imaginative ways of engaging young people in school music activities (D'Amore & Smith, 2016).

Our interest was to provide students – pre-service music teachers – with models and ongoing opportunities to practise with those models. We wanted to include aspects of informal and learner-centred teaching that involved high degrees of student autonomy over music choice and instruments and authentic learning and performance practices taken from popular and vernacular musicians in the United States and around the world, such as aural copying of songs and aural-based compositional practices in small groups.

The music education faculty were interested in opening our students' eyes to new possibilities for music education programmes and providing them with repeated opportunities to practise with pedagogical models involving electronic and digital technologies, broader concepts of musicianship and different pedagogical approaches. It is important to note that our intent was not to *replace* traditional methods and pedagogies, but instead to augment them with new experiences and opportunities for our students (and, therefore, for their students). While much has been written recently concerning the possibility that some of our traditional methods might be outdated (Bartel, 2004; Kratus, 2007; Randles & Muhonen, 2015; Randles & Smith, 2012; Williams, 2011), we were not yet at a point where we were ready to dismiss them all together.

Our initial proposal to the School of Music faculty began with the following 'background' information:

> *Through a several decades-long process examining the status and aims of music education in the schools, we realize that we must enact changes in our undergraduate curriculum to address the changing needs for musical understanding in public school students in the United States. We acknowledge that music-making has changed more dramatically*

than our prevailing instructional methods reflect. Recent research suggests approximately 90% of students presently do not participate in secondary school music programs.

We continue to be, first and foremost, concerned with achieving the highest levels of musicality, and in order to build on that which is well-represented in our current curriculum we accept that we must focus on increasing skills, knowledge and understanding in the following three areas:

- *Composition and improvisation abilities, as well as requisite aural skills*
- *World musics and the American music traditions*
- *Technologies and its uses in current music-making and music-teaching models*

These areas have been identified by NASM as well as our professional organization, Music Educators National Conference, as areas in which teacher education programs can be improved and expanded. We intend to join others in leading change in our profession. Thus, we propose changes to our curriculum, which our music education faculty has spent over a year refining.

This last paragraph was particularly significant because NASM (the National Association of Schools of Music) serves as an accrediting agency for Schools of Music in the US and has a remarkable influence over curriculum. The Music Educators National Conference (currently the National Association for Music Education) produced the aforementioned set of National Standards for K–12 music classes. Both these organizations recognized composition, improvisation, world and popular musics and digital technologies as being important areas for music teacher education programmes. Our most significant curricular change was the addition of two semesters of a methods course, *Progressive Music Education Methods*, and two semesters of a related ensemble we ended up naming *Creative Performance Chamber Ensemble*. Together, these courses amount to a sequence of methods courses each with a corresponding ensemble. Students are currently required to take a methods course concurrently with an ensemble class.

A new faculty line

I (Clint Randles) was hired in 2010 as an Assistant Professor of Music Education at the University of South Florida to prepare music teachers to teach classes in primary and secondary school that do not yet exist in most areas of the United States. I assumed the "space between spaces" (Randles et al., 2015), rather than the job of a typical instrumental, choral or general music teacher educator. Having just left a nine-year career as a secondary instrumental and primary-age general music teacher in the Midwest region of the US, I had been accustomed to the strong presence of the American wind band as a curricular offering in schools. As a doctoral student in music education at Michigan State University, I had been conceiving of a proliferation of all manner of changes in the curricular offerings of school music – everything from the inclusion of rock bands and technology-infused musical performance to bands and orchestras whose members composed as a regular, ordinary part of their school music experience. As I started my job at USF I did not realize that the rock band and technology in music performance areas of the change spectrum were going to be implementable as fully as they have been, in a relatively short period of time.

There was great pressure on me as I assumed this new faculty position. From day one I felt as if I had a target on my back, one at which many of the traditional music faculty might like to take aim. Even before I started teaching anything at USF, I felt as though many of the faculty members with whom I would be working thought that my position there was not necessary – a waste of a faculty line that could have been used to hire a new viola professor (which would have been a much better use of valuable resources, in their approximation). I must say here that it was a terrible feeling, not being wholly accepted by the school of music. Could I do anything to change their perceptions? What should I make of their perceptions? If they did not like the idea of electric guitars being in the building, did it matter how well I did my job? Whose opinions should I care about? I saw early on that I could not ever win with them. And so, with this fear and uncertainty, I went to work on something new in music teacher education, something that my colleagues had worked laboriously on before I had arrived, something that I believed in, something that could hopefully be beneficial to all those who prepare music teachers in the United States.

Progressive methods and creative performance chamber ensemble

My duties at USF now include teaching *Progressive Methods* (PM), a two-semester course sequence taken consecutively with *Creative Performance Chamber Ensemble* (CPCE), as mentioned above. PM is a class about putting pedagogical ideas surrounding change in school music education curricula on the table for students, while CPCE is a 'lab' class where students have the chance to exercise their musicianship in some of the under-represented areas in US formal music education. Prior to taking the *Progressive Methods* class sequence, all music education students must take an additional class, *Foundations of Music Education*, in which they are encouraged to see that while the world of music is very big, the world of normative US school music education represents only a small portion of it. *Progressive Methods* is where we introduce big, contemporary ideas in music education to students, including informal music-making practices (Green, 2002, 2008), presentational *vs* participatory music-making (see Table 5.1) (Turino, 2008) and improvisational *vs* ritualized performance (see Table 5.2) (Sawyer, 2012). All of these ways that humans interact with music are valuable to some sector of society. It stands to reason that if teachers of music in the schools would like to reach more of the population via/through the power of music, then these ways of being musical should be explored for the impact that they might have on future generations of (music) students. With these topics in mind, PM has been a place for us to incorporate both (1) adaptive change – doing things that we have always done, i.e. band, choir and orchestra, better and more creatively, perhaps (Randles & Stringham,

Table 5.1 Two different kinds of live performance – participatory and presentational

	Participatory	Presentational
Goal	Maximum sonic, kinesic participation of all present	Preparation of music for maximum interest for others
Conception	Music-making as social intercourse and activity among face-to-face participants; emphasis on the *doing* among all present	Music is an activity and object created/presented by one group (musicians) for another group (audience) in face-to-face situations; emphasis on the doing (artists) and listening (audience)
Rules/ Mediation	Little or no artist-audience distinction, only participants and potential participants; few or no physical barriers or markers distinguishing participants although activities (singing, dancing, playing instruments) can vary among participants	Clear artist-audience distinctions; artists and audience mediated by physical markers such as stages, lights, mics, video cameras and screens (e.g. in stadium concerts) within face-to-face situation
Time and Attention	Focus is inward among participants, is on the act of doing and is in the moment; sound-motion exists only in the moment	Focus for musicians is on themselves, the audience and the sound; for the audience is on the musicians and the sound, attention is in the moment, sound-motion exists only in the moment
Continua	less physical/semiotic separation among actors; less planning/control of musical sound; more attention to music as a social activity; less attention to music as art object; quality of social interaction is central to the conception of 'music' and 'good music'; sound-motion in the moment; immediate feedback as to how one is doing; sound is ephemeral; social focus is inward among participants	

Note: This table is taken directly from *Music as Social Life* (Turino, 2008, p. 90) and is used by permission of Thomas Turino

Table 5.2 Nine contrasting dimensions of ritualized and improvised performance

Ritualized	Improvisational	
Ossification	Revivalism	Ossified performances lose semantic meaning and are primarily a formal structure.
Low creative Involvement	High creative involvement	The degree of creative involvement of the performer
Indexically reflexive	Indexically entailing	The degree to which the performer's actions have implications for the next actions to follow
Narrow genre definition	Broad genre definition	If 'broad', then many different performances qualify as being of that type.
Large ready-mades	Small ready-mades	Ready-mades are the formulaic phrases and bits that all performers memorize.
Low audience involvement	High audience involvement	In many improvised genres, the boundary between performer and audience is fluid.
Resistant to novelty	Receptive to novelty	Improvised genres undergo more rapid historical change.
Changes long-lasting	Changes short-lived	But those changes don't stay in place very long
High cultural valuation	Low valuation	More highly valued genres are more ritualized on all of the above dimensions.

Note: This table is taken from *Explaining Creativity* (Sawyer, 2012)

2013), and (2) innovative change – incorporating new technologies, pedagogies and broad conceptions of musicality, including, for example, iPad musicianship (Randles, 2013a, 2013b; Williams, 2014).

Curriculum area 1: Performance

One of the first major curriculum areas that students in CPCE engage with is musical performance. They take part in three performances per semester, which take place outside all over the USF campus, wherever there are people (see Figure 5.1). In much the same way as the musicians in Green's (2008) book progress, students begin by working on arrangements of cover songs and then work their way to creating original songs, soundtracks and multimedia presentations. For many, this proves to be a difficult task, as they have never been asked to do such a thing before in their musical lives, nor have they sought to do it for fun at home in their spare time; most are performers from notation only on instruments that are

Navigating the space between spaces

Figure 5.1 CPCE performance (Fall 2014). Music education students at the University of South Florida perform a song by the band Tenacious D for students on the Tampa, Florida, campus. Among this group's members, four are percussion students and one is a saxophone student

found in traditional bands or orchestras. Over the past five years that I have been a part of the music education programme at USF, I have seen a shift from a culture of students being overall sceptical about change in music education to a culture of students being mostly welcoming to the idea of widespread change and expansion of curricular offerings in music programmes.

Curriculum area 2: Recording

As Turino (2008) details in his work, making recordings is one of the main ways that humans experience music. Thibeault (2015) explains how humanity has moved from what he calls a performance era to a recording era, and to a new media era. Each new era is additive, meaning that previous eras do not disappear; rather, they are added to as we engage with music in more ways. In CPCE, students must record all of the songs that they perform in public, taking a *Studio Audio Art* approach, to borrow from Turino (2008; see Figure 5.2). They multi-track record and layer their music in ways that might not even be possible in live performance, i.e. each player performing on multiple instruments while performing multiple vocal parts. Students are given time to record their music while my teaching assistants and I model what a teacher's role can be in such an environment – like a music producer (Randles, 2012). The role of a music teacher functioning as a producer is to bring out what is best in students, elements and attributes that are

55

Figure 5.2 CPCE recording as a part of class (Fall 2014). Music education students at the University of South Florida record a song by Katy Perry while four other groups record their music. A mixer, computer and headphone hub allow up to six groups to record and perform together at the same time in one room. While some might regard this practice as being inauthentic (Green, 2002) to ways that popular music is made in the 'real world', given the organization of school music spaces and the demands of teachers to limit sounds heard in adjacent rooms, this configuration makes practical sense

often already present (if hidden) to some extent, things that students have perhaps been longing to express.

Little Kids Rock and the Modern Band movement

A partnership between USF and national non-profit US organization Little Kids Rock (LKR) has been developing for more than a decade. LKR provides teacher training and instruments to schools along with pedagogical materials for students to learn, perform and create popular music (Powell & Burstein, chapter 20, this volume). Melanie Faulkner, the music supervisor for Hillsborough County (Florida) was one of the first music supervisors in the United States to adopt the programme as a part of the curricular offerings of the school district, which is currently the eighth largest in the country. Faulkner was a recent graduate of USF's Masters in Music Education programme when she instigated this partnership with LKR. Founder and CEO of LKR, David Wish, cites Faulkner's early adoption of the programme and ethos as being vital to the early spread and burgeoning success of LKR – 2,000 teachers and 187,000 students in 30 US cities (Wish, July 31, 2014).

Moving forward

Change in the music education programme at USF has occurred as a result of the diplomacy of a small group of music education faculty members acting on the vision of countless curriculum reformers in the field over the past several decades. By creating space for my (Clint Randles') position, having faith that I could work through the trials inherent to not being wanted or valued within a traditional school of music setting, and now seeing the success of the series of classes that I have helped pioneer, they (we) have forged a path for other institutions that might be similarly poised to navigate the space between spaces to follow. This chapter has been our sharing of a story of how popular music education – and, more broadly, adaptation and innovation in music education pedagogical practice (Randles, 2013b) – was added to the music teacher education programme of one institution in the US.

We recognize that our situation in the US is not reflected around the world. We are aware that the success of the Musical Futures project in the UK, Singapore, Canada, Brazil and elsewhere (D'Amore & Smith, 2016), the co-habitation of Western Art music with popular music at places of higher learning like the Sibelius Academy in Finland (Randles & Muhonen, 2015), and the prevalence of creative musical offerings in places like Brisbane, Australia, are extant examples of what we are trying to accomplish in the US. We have gathered much inspiration from colleagues involved in this work while undergoing the change that we have described in this chapter, and we are currently seeking further partnerships with our friends around the globe as we look to implement the next phases of change.

Popular music education is simply one component of a much larger and more nuanced movement that is necessary in schools of music all across the US. Creative thinking with music on the part of students, in all musical offerings (including theory and history, among a host of other areas), is the biggest shortcoming of the wider music education profession currently. In all aspects of music instruction, space and a higher place of honour for composition, improvisation and creative artistry must be given. Entrepreneurship – a staple of what has propelled the US forward over its history – has somehow been lost in trying to prepare all students of music, everywhere, in the same way. The idea of musicianship being much bigger than has been traditionally portrayed in school music education needs to be thoroughly explored and, more importantly, given room to grow and live in practice in the work of pioneer music teacher educators (Kaschub & Smith, 2014), so that future students of music can benefit from different ways of thinking and doing.

The Music Education faculty at USF is committed to providing musically and pedagogically rich experiences for pre-service music teachers, preparing them to expand primary and secondary curricular offerings in the US. We will continue to think and rethink, plan and re-plan, and implement meaningful change in our programmes at the undergraduate level as we seek to lead the profession by example. Not *all* change is possible *everywhere*. Context matters. However, relevant change that incorporates participatory music-making (Turino, 2008), informal music learning (Green, 2002, 2008) and improvisatory music-making (Sawyer, 2012) in the music curriculum can be achieved with careful planning and diplomacy. We are certain that there are others out there who think as we do. Future students of school music will reap the rich rewards of our and others' continued efforts in this area.

References

Bartel, L.R. (2004). *Questioning the music education paradigm*. Toronto: Canadian Music Educators' Association.

Bruner, J. (1977). *The process of education*. Cambridge, MA: Harvard University Press.

Byrne, C. & Sheridan, M. (2000). The long and winding road: The story of rock music in Scottish schools. *International Journal of Music Education, 36*, 46–58.

D'Amore, A. & Smith, G.D. (2016). Aspiring to music making as leisure through the Musical Futures classroom. In R. Mantie & G.D. Smith (Eds.), *The Oxford handbook of music making and leisure* (pp. 61–80). New York, NY: Oxford University Press.

Dewey, J. (1998). *Experience and education* (60th anniversary ed.). Indianapolis: IN: Kappa Delta Pi.

Finney, J. & Philpott, C. (2010). Informal learning and meta-pedagogy in initial teacher education in England. *British Journal of Music Education, 27*, 7–19.

Folkestad, G. (2006). Formal and informal learning situations or practices versus formal and informal ways of hearing. *British Journal of Music Education, 23*, 135–145.

Georgii-Hemming, E. & Westvall, M. (2010). Music education – a personal matter? Examining the current discourses of music education in Sweden. *British Journal of Music Education, 27*, 21–33.

Green, L. (2002). *How popular musicians learn: A way ahead for music education*. Farnham: Ashgate.

Green, L. (2008). *Music, informal learning and the school: A new classroom pedagogy*. Farnham: Ashgate.

Greher, G.R. (2008). Response to the panel: Dimensions and tensions of disconnect in music teacher preparation. *Visions of Research in Music Education, 12*, 1–3.

Hebert, D. (2009). Musicianship, musical identity, and meaning as embodied practice. In T.A. Regelski & J.T. Gates (Eds.), *Music education for changing times: Guiding visions for practice; landscapes: The arts, aesthetics, and education*, Volume 7. New York: Springer.

Karlsen, S. (2010). BoomTown music education and the need for authenticity – Informal learning put into practice in Swedish post-compulsory music education. *British Journal of Music Education, 27*, 21–33.

Kaschub, M. & Smith, J. (2014). *Promising practices in 21st Century music teacher education*. New York, NY: Oxford University Press.

Kratus, J. (2007). Centennial Series: Music Education at the tipping point. *Music Educators Journal, 94*(2), 42–48.

Mark, M. & Gary, C. (2007). *A history of American music education*. New York, NY: Rowman & Littlefield Publishing.

Piaget, J. (1970). *Science of education and psychology of the child*. New York, NY: Oxford University Press.

Price, D. (2005). *Musical Futures: An emerging vision*. London: Paul Hamlyn Foundation. Retrieved from: www.musicalfutures.org [Accessed 1 June 2015].

Price, D. (2006). *Supporting young musicians and coordinating musical pathways*. London: Paul Hamlyn Foundation.

Randles, C. (2012). Music teacher as writer and producer. *Journal of Aesthetic Education, 46*(3), 36–52.

Randles, C. (2013a). Being an iPadist. *General Music Today, 27*(1), 48–51.

Randles, C. (2013b). A theory of change in music education. *Music Education Research, 15*(4), 471–485.

Randles, C., Griffis, S., & Ruiz, J. (2015). "Are you in a band?!": Participatory (improvisatory) music making in pre-service music teacher education. *International Journal of Community Music, 8*(1), 59–72.

Randles, C. & Muhonen, S. (2015). Validation and further validation of a measure of creative identity among USA and Finland pre-service music teachers. *British Journal of Music Education, 32*(1), 51–70.

Randles, C. & Smith, G.D. (2012). A first comparison of pre-service music teachers' identities as creative musicians in the United States and England. *Research Studies in Music Education, 34*(2), 173–187. doi:10.1177/1321103X12464836

Randles, C. & Stringham, D. (Eds.) (2013). *Musicianship: Composing in band and orchestra.* Chicago, IL: GIA Publishing.

Rodriguez, C.X. (2004). *Bridging the gap: Popular music and music education.* Reston, VA: MENC.

Sawyer, K. (2012). *Explaining creativity: The science of human innovation.* New York: Oxford University Press.

Thibeault, M. (2015). The shifting locus of musical experience from performance to recording to new media: Some implications for music education, In C. Randles (Ed.), *Music education: Navigating the future* (pp. 63–90). New York: Routledge.

Tobias, E.S. (2013). Toward convergence: Adapting music education to contemporary society and participatory culture. *Music Educators Journal, 99*(4), 29–36. doi:10.1177/0027432113483318

Turino, T. (2008). *Music as social life: The politics of participation.* Chicago, IL: University of Chicago Press.

Williams, D.A. (2007). What are music educators doing and how well are we doing it? *Music Educators Journal, 94*(1). 18–23.

Williams, D.A. (2011). The elephant in the room. *Music Educators Journal, 98*(1), 51–57.

Williams, D.A. (2014). Another perspective: The iPad is a REAL musical instrument. *Music Educators Journal, 101*(1), 93–98.

Wright, R. (2008). Kicking the habitus: Power, culture and pedagogy in the secondary school music curriculum. *Music Education Research, 10*(3), 389–402.

Wright, R. & Kanellopoulos, P. (2010). Informal music learning, improvisation and teacher education. *British Journal of Music Education, 27,* 71–87.

6

Developing learning through producing

Secondary school students' experiences of a technologically aided pedagogical intervention

Aleksi Ojala

Introduction

As a practitioner-researcher I have gradually developed a pedagogical approach that has seen the teaching and learning in my classroom move from a one-size-fits-all education towards personalized learning paths. Through this approach, which I refer to as Learning Through Producing (LTP), students have been engaged in learning music through collaborative, technology-aided, creative music-making. As part of this project, the scope of student work was broadened from the reproduction of musical works to creative work such as arranging and songwriting, and from performance to producing shareable artefacts such as tracks and videos.[1] LTP was developed using design-based research (DBR) as a methodological toolkit. DBR allows the researcher to directly impact practice by developing and testing an innovation, in this case two e-learning materials, with the goal of generating approaches that can be generalized to other classrooms (Barab, 2014). In this chapter I first introduce the LTP approach and the e-learning materials that facilitate it, and then describe how the design-based research project was conducted. Following this, I share insights into secondary students' learning experiences during this technologically aided pedagogical intervention.

---

[1] In Finland, where popular music has been widely accepted as part of music curricula in schools and teacher training courses, general music education is often based on rehearsing easy-to-play pop hits in large group settings with traditional pop/rock band instruments such as drums, percussions, guitars and keyboards (Juntunen, 2011; Muukkonen, 2010; Väkevä, 2006; Westerlund, 2006).

Learning Through Producing, and the e-learning materials that facilitate it

The LTP approach has two stages: the initial *base-building* stage feeds into the producing stage (see Figure 6.1). These stages can take place either once or over multiple lessons. The *producing* stage sees musical knowledge, skills and identities constructed through sustained collaborative work that aims at creating shareable musical artefacts from the basic elements of music, using appropriate tools. As illustrated in Figure 6.1, this creative work of the producing teams takes place after the *base-building* stage, which can be further divided into common and personalized parts. A teacher-led, collective introduction of the most important basic elements and tools is targeted to all the students in a big group. After this, students can deepen their learning by creating personal learning environments and collaborating in producing teams. The teacher's role in this process is to create a warm, nurturing atmosphere and make sure that students have at least some kind of shared knowledge and skill base before they create their own goals and start working with musical material and tools that they find of relevance and interest to them. Figure 6.1 also shows how this process, which can take place once or several times during the course, moves from a formal, didactic approach towards a more informal pedagogical model (Green, 2008), recalling Folkestad's (2006) "continuum" of learning modes.

As part of the development and implementation of LTP, I came to the realization that my students were able to use their mobile devices[2] to consume, produce and share music and music-related knowledge (Partti, 2012; Salavuo, 2006). This inspired me to develop two e-learning materials that utilize LTP: an online video-based course and an e-book. When using LTP, the main aim of the online materials is to help students to develop their personal knowledge and skill bases by introducing elements and tools that they can use when they produce shareable musical

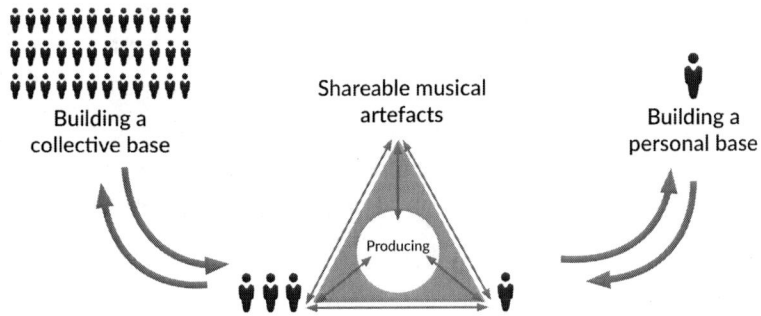

Figure 6.1 Twofold base-building stage in relation to the producing stage

---

2 In 2013, 77 percent of the students in Finnish general upper secondary schools had smartphones, and 80 percent laptops (Mikkilä, 2013).

Aleksi Ojala

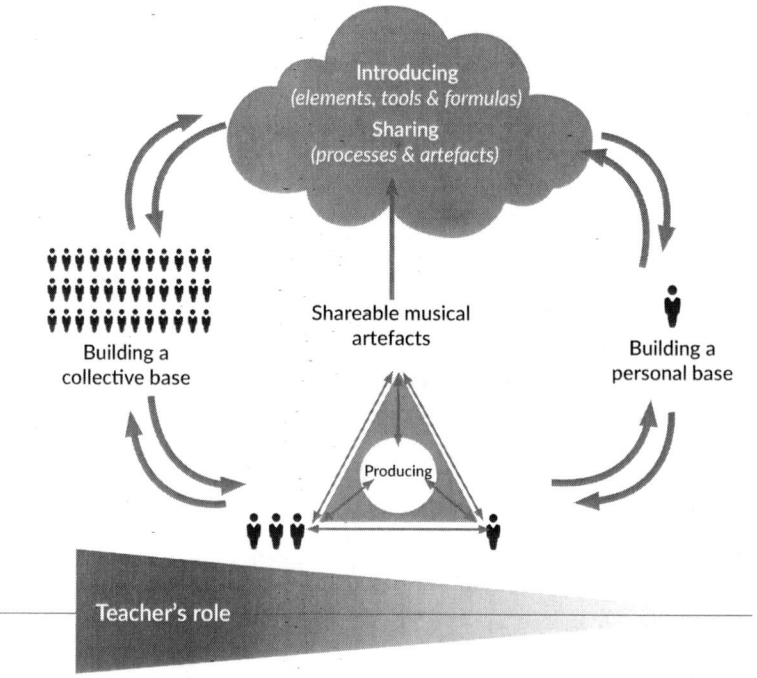

Figure 6.2 LTP approach in relation to the use of e-learning materials

artefacts. Furthermore, during and after the producing stage the use of cloud services offers myriad possibilities for students to share their creative processes and musical artefacts; in the LTP model this sharing can be used to support peer learning and to build collective knowledge and skill bases. Figure 6.2 illustrates the use of e-learning materials when using the LTP approach.

The online video-based course that utilizes LTP is called *Luova musiikin tuottaminen* (Creative Music Producing). It incorporates short videos produced by music educators, musicians, producers and students for the Rockway[3] online music platform for Finnish schools (Rockway, 2015). The material contains lessons on the basics of pop/rock band instruments and music theory, as well as on songwriting and music production techniques, such as how to use rhymes in creating lyrics, and lessons on recording acoustic guitar. The second developed e-learning outcome[4] is an e-book that focuses on using various free online applications that are curated for the *Tabletkoulu*[5] ('Tablet school') e-learning environment. Besides containing free

---

3 Rockway is a Finnish online music school based on video lessons.
4 This author developed the course with Mikko Myllykoski who is one of the leading experts and pioneers in the field of mobile music pedagogy in Finland.
5 The purpose of Tabletkoulu is to offer pedagogically innovative e-books for courses that a majority of the comprehensive school and general upper secondary school students in Finland will attend (Tabletkoulu, 2015).

digital tools for music production, the e-book offers an introduction to the basic elements of music using text, short videos and practical exercises in music-making.

Conducting the design-based research project: Context, methods and participants

The development and implementation of the LTP approach took place in the context of the only compulsory music course[6] in Finnish general upper secondary schools. In Finland about 50% of 15- to 16-year-old comprehensive school graduates continue their studies in general upper secondary school (grades 10–12), which provides eligibility for higher education (Ministry of Education and Culture, 2014; Statistic Finland, 2014). The Finnish general upper secondary schools' conception of learning emphasizes students' active knowledge creation (Finnish National Board of Education, 2003). This conception of learning requires schools and teachers to develop learning environments that enable students to set their own objectives and to work collaboratively in different groups and networks, also engaging with available technologies (Finnish National Board of Education, 2003).

I developed and tested the LTP approach and the e-learning materials that facilitate it with my own students during two research cycles of design, enactment, analysis and redesign. Four other teachers agreed to join the research team during the third research cycle, which took place during the autumn semester of 2014. The teachers were free to choose what elements and tools they introduced and how. Some teachers introduced the elements and tools mostly through hands-on music-making in a big group, whereas others utilized small-group work. Some teachers consistently used the e-learning environments in their music lessons, whereas others used the idea of the flipped classroom,[7] where students would go through introductory and/or optional e-materials before and after the actual classroom sessions in order to use the classroom time more efficiently for hands-on music-making and creative work. All teachers asked their students to create shareable musical artefact as final assignments for the course.

The four music teachers who joined the research team worked in different general upper secondary schools. Two of the schools were in the Southern capital area of Finland (Uusimaa), one in a Northern territory (Lapland) and one at the Eastern border (North Carelia). According to matriculation examination statistics (Tebest, 2014), the schools' ranking varied from being in the top 2% to the lowest 33% of the 442 general upper secondary schools in the country. Two of the schools provided personal iPad tablet computers for all of the students, whereas two other schools had 16 iPads permanently in the music class (for one or two students to

---

6 The general aim of this course, titled "Music and Me" – approximately 38 lessons long – is to help students to find their own ways of operating within the field of music (Finnish National Board of Education, 2003).
7 The 'flipped classroom', also known as 'flipped learning', 'inverted classroom' or 'reverted instruction' means a specific type of blended learning that uses technology to move traditionally class-based learning outside the classroom in order to use classroom time more efficiently for interactive, group-based, problem-solving activities (Sams & Bergmann, 2013; Strayer, 2012).

use at any given time[8]). The students were free to use these devices during music lessons or to bring their own devices. During the research the teachers shared experiences through email, a closed Facebook group and weekly Skype meetings. I also interviewed them either in person or through Skype approximately two months after the main research period.

A majority of the students took the compulsory music course during their first year in upper secondary school, at the age of 16. All the participants had free access to e-learning materials during the course. Besides using mobile devices to access the Rockway and Tabletkoulu online environments, the students used tablets, phones and laptops as musical instruments and as portable workstations for audio and video production. All the students were instructed to keep an electronic course diary and were encouraged to share their diaries with peers. The idea was that at the end of the course each student would have an electronic portfolio containing reflective essays and/or an audio-visual document about their activities that included work undertaken and artefacts developed during the course. The course diaries were intended to support students' active knowledge creation and peer learning, to work as an assessment tool for the teachers, and to provide data for the research project.

The student participants were asked to respond to surveys before and after the course. The aim of the short preparatory questionnaire was to provide an overall picture of students' musical backgrounds and expectations of the course, whereas the more detailed post-course survey aimed to provide an overall picture of their learning experiences during the course. This information was then clarified and verified through video-recorded and transcribed group interviews which took place within a week of the end of the course. Informed consent forms granting permission to use course diaries, surveys and interviews as data were signed by 97 students and their guardians. There were 52–71 respondents[9] to the preparatory questionnaire and 41 respondents to the post-course survey. Six students with different musical backgrounds and learning experiences from each music course were interviewed either individually or in small groups, depending on their teacher's preferences, to provide balance of representation from the participating schools.

It is important to realize that no 'polished' materials or pedagogical models were available to teachers and students during the data collection. Rather, guided by the idea of the DBR, new understandings brought about by this technologically aided pedagogical intervention were used to refine the e-learning materials and LTP approach. Hence, design work and theory building provided points of departure for the data collection and analysis. The data were analyzed following the typical qualitative analysis pattern of data reduction, data display and conclusion drawing and verification (Miles & Huberman, 2014). Since the compulsory music courses took place in different periods in different schools, I was able to organize the data collection and preliminary coding in a cyclical way, which made analysis

---

8 The student participants took the compulsory music course with 21–33 peers, depending on class size.
9 The discrepancy in sample size is due to the fact that not all students answered every question on the questionnaire.

an ongoing enterprise (Miles & Huberman, 2014). I considered first each student participant and then each music course as a case before looking at the whole group of participants and all the music courses for themes, such as the role of the teacher, peers, mobile devices and e-learning materials that were present for different students and schools[10] (Miles & Huberman, 2014). These overlapping themes allowed me to create the visual models presented in Figures 6.1 and 6.2, which became, in turn, essential tools when re-designing the e-learning materials.

According to the preparatory questionnaire, student participants reflected a wide variety of musical skills and attitudes towards music.[11] In addition, they reported different aims for their compulsory music course (Miles & Huberman, 2014). Since one of the aims of LTP is to generate possibilities for personalized learning paths, I wanted to find out a) what, and b) how, students with different musical identities report about their learning experiences. The analysis process led to the formation of the following five main categories, based on students' descriptions of their musical identities during and after the course:

1. Students who have a 'non-musician identity' have never had organized music-related hobbies and goals outside the music classroom, although they might sometimes make music or play a musical instrument during their free time.
2. Students who have an 'ex-musician' identity have at some point in their lives actively made music or played a musical instrument, including outside the music classroom, but report no longer being involved in musical activities.
3. Students who have an 'informally trained musician identity' actively make music or play a musical instrument without formal tuition. They have music-related goals outside the music classroom, but music-related hobbies do not necessarily occupy the majority of their free time.
4. Students who have a 'formally trained musician identity' have been actively taking part in extracurricular institutional music education for more than three years. Music-related hobbies take up the majority of their free time and they have ambitious music-related goals outside the music classroom.
5. Students who have a 'new musician identity' started or re-started actively playing an instrument or making music during or immediately following the course.

In what follows, I provide insights into the students' perspectives during and after their music course. I begin by providing an overview of the experiences of the whole group of participants. This picture is elaborated through the presentation of vignettes[12] that share narrative descriptions of the experiences of the five individual key participants (see vignette 1). The vignettes represent relatively

---

10 Miles and Huberman (2014, p. 103) write about "stacking comparable cases" when describing this kind of analysis technique.
11 This is in line with recent research that investigated Finnish comprehensive school leavers' musical skills and attitudes (Juntunen, 2011).
12 A vignette is a narrative, focused description of a series of events taken to be representative in the studied case (Miles & Huberman, 2014).

typical responses from the course participants. The data from participants' surveys and interviews have all been translated from Finnish by the author, and participants are all referred to by pseudonyms in order to maintain their anonymity.

Vignette 1 introduces each key participant's music course and describes their musical identities.

Vignette 1

Non-musician 'Ingrid' was a student of a technologically oriented teacher, who utilized a lot of iPads but also used traditional pop/rock band instruments during the course. In her music course, base-building and producing were done in small sections, one element and/or tool at a time. Ingrid describes her relationship with music: "I listen to music every day at home and when I work out . . . sometimes I play piano at home, even though it has never been my hobby and even though I am not good at it . . ." (survey).

Ex-musician 'Emma' was in a music course that was conducted in a regular classroom since the music classroom was used by another group. Hence, her teacher was forced to use mainly iPads instead of the traditional pop/rock band instruments that (s)he would normally use during the course. During the base-building stage they utilized e-learning materials and played cover songs. The producing stage took place during the last lessons of the course. Emma describes her relationship with music: "I love to listen to music and I listen to it a lot, mostly alternative rock . . ., I played piano for two years but quit it in fifth grade [five years ago]" (survey).

One of the informally trained musicians, 'Sarah', whose teacher utilized both iPads and traditional pop/rock band instruments during her course, describes her relationship with music: "I listen to all kinds of music from classical to K-pop [Korean pop]. . ., I started to play the piano when I was small but have never had a piano teacher" (course diary entry). Her teacher usually gave Tabletkoulu assignment as homework but students were free to use Rockway how they wished. Sarah studied constantly with her team members during the base-building stage, and they also played cover songs in the big group before the producing stage began.

'Joanna', who represents formally trained musicians, was in a course in which, according to her teacher "the solving of technical problems took too much class time during the music lessons" (interview). Since her group was really big, her teacher divided students into smaller groups. Some studied basics through online materials while others played together in the music class. Students produced their own songs individually, at home, at the end of the course. Joanna describes her relation to music: "Music has been and will always be an essential part of my life . . . I listen to lot of music, and study piano at the extracurricular music school. At home I also play guitar and accordion" (survey).

One of the new-musicians, 'Tina', was the author's own student during a course where we utilized both iPads and traditional pop/rock band instruments. She describes how the course changed her musical identity: "I listen to all kinds of music all the time . . ., I played classical piano for 11 years, but I quit the piano lessons last spring . . . I think it is thanks to this course that I got really excited about the guitar . . . my parents were astonished since I would just grab my brother's guitar and play it the whole evening. I also spent a lot of time with GarageBand and taught my brother to use it" (survey).

Tina's music course was divided into three equally long sections. After the introductory section that was based on hands-on music making in the big group, students were asked to make a cover version of an existing song in small groups that I had put together. At the end of the course students were asked to form producing teams and to produce a track or a music video. Throughout the course students were encouraged to deepen their learning with the use of e-learning materials.

Students' learning experiences in the base-building stage: Introduction of the elements and tools

Even though the participants had considerable musical information available through e-learning materials,[13] they underlined in their post-course survey responses that they felt that the teacher's presence was especially necessary in the beginning of the course to ensure that the creative work was accessible to all

---

13 There are altogether approximately 3500 online lessons available in the Rockway service.

students. This is not surprising considering that only a minority of the participants reported at the beginning of the course (preparatory questionnaire, 65 answers) that they could sing well (13 answers) or play an instrument well (17 answers).

The teachers had the opportunity to introduce elements and tools that the students needed when producing their own music either by the use of hands-on music-making, or through assignments that were completed in small groups or at home. However, some students were disappointed, feeling that they did not have enough time for hands-on musicking during the course. The students liked the basic idea of flipped classroom since "everybody has [a] phone and earphones all the time in their pocket anyway", as one student pointed out in interview. Still, only the most motivated students actively utilized the opportunity to deepen their learning through the use of e-learning materials during their free time [survey], and many students agreed that there should not be homework as part of a compulsory music course [survey].

Although the students reported that they were highly motivated to learn traditional pop/rock band instruments, they did not see the iPad as a real instrument (Randles, 2013; Williams, 2014). This view was particularly clear among the students who were forced to use iPad as their primary instrument during the course because they had no access to a music classroom (where the traditional instruments were kept). For instance, one of these students complained that "since we used mainly iPads I did not progress as a player" [survey]; another commented that "the students get more out of the course when playing real instruments than just touching a screen" [survey].

In vignette 2 the key participants describe in their course diaries their learning experiences during the base-building stage of the course.

Vignette 2

Ingrid (non-musician): Today was our third lesson. We uploaded the GarageBand application and everybody was supposed to compose a beat with a partner, which was really fun. At the end of the lesson we listened to what the others had done . . . During our fourth lesson we added virtual bass, piano and guitar tracks to our beat. It started to sound good! Then the teacher said that we should learn to play the product of our assignment with the real instruments. Luckily we had easy chords.

Emma (ex-musician): It has been fun playing with the iPads in the lessons, though sometimes it is a bit boring, depending on which instrument you play . . . during our three lessons in the actual music classroom I started remembering some chords on

> the guitar, which is funny since I've always thought that I'm useless with the guitar.
>
> Sarah (informally trained musician): Some students loved Rockway it but I only watched couple of videos about piano playing . . . Today we practised using GarageBand by making a short song. Some instruments sounded funny and we laughed a lot. After that we began to play and I found myself sitting behind the drums.
>
> Joanna (formally trained musician): The basic assignments were too easy for me, but I learned useful songwriting, guitar playing and vocal techniques from online videos.
>
> Tina (new musician): I learned the basics of the guitar during music lessons . . . I used Rockway to learn how to form barre chords . . . During the weekend I practised our arrangement a lot. I hope I have time to master F sharp major before we are supposed to perform the song in front of the class.

Students' learning experiences in the producing stage: Creating songs, tracks and videos in producing teams

Since tool selection has been seen to be a significant influence in shaping the creative processes when producing contemporary popular music (Partti, 2012) it is important to provide students with authentic technical tools. However, the educative use of LTP requires that students have an understanding of the relevant use of these tools in 'real world' cultural situations (Ojala & Väkevä, 2015). For instance, one of the teachers pointed out that students who did not have this understanding seemed to just "randomly play around with ready-made loops" [interview]. Furthermore, another teacher stated that after the students gained the basic understanding of the elements and tools during the base-building stage, they not only expanded their musical knowledge and skills during the producing stage but also "started to listen to music more analytically and critically" [interview].

Most of the student participants thought that they succeeded in songwriting, and produced tracks[14] that sounded "surprisingly good", as one student put it [interview]. In general, they reported a high level of peer learning, and stressed the benefits of a warm and trusting atmosphere when working in producing teams. However, the students emphasized that there should be enough time reserved for the producing process, and that the producing teams should not be too big or heterogeneous when it comes to musical taste and skills. Although the participants underlined the teacher's

---

14 To hear key participants' tracks, visit: https://soundcloud.com/keyparticipants/sets/tracks

significance during the introductory section of the course, they wanted the teacher to be available during the creative work in producing teams so that they could ask for help if they had problems. As soon as they got the first musical or lyrical ideas and overcame the first technical problems, the creative process "started to roll under its own weight", as one student described it [interview].

Although the students did not consider mobile devices as real musical instruments, the iPad seemed to function well as a portable (and virtual) studio for audio and video production. Most of the students used iPad's GarageBand application as their primary producing tool, but a couple of students preferred to work with other music software, such as FL Studio, on their own laptops. Smartphones were used mostly to capture and share unfinished musical ideas. The students who had enough time to make music videos used their iPads' iMovie application and thought the process was "funny" and "inspiring" [survey].

Vignette 3 describes the key participants' experiences during the producing stage of the course.

Vignette 3

Ingrid (non-musician): We had a really good team spirit . . . it was hard to get started, but after the first draft we progressed well . . . I enjoyed the making of the video – it was the climax of the course that really allowed us to use our creativity [survey].

Emma (ex-musician): It was fun to compose with a friend – we just tried different things and listened for what sounded good . . . I think we succeeded quite well, although we used a lot of loops [survey].

Sarah (informally trained musician): We all had our own roles in the team and everybody's ideas were respected. Sometimes somebody took the lead and others just commented . . . I tried composing for the first time and I think I will try it again after the course [survey].

Joanna (formally trained musician): I wrote a song for the memory of my father at home. He passed away four years ago . . . Lyrics just started to come and then also a melody, almost suddenly . . . After the song was written I just took a drum loop from GarageBand and recorded guitar, piano and vocal tracks on top of that [interview].

Tina (new musician): Our teamwork was really effective and we had a good time together . . . I ended up working a lot at home too, since I wanted to learn how to use GarageBand and

> iMovie properly, but it was worth it . . . I have shared our video with all my friends and I played our song on my grandfather's birthday to all my relatives; everybody wondered how on earth we were able to produce such a great song [survey].

Conclusion

Given the major transformations of the contexts of learning brought about by the digital revolution (Collins & Halverson, 2010; Prensky, 2010), and the contexts of global music culture (Hugill, 2008), it seems reasonable to claim that music educators should have an understanding of digital musical tools and their implications for the "democratization" of creativity[15] (Loveless & Williamson, 2013; Väkevä, 2006, 2009, 2010). In this chapter, I have introduced some possible ways to widen the perspective of institutional music learning from reproduction and performance to include arranging, songwriting, recording, mixing and sharing music, and to see music classrooms as hybrid spaces (Niknafs & Przybylski, chapter 32, this volume; Tobias, 2012) where students with different knowledge, skills, goals and identities learn music together. This introduces new ways to bridge the 'gap' between the 'real world' musical experiences of young people, and what is taught and learned in the school classroom. I have suggested that when musical knowledge and skills are constructed through producing, and when students are able to work with tools and musical material that they find relevant, opportunities arise for them to form music-related communities of practice (Wenger, 1998) and negotiate their musical identities (Burnard, 2012; Green, 2008). Furthermore, the findings of the study reported in this chapter suggest that in order to learn music effectively and purposefully through producing, many students benefit if they are introduced to musical elements and tools, together with the understanding of the relevant use of these tools in authentic cultural situations (Ojala & Väkevä, 2015), before the creative work in producing teams takes place.

While building a collective knowledge and skill base can be successfully accomplished through hands-on music-making in the music classroom, the use of e-learning materials and mobile devices can transform music learning in schools by offering ubiquitous affordances for personalized learning (Pachler, 2010). Therefore, for teachers, the use of LTP and e-learning materials can offer new pedagogical possibilities in moving from a one-size-fits-all model of instruction towards an education tailored to meet a learner's individual needs in achieving his or her goals (Sawyer, 2014) and achieving in his or her zone of proximal development (Vygotsky, 1978). The findings also indicate that e-learning materials and

---

15 Thus it is understandable and justifiable that technology-aided creative music making is going to be a prominent part of Finland's new core curriculum of music, taking effect in 2016 (Opetushallitus, 2015).

mobile devices cannot replace traditional instruments, the teacher or face-to-face interaction with peers, but, rather, that they can be used in ways that complement these established practices effectively.

Acknowledgements

I would like to thank the Finnish Cultural Foundation for financially supporting this work.

References

Barab, S. (2014). Design-based research: A methodological toolkit for engineering. In K.R. Sawyer (Ed.), *The Cambridge handbook of the learning sciences* (pp. 270–320). New York: Cambridge University Press.

Burnard, P. (Ed.) (2012). *Musical creativities in practice*. Oxford: Oxford University Press.

Collins, A. & Halverson, R. (2010). The second educational revolution: Rethinking education in the age of technology. *Journal of Computer Assisted Learning*, 26(1), 18.

Finnish National Board of Education. (2003). National core curriculum for upper secondary schools. National core curriculum for general upper secondary education intended for young people. Retrieved from: http://www.oph.fi/download/47678_core_curricula_upper_secondary_education.pdf [Accessed 9 September 2015].

Folkestad, G. (2006). Formal and informal learning situations or practices vs formal and informal ways of learning. *British Journal of Music Education*, 23(02), 135–145.

Green, L. (2008). *Music, informal learning and the school: A new classroom pedagogy*. Aldershot: Ashgate.

Hugill, A. (2008). *The digital musician*. New York, NY: Routledge.

Juntunen, M.-L. (2011). Musiikki [Music]. In S. Laitinen, A. Hilmola & M.-L. Juntunen (Eds.), *Perusopetuksen musiikin, kuvataiteen ja käsityön oppimistulosten arviointi 9. vuosiluokalla*. [Assessment of the learning outcomes in music, visual arts and crafts in the final 9th grade of basic education.] (pp. 36–94). Koulutuksen seurantaraportit 2011:1. [Follow-up reports 2011:1]. Helsinki, Finland: Opetushallitus [Finnish National Board of Education].

Juntunen, M. (2011). In A. Hilmola, S. Laitinen & M. Juntunen (Eds.), *Perusopetuksen musiikin, kuvataiteen ja käsityön oppimistulosten arviointi 9. vuosiluokalla* [Assessed learning outcomes in music, visual arts and crafts in the final 9th of basic education]. Helsinki: Opetushallitus.

Loveless, A. & Williamson, B. (2013). *Learning identities in a digital age rethinking creativity, education and technology*. London: Routledge.

Miles, M.B. & Huberman, M. (2014). In J. Saldaña (Ed.), *Qualitative data analysis a methods sourcebook*. Los Angeles, CA: SAGE.

Ministry of Education and Culture. (2014). Retrieved from: http://www.minedu.fi/OPM/Koulutus/lukiokoulutus/index.html?lang=en [Accessed 9 September 2015].

Muukkonen, M. (2010). *Monipuolisuuden eetos musiikin aineenopettajat artikuloimassa työnsä käytäntöjä*. [The Ethos of Versatility. Music Teachers Articulate Their Pedagogical Practices.]. Studia Musica, 42. Helsinki: Sibelius Academy.

Ojala, A. & Väkevä, L. (2015). Keeping it real: Addressing authenticity in classroom popular music pedagogy. *Nordic Research in Music Education, Yearbook*, 16, 87–99.

Opetushallitus. (2015). Lukion opetussuunnitelman perusteet 2015. [National core curriculum for upper secondary schools 2015.] Retrieved from: http://www.oph.fi/download/172124_lukion_opetussuunnitelman_perusteet_2015.pdf [Accessed 2 February 2015].

Pachler, N. (Ed.) (2010). *Mobile learning structures, agency, practices.* New York: Springer.

Partti, H. (2012). *Learning from cosmopolitan digital musicians: Identity, musicianship, and changing values in (in)formal music communities.* Studia Musica, 50. Helsinki: Sibelius Academy.

Prensky, M. (2010). *Teaching digital natives partnering for real learning.* Thousand Oaks, CA: Corwin Press.

Randles, C. (2013). Being an iPadist. *General Music Today, 27*(1), 48–51.

Rockway. (2015). Koulut. Retrieved from: http://rockwaykoulut.fi/ [Accessed 2 March 2015].

Salavuo, M. (2006). Open and informal online communities as forums of collaborative musical activities and learning. *British Journal of Music Education, 23*(3), 253–271.

Sams, A. & Bergmann, J. (2013). Flip your students' learning. *Educational Leadership, 70*(6), 16.

Sawyer, K.R. (2014). Introduction: The new science of learning. In K.R. Sawyer (Ed.), *The Cambridge handbook of the learning sciences* (pp. 27–56). New York: Cambridge University Press.

Statistic Finland. (2014). Retrieved from: http://tilastokeskus.fi/til/lop/2013/lop_2013_2014-06-12_tie_001_en.html [Accessed 9 September 2014].

Strayer, J.F. (2012). How learning in an inverted classroom influences cooperation, innovation and task orientation. *Learning Environments Research, 15*(2), 171.

Tabletkoulu. (2015). A new way to learn and teach. Retrieved from: https://www.tabletkoulu.fi/ [Accessed 1 March 2015].

Tebest, T. (2014). *Lukioiden ranking-lista julki – katso, miten oma koulusi sijoittui.* [General upper secondary schools ranking list published – see how your school ranked.] Retrieved from: http://yle.fi/uutiset/lukioiden_ranking-lista_julki__katso_miten_oma_koulusi_sijoittui/7258451 [Accessed 9 September 2014].

Tobias, E.S. (2012). Hybrid spaces and hyphenated musicians: Secondary students' musical engagement in a songwriting and technology course. *Music Education Research, 14*(3), 329.

Väkevä, L. (2006). Teaching popular music in Finland: What's up, what's ahead? *International Journal of Music Education, 24*(2), 126–131.

Väkevä, L. (2009). The world well lost, found: Reality and authenticity in Green's "new classroom pedagogy". *Action, Criticism, and Theory for Music Education, 8*(2), 7–34.

Väkevä, L. (2010). Garage band or GarageBand®? Remixing musical futures. *British Journal of Music Education, 27*(1), 59–70.

Vygotsky, L.S. (1978). *Mind in society the development of higher psychological processes* (Ed. M. Cole). Cambridge, MA: Harvard University Press.

Wenger, E. (1998). *Communities of practice learning, meaning, and identity.* Cambridge: Cambridge University Press.

Westerlund, H. (2006). Garage rock bands: A future model for developing musical expertise? *International Journal of Music Education, 24*(2), 119–125.

Williams, D.A. (2014). Another perspective: The iPad is a REAL musical instrument. *Music Educators Journal, 101*(1), 93–98.

7

A historical review of the social dynamics of school music education in Mainland China

A study of the political power of popular songs

Wai-Chung Ho

Introduction

With specific reference to Mainland China,[1] this chapter examines the relationships between social transformation, popular songs and school music education. Social changes have significantly influenced China's education policy and development and created imperatives and challenges for the content of school music education during the 20th and 21st centuries. As this chapter will show, politics has the power to influence culture, popular songs, the community, institutions and social order, which together condition individual and collective action. This chapter will examine the attempts made to shape cultural politics through the medium of protest, as well as how revolutionary songs have been used as a means of social integration through education during the 20th and 21st centuries.

The term 'popular songs' is vague, covering a wide field of musical endeavours and ranging over a long period of time in the mainland. On the one hand, there are songs that are popular but are not marketed with the intention of achieving sales, and these songs are principally for production and distribution purposes. Chinese

---

1 Mainland China (or simply known as China or the mainland) refers to the political and geographical terms under the direct jurisdiction of the People's Republic of China (PRC). Though Hong Kong and Macao are Special Administrative Regions (SARs) of the PRC, Mainland China does not include Hong Kong, Macao and Taiwan (the Republic of China).

popular songs such as these include the themes of reinforcing Chinese nationalism in the face of foreign aggression and fostering nation-building, as well as promoting communist values and praising the ruling Communist Party of China (CPC). Despite having little or no commercial value, these songs are popular, and they reach a broad audience via the Chinese government with support from the nation's official media.

On the other hand, since the 1980s, popular songs in popular culture in China have included Western music genres (largely American and British songs), Mandarin songs from Taiwan and Cantonese songs from Hong Kong, which have all become mainstream popular music in the mainland. In the 1990s and 2000s, respectively, China experienced a 'Japanese wave' and a 'Korean wave' in its conventional media, characterized by the popularity of Japanese and Korean popular music, television dramas, films, animation, cosmetics, food and lifestyles, online games and smartphones. Though the Chinese state has tolerated Western and other Asian popular songs, their production and reproduction may be limited by political and economic interventions. Schools, however, are encouraged to teach popular songs with 'healthy' lyrics approved by the current music curriculum guidelines (Ministry of Education, 2012).

This chapter challenges contemporary debates on popular songs in school music education, asking two key questions about the dynamics of developing a culturally relevant curriculum for students in China: (1) what was the relationship between power, cultural politics and popular songs in society and in school music education in the 20th century? and (2) what are the current perspectives on integrating popular songs into the music classroom in China in this global age? This chapter argues that music education is deeply implicated in the politics of culture, and the popular songs in its curriculum have always been part of a selective culture that has sought to exert a political group's power over the production and reproduction of the music's chosen and unchosen political meanings.

Popular songs and music education: From nationalism to communism in the 20th century

In response to the relationship between power, cultural politics and popular songs, this section presents a discussion on the analyses of popular songs in relation to political ideology in the cultivation of people's collective singing and identity with Chinese nationalism and communism to serve and to propagate the modern Chinese nation in society and in school music education in the 20th century.

Promotion of singing protest songs against foreign aggression

During the 19th century, the Imperial Qing Dynasty (1644–1911) faced international pressure from the European and Japanese powers, which extended their political influence into China. Foreign aggression resulted in unequal treaties, forcing China to open its doors to trading. The Sino-British War (also known as the Opium

War) of 1839–1842 marked the beginning of the West's demands to trade freely in China and for more access to ports. Songwriters in the early 20th century, such as Liang Qichao (1873–1929) and Zeng Zhimin (1879–1929), strongly recommended music education as an important element in the changing society. Liang strongly encouraged the promotion of foreign songs; he also wrote song lyrics such as "Loving Your Country" to cultivate children's feelings of nationalism. Chinese students and intellectuals such as Shen Xingong (1869–1947) and Li Shutong (1880–1942), who both studied in Japan and returned from musical training in 1903 and 1910, respectively, launched a school song campaign in China (Ho, 2010; also see Liu, 2010). The tunes of these early Chinese 'school songs' (*Xuetang yuege*) were not composed by Chinese composers but instead were adapted from some of the well-known Western folk songs and 'Japanese school songs' (*Syoka*) that were produced and disseminated in China during the Meiji period (1868–1912) (Ho, 2010; Lau, 2013; Melvin & Cai, 2004). Shen and Li, who believed that music could help save the country from foreign threats and Western imperialism, were the first 'modern' composers to synthesize European and Japanese songs with Chinese marches (Gild, 1998, pp. 111–112; Ho, 2010). According to Lin (2012, p. 74), Li Shutong wrote in the preface of the *Little Magazine of Music (Yinyue Xiao Zazhi)*, published in Tokyo in 1906, that music could be used to promote social change. Li stated that "[i]n Europe and America, [music] has a major influence [on society]; Asian countries should follow the achievements [of the West]. Music provokes the morality of a society and helps improve social integrity" (Qin, 1991, p. 3, translated by the author). For example, Shen Xingong's "Huanghe" ("Yellow River") called for self-discipline, self-strengthening and patriotism, and stressed the responsibility all Chinese people must bear for the nation.

The end of the First World War in 1918 coincided with the resurgence of Chinese nationalism. The first wave of modern Chinese nationalism reached its height during the May 4th Movement, also known as the New Culture Movement. The popular songs of the May 4th Movement featured melodies adapted from Chinese regional folk songs, local children's songs and even revolutionary songs from other countries, such as those from Russia's October Revolution; prominent in the lyrics was the theme of national humiliation. Military marches and singing were strenuously promoted, with a focus on teaching everyone "such political classics as 'The Internationale' ('*Guoji Ge*')"[2] (Judd, 1983, pp. 137–138), translated into Chinese by Qu Qiubai (1899–1935) in 1923 (Smith, 2002, p. 197).

Education reform (including music education) during the 1920s and the 1930s focused on the modernization of China and retaining Chinese identity to propagate state ideology. In 1922, the Chinese government attempted to design music syllabuses for primary and secondary schools. The goals of music education, as stated in the 1923 music curriculum, were to develop "emotional, spiritual, and

---

2 "The Internationale" is an anthem of Communist parties and many socialist movements and is available in many major languages throughout the world. It was originally a French song written by Eugène Pottier (1816–1887). It also became an official anthem of the Soviet Union, sung in Russian, in the years 1918 through late 1943.

ideological character traits in the child" (Ma, 1989, p. 72). The growth of nationalism in song lyrics in Mainland China was further reinforced by the invasion of China by foreign countries during the Second World War. The three important songwriters of the 1930s and the 1940s – Nie Er (1912–1935), Xian Xinghai (1905–1945) and Zhao Yuanren (1892–1982) – all created national-style tunes, the contents of which were determined not by musical quality but by political intention (Ho, 2006, p. 440). As observed by Kraus (1989, p. 49) and Wong (1984, pp. 121, 136), Chinese 'songs for the masses' (sometimes called mass songs and revolutionary songs) were produced as highly effective political propaganda and sung at political rallies. For example, "March of the Volunteers" (with lyrics by the left-wing writer Tian Han),[3] composed by Nie Er in 1934 for the patriotic movie *Children of the Storm*, was about an intellectual who left to fight in the Second Sino-Japanese War, and Nie's other mass songs "both represented and served as media for the expression of a class-inflected nationalism" (Howard, 2012, p. 5). The lyrics for "March of the Volunteers" were "clearly enunciated", and this song was particularly suitable for "mass movements" (Wong, 1984, p. 123). The song also included characteristics of European revolutionary songs and depicted Chinese intellectuals marching bravely to the front in the resistance against Japan during the Second World War:

> Rise up!
> Those who do not want to be enslaved!
> Let our flesh and blood fortify our new Great Wall.
> The people of China have faced their greatest danger.

The singing of anti-war songs became a significant musical activity and was promoted by China's Ministry of Education (MoE) from 1937 to 1945. With a view to developing school music education and group singing, the MoE published Chinese and English versions of the *Collection of Anti-War Songs* and trained students to sing the "Choral Work for Thousands of People" (Ho, 2003, p. 298; Ma, 2002, p. 65). Primary school music education in 1923 was proposed to encourage "contemporary and national spirits", a phrase that was replaced in 1947 by promoting a united spirit among Chinese children and addressing "both spiritual happiness and the development of bravery" (Ma, 1989, pp. 71, 73). The major aim of middle and senior elementary school music education was developing students' happiness in life and fostering "their spirit of progress and unity" (Ma, 1989, p. 75). The Chinese Communists' themes of anti-foreigners and revolutionary ideas, themes found in the song lyrics, were also integrated into a collective voice in

---

3 This song is believed to be the last piece composed by Nie Er. During China's Cultural Revolution, this song was forbidden to be sung, as Tian Han was imprisoned as a "counter-revolutionary". Another song, "The East Is Red", was adopted as the unofficial national anthem. The National People's Congress decided to restore the original version by Tian Han as the official national anthem on December 4, 1982; later, it made the song the official anthem of the PRC in a 2004 amendment of the PRC's constitution.

Chinese communism and propaganda songs

When Mao Zedong (1893–1976) officially proclaimed the founding of the People's Republic of China (PRC) on 1 October 1949, he attempted to destroy traditional Chinese culture with a view to creating a utopian communist state. During Mao's rule, between 1949 and 1976, music became an official instrument for the transmission of the beliefs and values needed to build a socialist revolutionary society. Communist propaganda songs such as "Without the Communist Party, There Would Be No New China" were popularized by the CPC. Propaganda songs and the arts in general were governed by Marxist-Leninist-Maoist ideology and were required to serve the interests of students, workers, peasants and soldiers, as well as to convey the messages of the government.

The Cultural Revolution (CR) was officially launched on August 8, 1966. As its name suggests, the CR was an attempt to transform Chinese culture by severing it from its feudal and bourgeois pre-Communist past and reforming it into a completely socialist model. The CR was anti-Western and opposed to regional and cultural differences; it also resulted in a complex social upheaval between Mao and other top party leaders for dominance of the CPC, and was identified as the "Ten Years of Turmoil" (Powers, 1997, p. 149; also see Spence, 2001). During the CR, the theme of revolutionary songs changed from national humiliation and revolutionary spirit to paeans for the Chinese revolution and Chairman Mao personally. Other types of popular songs were condemned as 'yellow music' and banned by the communists.[4] Composers such as Li Jinhui (1891–1967) (the 'Father of Chinese popular music'), who was known for creating a new form of Chinese popular music,[5] were persecuted and died during the CR. The CPC also depicted any Chinese popular music deemed to be associated with Western capitalist values as an inferior cultural form and condemned those Chinese who listened to American music or used American commodities as immoral. The musical fanfare that opened the CR was "The East Is Red", an old revolutionary song that had become the movement's anthem (Moskowitz, 2010, p. 19):

> The East is red.
> The sun is rising.
> China has brought forth Mao Zedong.
> He has a plan to bring the Chinese people good fortune.

---

4 Yellow music (*Huangse yinyue*) was a label used to describe the emergence of Chinese popular music and urban media culture in Shanghai's China, particularly during the 1920s and 1930s, and was also a reference to pornography.

5 His song "Dizzles" is often considered to be the very first Chinese popular song (or "Rock of China") that advocated "our Mandarin" and popularized the "folk musical form" (Li, 2014, p. 4). It was released in gramophone record format by the Pathé Records Company in Shanghai in 1926.

Hooray, he is the people's great saviour.

Besides "The East Is Red", which promoted the personality cult of Mao Zedong, other songs, such as "March of the Revolutionary Youth", "We Are Chairman Mao's Red Guards" and "Long Live Chairman Mao", were written to deliver the message of deifying Mao and establishing his authority in the country. Revolution-themed songs such as "Ode to the Motherland", "Without the Communist Party, There Would Be No New China" and "The People of the World Will Surely Be Victorious" were a notable part of propaganda to advocate or praise revolutions during the CR. These songs were promoted in communities and were encouraged to be taught in school music education.

Diversification of popular songs and education reform in school music education after the 1978 open door policy

In September 1976, Chairman Mao Zedong died. After the fall of the 'Gang of Four' (Chairman Mao's last wife, Jiang Qing, and her close associates Zhang Chunqiao, Yao Wenyuan and Wang Hongwen) and the end of the CR (1966–1976), Deng Xiaoping (1904–1997) regained power and adopted the Open Door Policy in 1978.[6] This policy stressed reforming and restructuring China's economic system and the utilization of capital, advanced technologies and management methods based on those in the rest of the world, including capitalist countries such as the United States. While propaganda songs and revolutionary songs lost their attraction among the Chinese populace, in the 1980s popular music influenced by cultural influences from foreign, particularly Western, countries began to resurge. The policy also facilitated the return of Western cultural influences and the acceptance of cultures from East Asian societies.

In the formation of Chinese popular music in the 1980s, there was a chronological progression that began with *Gangtaiyue* (popular songs produced in Hong Kong and Taiwan), proceeded to *Xibeifeng* (music influenced by Northwest folk

---

6 Deng Xiaoping was a Chinese revolutionary and politician. He was considered the most powerful figure in the PRC from the late 1970s until his death in 1997. He joined the Communist Party of China (CPC) in 1924 during a high school programme in France, from 1921 to 1924. Before returning to China in 1926, he studied for several months in Moscow. He was the CPC's general secretary in 1954 and a member of the Politburo (ruling party). However, Deng and Mao Zedong parted ways after disagreeing over the strategies of economic development and other policies in the 1960s. In 1966, Mao launched the Cultural Revolution and mobilized the youth group the Red Guards to root out and rid the party of 'capitalist roaders' (those who supposedly held 'right wing views'). Deng was stripped of political power and disappeared from public view. From 1969 to 1973, Deng and his family were exiled and were forced to undergo re-education in rural Jiangxi, located in the southeast of the country. In the spring of 1973, Deng returned to Beijing and was reinstated as a deputy premier, and in 1975 he became vice-chairman of the party's Central Committee. Despite carrying out various political reforms, Deng was forced from leadership and power by Mao. It was only after Mao's death and the fall of the Gang of Four in July 1977 that Deng began his political comeback.

songs) and culminated with *Yaogun Yinyue* (mainland Chinese rock) and its first popular idol, Cui Jian (see De Kloet, 2005a). New modern electronic appliances such as radios, cassette players and television sets provided the 'necessary infrastructure' for facilitating popular music's growth in the Chinese music market (De Kloet, 2005b, p. 231). Cassette tapes and compact discs by Hong Kong and Taiwanese singers, both legally imported and pirated, were even sold in state enterprises such as the Xinhua Bookstore,[7] as well as in privately run companies (Gold, 1993). During the 1980s and 1990s, Chinese cities were densely packed with karaoke bars, providing sites for one of the most popular leisure activities in the mainland.

The development of a market economy resulted in increased orientation among students towards materialist and individualist values. For a long time, popular culture had been prohibited in China's school music education for fear of spiritual pollution by 'Western culture', for example, the political campaign launched by the CPC in 1983 to eradicate "spiritual pollution" as a backlash against growing intellectual discourse promoting "humanism", advocating bourgeois liberalism and fostering "liberal tendencies in the arts" (Sum cited in Hong, 1998, p. 102). Thus, attempts were made to prevent the introduction of popular music into school curricula in the 1980s and 1990s.

Perspectives on the introduction of popular songs into globalized school music education

Globalization, without a doubt, has impacted education in China. The law on nine-year compulsory education took effect on 1 July 1986 to guarantee children the right to receive at least nine years of school education. This law facilitated tremendous progress in universalizing primary and junior secondary (i.e., grades one through nine) school education. Before 1986, there was no enforcement of compulsory education in the mainland. In order to enable itself to compete in the global economy, China, from the 1980s to 2000, enacted several major education reforms, including the universalization of compulsory education and teacher education. Another reform was launched on a trial basis in 2001, when the MoE issued a circular titled *Guidelines for Curriculum Reform of Basic Education*. The curriculum reform was aligned with social development and students' real-life experiences.

While China's economy has grown swiftly, popular culture and leisure activities have become more diverse and are increasingly supported by Chinese authorities. With the spread of the English language through globalization, learning English, including singing songs in English, has become a more valuable skill and practice, with impacts on cultural and educational developments in China. A survey conducted by Rupke and Blank (2009), involving 153 Chinese college students at the Anhui Institute of Education in Hefei, revealed that the three most preferred

---

7 The Xinhua Bookstore was formerly established as the Guanghua Bookstore in Yan'an under the Propaganda Department of the CPC in 1937. It is still the largest and only nationwide chain in China.

Western songs to listen to were "My Heart Will Go On" by Celine Dion, "Take Me Home, Country Roads" by John Denver and "Yesterday Once More" by The Carpenters. Most of the students also reported that they started listening to Western music during their high school education (Rupke & Blank, 2009, p. 133). According to Law and Ho's survey (2015) of 1,739 Shanghai students aged 12–17, the most preferred types of music were popular songs from the UK and the US, Taiwan and Japan and South Korea.

The 2011 reform of the Curriculum Standards for Primary Education and Junior Secondary Education marked the first time that the school music curriculum officially included learning a canon of popular songs (Ministry of Education, 2012). In spite of such changes in school music education, official songs found in the Chinese school curriculum attempt to espouse the relationship between popular songs, national education and traditional Confucian education. In response to the integration of popular songs into the school music curriculum in the global age of China, the following sections will highlight two forms of dynamic relationships: (1) a continual transmission of Chinese nationalism through popular music in school music education; and (2) a re-emphasis of Confucian education integrated into the learning of citizenship in popular music education.

Dynamics of the introduction of popular music, patriotism and nationalism into school music education

In response to the challenges of an increasingly interconnected and interdependent world, education reforms in China have had to address both global and national needs. The process of translating global imperatives for music education is increasingly intertwined with social changes, the cultural politics of the Chinese authorities and education reforms that are, in turn, both facilitated and constrained by national conditions and considerations.

The singing of the PRC's national anthem and other patriotic songs is a sign of how nationalization is emerging in the school music education programme. In October 2004, government ministries and other government organizations promoted a new patriotic education project titled "Three One Hundred for Patriotic Education" (i.e., 100 patriotic songs, 100 patriotic films and 100 patriotic books for young students) (Wang, 2008, p. 796). The singing of the PRC's national anthem, "March of the Volunteers", is encouraged in the Chinese school music curriculum. Even though the Second World War ended 70 years ago, there were other patriotic popular songs included that enlightened the spirit of Chinese students to fight against their Japanese enemies during the Sino-Japanese Wars, such as "We Are Not Afraid of Fighting" (People's Music Publishing House 2015, p. 4). As viewed by Wang (2014), the use of historical memory is "the prime raw material for constructing China's national identity" (p. 223) and cultivating a nationalistic and anti-Western victim mentality to provide Chinese youngsters with an understanding of who they are and how to comprehend the rest of the world in carrying out foreign relations.

In addition to the mainland's patriotic songs, other nationalistic or patriotic songs found in the music textbooks are drawn from popular songs composed by Hong Kong and Taiwanese artists to strengthen the relationship among the greater Chinese communities, as well as to stress the core identity marker of being Chinese. For example, the song "Descendants of the Dragon",[8] written by Taiwanese singer and songwriter Hou Dejian, uses the traditional symbol of the dragon to call for strong Chinese ethnic emotions (Jiangsu Juvenile and Children's Publishing House, 2012a, p. 12). The song "Pearl of the Orient", written by Taiwanese singer and songwriter Luo Da-you, praises the return of Hong Kong's sovereignty from the United Kingdom on 1 July 1997 (e.g. People's Music Publishing House, 2014a, p. 6). "My Chinese Heart", a 1982 song composed by Hong Kong songwriter Wang Fuling, with lyrics written by James Wong, protests the falsifying of information about the Second Sino-Japanese War in Japanese history books as mandated by the Japanese Ministry of Education (Hunan Literature and Art Publishing House, 2011, p. 43; Southwest China Normal University Press, 2012, p. 20). Such teaching materials as these much-loved and powerful patriotic songs drawn from the greater Chinese communities are intended to promote students' patriotism in the mainland.

Transmission of traditional Chinese values and global harmony in school music education

For thousands of years, Confucianism has shaped the ethical, social and political aspects of Chinese cultures and contributed to social and family harmony and well-being; thus, values in education are placed at familial, societal and individual levels. Chinese cultures value the role of collectivism, which affects family functions and behaviours within the five basic relationships of father-son, emperor-subject, husband-wife, elder-younger and friend-friend. In terms of popular culture, 'Confucius fever' has been growing since the 1990s (Alder, 2011; Hammond & Richey, 2015). The most evident sign of this phenomenon is that is has crossed the boundary between the scholarly and popular realms. Yu Dan, a professor of media studies at Beijing Normal University, gave a very popular series of TV lectures on the *Analects* of Confucius on China Central Television (CCTV, a predominant state television broadcaster in the mainland) and published a book on the *Analects*,[9] first in Chinese (2006) and later in English, titled *Confucius from the Heart* (2009).

In this global age in the mainland, the nuclear family still remains the basis for traditional Chinese values in school education. These values advocate harmony

---

8 The song was composed in 1978 in response to the American decision to break off diplomatic relations with the Republic of China (Taiwan) and establish relations with the PRC. When the song was popular in Taiwan, most Taiwanese people had never visited the mainland. The song has remained a symbol of their collective memory.
9 The *Analects* (also known as the *Analects of Confucius*) is a collection of sayings and ideas attributed to the Chinese philosopher Confucius and his contemporaries.

and order among individuals, the family and society, and they include the order of relationship by status, filial piety, obedience to the social hierarchy, respect for tradition and pride in one's cultural heritage. Despite the emphasis on a mother's love (rather than a father's love) in the mainland, the encouragement of filial piety is one of the paramount guiding ethics regulating students' social behaviour through school music education (Ho, 2013; Law & Ho, 2011).

Moreover, popular song lyrics selected from both local and foreign literatures affirm friendship, peace-building and global harmony in school music education. Friendship is the only human relationship based on mutual respect, fidelity and faithfulness that can be non-hierarchical among the five key relationships of Confucianism. Song lyrics that delineate the beautiful qualities of friendship (e.g. mutual understanding, affection, compassion, kindness to others and empathy), such as "Come Together, My Friends" (Lei, 2009, pp. 46–47) and "The More We Get Together" (a traditional British folk song and popular children's song) (Jiangsu Juvenile and Children's Publishing House, 2012c, p. 14), are found in mainland textbooks. In addition, "Auld Lang Syne" (originally a traditional Scottish folk song with lyrics written by the Scottish poet Robert Burns, but popularized as the theme song of the movie *Waterloo Bridge* released in 1940), a song about remembering friends from the past and not letting them be forgotten, has been included in Chinese music textbooks (e.g. see Jiangsu Juvenile and Children's Publishing House, 2012b, pp. 32–33).

Chinese songs such as "Let the World Be Filled with Love" (Jiangsu Juvenile and Children's Publishing House, 2012a, p. 51), "You and Me" (a theme song for the 2008 Beijing Olympics, written by Chen Qigang and performed in the opening ceremony of the Olympics by Liu Huan and Sarah Brightman) (Southwest China Normal University Press, 2013, p. 4), and other Chinese songs adapted from foreign tunes such as "Happy Choral Praise" (the theme song adopted from Beethoven's Ninth Symphony) (Jiangsu Juvenile and Children's Publishing House, 2012a, p. 50) and "We Are the World" (a song written by Michael Jackson and Lionel Richie and recorded by the supergroup USA for Africa in 1985) (People's Music Publishing House, 2014b, pp. 6–7) are included with the intention of showing how some popular songs relate world peace to social harmony.

All of these songs call on students to make the world a better place, one full of hope and love, and to treasure friendship and unity between people. They are also used as collectivist elements that emphasize family and work group goals above individual needs or desires. With a view to constructing a new value system in school music education, song lyrics in today's school music curricula attempt to create a distance from Mao's revolutionary ideology.

Conclusion

Over the past three decades, China's political reforms, Open Door Policy, dramatic economic growth, and increasingly assertive foreign policy have had an unprecedented impact on school education. This chapter has addressed the power and potential use of popular songs in school music education as a producer and reproducer of cultural politics in the mainland. It first examined how songs that are popular are taught in China's school music education to empower social and collective values and to serve as a mechanism for political indoctrination, particularly in its selection of anti-Japanese popular songs and in praising the construction of Chinese revolutionary ideology in the 20th century. In line with the development of the market-oriented economy, the most significant changes occurred in 2011, when the reform of the Curriculum Standards for Primary Education and Junior Secondary Education marked the first time that the school curriculum officially included popular songs (Ministry of Education, 2012).

With the complex and dynamic nature of the processes of socialization and globalization, music production is continually affected and shaped by the consideration of power and social agencies. When the Chinese government launched a campaign to assimilate popular songs into school education, and music education in particular, what remained unchanged was the zeal with which the state strove to make popular songs in school music education conform to its Confucian and nationalistic education values. The political ideologies that have driven the use of popular songs in school music education in China serve to reproduce that political order which is believed to be best for society as a whole.

Globalization is not simply a new conceptual framework through which cultural change via the introduction of popular songs in China's school music education can be understood; it is also a historical and sociopolitical context in which the nation has enfolded its values in providing its own cultural identity to a dynamic and context-bounded sociopolitical construction of school music education in the new age of China. In the end, messages delivered in popular songs that convey students' loyalty and love for their homeland will continue to be the main theme in school music education throughout China as the globalization process unfolds in the 21st century.

Acknowledgement

The author would like to express her gratitude to Hong Kong Baptist University for the generous support of the Faculty Research Grants.

References

Alder, J.A. (2011, April 11). Confucianism in China today. Pearson living religions forum. Retrieved from: http://www2.kenyon.edu/Depts/Religion/Fac/Adler/Writings/Confucianism%20Today.pdf [Accessed 20 March 2015].

De Kloet, J. (2005a). Popular music and youth in urban China: The Dakou generation. *China Quarterly*, *183*, 609–626.

De Kloet, J. (2005b). Authenticating geographies and temporalities: Representations of Chinese rock in China. *Visual Anthropology*, *18*, 229–255.

Gild, G. (1998). Dreams of renewal inspired by Japan and the West: Early 20th century reforms in Chinese music. *Chime*, *12–13*, 116–123.

Gold, T.B. (1993). Go with your feelings: Hong Kong and Taiwan culture in greater China. *The China Quarterly, 136,* 907–925.

Hammond, K.J. & Richey, J. (2015). *The sage returns: Confucian revival in contemporary China.* Albany: State University of New York.

Ho, W.C. (2003). Westernization and social transformations in Chinese music education, 1895–1949. *History of Education, 32*(4), 289–301.

Ho, W.C. (2006). Social change and nationalism in China's popular songs. *Social History, 31*(4), 435–453.

Ho, W.C. (2010). China: Socio-political constructions of school music. In G. Cox & R. Stevens (Eds.), *The origins and foundations of music education: Cross-cultural historical studies of music in compulsory schooling* (pp. 189–204). London and New York: Continuum.

Ho, W.C. (2013). Social challenges and cultural influences on China's music education: Practices and issues in teaching popular music in schools. In X.M. Li (Ed.), *Education in China: Cultural influences, global perspectives and social challenges* (pp. 89–105). New York: Nova Publishers.

Hong, J.H. (1998). *The internationalization of television in China: The evolution of ideology, society, and media since the reform.* Westport, CT: Praeger Publishers.

Howard, J.H. (2012). The making of a national icon: Commemorating Nie Er 1935–1949. *Twentieth-Century China, 37*(1), 5–29.

Hunan Literature and Art Publishing House. (2011). *Gechang (Singing)*. Hunan: Author.

Jiangsu Juvenile and Children's Publishing House. (2012a). *Yinyue (Music)* [*Grade 7, vol. 1*]. Nanjing: Author.

Jiangsu Juvenile and Children's Publishing House. (2012b). *Yinyue (Music)* [*Grade 7, vol. 2*]. Nanjing: Author.

Jiangsu Juvenile and Children's Publishing House. (2012c). *Yinyue (Music)* [*Grade 9, vol. 2*]. Nanjing: Author.

Judd, E.R. (1983). Revolutionary drama and song in the Jiangxi soviet. *Modern China, 9*(1), 127–160.

Kraus, R.C. (1989). *Pianos and politics in China: Middle-class ambitions and the struggle over Western music.* New York: Oxford University Press.

Lau, F. (2013). Voice, culture, and ethnicity in contemporary Chinese compositions. In C. Utz & F. Lau (Eds.), *Vocal music and contemporary identities, unlimited voices in East Asia and the West* (pp. 99–115). London: Routledge.

Law, W.W. & Ho, W.C. (2011). Music education in China: In search for social harmony and Chinese nationalism. *British Journal of Music Education, 28*(3), 371–388.

Law, W.W. & Ho, W.C. (2015). Popular music and school music education: Chinese students' preferences and dilemmas in Shanghai, China. *International Journal of Music Education, 33*(3), 304–324.

Lei, Y. S. (ed.) (2009). *Yinyue (Music)* [*Grade 4, vol. 1*]. Guangdong: Guangdong Education Publishing House and Guangdong Flower City Publishing House.

Li, A. (2014). Yellow music: A transcultural musical genre's role in heterogeneous community unification. *Wellesley College Digital Scholar and Archive.* Retrieved from: http://repository.wellesley.edu/cgi/viewcontent.cgi?article=1007&context=library_awards [Accessed 21 March 2015].

Lin, T.H.L. (2012). *The development and conceptual transformation of Chinese Buddhist songs in the twentieth century.* Unpublished PhD thesis. San Diego: University of California. Retrieved from: https://escholarship.org/uc/item/3fx0q1pd [Accessed 1 September 2015].

Liu, C.C. (2010). *A critical history of new music in China* (Translated by C. Mason). Hong Kong: The Chinese University of Hong Kong.

Ma, D. (2002). *Ershi shiji zhongguo yinyue jiaoyu* (*China's school music education in the twentieth century*). Shanghai: Shanghai Education Publishing House.

Ma, S.H. (1989). *The curricular content of elementary music in China between 1912 and 1982* (PhD Dissertation, University of North Texas). Ann Anbor, MI: University Microfilms International.

Melvin, S. & Cai, J.D. (2004). *Rhapsody in red: How western classical musical music became Chinese*. New York: Algora Publishing.

Ministry of Education, the People's Republic of China. (2012). *Yiwu jiaoyu yinyue kecheng biaozhun [Curriculum standards for primary education and junior secondary education: Music]*. Beijing: Beijing Normal University Press.

Moskowitz, M.L. (2010). *Cries of joy, Songs of sorrow: Chinese pop music and its cultural connotations*. Honolulu: University of Hawai'i Press.

People's Music Publishing House. (2014a). *Yinyue (Music)* [Grade 8, first term]. Beijing: Author.

People's Music Publishing House. (2014b). *Yinyue (Music)* [Grade 9, first term]. Beijing: Author.

People's Music Publishing House. (2015). *Yinyue (Music)* [Grade 3, second term]. Beijing: Author.

Powers, J. H. (1997). Conflict centres and management strategies during China's "Ten Years of Turmoil". *Intercultural Communication Studies*, 7, 149–168.

Qin, Q.M. (1991). *Hongyi dashi Li Shutong yinyue ji (Selected works of Master Hongyi, Li Shutong)*. Taipei: Huiju.

Rupke, H.N. & Blank, G. (2009). "Country roads" to globalization: Sociological models for understanding American popular music in China. *Journal of Popular Culture*, 42(1), 126–146.

Smith, S.A. (2002). *Like cattle and horses: Nationalism and labor in Shanghai, 1895–1927*. Durham, NC: Duke University Press.

Southwest China Normal University Press. (2012). *Yinyue (Music)*, [Grade 8, vol. 1]. Chongqing: Author.

Southwest China Normal University Press. (2013). *Yinyue (Music)*, [Grade 8, vol. 2]. Chongqing: Author.

Spence, J. (2001). *The search for modern China*. New York: W.W. Norton and Company.

Wang, Z. (2008). National humiliation, history education, and the politics of historical memory: Patriotic education campaign in China. *International Studies Quarterly*, 52, 783–806.

Wang, Z. (2014). *Never forget national humiliation: Historical memory in Chinese politics and foreign relations*. New York, NY: Columbia University Press.

Wong, I.K.F. (1984). Geming gequ: Songs for the education of the masses. In B.S. McDougall (Ed.), *Popular Chinese literature and performing* (pp. 112–143). London: University of California Press.

8

Towards 21st-century music teaching-learning

Reflections on student-centric pedagogic practices involving popular music in Singapore

Siew Ling Chua and Hui-Ping Ho

Introduction

This chapter discusses the teaching-learning of popular music in Singapore's general music classrooms, focusing on issues of music pedagogic practices and, perhaps more critically, the music teacher's role in effecting these practices. Green's (2006, 2008) work in highlighting issues of autonomy, authenticity and music pedagogy has stimulated vibrant discussion in the field (Folkestad, 2006; Green, 2008; Ho & Law, 2014; Smith, 2013; Väkevä, 2006). A significant impact of these developments is that they have opened up the music teacher's pedagogical repertoire.[1] Running in tandem with these exciting developments is the pan-Ministry call for a "student-centric" education and the nurturing of 21st-century competencies (MOE, Singapore, 2010). Drawing from vignettes in Singapore's music classrooms, we suggest that 21st-century music teaching-learning involving popular music needs to be student-centric, give students autonomy and empower the student voice (Finney & Harrison, 2010). We call for highly nuanced and thoughtful facilitation by teachers, so that students are meaningfully guided towards their learning goals.

---

1 Along with Green's informal learning, discussions include non-formal teaching, which together became part of the pedagogical package that was produced by Musical Futures (D'Amore, n.d.). Ho & Chua (2013) looked at case-study contextualizations of this range of music pedagogies in the Singapore classrooms.

Notions and definitions

Formal and informal approaches

We begin by putting forth some key notions and definitions that will guide the discussion. The first relates to the pedagogic practices of formal and informal learning. In formal teaching approaches, the teacher generally makes most of the curricular and pedagogical decisions, scaffolds a structured progression of learning for the students and generally relies on notation in the teaching-learning process. In informal learning, which is a practice adapted from how musicians learn on their own, outside formal music instruction (Green, 2008), students decide on the music to learn, with whom they learn and how they learn (often by aural copying), with the teacher facilitating them to reach their learning goals. Through adapting informal learning in music teaching, the teacher draws out learning from students rather than directing the learning, and usually with a greater focus on oral-aural processes. It is worth noting Folkestad's comment that "accordingly, informal learning typically involves more than just the core subject of learning, in this case the music; it features an integrated learning on a more holistic level" (2006, p. 137). While formal teaching and informal learning approaches are often juxtaposed like binary opposites, this paper takes the notion of them being situated along a continuum (Folkestad, 2006, p. 135), because practices in the classroom can be rather nuanced (D'Amore & Smith, 2016; Powell et al., in press).

Orientation

The second notion is in regard to the teacher's 'orientation' in music teaching-learning; Finney and Philpott (2010) delineated the *intentionality* of informal learning orientation towards *playing and making music*, while "the formal moment is an orientation to learning *how to play music*" (Folkestad, 2005; cited in Finney & Philpott, 2010, p. 9; emphasis added). Similarly, the teacher's orientation towards learning impacts how students will experience music learning. For example, informal learning when undertaken by a teacher with formal 'orientation' may result in the teacher disrupting the students' natural flow of music learning. Given the significance of these ideas, we wish to build upon them in order to create a 'student-centric' orientation, where the *intentionality* is on the learning needs of the students, which would anchor decisions regarding the direction in which pedagogic practices would lean in the continuum of formal teaching and informal learning.

Autonomy and flow experiences

The third notion that we would like to put forth concerns how autonomy is balanced between students and teachers. In informal learning, students are given a choice of what music to play, how to play it and with whom they play (Green, 2006, 2008). This autonomy seems to create a heightened level of student engagement and motivation in learning (Green, 2008; Wright, 2008). Ho (2013a) suggests that this resonates with how autonomy is seen through the lenses of Self-Determination

Theory, which, in the educational context, posits that when basic psychological needs of autonomy, competence and relatedness were met, students experienced greater engagement in learning (Reeve et al., 2004; Turner et al., 1998, cited in Stefanou et al., 2004). We propose three types of autonomy: procedural, organizational and cognitive. Out of the three dimensions of autonomy proposed by Reeve et al. (2004), the one that is most relevant here is *cognitive autonomy*.

We suggest that cognitive autonomy support is crucial when it comes to facilitating students to reach their learning goals. Cognitive autonomy support

> encourages student ownership of the learning and can include teacher behaviours such as asking students to justify or argue for their point, asking students to generate their own solution paths or asking students to evaluate their own and others' solutions or ideas.
>
> *(Logan et al., 1995; cited in Stefanou et al., 2004, p. 101)*

This can be done through facilitation of student learning through questions and conversations. Skilful facilitation allows autonomy to develop in the students and may help to arrest issues of students not being on-task and focused (if and when that happens). Connected to autonomy is the fourth notion – that of *flow*. Flow experiences are created when students are in "a state in which . . . (they) are so involved in an activity that nothing else seems to matter" (Csiksentmihalyi, 1990, p. 4). Such an experience is created when students feel sufficiently challenged and competent in performing an authentic task that they find to be relevant and purposeful.

The context of Singapore's music education

Popular music has been part of Singapore's general music[2] curriculum content since the 1993 syllabus revision (at which point it was referred to as "pop music"). All students take up General Music as part of their education for at least the first eight years of their schooling. The latest General Music syllabus (MOE, 2014), which applies across primary and secondary levels, states that opportunities must be offered for students to engage with diverse musical styles, traditions and genres, including "Art Music [and] Popular Music" (p. 19). Definitions of popular music are rarely unproblematic and this is not the place to debate them (Jones, chapter 27, this volume; Moir & Medbøe, 2015; Smith, 2013, 2014). We take, as a point of departure, Frith's (2001) definition of popular music as a term that primarily denotes music that is "accessible to the general public", "produced

---

2 Music is a subject in schools' curricula, requiring that every child is provided a basic music education. This aims to develop awareness and appreciation of music in local and global cultures, develop ability for creative expression and communication through music, and provide the basis to develop an informed and lifelong involvement in music (MOE, 2014). Students with inclinations and interest in music can also take music in a co-curricular activity such as Band or Choir, or as a subject leading to national examinations at the upper secondary and junior college levels.

commercially, for profit, as a matter of enterprise not art", and which "includes all contemporary popular forms – rock, country, reggae, rap, and so on" (2001, p. 94). While Anglo-American popular music is popular among students in Singapore, their lived experiences often include pop music of diverse languages and styles, such as Mandarin pop, Malay pop, Bollywood, J-pop and K-pop. This musical environment among students in Singapore is indicative of the larger popular music soundscapes in Singapore, reflecting our multi-ethnic society, which is 74% Chinese, 13% Malay, 9% Indian and 3% others (such as Eurasians) (Ministry of Trade & Industry, 2014, p. 5).

Moving in tandem with the Ministry's strategic direction of a student-centric education, a tenet driving the work of the Singapore Teachers' Academy of the aRts (STAR)[3] is also to nurture in students 21st-century outcomes of being a "confident person, self-directed learner, active contributor and a concerned citizen" (MOE, 2010, p. 3). The Ministry identified three key competencies (21CC) – Civic Literacy, Global Awareness and Cross-cultural Skills; Critical and Inventive Thinking; and Information and Communication Skills – which will "underpin the holistic education that our schools provide to better prepare our students for the future" (MOE, 2010). These are some of the key impetuses behind the research of pedagogic practices by STAR, which was set up in 2011 with the aim of strengthening the pedagogic knowledge and practices of teachers so that they are able to understand and implement the music syllabi effectively.

Among the research of pedagogic practices by STAR, two are of significance to our discussion in this chapter. First, the piloting of informal music learning and non-formal music teaching approaches with five case studies in 2012 led to an understanding of how these approaches hold potential for developing students' confidence, creativity, collaboration and self-directed learning, and how these pedagogies could be put into practice in our classrooms (Chua & Ho, 2013a/2013b; Chua, 2013a/2013b; Ho, 2013a/2013b; Onishi, 2013). Second, a research project completed in 2014, in collaboration with the National Institute of Education and other divisions in the Ministry of Education, led to findings on Physical Education, Art and Music pedagogical practices that nurture 21CC. The latter project used a case study approach in which researchers examined 12 music teachers on their pedagogic practices over a two-year period (2013–14), with the aim of exploring student-centric pedagogic practices. The findings confirmed the importance of empowering students' musical voices by providing them with opportunities to engage in critical thinking in music, creative and collaborative music-making and musical communication (MOE, 2016, p. 72–95). The findings, together with these pedagogic approaches, were then shared through two workshops with 31 teacher-leaders, who were to trial these approaches in their own classrooms in 2015 so

---

3 The Singapore Teachers' Academy for the aRts (STAR) was established in 2011 to enhance the professional excellence and practice of art and music teachers in order to improve the quality of art and music education in schools in Singapore. It is a part of the Ministry of Education. Further details are available at http://www.star.moe.edu.sg/.

that they could, in turn, share them with other teachers. Their lessons were video-recorded either by themselves or by teacher educators at STAR for professional development purposes.

Situating these findings and considerations in light of pedagogy for popular music in Singapore, we posit that the critical success for students' engagement in authentic musical experiences and autonomy in learning lies very much in the role of the music teacher in the following three areas: (1) autonomy negotiation and 'balance' between teacher and students, (2) facilitation of students' music-making and group work and (3) facilitation of student reflection in a community of learners. We discuss these, below, through vignettes of lessons conducted by one of the music teachers in early 2015.

Reflections on pedagogic practices

This section discusses the three areas of pedagogic practice from the aforementioned studies at STAR. Excerpts from the pedagogic practices of the teachers in the 2012 pilot, as well as from those of the 2015 teacher-leader, are included for the purpose of our discussion. The names given in the vignettes are fictitious in order to maintain confidentiality.

Autonomy: Negotiations of balance

Findings from our 2012 pilot and 2015 trial suggest that autonomy can be balanced between students and teacher. For example, where students were free to choose their own songs, they had to *inform* the teacher of their choices of songs, which they made as a group. The act of informing the teacher indicated a level of accountability to a key member of the learning community – the teacher. Where students were free to select their friendship groups, the teachers had to manage situations where some students could not find a group. One teacher, instead of assigning these students to existing groups, drew upon the school values of 'care' and 'responsibility' to encourage groups to 'invite' those who might be left out to join their groups. This positioned the class as *one community* of music-makers (Lave & Wenger, 1991).

From the pilot and trial, we have also found how the informal learning process provided opportunity for the social dimension of learning, which is important in student-centric pedagogical practices (Chua & Ho, 2013b; Niknafs & Przybylski, chapter 32, this volume). While much learning is socially constructed (Vygotsky, 1978), through 'group learning' (Green, 2008) we suggest that the teacher plays a different but nevertheless important role in the 're-configured' learning classroom community. Autonomy could thus be seen as a shared 'entity' between the learners *and the teacher*, enabling negotiations to take place so that there is a sense of comfortable balance for all concerned. Thus, "it is not that the teacher no longer has a role, but the role is more complex and nuanced than transmission and credentialling" (Lebler, 2007, p. 213). We will continue to discuss this role in the sharing of two vignettes about teacher facilitation.

Facilitation of music-making and group work

The facilitation of music-making in informal learning includes the modelling of problem-solving in group work. In one of the trials, a teacher-leader, Ms Soh, was facilitating with an informal learning approach where students worked in groups in different workstations in the music classroom, where each workstation was a 'jam hub', comprising electric guitars, keyboards, electronic drums, iPads and headphones. One of the groups had a dispute as two of the members who were playing the guitars were unable to coordinate. The group was working to perform the keyboard and guitar parts of a pop song they had chosen. Ms Soh approached the group and the following dialogue ensued:

MS SOH: OK OK. OK. We will not quarrel among ourselves. Let's try to solve the problem. OK. Number one ...
1ST BOY ON GUITAR: Finger pain.
MS SOH: Finger pain? Massage ... [she started rubbing her own fingers to demonstrate to the student how he could massage his fingers]
2ND BOY ON GUITAR: No. He says changing chords is very difficult.
MS SOH: OK. If changing chords is difficult, what do you think he can do to help?
2ND BOY ON GUITAR: Keep the guitar and then play keyboard.
MS SOH: If he wants to keep to the guitar, then how?
[2nd boy on guitar shrugged his shoulders]
BOY ON BASS: Just play one beat for the whole thing [gesturing a strum]. Play one note for the whole song.
BOY ON KEYBOARD: He can just play A minor first and then wait for [2nd boy on guitar].
MS SOH: Yes, he can.
BOY ON BASS: OK. [Facing the 1st boy on guitar] You play A minor only. [Then turning to the teacher]. Let him play A minor only.
MS SOH: He can play A minor.
BOY ON KEYBOARD: He needs to do two [chords].
MS SOH: He needs to do two, and then you [the 2nd boy on the guitar] need to do two. Is that the plan?
2ND BOY ON GUITAR: I don't get it.
BOY ON KEYBOARD: Because there is A minor, C and G.
BOY ON BASS: He can only play A minor.
[The boys eventually worked out the chord(s) that each of the students on the guitar would play.]
MS SOH: Try it. Sounds like an idea.
[Boy on bass was looking proud of himself]
MS SOH [TO THE 2ND BOY ON GUITAR]: Find your G chord first.
[The boy tried to work it out.]
MS SOH: You are getting there!
2ND BOY ON GUITAR: By changing A minor to C, I'm not so good.

MS SOH: Am I asking for perfection here? Remember, we said last week, this is work in progress. So, don't worry if you cannot do it perfectly.
[Boy on bass then suggested adding a rest after the seventh strum (in the eight strumming pattern phrase) so as to allow the boy on the guitar time to change the chord after the eighth count.]
MS SOH: Yes, no one will notice. Yes, ready? Start!
[The 2nd boy on the guitar started to strum, as boy on bass counted the beats next to him: "one, two, three, four, five, six, seven, change!" They repeated the cycle of chord changes for a few rounds successfully.]
MS SOH: Very good! You coordinated!
BOY ON BASS: See? My idea works! [Looking very pleased]

Examining the role of the teacher above, it is clear that she played the facilitator and the mediator to resolve the dispute between students by empowering them to make decisions and value one another's suggestions. She modelled a process in which students could learn to work together by affirming their suggestions, so that students would, in turn, value and try out suggestions made by their own peers. In this way, the students owned their learning process as they made suggestions to resolve the technical difficulty they faced. The teacher also acknowledged the "work in progress", emphasizing the process (rather than the product) – recalling Powell and Burstein's discussion of "approximation" (chapter 20, this volume). When given the opportunity, students demonstrated that they were able to assess and monitor themselves, as seen when they understood that they had difficulties with chord changes.

As demonstrated by Lebler (2007), the notion of self-monitoring or reflecting on one's practice is a key driver of learning in popular music practice. Although Lebler was referring to it in the context of higher education, one can see how informal learning, and the way the teacher facilitated the students' learning, generated an almost "natural" (Green, 2008, p. 42) need to self-monitor, which is crucial to the development of students' self-management and critical thinking, among the 21st-century competencies sought by Singapore's MOE. In the brief excerpt above, it can be observed that students took ownership of their own work, and this was made possible by the teacher helping to give voice to the students through their collaborative work.

Facilitation of student reflection in a community of learners

At the end of the lesson described above, Ms Soh invited a few groups to perform for the others as a mid-point check. The first group started pounding out the chords on the keyboard for Bruno Mars' "Just the Way You Are". As the keyboardist negotiated a chord change, he missed a chord, cried out "shit!" and carried on. The singer started singing as he looked down on his mobile, deciphering the lyrics from his mobile phone. He was emotionless, and as he hit the high notes he sounded rather flat. Some of his classmates started to sing along with him at the chorus section. There was a lot of excitement and laughter in the class although the performance was mediocre. At the end of the performance, the whole class cheered. Ms Soh had to calm them down as she started to facilitate a short reflection on their work.

MS SOH: Hey, you got a fan base! [The students cheered.] Can you all take one moment to think (about) what you like about the performance?
STUDENTS: Yang! [This was the name of the singer]
MS SOH: Everybody shouted out "Yang". OK. Just take one moment to write what you like about this performance. [Then, turning to Yang's group.] Yang, your group – also think about what you like about your own performance.
A STUDENT FROM YANG'S GROUP: I don't like it!
MS SOH: Find something you like about your performance.
[After 1 minute, the teacher picked a student at random to respond to her question.]
STUDENT: Just now, even though they made a mistake, they continued.
MS SOH: You like it that they continued even though they made a mistake? So, what criteria do you think they were meeting there?
[In this, the teacher drew students' attention back to the earlier criteria upon which they had agreed.]
SEVERAL STUDENTS: Coordination!
MS SOH: The show must go on. OK. Now, this group, I am going to ask you a simple question. What was difficult in coming up with this performance?
ONE STUDENT FROM THE GROUP: Got no "auto-tune".
MS SOH: Got no "auto-tune". So, besides the singing?
ONE STUDENT: Fingering.
ANOTHER STUDENT: We stopped halfway.
YANG: We decided to finalize everything just today only but we managed to [do the] basic first.
MS SOH: Oh. So you want to take it as basic as you can. OK. I thought that was quite a good decision because by taking it as basic as they can, they are starting from ground zero so everyone can still play together as a group. Good choice! Now, if you want to improve on this, what would you do?
[Yang shrugged his shoulders.]
ONE STUDENT: Playing the music properly because just now, when I played halfway, I got lost because suddenly stopped. I do not know what is the beat after that.
MS SOH: So, playing it properly means you want to make sure you can play everything accurately. Is that what you are trying to say? So, the next step is, still keep it basic but make sure everyone can play accurately.

In this facilitation process, Ms Soh had asked the students to identify an area for improvement that became the goal towards which they would work the next time they practised. This encouraged self-directed learning, as students owned their learning goals. This mid-point check on the students' progress by getting groups to perform for one another provided a structure to help pace student learning. Ms Soh had to decide whether to allocate time for all the groups to perform by the end of the lesson, and in the moment decided that she would only have some groups perform. All then spent time reflecting on their progress and making references to the criteria they had agreed on as a class (Chua, personal communication, 13 March 2015).

In this second vignette, there was evidence of peer support and enjoyment that were the result of the positive learning environment established by the teacher. The informal/non-formal learning approach provided the opportunity for students to learn in groups. Extending from this, the teacher created a sense of class community where the groups supported one another in their performing efforts. Her students were clearly engaged. One student requested to stay back after the class to practise on the keyboard, as he did not have to attend the next lesson, unlike the other students. The teacher also cited other examples where students requested to practise, in response to which she made the room available for students' use.

Discussion

Similar to findings in our earlier work on the trialling of informal and non-formal approaches involving popular music (Chua & Ho, 2013a/2013b), we found that while the opportunities provided through these approaches in the above pedagogic trials fostered a learning environment that engaged students musically and developed their musical behaviours and musical understandings, the effectiveness of these approaches depended on the teacher's student-centric orientation and facilitation. What we have highlighted through the vignettes is the critical role of the teacher as a facilitator, as evidenced through the interventions in the learning process described above, in supporting the cognitive autonomy of the students. The teacher needs to be acutely aware of his/her students' profiles and levels of attainment in order to motivate students in their learning by guiding them to experience small successes throughout their work, asking questions to help them reflect and providing encouragement and affirmation so as to give students confidence. Such reflection on learning is crucial in developing the ability to self-monitor and self-direct learning (Lebler, 2007).

Through the vignettes in which the teachers supported cognitive autonomy, thereby empowering the student voice, the following 'teacher moves' were observable, also corroborating our earlier findings from research on pedagogical approaches that nurture 21st-century competencies (MOE, 2016, p. 72–95). They include:

a   *Facilitation of students' musical choices and decisions*

   The informal/non-formal approach allows students greater control of their learning. Teacher facilitation can be appropriately applied to give voice to students' musical decisions. The teacher modelled a process in which teacher and students collaborating on music-making activities could respect one another's musical decisions, drawing from students' suggestions to resolve technical problems, then validating these suggestions by having students act on them. This process empowered students to appreciate and consider suggestions and from themselves and their peers as they developed competence and confidence in music performance.

b   *Facilitation of musical creativity and critical thinking*

   The facilitation of reflection on students' music-making as demonstrated in the vignette is an example of how critical thinking can be facilitated in music lessons.

c   *Facilitation of collaborative group work and leveraging technology*

   In creating a collaborative learning environment, Ms Soh's set-up of workstations that use electronic instruments, iPads and headphones mimicked learning outside school contexts that leverages the use of technology (see also Williams & Randles, chapter 5, this volume). Apart from the use of hardware, Ms Soh's modelling of how disputes could be resolved by appreciating and validating one another's suggestions also contributed to students' understanding of how they could develop 'soft skills' to collaborate effectively.

There is evidence in the above vignettes that students were engaged in their musical discourses and experienced musical fluency (Swanwick, 1999) as they took ownership in order to tackle the musical challenges they set for themselves in the task. This was made possible when students participated in the authentic processes of learning (Green, 2002), and the teachers provided clear goals and immediate feedback through group work as well as mid-point checks with students performing for one another to help pace and develop their learning.

Conclusion

In the context of 21st-century teaching and learning in Singapore, pedagogy involving popular music needs to be student-centric, give students autonomy and empower the student voice. This gives students opportunities to grow in confidence as self-directed learners and active contributors, as they nurture their 21st-century competencies in critical thinking and collaborative work, as highlighted above. This necessitates a very highly nuanced and thoughtful facilitation from teachers with a student-centric orientation. As discussed in this chapter, three key areas of teaching practice important for a student-centric, informal learning approach are: (1) autonomy negotiation, (2) facilitation of students' music-making and group work and (3) facilitation of student reflection in a community of learners.

As the music education community continues to discuss pedagogy for popular music (Mantie, 2013), facilitative approaches and the critical role of the teacher as a facilitator, need to be more foregrounded to help practitioners realize the aims and objectives integral to these approaches. A key point is the need to understand more about how cognitive autonomy could be better supported in music classrooms. As the transmission and consumption of popular music is varied, pedagogical processes could leverage media and technological advances in the classroom. Further research could throw light on the facilitation of an informal learning approach, investigating, for example, how media and technology in popular music production and consumption could give insights into music pedagogy that is more connected with the living experiences of students and contemporary industry practices (Powell & Burstein, chapter 20, this volume; Thompson & Stevenson, chapter 17, this volume).

References

Chua, S.L. (2013a). Informal learning for song writing. In S.L. Chua & H.P. Ho (Eds.), *Connecting the stars: Essays on student-centric music education*. Singapore: Singapore Teachers' Academy for the aRts, Ministry of Education. Retrieved from: http://www.star.moe.edu.sg/star/slot/u1050489/chapter11.pdf [Accessed 21 March 2015].

Chua, S.L. (2013b). STOMPing up musical engagement the non-formal and informal ways. In S.L. Chua & H.P. Ho (Eds.) *Connecting the stars: Essays on student-centric music education*. Singapore: Singapore Teachers' Academy for the aRts, Ministry of Education. Retrieved from: http://www.star.moe.edu.sg/star/slot/u1050489/chapter14.pdf [Accessed 21 March 2015].

Chua, S.L. & Ho, H.P. (2013a). Articulating 21st century music teaching and learning: contextualising pedagogies in Singapore. Paper presented at 9th Asia-Pacific Symposium on Music Education Research and Arts Education Conference, Singapore.

Chua, S.L. & Ho, H.P. (2013b). Connecting findings, reflections and insights: Student-centricity musically, creatively. In S.L. Chua & H.P. Ho (Eds.), *Connecting the stars: Essays on student-centric music education*. Singapore: Singapore Teachers' Academy for the aRts, Ministry of Education. Retrieved from: http://www.star.moe.edu.sg/star/slot/u1050489/chapter15.pdf [Accessed 21 March 2015].

Csikszentmihalyi, M. (1990). *Flow: The psychology of optimal experience*. New York: Harper and Row.

D'Amore, A. (Ed) (n.d.) *Musical futures: An approach to teaching and learning* (Resource Pack, 2nd ed.). London: Paul Hamlyn Foundation.

D'Amore, A. & Smith, G.D. (2016). Aspiring to music making as leisure through the Musical Futures classroom. In R. Mantie & G.D. Smith (Eds.), *The Oxford handbook of music making and leisure* (pp. 61–80). New York: Oxford University Press.

Finney, J. & Harrison, C. (Eds.) (2010). *Whose music education is it?: The role of the student voice*. UK: National Association of Music Educators.

Finney, J. & Philpott, C. (2010). Informal learning and meta-pedagogy in initial teacher education in England, *British Journal of Music Education*, 27(1), 7–19.

Folkestad, G. (2006). Formal and informal learning situations or practices vs formal and informal ways of learning. *British Journal of Music Education*, 23(2), 135–145.

Frith, S. (2001). Pop music. In S. Frith, W. Straw & J. Street (2001). *The Cambridge companion to pop and rock*. Cambridge: Cambridge University Press.

Green, L. (2002). *How popular musicians learn: A way ahead for music education*. Aldershot: Ashgate.

Green, L. (2006). Popular music education in and for itself, and for "other" music: Current research in the classroom. *International Journal of Music Education*, 24(2), 101–118.

Green, L. (2008). *Music, informal learning and the school: A new classroom pedagogy*. Hampshire and Burlington: Ashgate.

Ho, H.P. (2013a). Rollin' in at the deep end: Choice, collaboration and confidence through informal learning with the guitar. In S.L. Chua & H.P. Ho (Eds.), *Connecting the stars: Essays on student-centric music education*. Singapore: Singapore Teachers' Academy for the aRts, Ministry of Education. Retrieved from: http://www.star.moe.edu.sg/star/slot/u1050489/chapter10.pdf [Accessed 21 March 2015].

Ho, H.P. (2013b). Connecting the curricular and co-curricular through formal and non-formal teaching. In S.L. Chua & H.P. Ho (Eds.), *Connecting the stars: Essays on student-centric music education*. Singapore: Singapore Teachers' Academy for the aRts, Ministry of Education. Retrieved from: http://www.star.moe.edu.sg/star/slot/u1050489/chapter13.pdf [Accessed 21 March 2015].

Ho, H.P. & Chua, S.L. (2013). Piloting informal and non-formal approaches for music teaching in five secondary schools in Singapore: An introduction. In S.L. Chua & H.P. Ho (Eds.), *Connecting the stars: Essays on student-centric music education*. Singapore: Singapore Teachers' Academy for the aRts, Ministry of Education. Retrieved from: http://www.star.moe.edu.sg/star/slot/u1050489/chapter9.pdf [Accessed 21 March 2015].

Ho, W.C. & Law, W.W. (2014). Gender, popular music, and music learning in China's Shanghai. *Visions of Research in Music Education, 25*. Retrieved from: http://www.rider.edu/~vrme.

Lave, J. & Wenger, E. (1991). *Situated learning: Legitimate peripheral participation*. Cambridge: Cambridge University Press.

Lebler, D. (2007). Student-as-master? Reflections on a learning innovation in popular music pedagogy. *International Journal for Music Education, 25*(3), 205–221.

Mantie, R. (2013). A comparison of "popular music pedagogy" discourses. *Journal of Research in Music Education, 61*(3), 334–352.

Ministry of Trade & Industry (2014). *Population trends 2014*. Retrieved from: http://www.singstat.gov.sg/docs/default-source/default-document-library/publications/publications_and_papers/population_and_population_structure/population2014.pdf [Accessed 21 March 2015].

MOE (2010). *Nurturing our young for the future: Competences for the 21st century*. Singapore: Ministry of Education.

MOE (2014). *2015 Syllabus: General music programme (primary/secondary)*. Student development curriculum division, Ministry of Education. Retrieved from: http://www.moe.gov.sg/education/syllabuses/arts-education/files/2015-general-music-programme-syllabus.pdf [Accessed 21 March 2015].

MOE (2016). *Enhancing 21st century competencies in physical education, art and music: PAM research report*. Singapore: Ministry of Education. Retrieved from: http://www.star.moe.edu.sg/star/slot/u3049/doc/PAM-full-single.pdf [Accessed 20 October 2016].

Moir, Z. & Medbøe, H. (2015). Reframing popular music composition as performance-centred practice. *Journal of Music, Technology and Education, 8*(2), 147–161.

Onishi, P. (2013). Negotiating the boundaries of formal and informal learning. In S.L. Chua & H.P. Ho (Eds.), *Connecting the stars: Essays on student-centric music education* (pp. 66–85). Singapore: Singapore Teachers' Academy for the aRts, Ministry of Education. Retrieved from: http://www.star.moe.edu.sg/star/slot/u1050489/chapter12.pdf [Accessed 21 March 2015].

Powell, B., Smith, G.D., & D'Amore, A. (in press). Challenging symbolic violence and hegemony in music education through contemporary pedagogical approaches. *Education 3-13: International Journal of Primary, Elementary and Early Years Education*.

Reeve, J., Jang, H., Carrell, D., Jeon, S., & Barch, J. (2004). Enhancing students' engagement by increasing teachers' autonomy support. *Motivation and Emotion, 28*(2), 147–169.

Smith, G.D. (2013). Seeking "Success" in popular music. *Music Education Research International, 6*, 26–37.

Smith, G.D. (2014). Popular music in higher education. In G. Welch & I. Papageorgi (Eds.), *Advanced musical performance: Investigations in higher education learning* (pp. 33–48). Farnham: Ashgate.

Stefanou, C.R., Perencevich, K.C., DiCintio, M., & Turner, J.C. (2004). Supporting autonomy in the classroom: Ways teachers encourage student decision making and ownership. *Educational Psychologist, 39*, 97–110.

Swanwick, K. (1999). *Teaching music musically*. London and New York: Routledge.

Väkevä, L. (2006). Teaching popular music in Finland: What's up, what's ahead? *International Journal of Music Education, 24*(2), 126–131.

Vygotsky, L. (1978). *Mind in society: Development of higher psychological processes*. Cambridge: Harvard University Press.

Wright, R. (2008). Kicking the habitus: Power, culture and pedagogy in the secondary school music curriculum. *Music Education Research, 10*(3), 389–402.

9

Popular music education in Hong Kong

A case study of the Baron School of Music

Hei Ting Wong

Introduction

Cantonese popular music – Cantopop – is unique to Hong Kong, penetrating local lives and spaces through various media. Until recently, locals considered Cantopop as a means of entertainment and a source for identity construction, but not as a topic for study at college or school. Similarly to the inclusion of popular music education in other parts of the world (Till, chapter 2, this volume), Cantonese popular music was implemented much more recently in local schools than Western classical music. Prior to popular music elements being introduced to the music curricula of local mainstream secondary schools in 2009, popular music industry insiders began operating private music schools to teach instruments and singing in the Cantopop style. Currently five of these schools remain in operation; one of these is the Baron School of Music (BSM).

After providing some background to music education in Hong Kong, this chapter presents a discursive case study of BSM as the first private popular music school in Hong Kong structured and organized for the study of local popular music (Cantopop), and the only school to offer programmes that qualify for the government's Continuous Education Fund (CEF) (explained below). This chapter is the first academic study of BSM; below I compare elements of BSM with private popular music schools in the United Kingdom and the United States. This chapter reports on archival research and draws on in-depth interviews with former students of BSM, hoping to shed light on a unique case and context of popular music education in Hong Kong.

Music education in Hong Kong

Mainstream (government-funded) school education

Due to British colonial rule in Hong Kong (1841–1997) and the missionary-initiated education during that time, Hong Kong schools' music curriculum was – and largely remains – Eurocentric, with a focus on Western classical music. The curriculum has been revised over time, as the political environment and the relationship between Hong Kong, China and the UK continued and continues to shift (Ho, 2011). Ho describes in detail the structure and contents of music education in Hong Kong, pointing out that the first official music curriculum for Hong Kong primary and secondary schools was set up by the Music Department of the Education Department[1] in 1952 (2011, p. 73). Traditional Chinese music was first provisionally listed in the music curriculum for junior students in secondary school in 1983, and Hong Kong contemporary classical music was not included in the syllabus until 1987, for form four and five students[2] (Ho, 2011, pp. 76, 81). Even so, Ho notes, "Hong Kong classical music was less prominent than both Western and Chinese classical music" (Ho, 2011).

Cantonese is the primary dialect of Hong Kong, as well as Canton (Guangdong) province and its vicinity, and Hong Kong has been the main production site for Cantopop. However, Cantopop was historically widely viewed as inferior by comparison to Mandarin popular songs imported from Shanghai, or Cantonese opera – until it was popularized in 1974 due to the success of the television drama theme song "The Fatal Irony"[3] (Wong, 2003, pp. 89, 92). The success of Cantopop was primarily seen in the working class of the 1970s. Ho explains:

> Cantonese popular songs were viewed as "low-class" by the government and some social organizations. Local popular songs were never formally introduced into the curriculum; indeed, some teachers regarded their use in school as a waste of time because students already knew a lot about them from the mass media. Many teachers did not teach popular music because they did not know much about them [Cantopop songs, Cantopop structure/theory or/and Cantopop production as they were trained in western classical music] and were not familiar with their style.
>
> *(2011, p. 82)*

---

1 The current Education Bureau was previously named the Education Department (before 2003) and the Education and Manpower Bureau (2003–2007).
2 Form four and five students are about 14 or 15 years old, with variations due to the admission age of primary school or transfer from non-local education systems.
3 "Fatal Irony" is composed by Kar Fai Joseph Koo, with lyrics written by Cantonese Opera writer Shiu Tak Yip, and sung by Sandra Lang (who used to sing English songs).

It was not until 2009, with the education reform of the "3–3–4 Scheme", that both local and Western popular music became part of the curriculum in schools.[4] A new public examination, the Hong Kong Diploma of Secondary Education (HKDSE), was introduced, with a new curriculum for each subject, and popular music was included for the first time.

'Popular music' and 'pop songs' appear in the study guidelines in various modules of the HKDSE music curriculum from 2009. This breakthrough, however, was limited and the materials included are somewhat outdated. For example, Compulsory Module 1 (Listening) lists popular music compositions by locals Joseph Koo and Sam Hui, and Western hits performed by Elvis Presley and the Beatles, worth 6% of the entire exam (CDC & HKEAA, 2014, p. 8). These four acts are from 1970s–1980s Cantopop and 1950s–1960s Western popular music, respectively, revealing a focus on reified popular music canon, rather than the recognition that other, contemporary, music that may currently be more popular among students or in the local society in general; this arguably reflects a 'cultural lag' among government officials. Popular music is also listed in Compulsory Modules 2 (Performing I) and 3 (Creating I), and in Elective Module 4 (Special project) and 5 (Performing II) of the music curriculum, in which students perform, compose and research Cantopop or popular music in general (pp. 8–10). Though Western classical music still has a heavy weight in the exam (20% is on Western music listening skills), the inclusion of popular music, specifically Cantopop, in local school curricula is encouraging in that it emphasizes local culture for the first time in the history of institutionalized music education in Hong Kong.

Alongside the late adoption of popular music in secondary education, popular music has become a niche area in music departments in Hong Kong's universities. Five tertiary institutions have music departments – Chinese University of Hong Kong (CUHK), Hong Kong Baptist University (HKBU), University of Hong Kong (HKU), The Education University of Hong Kong (EdUHK)[5] and Hong Kong Academy of Performing Arts. All offer music programmes from Diploma to Doctorate, but none of them has a programme specializing in popular music. "Popular Music Production" and "Technology in the Popular Music Industry" are the only two modules offered in the Bachelor of Music Education programme at HKIEd[6] (Hong Kong Institute of Education, 2014) that focus on popular music, and a lyric-writing course is offered by the Department of Humanities and Creative

---

4 The "3–3–4 Scheme" is an education reform of the secondary and tertiary education in Hong Kong, from 13-year pre-tertiary education and three-year tertiary education to 12-year pre-tertiary education (three-year junior secondary and three-year senior secondary) and four-year tertiary education. The corresponding HKDSE is recognized in many overseas countries; it is especially packed with the tariff system of the Universities and Colleges Admissions Service (UCAS) and the International English Language Testing System (IELTS) in the UK (HKEAA website, 2015).
5 EdUHK was officially renamed from Hong Kong Institute of Education (HKIEd) in May 2016.
6 More details of the education reform and the new music-related programmes developed by HKIEd due to the reform can be referred to Leong, 2014.

Writing at HKBU. Instead of being included in music departments, research on popular music is conducted by other departments in local universities, such as Cantopop lyrical analysis in Chinese, English or Cultural Studies departments by Prof. Yiu Wai Chu of HKU[7] and Prof. Ching Kiu Chan of Lingnan University,[8] and functions of Cantopop with media in Sociology or Journalism departments by Prof. Chun Hung Ng of HKU and Prof. Kit Wai Ma of CUHK. Cantopop was not a research interest among local scholars until the 1990s, and the first local conference on Cantopop was held in 1991 (Wong, 2003, p. 2). As popular music education is not commonly found in local schools, Hong Kong locals need to seek alternative ways to formally train in popular music performance or production; attending private music schools such as BSM is one option.[9]

Young indicates that modes of informal music learning from outside the traditional structures of school and the formal curriculum have gained recognition in formal UK education in recent years (2012, p. 242). Green observes the complexities intrinsic to bringing 'outside' music into schools:

> The classroom context has a tendency to change pupils' perceptions of music's delineations, and that the delineations of popular music do not fit well in the classroom. Additionally, popular music's inherent meanings have been rather distorted by a pedagogy that has been slow to recognize the demands of popular music's informal learning practices.
>
> *(2006, p. 113)*

Approaches such as Musical Futures in the UK, Australia, Canada, Australia, Singapore, Brazil and elsewhere, and Little Kids Rock's Modern Band in the US, are successfully bringing popular music and informal learning into mainstream schools (Powell et al., in press). BSM provides examples of incorporating informal music learning in popular music into a formal institutional setting – what Smith identified as taking place in higher popular music education, and called "formalization of informalization", as part of a trend in some institutions towards "hybridized" music learning (2013, p. 32) (see also Lebler & Hodges, chapter 22, this volume).

Private (for-profit) music schools

As shown in Table 9.1, seven for-profit music schools have provided popular music education in Hong Kong alongside mainstream music education provision. Several, including BSM, were started or sponsored by insiders from the local popular

---

7 Chu started working on Cantopop research when he was at HKBU; now he is affiliated with HKU.
8 Chan started working on Cantopop research when he was at CUHK; now he is affiliated with Lingnan University.
9 The privatization of (higher) education is linked to the global growth of neoliberalist ideologies (see e.g. Giroux, 2014, pp. 45–49).

Table 9.1 For-profit popular music education schools in Hong Kong

School Name	Year Established	Industry Insiders Related (selected)	Popular Music Programmes (selected)	Status
音樂農莊 The Music Farm	1987	區瑞強 Albert Au (singer), 曾路得 Ruth Chen (singer)	Singing	Active
Ricky Music Factory	1998	朱翰博 Ricky Chu (drummer)	Drumming, composing, guitar	Active
音樂人教室 Music Man Productions	2002	張崇德 Peter Cheung (singer), 張崇基 Andrew Cheung (singer)	Singing, guitar	Active
杜麗莎國際演藝學院 Teresa Carpio International School of Performing Arts	2004	杜麗莎 Teresa Carpio (singer)	Singing	Not in business
伯樂音樂學院 Baron School of Music	2006	伍樂城 Ronald Ng (composer, producer), 雷有暉 Patrick Lui (singer), 林夕 Lin Xi (lyricist), 黃丹儀 Dennie Wong (singer, composer), 金培達 Peter Kam (composer, film scorer)	Singing, lyrics writing, songwriting, production, DJ, pop instrumental performance	Active
博丞音樂專業學院 Pops School of Music	2007	張家誠 Alan Cheung (composer), 嚴勵行 Johnny Yim (producer, composer)	Singing, song writing, production	Not in business
英皇娛樂演藝創意學院 Emperor Entertainment Academy for Performing Arts	2011	Related to the local music label/film production company, Emperor Entertainment Group (EEG; 2014)	Singing	Active

music and entertainment industries, such as producers, singers, songwriters or instrumentalists. The Emperor Entertainment Academy for Performing Arts, for example, is supported by the local Emperor Entertainment Group (EEG), which operates music labels and film production companies (The Emperor Entertainment Group, 2014).

Some of these schools have closed, perhaps seeking only to serve shorter-term ends for students and the institutions instead of offering the recognized qualifications that BSM awards. BSM has earned governmental recognition through offering diploma and professional certificate programmes that qualify for CEF (explained below).

A tailwind of the local popular music industry and BSM: Continuing education fund (CEF) in Hong Kong

Established in June 2002, CEF is operated by the Student Financial Assistance Agency of the Hong Kong government.[10] It was designed to alleviate the financial burden for people who would like to learn new skills for working purposes, and promotes continuous learning in eight domains: Business Services, Financial Services, Logistics, Tourism, Creative Industry, Design, Language and Interpersonal and Intrapersonal Skills for the Workplace (Continuing Education Fund, 2014). CEF supports the development of popular music skills under the banner of Creative Industry. To qualify as CEF course providers, institutions need to customize courses to suit one of the eight domains and the Specifications of Competency Standards (SCSs) under the Qualifications Framework (QF). The QF is:

> A hierarchy that orders and supports qualifications of academic, vocational and continuing education. To strengthen the industries' leading role in the development of vocational training so as to enhance the effectiveness of the latter, SCSs are formulated by the respective industries. To ensure wide acceptance of the qualifications conferred by various educational and training bodies under the QF, a quality assurance mechanism is set up. All QF-recognized qualifications are quality assured.
>
> *(Qualifications Framework, 2014)*

This government-led sponsorship echoes higher education policy elsewhere, such as in the UK, where emphasis is placed on vocational training with the matters of "global competitiveness, knowledge to wealth creation, and employability" at the heart of higher education policy (Parkinson & Smith, 2015, p. 95). Employability is understood as conceptually different from employment;

---

10 CEF applicants need to be Hong Kong residents, aged between 18 and 65, who have "the right of abode or the right to land or to remain in Hong Kong without restriction", and who are enrolled in certified, reimbursable course(s) for the maximum amount of HKD$10,000 (USD$1,290) (Continue Education Fund, 2014).

it is "a set of achievements" to benefit oneself and the economy and "about learning... [focusing] less on 'employ' and more on 'ability'" (Parkinson, 2014, pp. 28–29). This trend is apparently widespread globally (e.g. Morrow et al., chapter 26, this volume; Sylvester & O'Reilly, chapter 24, this volume). Participating in CEF, BSM thus also "inculcate[s] values that align with the government's macroeconomic strategy" and embeds and embraces "aims and learning outcomes that are devised in awareness of these policy agendas" (Parkinson & Smith, 2015, p. 95).

BSM exemplifies a national tendency in Hong Kong and internationally towards neoliberalization of education systems, "correspond[ing] to market principles, [...] consumer choice and economies of scale" and "support[ing] the government's ideology of governance by market principles" (Jones, chapter 27, this volume; McLaughlin, chapter 10, this volume; Smith, 2015; Parkinson, 2014, pp. 34, 35).

Six programmes offered by BSM are eligible for CEF:

- MIDI and Digital Audio
- Composition I
- Certificate in Lyric-Writing
- Advanced Certificate in Modern Audio Production
- Advanced Certificate in Vocal Techniques and Performing Vocals
- Professional Diploma or Professional Certificate in Music Marketing and Management (in collaboration with the Li Ka Shing Institute of Professional and Continuing Education of the Open University of Hong Kong (LiPACE))
(Continuing Education Fund, 2014)

These are in the CEF domain of Creative Industry and are designed to help students achieve and demonstrate a certain level of skills and knowledge for application in the music industry. Some other organizations also offer courses related to popular music; LiPACE has a lyric-writing course, for example, but none of the courses on the list at BSM are offered by other local popular music schools. As the CEF offers financial assistance for continuous education, BSM President Ronald Ng has stated that BSM courses are designed to build up the professional credentials of local popular music industry workers, enhance teaching quality by having industry insiders as instructors and attract talents who might not otherwise be able to join the industry (cited in Yu, 2013, pp. 189–190).

Baron School of Music

BSM was established in 2006 by Ronald Ng, the School's president and a well-known Cantopop composer and producer, with music industry colleagues including Patrick Lui, the lead singer of the local rock band *Taichi*. Famous local lyricist Xi Lin is the Honourable Director, and around 40 industry insiders from different professions are the instructors (Lui, 2006, C07; Tse, 2006, C01). BSM is structured into seven divisions, each of which offers classes ranging from one-day master classes or talks to a two-year part-time Diploma.[11] Classes include Classical Music Performance, Pop Music Performance, Vocals, Lyric-writing, Recording and Mixing, Music Production and Technology, DJ (Scratching/Mixing), Beatbox and Rap and Junior Music School (Baron School of Music, 2014). Each division is led by an experienced industry insider, and students are trained by industry professionals (Baron School of Music, 2014). For example, in the Lyric-writing Division, Xi Lin is the Director, while award-winning lyricists Yat Yiu Yu, Kin Yan, Joe Lei and Jone Chui are teaching staff (Baron School of Music, 2014).

Comparing BSM with its western counterparts

The programme structure at BSM is relatively different from those of other programmes at the same level in popular music schools in, for instance, the US and the UK. (I mention examples of popular music education institutions from these two countries in particular, as Ronald Ng is a graduate of the Berklee College of Music [Boston] in the US, and therefore much of the ethos of school arguably derives from his experiences there, and UK qualifications are highly regarded in Hong Kong.) Ng stated in an interview that BSM's course designs reference those of Berklee; however, as the popular music industries of the US and Hong Kong are different in many ways, such as the preferred musical styles and singers' images, he claims that he does not directly transfer the "Berklee model" – emphasis on the training in both Western musical theory and practical skills with a longer study duration for a certificate or higher qualification – to BSM. Ng claims that BSM balances time between lessons, practices and internship opportunities (cited in Yu, 2013, pp. 188–189). As diploma is the highest level of qualification granted by BSM, the following compares roughly equivalent levels of programmes.

One noticeable area of difference is entrance requirements. BSM states that new students applying to study vocal and instrument majors are required to attend auditions and interviews (Baron School of Music, 2014). Applicants for other programmes are required to meet certain prerequisites such as external examinations (Baron School of Music, 2014). For example, among CEF-qualified programmes, only the Diploma in Music Composition and Production has prerequisites.[12] Compared to the low/no requirements of BSM, UK schools are more demanding even at the diploma level, requiring five passes in five GCSEs[13] with grade C or above

---

11 Diploma is an education qualification designed by the British colonial government in Hong Kong, and diploma programmes are considered part of tertiary education. Higher Diploma programmes in universities are subsidized by the Hong Kong government and are highly regarded by local employers. Study time is two years, compared to the bachelor's degree programmes of three years (prior to 1012) and four years (post-2012).
12 According to BSM's website, the prerequisites of the Diploma programme are: 1. Passed Grade 5 Theory and Grade 6 on any instruments of the Associated Board of the Royal Schools of Music (ABRSM), UK, or; 2. Completed the 'Foundation music production' course [at BSM] and passed Grade 5 Theory of ABRSM by the start of phrase four of the Diploma.
13 GCSE, the General Certificate of Secondary Education, is a public examination for students who completed the compulsory school education (about 16 years old) in England, Wales and Northern Ireland.

(Academy of Contemporary Music, 2014; Institute of Contemporary Music Performance, 2014). All UK schools require an audition/interview at the initial stage of the admission; the Institute of Contemporary Music Performance (ICMP) states a requirement of at least two years' experience in the majoring instrument for diploma (pre-undergraduate) applicants (Institute of Contemporary Music Performance, 2014). Berklee and Musicians Institute (MI) do not offer diploma programmes, but, like ICMP, have either short-term summer or certificate programmes, respectively, which have low to no prerequisites (Berklee College of Music, 2014; Musicians Institute, 2014). MI offers associate's degrees that require a high school diploma and audition with audio example (Musicians Institute, 2014). The admission requirements for CEF-qualified certificates or diploma programmes at BSM appear lower than programmes of similar levels in the UK and the US.

There are further differences, present in the curricula of comparable programmes. The performance programmes of the UK and US schools all provide music theory and ear/aural perception training courses. BSM's Advanced Certificate in Vocal Techniques and Performing Vocals seems to be more practical, embedding theory in practice-based classes, listing the only theoretical courses in Phase One as "Structure and Principles of Voice Production of Body" and "13 Voice Control Methods" (Baron School of Music, 2014). BSM's Diploma in Music Composition and Production programme has still fewer elements in music theory, focusing on the hands-on skills of music production (Baron School of Music, 2014). BSM assumes the students of this diploma programme have prior musical and theoretical knowledge for song-arranging and producing; the "four-tier education goal" of BSM states students should pass the first three tiers of music theory and aural training before they enrol in professional diploma programmes (2014). BSM evaluates students ' performance per semester through in-class and concert performances and the results of external examinations with ABRSM, Trinity or Rock School (2014).[14]

Overall, given that the duration of programmes of study at BSM is considerably shorter, BSM's programme structures appear to be more intensely practical and vocationally orientated than those of schools in the UK and the US. Based on the length and content of the programmes, graduates may not be highly theoretically knowledgeable, but are provided with practical experience and practical, applicable knowledge and skills for the local music industry (see Hooper, chapter 13, this volume). Hannan suggests the requirement of skills among different types of musicianship is different; even though both Western classical and popular musicians need a certain level of reading skills in Western musical notation, popular musicians need more support in music technology, such as the application of computer technologies to assist in music-writing and arranging (2006,

---

14 As music learning is mainly an out-of-curriculum experience in Hong Kong, many local music learners who learn Western classical music take the grade examinations from either the Associated Board of the Royal Schools of Music (ABRSM; 2014) or Trinity College London (Trinity; 2014) to certify their learning progress. A preference for taking examinations from these two British schools reflects the high regard in which the British education system is held, recalling Hong King's colonial heritage. Refer to the websites of ABRSM and Trinity.

pp. 148–149) – notwithstanding the over-simplification of an implied binary opposition between classical and popular music learning (see Fleet, chapter 14, this volume, for discussion of the importance of notation and proficiency in music reading).

BSM niche – bridging the classroom to the job market

The key selling points of BSM are: providing students with opportunities to learn from experienced popular music industry insiders, getting connected to the industry and networking with insiders through working on commercial projects and providing opportunities for instructors to discover new talents in the student pool – all in the local, regional context of Hong Kong and Cantopop. In the current prevailing neoliberal economic-ideological environment, education as an investment becomes a form of consumerism, and "[c]elebrity has become the principal expression of value in a society in which only commodified objects have any value" (Giroux, 2014, pp. 48–49; McLaughlin, chapter 10, this volume; Morrow et al., chapter 26, this volume). This is proved by the selling points of BSM as well as the intervention to the creative industry by the CEF and QF operated by the Hong Kong government.

With the network of Ronald Ng and other industry insiders teaching at BSM and running the school, BSM has developed various methods for promotion and marketing. For instance, BSM hosts local and international singing competitions to promote the school and distributes as prizes vouchers to study at BSM. An informant interviewee for this chapter participated in a singing contest hosted by the Success in Music Charity Foundation (founded by Ronald Ng) in conjunction with BSM and other related companies as some of the lead sponsors (Success in Music Charity Foundation, 2014). The 10 finalists received study vouchers for BSM and the opportunity to perform in Ronald Ng's concert of his own compositions, singing for Cantopop stars at the Hong Kong Coliseum (the foremost Cantopop venue) along with 30 vocal students of BSM.

As BSM's programmes aim to strike a balance between theory and practice, 'real-work' opportunities are essential before entering into the industry – a notion that pervades similar provision internationally (see Lebler & Hodges, chapter 22, this volume; Morrow et al., chapter 26, this volume; Smith, 2014; Smith & Shafighian, 2013). BSM has at least two affiliated production companies – Solid Sound Production Ltd and Baron Productions and Artiste Management Ltd – that seek commercial projects for BSM students and contracted BSM graduates (Baron Music, 2012).[15] These two companies are either owned by BSM-related person-

---

15 There is not room here to debate the numerous ethical issues presented by the student/teacher/school/industry interconnectivity that is a feature of many popular music programmes. Donna Weston's (2015) paper on the Seed project at Queensland Conservatorium, for instance, provoked heated debate among delegates at the Research in Popular Music Education One-Day Symposium at University of Huddersfield, in association with IASPM and the Institute of Contemporary Music Performance. (http://www.iaspm.org.uk/research-in-popular-music-education/) and ICMP (icmp.co.uk).

nel or led by BSM teachers. Through providing some students with six-month employment contracts, the companies help students to understand expectations of the industry as a working environment (Yu, 2013, pp. 190–191).

An informant for this chapter spent two years completing BSM's Diploma in Music Composition and Production. He attended BSM in the hope that the school would help him to become a Cantopop songwriter and producer. He felt the cost of the course was high, but was grateful for the hands-on experience, especially with professional music recording applications, and for instruction in a small-class setting. He received a short-term contract with a company affiliated to BSM in the middle of his studies, where he mainly helped in scoring and arranging. He later entered the local famous CASH SongWriters Quest, hosted by the Composers and Authors Society of Hong Kong Ltd (CASH), and was one of the finalists after graduating from BSM. He is now a contracted songwriter with a local production company, and feels confident that the knowledge and real-world experience gained during his time at BSM ensured his path to becoming the 'new blood' of the local popular music industry.

BSM seems to have a good record in bridging graduates into the music industry and professions (Baron School of Music, 2014). However, one particular instance highlights some of the complexities inherent in a marketized, market-focused, neoliberal music education (especially HPME) environment (Jones, chapter 27, this volume; McLaughlin, chapter 10, this volume). Following the first episode of singing competition *The Voice*, hosted by the local Television Broadcasts Limited (TVB) in 2009, a local magazine printed a story revealing that a participant in the show was a vocal student of BSM. Ronald Ng was one of the judges in the initial stage of the show. This became a headline story; Shing Ming Tsang from the external affairs of TVB clarified to the magazine that "We knew about Ronald Ng's student[s] being in the competition in advance, [but] we believe our judges are professional. We checked the scores afterwards, Ronald Ng did not practise favouritism" (FACE Weekly, 2009, F048). Chun Tung Mak, executive producer of *The Voice*, commented that "One judge cannot control the entire result!" (Sudden Weekly, 2009, SW081). After this, Ronald Ng was not on the judge's panel for the rest of *The Voice*. The story quickly 'died', as the student in question only went on to become one of 19 finalists. BSM, like other popular music schools and departments around the world, has an intriguing and complex balance of roles to play between education, promotion, markets and the industry.

Tuition fees at a glance

The tuition fees for BSM's courses are quite high, targeting middle-class families, although studying at BSM is still cheaper than comparable schools in the UK and the US. For a local citizen to enrol in a full-time undergraduate programme sponsored by the Hong Kong government in any local universities (i.e. not BSM – a private, for-profit institution), costs HK$42,100 per year. Table 9.2 compares tuition fees between BSM and similar programmes in schools in the UK and the US.

Besides the cost of tuition, studying popular music production outside of Hong Kong is possibly unattractive to prospective students of BSM because it would be

Table 9.2 Tuition fees among comparable programmes of the five schools[16]

School	Level	Programme	Length	Tuition Fee
MI	Certificate	Independent Artist	2 quarters	US$15,990
MI	Associate of Arts	Combined Emphasis	6 quarters	US$47,970
Berklee	Diploma	Contemporary Writing and Production	8 semesters	US$134,264
ACM	Certificate of Higher Education	Commercial Music (Songwriting and Artist Development)/ Contemporary Music Production	1 year (2 terms)	£5,995 (~US$9,177)
ACM	Accredited / Industry Qualification Courses	Music Production/ Contemporary Songwriting & Artist Development	6 months (2 terms)	£5,995 (~US$9,177)
ICMP	Certificate of Higher Education	Songwriting	1 year	£8,200* (~US$12,553)
BSM	Diploma	Production and Composition	5 phases (can be completed in 1.5 years)	HK$75,000 (~US$9,677)

* Specific for International students

less likely to provide either the knowledge applicable to working with local audiences or the network of the local music industry.

Conclusion

BSM is a private music school in Hong Kong focusing on popular music education and is the first and currently the only school providing organized vocational and continuous education for newcomers to and current professionals in the local popular music industry. The provision by BSM of programmes recognized by the government for the CEF matches the ideologically neoliberal development direction of the Hong Kong government, as well as meeting student-consumers' needs

16 Information taken from websites of respective schools; currency exchange rate as of 7 October, 2015.

for qualifications and networking opportunities to enter or remain and compete in the industry. Through offering lectures, practical, vocational study modes and internships, it is hoped that BSM will bring more and a greater diversity of production talents and influences to the local Cantopop industry, helping Hong Kong to emerge from the heavy shadow of a culturally oppressive colonial past.

References

Academy of Contemporary Music. (2014). Prospectus 2015/16. Retrieved from: http://www.acm.ac.uk/wp-content/downloads/ACM-Prospectus-2015-Web.pdf [Accessed 16 December 2014].
Baron Music. (2012). [Website of Baron Productions and Artiste Management Ltd and Solid Sound Production Ltd]. Retrieved from: http://www.baronpro.com/web/html/index.html [Accessed 16 December 2014].
Baron School of Music. (2014). [Website]. Retrieved from: http://bsm.com.hk/b5/index.htm [Accessed 16 December 2014].
Berklee College of Music. (2014). The core music curriculum. Retrieved from: http://www.berklee.edu/core [Accessed 16 December 2014].
Continuing Education Fund, The Government of the Hong Kong Special Administrative Region. (2014). [Website]. Retrieved from: http://www.sfaa.gov.hk/cef/ [Accessed 16 December 2014].
Curriculum Development Council and the Hong Kong Examinations and Assessment Authority. (2014). *Music Curriculum and Assessment Guide (Secondary 4–6)*. Retrieved from: http://334.edb.hkedcity.net/doc/eng/curriculum/Music%20C&A%20Guide_updated_e.pdf [Accessed 16 December 2014].
The Emperor Entertainment Group. (2014). [Website]. Retrieved from: http://www.eegmusic.com/ [Accessed 16 December 2014].
Giroux, H. (2014). *Neoliberalism's war on higher education*. Chicago, IL: Haymarket Books.
Green, L. (2006). Popular music education in and for itself, and for "other" music: Current research in the classroom. *International Journal of Music Education*, 24(2), 101–118.
Hannan, M. (2006). Contemporary music student expectations of musicianship training needs. *International Journal of Music Education*, 24(2), 148–158.
Ho, W.C. (2011). *School Music Education and Social Change in Mainland China, Hong Kong and Taiwan*. Leiden, The Netherlands: Koninklijke Brill NV.
Hong Kong Examinations and Assessment Authority. (2015). Recognition of HKDSE. Retrieved from: http://www.hkeaa.edu.hk/en/recognition/hkdse_recognition/overseas/ [Accessed 15 April 2015].
Hong Kong Institute of Education. (2014). Course list of bachelor of music education. Retrieved from: http://www.ied.edu.hk/bme/std_prolist_4yr.html [Accessed 16 December 2014].
Institute of Contemporary Music Performance. (2014). Diploma overview. Retrieved from: http://icmp.co.uk/courses/diploma-overview [Accessed 16 December 2014].
側田喪冧《巨聲》索女　何雁詩猛料起底　(2009.8.7)。忽然一周，SW080–081頁。[Justin Lo likes *The Voice* beauty, Stephanie Ho's background is revealed. (2009, August 7). *Sudden Weekly*, SW080–081.]
Leong, S. (2014). Education policy reform: Cultures, creativities and conditions in Hong Kong post-1997. In P. Burnard (Ed.), *Developing creativities in higher music education: International perspectives and practices* (pp. 37–49). Abingdon, Oxon: Routledge.

Musicians Institute. Admissions. Retrieved from: http://mi.edu/admissions-financial-aid/how-to-apply/ [Accessed 16 December 2014].

Parkinson, T. (2014). *Values of higher popular music education* (PhD Dissertation). Reading: University of Reading.

Parkinson, T. & Smith, G.D. (2015). Towards an epistemology of authenticity in higher popular music education. *Action, Criticism, and Theory for Music Education, 14*(1), 93–127.

雷有暉籌辦歌唱學校 (2006.1.3)。大公報，C07頁。[Patrick Lui is preparing for a music school. (2006, January 3). *Ta Kung Pao*, C07.]

Powell, B., Smith, G.D. & D'Amore, A. (In press). Challenging symbolic violence and hegemony in music education through contemporary pedagogical approaches. *Education 3–13: International Journal of Primary, Elementary and Early Years Education*.

Qualifications Framework, Education Bureau, The Government of the Hong Kong Special Administrative Region. (2014). Introduction. Retrieved from: http://www.hkqf.gov.hk/guie/HKQF_intro.asp [Accessed 16 December 2014].

Smith, G.D. (2015). Neoliberalism and symbolic violence in higher music education. In L. DeLorenzo (Ed.), *Giving Voice to democracy: Diversity and social justice in the music Classroom* (pp. 65–84). New York, NY: Routledge.

Smith, G.D. (2014). Popular music in higher education. In G. Welch & I. Papageorgi (Eds.), *Advanced musical performance: Investigations in higher education learning* (pp. 33–48). Farnham: Ashgate.

Smith, G.D. (2013). *I drum, therefore I am: Being and becoming a drummer.* Farnham: Ashgate.

Smith, G.D. & Shafighian, A. (2013). Creative space and the "silent power of traditions" in popular music performance education. In P. Burnard (Ed.), *Developing creativities in higher music education: International perspectives and practices* (pp. 256–267). London: Routledge.

Success in Music Charity Foundation. (2014). [Website]. Retrieved from: http://www.simusic.org.hk/eng/index.html [Accessed 16 December 2014].

Trinity College London. (2014). [Website]. Retrieved from: http://www.trinitycollege.com/site/?id=55 [Accessed 16 December 2014].

謝慧心 (2006.5.4)。伍樂城 K歌以外的心願 創作概念碟，香港經濟日報，C01頁。[Tse, W. S. Ronlad Ng's wish besides K-song: produce a concept album. (2006, May 4). *Hong Kong Economic Times*, C01.]

爆《超級巨聲》超造馬 評判伍樂城薦愛徒入局 (2009.8.5). FACE, F046–048頁. [*The Voice* is unfair, Ronald Ng the judge puts beloved student in the game. (2009, August 5). *FACE Weekly*, F046–048.]

Weston, D. (2015, July). *Seeds of change: Connecting learning with industry through entrepreneurship.* Paper presented at the Research in Popular Music Education One-Day Symposium, Huddersfield, UK.

黃湛森。2003年。《粵語流行曲的發展與興衰：香港流行音樂研究（1949–1997）》。香港：香港大學博士論文。[Wong, J.S. (2003). *The rise and decline of Cantopop: A study of Hong Kong popular music (1949–1997)* (PhD Dissertation). Hong Kong: The University of Hong Kong.]

Young, V. (2012). Professional development and music education. In C. Philpott & G. Spruce (Eds.), *Debates in music teaching* (pp. 242–258). Abingdon, Oxon: Routledge.

于逸堯 (2013)。香港好聲音。香港：三聯書店。[Yu, Y.Y. (2013). *Hong Kong talks music.* Hong Kong: Joint Publishing.]

10

Mediations, institutions and post-compulsory popular music education

Seán McLaughlin

Introduction

This chapter draws on two main pieces of research – first, my doctoral thesis, which examined the processes of professionalization in Scottish folk/traditional music and the way in which this impacts ideology and conceptualization (McLaughlin, 2012). This work involved a study of mediation/mediators and examined the role of Further and Higher Education (FE & HE)[1] institutions in shaping understandings of folk and traditional Scottish music. Second, this chapter draws on an ongoing piece of research, funded by the Royal Society of Edinburgh, examining the teaching and assessment of creative practice in Scottish post-compulsory (FE and HE) popular music education. While my focus is primarily on FE and HE institutions in Scotland, discussion also includes HE institutions from other parts of the UK.

I first present a theoretical framework for discussion (in mediation) before moving on to wider discussion on institutions, popular music programmes and vocationalism. The lens of mediation/mediators is integral to discussions of definition, institutions and values, and will hopefully be useful in future research on the role of popular music's educational and industrial organizations – viewing these bodies as forces of construction rather than interpretation. I argue here that popular music

---

1 Further Education (FE), in the UK, is for those beyond the age of compulsory education (currently 16 years old), continuing studies below the level of first-year of university. Examples of these are English Access to Music (Access to Music, 2015) and BTEC qualifications (Pearson Qualifications, 2015), and Scottish Qualifications Authority (SQA), NQ, NC and NPA qualifications (Sqa.org.uk, 2015). These programmes usually take place in what are termed FE colleges. Higher Education (HE), in the UK, refers to any programme of study that, at its lowest level, aligns with that of first-year university.

programmes are ideologically constructing popular music, and that this should be acknowledged and discussed in terms of both pedagogical and wider cultural impact (see also Lebler & Hodges, chapter 22, this volume; Morrow et al., chapter 26, this volume; Wong, chapter 9, this volume).

Mediation

In Marxist and Hegelian theories, mediation is not simply a process of transmission, but a means of construction; hence the concept has been presented as central to discussions of dialectical process (Hegel & Knox, 1988; Hegel, Miller & Findlay, 1977; Marx, Engels & Stedman Jones, 2002). In the cases of both the popular music industries (as one set of institutions) and FE and HE institutions (as another), we find examples of mediating bodies that play active roles in the construction of definitions of popular music and, hence, the ideology that underpins assessment and evaluation. Green (1988) observes that the sociology of music:

> Must construct its objects, in full recognition of the complexities of individual and social mediation. It must therefore consciously construct both the institutions in which individuals think and act, and the subjectivity of individuals themselves in connection with musical structure; it must negotiate with thinking and interpreting actors who have their own ideas and experiences, being confronted with various styles of music in different settings; but it must remember that the coexistence of all these spheres creates the phenomena that are its objects of study.
>
> (p. 10)

Green here presents an argument that is central to many approaches to the cultural and sociological study of popular music (Clayton, Herbert & Middleton, 2003; Frith, 1981, 1998; Harker, 1980; Longhurst, 1995), and from which the development of methodologies for popular music pedagogical studies and practices can easily draw influence.

The study of mediations and mediators should be central to an exploration of the role of FE and HE institutions in popular music education. For a general theory of mediation, this chapter turns to Negus (1996), who presents the concept as it applies in the wider context of popular music and social theory. Negus (1996, p. 66) divides the analysis of mediation into three connected ideas – the first is that of *coming in between*, or intermediary action; the second is mediation as a means of transmission or an agency that comes in between reality and social knowledge; and the third is that all objects, particularly works of art, are mediated by social relationships. He explains that the analysis of what is here classified as "intermediary action" would involve the study of the "practices of all the people who intervene as popular music is produced, distributed and consumed" (1996, p. 66). Negus primarily focuses on the popular music industries, citing "staff within record companies", DJs, "journalists", "video directors", those who collect revenue generated by copyright and "retail staff in record shops" as examples of this first category (1996, p. 67). In the second category, "mediation as transmission", he refers to the relationship communication technologies have with music. Negus separates this group of mediation devices into six types that very loosely correspond to chronological advances in technological development. The first of these, "the printed word" (which, by extension, also includes printed music), is capable of presenting representative symbols, but not the *music* itself (1996, p. 71). The second, "sound carriers", are incredibly important, as they were the first to present the actual audio, shifting the understanding of music and offering potential changes in the way in which it was "created, distributed and listened to" (1996, p. 68). The third category, radio broadcasting, is argued (by many) to be one of the most influential transmission media for music, opening up the possibilities of *space* for music. At this point, as Frith (1998) observed, the listener/consumer herself becomes something of a mediating force for her own consumption; she is now the interpreter and has control; with advancements in sound reproduction technology of stereo image, time and frequency with the introduction of the graphic equalizer on the home hi-fi, she has massively increased control of musical properties and "musical space-time" (Frith, 1998, p. 234).

It should be stressed here that these developments do not simply supersede and replace one other, but instead cause a re-negotiation of existing modes of production, transmission (or distribution/dissemination) and consumption. Though the novelty of graphic equalizers has possibly worn off, there have been numerous commercial experiments (perhaps following Radiohead's *In Rainbows* (2007), which gave the consumer complete control over price for three months) that continue to re-negotiate the level of consumer engagement with various points in the production-to-consumption chain. Examples include Bon Iver's Stems Project (Paste Magazine, 2015), or The Kaiser Chiefs' Choose Your Own Track Listing (Sherwin, 2011). These types of experiments have often been cited as PR stunts (Bray and Cripps, 2011); however, this is perhaps oversimplifying an issue that is more indicative of cultural, and consequent ideological, shifts in modes of mediated music consumption resulting from advances in technology.

Negus's (1996) fourth type of transmission mediator is the "moving image of film and television", which was crucial in developing ideas of the visual and physical contextual space of music – in particular popular music – through developments such as Music Television (MTV) in 1981. A fifth category, somewhat downplayed by Negus (understandably, given the date of publication) is that of "telecommunications technologies", which in his study focuses on the transmission of data through phone lines (Negus, 1996, p. 68). For our purposes, this category should be more usefully clarified and updated as *the internet* – now a ubiquitous, powerful and incredibly important part of music transmission and consumption, as well as increasingly influential in modes of production with the growing possibilities of sharing larger files such as high sample- and bit-rate audio (Negus, 1996). This category also goes some way towards swallowing the fourth, given that YouTube has become the biggest streaming service in the West (Ingham, 2015), positioning music videos as a resurgent and increasingly important part of music marketing campaigns (Edmond, 2012). Jones suggested that the internet would become an increasing concern for popular music scholars in three particular areas – production (particularly in "overcoming distance between performers"), consumption and distribution (2000, pp. 217–218). Indeed, the internet as a transmission mediator also has the ability to encompass all the modes of transmission mentioned above, and so serves as a dual mediator of sorts; for example, any study of a streamed performance could involve the examination of music and film/moving image, and of the internet as a space, context and transmission mediator in itself.

The sixth and final transmission mediator proposed by Negus (1996, p. 68) is that of musical instruments, which have "enabled different types of musical communication to take place". In this, Negus positions all technological advancements in sound producers – as opposed to sound carriers – although this distinction becomes a little hazy with the inclusion of both recording studio/live performance equipment (some of which could perhaps more comfortably sit with *non-consumer* or *professional* electronic sound production and manipulation devices), and the previous category (here re-construed to include the internet and related communications technologies).

An issue in Negus's work, however, is that he places the ideas of "reality" and "social knowledge" at opposite ends of a mediated spectrum where *reality* could be read as absolute (1996, p. 68). In using mediation to understand ideological construction in the case of popular music within a given institution, it would be unhelpful to attempt to position this object (social knowledge) as having undergone a transformative process (through mediation), leaving behind an absolute reality. While many interpreted *starting points* for definition could be uncovered, the presupposition of an initial or objective *reality* for popular music is unhelpful. It is, then, likely to be far more powerful and appropriate to consider how institutions (in our case education institutions) and institutional processes construct popular music (rather than interpret it) (see also Wong, chapter 9, this volume).

Returning to the third of Negus's initial three ideas – that of the "mediation of social relationships" (1996, p. 66) – he also refers to the way in which power is exercised (and ideological judgements manifested) by those who have a degree of control over the aforementioned processes and devices for mediation. Though the previous two ideas (intermediary action and transmission, and their subsets) are immeasurably important to popular music pedagogy, it is this third idea that provides the most useful thread for beginning the analysis of institutional approaches to popular music education. Indeed, the examination of social relationships, in this context, allows (or even necessitates) the study of intermediary action and, in turn, transmission.

Vocationalism

Most FE and HE institutions delivering programmes in popular music make some claim towards preparing students for careers in the popular music industries[2] (Krikun, chapter 4, this volume; Parkinson & Smith, 2015). Though this has arguably always been seen as the primary objective of FE programmes, solid graduate

---

2 This pluralization is a reference to the work of Williamson and Cloonan (2007).

employment pathways are also becoming increasingly important in HE, perhaps as a result of obligations to the Key Information Set (KIS) and other recent UK government objectives and initiatives (Parkinson & Smith, 2015). This said, employability seems to remain somewhat less present in the rhetoric of other arts programmes – fine art, for example (Glasgow School of Art, 2015a). Though the long-term situation in regard to other arts is uncertain, given increasing governmental pressure on HE that directly links education to employment (Conservative Party, 2015), there is a noticeable distinction between the marketing language of popular music programmes and that of the visual arts. Training in songwriting, production, live and studio performance are common to practical popular music programmes, and degrees are often advertised as equipping undergraduate students with the skills required for specific roles in the industries (Parkinson & Smith, 2015).[3]

These observations are not necessarily intended to call into question the ideological relationship between practical popular music undergraduate programmes and the music industries, but rather to provide context to our discussion of mediation. There is no intended hard-line Marxist/Neo-Adornian argument here, yet, by the same token and as a backdrop to discussions, it should also be noted that popular music practices are not all inescapably driven or determined by a desire for some level of commercial success (Smith, 2016). By extension, it can comfortably be argued that not all skills and knowledge taught and practised within educational institutions need necessarily map directly against hypothetical industrial scenarios. As Frith et al (2001, p. 26) state, "the starting point for an understanding of the music industry . . . must be the fact that 'popular music' is not the same thing as the sum of the products of the popular music industry". They argue that popular music is, in many ways, tied to the industries that gave rise to it, but that there are many popular music phenomena that do not centre on the creation of a commercial product.

The art/commerce tension is an old issue (see e.g. Becker, 1982; Bourdieu and Johnson, 1993) but still a highly relevant one facing UK HE, as Parkinson and Smith (2015, p. 95) observe:

> HE policy in the UK is increasingly characterized by themes of global competitiveness, knowledge to wealth creation, and employability . . . measured in terms of paid graduate employment. Popular music programs operating within this policy framework must be seen to address these imperatives, advocating good economic citizenship and inculcating values that align with the government's macroeconomic strategy.

The authors, referring to Giroux (2007, 2014) and Hewison (2014), also suggest that:

> [Popular music] Program teams are obliged to subscribe, outwardly at least, to a conception of educational value traceable to a dominant neoliberal meta-policy that totemizes global competition, in which "citizenship is narrowed

---

3 For further discussion see Hewison (2014).

to the demands of consumerism" (Giroux, 2007, p. 25), where neoliberalism is so pervasive that "it [is] now more than common sense that the only way to increase the common good [is] by maximizing individual freedom in the market" (Hewison, 2014, p. 3), "leading to the neoliberal utopian notion that paradise amounts to a world of voracity and avarice without restrictions" (Giroux, 2014, p. 13). To decline to do so would be to jeopardize funding.

(p. 105)

Following on from debates on popular music's potential aesthetic principles from a pedagogical perspective, there is also a much deeper lack of a consensus on the term *popular music* itself (Hooper, chapter 13, this volume; Krikun, chapter 4, this volume).[4] On the one hand is a set of phenomena that potentially occur with or without the objective of creating a commercial product; on the other, many of these phenomena will have been influenced by popular music as a commodity (such as ticketed live music or records) in the first place. Is the '*not folk* and *not Western art*' argument sufficient (Middleton, 1990, p. 4)? Tagg's approach in 1983 was to categorize the 'popular' in popular music as that which was "traditionally excluded from conservatories, schools of music, university departments of musicology, in fact generally excluded from the realms of public education" (Tagg, 1983), though this, too, is hardly watertight or stable. To conflate a broad spectrum of aesthetic principles, business-models, practices and ideas into one ambiguous term is problematic enough, without then using it as the foundation upon which to build tertiary education programmes.

Although many might argue that there are no inherent problems with the creation of FE and HE education programmes in popular music, this chapter argues that there are three fundamental issues that require further (or potentially constant) examination. The first of these problems is the general focus on vocationalism and the all too common and outdated association this has with technical proficiency on a chosen musical instrument. The second is in the very definition of the term *popular music* itself – many institutions opt in and take on board any assumptions/ ambiguity the term may create, while others seem actively to attempt circumnavigation and aim squarely at music as a commodity, with titles such as *Commercial Music*, or as a set of skills, ideas and approaches that could be utilized for the purposes of industrial employment, i.e. *Music Business* (Cloonan & Hulstedt, 2012; Jones, chapter 27, this volume). The third, related, issue is that of the ideological assumptions of institutions, or the ways in which an institution's historical relationship with popular music is articulated in its system of values (Smith, 2014). It is in this context that I present some thoughts on the comparative roles of educational and industrial institutions, their function as mediators for assessment/evaluation, and more generally on how these might construct popular music as an idea.

---

4 For more on this debate see: Can we get rid of the 'popular' in popular music? A virtual symposium with contributions from the International Advisory Editors of *Popular Music* (1999).

Institutions

North (1990, pp. 3–10) suggests a tiered distinction between *institutions* (citing them as having more global formal or informal "codes of behaviour") and lower *organizations* such as "political bodies", "economic bodies", "social bodies" and "educational bodies". This model essentially deals with institutional rules and an organizational ideology that has reacted to, or is informed by, those rules. Giroux (2007) Parkinson and Smith's (2015, p. 105) earlier cited "neo-liberal meta-policy" can be seen as currently exerting economic and ideo-political institutional pressure on educational organizations. These organizations, in turn, present knowledge and rules that, although somewhat less static and dominant, have a real and tangible impact on the construction and/or perpetuation of ideas. However, if in North's definition, institutions exist to present constraints to our choices, do HE popular music programmes not then function as powerful and persuasive institutions for students?

Searle (1995, p. 96) presents an alternative discourse, in accepting a broader view of the definition of institutions (as social objects), and suggests that rules imposed by such institutions can be either "regulatory" or "constitutive". In this definition, driving on the left-hand side of the road could be seen as an example of a regulatory institutional rule – in that one could still be seen as driving while doing so on the 'wrong' side of the road. Conversely, playing chess necessitates an adherence to a particular set of 'constitutive' rules – should you fail to adhere to these rules you are no longer playing chess. This discourse is perhaps useful when considering the roles played by popular music education programmes. The typology of rules (as tools for developing an understanding of institutional power) is important for thinking about institutions and conceptualization – does popular music education, as a force of construction through mediation, present regulatory or constitutive rules, or both?

Institutions and vocationalism

Although Cloonan (1999, p. 78) suggests that the development of popular music studies in the UK can be traced back to the 1960s, the phenomenon of FE and HE programmes in popular music performance *practice* is still relatively new. As Birkett (1992, p. 239) documented, in September 1991 "it became possible to undertake a study programme in jazz, popular and commercial music at Higher Education level which carries full, mandatory funding".[5] While this is to an extent accurate, the SQA rolled out HNC (HE) and NC (FE) qualification modules in Rock Music Performance in 1990 (SQA, 2015), perhaps following the success of the *Rock School* television programme (IMDb, 2015). The University of Salford, too, "launched a BA in Popular Music and Recording in

---

5 Prior to 1998, higher education tuition fees in the UK were paid by the UK government. Student contribution towards tuition fees were introduced in 1998, and since then fees incurred by students in England have increased from around £1,000 to over £8,000 per annum.

1990", and Cloonan (1999, p. 81) has cited other "important pioneers" in Leeds University, with its BA in Popular Music, and University of Westminster's BA in Commercial Music – although notably neglected are independent HE providers such as the British and Irish Modern Music Institute (BIMM), the Institute of Contemporary Music Performance (ICMP) and the Academy of Contemporary Music (ACM).

The largest validation body for the early post-compulsory popular music Further Education programmes, the Business and Technical Education Council (BTEC) – owned by Pearson PLC – (Pearson Schools and FE Colleges, 2015) is important, as it indicates that many college popular music programmes have historical roots in *business and technical* practices, rather than, say, those of the *arts* (ideologically, if not necessarily in practice and pedagogy). Evidence of these roots can arguably still be seen in many current popular music programmes, particularly in the underlying assumptions that (a) success is at least partially measured by technical proficiency, or (b) a financially sustainable career in music is the main driving force for most students (Parkinson & Smith, 2015). Edinburgh Napier University's Music (Popular) BA (Hons) undergraduate programme, for example, expects students to "achieve a high degree of competence on (their) principal study (voice, guitar, bass guitar, drums or composition)" (Edinburgh Napier University, 2015), while the University of the Highlands and Islands claims that a "focus on music industry", "individual instrument study" and "real live scenarios of performance situations" are "special features" of the programme[6] (University of the Highlands and Islands, 2015). Middlesex University states in its prospectus:

> Our course will develop your knowledge of popular music while enhancing your musical skills and preparing you for success in the music industry and beyond. Our dedicated staff team bring experience from a range of music industry backgrounds, including songwriting, performance, production, management and journalism. You will learn from their expertise and benefit from their industry links.
>
> *(2015)*

The stress placed on industry is obvious here, as the term appears three times in so many sentences. The University of Sunderland similarly states:

> The range of career paths for our graduates includes freelance performance, recording, broadcasting, composition, arranging, production, publishing, management and teaching. This course is aimed at people who have achieved Grade 8 or an equivalent standard in music performance.[7]
>
> *(University of Sunderland, 2015)*

---

6 'Course' is used in the UK as synonymous with 'programme'; where, for example, US English authors refer to 'courses', UK authors would usually refer to 'modules'.
7 Graded performance exams in the UK focus largely on the development of technical proficiency.

The initial BTEC FE qualifications and early HE focus on commercial music in institutions such as the University of Westminster and the University of Paisley (Cloonan, 1999, p. 81), coupled with a continuing localized institutional (legislative) pressure on universities and colleges to produce positive employment statistics, have a strong impact on the development and reinforcement of institutional values. These values, for example, often emphasize a) development of technical skills construed in terms of technical mastery of a given musical instrument, or b) more broadly the potential for industrial and financial success. This ideological assumption is fairly widespread; Green (2001, p. 28) goes some way towards suggesting that the ultimate goal for a musician (or "end-point") is to "acquire the knowledge and skills required of a successful popular musician – successful in the sense of being able to maintain a playing career – in a variety of contexts"; success, as a concept in itself, is particularly limited here. Cloonan (1999) and Parkinson and Smith (2015) have noted that such notions are also perpetually constructed by the press as a mediating force. As an example, Cloonan (1999) discusses the response to Edinburgh Napier University's creation of a Music (Popular) BA (Hons), stating that press articles assessed the programme entirely on "what it might lead to commercially" for its graduates (Cloonan, 1999, p. 85).

There are exceptions to this heavy emphasis on vocationalism, however. Newcastle University's Contemporary and Popular Music BA Honours programme prospectus, for example, states that the programme places "strong emphasis on creativity, experimentation and artistic risk-taking. There are also plenty of opportunities to develop your performance skills, helping you to grow as an accomplished musician" (Newcastle University, 2015). Creative practice, technical performance skills and musicianship are presented as opportunities, rather than requirements or concrete objectives. It seems that, although acknowledged, industry-focused practices are not necessarily at the forefront of the programme aims. Notwithstanding the need for further study of pedagogical practices and the day-to-day articulation and enactment of values, very few institutions offering popular music programmes appear to place this amount of emphasis on creative practice and the development of new work/s in their prospectuses or on their websites – certainly not without then positioning creative practice against future industrial/employment roles.

Projected values parallel to those on Newcastle University's undergraduate Contemporary and Popular Music programme can be seen in institutions outside of popular music, such as the Glasgow School of Art, which states that its fine art programme "aims to equip students with the necessary skills and expertise to realise their full creative potential and to pursue a career in the visual arts or other chosen professions" (Glasgow School of Art, 2015b). The focus on the student as a *creative* (as opposed to a *technician*), coupled with the flexibility allowed here for interpretations of what it means to be a musician (Newcastle University, 2015b) or visual artist (Glasgow School of Art, 2015b), implies value systems that see industry as a part of, although not necessarily central to, defining popular music and fine art in education. Frith and Horne (1987, p. 27) have suggested that the "art school is unique in British higher education" in that it "condones and encourages an attitude of learning through trial and error, through day-to-day experimentation rather than through instruction". It is possible that, where institutionally viable, popular music programmes have attempted an integration of this or a similar ethos – this is certainly an area worthy of further research.

Though on the surface it may appear that this focus on the development of the musician as a creative sits on one side of the *art versus commerce* debate, such binaries are almost always unhelpful. Indeed, Toynbee (2000, p. 32) has suggested that creative "institutional autonomy" may more helpfully be considered in terms of organization of creative labour in the popular music industries than the structuring of programmes around specific technical skill sets. For Toynbee (2000, p. 32), institutional autonomy is a conceptualization of the "massive oversupply and indiscipline of musical labour", coupled with a level of consumer demand meaning that the "music makers" are also "creators" (an idea central to many popular music and authenticity arguments). In order for industries revolving around intellectual property to function as they do, they must guarantee a certain level of creative autonomy. Autonomy, as a mediating idea and pedagogical practice, is not new to popular music education (Green, 2008); however, the ways in which it manifests in the development of skill sets, creative practice, peer-interaction, tutor-student power relationships and learning environments in post-compulsory education institutions is worth further examination.

Conclusion

In all cases, institutions delivering programmes in popular music articulate an ideology, or set of ideologies, that construct popular music/s. In the brief examination of UK further and higher popular music education, I have demonstrated that many programmes have strong roots in vocationalism. These programmes have mostly focused on selling the possibilities of employment to prospective students of popular music, trumpeting primarily their industry links and industry-focused programme design. But this is not simply an ideology created and reinforced internally or collectively – the most recent pressures (since 2010) from the Liberal-Conservative coalition and Conservative governments in the UK have perhaps made this all but mandatory for survival. Following on from these initial observations of outwardly projected ideals, it is important that research now takes place that assesses ideology in the actual pedagogical practices on popular music programmes, and, more specifically, examining ideologies pertaining to *creative practice* and *industry*. What are the definitions and constitutive or regulatory rules (Searle, 1995)? Are there internal debates and tensions? How is popular music, as an idea, being constructed for students, and does it espouse this outwardly projected focus on vocationalism (Giroux, 2014; Parkinson & Smith, 2015)? Is popular music presented as a performance practice, a set of traditions, a creative practice, an industrial practice, or a set of social/cultural phenomena? If it is presented as all of these things, what is the balance, and what impact does this have on students' practices, work, thoughts and outlooks?

The study of institutions as mediating forces in popular music education is useful in several ways. Most generally it allows us to examine the roles popular music programmes may play in constructing popular music, both ideologically and within its own area of the music industries – being a component of Williamson, Cloonan & Frith's (2003) Education Sector in their proposed division of the industrial landscape. It also helps us to examine the nature of this process of construction and regulation within institutions, and assists in the study of institutional value systems and how they may manifest in everything from programme design and marketing/prospectuses, through to teaching, learning and assessment practices.

References

Access to Music. (2015). *Music courses | music technology | music business | performance*. Retrieved from: http://www.accesstomusic.co.uk/courses/further-education-music-courses/music-courses [Accessed 12 June 2015].

Becker, H. (1982). *Art worlds*. Berkeley, CA: University of California Press.

Birkett, J. (1992). Popular music education – the dawning of a new age. *Popular Music*, *11*(02), 239–241. Retrieved from: http://dx.doi.org/10.1017/s0261143000005043

Bourdieu, P. & Johnson, R. (1993). *The field of cultural production*. New York, NY: Columbia University Press.

Bray, E. & Cripps, C. (2011). *The fans chose the album, but how many will actually buy it? The Independent*. Retrieved from: http://www.independent.co.uk/arts-entertainment/music/features/the-fans-chose-the-album-but-how-many-will-actually-buy-it-2301743.html [Accessed 8 June 2015].

Clayton, M., Herbert, T. & Middleton, R. (2003). *The cultural study of music*. New York, NY: Routledge.

Cloonan, M. (1999). What is popular music studies? Some observations. *British Journal of Music Education*, *22*(1), 77–93. Retrieved from: http://dx.doi.org/10.1017/s026505170400600x

Cloonan, M. & Hulstedt, L. (2012). *Taking notes – mapping and teaching popular music in higher education*. The Higher Education Academy. Retrieved from: https://www.heacademy.ac.uk/sites/default/files/Cloonan_2012.pdf [Accessed 7 June 2015].

Conservative Party. (2015). *The Conservative party manifesto 2015*. Retrieved from: https://www.conservatives.com/manifesto [Accessed 17 August 2015].

Edinburgh Napier University. (2015). *Music (popular) – BA (Hons) at Edinburgh Napier University*. Retrieved from: http://www.courses.napier.ac.uk/courses.aspx?ID=%2fu54111.htm [Accessed 3 January 2015].

Edmond, M. (2012). Here we go again: Music videos after YouTube. *Television & New Media*, *15*(4), 305–320. Retrieved from: http://dx.doi.org/10.1177/1527476412465901

Frith, S. (1981). *Sound effects*. New York, NY: Pantheon Books.

Frith, S. (1998). *Performing rites*. Oxford: Oxford University Press.

Frith, S. & Horne, H. (1987). *Art into pop*. London: Methuen.

Frith, S., Straw, W. & Street, J. (2001). *The Cambridge companion to pop and rock*. New York, NY: Cambridge University Press.

Giroux, H. (2007). Utopian thinking in dangerous times: Critical pedagogy and the project of educated hope. In M. Coté, R. Day & G. de Peuter (Eds.), *Utopian pedagogy: Radical experiments against neoliberal globalization* First ed.; pp. 25–42. London, Ontario: Toronto University Press.

Giroux, H. (2014). *Neoliberalism's war on higher education*. Chicago: Haymarket Books.

Glasgow School of Art. (2015a). *The Glasgow school of art*. Retrieved from: http://www.gsa.ac.uk/ [Accessed 8 July 2015].

Glasgow School of Art. (2015b). *Undergraduate study*. Retrieved from: http://www.gsa.ac.uk/study/undergraduate-degrees/ [Accessed 5 January 2015].

Green, L. (1988). *Music on deaf ears: Musical meaning, ideology, education*. Manchester: Manchester University Press.

Green, L. (2008). *Music, informal learning and the school: A new classroom pedagogy*. Farnham: Ashgate.

Green, L. (2001). *How popular musicians learn – A way ahead for music education*. Burlington, VT: Ashgate.

Harker, D. (1980). *One for the money*. London: Hutchinson.

Hegel, G. & Knox, T. (1988). *Aesthetics*. Oxford: Clarendon Press.

Hegel, G., Miller, A. & Findlay, J. (1977). *Phenomenology of spirit*. Oxford, England: Clarendon Press.

Hewison, R. (2014). *Cultural capital*. London: Verso.

IMDb. (2015). *Rockschool (TV Series 1985–)* . Retrieved from: http://www.imdb.com/title/tt0242229/ [Accessed 9 January 2015].

Ingham, T. (2015). *YouTube is the no.1 music streaming platform – and getting bigger – Music business worldwide. Music Business Worldwide*. Retrieved from: Retrieved from: http://www.musicbusinessworldwide.com/youtube-is-the-no-1-music-streaming-platform-and-getting-bigger/ [Accessed 6 July 2015].

Jones, S. (2000). Music and the internet. *Popular Music, 19*(2), 217–230. Retrieved from: http://dx.doi.org/10.1017/s026114300000012x

Longhurst, B. (1995). *Popular music and society*. Cambridge: Polity Press.

Marx, K., Engels, F. & Stedman Jones, G. (2002). *The communist manifesto*. London: Penguin Books.

McLaughlin, S. (2012). *Locating authenticities: A study of the ideological construction of professional folk music in Scotland* (PhD Dissertation). Scotland: The University of Edinburgh.

Middlesex University. (2015). *Popular music | Middlesex University London*. Retrieved from: http://www.mdx.ac.uk/courses/undergraduate/popular-music [Accessed 3 January 2015].

Middleton, R. (1990). *Studying popular music*. Milton Keynes: Open University Press.

Negus, K. (1996). *Popular music in theory*. Cambridge: Polity Press.

Newcastle University. (2015). *Contemporary and popular music BA honours: Course overview – undergraduate study – Newcastle University*. Retrieved from: http://www.ncl.ac.uk/undergraduate/degrees/w301/courseoverview/ [Accessed 9 January 2015].

North, D. (1990). *Institutions, institutional change, and economic performance*. Cambridge: Cambridge University Press.

Parkinson, T. & Smith, G. (2015). Towards an epistemology of authenticity in higher popular music education. *Action, Criticism & Theory for Music Education, 14*(1), 93–127.

Paste Magazine. (2015). *Bon Iver, Bon Iver: Stems project winners announced*. Retrieved from: http://www.pastemagazine.com/articles/2012/10/bon-iver-stems-project-winners-announced.html [Accessed 17 May 2015].

Pearson Qualifications. (2015). *Welcome to BTEC | Pearson qualifications*. Retrieved from: http://qualifications.pearson.com/en/about-us/qualification-brands/btec.html [Accessed 12 June 2015].

Pearson Schools and FE Colleges. (2015). *Pearson schools and FE colleges | Pearson education | Resources for primary, secondary and FE colleges*. Retrieved from: http://www.pearsonschoolsandfecolleges.co.uk/ [Accessed 12 August 2015].

Radiohead. (2007). *In rainbows*. London: Xurbia Xendless Ltd.

Searle, J. (1995). *The construction of social reality*. New York, NY: Free Press.

Sherwin, A. (2011). *Kaiser Chiefs' fans invited to design album. The Independent*. Retrieved from: http://www.independent.co.uk/arts-entertainment/music/news/kaiser-chiefs-fans-invited-to-design-album-5882641.html [Accessed 29 September 2015].

Smith, G.D. (2016). (Un)popular music making and eudaimonia. In R. Mantie & G.D. Smith (Eds.), *The Oxford handbook of music making and leisure* (pp. 151–170). New York, NY: Oxford University Press.

Smith, G.D. (2014). Popular music in higher education. In I. Papageorgi & G. Welch (Eds.), *Advanced musical performance: Investigations in higher education* (pp. 33–48). Farnham: Ashgate.

SQA. (2015). *SQA*. Retrieved from: http://www.sqa.org.uk/sqa/70972.html [Accessed 9 January 2015].

Tagg, P. (1983). *Philip Tagg | Why IASPM? Which tasks? (Reggio Emilia 1983). Tagg.org*. Retrieved from: http://www.tagg.org/articles/iasptask83.html [Accessed 24 July 2015].

Toynbee, J. (2000). *Making popular music*. London: Arnold.

University of the Highlands and Islands. (2015). *Popular music – University of the Highlands and Islands*. Retrieved from: http://www.uhi.ac.uk/en/courses/ba-hons-popular-music#tab-summary [Accessed 3 January 2015].

University of Sunderland. (2015). *Jazz, popular and commercial music BMus (Hons) – University of Sunderland*. Retrieved from: http://www.sunderland.ac.uk/courses/artsdesignandmedia/undergraduate/jazz-popular-commercial-music/ [Accessed 9 January 2015].

Williamson, J. & Cloonan, M. (2007). Rethinking the music industry. *Popular Music, 26*(02), 305–322. Retrieved from: http://dx.doi.org/10.1017/s0261143007001262

Williamson, J., Cloonan, M. & Frith, S. (2003). *Mapping the music industry in Scotland*. Glasgow: Scottish Enterprise.

11

Where to now? The current condition and future trajectory of popular music studies in British universities

Simon Warner

Introduction

On 25 July 2014 the final cohort of a popular music degree graduated in a University of Leeds ceremony in the campus's historic Great Hall. These graduates represented the last remnants of a higher education programme that had enjoyed a more than 20-year history. Although this particular bachelor's degree – in Popular and World Musics – had only existed under that name since 2001, it had grown out of a BA (Hons) in Popular Music Studies founded in 1992. While the concluding moments of this educational programme would be maybe no more than a minor footnote in the long arc of British higher educational history, it was, I argue, a marker within the progress of the multidisciplinary field dealing with popular music as a realm of serious study, one which had existed for barely a quarter of a century in the UK's undergraduate sector. The demise of a well-established undergraduate popular music studies programme appeared to indicate something about the condition of this realm of academic enquiry. Thus, it seemed a suitable moment to reflect on the recent past in this area of study, consider its present condition and possible future. Is the study of popular music in higher education Britain in good health or in decline? Or has a relatively brief flowering been pruned back by a range of, for example, institutional and economic, financial and cultural, pressures?

In this chapter I draw upon recent interviews with prominent academics engaged in popular music studies, and on personal experience as a teacher, researcher and programme designer/leader in popular music studies, in considering the history of the two Leeds University BAs on which the curtain has now fallen. My intention is thus to 'take the temperature' of popular music studies in higher education in the UK, and to look at where it may be heading in the years to come.

We might see the origins of the field of popular music studies (including a range of multidisciplinary approaches – see Cloonan, 2005; Hesmondhalgh & Negus, 2002, p. 1) as dating back to the 1970s and early 1980s, when books by Dave Laing (1970) and Charlie Gillett (1971), Simon Frith (1978/1981) and Dick Hebdige (1979), made claims that popular music was more than mere commercial, mass entertainment and, rather, a powerful historical and social force that required the tools of sociology and the new techniques of cultural studies to expose its messages and meanings, drawing on the Birmingham Centre for Contemporary Cultural Studies' intellectual momentum since its inception in 1964. For some time, the musicological dimension was regarded more warily, although key figures such as Philip Tagg (1979) attempted to bridge the gap between the sounds of music and its signs. Most important, however, in terms of a book-length text, was *The Sociology of Rock* (1978), quickly reissued as *Sound Effects: Youth, Leisure and the Politics of Rock 'n' Roll* (1981), Frith's in-depth, sociological study of popular music set against various backdrops – Adorno's Frankfurt School critique, folk music, the mass media and more.

Frith's volume and the supporting impetus – including the establishment of the International Association for the Study of Popular Music (IASPM) at an Amsterdam conference in 1981 – gave encouragement to some visionary British university departments to introduce popular music to higher education programmes and syllabi over the following decade. We should credit two particular developments here: a commitment to focused postgraduate study at Liverpool University which, via its new Institute of Popular Music, founded in 1988, launched the world's first Master of Arts degree in Popular Music Studies in 1990, and the introduction of popular music components in Salford University's music degree at the start of the 1990s. Out of these key initiatives, the final 10 years of the century would see a gradual, steadily increasing engagement with popular music studies in both the new universities and, more tentatively, some longer-established institutions (it is worth pointing out that Liverpool University was a member of the UK's elite Russell Group of research-active universities, and the Greater Manchester-located University of Salford, although a former technical college, had been awarded university status by 1967). For a fuller discussion of the emergence of higher popular music education (HPME) in the UK, see for example Till (chapter 3, this volume) and Parkinson and Smith (2015).

I became a small part of the story when, in 1990, I joined the first small cohort of students – a group numbering four – in the initial popular music studies MA at Liverpool's Institute for Popular Music. Like a number of those earlier trailblazers in the popular music studies field – such as Frith, Laing and Gillett (see Warner, 2015, p. 444) – I had a journalistic background and had written about popular music for the provincial evening press. By the time I was completing my postgraduate Liverpool studies at the end of 1992, I had become the regional live rock critic for national newspaper *The Guardian*. In autumn 1994, the West Yorkshire liberal arts institution, Bretton Hall College, whose degrees were validated under the auspices of the University of Leeds, advertised for a lecturer to teach in its recently established BA in Popular Music Studies. I was appointed to the role and, in November of that year, I began teaching in the programme.

Where to now?

The popular music studies degree at Bretton formed part of a portfolio of degrees offered by the college's School of Music. It was inaugurated in 1992 and attracted an initial cohort of around 25 students, who were in their final year as I arrived. The programme was wide-ranging, covering performance, composition and technology alongside critical and historical studies, and attempted to connect members of the programme with employment opportunities via self-devised business projects, ideas of entrepreneurship and helping to organize industry placements. The programme subsequently continued to recruit well, with year groups generally hitting the mid-20 mark. After going through various iterations at locations in and around Leeds, a decision was taken by the university's School of Music to close this distinctive degree programme in 2014, while retaining popular music-oriented modules (courses) within the other, more traditional, music degrees on offer. This is only one example of a programme that has lived and died. There have been many other programmes – and even dedicated institutions – that have emerged in the UK over the last quarter century and often survived. Today, many UK programmes include popular music in their title or their syllabus (Cloonan & Hulstedt, 2013; Smith, 2014).

Method

I wrote to 34 established academics in the PMS field (Cloonan & Hulstedt, 2013; Smith, 2014) – principally in music departments, and all in institutions that had established reputations as leaders in this educational area – to gauge their perception of the current condition of PMS in the UK. Twenty-four responded, from 21 institutions. Seven old universities and 14 post-92 new universities are represented. Two respondents requested anonymity and are anonymized below. Most of those who were generous enough to supply answers are quoted in this chapter, but not, for reasons of space, everyone.

I asked my interview subjects seven questions via email:

- How would you describe yourself (e.g. musicologist, historian, cultural theorist, sociologist, musician, composer, technologist, etc.)?
- To which university are you attached and what is your title?
- To which undergraduate courses with popular music content have you contributed?
- If relevant, does your institution have a degree programme with popular music in its title?
- If so, how long has it run and what is it called?
- If your current (or past) institution previously had a programme with popular music in its title, when did it run and why did it end?
- And, how would you assess the present health of popular music studies in the area of undergraduate degree programmes in the UK?

As my principal question related to the 'health' of the subject within the HE sector, I focus on the responses to the last question that I asked participants. I identified four main and recurring themes which emerged from among the exchanges. These I have characterized as: (1) tensions between practical activity and critical studies, (2) art music traditions and discourses of the popular, (3) the vocational emphasis of degree courses, and (4) the rise of private provision in the sector and its potential implications for the field of study. I have utilized these headings and arranged material accordingly, following an iterative coding process while reading and re-reading participant responses. As such, this study was conducted in line with normative expectations in qualitative enquiry (e.g. Lincoln & Guba, 1985; Smith et al., 2009).

Findings and analysis

Tensions between practical activity and critical studies

A number of commentators raise the issue and place of practical activity – performance, composition, technology and business – in this sphere and its relation to the intellectual or critical dimension that was originally at the core of popular music studies as established in some institutions. Some respondents felt that this remains an area of contention, blurring the original academic aspirations of those at Liverpool University, IASPM, etc.; others believed that a consensus is gradually being established, and that accommodation of practice and theory as complementary models is in process (see e.g. Hooper, chapter 13, this volume; Parkinson & Smith, 2015).

On the general status of PMS, Bob Davis, Senior Lecturer in Popular Music/Music Technology at Huddersfield University, remarked:

> Tricky one. I teach across courses which have a strong practical – performance/composition – content rather than a bias towards academic work, so my impression is that PMS, in that wider sense, is very much alive and well, given the numbers we continue to recruit, but I do worry that PMS as a "study" might not have broadened its scope sufficiently to study popular music in the here and now but instead is studying its (self-referential) self. Recent articles in [the UK scholarly journal] *Popular Music* – used here as a test of where we might be at the moment – seems to be covering very similar ground (genre analysis, something on rock, punk, maybe lyric analysis, masculine/feminine, race, authenticity) and I don't necessarily see a discourse that is addressing the here and now of the students we teach.

The late Sheila Whiteley, Professor Emeritus in Popular Music at the University of Salford, stated:

> With institutions such as BIMM [British & Irish Modern Music Institute], PMS is still expanding and their degree courses [programmes] also have an emphasis on performance, composition, and studio production. However, it does appear that specialist undergraduate courses, obviously important [...] in terms of producing erudite graduates who can defend the continuing importance of the field, not least globally and virtually, are decreasing.

Whiteley's observations regarding the erudition of graduates from undergraduate popular music programmes certainly would welcome critique and begs further research, although this chapter contains space for neither.

Simon Zagorski-Thomas of the University of West London expresses this view, emphasizing the value of the field to institutions, rather than in terms of graduate attributes:

> One big shift in the past five years that I see is the expansion of popular music practice in music – performance and production. That certainly seems to be expanding at full tilt – and there is also an increase in musicology and ethnomusicology departments engaging with popular music, and perhaps even ideas taken from Popular Music Studies. I think that if the study of popular music is moving up the hierarchy of subject prestige at all, it's as much to do with this acceptance in traditional music departments as it is to do with the hard work of popular music studies academics.

Anonymous A, a lecturer at a post-1992 university, said:

> Some programmes are shifting towards an emphasis on practice. For me, I don't think that's the direction to go in. We need to produce good practitioners, yes, but also produce those who can think about their practice, able to argue their particular approaches. Practice needs to be contextualized in an academic context.

Attempts are being made to integrate practice and research as he suggests, in, for instance, the (albeit postgraduate) MMus Popular Music Performance programme at London's Institute of Contemporary Music Performance (Institute of Contemporary Music Performance, 2015). Participants' responses perhaps indicate a trend in this young field, where academics are not aware of one another's programmes; one of the other aims of publications such as this volume is to bring diverse practices and perspectives together for dissemination among the community.

Art music traditions vs the popular

One of the principal problems that popular music studies has faced in its short tenure in the academy, particularly when it has endeavoured to cultivate a place in university music departments, is the powerful and dominating presence of the Western Art music tradition, which has enjoyed a central and privileged place in UK higher education for centuries (Parkinson, 2014; Parkinson & Smith, 2015). Kassabian argues that debate over the 'popular' "continues to be a focal point for a set of institutional struggles [. . .] aimed at opportunities for scholars to study mass-mediated culture within universities" (1999, p. 113). He finds that the forces of the cultural establishment have rallied to protect their territory, not just to underpin and propagate the intellectual pre-eminence of their research and study, but also to protect the physical representation of that older school of thought within the academic corridors, fighting not just over ideas but also a campaign for space – in terms of contracted jobs, office allocation and scheduled time – to present perspectives on a version of music that is mass-produced, mass-consumed and mass-mediated. The notion of the popular is, however, perpetually under debate – a discussion that likely affects and reflects institutional and programme-level attitudes in the field – with other scholars understanding popular to mean far more than the commoditized culture that Kassabian, for example, implies (Kirschner, 1998; Smith, 2013, 2016).

This particular locking of horns is perhaps less prevalent in institutions where younger disciplines bring popular music studies into their own original and developing contexts. Departments with interests in media communications, sociology or cultural studies, for example, may feel their hegemony is less under threat from such *arriviste* pursuits as popular music studies, and instead see their particular interests stimulated and strengthened by the addition of such cutting-edge and up-to-date forms of enquiry, producing and teaching and learning materials as PMS is prone to employ. Derek B. Scott, Professor of Critical Musicology at the University of Leeds shared this view, arguing that:

> PMS is healthy. I like the fact that most university music degrees now have popular music content. Popular music programmes as separate entities may be in decline, however, [mergings of music programmes have recently taken place at Liverpool and Salford Universities as well as Leeds] but there's nothing like the problem facing, say, the decline of baroque music courses.

Rupert Till, Senior Lecturer in Music Technology at the University of Huddersfield, commented:

> PMS is very strong in new universities and developing in old universities. It's still a minority activity in old universities, despite being the majority music. Classical music degrees are still better funded; for example, popular music performance students are taught 10 hours of individual tuition, classical performers get 22 hours, on almost identical modules. Class sizes are smaller in classical music modules, and essentially popular music is cross-subsidising classical music teaching. "Music" is still regarded at Huddersfield University as classical music. This makes my blood boil.

Zagorski-Thomas, on the other hand, was under "the impression that there is more snobbery and conservative intransigence about popular music in the non-musicians who manage universities than there is among the musicologists and classical composers/performers who work in them".

Dai Griffiths, Senior Lecturer in Music at Oxford Brookes University, explained that in his institution there has been

> A lot of Popular Music activity without there ever being a course named Popular Music. The reason for that is that we (me primarily, but also my

colleagues) resisted the fragmentation of the title "Music", and were resistant to the split cohort. The thought was always there to invent the pop music degree – "thought" rather than "pressure". It might change in the future.

Nathan Wiseman-Trowse, Associate Professor in Popular Music at the University of Northampton, opined:

> The sector seems to be riding out changes to higher education. Programmes are diverse and there is little in the way of a core curriculum but this is allowing universities to recruit on distinctiveness. That said, a set of core principles or areas under the banner of Popular Music Studies seems to be coalescing.

However, Simone Krueger, Programme Leader in Popular Music Studies at Liverpool John Moores University, reported another PMS casualty:

> Our current programme will cease to exist in 2015 . . . The "official" reasons that were named to us included poor stats (number of [upper second class honours] degrees; retention; student satisfaction, etc.) and lack of fit into overall strategic plan of the School of Art and Design, ironically now located in the John Lennon Art and Design Building.

Richard Osborne, Senior Lecturer in Popular Music at Middlesex University, summed up the discussion succinctly, saying he regarded PMS's status as 'mixed'. He argued:

> Where institutions have a popular music degree amongst other music degree programmes, the popular music programme usually attracts more students than degrees in classical music or in jazz. At the same time, popular music degrees are diminishing in number, particularly in universities. There appears to be a regional bias to this as well. I work in London, where popular music degrees appear to be relatively healthy. At the same time, however, I do live in fear that my university will decide that this type of provision is too expensive to run and isn't bringing in enough research money.

Pete Astor, Senior Lecturer in Music at the University of Westminster, was more optimistic about the field of popular music education, explaining:

> When people ask what I teach, I always say "Music". However, I am also very aware of the fact that, when I say this, people immediately assume it's classical or jazz, which, of course, is a political distinction right there! In an ideal world, it's music and, over time, I think what we teach will become music and the value judgements attached to it will fall away. But not for a while, unfortunately!

Simon Warner

Hillegonda Rietveld, Professor in Music and Sonic Media at London South Bank University, believes that PMS is

> an important component in most university portfolios, whether as a stand-alone [programme] or as a component of a wider programme. I do think, though, that the phrase "popular music" is disappearing in favour of just "music," in order to evade stereotyping.

She goes on to explain:

> Popular music has been meshed into various HE curricula, and is now . . . normalised by the term "music studies". The advantage of "music studies" is that it can include both popular and unpopular music, including experimental crossovers between avant-garde and "popular" music and rare-to-find indie releases. Another term I have come across is the study of "audio cultures", which can then also include sound design of a wide range of media environments, such as computer games and cinema.

The perceived value of popular music in higher education seems as contended as the meaning of 'popular music' in this context, and the national picture certainly appears rich and complex, with issues centring around the nature, purpose and worthiness of popular music study in its various guises.

The vocational emphasis of degree programmes

In the post-millennial period, higher education in the UK has moved from being a fundamentally free 'service' (to the user) to becoming increasingly viewed – at a national governmental level – as a market-driven commodity, coming with an ever-higher price tag for the 'consumer'. Angus (2007, p. 64) describes this as a shift towards higher education being required to operate primarily as a "private-public or corporate-state joint economic institution that produces training and credentials recognized in the global corporate economy or the national bureaucracy". This is the new global normal, in which governments and mainstream media perpetuate an ideology in which "it [is] now no more than common sense that the only way to increase the common good [is] by maximizing individual freedom in the market" (Hewison, 2014, p. 3). This initial, significant philosophical shift and subsequent escalation in undergraduate charges has prompted an intense debate about higher education's purpose, ethos and value (Allsup, 2015; Parkinson & Smith, 2015; Smith, 2016).

Allan F. Moore, Professor of Popular Music at the University of Surrey, argues that

> PMS seems widespread, but that's not the same thing as "health". My perspective is that much PMS teaching is "unhealthy" in that it tends to emphasize directly vocational knowledge and content at the expense of the prior aim, which is to teach students to think for themselves.

Thus Moore recalls Parkinson and Smith's observation regarding "the instrumentalism inherent in the employability-focused pedagogies" now prevalent in higher popular music education (2015, p. 114). Sue Miller, Senior Lecturer/Course Leader in the BA of Popular Music at Anglia Ruskin University, Cambridge, comments:

> I think [PMS courses] are too narrow in remit and are often marketed solely at BTEC[1] male guitarists – this then gets reflected in the curriculum with an emphasis on music business, "hands-on industry experience" and songwriting (with some music tech thrown in). Additionally I worry that selling the idea that all students will be successful as performing artists and/or songwriters (in terms of earning a living) is a little dishonest. The emphasis on employability at my current institution makes it hard to argue for the value of a popular music degree as an arts degree rather than a vocational course mapped on to one or two specific careers on graduation.

Meanwhile, Martin Cloonan, Professor of Popular Music Politics Glasgow University, is emphatic regarding the idea that

> the big divide is between pre- and post-92 institutions. There is a real need to show that PMS is not (just) about getting jobs, especially as the main mode of employment is self-employment, about which most universities don't have a clue.

Mark Duffett, Senior Lecturer in Media and Cultural Studies, Chester University, shares a more general concern for "all the 'pure' subjects right now", suggesting, "if they do have a future in the UK at undergraduate level, given the current climate, it seems to be in combination with applied and vocational subjects".

Richard Osborne (Middlesex) adds:

> This is a crucial period for popular music degrees. The sector has come under threat just as it was becoming established. In my ideal world, I would have loved to have seen various types of popular music degree – some that are very practically orientated, whereas others might have no practical component whatsoever making the courses more akin to film studies. The latter now feels as though it's a long way off and might never happen, as the focus for provision is on training students for the marketplace.

Private *versus* public provision

The meteoric rise of a market economy among England's universities in the 2000s has led to the almost inevitable emergence of private institutions wanting to replicate higher education courses but sell them profitably to their undergraduate

---

1 BTEC, or the British and Technology Education Council, is the name attached to a UK FE (Further Education) qualification.

clientele – embodying what Giroux (2014, p. 54) describes as "the [societal] shift from the social contract to savage forms of corporate sovereignty". These institutions may be able to sell programmes and qualifications at lower and more competitive prices, an outcome that could unbalance this emerging marketplace. This concerns some of my respondents – academics in the public sector – who felt that it may not be long before they face the full and fierce challenge of independent operators who stress competitive fees and close industry relationships (e.g. BIMM, Academy of Contemporary Music), alongside those public universities that have for decades also stressed industry connectivity and graduate employability among the principal offerings of their undergraduate popular music programmes (e.g. University of Westminster).

Anonymous A, a lecturer at a post-92 university, took a more balanced view, observing:

> Some private music institutions will ultimately secure their own degree awarding powers on the basis of the size of the student body. And they are far cheaper providers, perhaps half the price. This has real potential to impact the university sector hard in the years to come . . . But I have to stress that there are also good things about private provision. Private providers could make universities make sure they continue to offer a good service; we cannot just rest on our laurels. The private sector is not all about negatives – there are some positives, too. I've seen clear assignment briefs, industry relevant people delivering courses, and involvement by cutting-edge members of the business.

Reflecting the customer orientation of current discourse around higher education, Anonymous B, who teaches at a private institution, said:

> Popular music performance and music business degrees seem ideally suited to private providers partly because performance undergraduates are often looking for a practical rather than an academic experience, and partly because they can offer unrivalled industry connectivity. I think the way forward for the subject is to situate popular music and all its guises in its rightful place at the heart of our culture and as a significant contributor to the economy.

From my small sample, however, it seems that most academics side with Allsup (2015, p. 258), feeling a strong conviction that "education must encompass more than training", embracing a liberal ideal of education that recognizes "a theory of self-formation that is more ancient".

Conclusions

It appears that while degree programmes specifically named Popular Music or Popular Music Studies may be in decline in the university sector in the UK, the field is far from disappearing from the country's broader higher education sector. We may be witnessing the expansion of more practically orientated programmes and the more intellectual study of the subject shrinking to some extent, although such a dichotomy is of course simplistic and would deny the complexity of inter-disciplinary study and 'outcomes' required to achieve a (nationally benchmarked) undergraduate music degree anywhere in the UK.

The pernicious spread of neoliberal marketization of education across the sector (Giroux, 2003) may have a disproportionate impact on the status or viability of subject areas like popular music studies. In an educational realm where the market has become a powerful and influential ingredient, the arrival and growth of the private provider has been, perhaps, inevitable. It is possibly the emergence of this player in the drama that will most affect the next decade of the PMS narrative. Private institutions are likely to continue to carve out a piece of this potentially lucrative sector. Meanwhile, public sector universities may struggle to impart the 'added value' of a higher education experience – arguably at the heart of a liberal education (Allsup, 2015; Angus, 2007; Giroux, 2003, 2014; Smith, 2015) – under the weight of increased pressure to provide professional training, work experience and internship opportunities geared towards employment in the music industry. Perhaps the onus is on us, the lecturers, as Smith (2015, p. 79) suggests:

> Our job as educators is to lead by example. Where curricula and mission statements are instrumentalist in focus, we have to show students by engaging them critically, helping them to see Oz from different perspectives by removing the green glasses of neoliberalism and discussing that there is an alternative possibility to the normative, self-defeating crush of the omnipotent capitalist, neoliberal paradigm.

References

Allsup, R.E. (2015). The eclipse of a higher education or problems preparing artists in a mercantile world. *Music Education Research*, *17*(3), 251–261.

Angus, I. (2007). Academic freedom in the corporate university. In M. Coté, R.J.P. Day, & G. de Peuter (Eds.), *Utopian pedagogy: Radical experiments against neoliberal globalization* (pp. 64–75). London, ON: Toronto University Press.

Cloonan, M. (2005). What is popular music studies? Some observations. *British Journal of Music Education*, *22*(10), 77–93.

Cloonan, M. & Hulstedt, L. (2013). Looking for something new: The provision of Popular Music Studies degrees in the UK. *IASPM Journal*, *3*(2), 63–77, Retrieved from: www.iaspmjournal.net.

Frith, S. (1981). *Sound effects: Youth, leisure and the politics of rock 'n' roll*. New York: Pantheon.

Gillett, C. (1971). *The sound of the city: The rise of rock 'n' roll*. London: Sphere.

Giroux, H.A. (2003). Utopian thinking under the sign of neoliberalism: Towards a critical pedagogy of educated hope. *Democracy and Nature*, *9*(1), 91–104.

Giroux, H.A. (2014). *Neoliberalism's war on higher education*. Chicago, IL: Haymarket.

Hebdige, D. (1979). *Subculture: The meaning of style*. London: Methuen.

Hesmondhalgh, D. & Negus, K. (2002). Introduction – Popular music studies: Meaning, power and value. In D. Hesmondhalgh & K. Negus (Eds.), *Popular music studies* (pp. 1–10). London: Arnold.

Hewison, R. (2014). *Cultural capital: The rise and fall of Creative Britain*. London: Verso.

Institute of Contemporary Music Performance (2015). Masters degree overview. Retrieved from: http://icmp.co.uk/courses/masters-degree-overview [Accessed 23 August 2015].

Kassabian, A. (1999). Popular. In B. Horner & T. Swiss (Eds.), *Key terms in popular music and culture* (pp. 113–123). London: Blackwell.

Kirschner, T. (1998). Studying rock: Toward a materialist ethnography. In T. Swiss, J.M. Sloop & A. Herman (Eds.), *Mapping the beat: Popular music and contemporary theory* (pp. 247–268). Malden, MA: Blackwell.

Laing, D. (1970). *The sound of our time*. Chicago: Quadrangle Books.

Lincoln, Y. & Guba, E. (1985). *Naturalistic inquiry*. Beverly Hills, CA: Sage Publications.

Parkinson, T. (2014). Values in higher popular music education. Unpublished PhD dissertation, University of Reading.

Parkinson, T. & Smith, G.D. (2015). Towards an epistemology of authenticity in higher popular music education. *Action, Criticism, and Theory for Music Education, 14*(1), 93–127.

Smith, G.D. (2013). Seeking "success" in popular music. *Music Education Research International, 6*, 26–37.

Smith, G.D. (2014). Popular music in higher education. In G. Welch & I. Papageorgi (Eds.), *Advanced musical performance: Investigations in higher education learning* (pp. 33–48). Farnham: Ashgate.

Smith, G.D. (2015). Neoliberalism and symbolic violence in higher music education. In L. DeLorenzo (Ed.), *Giving voice to democracy: Diversity and social justice in the music classroom* (pp. 65–84). New York, NY: Routledge.

Smith, G.D. (2016). (Un)popular music making and eudaimonia. In R. Mantie & G.D. Smith (Eds.), *The Oxford handbook of music making and leisure* (pp. 151–170). New York, NY: Oxford University Press.

Smith, J.A., Flowers, P., & Larkin, M. (2009). *Interpretive phenomenological analysis: Theory, method, and research*. London: SAGE.

Tagg, P. (1979). *Kojak: 50 seconds of television music (towards the analysis of affect in popular music)*. Göteborg: Skrifter från Musikvetenskapliga institutionen, 2.

University of Buckingham. History of the University. Retrieved from: http://www.buckingham.ac.uk/about/history [Accessed 3 January 2015].

University of Salford. History of the University. Retrieved from: http://www.salford.ac.uk/about-us/heritage [Accessed 3 January 2015].

University of Westminster. Music courses. Retrieved from: http://www.westminster.ac.uk/courses/subjects/music [Accessed 24 August 2015].

Warner, S. (2015). In print and on-screen: The changing face of popular music journalism. In A. Bennett & S. Waksman (Eds.), *The Sage handbook of popular music* (pp. 438–454). London: SAGE.

12
Parallel, series and integrated
Models of tertiary popular music education

Gavin Carfoot, Brad Millard, Samantha Bennett and Christopher Allan

Introduction

A wide range of tertiary institutions offer popular music curricula, from those with well-established Western Art music traditions, through to those specifically focused on popular music education. Various scholarly studies of learning and teaching have documented and developed new approaches to pedagogy, curriculum and assessment, such as those by Green (2001), Lebler (2007, 2013) and Smith (2013). However, due to the fact that most of these studies are based in singular programmes or departments, few have been able to provide broad, multi-institutional analysis and critique of popular music education practices, perhaps with the exception of the UK-based report by Cloonan and Hulstedt (2012). Different institutional contexts may include a range of factors that impact upon learning experiences and outcomes for students, such as the overall vision and objectives of the institution and programme; departmental history and context; whether the programme includes popular music education alone, or delivers it in combination with other areas of music; the degree to which learning and teaching practices are embedded in established models, or are informed by pedagogical developments and innovations; and ways in which the background, orientation and attitudes of faculty members can shape pedagogy.

This chapter provides a comparative examination of these issues, conceived via three main models: parallel, series and integrated. Examples from within the Australian tertiary sector are presented for each model, from Queensland Conservatorium Griffith University (QCGU), Queensland University of Technology (QUT), Australian National University (ANU) and University of Newcastle (UoN). Each example refers to different three-year specialist Bachelor of Music (BMus) programmes, or programmes that have developed into a BMus from precursors in a more generalist Bachelor of Arts (BA) structure. The institutional contexts mentioned may resonate with, for example, UK- and US-based programmes, although international relationships can be complex (Mantie, 2013). Nonetheless, comparison of the examples can contribute to an understanding of institutional issues that popular music education has faced – and may continue to face – in changing tertiary environments.

Following early research studies in music education, which looked at the impacts of popular music on pedagogy (Campbell, 1995; Dunbar-Hall, 1996), and Green's seminal work on informal learning in popular music (2001), the number of institutions offering popular music education has increased significantly (Cloonan & Hulstedt, 2012). Although this has been less so in the United States (Krikun, chapter 4, this volume), there is evidence that this is changing (Hebert & Campbell, 2000; Powell et al., 2015; Smith, 2014a), along with ongoing consolidation of the area in the UK and Europe (Smith, 2014b). As the opportunities for studying popular music have increased, so too has the study of popular music pedagogy, often building on Green's work as a kind of disciplinary 'ground' or set of themes. Despite such momentum, there has also been evidence of significant ambiguities about the relationship between popular music studies, education and performance practice, indicating that these terms are employed in blurry and overlapping ways dependent on differing contexts (Smith, 2014a, pp. 187–188). In the US context, Mantie offers a pointed analysis of the discourses that conflate popular music studies as a scholarly discipline with education-focused work on popular music pedagogy (2013, p. 347). Other reports on tertiary popular music education in the UK have identified how popular music is found in the sector in three main areas: 'practical' studies that incorporate performance, musicianship, songwriting, composition modules and production; 'vocational' studies of the business sectors and industries covering areas of popular music not directly related to performance and performance skills; and 'critical' perspectives typified by the social, cultural and historical study of popular music (Cloonan & Hulstedt, 2012). These terms are prone to considerable overlap, all of which has made it difficult to position the serious study of popular music pedagogy. Consequently, scholars have tended to present descriptions and evaluations of specific programmes, at the expense of broader issues such as multi-institutional analysis and critique.

About the models and examples

In this chapter, we present the concept of *parallel, series* and *integrated models* as a way of understanding how popular music has entered the tertiary music environment. The *parallel* model refers to scenarios in which the introduction of tertiary popular music education has been segregated from existing study options in Western classical or jazz music. Under this model, traditional pedagogical approaches associated with Western Art music tend to be protected through parallel institutional and faculty structures: in such cases, discourses of musical value are reflected in pedagogical differences and justified by belief that different musical styles, genres and traditions should be taught in different ways. The *series* model can be found in cases where institutions have proceeded through multiple processes of review, planning and implementation, resulting in the adoption of new methods or pedagogies that supplant previous approaches, or indeed in the establishment of completely new degrees or programmes of study. In some cases, the series model can be seen as following social and cultural changes in musical style and taste, as well as a shift in faculty expertise, departmental focus or funding pressures and concerns. This model is especially applicable in smaller or younger tertiary institutions where faculty have been forced or have chosen to implement changes in response to sustainability issues such as the need to attract students.

Situations in which popular music education has been *integrated* more holistically are less common, although there are increasing instances where this is the case. Such an approach relies on a substantial willingness for change on the part of institutions and faculty members, particularly regarding discourses about the links between musical styles, values and pedagogical approaches. In theory, a *radically integrated* approach to pedagogy would involve the coexistence and cross-fertilization of approaches from many music styles and genres: in this concept, an integrated approach to *popular music education* might be more simply described as an integrated approach to *music education* overall, irrespective of style or tradition. This type of integration may be conceived of through overlapping discourses of musical *universality* on the one hand (in which aspects of music as a common language are emphasized) and *difference* on the other hand (in which a diversity of musical contexts and approaches is emphasized). In practice, it is common that integrated approaches to popular music education involve negotiations between such discourses, resulting in integration at some levels and parallel specializations at others.

Parallel, series and integrated models often exist in complex and contiguous ways; for example, it is possible that different approaches to pedagogy (embedded in popular music or Western Art music) may function in parallel with each other, while models of assessment are more integrated, or indeed the opposite may be the case: popular musicians and Western Art musicians may experience learning together in integrated ways, but be assessed in parallel ways by different criteria according to musical style and tradition. Overall, the parallel, series and integrated models are mostly useful as fluid concepts for identifying the general circumstances that have arisen through the introduction of popular music and popular music pedagogy in tertiary education. The models are also useful in encouraging us to think about popular music pedagogy in cross-institutional terms. The following sections describe four institutional examples, including some interpretation in terms of the parallel, series and integrated models. The authors have each been intimately involved with popular music education in at least one of these institutions. Following description of the individual examples, we provide analysis and critique of various issues, identifying factors that are highlighted through each model.

Example 1: Queensland Conservatorium, Griffith University

The QCGU case study involves a three-year Bachelor of Popular Music degree, distinguished by the explicitness of the term 'popular music' in its name: students and faculty refer to the degree as the 'BPM', although on completion students are awarded a 'BpopMus' qualification. The BPM programme is the youngest of three degree pathways at QCGU, offered in parallel to a BMus that focuses on Western classical and jazz traditions, and a Bachelor of Music Technology (BMuTech) programme. Since its establishment in 1999, the BPM degree has been delivered on the Gold Coast campus, in isolation from the main QCGU campus, which is located 70 kilometres north in the city of Brisbane. The BPM has undergone a number of reviews and refinements since its inception, following the early adoption of self- and peer-assessment models and elimination of one-to-one instrumental and vocal lessons. Conceived of as a response to how popular musicians learn in self-directed and informal ways, this model utilizes the recording process as the key pedagogical tool, with less emphasis on the recitals and live performances typical of most music degrees. Lebler has documented the effectiveness of this pedagogical approach, predominantly through analysis of student survey data (Lebler, 2006, 2007, 2008, 2013). Processes of review have refined the degree structure and curriculum, creating new elective study pathways, live performance opportunities (Anthony, 2015; Lebler & Weston, 2015) and work-integrated learning projects with industry and community partners (Bartleet & Carfoot, 2013). The pedagogical innovations of the BPM degree have not been incorporated into reviews of the more classically orientated BMus, indicating that to a large extent the degrees are conceived of, delivered and reviewed in parallel ways (Carey & Lebler, 2012).

By operating in parallel and being physically removed from the classical, jazz and music technology areas of QCGU, BPM students have benefitted from bespoke learning and assessment approaches that are closely aligned with the informal learning practices of popular music. However, this has also resulted in a range of issues for students and staff, including a sense of isolation from students of Western classical music, jazz and music technology. Faculty members have attempted to address such issues through a variety of initiatives and projects, including promoting student work through regular music releases and a related concert series on the Brisbane campus (Lebler & Weston, 2015). Nonetheless, it is probably accurate to say that the nature and design of these parallel degrees – represented by significant literal and metaphorical distance – presents a major barrier to the integration of pedagogical approaches across musical styles.

Example 2: Queensland University of Technology

The BA (Music) degree offered at QUT was established in 1990 (Thomas, 1990) and has gone through a series of changes, initially with a basis in one-to-one lessons organized in streams or strands: *Jazz and Popular Music* and *Vocal and Instrumental Music*. By 1996 the stream structure was discontinued in favour of a more holistic approach, and students chose their principal instrument and area of specialization within their 'Principal Studies'. However, when the BA (Music) was replaced by a BMus in 1997, the practical components of the programme were again delivered through streams of jazz/popular music and Western classical music, while academic units of study (music theory and history) were offered in a more integrated fashion across streams. By 2002, parallel streams of Performance and Production had been developed, with a total of up to seven pathways – three within Performance (Instrument or Voice, Music Theatre, Associate Artist) and four within Production (Singer-Songwriter, Composing for Mixed Media, Digital Media, Recording and Sound). At this time, a somewhat integrated model was in place, in which students specialized in a particular performance tradition but frequently performed in stylistically diverse ensembles for credit, resulting in communities of practice across styles and traditions.

Following this model, the degree flourished for a sustained period, through to the late 2000s, at the same time that popular music education was burgeoning in the tertiary environment in the UK (Cloonan & Hulstedt, 2012). In 2006, 20 arts disciplines, including music, were consolidated under the term 'creative industries', a category of academic and industry discourse at that time (Cunningham, 2002; Hewison, 2014). From 2010 onwards, informal learning practices of popular music were more fully adopted, resulting in one-to-one lessons being supplanted by weekly workshops, and assessment practices that moved from individual student recitals to group-based performances. Overall, changes in the programme have occurred in terms of the series model, given that there has predominantly been one main degree pathway (BA or BMus) and that changes in structure and approach have often supplanted previous arrangements (the most significant of these being the relatively recent abandonment of one-to-one lessons). Despite the overall appropriateness of the series model, the context of popular music education at QUT provides an example of how parallel, series and integrated models can exist simultaneously at different levels of curriculum, pedagogy and assessment.

Example 3: Australian National University

The ANU School of Music's BMus represents a predominantly integrated model of popular music education, devised by newly appointed faculty members in 2012 following a complete and radical school restructure (Bennett, 2014; Tregear, 2014). The revised BMus takes a more holistic approach to curriculum in which popular music (performance and popular musicology) is integrated with the study of other musical traditions. The degree features majors and minors in Performance, Musicology and Creative Musicianship, with a further Music Technology minor incorporating three main areas of content specific to popular music. These areas are: (1) the study of popular music history, culture and context (including audience reception, phonography, gender and sexuality, culture and subculture), along with the techniques of popular music analysis (Moore, 1993; Tagg, 1982); (2) studies in music and digital media, which – drawing on precedents at Harvard University and UoN (Bennett, 2014) – combine practical and theoretical approaches to music and social media, music and the internet, podcasting, copyright law and online IP management; and (3) studies in music recording and production techniques, designed to introduce students to the fundamentals and science of sound and recording. Along with the development of these part-parallel/part-integrated minors, popular music performance has been integrated into the performance major and minor, as well as into ensemble practices.

This example demonstrates the kind of integrated approach less common in many institutions. However, somewhat in keeping with the school's traditional background, the revised degree structure has continued to incorporate one-to-one tuition for all performance majors. Lessons are augmented by weekly performance seminars and compulsory ensemble performances, with a Popular and Contemporary ensemble offered for the first time in 2014. This ensemble has been keenly subscribed to by students with traditional Western Art music backgrounds, and it attracts non-music majors from other areas of the arts and social sciences. These changes might be characterized as occurring in series, given the major reforms that occurred simultaneously across the entire School of Music through a re-positioning and 'rebranding' intended to attract students from non-traditional music performance backgrounds. Keeping in mind that the School is still in a period of transformation, early signs point to benefits of an integrated and inclusive curriculum designed to cater to the holistic experience of life as a musician, in contrast to previous emphases on niche instrumental and performance traditions.

Example 4: University of Newcastle

Until 2008, the UoN BMus followed a traditional conservatoire model including one-to-one lessons, study of traditional Western harmony, historical musicology and traditional ensemble studies. Following a review of the BMus, the decision was made to open the degree to a variety of musical styles other than Western classical music, and since 2009 students have been able to study the styles and genres that most interest them. Following the same general structure as previous iterations of the degree, students study three core areas: Principal Study (one-to-one lessons), Collaborative Music-Making (ensemble-based learning) and Creative and Analytical Studies in Music (harmony and aural studies). Echoing models from the other example institutions, music theory and aural studies have been positioned and delivered as core curricula across musical styles and traditions. However, curricula in these areas have undergone major shifts, along with the addition of new pathways of study through majors in Creative Production, Songwriting, Composition and Music in the Creative Industries. Students in these new majors learn through collaborative work in small groups, rather than one-to-one lessons. A number of electives are also available in traditional and non-traditional areas, including the option to study performance in Western classical, popular, jazz and world music traditions along with electives in pedagogy, sound engineering and film music. These offerings embed diversity across the degree programme, reflected in the fact that, in their second semester of Principal Study, students are required to present a recital entirely outside their main genre. This represents a major departure from models of specialization in conservatoire music degrees and is a clear example of integration across music styles. This has occurred mostly within degree structures inherited from a traditional context, although further reviews are expected to consolidate such integration through changes to these structures.

Identifying the issues

The examples presented above are multifaceted and situated within myriad variables that may only be relevant to specific institutional, social, cultural and personal contexts. Nonetheless, we have identified some recurring themes resulting from the parallel, series and integrated models, including the effect of institutional transitions and competition, the influence of faculty member expertise, approaches and conceptions of music practice and assessment, and responses to changes in the music industry and professional careers of musicians. These are just some of the issues that have faced popular music education in tertiary contexts, influencing the practices and pedagogies that tend to be employed across different models.

Institutional transitions and competition

Institutional factors at ANU and UoN have meant that popular music education was introduced through substantial internal reviews, in both cases resulting in major and at times controversial changes of approach (Powles, 2012; Tregear, 2014). In some cases, the controversy has been rooted in the desire to maintain perceptions of excellence in Western classical performance, echoing discourses of elitism well documented in music education research (Martin, 2012; Williams & Randles, chapter 5, this volume). For the examples of QCGU and QUT, the introduction has been less controversial, although the QUT degree has also gone through substantial changes in focus. Of the four examples presented here, only the parallel BPM programme from QCGU has proceeded solely in the area of popular music education, illustrating a 'path of least resistance' for an institution with a substantial investment in traditional approaches to music education. The ANU and UoN programmes – and past iterations at QUT – have brought popular music together with other styles, attempting to circumvent sometimes-artificial divisions in pedagogy. The current QUT BMus functions more as a popular music programme, typifying the series model whereby popular music education has supplanted previously more-integrated approaches. However, ANU and UoN's recent commitment to integrated models reveals that it is possible to bring together musicians from various backgrounds in an open-ended pedagogical framework not overly determined by musical style and genre.

Although aspects of institutional competition can be overstated in music education markets, competition nonetheless has the capacity to influence or serve as a catalyst for change. For example, part of the redesign of the QUT degree in 2010 resulted in a market position alongside QCGU and another degree at the University of Southern Queensland, with all three institutions situated within a

90-minute drive of one other. Competition between popular music education providers beyond city and state borders in Australia exists only to a very small degree, and there is limited competition for student enrolments between the Queensland-based example programmes and the degrees offered by ANU and UoN. As the only regional institution in these case studies, UoN's major competition is not from other universities but from vocational education providers who do not offer one-to-one lessons. Articulation arrangements have been put into place between the two sectors, allowing graduates from vocational education to articulate into higher degrees or gain credit for prior studies. The pathways between these sectors are one area in need of further study; evidence has suggested that popular music education offerings across sectors in Australia are growing through private providers, although the degree of competition or accord between sectors is not well-known (Hannan, 2001).

Faculty member expertise

Faculty member background and experience often has a distinct influence on how popular music education is incorporated into tertiary institutions. This influence is intensified by the small number of faculty members employed in many institutions; for the fewer than 10 full-time faculty members at both QCGU and QUT, staff expertise is primarily focused in popular music styles and genres, with some limited evidence of diversity of background in other areas (including jazz and Western classical music). In QCGU's parallel model, current faculty members are almost exclusively focused on various areas of popular music education. This is also the case at QUT, although the makeup of QUT faculty has changed in series over time, in response to changes in programme structure and focus. At ANU and UoN, the staff profiles have undergone changes with the appointment of new faculty members who have expertise in popular music styles, reflecting a pattern through which curriculum review has necessitated major changes in faculty profile. This played out at ANU through radical and controversial reforms whereby the number of academic faculty members was halved, and a subsequent process wherein existing faculty were required to reapply for positions (Martin, 2012). At UoN, faculty members with a background in Western classical music have had to integrate their existing skill sets alongside those of new staff members, and/or be involved in retraining initiatives.

Changes in faculty profile can impact a variety of areas, including the way that students are admitted to study; for example, audition panels have historically relied on faculty members' instrumental or vocal specializations. More recently, audition panels tend to rely on a more 'generalist' approach to assessing students' readiness to learn. Overall, the makeup of faculty members appears to correspond to the three models: parallel degrees such as QCGU rely on a parallel cohort of faculty members; degrees such as those at QUT have changed in series over time, as have their faculty; more integrated programmes as those found at ANU and UoN demonstrate an integration of various faculty members with diverse areas of specialization.

Approaches to music practice and assessment

Whereas traditional conservatoire approaches have placed particular value on individual instrumental and vocal virtuosity, models of popular music education have tended to encompass a broader range of skills, from areas such as music technology and industry to entrepreneurial practices (Lebler & Hodges, chapter 22, this volume; Morrow et al., chapter 26, this volume). These kinds of musical literacies, "creativities" (Burnard, 2012) or "Track Imperatives" (Bennett, 2015, p. 45), involve different values than are often reflected in institutional priorities and approaches (Perkins, 2014; Smith & Shafighian, 2013). One major difference in popular music education has been the recognition of informal ways of learning: in this regard, the QCGU BPM degree has been designed without one-to-one lessons in any form, instead embedding informal approaches to pedagogy within formal structures. However, each of the other case studies has relied at some point on the traditional conservatoire approach where students are expected to excel in instrumental or vocal performance (or in an area of specialization such as composition), and where they are assessed through performance recitals (Thomas & Millard, 2006). The QUT BMus has historical precedents in traditional models of one-to-one lessons, although the current model has seen a shift to practical work in small ensembles, which encourages self-directed learning and peer feedback, alongside formative feedback from mentoring faculty members (Hall, 2015; Pulman, 2014). This approach has some similarities to QCGU, although the QCGU BPM degree has until recently been more focused on recorded music and includes more structured scaffolding of self and peer assessment.

Both ANU and UoN programmes continue to utilize one-to-one lessons. At ANU, one-to-one tuition is blended with performance seminar and ensemble practice, continuing a conservatoire-style model although without separation based on musical style or genre. In a similar fashion, instrumental and vocal studies at UoN are delivered through weekly techniques and performance practice classes regardless of style or genre; all instrumental and vocal students participate in a combined techniques class whereby students come together around technical issues and topics, an approach that has led to an inclusive community of practice across music styles. This model encourages scenarios in which classical pianists accompany popular singers, classical singers act as backup singers for popular singer-songwriters, brass and woodwind instrumentalists with classical backgrounds form jazz ensembles, and so on. As mentioned above, this is similar to an earlier iteration of the QUT programme in which students were encouraged to participate in a range of ensemble activities across genres. Approaches to assessment in each of these scenarios tend to rely on performance recitals, although this is contrasted with the bespoke approach to assessment found at QCGU, which involves extensive use of peer assessment through recordings rather than live performance (Lebler, 2007). Assessment models at ANU were traditionally defined in two forms: performance- and essay-based assessment. Where these forms were combined or integrated with other types of assessment relevant to popular music pedagogy (such as multimodal assessment formats), students have found such innovations challenging, not least because the assessment tasks forced them 'out of their comfort zone'. This illustrates the kinds of problems that attempted integration in assessment can present, and ways that integration at different levels of curricula and assessment can present different issues.

Responses to changes in the professional prospects of music graduates

The introduction of popular music education is often justified as a response to the diverse portfolio careers common among professional musicians in the 21st century. This area has been the topic of extensive research indicating how music graduates are presented with a "prevalence of portfolio careers incorporating both creative and non-creative roles" rather than narrowly defined performance-based employment (Bennett, 2012; Bennett & Bridgestock, 2014, p. 1). Recognition of these career prospects is reflected in the QCGU programme through the alignment of curriculum and assessment tasks with a range of professional roles and skills. At QUT the influence of this perspective has been especially strong, given the institutional emphasis on, and investment in, the notion of the creative industries (Cunningham, 2002; Turner, 2011). As such, historical changes occurring in series at QUT can be seen as an example of how pedagogy and curriculum have responded in a reflective and dynamic way to social, cultural and industrial changes in the music professions, without the need for sudden or radical change for reasons of sustainability or other pressures. For institutions like ANU and UoN, changes in programme structures have been arrived at through difficult circumstances and major review, although in both cases these challenges appear to have presented opportunities to develop innovative and holistic ways of responding to changes in the professional careers of musicians. At UoN, this process of musical inclusiveness has resulted in doubled enrolments and renewed evidence of sustainability in the BMus programme.

Summary

The examples and analysis presented here hopefully reflect issues that are also common internationally, or that offer useful contrast to international contexts. One broad, remaining question might be: How can we assess cross-institutional structures and models of popular music education in terms of notions of 'best practice'? In this regard, each of the conceptual models has its own advantages and disadvantages in various contexts, its own paradigms and problems. In the parallel model in place at QCGU, the advantage of bespoke curriculum and assessment in popular music is countered by a structural reinforcement of separation and segregation between musical styles and genres. The series model associated with the QUT programme represents a reflective and dynamic approach to music education, although does not in itself guarantee the development of innovative or integrated pedagogical approaches. The integrated approach associated with programmes at ANU and UoN meets some of the larger challenges and problems through compromise and a need or desire to bring together music students in a holistic study pathway. Whether or not any one of these models represents best practice models for popular music education is open for discussion. Hopefully, an understanding of the models might enable popular music educators to better understand institutional contexts that may both positively influence and adversely constrain innovations in popular music education.

References

Anthony, B. (2015). Creative conceptualisation: Nurturing creative practice through the popular music pedagogy of live recording production. *IASPM Journal*, *5*(1), 139–156.

Bartleet, B.-L. & Carfoot, G. (2013). Desert harmony: Stories of collaboration between Indigenous musicians and university students. *International Education Journal: Comparative Perspectives*, *12*(1), 180–196.

Bennett, D.E. (Ed.) (2012). *Life in the real world: How to make music graduates employable*. Common Ground Publishing Pty, Limited.

Bennett, D.E. & Bridgstock, R. (2014). The urgent need for career preview: Student expectations and graduate realities in music and dance. *International Journal of Music Education*, *32*(2), 1–15.

Bennett, J. (2015). Creativities in popular songwriting curricula. In P. Burnard & E. Haddon (Eds.), *Activating diverse musical creativities: Teaching and learning in higher education* (pp. 37–55). London: Bloomsbury.

Bennett, S. (2014). An imaginary subject? Designing "Music and Digital Media" for a post conservatorium BMus programme. In E. Himonides & A. King (Eds.), *Proceedings of the SEMPRE MET 2014: Researching music, education, technology: Critical insights* (pp. 41–44). London: Institute of Education, University of London.

Burnard, P. (2012). *Musical creativities in practice*. Oxford: Oxford University Press.

Campbell, P.S. (1995). Of garage bands and song-getting: The musical development of young rock musicians. *Research Studies in Music Education*, *4*, 12–20.

Carey, G. & Lebler, D. (2012). Reforming a Bachelor of Music programme: A case study. *International Journal of Music Education*, *30*(4), 312–327.

Cloonan, M. & Hulstedt, L. (2012). *Taking notes: A mapping of HE popular music and an investigation into the teaching of theory and analysis*. York: The Higher Education Academy.

Cunningham, S. (2002). From cultural to creative industries: Theory, industry and policy implications. *Media International Australia, Incorporating Culture & Policy*, *102*, 54–65.

Dunbar-Hall, P. (1996). Designing a teaching model for popular music. In G. Spruce (Ed.), *Teaching music* (pp. 216–226). London: Routledge.

Green, L. (2001). *How popular musicians learn: A way ahead for music education*. Burlington, VT: Ashgate.

Hall, R. (2015). Enhancing the popular music ensemble workshop and maximising student potential through the integration of creativity. *International Journal of Music Education*, *33*(1), 103–112.

Hannan, M. (2001). The future of tertiary music training in Australia. *Music Forum*, 7 (3), 14–17.

Hebert, D.G. & Campbell, P.S. (2000). Rock music in American schools: Positions and practices since the 1960s. *International Journal of Music Education*, *36*(1), 14–22.

Hewison, R. (2014). *Cultural capital: The rise and fall of creative Britain*. London: Verso.

Lebler, D. (2006). The master-less studio: An autonomous education community. *Journal of Learning Design*, *1*(3), 41–50.

Lebler, D. (2007). Student-as-master? Reflections on a learning innovation in popular music pedagogy. *International Journal of Music Education, 25*(3), 205–221.

Lebler, D. (2008). Popular music pedagogy: Peer learning in practice. *Music Education Research, 10*(2), 193–213.

Lebler, D. (2013). Using formal self and peer-assessment as a proactive tool in building a collaborative learning environment: Theory into practice in a popular music programme. In H. Gaunt & H. Westerlund (Eds.), *Collaborative learning in higher music education* (pp. 111–121). Farnham: Ashgate.

Lebler, D. & Weston, D. (2015). Staying in sync: Keeping popular music pedagogy relevant to an evolving music industry. *IASPM Journal, 5*(1), 124–138.

Mantie, R. (2013). A comparison of "popular music pedagogy" discourses. *Journal of Research in Music Education, 61*(3), 334–352.

Martin, D. (2012). ANU school of music cuts to go ahead. *ABC News.* Retrieved from: http://www.abc.net.au/news/2012-06-15/anu-school-of-music-cuts-to-go-ahead/4073276

Moore, A. F. (1993). *Rock, the primary text: Developing a musicology of rock.* Philadelphia; Buckingham: Open University Press.

Perkins, R. (2014). Learning cultures, creativities and higher music education institutions. In P. Burnard (Ed.), *Developing creativities in higher music education: International perspectives and practices* (pp. 223–233). New York, NY: Routledge.

Powell, B., Krikun, A. & Pignato, J. M. (2015). "Something's Happening Here!": Popular music education in the United States. *IASPM@Journal, 5*(5), 4–22.

Powles, J. (2012). ANU music school cuts: Musicians need to keep in time. *The Conversation.* Retrieved from: https://theconversation.com/anu-music-school-cuts-musicians-need-to-keep-in-time-7731

Pulman, M. (2014). Popular music pedagogy: Band rehearsals at British universities. *International Journal of Music Education, 32*(3), 296–310.

Smith, G.D. (2013). Pedagogy for employability in a foundation degree (FdA) in creative musicianship: Introducing peer collaboration. In H. Gaunt & H. Westerlund (Eds.), *Collaborative learning in higher music education* (pp. 193–198). Farnham: Ashgate.

Smith, G.D. (2014a). Seeking "success" in popular music. In C. Randles (Ed.), *Music education: Navigating the future.* New York, NY: Routledge.

Smith, G.D. (2014b). Popular music in higher education. In G. Welch & I. Papageorgi (Eds.), *Advanced musical performance: Investigations in higher education learning* (pp. 33–47). Farnham: Ashgate.

Smith, G.D. & Shafighian, A. (2013). Creative space and the "silent power of traditions" in popular music performance programmes. In P. Burnard (Ed.), *Developing creativities in higher music education: International perspectives and practices* (pp. 256–267). New York, NY: Routledge.

Tagg, P. (1982). Analysing popular music: Theory, method and practice. *Popular Music, 2*, 37–67.

Thomas, A. (1990). Tertiary music education – Responding to change? In *Proceedings of the VIIth National ASME Conference* (pp. 79–81): Australian Society for Music Education.

Thomas, A. & Millard, B. (2006). Towards enhancing student learning and examiner reliability with criterion-referenced assessment in the creative arts: The case of music. In B. Shortland-Jones (Ed.), *Enhancing student learning 2006 evaluations and assessment conference refereed papers.* Perth, Western Australia. Retrieved from: https://eprints.qut.edu.au/24868/

Tregear, P.J. (2014). *Enlightenment or entitlement? Rethinking tertiary music education.* Strawberry Hills, NSW: Currency House.

Turner, G. (2011). Surrendering the space: Convergence culture, cultural studies and the curriculum. *Cultural Studies, 25*(4), 685–699.

Part III
Curricula in popular music

13

Do the stars know why they shine?

An argument for including cultural theory in popular music programmes

Emma Hooper

> A study that focuses on music but refuses to isolate it.
> (Middleton, 1990, v)

When literary critic Roland Barthes declared the "death of the author" (1977, p. 142) his intended subject was not just traditional authors of written text, but also the 'author' as creator of all forms of cultural text, from books to ballet, musicals to macramé. Barthes' 'dangerous' idea – that the 'meaning' (and even, arguably, the value) of such a text is not necessarily imparted from or by the authors themselves (their biography or their intentions), but is, instead, imbued from "a multi-dimensional space in which a variety of writings, none of them original, blend and clash ... drawn from innumerable centers of culture" (p. 146) – certainly shook things up in academic and critical circles, particularly in university departments, opposed as it was to many tenets of traditional, text-centric methods of literary criticism.

The importance and impact of Barthes' claim, and the controversy surrounding it, are particularly relevant within the realm of popular music, where, with ghost-writing as the norm, the idea of 'author' itself is slippery – how many fans know the name of the person(s) who actually *wrote* Britney Spears' "Work Bitch" (2013) or Celine Dion's "My Heart Will Go On" (Horner, 1997)? – and where receptive context is implied by the very title of the genre itself: *popular* music. In short, popular music is largely defined by the context from which it springs and through which it is received – that which makes it *popular*. It is a keen example of Barthes' theory in action. This is why I find it more than a little strange and

153

rather regrettable that the average undergraduate student in many UK universities' popular music programmes[1] has no idea who Barthes is, and why they should care. These programmes too often still adhere, as Georgina Born states, to "the assumption that the score [or popular music equivalent] and its apparent embodiment of composers' intentionality can be taken as tantamount to musical experience" (2010, p. 218). In this chapter I argue that cultural, critical and, therein, sociological, theory are important and necessary components of any popular music programme, making the case that this is, perhaps, the true distinction of our field: a charged and current space for discovery, discussion and dissemination of inextricable links between contemporaneous culture and context, for contextualizing, therefore, both the art and the artist. In the words of Abramo,

> If educators acknowledge and then engage with the influences of discourses and identities, then new avenues in popular music pedagogy will reveal themselves. This may provide opportunities to educate students about the function of music in the formation of their identities as well as introduce them to new experiences that may transform their musical understanding.
>
> *(2011, p. 476)*

Why us? The unique situation of music among art forms

For various reasons, music has historically been, and indeed still often is, held apart from, or even above, other art forms, for its (arguably) unique feature of primarily evoking emotion as opposed to representing concrete things. German philosopher Arthur Schopenhauer is a notable advocate of this idea, proclaiming music's unique status among art forms, stating that, "Depicting individual things . . . is the aim of all the other non-musical arts . . . [but] music, since it passes over the ideas, is . . . quite independent of the phenomenal world, positively ignores it" (1969, p. 257). Further supporters of this pervasive school of thought include the Symbolist poets of the 19th century, who "were often in love with the idea of music as a higher art form, floating free of worldly encumbrances and capable of expressing the ineffable" (Frolova-Walker, 2002, p. 507).

Whether or not one agrees with this idea, the connection between its pervasiveness and the arm's-length relationship music studies has largely maintained with cultural studies and sociology, these by-nature earth-bound perspectives of investigation, is strong. As Philip Böhlman states, "The reason for the field's imagined escape into a world without politics results from its essentializing of music itself. This act of essentializing music, the very attempt to depoliticize it, has become the most hegemonic form of politicizing music" (1993, p. 419). Of course, while much of this is also relevant to traditional music departments and musicology, I look

---

1 Within this chapter I will be mainly focused on higher education within the UK; nevertheless, the majority of points made may well be relevant to popular music teaching and courses of all levels and nationalities.

to how and why the situation can and arguably should differ in popular music schools, departments and programmes specifically in the next section.

Why here? Traditional *vs* popular: Does it matter to them, and should it matter to us more?

> Popular music simply cannot be studied in the same way as art-music; scholars applying traditional methods to popular music produce distorted readings.
>
> (Covach, 1999, p. 452)

As an undergraduate student, milling around a traditional Western university music department, I learned a lot about music theory, music performance and music history. All three are, arguably, important tenets of a well-rounded music education. However, it was not until my exotic forays way across campus into the English literature department that I ever heard speak of Barthes, or the idea that cultural artefacts could be understood through *current* contextual or sociological lenses. As Born suggests, "The mutual mediation of musical sounds and social processes is placed outside the conceptual bounds of musicology" (2010, p. 214). However, as Horn describes, "Over the years . . .[I] became used to thinking of music in social, economic and ethnographic terms as well as 'musical' ones, as the word trickled down from other students [in other departments]" (2008, p. 17).

Note that many of the first serious inklings of attention paid to sociological and cultural studies contexts within music departments arose around the same time as popular music programmes began to crop up as viable academic options from respectable institutions. Liverpool University's Institute of Popular Music (founded in 1988) was "the first academic centre in the world created specifically for the study of popular music" (University of Liverpool, 2014). The deluge followed, and, by 2004, the Universities' Central Admission Services (UCAS) Student Guide listed 18 institutions across the UK as having degree programmes in Popular Music Studies (PMS). Closer inspection revealed that the same subject area is listed in numerous other places under headings such as Commercial Music (Universities of Paisley and Westminster and Bath Spa University College), Popular and Contemporary Music (University of Newcastle), Music Culture (University of East London) and Jazz Studies (University of Exeter) (Cloonan, 1999, p. 77), to say nothing of the numerous private providers such as the British and Irish Modern Music Institute, the Academy of Contemporary Music and the Institute of Contemporary Music Performance.

With this formal recognition of popular music as a subject able to be studied and *worth* studying, a need for new and different tools in analysis was quickly recognized. "The relationship between classical musicology and popular music was fraught with difficulty and has been much commented upon" (Cloonan, 1999, p. 79); features such as texture and production-as-art-form begged exploration and emphasis, and the hegemony of things such as melody and pitch in traditional musicological methods was called into question.

> At its core was the problem that a methodology based on notation and assessment of music on the printed page is ill-equipped to deal with a medium in which notation plays little or no part, where the sounds of musicians (such as James Brown's whoops) are more important than the notes played and where improvisation (rather than strict adherence to the text) is highly prized.
>
> *(Cloonan, 1999, p. 79)*

At the same time, popular music's deep, fluid and current relationship with the cultures and societies that surround and produce it called further attention to the need for not just new formal analytic tools, but also sociologically critical ones. Born (2010, p. 219) notes, "It is popular music studies and music sociology that have more reliably connected this [musicology and ethnomusicology] to a macro-social analytics of music, bringing to the fore the large-scale political, economic, institutional and cultural processes that condition musical experience". This new scope suggested by popular music studies is now, albeit gradually, leading to the necessary undermining and revolution of musicology and musicological method in general: "The history of musicology and music theory in our generation is one of loss of confidence: we no longer know what we know" (Cook & Everist, 1999, Preface).

For many musicologists, a useful bridge to this new sense of musical scope was to be found in ethnomusicology, and, as such, many began to apply ethnomusicological theories and approaches, as well as the 'ethnomusicology' label itself, to this practice of considering Western music works within sociological contexts. Brackett stated that "ethnomusicology is the discipline that has grappled with the issue of the relationship between context and text in the most sustained and explicit fashion" (1995, p. 22), while Cook noted that it "act[s] as marriage broker, declaring that we are all ethnomusicologists now" (Cook, 2008, cited in Born, 2010, p. 215).[2] As Born observed:

> Changes were happening in the early 1990s . . . and depending upon one's perspective, they were fed by a pincer movement in which the impact of humanistic feminist and critical theory in musicology was being matched by that of the emergent field of popular music studies . . . influenced in turn by British cultural studies and its sociological orientation.
>
> *(2010, p. 207)*

Regardless of the degree to which the impetus stems from the rise of popular music programmes, that music departments of all kinds began opening up to ideas of culturally contextual frameworks of interpretation and analysis is, in my

---

2 It is interesting to note that Barthes himself, in the aforementioned "The Death of the Author" essay, makes this connection with the methods of ethnomusicology: "In ethnographic societies, the responsibility for a narrative is never assumed by a person" (Barthes, 1977, p. 142).

opinion, encouraging. However, the need for such ideas and approaches within popular music programmes was perhaps the most vital and necessary, both in terms of faculty research, where it has now largely been embraced (see above), and, notably, pedagogical practices, where it too often, still, has not.[3] The key to popular music pedagogy is, I believe, in the name. What do we mean by 'popular', exactly? It is a societally or culturally defined term. As opposed to the labels 'Classical', 'Baroque' or 'Renaissance', which are retro-actively named and classified (and therefore knowable, containable beasts), by its very nature and definition, *popular music* is a current, changing and contemporarily culturally defined area.[4] It is both more precarious and more liberated for its newness, and the uneasy freedom that comes from not being tied down by the long, stubborn roots of its neighbours, the traditional music and musicology departments. It is dangerously lazy, therefore, to approach the structure and formatting of popular music programmes with the same old formula; while there are certainly a number of useful crossovers with and from traditional musicology, it is both our responsibility and privilege, as relative pioneers on this particular pedagogical landscape, to ensure that the integral cultural and sociological contexts of the field are acknowledged, discussed and explored with students as a matter of course. Treating these areas and approaches as optional or secondary, is, I believe, an injustice to students and institutions. It is our responsibility as educators "to provide a non-essentialist, non-notation focused socio-cultural analytics of music" (Born, 2010, pp. 218–219). As Middleton succinctly put it, "Since music comes to us through the 'grapevine' of culture, it is, as we have seen, vital to study it 'as culture' and 'in culture'" (1990, p. 128).

Why them? What's in it for the students?

> A teacher . . . must help students construe the "relationships between musical material on one hand, and other things existing outside the music on the other hand".
> —(Green, cited in Abramo, 2011, p. 467)

This argument for the inclusion of sociological and cultural context in popular music education breaks down into two main threads along the lines of the main division in creative arts study in general: practical and theoretical. The latter schools of thought include such more traditional fields as music theory, analysis, history and even ethnomusicology. The reasoning for sociological and cultural theory here is perhaps the more easily explained, following on from arguments made above, as any theoretical examination of popular music would certainly be remiss not to engage with the nature of the beast itself, that is to say, that current context which

---

3 For a more rigorous and comparative study of popular music pedagogical practices, see Roger Mantie's "A Comparison of 'Popular Music Pedagogy' Discourses" (2013).
4 For a full discussion of the intricacies of defining 'popular music', see the first chapter of Richard Middleton's *Studying Popular Music* (1990, p. 1–33).

makes the music popular. Take, for example, if a class were looking to discuss Lady Gaga's song "Born This Way" (2011). As well as considering the formal musical components (harmonic, rhythmic and textural analyses) and the historic lineage that lead up to this song from this performer – tracing a line from Laurie Anderson and Madonna to Gaga as we could from Bach to Mozart to Mahler – it is also entirely sensical that, in order to gain a full understanding of the song-as-artwork, students should examine the external factors that put this song on their cultural radar in the first place. As Brackett explains, with pop opuses, "Their 'importance' fluctuates continually depending on the human context in which they are embedded. In this way, analytical metalanguage and the process it describes remain inextricable both from their socio-historical context and from any act of aesthetic evaluation" (1995, p. xii). In this case, "Born This Way" is deeply and fundamentally embedded in a context of contemporary queer and gender studies; to understand one is to understand the other, both in terms of the work itself and its success. Further examples could include Billie Holiday's "Strange Fruit" (Meeropol, 1939) within a framework of contemporaneous race-politics, or much of Tracy Chapman's work within a framework of social and economic class (particularly in the United States). As Frith writes, "the music industry cannot be treated as being somehow apart from the sociology of everyday life – its activities are themselves culturally determined" (2001, p. 27). If we are looking to teach students comprehensively about this industry and its artefacts, this "sociology of everyday life" that makes popular music 'popular' needs to be addressed, explained and explored.

Students need to be equipped with these sociological tools reaching beyond standard musicology to criticize and contextualize popular music, for the same reason that popular music analysts have recognized the need for new methods within the realm of pop culture. A useful example is Larry Starr's rather traditional analysis of Gotye's "Somebody That I Used To Know" (2011) for a piece in *The Stranger* titled "Ask A Musicologist: Why is that Gotye Song so Catchy?" wherein staunchly traditional modes of analysis ignore much of what makes this song and much of contemporary pop tick (for example, texture, and production in general). This leads Starr to the awkward conclusion that "If there is anything at all noteworthy about this song from a musical point of view, it certainly escapes me" (Graves, 2012). Withholding such avenues of understanding would be akin to leaving student learners with only half the pieces of a puzzle, forming a less-than-complete picture. "Music is not just the product of harmony, melody and rhythm relations, but perhaps more importantly, a *social* product" (Kortoba & Williams, 2013, p. xi).

What if one's department or school is performance-based, focused more on the vocational than the analytic? In this case, the general pedagogical goal is to produce graduates prepared to succeed within the popular music industry, or – as Parkinson and Smith explain in their detailing of a Higher Education Academy-commissioned study by Cloonan and Hulstedt (2012) – to design programmes teaching "students to 'do' popular music – that is, make it or work with it – as opposed to study it in the manner of a humanities subject" (Parkinson & Smith, 2015, p. 99). This industry is succinctly defined by Frith: "The music industry question is straightforward: how to make money out of music? . . . The underlying issue is metaphysical. Music is, by its nature, non-material . . . Popular music culture is, if you like, an immense communication network" (2001, pp. 26–28). As Frith highlights, popular music exists in a climate of fluid cultural exchange, now more than ever. Songs are uploaded to accompany political videos, and pop stars live tweet everything from elections to the Olympics. In this highly publicized environment, every performance decision, from lyric innuendo (such as in Robin Thicke's song "Blurred Lines" [2013]) to footwear (electro-pop star Robyn's shoes have their own Facebook fan page; Facebook, 2011), is part of a fast-moving, intricate, delicate semiotic system of persona, politics and communication. Within popular culture, the artefact is only a small portion of the art. There is an expectation that our pop music and pop musicians will participate in this culture as simultaneous creators and commentators. The binary mindset of "doing" versus "thinking about" observed in Cloonan and Hulstedt's study, wherein "some educators find the term 'popular music studies' to be unrepresentative of the reality of what they do, with one questionnaire respondent declaring 'we don't teach popular music studies, we teach popular music'" (Cloonan & Hulstedt, 2012, p. 20) is therefore nonsensical in the current popular music industry. Students need to be aware not just of what chord they are playing and how to play it, but also how its reception will be altered dependent on innumerable 'meta-musical' choices, sociologically contextualized, championed or critiqued.

One pervasive example of this phenomenon is YouTube. YouTube, a *video* site, is now one of the biggest current distributors of music worldwide; according to online statistics site Statista, 81% of Americans aged 12–24 have "used YouTube to watch music videos or listen to music as of February 2014", with 64% having done so in the month preceding the study (Statista, 2014). Of course, phenomena such as MuchMusic, MTV and other music-video media have been around for decades; however, their scope balks in comparison; at its peak in 1999, MTV had "almost 800,000 daily viewers" (Luckerson, 2013), while YouTube currently handles more than 33 *million* unique views a day (Statista, 2014). One notable and partial explanation of this remarkable difference in scale is that the formats and functions of the two differ; MTV (and other music video channels) consisted of pre-set, commissioned programming, while YouTube is an on-demand, and, with the marked prevalence of internet-enabled mobile devices, portable service, arguably currently the world's biggest and most versatile video-jukebox. Therefore, much as the Syd Barretts[5] out there would like to disappear from sight (and site[s]) and exist only in sound, this is simply not a viable position for current performers. More and more, to be heard *is* to be seen, and to be tweeted and retweeted, and instagrammed, and interviewed, as "in myriad encounters . . . people of every kind and taste engage every day in dialogues about popular music's meanings and effects" (Middleton, 1990, p. 1). Today's popular music and musicians exist "as part of a web of broader cultural activities" (Brackett, 1995, p. xi). It is therefore keenly important that if

---

5 Barrett, a founding member of Pink Floyd, was notably reclusive, shying away from limelight and the public view.

student performers are to be expected to succeed, that they are taught fluency in the language of sociology and semantics, not as abstract tools for theory and criticism, but as active components of their own performance and a way to understand their potential professional life.

Lady Gaga is, again, one of the more obvious examples of this sort of socially aware performer in action, having acknowledged at the 2011 MTV awards, "I am not real. I am theater" (Gaga, 2011, cited in Halberstam, 2012, p. xi). Another such act is Macklemore (AKA Ben Haggerty) and Ryan Lewis, whose two YouTube hits, "Same Love" (2012a) and "Thrift Shop" (2012b), despite topical differences (the former being pro gay-marriage/equality, and the latter a gentle satire of R&B consumer culture) both project a clear liberal-left viewpoint and both function as considered cultural commentary in their musical, lyrical and visual presentations.[6] The manipulation and power of this sort of careful semantic crafting trickles down to less overtly socially self-aware performers as well, from Ed Sheeran's just-out-of-bed hair, comforting boy-next-door hoodies and lyrics ("I saw a shooting star/ And thought of you" [Sheeran, 2014]) to Lana Del Ray's 'noir' stylings – lyrics, visuals and interview demeanour (see, for example, a recent *Guardian* interview with the performer, titled "Lana Del Ray: 'I Wish I Was Dead Already'" [Jonze, 2014]). Although there is a sliding scale of active politicization, every detail of a pop musician's persona is culturally contextualized and significant; each decision, whether intentional or not, is a megaphone to the world, broadcasting: "This is who I am, what I believe, what I'm for . . . " It is therefore indispensable, for reasons personal, practical and political, that we equip our student popular musicians with the sociological understanding and tools to negotiate this erratic landscape.

> If educators acknowledge and then engage with the influences of discourses and identities, then new avenues in popular music pedagogy will reveal themselves. This may provide opportunities to educate students about the function of music in the formation of their identities as well as introduce them to new experiences that may transform their musical understanding.
>
> *(Abramo, 2011 p. 476)*

Why today? Is now so different to ever before?

Of course, to some extent at least, the importance of cultural and sociological contextualization in popular music is not new, and Bob Dylan's decision to go electric at the Newport Folk Festival in 1965 is as relevantly resonant as Miley Cyrus's twerking incident at the 2013 MTV Video Music Awards; however, I believe

---

6 Although there is no evidence to suggest this is the case with Macklemore and Lewis, it is worth considering the fact that a significant portion of the music made within this industry is, in fact, all or partially ghost-written, as with our earlier Britney Spears example. The need for cultural and sociological literacy is no less valid in these cases, as both the ghost-writers themselves and the performers delivering, and embodying, the music and musical messages will benefit from a semiotic firm footing.

there are three crucial reasons why these critical skills need to be pedagogically addressed *now* more than at any other period in history. The first is the simple fact that popular music programmes are still a relatively new phenomenon in higher education. As discussed above, the newness of this area of study comes with a certain academic freedom, as these programmes look for ways to come into their own, and be distinct from traditional music departments and programmes of study. With this freedom comes responsibility, as Henry Giroux emphatically states, to "address education as a crucial means for expanding and enabling political agency" (2003, p. 96).

The second reason, as alluded to above, is the current, and increasing, pervasive multimedia nature of popular music and the popular musician persona. This has snowballed into the current climate where, either to understand *or* succeed in the popular music industry, a scholar and performer must be plugged into this "immense communication network" (Frith, 2001, p. 28), confidently able both to read and to produce culturally significant signs and symbols through and beyond their music: "Music making is not merely the manipulation of sound in a social vacuum, but instead influences and is influenced by society" (Abramo, 2011, p. 466).

The third reason for the current need for this particular sociologically aware curriculum in popular music departments, classrooms and schools is especially resonant for student performers, and is closely tied to the second reason, with its nod to the ongoing march of technology. In the past, much of popular music's public engagement was via carefully controlled marketing and branding departments. Today, however, the rise of personal access to digital technology and internet have put much more of the control, and onus, in the hands of popular musicians themselves, professionals and students alike. As Kristen Schweizer points out in a late 2013 edition of *Bloomberg Businessweek*,

> Megastars such as Macklemore and Lewis relied on YouTube to build a fan base, while Adele was offered a recording contract by a small indie label after a friend posted her demo on Myspace. Miley Cyrus and One Direction got their start on TV shows ... What you need is TV exposure, social media, and advertising. Few acts are successful today just because radio decided to play them.
>
> *(Schweizer, 2013, p. 25)*

While the big-name music labels have continued to find ways to maintain significant financial power (the 'big three's' controversial sub-minima agreements with Spotify are good examples of this), they have undeniably lost their grip on and/or wilfully out-sourced many of the public-facing elements of the industry. The results vary from indie- or even self-recorded and produced artists cracking the top 40 – like Essex band Koopa, who were the first unsigned band to make the UK top 40, in 2007, doing so almost exclusively through online downloads (BBC News, 2007) – via the pocket-companion model of artist-maintained social media outlets such as Instagram, Twitter, Vine and Facebook, to homemade music videos hitting millions of views. A notable example of this latter phenomenon is American band OK GO!'s initial lo-fi 'treadmill' video for their single "Here It Goes Again" (2006), choreographed and directed by the band, along with lead singer Damian Kulash's sister Trish Sie. The homemade video received over 50 million YouTube views, won a Best Short-Form Music Video Grammy and was named one of *Time Magazine*'s "30 All-Time Best Music Videos" (Suddath, 2011).

The current state of the industry is at once so broad and so personal that big-label branding departments are helpless to contain and control their product as they once could, instead now often intentionally opting to out-source the task to culturally aware artists themselves.

> For their eighth studio release, *In a World Like This*,[7] the Backstreet Boys – now middle-aged men – abandoned the classic record company contract, turning to what the industry calls a label services company, which works almost like a consultant. Under these deals, bands call the shots on marketing and distribution ...The success of label services has spurred traditional record companies to open similar divisions.
>
> *(Schweizer, 2013, p. 25)*

All this, ultimately, means that the contemporary aspiring popular music performer who is socially and sociologically aware enough to be able, for example, to write editorials for *The Guardian* on their position regarding the feminist-problematics of pop, like Chvrches' Lauren Mayberry (2013), or to understand the implications of their statements, such as Kanye West and his 2005 televised uttering "George Bush doesn't care about black people" (Breihan, 2010), or give eloquent public reasoning on their websites regarding the banning of mobile phones at their concerts like Kate Bush (Ellis-Petersen, 2014), is and will continue to be at a distinct advantage in the current, historically unique popular music machine. Now, more than ever,

> Popular music culture isn't the effect of a popular music industry; rather, the music industry is an aspect of popular music culture. The industry has a significant role to play in that culture, but it doesn't control it and, indeed, has constantly to respond to changes within it.
>
> *(Frith, 2001, p. 27)*

Conclusion: We must be the change we wish to see . . . are popular musicians always activists?

> Popular music affects all major social institutions.
> —(Kortoba & Williams, 2013, p. xi)

I have argued for the importance of including cultural theory, in its many guises, as an integral part of higher education popular music programmes, highlighting

---

7 Released in 2013.

the importance of arming graduates with the tools to be sociologically active and aware as commentators, consumers *and* creators. Considering this, a pertinent companion question might be: *must* pop musicians, by the nature of the current game, be social activists? While it is certainly true that "Popular music, in its capacity to draw and form communities, may then be said to be a social and political force" (Kortoba & Williams, 2013, p. 112), I would propose the answer to this question is: no. Popular musicians are just as capable of using (and perhaps much more likely to use) the social megaphone of their position to uphold the status quo as to challenge it. Of course, the concept of 'status quo' is a vast and hazy one, wherein, for example, the recent 'bad-boy' behaviour of former pop sweetheart Justin Bieber could be seen as against it (due to his drug use and general law-breaking, for example) or very much in line with it (upholding standard stereotypes of rock 'n' roll and 'manliness' through disregard for authority, or traditional big-label methods of music-making and distribution, for example). For the purposes of brevity and focus, I will save the full discussion and definition of 'status quo' for elsewhere, relying here on a more broad-strokes definition of the term. In brief, for every Macklemore and Lewis taking a political stand there are a dozen or more Taylor Swifts, 'small-c' conservative musicians who do not challenge the status quo. That said, it is important to note that popular music and associated personas are always *potential* activists, existing as they do within a frenetic and fluid space where "Politics enters music, and music enters politics, in numerous and often subtle ways" (Kortoba & Williams, 2013, p. 112). Regardless of whether they foster dreams of LiveAid, Indies-only and political revolution or of going-with-the-flow and bookishness behind the scenes, it is the responsibility of educators and institutions to arm students of popular music with the sociological fluency with which both to study and to participate in this culture in either, or any, capacity. It is important to emphasize that it is not just politically interested students who are set to gain from the inclusion of cultural theory on popular music programmes, but all students, be they focused on performance, theory or history, self-identifying as conservative, moderate, liberal or, indeed, revolutionary.

By virtue of the newness and perpetual, inherent relevance of popular music education, and the state of the contemporary world and industry that surround it, my firm conclusion is that it is the exciting privilege and the important responsibility of current popular music departments, colleges and programmes to offer students, "a study that focuses on music but refuses to isolate it" (Middleton, 1990, v).

References

Abramo, E.J. (2011). Queering informal pedagogy: Sexuality and popular music in school. *Music Education Research*, *13*(4), 465–477.

Back Street Boys (2013). In a world like this [Compact disc]. London, Los Angeles: K-BAHN. (2012–2013).

Barthes, R. (1977). The death of the author. In *Image Music Text* (pp. 142–148). Stephen Heath (translator). London: Fontana Press.

BBC News. (2007, January 10). Unsigned band set to crash charts. Retrieved from: http://news.bbc.co.uk/1/hi/entertainment/6248535.stm [Accessed 1 December 2014].

Bohlman, P. (1993). Musicology as a political act. *The Journal of Musicology, 11*(4), Autumn, 411–436.

Born, G. (2010). For a relational musicology: Music and interdisciplinarity, beyond the practice turn. *Journal of Royal Musicological Association, 135*(2), 205–235.

Brackett, D. (1995). *Interpreting popular music*. Berkeley: University of California Press.

Breihan, T. (2010, November 3). George W. Bush calls Kanye West Katrina diss the worst moment of his Presidency. *Pitchfork Magazine*. Retrieved from: http://pitchfork.com/news/40587-george-w-bush-calls-kanye-west-katrina-diss-the-worst-moment-of-his-presidency/ [Accessed 3 December 2014].

Cloonan, M. (2005). What is popular music studies? Some observations. *British Journal of Music Education, 22*(1), 77–93.

Cloonan, M. & Hulstedt, L. (2012). Taking notes: A mapping of HE popular music and an investigation into the teaching of theory and analysis. A report for *the Higher Education Academy*. Retrieved from: https://www.heacademy.ac.uk/ sites/default/files/Cloonan_2012.pdf [Accessed 30 November 2014].

Cook, N. (2008). We are all (ethno)musicologists now. In H. Stobart (Ed.), *The new (ethno) musicologies* (pp. 48–67). Lanham, MD: Scarecrow Press.

Cook, N. & Everist, M. (Eds.) (1999). *Rethinking music*. Oxford: Oxford University Press.

Covach, J. (1999). Popular music, unpopular musicology. In N. Cook & M. Everist (Eds.), *Rethinking music* (pp. 452–470). Oxford: Oxford University Press.

Ellis-Petersen, H. (2014, August 19). Kate Bush asks fans not to use phones or tablets at London comeback gigs. *The Guardian*. Retrieved from: http://www.theguardian.com/music/2014/aug/19/kate-bush-asks-fans-no-phones-tablets-london-gigs [Accessed 1 December 2014].

Facebook. (2011). Robyn's shoes. *Facebook*. Retrieved from: http://www.facebook.com/pages/Robyns-Shoes/151591034946390 [Accessed 1 December 2014].

Frith, S. (2001). *The Cambridge companion to pop and rock*. Cambridge: Cambridge University Press.

Frolova-Walker, M. (2002). Review of *Russian opera and the symbolist movement*, by Simon Morrison. California Studies in 20th-Century Music, 2.

Giroux, H.A. (2003). Utopian thinking under the sign of neoliberalism: Towards a critical pedagogy of educated hope. *Democracy and Nature, 9*(1), 91–104.

Gotye (2011). Somebody that I used to know. *Making Mirrors* [CD]. Melbourne: Eleven.

Graves, J. (2012, August 29). Ask a musicologist: Why is that Gotye song so catchy? *The Stranger*. Retrieved from: http://lineout.thestranger.com/lineout/archives/2012/08/31/ask-a-musicologist-why-is-that-gotye-song-so-catchy [Accessed 15 November 2014].

Halberstam, J. (2012). *Gaga feminism: Sex, gender and the end of normal*. Boston, MA: Beacon Press.

Horn, D. (2008). The origins and development of the Institute of Popular Music: An interview. *Popular Music History, 3*(1), 9–38.

Horner, J. (1997). My heart will go on [Recorded by Celine Dion]. *Let's talk about love* [CD]. New York: Columbia.

Jonze, T. (2014, June 12). Lana Del Ray: "I wish I was dead already". *The Guardian*. Retrieved from: http://www.theguardian.com/music/2014/jun/12/lana-del-rey-ultraviolence-album [Accessed 16 November 2014].

Kortoba, J. & Williams, J. (2013). *Understanding society through popular music*. New York, NY: Routledge.

Lady Gaga & Laursen, J. (2011). Born this way [Recorded by Lady Gaga]. *Born this way* [CD]. London: Interscope.

Luckerson, V. (2013, April 2). Internet saved the video star: How music videos found new life after MTV. *Time Magazine*. Retrieved from: http://business.time.com/2013/04/02/internet-saved-the-video-star-how-music-videos-found-new-life-after-mtv/ [Accessed 17 November 2015].

Macklemore & Lewis, R. (2012a). Same love [Digital Download]. *The heist*. Seattle, WA: Macklemore LLC.

Macklemore & Lewis, R. (2012b). Thrift shop [Digital Download]. *The heist*. Seattle, WA: Macklemore LLC.

Mantie, R. (2013). A comparison of "popular music pedagogy" discourses. *Journal of Research in Music Education, 61*(3), 334–352.

Mayberry, L. (2013, September). Chvrches' Lauren Mayberry: "I will not accept online misogyny'. *The Guardian*. Music blog. Retrieved from: http://www.theguardian.com/music/musicblog/2013/sep/30/chvrches-lauren-mayberry-online-misogyny [Accessed 14 November 2015].

Meeropol, A. (1939). Strange fruit [Recorded by Billie Holiday]. *Fine and mellow* [78]. New York: Commodore.

Middleton, R. (1990). *Studying popular music*. Milton Keynes: Open University Press.

OK Go! (2006). Here it goes again. [CD] *Here it goes again*. Los Angeles, CA: Capitol.

Parkinson, T. & Smith, G.D. (2015). Towards an epistemology of authenticity in higher popular music education. *Action, Criticism, and Theory for Music Education, 14*(1), 93–128.

Schopenhauer, A. (1969). *The world as will and representation*. New York: Dover Publications.

Schweizer, K. (2013, December 23). Pop stars in search of a better record deal. *Bloomberg Businessweek*, 25–26.

Sheeran, E. (2014). All of the stars [Digital Download]. London: Atlantic.

Spears, B., Jettman, W., Jettman, O., Ingrosso, S., Preston, A., & Cunningham, R. (2013). Work bitch [Recorded by Britney Spears]. On *Britney Jean* [CD]. California: RCA.

Statista. (2014, February). Share of U.S. population who have used YouTube to watch music videos or listen to music as of February 2014, by occurrence. Retrieved from: http://www.statista.com/statistics/291018/us-users-who-use-youtube-to-watch-or-listen-to-music/ [Accessed 30 October 2015].

Suddath, C. (2011, July 6). The 30 All-TIME best music videos: OK go "Here it Goes Again". *TIME*. Retrieved from: http://entertainment.time.com/2011/07/28/the-30-all-time-best-music-videos/slide/ok-go-here-it-goes-again-2006/ [Accessed 30 October 2015].

Thicke, R., Williams, P. & T.I. (2013). Blurred lines [Recorded by Robin Thicke]. *Blurred lines* [CD]. Santa Monica, CA: Interscope.

University of Liverpool. (2014). Institute of Popular Music. Retrieved from: http://www.liv.ac.uk/music/research/institute-of-popular-music/ [Accessed 1 December 2015].

YouTube. (2014). Statistics. Retrieved from: https://www.youtube.com/yt/press/en-GB/statistics.html [Accessed 1 December 2015].

14

'I've heard there was a secret chord'

Do we need to teach music notation in UK popular music studies?

Paul Fleet

Introduction

Much of what follows is born from my experience as a student, a popular musician and a teacher in further and higher education.[1] The chapter, then, follows a more emic trajectory, as opposed to an etic means of consideration (Fetterman, 2008). I firmly acknowledge that the discussion of musical notation is a difficult and contentious issue within popular music studies; this chapter is designed to explore what I will go on to argue is the inherent value of notation to a popular musician who has chosen to study their discipline within an institution; and I hope to offer guidance to those designing popular music curricula to prevent, as the title suggests, any student from feeling that there are elements of music that are somehow secret and only known to those who can read and write.

There are two significant forces at play when considering the role of notation in musical practice: one is the distinction between those who choose, and those who choose not to, notate a musical object; and the other is *in extremis* between music that has notation as an integral part of the musical object itself and music which transmits and communicates through purely aural means.[2] The tensions between these forces are magnified in an educational environment where there is increasing

---

1 In the UK, further education is extra to compulsory education; students usually complete further education programmes aged 16–18, before studying in higher education (at university or college).
2 The use of aural here does not preclude its related term oral; rather I am using the word aural in its widest sense to include orality.

engagement with music from a wide range of practices. Two short opposing examples of differing musics should help to illuminate this matter further.

In one corner, the notation of Western European art music has considerable standing due to its cultural and social history. The value of notation to musicians operating in this field is that they can be separated from the composer by both geography and time and yet the composer's intentions can still be realized. Further, the writing of such music is a way to preserve collections of materials larger than any group of living performers, and also, from the 18th century onwards, it was a useful commercial activity for composers/arrangers (Kelly, 2015). In the opposing corner, the *guru-shishya* tradition of North Indian classical music is exclusively an aural-based practice. Here, the transmission of musical materials relies upon a master-apprentice relationship where the guru (the teacher) holds the music internally – embodying its history and potential – ready to transmit to the shishya (the student). The binarism at play is the sense of the musical material standing either inside (between people) or outside (in a document) the mode of communication. There are of course subtleties to these positions. Those who consider the relationship outside (e.g. a document of music such as a score) require an act of inside (e.g. a performance) to realize the music; and those who consider the relationship inside (e.g. transmission between performers) can find the practice challenged by external forces.[3] But as examples they help show the polarities that can create difficulties for the student and teacher if both parties are not sensitive to these issues when studying the materials of music as part of a formal educational programme.

Such tensions become even more problematic – and one may argue that they may even become a barrier to educational pathways – in the study of popular music within degree-awarding institutions. The above forces and their separation are augmented by another element: those who believe that musical notation should or should not be taught as part of an educational curriculum. If there is one topic that can be sure to cause lively debate among colleagues at a conference considering popular music it is the question of notation. This is not a new consideration; it is an issue that has been part of the question of provision since the inception of popular music degrees. In the early years of popular music provision, Alf Björnberg (1993, p. 74) shortlisted "notation vs the ear" as one of the "areas of conflict" in the teaching of popular music. Part of the root of this debate comes from the diverse entry paths of students wishing to undertake a music degree. Roughly 25 years ago, before the emergence of degrees in popular music,[4] the standard UK entry requirement would be three A levels[5] (one of which being music) and a high practical grade on an instrument. In a very short space of time this traditional route has exploded into a

---

3 It is perhaps noteworthy that the *guru-shishya* relationship is being challenged due to the rethinking of contemporary society in India and the interest of the West in its music. For example see Schippers (2007).
4 The nature and genesis of popular music degrees is also a complicated issue (Cloonan & Hulstedt, 2012; Krikun, chapter 4, this volume; Parkinson & Smith, 2015).
5 A Level (also known as GCE Advanced Level) qualifications are a secondary school leaving qualification offered in further education in the UK.

network of entry paths that not only takes into account A levels, Scottish Qualifications, Irish Leaving Certificate, International Baccalaureate, BTEC Level 3 Extended Diplomas and Access Qualifications, but also involves many admission officers being given room to accept students who have none of these but whose learning can be evidenced with accreditation of prior experiential learning (APEL).

As a hypothetical example, two students may be sitting next to each other in the same lecture where they have been through the same education system in England and have been taught to "use and understand staff and other musical notations" at Key Stage 2 (Music Programmes of Study, 2013, p. 2). However, one student took music as part of their secondary school exams (General Certificate of Secondary Education: GCSEs) and then an A Level where they demonstrated the required levels of musical notation in these qualifications; they also sat and passed the Associated Board of the Royal Schools of Music (ABRSM) Grade 5 theory qualification (ABRSM Music Theory Grade 5 Syllabus, 2015), which contains questions about different clefs, ornamentation of melodies, harmonic progressions, transpositions, etc., as this is a prerequisite of being entered for practical instrumental exams above Grade 5. In short, this student's musical education had a substantial emphasis placed on the reading and comprehension of musical notation.

The other student did not take music among their GCSEs and in a parallel educational trajectory went to college to study music, where their BTEC Higher National studies (BTEC Higher Nationals: Music, 2010) did not include the unit in Music Notation (it is not a mandatory core unit and, in this example, was not part of the college's rules of combination). In short, the student who has graduated from college has not needed any music notation skills to meet the entry requirements that were set by the same Higher Education Institution (HEI) that accepted the student who has just completed their A levels. From these educational trajectories (notwithstanding learning outside of school contexts) it may appear that these students should be on different programmes, with one undertaking a music degree exclusively focusing on Western European art music and the other undertaking a degree exclusively in popular music. But this is not what is happening across HEIs. Provision is as mixed as the student body that encounters it. This is no bad thing when considering the education and training of musicians in such institutions, but it does make ideas of benchmarking and consistency across the student experience deeply problematic in a sector where there are independent bodies that monitor and advise on standards and quality across UK HEIs.[6]

Investigating the provision of notation as part of popular music degrees in UK HEIs

Within the UK institutions that advertise undergraduate programmes in popular music, there is an interesting matrix of those who do and those who do not ask for fluency in reading and interpreting music notation as part of their

---

6 One such independent body is the Quality Assurance Agency for Higher Educations (QAA): http://www.qaa.ac.uk/en.

entry requirements, and those who do and those who do not go on to teach music notation as part of their programme. I carried out this research in October 2014 using both a generic internet search engine and entering the search terms "popular+music+degree", and the Universities and Colleges Admissions Service (UCAS) search engine with the search term *music*. The results were cross-referenced and each website of the triggered institution visited in order to gather more detailed data. The reason for using this mode of investigation was to mirror the activities of a potential student and therefore ground this snapshot from such a perspective. It would be one thing to collect such data as an academic contacting colleagues across the sector, but this may have led to the research telling us 'what we already think we know', and I would argue that by behaving as a student searching the web one might stand a better chance of capturing the nature of this provision across popular music studies.[7]

Out of 57 undergraduate degrees in popular music studies, 10 institutions asked for some level of musical notation as an entry requirement and continued to teach notation during the programme; 16 did not mention it as an entry requirement yet taught some form of notation; 31 did not list it as an entry requirement and did not list the teaching of notation on their programmes; and no one listed it as an entry requirement and then did not make it part of their assessed provision (Figure 14.1 shows these data as percentages).

A significant number of popular music degrees do not ask for any evidence of a student's understanding of music notation and do not go on to consider this area within their programme of study. I comment further on this issue as the chapter progresses, but for the moment let it stand that teaching and learning of music notation are not formal requirements of roughly half the popular music degrees in

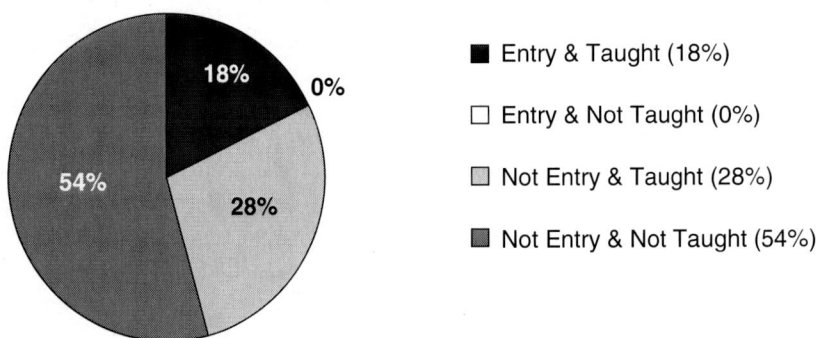

Figure 14.1 Notation entry requirement / taught matrix

---

7 While it will be of little surprise to anyone involved in the recruitment and selection of students, it is useful to note that the most recent report by the education solutions company Hobsons reinforces that for just under 10,000 respondents representing 179 countries, institutional websites were their first and preferred sources of information on degree programs (Marketing Channel Optimisation, 2014). Thanks to Kerry Ellis Byrne (Marketing Officer at Newcastle University) for directing me towards this document.

the UK. However, 18% of all popular music degrees in UK institutions *do* require evidence of some form of music notation knowledge from their prospective students and then go on to teach notation.

For many years, the benchmark of music notation required by a UK degree-awarding institution was the ABRSM Grade 5 Theory certificate. This qualification (which deals principally with what may be described as theories of common-practice, Western classical music) enabled musicians to take post-grade-5 ABRSM practical exams and became an adopted entry requisite to the study of music in higher education. The merits of this benchmark were unproblematic in an environment where music degrees placed a significant if not complete emphasis on Western European art music. But in the current environment, where very few music degrees have this emphasis, such a benchmark can become unwelcome and misguiding for both prospective and current students. One may argue that, to an extent, this has been mitigated by the introduction of other music theory qualifications, such as the Popular Music Theory grades from the London College of Music Exams (LCM). The LCM qualifications, like the ABRSM qualifications, are regulated by the governmental Office of Qualifications and Examinations Regulation (Ofqual) and from Grade 6 onwards carry UCAS points that count towards undergraduate entry requirements. However, those HEIs that request an entry requirement of some form of music notation ability either explicitly state the ABRSM Grade 5 or simply ask for 'Grade 5 or 6' theory which, given the dominance of the ABRSM in the UK, notionally defaults to the ABRSM's standard certificate in music theory/literacy.

I must state that I am not against the ABRSM qualification; it has stood the test of time as a useful indicator of a specific skill set in music. Nor am I against the LCM qualification. I do suggest, however, that there may be an unhealthy cultural dominance of these qualifications as benchmarks, or – worse – barriers, to further study. From the data gathered, only a few institutions stated that they set a theory test at interview, and it is these in-house diagnostics that are the more useful indicators of institutional attitudes. There needs to be an overarching principle of 'fit for purpose' for these pre-entry theory tests. If the staff responsible for setting the tests believe they are useful indicators of student suitability, then the tests can also be used to signal the programme content to students before admission. The test can therefore give both parties a better sense of understanding about suitability (institution/academic-specific) and relevance both during and after the programme of study (musician/vocation-specific).[8] In respect to the 18% of degree-awarding institutions who set a test and then continued to teach music notation, and also to those who have considered this as a possible action, I would argue that the test needs to act as this two-way signal. For example, the ability to transpose is part of a Grade 5 Theory syllabus and this skill often forms part of similar level music theory tests. The ABRSM Grade (ABRSM, 2015) asks candidates to write "at concert

---

8 I am not discounting the possibility that some institutions already follow this practice, but that it is not something gained from the data capture.

pitch a melody notated for an instrument in B♭, A or F, and vice versa", while the LCM Grade (LCM, 2015) requires candidates to transpose "a chord progression, presented in chord symbols, into any key within a range of keys up to 4 sharps and 4 flats". The first considers the transposition a melodic task and the second as a harmonic task. As a practising popular musician I have needed to do both of these actions and rarely in isolation from each other. As a result of informed practice, when devising a test for potential students I have combined these skills to form a 'real-world' example: I ask candidates to transpose a provided four-bar phrase from concert pitch for three horns (B flat trumpet, E flat saxophone and B flat trombone) into their respective instrumental pitches. The test checks whether the correct clefs and keys are being used, checks if there is awareness of harmonic coherence between instrumental voices and measures the fundamentals of transposition. It ceases to be a theory test by numbers and becomes more transparent to the candidate that what they are writing is a skill they can deploy outside of their studies.

As mentioned above (and perhaps unsurprisingly), no HEI requests some form of entry requirement of musical notation and then does not consider it within its curricula. While on the surface this particular part of the matrix may seem obvious (why would anyone ask for evidence of something and then not go on to explore it?), it is worth highlighting these data in reference to the other parts of the matrix and in particular the previously considered tension between notational ability being an entry requirement and it also then being taught. The data indicate that no institution believes that the ability to read and write music is something that can be considered a given either within a student's ability or with evidence from an external provider. This information is encouraging inasmuch as there is no sense of *laissez-faire* towards this issue, and perhaps this is partly why the debate has continued to rumble since the inception of popular music degrees. So, what would happen if this issue were to become polarized and the data were asked a very simple question: how many institutions mention notation and how many do not? There is an almost even balance: 46% (18% before and during the degree programme, 28% only during the degree programme) consider notation, and 54% do not.[9]

Among the 28% of institutions that teach musical notation within their popular music degrees but do not ask for evidence at entry, there is a remarkable variety of module/course titles. There are those that signal awareness that a student may not have studied notation before, such as "Introduction to Music Theory"; those titled "Music Theory", "Harmony" or "Written Musicianship", which imply the theoretical consideration of musical materials, as in "Music Literacy"; and those that ground the skills within a practice, such as "Arranging and Scoring", "Musicianship" or "Songwriting". These three broad areas cover the provision of approaches

---

9 For the sake of clarity I shall not open the investigation to the role of graphic scores and non-notation representations of music, although I acknowledge that they are part of many popular music studies (Stone, 1980).

to the study of musical notation in UK HEIs – the introductory, the theoretical and the practical. Without actually studying these modules or drilling down further into their content from their respective module handbooks, it is impossible to consider where these areas may overlap. It may well be that a theoretically titled module has practical considerations throughout its delivery (and, as I go on to argue, one would hope that it does), but given this evidence and that these titles are designed to be indicative of their content, what can be reasonably gathered from this information? The introductory modules are in the minority in this section, and while we must be mindful of the need not to presume the knowledge base of students, we must also be careful not to undermine their experience. For many students participating in an introductory music theory class, learning the principles of clefs, keys and time signatures (among other elements of music theory) can be a somewhat uncomfortable experience. It can feel overtly rudimentary within a further or higher educational setting.

Further complications in this matter are issues of differentiation and transition management. The musical notation skill base of a cohort undertaking an undergraduate entry-level module can be as wide as one could imagine, and their movement from either a prior educational establishment (e.g. school or college) or, in the case of some students, a professional environment, can be equally diverse. It is also worth remembering that these are variables in a learning environment that includes a wide range of skill levels, with students who come from a variety of backgrounds, and is an ongoing reconsideration. Students in each year group may have different skill sets, so the content explored with students needs to be responsive rather than prescriptive.

I would suggest that the overtly theoretical module titles (see above) are also not conducive to an inclusive teaching environment in a subject that deals with both performance and theory, as they have the tendency to conjure up reclusive images of sitting with pencil and paper in a discipline that is, at its heart, practical. I do not suggest that the theory of music should not be taught (far from it), but I am concerned about the signals that such module titles have the potential to show. For example, as an undergraduate I recall sitting in a compulsory "Music Theory Aural Transcription" module which, as its name suggests, was a module designed to teach interval recognition from a theoretical perspective; one of its prescribed tasks was to transcribe a tone-row by ear. For the person sitting next to me with perfect pitch the task was very easy, but I found the whole experience difficult and demoralizing. Years later, as a lecturer, when I was constructing music theory and aural modules, I was thinking about differing teaching methods and was reminded of this experience. What had I gained in that tone-row session, what pedagogy was at play and had I ever needed that skill which I was unable to demonstrate in that session? The conclusions were startling: my sense of interval recognition had not been strengthened by the experience; in fact, it had been the reverse. It was a non-interactive session, as the lecturer did not need to engage in the experience and the students were either able to succeed or became lost in the row of notes. Importantly, I have never once needed to transcribe a tone-row by ear without recourse to an instrument or with reference to a printed score. This case highlighted for me the need for the musical materials with which students engage to be active and transferrable outside of the teaching environment – active in the sense that there is dialogue in the learning environment between the students and lecturer, where both parties bring their prior learning experiences to bear on the intended learning outcome; and transferrable in the sense that both the students and lecturer(s) remain conscious of the practical value and application of theoretical knowledge. As a parallel, one may, for example, consider the hypothetical case of a medical student learning the internal structures of the human body from a textbook, never to apply them to a living body.

Those modules which signal the practical application of the theory in their title, hold, I would argue, the key to the delivery of not just musical notation skills but also music theory skills in general. This should not soften the theoretical input nor dumb down the depth of the theory; quite the reverse. For example, and to contextualize this process outside of music for the purposes of greater clarity, to *theorize* what 20% of a given figure is remains nonrepresentational until it is placed in a *practical* consideration, such as it being the basic rate of income tax on your salary. Such holds true for notational skills, as they do not serve an end in themselves.

I have repeatedly heard from peers two objections to teaching notation on popular music degrees. The first, lecturers state, is that they were taught the skills but have never needed them in their practice; and the second is that many successful popular musicians have never needed theoretical skills such as notation.[10] The first argument is weak at best, as it suggests that the theoretical knowledge they engaged with in their formative years has never driven their creativity consciously or subconsciously, actively or passively, or in acceptance or rejection of that knowledge. The second argument is misleading, as it does not take into account the possibility that the very reason students have undertaken a degree programme in popular music may be to enrich their knowledge alongside their creativity, and to challenge and explore new territories in their chosen discipline.

One need only consider the Quality Assurance Agency for Higher Education Benchmark for Music (QAA, 2008), which states:

> Students of music, in whatever context, are required to engage with their own experience of musical materials and objects, and to develop their own understanding of how theory and practice come together, while also opening themselves up to the full range of critical opinion.

That a popular musician may not need notation skills in order to create musical works is not contestable, but it should not be confused with the trajectory of a popular musician in an undergraduate programme, who has chosen to enrich their understanding in a scholarly environment. So, to return to the last label of music theory modules: the most appropriate would be those that explore the theory from

---

10 At this point the Beatles are usually mentioned, but commonly without reference to the music notation skills of one of the contenders for being the 'fifth Beatle': George Martin.

a practical perspective, and vice versa, and that position content from the perspective of learning both inside and outside of the teaching environment.

Looking through a Johari window of these tensions of entry/not entry and taught/not taught, it is interesting to note that there is no trend to the degree programme titles or to programme content at the HEIs. The foci of popular music degrees including Popular Music, Music Technology, Commercial Music, Songwriting and Music Production, etc., and the pre- and post- '92 universities and the colleges that deliver undergraduate programmes, are evenly represented in each of the categories within the matrix.[11] This is a real strength within the overall provision as it shows that there is no social or historical agenda and that nobody can suggest that, for the sake of argument, 'only the pre-'92s consider notation'. More importantly, it opens up the idea of music notation benchmarking as something that can be considered by all popular music study providers. Put simply, this is an issue that anyone involved in popular music studies at degree level shares, regardless of subject or site.

A future for music notation within popular music studies

I turn now to a suggestion of how those responsible for provision of teaching and learning in popular music studies could move forward as a collective of providers. John Brewer (2013, p. 169) proposed that to be of public good, social science must transgress the boundaries between research, teaching and engagement. His point goes further into cross-disciplines and across nations, but I would like to suggest that this idea of 'transgression' in academic disciplines is highly relevant to the study of popular music. Transgression is meant in the sense of overstepping presupposed boundaries of research into what it means to be a popular musician both during and after studies at an HEI; of teaching the skills and creating the learning environment to engage with the plurality of music; and of engagement in encouraging students to consider the wider reception and opportunities of their music and the music of others.

These transgressions can be reframed for students in popular music degree programmes if educators take on the position of enablers and facilitators for empowerment (Askerøi & Viervoll, chapter 19, this volume; Hooper, chapter 13, this volume; Partti, 2012; Smith, 2013). As I have suggested, with reference to the QAA, the reason a student undertakes a programme of study within a degree-awarding institution may be to challenge and increase his or her knowledge base. I would suggest that the act of placing the notation of music at the heart of a popular music degree's curriculum is not *necessarily* a good thing, but I would strongly suggest that not placing it within the learning environment at all is to perform a disservice to students. It should not sit against the working practices of a popular musician

---

11 For a critical discussion regarding the pluralistic nature of degrees across UK institutions delivering popular music studies, and in particular the 'authenticity' of such provision, see Parkinson & Smith (2015).

as a skill that they do not possess and therefore might deny them the equal ability to work with other musicians who do work with music notation. To deploy a deliberately provocative metaphor, notation should become a weapon in a graduate's armoury. The strength of notation is that, since its inception, it has acted "as a means to record the sounds of time" (Kelly, 2015, p. 4). It was never meant to replace sound, and to this extent the advancement of written notation alongside that of recording media is a parallel evolution, not a replacement of the former by the latter.

That notation can represent pitch and rhythm across the x and y axes of the stave, and has been developed to include timbre, expression, dynamics, microtonality and graphic representations of sound, means that it only reaches an end-point of possible sonic inclusions if those who deliver these programmes consider notation to have been superseded by recording media. But these are related recording technologies that can serve different purposes. Notation is a tool for the capture of musical materials that not only notates the music but also *an*notates it. It is this difference that is the key to understanding its parallel track to recording media and its continued value. The music in both notated form and recorded form can be, for example, cut, spliced and/or copied so that the seeming linearity of its presentation can be manipulated. But a strength of notation is the value added, the commentary that connects the dots on the page to the sounds in the air. There is a wealth of theoretical language that forms a common tongue of understanding in and of musical materials.

Music notation in popular music studies is therefore not something that should remain a "secret" known only to some students, leaving others "baffled" by the implications of "the fourth, the fifth, the minor fall and the major lift" (Cohen, 1984). Notation and the teaching of this area of music need to be fit for purpose, not learned as a skill to stand outside of musical practice. The inherent strengths of notation need to be deployed in the learning environment, not ignored or considered irrelevant when they can enhance the subject area. It should not be left to Western European art music programmes alone, as – to refigure the point made by Christopher Small (1998, p. 111) that "The Great Composers . . . all were fluent nonliterate as well as literate composers and performers" – there should be no reason to prevent popular musicians being fluent literate as well as nonliterate composers and performers. In short, teachers as enablers of knowledge and understanding have a duty of care to their students to ensure that when their students leave HEIs nothing is left out of the provision that is tangibly and/or potentially part of their potential wider practice. Instead, students who elect to study their chosen discipline within a UK HEI are empowered, their skills are enriched and they leave as musicians who are able to engage with the wealth of opportunities available to 21st-century musicians.

References

Associated Board of the Royal Schools of Music. (2015). *ABRSM music theory grade 5 syllabus*. Retrieved from: http://us.abrsm.org/en/our-exams/music-theory-exams/music-theory-grade-5/ [Accessed 14 October 2015].

Björnberg, A. (1993). 'Teach you to rock'? Popular music in the university music department. *Popular Music 12*(1), 69–77.

Brewer, J. (2013). *The public value of the social sciences*. London: Bloomsbury Academic.

BTEC Higher Nationals: Music. (2010). Retrieved from: http://qualifications.pearson.com/en/qualifications/btec-higher-nationals/music-2010.coursematerials.html [Accessed 16 June 2011].

Cohen, L. (1984). Hallelujah. *Various Positions* [Record]. Columbia.

Cloonan, M. & Hulstedt, L. (May 2012). Taking notes: Mapping and teaching popular music in higher education. *Higher Education Academy*, 1–46. Retrieved from: https://www.heacademy.ac.uk/sites/default/files/cloonan_2012.pdf [Accessed 14 October 2015].

Department of Education. (2013). Music Programmes of Study: Key Stages 1 and 2 National Curriculum in England. Retrieved from: https://www.gov.uk/government/uploads/system/uploads/attachment_data/file/239037/PRIMARY_national_curriculum_-_Music.pdf [Accessed 14 October 2015].

Fetterman, D. (2008). Emic/etic distinction. In L.M. Given (Ed.), *The Sage encyclopedia of quantitative research methods* (p. 289). Los Angeles, CA: SAGE.

Kelly, T.F. (2015). *Capturing music: The story of notation*. New York, NY: Norton.

London College of Music. (2015). *LCM popular music theory grade 5 syllabus*. Retrieved from: http://www.popularmusictheory.org/grades/grade-5-music-theory.php [Accessed 14 October 2015].

Marketing Channel Optimisation: Achieving competitive advantage in higher education recruitment. (2014). Australia: Hobsons Australia Pty Ltd.

Parkinson, T., & Smith, G.D. (2015). Towards an epistemology of authenticity in higher popular music education. *Action, Criticism, and Theory for Music Education, 14*(1), 93–127.

Partti, H. (2012). *Learning from cosmopolitan digital musicians: Identity, musicianship, and changing values in (in)formal music communities*. Helsinki: Sibelius Academy.

Quality Assurance Agency for Higher Education (2008). *Music: Subject benchmark*. Retrieved from: http://www.qaa.ac.uk/en/Publications/Documents/Subject-benchmark-statement-Music-.pdf [Accessed 14 October 2015].

Schippers, H. (Spring 2007). The guru recontextualized? Perspectives on learning North Indian classical music in shifting environments for professional training. *Asian Music, 38*(2), 123–138.

Small, C. (1998). *Musicking: The meanings of performing and listening*. Hanover: University Press of New England.

Smith, G.D. (2013). Seeking "success" in popular music. *Music Education Research International, 6*, 26–37.

Stone, K. (1980). *Music notation in the twentieth century: A practical guidebook*. New York, NY: W.W. Norton.

15
'Art' to artistry
A contemporary approach to vocal pedagogy

Diane Hughes

Introduction and context

This chapter discusses a contemporary approach to teaching singing. It draws on my professional practice as a performer and teacher, and highlights the value of reflexive practice in music education (Nelson, 2013). The discussion builds on my research into contemporary vocal artistry and transformative learning in tertiary music education. My pedagogical approach is therefore both research-based and practice-led, and was recognized with a national award from the Australian Office of Learning and Teaching in 2014. The progressive development of curricula and their refinement have occurred in light of my research on subjects including: investigating contemporary vocal artistry (2010–2012) (Hughes, 2010, 2012, 2013a, 2013b, 2014); designing and implementing a vocal journal (2009–2011, 2014) (Hughes, 2010, 2015a); assessment in contemporary vocal studies (2009–2014) (Hughes, 2015a); career development in the contemporary music industries (2013–2014) (Hughes et al., 2013; Hughes et al., 2014; Hughes et al., 2016; Keith et al., 2014); and reflection and reflexivity in vocal/musical studies (2014 to present). The inclusion of student and teacher perspectives on curricular content and delivery provide additional viewpoints that help to balance author subjectivity.

My approach to teaching contemporary singing has been developed, incorporated and included in a tertiary music course (a qualifying Major within a Bachelor of Arts degree) since 2008, and is one that challenges stereotypical notions of singing pedagogy. It draws on a range of practices and understandings including pedagogical principles (e.g. a variety of learning strategies), developments in voice science (e.g. to enable healthy vocal production) and popular music practices (e.g. informal learning; practitioner experiences). Traditional vocal pedagogy typically concentrates on teaching in a master-apprentice (one-to-one) model. In such an approach, the teacher is the sole or principal person directing the student and, in this context, instruction in appropriate vocal technique typically features (e.g. Greene, 1912). While vocal technique is highly relevant for effective contemporary singing and vocal longevity (Sataloff et al., 2014, p. 3), contemporary vocal pedagogy also needs to comprehensively address the evolutionary nature of popular musics, encompass a range of stylistic nuances and include complex technologies that have brought about significant changes to the ways in which the contemporary singing voice may be conceptualized sonically.

Technologies enabled the singing voice to be more intimate, audible and individual, as Potter and Sorrell (2012) explain:

> The microphone [and associated amplification and recording technologies] also offered the possibility for singers to personalize their delivery: relieved of the need to maximise their acoustic potential they were much less likely to sound like generic sopranos, altos, tenors and basses. The microphone created a previously unknown kind of charismatic vocal persona.
>
> *(p. 245)*

The progression from acoustic instrument to the technologically processed contemporary singing voice is pedagogically significant. It requires contemporary singing teachers to implement critical listening skills and facilitate understanding in such things as spectral sound properties so that singers are able to recognize their optimal processed, resultant sound (Hughes, 2010, 2014). A range of technologies must therefore be viewed as extensions of the contemporary singing voice (e.g. amplification; applied effects) and pedagogical strategies need to be developed to enable comprehensive vocal exploration and use of technologies (Hughes, 2014, p. 293).

This chapter focuses on curricular components that address the complexities of singing in a range of contemporary popular music practices. In doing so, it speaks to the contextual challenges of developing and maintaining contemporary vocal artistry. Before outlining specific contemporary curricular components and situating singing in popular culture musics, the chapter defines what is traditionally regarded as artistic singing, with the aim of providing points of contrast to highlight important ways in which contemporary vocal artistry differs from the typical notions of vocal artistry associated with the Western classical singing tradition.

Artistic singing

There is an established tradition of classical singing as a Western Art form, with several publications that specifically document the 'art' of singing (e.g. Caruso & Tetrazzini, 1909; Hamady, 2009). One such publication, a recorded lecture *On the Art of Singing* (Greene, 1904), exemplified the view that the singing voice is preeminent among musical instruments. Greene (1904) asserted that to be preeminent in classical vocal performance required extensive vocal training, which he later documented in his pedagogical method, *Interpretation in Song* (Greene, 1912). Unlike other pedagogical methods that concentrated on singing

Table 15.1 Teaching components in *Interpretation in Song*

Components	Related pedagogical content
1. Composer's intent	The score, reconciliation of phrasing to text
2. Perfected vocal technique	Resonant production, correct breathing
3. Magnetism	Stage presence, sustained focus
4. Musicality	Notation, piano accompaniment, study of song
5. Intelligible articulation	Inclusion of prosodic or poetic meters
6. Recital programmes	Creating atmosphere, avoiding fatigue

Source: Greene (1912)

as musical training (e.g. Curwen, 1876) or solely on vocal technique (e.g. Evetts, 1928), Greene's pedagogy focused on interpretation of a composer's intent in song delivery. This he labelled as the singer's "equipment" (pp. 1–28) which included perfected technique, "magnetism" (stage presence) (pp. 8–12), atmosphere in performance and command of tone-colour. 'Art' song, with its "musical response" (Kimball, 2013, p. 16) set to existing poetry or prose, was Greene's preferred repertory, as it communicated "the great human emotions in the language of poets enabled by music" (Greene, 1912, p. 1). Greene's pedagogical components and related content (see Table 15.1) are cited in this discussion to highlight the transition from the art of singing to what is increasingly referred to as the 'artistry' of contemporary singers.

At the time of finalizing this chapter, dialogue between judges in an episode of *The Voice* (Australia) (Nine Network, 2015) drew heated debate as to what constitutes contemporary vocal artistry. English singer and songwriter Jessie J sparked the debate with contentious remarks about singer-entertainers versus singer-artists. She related the latter to those singers who were able to be true to themselves, to be individual and to be 'authentic'. While Joel Madden (lead vocalist for American band Good Charlotte) responded with the view that contemporary artistry is the ability to perform a song with a high level of individual expression, Puerto Rican singer and fellow judge, Ricky Martin, stated that "artistry is to make people [the audience] feel". Jessie J also alluded to this when she said "I know how hard it is to live your life with your wounds exposed to heal other people". Collectively, these sentiments are encompassed in my research-based definition of contemporary vocal artistry as "expressivity, individuality and stylistic integrity" (Hughes, 2014, p. 299) in which musical creativities (e.g. individual phrasing, vocal embellishment) are central. Given *The Voice* debate and the continual, wider references to singers as artists, discussion of contemporary vocal artistry, and related pedagogy, is timely.

Contemporary vocal practices

While everyone who possesses a functioning voice can sing, degrees of inherent vocal proficiency are often related to the reasons why people sing. We collectively sing at celebrations, sporting events and various ceremonies; we do not always wish to sing individually. Bithell (2014) refers to the natural voice as "a voice that is not classically trained" (2014, p. 16). Perhaps this description and its reference to classical training relate to the desired 'authentic' aesthetic of many contemporary singers (Hughes, 2014, p. 290). Every voice has its own signature or vocal 'print'. It expresses who we are culturally, socially and ethnically. It is typically indicative of gender and age range, is highly expressive and is reflective of enculturation and experience (Hughes, 2013a).

In addition to the enculturation process, phonation, voice function and effective production are reliant on the coordination of a range of anatomical and physiological components. When the coordination is impeded, the voice can suffer temporary or permanent damage. Singers who are unaware of, for example, overloading the vocal mechanism (e.g. singing excessively loudly with a level of constriction) are potentially susceptible to vocal damage. Such singers may be resilient for a period of time, but their voices may suffer from extreme and prolonged use, from poor ingrained habits or from a lack of effective technique. There are several examples of high-profile popular singers who have suffered vocal health issues (e.g. Adele, Keith Urban, Celine Dion, John Mayer) (Hughes, 2013b). Voice science affords understanding of vocal anatomy and physiology, which can be utilized to develop appropriate curricula; learning to sing with healthy function and production may help circumvent or prevent vocal health issues from occurring. Certainly, vocal health and optimum voice function should be considered in the development of effective vocal pedagogy for contemporary singers. Together with the aim of fostering individuality and expressivity, vocal health and care strategies underpin the curricular components outlined below.

For the purposes of this discussion, the study of the contemporary singing voice is framed within "popular culture musics" (PCM) (Hughes, 2010, 2014). This term was introduced into the literature with the explicit purpose of distinguishing between contemporary and classical styles of singing and their respective repertoires. The use of 'classical' and 'contemporary' for classification is admittedly problematic, in that 'contemporary' also refers to vocal music such as art song. Up until PCM's introduction, the distinction between classical and contemporary singing had been determined as the singing of classical music or the singing of contemporary commercial music (CCM). CCM was a term introduced by LoVetri in 2000 to distinguish between "the styles formerly referred to as 'non-classical'" (LoVetri, 2014). While I support the need for differentiation between these two principal methods of voice production and associated repertoire, PCM is used in this discussion as it not only encompasses the broad gamut of musical styles in popular culture, but also emphasizes the sociocultural and artistic underpinnings of contemporary singing practices instead of accentuating their potential commerciality.

Vocal pedagogy in PCM

While informal music practices can provide a framework for vocal learning inside and outside of institutional settings (Green, 2010), more formal practice-led methodologies for singing in PCM evolved in the latter decades of the

20th century (e.g. Riggs, 1985). Contemporary methodologies have developed, along with a plethora of online opportunities, despite a lack of institutional training opportunities for vocal pedagogy in PCM. This may be due, in part, to the notion that everyone can sing and the attendant popular myth that undergoing singing training may change the often-prized and 'natural' or individual sound of the voice in PCM styles. As Sataloff et al. note (2014), pop singers "are often afraid that singing lessons will make them sound 'operatic' and will interfere with their style" (Sataloff et al., 2014, p. 3). An aversion to singing training may also be due to informal learning situations that lead to "emphasizing aural, improvisatory and creative aspects" (Green, 2010, p. 227). Undoubtedly, informal situations facilitate many PCM singers to learn as they explore and practice with other musicians.

Singing in PCM has transitioned from the early 20th-century vaudeville performance, through crooning, being broadcast live, being captured in recordings and amplified in performances, to contemporary popular singing and its treatment and processing via digital software and hardware (Hughes, 2015b). As such, specific vocal curricula for PCM require consideration of the acoustic instrument in ways that facilitate understanding of its conversion to electrical signal and applied effects. Curricula for the teaching and learning of singing in PCM are multifaceted. The curricular components below have been designed to address the complexities of practice while facilitating contemporary vocal artistry as "expressivity, individuality and stylistic integrity" (Hughes, 2014, p. 299). In their design and implementation, the recognition and fostering of individual vocal sound is given precedence over fostering a sound to suit particular voice classifications and repertoire. Exceptions to this can be made for those such as singers aiming to be in tribute bands or aiming to sing specific characterizations or roles.

Curricular components

While detailing curricula for contemporary vocal studies in their entirety is beyond the scope of this chapter, the following essential curricular components have been designed to facilitate development of contemporary artistry. They account for the opportunities and challenges of singing in PCM that formed the emergent themes of individual expression, technical and musical ability, stylistic integrity, technological applications, artistic image and confidence/presence reported in research findings on contemporary vocal artistry (Hughes, 2014, pp. 290–295). The curricular components are specific to the learning and teaching of vocal studies (contemporary singing) in PCM, which is delivered to groups of students in three levels of tertiary study – foundation, intermediate and advanced. Each level of study is delivered over a 15-week session in which 13 weeks of classes are undertaken. Formative assessment tasks are aligned to specific learning outcomes in each level of study (Hughes, 2015a). The following curricular components underpin effective vocal technique for singing at the foundation level. They facilitate exploration of vocal nuances and musical styles at the intermediate level and emphasize the relevance of individual artistry for advanced-level students.

Table 15.2 Components and content examples in popular music vocal pedagogy

Components	Related pedagogical content
1. Vocal and musical creativities	Vocal embellishments, improvisation, musical arrangements, songs, collaboration
2. Individuality	Vocal tone, 'authentic' voice – using vocal modelling only as a springboard for exploration, reflection, expressivity, vocal health
3. Artistic development and presence	A consolidation of vocal, musical and performative learning
4. Musicality	Delivery, accompaniment choices, critical listening
5. Technologies	Vocal processing, amplification, effects. Recording, looping, online platforms and strategies, social media
6. Industry practices	Digital distribution, streaming, touring, recording, live performances, networking, copyright, revenue streams, music publishing

The following sections detail each curricular component and related examples of pedagogical content (see Table 15.2). The inclusion of research findings in the discussion allows for additional perspectives on the implementation, realization and delivery of the curricular content and learning. The findings are drawn from current research on reflection and reflexivity in contemporary vocal curricula. Research participants include students (2014; N=18; S1–18) and tutors (2014–2015; N=4; T1–4). In addition to anonymously completed surveys, examples of student journal entries are also included. These are cited with permission. To ensure participant anonymity, a research assistant was employed to collect data and liaise with participants; ethics approval to undertake the research was obtained from Macquarie University's Human Research Ethics Committee.

Component 1: Vocal and musical creativities

Singers in PCM often display a multiplicity of creativities (Burnard, 2012). These can be in the creative use of technologies in performance (e.g. using looping technologies) (see Hughes, 2015b), in expressive techniques (e.g. a range of vocal tone and/or registers) and in vocal delivery (e.g. improvisation). For these reasons, facilitating creativity is integral in the teaching of contemporary singing and in the assessment of student learning (Hughes, 2015a). Teaching strategies include singing exercises to aid the development of effective and healthy vocal production (at all levels), the embellishment of melody and improvisation (at the intermediate and advanced levels) and fluidity in melisma and expressivity (advanced level). Exercises are introduced to each level of study with increasing complexity. Students explore possibilities through melodies and sounds they create using a range of purposefully created instrumental backing tracks and rhythm tracks. Individual reflection plays an important role in this exploratory stage of the learning process, as a tutor explains:

> The process of learning to reflect fosters an innate understanding of one's own voice and students take responsibility for their own vocal development and vocal health. In other models of teaching, students are often expected to simply do what their teacher has told them to do.
>
> *(T1)*

Component 2: Individuality

As the singing voice is "physical, cultural, psychological and emotional, all at the same time" (Cook, 2004, p. 10), curricular components and content focus on the uniqueness of each voice and encourage individuality (Hughes, 2010, 2013a, 2014, 2015a). Popular musics are also constantly evolving, so unless singers strive to front a tribute band or work in musical theatre, individuality is a desirable learning outcome at each level of study. The discussion by *The Voice* judges cited above highlights the relevance of individuality in industry practices. In recognition of individual vocal quality and the uniqueness of each voice, students are urged not to view their voices in terms of traditional classifications such as alto or soprano, tenor or bass. Rather, students are encouraged to become kinaesthetically aware of how their voices convey sound and then to 'listen' to the sound of their voices. In learning to identify their individual vocality, students are encouraged to listen critically to their monitored singing voice via amplification (all levels) or through recorded playback (advanced level) (Hughes, 2014). As students progress through the intermediate and advanced levels, they are assigned critical listening exercises with increasing complexity (e.g. to identify vocal nuances in relation to musical styles). These listening exercises are used as a formative tool to heighten aural skills and to assist in reflexivity.

Enabling others to hear the individual voice in a group context can be done through development of specific pedagogical strategies (Hughes, 2015a). These strategies pertain to monitoring and assessing individual students' progress through the practical learning tasks that occur in group tutorials of up to 20 students (Hughes, 2015a); tutorials are in addition to weekly lectures. In the practical sessions, the tutor is required to facilitate both group and individual tasks. The tutor will typically listen to individual students singing as well as the group singing together. Students are required to sing collectively and to sing solo lines in group singing exercises and performances; they are assessed using a range of criteria including effective technique, expressive techniques, individuality and originality (Hughes, 2015a). Individuality in phrasing, interpretation, stagecraft and accompaniment choices is encouraged in each level of study. Individuality in song interpretation is fostered through each student's emotional connection or response to repertoire. For this reason, students choose their own repertoire to sing in tutorials and for performance assessments. They are also encouraged to write and perform their own songs (see also Bennett, chapter 23, this volume).

Research findings on the role of reflection in learning have identified that the process of reflection assists students to focus on their individuality, aspirations and abilities. Students typically comment that maintaining reflective journals (documenting and analyzing reflection and reflexivity), including goal-setting and associated actions, deepens their level of understanding. Linking reflection to unit content is viewed by students and tutors as strengthening learning:

> Reflection may be the key part of learning since it is the process which facilitates the consolidation of learning and the building on previous learning.
> *(S2)*

> Reflection on me allows me to critically analyze what I already know and add the new experience somewhere in the spectrum.
> *(S18)*

> [Reflection is] a student's own perception of their learning experience and learning and/or creative process. It may also include a student's perception of the learning experience and process of other students and how this relates to their own experience and process.
> *(T2)*

In written tasks, students are asked to progressively and reflectively describe and/or analyze their singing voices (Hughes, 2015a). At times, this involves analyzing their performances. Students' vocal health is also progressively monitored through their respective journals, and in all practical sessions and performance assessments. Students are encouraged to explore stylistic and creative nuances utilizing the effective and healthy technique emphasized in curricular content.

Component 3: Artistic development and presence

For advanced-level vocalists, the curricular content and delivery emphasize defining and expressing individual artistry. At this level, the transformative capabilities of popular music education become increasingly evident. Advanced students are typically confident singers, individually able to describe their voice and/or identity as a singer:

> My voice has found its sound. It knows where to sit now, and what sounds good.
> *(2014 Journal Reflection, Student 12, Week 11)*

> Overall this unit [Advanced Vocal Studies] has helped me understand who I am as an artist; I know that I am a technologically driven artist.
> *(2014 Reflection, Student 7, Week 12).*

Throughout the advanced level of study, students become more adept at referring to themselves as artists. When asked to either describe 'the singer as artist' or to identify a time or a defining moment when students in vocal studies began to think of themselves as 'singer-artists', research participants responded:

> I can . . . when I started vocal studies I was a guy who wants to sing, but by third year I was a singer.
>
> *(P8)*

> The voice is an instrument. Being able to manipulate your voice, in the same expressive ways as a musician in order to creatively present yourself, makes you an artist.
>
> *(P7)*

A consolidation of learning is typically evident at this advanced level of vocal study, highlighted in this example:

> This unit [Advanced Vocal Studies] has been particularly amazing for me . . . I have learned so much about my voice. About my artistry. My connection to music. My music making.
>
> *(2014 Reflection, Student 12, Week 11)*

Component 4: Musicality

Curricular content also addresses creativity in relation to musicality, the song and elements of musical styles in PCM. Learning about 'song' occurs both in an ensemble context and for solo performances. In the various levels of study, students are encouraged to explore a range of songs and styles for their respective ensembles and to collaboratively create harmony and musical arrangements. Creating a musical 'feel' for an ensemble performance often replaces the necessity for pre-determined dynamic markers or other notated markers of musical expression as expressive techniques usually evolve through the creative process. At the intermediate level, students are also encouraged, both individually and collectively, to create melody and lyrics as part of their ensemble work. The collective collaboration in the songwriting process mirrors the community of musicians singers typically need to find in their professional lives:

> [The formative assessment tasks that were beneficial to my learning] got me working with musicians I would not usually work with.
>
> *(S9)*

For many in popular music education, the focus on sound and aurality places less emphasis on written notation. For example, chordal understanding (e.g. chord voicings, progressions) and musical arrangement may be acquired through creative processes. With emphases on aurality, the concept of musical literacy for singers in PCM is very different from concepts of traditional musical literacy and notation (see Fleet, chapter 14, this volume).

Component 5: Technologies

Musical sound is, at times, in the background of our daily lives. Instead of being foregrounded as a participatory activity, much musical listening is now passive. Digital technologies have afforded us the opportunity to listen to music on portable devices; we 'listen' to our musical preferences on our phones while doing such things as commuting, filling in time or multitasking. Spatial qualities, sound mixes, real-time, relayed time, various formats and listening devices impact on how we listen and what we hear. Critical engagement in musical listening therefore often requires the stimulation and development of active listening capabilities (e.g. critical listening exercises in lectures, allocated time for individual student research and listening). The development of aural awareness and critical listening skills are interrelated. The relevance of critical listening in vocal and musical learning is evident in several ways:

> Listening to my own recordings after a session in a recording studio; listening to my voice led me to improve my singing techniques.
>
> *(P7)*

> I learned a lot from listening to other artists – students but also professionals – with ears and mind tuned to the techniques addressed in class.
>
> *(P3)*

I have argued that PCM singers should be encouraged to 'own' their sound (Hughes, 2010). This can include such aspects as the vocal level or volume in the context of other musicians and/or methods of accompaniment, as, for singers, learning how to be heard is a fundamental skill. Effectively conveying vocal sound through amplification or when recording is underpinned by understanding of spectral qualities and room acoustics. Singing in popular music education (at all levels and in all educational settings) should address these aspects and include instruction in appropriate pre-performance sound-checks, monitoring of the voice onstage and in recording, microphone types and placement, various applied effects and treatments (Hughes, 2012). Consequently, tutorials or specifically designed teaching sessions (e.g. recording studio workshop) can facilitate experience in reverberant sound, dry sound, effected sound, altered sound (e.g. graphic equalization, pitch correction), layered or looped sound and compressed sound. Exploration of technologies and the singing voice is introduced in vocal studies at the foundation level; further exploration of technologies and the singing voice is facilitated in intermediate and advanced levels with increasing complexity.

Component 6: Industry practices

The contemporary opportunities for artists to create and share their music are vast and numerous (Hughes et al., 2013b). These include the use of social media and other online platforms and opportunities for music streaming. While the shift to enable consumer access to individual songs creates opportunities (e.g., it costs much less to produce a single than an album, particularly benefitting early-career singers), the ability for singers to stand out among their peers is challenging both online and in real-time, as well as in physical environments (Keith et al., 2014). While it has been customary in the offline space for such challenges to be handled by recording labels and artist managers, many contemporary singers now assume a range of responsibilities as do-it-yourself (DIY) artists (see Lebler & Hodges, chapter 22, this volume). This has been largely enabled by the digital musical ecology and the democratization of technologies (Keith et al., 2014). While some singers still may aspire to be recording artists (as per the 20th-century recording label-centric model – see also Bennett, chapter 23, this volume), funding opportunities (e.g. crowd-funding), a range of recording facilities (including home studios), and independent labels or self-releases now make it possible for many singers to fund their own recording projects and to maintain creative control. Therefore, within the focus of networking and industry practices (Keith et al., 2014), there are a number of educational strategies and skills that extend beyond – and remain complementary to – the singing voice in PCM (e.g. artistic image, branding, copyright, revenue streams, publishing). Similarly, workplace health and safety issues and the overarching concept of artist well-being should be included in curricular content where relevant (e.g. vocal overload in relation to extended periods of singing or sustained loud singing; touring demands and vocal health; recording demands and vocal health; inadequate amplification) (Hughes et al., 2014).

Conclusions

Research indicates that curricular components may be designed and implemented to facilitate contemporary artistry and artistic 'ownership' (Hughes, 2010). This is evident in the transformative elements identified in participant responses. Rather than pedagogy or teaching methods to 'direct' singers, the aim of the curricular components is to facilitate artistry, artistic vision and practice through a range of exploratory and creative processes. In some ways (e.g. through the student-devised ensemble tasks), the curricular components and group learning incorporate informal learning into formal processes through peer interaction and collaboration. Cumulatively, the curricular components are significantly different to those discussed by Greene (1912) (see Table 15.3); a century ago, a singer would typically be taught the 'art' of how to sing a song in a particular way, and the teacher would be the unquestionable authority in a one-to-one relationship. While the one-to-one approach is still the model for instrumental learning in most conservatoires, it is also a model that may limit autonomy in learning. As Gaunt (2011) identified, "there was also evidence of a possible connection between dynamics of power in the [one-to-one] relationship and students' reluctance to develop artistic and professional self-direction" (p. 159).

While the intent of the respective curricular components is aligned in the premise of communicating through song, the inherent difference between the two approaches is the preferred level of individuality. The 'art' of singing a song in the early 19th century, as Greene's example highlights, was primarily focused on

Table 15.3 A comparison of traditional and contemporary

The 'art' of singing (Greene, 1912)	Contemporary artistry (Hughes, this volume)
1. Composer's intent	1. Vocal and musical creativities
2. Perfected vocal technique	2. Individuality
3. Magnetism	3. Artistic development and presence
4. Musicality	4. Musicality
5. Intelligible articulation	5. The use of technologies
6. Recital programmes	6. Industry practices

technical skill and ability in representing a composer's intent. Related pedagogy was therefore designed to communicate and uphold integrity of compositions in performance. In contrast, artists in PCM typically either perform original songs or offer new interpretations and versions of existing repertoire. In contemporary artistry we hear and see an individual communicate. It is artistry that is not so much concerned with *perfected* technique, but rather *effective* technique, which conveys emotion and intent. The contemporary curricular components outlined in this chapter are designed to foster individuality and to develop "artistic and professional self-direction" (Gaunt, 2011, p. 159). Their pedagogical contextualization identifies the fact that the contemporary singing voice in music education extends well beyond acoustic output to include a plethora of creative and industry practices. While discussion surrounding singer-entertainers *versus* singer-artists in PCM (Nine Network, 2015) has been beyond the scope of this chapter, it is relevant to note that an entertaining performance need not preclude the performance or the performer from being artistic. That on-air debate does, however, exemplify aspects of the complexity of contemporary vocal artistry in PCM and the multiplicity of contexts and practices it underpins.

References

Bithell, C. (2014). *A different voice, A different song.* Oxford: Oxford University Press.
Burnard. P. (2012). *Musical creativities in practice.* Oxford: Oxford University Press.
Caruso, N. & Tetrazzini, L. (1909). *Caruso and Tetrazzini on the art of singing.* Project Gutenberg. Retrieved from: http://www.gutenberg.org/files/20069/20069-h/20069-h.htm [Accessed 2 August 2015].
Cook, O. (2004). *Singing with your own voice.* London: Nick Hern Books Limited.
Curwen, J. (1876). *The standard course of lessons and exercises in the tonic sol-fa method of teaching music.* London: Tonic Sol-fa Agency.
Evetts, E. (1928). *The mechanics of singing.* London: J. M. Dent and Sons.
Gaunt, H. (2011). Understanding the one-to-one relationship in instrumental/vocal tuition in higher education: Comparing student and teacher perceptions. *British Journal of Music Education, 28*(2), 159–179.
Greene, H.P. (1904). *On the art of singing.* [Columbia Records International Educational Society series (Lecture 75)] Disc numbers D40149–40150.
Greene, H.P. (1912). *Interpretation in song.* London: Macmillan.

Green, L. (2010). Informal learning in the music classroom: A seven-stage program. In J. Ballantyne & B.L. Bartleet (Eds.), *Navigating music and sound education* (pp. 227–245). Newcastle upon Tyne: Cambridge Scholars Press.

Hamady, J. (2009). *The art of singing – discovering and developing your true voice (vocal instruction)*. Milwaukee: Hal Leonard.

Hughes, D. (2010). Developing vocal artistry in popular culture musics. In S. Harrison (Ed.), *Perspectives on teaching singing: Australian vocal pedagogues sing their stories* (pp. 244–258). Bowen Hills, QLD: Australian Academic Press.

Hughes, D. (2012). Mediocrity to artistry: Technology and the singing voice. In J. Weller (Ed.), *Educating professional musicians in a global context. Proceedings of the 19th International Seminar of the Commission for the Education of the Professional Musician* (CEPROM) (pp. 64–68). Athens, Greece: International Society for Music Education, Philippos Nakas Conservatory.

Hughes, D. (2013a). An encultured identity: Individuality, expressivity and the singing-self. *Australian Voice, 15*, 13–19.

Hughes, D. (2013b). 'OK, great sound, what are you experiencing as you're singing that?' Facilitating or interrupting the flow of vocal artistry. In O. Wilson & S. Attfield (Eds.), *Shifting sounds: Musical flow. A collection of papers from the 2012 IASPM Australia/New Zealand Conference*, December 5–7, 2012 (pp. 80–87). Hobart, Australia.

Hughes, D. (2014). Contemporary vocal artistry in popular culture musics: Perceptions, observations and lived experiences. In S. Harrison & J. O'Bryan (Eds.), *Teaching singing in the 21st Century* (pp. 287–302). New York: Springer.

Hughes, D. (2015a). Assessment and feedback in curricula design for contemporary vocal studies. In D. Lebler, G. Carey & S. Harrison (Eds.), *Assessment in music education: From policy to practice* (pp. 251–268). Zurich: Springer.

Hughes, D. (2015b). Technologized and autonomized vocals in contemporary popular musics. *Journal of Music, Technology and Education, 8*(2), 163–182.

Hughes, D., Evans, M., Keith, S. & Morrow, G. (2014). A "duty of care" and the professional musician/artist. In G. Carruthers (Ed.), *Proceedings of the commission for the education of the professional musician* (CEPROM), July 2014 (pp. 31–41). Bello Horizonte, Brazil.

Hughes, D., Evans, M., Morrow, G. & Keith, S. (2016). *The New Music Industries: Disruption and Discovery*. London: Palgrave Macmillan.

Hughes, D., Keith, S., Morrow, G., Evans, M. & Crowdy, D. (2013). What constitutes artist success in the Australian music industries. *International Journal of Music Business Research, 2*(2), 61–80.

Keith, S., Hughes, D., Crowdy, D., Morrow, G. & Evans, M. (2014). Offline and online: Liveness in the Australian music industries. *Civilisations: The State of the Music Industries, 13*, 221–241.

Kimball, C. (2013). *Art song: Linking poetry and music*. Milwaukee, WI: Hal Leonard.

LoVetri, J. (2014). Jeanette L. LoVetri Biography – 2014. *The Voice Workshop*. Retrieved from: http://www.thevoiceworkshop.com/lovetri.html [Accessed 5 September 2016].

Nelson, R. (2013). *Practice as research in the arts: Principles, protocols, pedagogies, resistances*. London: Palgrave McMillan.

Nine Network. (2015). *The voice (Australia)* Season 4, Episode 16 [Aired 16 August 2015, Nine Network.] Retrieved from: http://www.9jumpin.com.au/show/thevoice/episodes/season-4/episode-16/live-show/#autoplay [Accessed 27 August 2015].

Potter, J. & Sorrell, N. (2012). *A history of singing*. Cambridge: Cambridge University Press.

Riggs, S. (1985). *Singing for the stars: A complete program for training your voice*. Van Nuys, LA: Alfred Publishing.

Sataloff, R.T., Hawkshaw, M.J., Moore, J.E. & Rutt, A.L. (2014). *50 ways to abuse your voice*. Oxford: Compton.

16
Defeating the muse
Advanced songwriting pedagogy and creative block

Jo Collinson Scott

Introduction

In her important text on popular music education, *How Popular Musicians Learn*, Lucy Green has highlighted that despite popular music's inclusion in university programmes in the UK for the last 30–40 years, there is still little formal knowledge regarding how popular musicians learn, what their attitudes are to learning and how this relates to popular music pedagogy. Pamela Burnard has made the most comprehensive case for more research into the pedagogy of popular music creativities, demonstrating that "the way in which teachers of different subject domains judge, or capture and report formatively and summatively, the multiplicity of musical creativities and the creative learning processes or the creative product outcomes, still remains unclear" (Burnard, 2012, p. 259; Burnard & Power, 2013). She makes a direct call for the development of new pedagogies and understandings of musical creativities that are inspired by contemporary popular music practice.

More recently, Martin Isherwood's (2014) scoping exercise of songwriting in Higher Education in the UK, *Sounding Out Songwriting*, concluded with similar concerns about lack of knowledge surrounding popular music teaching practices and their relation to songwriting practice. It describes how, "despite the centrality of songwriting to popular music Higher Education", the teaching and learning of songwriting practice has developed across the field "in an isolated, unplanned, uncoordinated and organic manner in a range of institutions and programmes" (p. 9). With this in mind, the research presented in this chapter begins to explore pedagogy of songwriting in the UK through a focus on creativity assessment.

As acknowledged by Shuker (1994), there has been very little research into creativity and creative processes in popular music. There are also a number of inherent difficulties in defining and examining creative processes and creative outcomes in an educational setting, which means that *creativity* related to popular music product (in this case, song) is somewhat difficult to describe, evaluate, assess and contribute to with learning (Burnard & Power, 2013; Cowdroy & de Graaff, 2005; Hickey & Lipscombe, 2006). The primary focus on *the individual* and individual *insight* as the locus of creativity – which was highly prevalent in creativity research up until the 1990s – and the resultant reliance on introspection for answers regarding the nature of the creative process has added to an idea of the unknowability or singular specificity of the process. This difficulty in understanding has led to the development of a culture and literature of 'mystery' around creative processes. It has also allowed what are now commonly referred to (e.g. by Weisberg, 1993) as inspirational and romantic 'myths' of creativity to come to hold sway in understandings of the creative process in songwriting. These conceptions of the creative process as something magical, indescribable, unconscious, passive and born out of a flow of mystical inspiration are particularly promoted by literature surrounding the commercialization of pop songs (Brennan, 2006; McIntyre, 2008; Shuker, 1994; Wicke, 1990). They are also perpetuated by songwriters themselves, encouraged by the music press, who frequently buy into (or sell) ideas of authenticity, intrigue and personal genius associated with these notions (Bilton, 2013; Burnard, 2012; McIntyre, 2008). This means that understandings of processes of creativity within popular music-making have traditionally been largely tacit.

There is also an inherent difficulty in defining and describing what is meant by *creativity* or *the creative process*. Attempts have included the four-stage model (Hadamard, 1949; Wallas, 1926), which focuses around a moment of insight; the conceptual definition posited by Margaret Boden (1992), which describes a product as creative if it is novel, valuable and surprising; and, more recently, social process models or systems theories of creativity, based in the work of Bourdieu and expanded by theorists such as Csikszentmihalyi (1996, 1999). They define multiple creativities and describe these at work not within a singular songwriter, but in relationship between the songwriter as "individual", the songwriter's "domain" and the wider "field". The first detailed studies on creativities in popular music-making, by Toynbee (2000), McIntyre (2008) and Burnard (2012), have all focused on these social theories.

When it comes to examining creativity in the context of teaching, learning and assessment, the development of systems theories of creativity has led some researchers (e.g. Bindeman, 1998) to suggest that phenomenology is the most appropriate method for its study, because its focus is on lived and shared experience – such as between artists, their audiences and critical structures – rather than on examination of objects (i.e. 'objective' examination of product). As such, a phenomenological approach that aims to identify and describe the common aspects of the experience of the "abiding concern" (van Manen, 1990, cited in Creswell, 2013, p. 79) via an interpretive process is an appropriate approach. It is for these reasons that, rather than attempt to navigate this range of difficulties and varied approaches in setting out a *conceptual* definition of creativity at the outset of this paper, the approach here has been to attempt to understand *operational* definitions of creativity as they are practiced within advanced-level songwriting pedagogy.

Jo Collinson Scott

This chapter aims to explore how songwriting pedagogues understand creativity and creative processes operationally in their teaching and learning practices. Since myths surrounding creative processes hinder verbal articulation of students' (and pedagogues') understandings of what creativity is and how the processes of creation in songwriting proceed, I suggest here that focusing this investigation on the point at which these myths are challenged can help to demonstrate important aspects of operational understandings of essential creative processes in songwriting. I contend that the experience commonly described as 'creative block' (or 'creative frustration') is a point at which the romantic notions of creative 'mystery' or 'genius' are challenged, and where conscious, informed focus needs to be brought to bear on creative processes. This experience (which I discuss further, below) has been described as one that "perhaps more than any other ... seem[s] to demystify the creative act" (Sapp, 1992, p. 24).

Methods

With such a proliferation and variety of approaches to popular songwriting pedagogy across a large number of HE institutions and courses in the UK (Isherwood, 2014), the approach I take here is to isolate initial examinations to the most advanced forms of songwriting pedagogy – in this case, teaching at a master's degree level – and to concentrate in detail on a small cohort of pedagogues covering the UK's two dedicated songwriting master's degrees.[1] Using a phenomenological approach, this research focused on in-depth, semi-structured interviews with master's level songwriting pedagogues, augmented where possible with reference to relevant assessment criteria, guides and briefs provided by participants.

Research by Susan Orr into assessment practices in arts in Higher Education (2005, 2007, 2010) has concluded that "interview-based studies can elicit 'an espoused generalist view of assessment' that may not relate directly to actual practice", but that "the reported representations are still of value" in that they reflect important aspects of tacit experience and the social field within which songwriting pedagogy is operating (2010, p. 8). Similar conclusions were reached by Janice Orrell (2003). With this in mind, I interviewed four songwriting pedagogues. Participants were selected in order to attain a depth of information on the only two UK-based songwriting-focused master's degrees (both course leaders were included in the cohort), with one extra participant selected because of their intended development of a forthcoming master's programme as well as their eminent experience in the sector. All of the participants were professional songwriters

---

1 There are a number of general popular music master's courses in the UK that offer songwriting as a strand, but for the purposes of clarity and simplicity this research focuses primarily on pedagogues from songwriting-specific master's degrees. The two degrees in question are the MA in Songwriting from Bath Spa University, and the MA in Songwriting and Performance from the University of the West of Scotland. Although this research is based in the HE sector of the UK, its implications are, I suggest, clearly applicable to songwriting pedagogy more widely, where the same or related romantic myths surrounding creative practice in popular music prevail.

(three of the participants have been writing professionally for over 30 years, and two are responsible for top 40 singles). I also include here my own experience as a professional songwriter over the past 11 years. I have been a community songwriting pedagogue for over 14 years, am a master's degree level songwriting pedagogue and was the co-developer of the MA in Songwriting and Performance at the University of the West of Scotland. All interview data have been anonymized, although participants were made aware of the limitations of this anonymization in such a small and specific cohort.

Within the context of this as a phenomenological study, definitions of the phenomenon in question will be drawn from the respondents' experiential understandings. Our interest then lies in how pedagogues of advanced songwriting understand the definition of creativity *as it is worked out in experience* through their teaching and assessment practice, as they clearly already work within an operational definition of creativity. Pedagogues were asked to define creativity as it was practically applied as an assessment criterion in their modules.[2] They were also asked to describe specific examples of approaches they had taken in their learning and teaching practices to help students overcome periods of creative block.

Findings: Operational definitions of creativity

All participants, labelled A-D, explored the question of whether or not their teaching and assessment practices concerned 'creativity' in songwriting specifically. Where respondent A's significant statements communicated ambiguity towards the assessment of creativity as part of his practice, the other respondents all agreed that what they understand to be 'creativity' is either specifically assessed (as evidenced by assessment criteria across modules that asked for 'evidence of creative control', provided by respondents B and C) or, as respondent D described it, 'generally inherent' in all assessment considerations, if not required specifically within criteria.

Respondent A was initially reluctant to discuss 'creativity' specifically as being a part of the assessment process with regards to songwriting, and instead described his practice of assessing songs primarily with regard to how well they communicate emotion to the listener.

> I think that songs are heightened human emotion, a communication of heightened . . . you know, like: I love you, I hate you, I wanna die, or whatever . . . And the key criteria [sic] if you like, is how effectively do you get that feeling across to an audience. How do you communicate that?

Such assessment is done within the understanding of songwriting as a functional craft (the function being communication) and where the song can be judged against specific constraints.

---

2 'Module' in the context of UK higher education translates to 'course' in other HE contexts, such as the US.

Respondent B had the most formalized understanding of creativity (i.e. closest to a conceptual definition):

> It's up to the listener to be surprised or to value something that the songwriter does. So, by that token, I don't think a songwriter can ever say that they are creative, I think only a listener can say that a songwriter is creative . . .
>
> It goes back really to, again, a philosophical realization that creativity is in the eye of the beholder, because of newness, surprise and value.

In this sense, assessment of creativity is done by the assessor, using his or her expertise in the field to gauge the product's relative surprise, newness and/or value to an audience (Boden, 1992), with the audience defined relative to the genre or style of the song.

Respondent C succinctly described his understanding of creativity as 'synthesis':

> Synthesis in that context would include the use of stimulus materials of one kind or another, sometimes collaborative processes, experience – in terms of what you have been immersed in as a musician, what your specifically musical influences might be said to be – and also your skill, or your skill-set as a musician. . . . I think something [is creative] that brings some or all of those elements together in an unexpected way given the domain.

This can be related to the theoretical understanding of the importance of divergent thinking in creativity, which defines how well a thinker can productively connect disparate ideas or concepts together as a measure of creativity (see Kaufman et al., 2008, p. 32). In terms of assessment of creativity, this definition places emphasis on documentation of process and domain as well as final product.

Finally, respondent D found the significance of the distinction between art and craft important in his understanding of creativity. In this understanding, 'art' signifies the underlying meaning of the word 'creativity', whereas 'craft' acts as an important part of the pre- and post-creative process. It is in this distinction – between 'art' and 'craft' – that aspects of the aforementioned inspirational or romantic ideas of songwriting practice come to the fore. For example, it was key in respondent D's description of his understanding of creativity that this 'artistic' aspect of the creative process cannot be understood or rationally apprehended:

> As soon as you use the word creativity, you're reducing your argument to meta-physics. This is my fundamental point of view on it. And I'm not trying to be facetious. I'm simply trying to state my point, which is that the creative process is a mystery to me. I understand a lot of it I think, because I've been involved in it for so long, but there's a fundamental aspect of it which I don't think I'll ever understand, nor do I particularly think it's in my interest to understand, to be honest. I just get upset when people use the word "creativity" . . . Use the word "mystery" instead . . . a mysterious process . . . it's a mystery isn't it?

Respondent C also described his experience of aspects of the creative process as inherently mysterious. However, his descriptions communicated a struggle between this view and his worldview or role as an academic:

> I think I probably (given how I earn my living) I think I would have to argue that one can understand every part of the creative process. But honestly, I think there are unknowable things. That does not mean that we shouldn't seek to understand them. And well, bluntly, that's the point of being in a university – is to seek to understand things.

The tension between, on the one hand, aspects of creative processes within songwriting that are enjoyed or valued as 'unknowable' or 'mysterious' and, on the other, their place within a formal academic teaching environment, with its requirement for critical reflection, is the key to the importance of an investigation of creative block in understanding operational definitions of creativity within songwriting pedagogy. When creative flow is easy there is no need to reflect consciously on the processes involved, but when it becomes problematized this can potentially be the starting point for different forms of learning about the songwriting process – for both songwriters and songwriting pedagogues.

Understandings of creative block

Using Rose's 1984 definition of writer's block as a basis, but applying it to creativity in songwriting rather than essay writing, we can define this phenomenon as an inability to begin or continue writing/completing a song that lasts for a prolonged period and comes with associated feelings of frustration, anxiety or lack of control over the process.[3] The existence of creative block as an experiential phenomenon in songwriters was confirmed by all interview respondents and their descriptions of their understandings of its causes in students and themselves both verified and augmented Rose's conclusions on the matter. These causes can be summarized under the following headings: lack of stimulus; lack of space; editing too early or applying inappropriate criteria; and a lack of strategies to overcome creative frustration or pain.

Lack of stimulus

Pedagogues described experiencing creative block most obviously within a vacuum, i.e. in a situation where there is no one to write for, no given brief or deadline and therefore nothing to force the writer beyond indecision in the face of an endless array of options. In this context, respondents B and C both described

---

3 Rose's book *Writer's Block: The Cognitive Dimension* (1984) is one of the only in-depth academic studies of the phenomenon to-date.

the importance of encouraging the collection of potential ideas in sketchbooks, or by other means, so that creativity can be stimulated at any time by attempts to connect selections from these archives. All respondents also noted the importance of the stimulus provided by a deadline or brief. Respondent A stated, "I think deadline is really important. Pressure is really important. And students find that. As I say, I only observe creative blocks when they have to do it [impose timeframes] themselves".

Most respondents noted specifically that where songwriters are invested in notions of creativity arising as an uncontrolled flash of inspiration, i.e. something that happens passively and cannot be planned or controlled, it is more likely that songwriters will resist the setting of activities or actions that would serve to provide them with stimulus materials. I would also add that belief in the ideals of creative genius could exacerbate circumstances where students lack stimulus material. For example, in the context of the myth of creative genius, many helpful and frequently used songwriting stimulus techniques (such as 'ghost-song writing') seem shamefully derivative: few songwriters would feel free to admit that the starting point of their amazing creation was the alteration of the chord structure of a song belonging to an influential peer.

Lack of space

The second potential cause of creative block is a lack of space to contemplate and practice creative thinking. Respondent D described the importance of solitude for his creative practice and noted that periods of creative block for him were precipitated by life events that did not allow him the time, space or solitude within which to create.[4] Respondent C also described periods of being tired, having written too much and needing to 'let the well fill up' again before he could work effectively.

No specific pedagogic techniques were suggested for overcoming this particular cause of creative block; however, there was recognition that the existence of MA programmes focused specifically on songwriting practice creates a space where it is socially acceptable for students to spend considerable time focusing on creativity when doing so in pursuit of educational attainment. Studies into the effect of environment have consistently shown that factors such as a lack of workload pressure, freedom, time and space for playfulness/risk-taking or humour are key to encouraging creativity in work environments (e.g. Amabile, 1996; Ekvall & Ryhammar, 1999; Reiter-Palmon et al., 2014). Although highlighting the role of freedom and time in encouraging creativity might seem to contradict notions of the importance of deadline and pressure in overcoming creative block, the context of these constraints in the advanced songwriting course is one where *all* activities are focused on developing and encouraging creativity.

---

4 Csikszentmihalyi and Sawyer (1995) have discussed the importance of solitude during the creative process and found it to be particularly important for artists.

Applying inappropriate criteria and/or editing too early

Rose's key conclusions on the causes of creative block included the contention that students who block tend to evaluate their writing against inappropriate criteria and edit too early in the writing process. It is clear that students often work to criteria based on romantic or inspirational myths of creativity: for example, models of creative 'genius', where the work should simply flow out all at once, perfectly formed, rather than coming out in seemingly inadequate pieces that are slowly edited together and made better (Bennett, 2015). These constitute 'inappropriate' criteria in a songwriting context and result in the fear, anxiety and defensiveness that respondents described as being factors in the causation of creative block. Respondent B clearly described such effects on students' attitudes to feedback:

> This relates, I think, to the romantic idea of the song sounding like it should come out fully formed, and therefore the non-sequitur that therefore the first idea that you had needs to be the one. . . . So for example, you might say "well your verse two is a bit long and loses the narrative a bit" and a student might say, "but that's how I was feeling that day" and that becomes the truth that they're trying to communicate back to the group.

Judged under such inappropriate criteria, sub-standard initial songwriting efforts are seen as a sign of a lack of creative ability rather than as starting points that can be worked at and shaped into something more successful. Furthermore, respondent B suggests here that the quality of the work may be taken very personally, i.e. producing a 'bad' song means not only that the writer herself is uncreative, but that the personal emotion or circumstance that inspired the song is also somehow bad or worthless. My own personal experience of typical student responses to feedback backs this up, and furthermore, I would note that such personalization of elements of songs often results in fear or anxiety, which manifest themselves in specific behaviours, such as writing many beginnings or parts of sections of songs that are subsequently discarded. These constitute what Rose describes as 'early-editing' behaviour. Ingegerd Carlson has documented the potentially negative effects of internalized critique in her recent research on neurophysiological aspects of creativities, where she describes the delicate balance between the crucial need for rational editing practices and the danger of the lowering of self-esteem that can result from this:

> A problem with an exceedingly dominant evaluative function is that too many negative and self-critical thoughts will risk lowering self-esteem. Since highly creative ideas are often confronted with a sceptical environment, and since creative people have an inbuilt sensitivity to impressions, this may cause big trouble.
>
> *(Carlson, 2014, p. 64)*

Lack of strategies to overcome creative frustration/pain

The final suggested cause of creative block is related to what songwriters describe as the natural 'pain' or frustration of the creative process. Respondent A used the analogy of exercise, the pain of which is frequently the overriding memory of the experience, despite the ultimately rewarding nature of the activity. Sapp (1992) understands this pain in terms of frustration and describes it as an important part of every experience of creative processes. He notes that on reaching the point of creative frustration, individuals can respond in a number of ways: *denial* (abandoning the current song, or part of a song), *rationalization* (not having overcome the problem satisfactorily, but settling with the product as-is and justifying or defending it), *acceptance* (acceptance of the stagnant position), or *new growth*. New growth is, according to Sapp, the desired response – the one that moves past the creative block. Importantly, he observes that students who lack the flexibility of being able to choose from a range of alternatives to an unsatisfactory or stagnant creative position often find that they experience creative frustration more frequently, or that they cannot overcome it satisfactorily.

Several respondents described a perceived relationship between youth and inexperience in songwriters and subsequent creative block. Reliance on one 'natural' or instinctive compositional practice soon wears thin, becomes repetitive, or leads to over-similar results. As respondent A described it, "you can sort of like create maybe a hundred variations on that, you know, and it sounds brilliant for a while but then you've got to move past that". When this moment arrives, inexperienced songwriters can find themselves blocked as a result of a paucity of alternative approaches from which to draw. Believing in the myth of genius means that such young songwriters find difficulty in developing the skills to overcome this problem.

Helping students to move beyond creative block

Developing an appropriate approach to editing song materials and removing fear and anxiety related to personalization of the editing process can be important elements in creative process. The difficulty here, however, is that students have been shown to lack a model of how to assess creative practice or to describe and rationalize it (Bennett, 2015; Toynbee, 2000; McIntyre, 2008). This is partly a product of the way in which songwriters tend to learn their craft: in an informal manner and therefore via tacit means (Green, 2002).

Don Lebler (2008) has explained the importance of popular music students developing the ability to self-assess and peer-assess. Lebler's approach puts editing and self-assessing behaviour at the heart of the learning experience through the use of assessment-*as*-learning. In this model students are asked to continually assess their own work as it continues, and at the end of the module are included on a panel of six or seven other students and one tutor who contribute equally to marks for other students' creative portfolios. Part of each participant's overall mark comes from this panel assessment, and a smaller percentage is based upon teachers' assessment of how well the student gave feedback and assigned marks. Lebler's model places self-assessment, peer-assessment and editing practice at the heart of the learning experience and of pedagogical practice.

Respondents identified a number of other teaching and assessment approaches that could help towards overcoming these problems and could allow students to self-assess and edit in ways that serve their creative processes. Foremost among them was the use of formative assessment in pedagogic practice, largely through peer-feedback sessions and 'songwriting circle' events. The perceived value of these events was in students learning about editing processes and practising/developing the use of descriptive terms and specific vocabulary to describe their creative decision-making processes.[5] Orr has also discussed how studio-based assessment techniques (i.e. groups of experts joining together in assessment of a creative product) can facilitate the transfer of previously tacit knowledge between participants. She, along with Sadler, concludes that, "standards based on tacit knowledge commonly exist in an unarticulated form but can be shared amongst experts . . . by joint participation in evaluative activity" (p. 10, quoting Sadler, 2005, p. 192).

There are, however, two potential dangers associated with these types of approaches. The first is that too much formative assessment activity too early on in the creative process might serve to reinforce the practices of early editing that Rose describes as potential contributors to creative block. Some students who block have a tendency to focus an overly critical eye on their work too early on in the process of development, which leads to discarding ideas rather than working them through. It will perhaps depend on the skilfulness of the chairing of the feedback sessions as to whether such students gain a healthy example of flexible and helpful attitudes to editing or internalize over-zealous critical practices as a result. The second danger is that bringing rational understandings to bear on previously unexamined aspects of creative processes will 'demystify' them in such a way as to reduce enjoyment and therefore motivation to create. There is an important rewarding feeling that comes along with the experience of creation that Csikszentmihalyi and Csikszentmihalyi (1988) describe as 'flow'. For some songwriters, the experience of flow may be disrupted by knowledge of the origins and mechanisms of a previously mysterious and exciting process. Respondent C raised the possibility that perhaps, for those songwriters who espouse this view, examining their own creativity could indeed be harmful to the process.

Weisberg advises that instead of teaching general 'creativity-enhancing skills' (the method arguably implied by the genius myth), pedagogues should "emphasise development of deep expertise in a particular domain" (p. 262). Methods that seek to expand domain can help to provide a broader range of skills and methods from which to draw when encountering a problem, and this ability is key to allowing writers to overcome blocking. All respondents discussed the importance of teaching that focuses on broadening the listening practices and range of writing habits of students.

---

5 Joe Bennett (2015) has described the development of an approach to such peer-feedback sessions in order to avoid defensive and personalized responses to suggested edits.

Three out of four respondents also described the setting of time- or deadline-based constraints on songwriting tasks as being particularly effective in challenging students to realize that creative frustration doesn't signal the end of the creative process. Many students have never experienced the result of pushing through the process of creation under time constraint, having worked generally in informal songwriting settings and often mainly for pleasure. This approach also forces those students who have come to think of creativity as a passive process of waiting for inspiration to recognize that songwriting can proceed via active means when required. As respondent C noted, this technique is also helpful for assessment of creativity, as it allows assessors to observe the whole songwriting process happening in real time and, in particular, to focus on the range of creative problem-solving techniques easily at the students' disposal.

Although there are advantages to the use of constraint-based tasks in this way, it is important to note that there is a potential risk in relying too heavily or primarily on tasks involving short time-scales (such as those described by respondents B and C as some of their most effective pedagogic tools). Exercises where songwriters have only a few hours to finish a song and present it for critique can serve to reinforce less satisfactory practices with relation to creative frustration (such as rationalization or acceptance). The luxury of extra time to work through the creative process allows the songwriter to explore a larger number of creative solutions to a specific frustrating problem and practice discerning selection techniques over which is the most appropriate solution.

Conclusions

While their conceptual definitions of creativity differ considerably, songwriting pedagogues describe using similar teaching, learning and assessment techniques, which include constraint-based tasks, domain expansion techniques, peer feedback sessions focused on developing self-assessment abilities and the use of assessment techniques that rely on the consensus of a group of experts. This chapter has shown how these techniques – resulting from points of convergence in operational understandings of creativity – relate to the key points in creative processes where creative block can arise. This demonstrates the importance of the development and implementation of approaches to songwriting pedagogy, which can be seen to help songwriters develop and expand their songwriting methods in ways that some informal (and often only tacitly understood) learning practices centred around normalized romantic assumptions might not allow. A number of assessment approaches, such as peer- and consensual-assessment techniques, have been highlighted as having the potential to be helpful for songwriting pedagogues in order to formalize (and perhaps in time to standardize) some of the techniques that are already prevalent within the sector. It is an interesting irony that where previously creative block might have been seen to be *caused* by the defeat of a mystical muse, it seems that the defeat of the idea of the muse (its ideological effect on our understandings of the processes of creativity) may actually hold the key to overcoming it.

References

Amabile, T. (1996). *Creativity in context: Update to the social psychology of creativity*. Colorado: Westview.
Bennett, J. (2015). Creativity in popular songwriting curricula – Teaching or learning? In P. Burnard & L. Haddon (Eds.), *Activating diverse musical creativities: Teaching and learning in higher education* (pp. 37–56). London: Bloomsbury.
Bilton, C. (2013). Playing to the gallery: Myth, method and complexity in the creative process. In K. Thomas & J. Chan (Eds.), *Handbook of research on creativity* (pp. 125–137). Cheltenham: Edward Elgar.
Bindeman, S. (1998). Echoes of silence: A phenomenological study of the creative process. *Creativity Research Journal, 11*(1), 69–77.
Boden, M. (1992). *The creative mind: Myths and mechanisms*. London: Abacus.
Brennan, M. (2006). The rough guide to critics. Musicians discuss the role of the music press. *Popular Music, 25*(2), 221–234.
Burnard, P. (2012). *Musical creativities in practice*. Oxford: Oxford University Press.
Burnard, P. & Power, A. (2013). Issues in conceptions of creativity and creativity assessment in music education. In K. Thomas & J. Chan (Eds.), *Handbook of research on creativity* (pp. 212–228). Cheltenham: Edward Elgar.
Carlson, I. (2014). Biological and neurophysiological aspects of creativity. In E. Shiu (Ed.), *Creativity research: An inter-disciplinary research handbook* (pp. 51–67). Abingdon: Routledge.
Cowdroy, R. & de Graaff, E. (2005). Assessing highly creative ability. *Assessment and Evaluation in Higher Education, 30*(5), 507–518.
Creswell, J.W. (2013). *Qualitative inquiry and research design: Choosing among five approaches* (3rd ed.). Thousand Oaks, CA: SAGE.
Csikszentmihalyi, M. (1996). *Creativity: Flow and the psychology of discovery and invention*. New York: HarperCollins.
Csikszentmihalyi, M. (1999). Implications of a systems perspective for the study of creativity. In R. Sternberg (Ed.), *Handbook of creativity* (pp. 313–335). New York, NY: Cambridge University Press.
Csikszentmihalyi, M. & Csikszentmihalyi, I. (Eds.) (1988). *Optimal experience: Psychological studies of flow in consciousness*. New York, NY: Cambridge University Press.
Csikszentmihalyi, M. & Sawyer, K. (1995). Creative insight: The social dimension of a solitary moment. In R.J. Sternberg & J.E. Davidson (Eds.), *The Nature of insight* (pp. 329–363). Cambridge, MA: MIT Press.
Ekvall, G., & Ryhammar, L. (1999). The creative climate: Its determinants and effects at a Swedish university. *Creativity Research Journal, 12*, 303–310.
Green, L. (2002). *How popular musicians learn: A way ahead for music education* [Kindle version]. Aldershot, UK: Ashgate.
Hadamard, J. (1949). *The psychology of invention in the mathematical field*. Princeton, NJ: Princeton University Press.
Hickey, M. & S. Lipscombe (2006). How different is good? How good is different? The assessment of children's creative musical thinking. In I. Deliege & G. Wiggins (Eds.), *Musical creativity multidisciplinary research in theory and practice* (pp. 97–110). East Sussex: Psychology Press.
Isherwood, M. (2014). *Sounding out songwriting: An investigation into the teaching and assessment of songwriting in higher education*. Higher Education Academy Report. Retrieved from: http://www-new1.heacademy.ac.uk/assets/documents/disciplines/ddm/ISHERWOOD(2014)SoundingOutSongwriting.pdf [Accessed 2 December 2014].

Kaufman, J.C., Plucker, J.A., & Baer, J. (2008). *Essentials of creativity assessment*. New York, NY: Wiley.

Lebler, D. (2008). Popular music pedagogy: Peer learning in practice. *Music Education Research*, *10*(2), 193–213.

McIntyre, P. (2008). Creativity and cultural production: A study of contemporary Western popular music songwriting. *Creativity Research Journal*, *20*(1), 40–52.

Orr, S. (2005). 'Justify 66 to me!' An investigation into the social practice of agreeing marks in an HE Art and Design department. In C. Rust (Ed.), *Improving student learning through assessment: Proceedings of the 2005, 13th International Symposium* (pp. 283–294). Oxford: Oxford Brookes University Press.

Orr, S. (2007). Assessment moderation: Constructing the marks and constructing the students. *Assessment and Evaluation in Higher Education*, *32*(6), 1–12.

Orr, S. (2010). "We kind of try to merge our own experience with the objectivity of the criteria": The role of connoisseurship and tacit practice in undergraduate fine art assessment. *Art, Design & Communication in Higher Education*, *9*(1), 5–19.

Orrell, J. (2003). *An exploration of congruence and disjunctions between academics' thinking when assessing learning, and their beliefs about their assessment practice*. Paper presented at the 11th Improving Student Learning Symposium, Hinckley, Leicestershire.

Reiter-Palmon, R., Beghetto, R.A., & Kaufman, J.C. (2014). Looking at creativity through a business-psychology-education (BPE) lens. In E. Shiu (Ed.), *Creativity research: An interdisciplinary research handbook* (pp. 9–30). Abingdon: Routledge.

Rose, M. (1984). *Writer's block: The cognitive dimension. Studies in writing and rhetoric*. Carbondale, IL: Southern Illinois University Press.

Sadler, D. (2005). Interpretations of criteria-based assessment and grading in higher education. *Assessment and Evaluation in Higher Education*, *30*(2), 175–194.

Sapp, D. (1992). The point of creative frustration and the creative process: A new look at an old model. *Journal of Creative Behaviour*, *26*(1), 21–28.

Shuker, R. (1994). *Understanding popular music*. London: Routledge.

Toynbee, J. (2000). *Making popular music: Musicians, creativity and institutions*. London: Hodder.

Wallas, G. (1926). *The art of thought*. New York, NY: Harcourt Brace.

Weisberg, R. (1993). *Creativity: Beyond the myth of genius*. New York, NY: Freeman.

Wicke, P. (1990). *Rock music: Culture, aesthetics and sociology*. Cambridge: Cambridge University Press.

17

Missing a beat*

Exploring experiences, perceptions and reflections of popular electronic musicians in UK higher education institutions

Paul Thompson and Alex Stevenson

Introduction

Although formal educational institutions, particularly Higher Education (HE) institutions, in the UK have begun to acknowledge aspects of dance and hip-hop styles of music as useful inclusions in their curricula, there is still a notable lack of research into the relationship between popular electronic music production and formal education, with only a handful of studies in this area (e.g. Söderman & Folkestad, 2004; Snell & Söderman, 2014). Thompson (2012) argues that Western Art music pedagogy and its related conventions, as observed by Campbell (1991), are still evident in formal institutions today. Consequently the integration of popular electronic styles of music, such as hip-hop and house, into the curricula of formal educational syllabi has been decidedly slow. The popular electronic musician is "broadly defined through the notion that technology, such as the turntable or computer, is central to the interaction, performance and production of popular styles of electronic music such as dance and hip-hop" (Thompson, 2012, p. 46). The difficulty in integrating the popular electronic musician into formal educational and musical structures is generally linked to the use of music and recording technologies (Thompson, 2012). Consequently, popular electronic styles of music are often discounted in studies of musical practice, because an instrument is not 'played' in the traditional sense,[1]

---

* A longer version of this study was previously published: Thompson, P. & Stevenson, A. (2015). Exploring the experiences, perceptions and reflections of popular electronic musicians at UK higher education institutions. *Journal of Music, Technology and Education*, 8(2), 199–217.
1 Both Randles (2013) and Williams (2014) explore this issue in relation to the use of iPads as instruments within educational settings.

and are overlooked in musical analysis due to a lack of pertinent and appropriate musicological and contextual frameworks.[2] Moreover, the experiences of popular electronic musicians have been largely ignored in studies of popular music learning, which typically focus on rock-based[3] popular musicians (Green, 2002; Powell & Burstein, chapter 20, this volume). In order to illuminate the experiences of popular electronic musicians in formal education, the following study surveyed popular electronic musicians studying music-related[4] programmes at HE institutions across the UK, capturing some of their experiences, perceptions and reflections.

Context

Music education is often grouped into three broad forms: formal, non-formal and informal, which are characterized by their methods of learning (Mok, 2011). Formal music education is delivered within an educational institution and employs a structured curriculum (Boekaerts & Minnaert, 1999) based upon the framework of "Western Classical music pedagogy" (Green, 2002, p. 4). Non-formal education takes place inside or outside of an institutional context and often employs a tailor-made or loosely designed curriculum to suit learners' needs (Rogers, 2004). It typically involves the use of aural and oral methods of teaching and learning, often with musical notation to supplement the guidance of a teacher or mentor.[5] Informal music education typically involves developing musical skills and acquiring musical knowledge without a structured curriculum (Rennie & Mason, 2004) and often employs the approach of watching and copying teachers, family, friends, recordings or performances (Green, 2002; Thompson, 2012). These educational categories have been usefully described on a continuum (Folkestad, 2006); however, there is still much debate on the boundaries of each educational category because it is often unclear where formal education ends and non-formal or informal education begins (Rogers, 2004). Although an in-depth debate is beyond the focus of this study, the contested definitions of educational categories provide a useful starting point in acknowledging the complexities of musical learning both inside and outside educational institutions (Lebler & Hodges, chapter 22, this volume).

The experiences of learners in formal educational settings show how these distinctions and their traits are often porous. For example, an often-identifiable trait of informal music education is learning with peers in a cooperative manner. Studies into peer and cooperative learning[6] identify that this often takes place in formal educational settings implicitly and recognize there are benefits of incorporating these practices into HE music provision more explicitly (Chua & Ho, chapter 8, this

---

2 Exceptions include Rambarran's (in press) study of laptop musicians.
3 The term 'rock-based' here refers to guitar, bass, piano, drum and vocal musicians.
4 The term 'music-related' used here and elsewhere in this chapter refers to educational programmes that include music such as music, popular music, or sound and music technology.
5 Although this is not always the case; see Mok (2011) for further discussion of non-formal learning.
6 For an overview of the literature, see Burnard (2013), Topping (2005) and Westerlund and Gaunt (2013).

volume; Jones & King, 2009; Lebler & Hodges, chapter 22, this volume; Smith, 2013; Thompson, 2012). Green's (2002) analysis of how popular musicians learn highlights that the popular musicians in her study "were able to make connections between many of the skills and knowledge they were acquiring through formal and informal means. In spite of this . . . their informal learning practices continued unabated" (2002, p. 175). These connections were often made by the musicians themselves rather than purposely embedded into a specifically designed music curriculum.

In their overview of HE music programmes in the UK, Gaunt and Papageorgi recognized "a growing awareness of . . . peer learning . . . [leading to] an emphasis on collaborative creative projects driven by students' own ideas . . . supporting a move . . . towards a more student-centred approach" (2010, p. 267). However, they note that this was more evident in "chamber music or small band playing" (2010, p. 267) rather than in popular music education programmes such as music production and music technology. In another study Papageorgi et al. (2010) uncovered tensions between some of the popular musicians and formal education. These tensions occurred because of their often-opposing teaching and learning methods and focus. For example, students predominantly studying popular music programmes reported "a [cultural] clash between practical and academic aspects of music learning" (2010, p. 159).

This cultural clash between popular musicians and formal music education is also evident outside the UK. In his analysis of formal popular music programmes, Mantie (2013) identified a difference in focus between the USA and other countries such as the UK, Australia and Finland. His findings indicated that outside of the USA, there is a well-established incorporation of popular music in the music education system; however, paraphrasing Green (2002), Mantie also suggested that despite this adaptation, "teaching strategies and methods in the United Kingdom did not change accordingly" (2013, p. 348). As evidenced by this study, this lack of pedagogical change has, we argue, resulted in some popular music styles – particularly those that use traditional instrumentation or existing theoretical frameworks – to be prioritized over other musical styles, such as electronic and sample-based popular music (see also Powell & Burstein, chapter 20, this volume). In a more recent study of music education in UK schools, Green suggested that this prioritization occurs because "no teachers elected to buy twin decks for scratching. This is probably because scratching is that much further removed from the popular music into which the teachers were themselves enculturated than guitars and drum kits" (2009, p. 48). McQueen and Hallam support Green's suggestion, explaining that prioritization occurs "because music teachers have traditionally experienced a more formal training themselves, and popular music has been seen as a motivating means to a more traditional end" (2010, p. 234). Consequently, popular electronic styles of music are often overlooked in preference for popular music styles that are more closely related to traditional musical instrumentation and traditional musicological frameworks.

Methodology

This study draws upon data gathered from an electronically distributed questionnaire and a series of semi-structured interviews, with the specific aim of focusing on popular electronic musicians' musical practices, processes and experiences within HE in the UK. As such, we have drawn on Papageorgi et al.'s (2010) approach to capturing students' perceptions of the pervading philosophy within their respective educational institutions. This helped to connect the musicians' perceptions with their approaches to musical learning and performance as they develop their skills as musicians. It has been argued that concentrating on experiences, rather than documents or artefacts, "increases our knowledge of the details of cultural processes and practices" (Cohen, 1993, p. 135); in this instance, it allowed a qualitative analysis of the musicians' experiences.

The study was conducted over a five-month period, from August 2014 to December 2014, beginning first by distributing a questionnaire link via programme leaders to current students and recent graduates of music-related programmes at eight HE institutions across the UK. The entire investigation included 41 musicians, who were either current students or recent graduates of music-related undergraduate degree programmes. As the study included a relatively small number of musicians, every effort was made to represent the breadth of popular electronic music-making, and each musician first undertook a survey where they identified which category of popular electronic musician they were (e.g. DJ, turntablist, dance or hip-hop producer). In order to gain a perspective on a range of experiences, all ages, from 18 to 41 and above,[7] were included and the study included both male and female musicians,[8] a minority of whom were educators and professional, part-time popular electronic musicians. Also included in the study were commercially established, UK-based hip-hop and dance music producers and popular electronic musicians who had experienced some commercial success releasing their music on independent record labels.

In the first stage of the study, all 41 musicians completed the online questionnaire. Responses were captured through Google forms, which allowed the results to be grouped by age, experience or a question-related theme. The questionnaire was split into three sections: "About You", "About Your Course"[9] and "About Your Practice". The "About You" section captured general demographic information and data more pertinent to the individual's musical education and experience. The "About Your Course" section captured information on each musician's experience while studying their chosen music-related programme. The final section, "About Your Practice", gathered information on the development of each musician's practice as a popular electronic musician.

From the 41 musicians, six were selected for interview. In selecting the six interviewees, an effort was made to represent each of the four main categories of popular electronic musician (DJ, turntablist, hip-hop and dance music producers). Therefore, each category has been represented by at least one of the interviewees. Of the six interviewees, two were hip-hop producers, one was a DJ, one was a

---

7 41 and above was the highest selectable age category on the questionnaire.
8 Participants did not have to declare their gender in the questionnaire, although the majority of the musicians did.
9 The term 'course' here refers to the 'programme' of study.

turntablist and two were dance music producers. The musicians' responses from the questionnaire provided a useful starting point on which to base the questions for the interviews. A semi-structured interview approach was adopted to allow flexibility in exploring the issues and experiences of each musician while maintaining a commonality to each interview by posing the same questions (Priest, 1996). The interviews were recorded on a digital Dictaphone and later transcribed. The responses were then grouped in relation to the three broad areas of the questionnaire in order to highlight the development of particular themes. In this way responses could be more easily analyzed and common themes more readily identified and coded. Responses from the musicians in this study have been made anonymous, and each respondent has been assigned a given number. The majority of conversational utterances, such as 'errs' and 'ums', have been removed to maintain clarity. Responses included in the main body of the text are from all of the participating musicians, as far as possible. In terms of the general themes of the study, the musicians' answers generally reflected the experiences of all 41 musicians.

The musicians' previous experience of music education

In order to contextualize the popular electronic musicians' perceptions and experiences of formal education, the interviews began by exploring their experiences of music education prior to their HE studies. The majority of the participants had experienced compulsory music education relatively recently, although two of the musicians were 41 or above and had therefore attended school in the 1960s and 1970s. Of particular note, 25 of the 41 musicians in this study had not learned or studied popular styles of music in school prior to HE. A number of the responses regarding formal, compulsory music education were also notably negative:

PARTICIPANT 20: I learnt very little music at school. Music lessons in school were always difficult – a subject I feel a lot of children struggled to get to grips with, which meant a lot of pupils didn't bother trying.

PARTICIPANT 19: [Music education in school included] some appallingly boring lessons on elementary music theory and one small man's highly opinionated view of what we should listen to.

Responses from the musicians also showed that the majority of formal, compulsory music education only included the study of Western classical music, as in this example:

PARTICIPANT 10: I studied GCSE[10] music in secondary school, but this didn't really address popular styles of music at the time (I only really remember covering Baroque music a lot!).

---

10 General Certificate of Secondary Education is a qualification undertaken in secondary school between the ages of 14 and 16.

Music technology was introduced mainly to support composition within the Western classical musical tradition:

> PARTICIPANT 32: I studied music all the way up to A Level.[11] From what I can remember from the earlier years we were taught basic melodies on piano, and classical music at GCSE. Also during GCSE we were introduced to Cubase[12] where we worked on compositions, so I guess this is where I was first introduced to electronic music-making. Throughout A Level the lessons were very theory based, looking at music in history and working on harmony arrangements. We also studied jazz and listening techniques. It was only through my own desire that in my free time I played around with Logic[13] and different synths.

Despite the frequent absence of popular electronic music from the curriculum, some of the musicians in this study highlighted that learning about music production and music technology on their programme of study had sparked their interest in popular electronic music:

> PARTICIPANT 15: I was introduced to the world of music production while studying music technology at AS and A level during sixth-form[14] study. I was a complete novice in the area, having only having a background in music theory and performance. I quickly became enthusiastic about this area of music production as it was a world that was completely new to me.
>
> PARTICIPANT 29: Through college in Cornwall, where I took a music technology course, I started experimenting with making my own style of chilled house music with washy vocals. This style was derived from my years playing in a shoegaze/psych-rock band.
>
> PARTICIPANT 11: I began producing through studying music technology at A Level. At the same time I took an interest in electronic music and dance music.

Despite the formal study of music technology and music production influencing some of the musicians' interest in popular electronic music, the vast majority of responses in the study highlighted a perceived disconnect between the musicians' own personal experiences of popular electronic music and the content of their programmes' curricula. For example, a number of the musicians noted that popular music within their programmes was limited to guitar-based rock music. Consequently, access to electronic musical instruments and software

---

11 AS and A-Levels are qualifications taken by 17–18-year-olds in years 12–13 in the English education system, prior to University.
12 Cubase is a Digital Audio Workstation software programme made by Steinberg.
13 Logic is a Digital Audio Workstation software programme made by Apple.
14 'Sixth form' is a term for years 12 and 13 in the English, Welsh and Northern Irish education system.

was an important factor in developing the musicians' musical interest, skills and knowledge:

PARTICIPANT 10: I first started getting into electronic music after I bought Logic ... I loved being able to compose for a huge array of instruments which I otherwise would not have had access to. As I learned more about music and new genres of music, I started to experiment with new sounds and textures, moving away from traditional instrumentation (drums, guitars, keys and bass) to more heavily sampled work using more abstract sounds such as percussive elements (like vocal snippets and SFX).[15]

PARTICIPANT 37: Once I found out about electronic music I really enjoyed it and felt like I wanted to be a part of that culture so I decided to start making electronic music. Also it was easy to get access to a DAW[16] and to have electronic elements at the ready rather than having to record instruments, which I wasn't able to do at home. I knew I could start making music wherever then as it was just on my laptop/computer and I didn't need much equipment to do it.

In summary, although the musicians' previous experiences within formal music education were mixed it is clear that only a minority were able to engage with popular musical styles – and, in particular, popular electronic music – in school. The musicians predominantly experienced Western classical music in formal music education in schools, and in common with other studies (Bennett, 1980; Berkaak, 1999; Cohen, 1991; Finnegan, 1989; Green, 2002; Horn, 1984; Lilliestam, 1996) we found that popular electronic styles of music were overlooked in the curriculum. However, some music-related programmes within sixth-form and FE institutions offered some of the musicians the opportunity to engage with popular electronic music within formal education. All but one of the musicians who stated that popular electronic music was included in their school curriculum were between the ages of 18 and 21, which signals a potential change in approach towards the inclusion of popular electronic music in school curricula. The results of the study show that outside of this age group, however, popular electronic musical styles were more likely to be included later on (in 'sixth' form, or 'Further Education') in formal educational programmes, and that popular electronic styles were included within music technology, rather than traditional music, programmes.

The Musicians' programmes of study

Twenty-three of the 41 musicians in the study noted that popular electronic styles of music were included in the curriculum at the HE institution they attended. However, in-depth responses highlighted that the majority of this inclusion was

---

15 SFX is an abbreviation of Sound Effects.
16 DAW is an abbreviation of Digital Audio Workstation.

on a contextual basis in which the history and culture of popular electronic styles of music were taught:

PARTICIPANT 35: We touched upon the history of early hip-hop, from DJ-ing in the '70s up to heavy use of sampling in the late '80s.

A minority of the musicians noted that they were taught some of the practical aspects of popular electronic music:

PARTICIPANT 17: They were taught in the context of computer-based music-making somewhat generally.
PARTICIPANT 9: Some lessons focused on sequencing and synthesis, so dance music production techniques were covered. However, these techniques are not dance music exclusive, and overall, the course had a rock focus.
PARTICIPANT 13: Basic production values, structural aspects and timbre were taught through building a short track in a workshop style lecture.
PARTICIPANT 30: Through live performance using Ableton Live,[17] part of the module was to create a track.

Fifteen musicians noted that popular electronic styles of music were not included in the curriculum. Some of the musicians suggested that this might be, in part, due to a lack of recognition that popular electronic styles of music are worthy of study:

PARTICIPANT 7: I feel electronic and sample-based music is not considered as academically significant as other styles of popular music due to a perceived lack of compositional prowess.
PARTICIPANT 34: I think that academic [popular] music still revolves around the idea of bands/live music being the only credible form. Electronic music and especially up-pace dance seem to be viewed as adolescent. I think this could be down to the music still being quite young by comparison to traditional styles. This could also be impacted by some tutors having interests that are more akin to their age group [sic]. Therefore electronic music is not viewed as something as credible, due to the stereotypes that were made during the music's infancy.

In summary, over half of the musicians experienced popular electronic music within their programme of study through cultural and historical analysis, with a smaller minority engaging in practical study through lessons and workshops on composition and production. Some of the musicians noted that the practical study of popular electronic music was not considered as academically significant, and this was potentially due to a lack of tutor knowledge and experience.[18] However,

---

17 Ableton Live is a Digital Audio Workstation software programme designed specifically for use in live music performance as well as recording and production.
18 For an in-depth discussion of this issue in relation to hip-hop, see chapter 13, 'How critical pedagogy and democratic theory can inform teaching music, and especially hip-hop' in Snell and Söderman (2014).

some of the musicians' responses echo Papageorgi et al.'s (2010) findings, in which the musicians' musical tastes were broadened as a result of studying popular music in formal education.

Musicians' perceptions of what is missing from HE

We sought to capture the reflections of popular electronic musicians on what they perceived to be missing from the curriculum of their HE programmes. These reflections were mixed, but suggested that there was a general lack of acknowledgement that popular electronic styles of music are worthy of study. There was a shared expression that there could be a more appropriate use of musicological frameworks for analyzing popular electronic music:

PARTICIPANT 17: I felt that a greater emphasis on understanding electronic music would be particularly useful, though it remains a field which receives little musicological attention and several possible models emerge from the electro-acoustic tradition and are not greatly applicable.

Some musicians' reflections highlighted how practical teaching (or facilitation) of music technologies could be more usefully integrated into their music curriculum:

PARTICIPANT 11: Creating a live setup as an electronic music producer has been very important, through the use of Ableton and similar programmes. There is a huge range of possibilities that can be explored through the use of live instrumentation and electronic music within programmes such as Ableton, I feel this area could be explored, as it is a popular area of interest within the electronic music scene.

PARTICIPANT 10: Musicianship and DJing. I feel that had the course been taught with a more musical slant to it then the same information and skills would appear much more applicable. I also feel that DJing helps producers and musicians immensely as it helps greatly with reaffirming music theory knowledge (for instance, harmonic mixing using the circle of fifths).

PARTICIPANT 28: Just general electronic music production is not really talked about. Deconstruction of tracks as a class would be interesting.

A number of the musicians also noted that the curriculum could focus more specifically on the music industries in relation to popular electronic music practice:

PARTICIPANT 34: I would implement a business element to the course. This is because a lot of electronic producers are freelance practitioners and I can imagine a lot of people give up before they get that far as they cannot seem to make a living from it.

PARTICIPANT 7: Electronic music production is a relatively specialist practice, in which finding a job within the industry is fiercely competitive . . . I believe there needs to be a marriage of education and practical experience to stand a chance of fulfilling the goal of achieving a job within the industry.

The musicians' comments highlighted a range of missed opportunities within current academic practice, such as a need for electronic popular music examples to be critically analyzed alongside other popular music examples within the curriculum. They also recognized an opportunity to incorporate the innovations in live performance applications of electronic music production, alongside the use of more appropriate theoretical and musicological frameworks. Some of the musicians also emphasized the need to include relevant entrepreneurial aspects within the curriculum. Entrepreneurialism, for example, has been identified as a key aspect of hip-hop culture in which hip-hop musicians "recognized the importance of being self-employed, providing innovative goods or services, and attaining self-reliance and self-determination" (Price, 2006, p. 40).

In summary, although a minimal amount of practical tuition was included in some of the musicians' programmes, the responses indicate that the general absence of practical popular electronic music could be due to a lack of recognition that popular electronic styles of music are worthy of study. Consequently, the musicians in this study noted that Higher Popular Music Education (HPME) could include not only more practical teaching or facilitation of music technologies, but also study of the music industries as they apply to popular electronic music practice. The centrality of entrepreneurship, business and industry to HPME is recognized in other contexts (Lebler & Hodges, chapter 22, this volume; Morrow et al., chapter 26, this volume; Warner, chapter 11, this volume); and so incorporating more entrepreneurship, business and industry into popular electronic music education would bring it into line with other music styles.

Discussion

The responses from the musicians in this study highlight a number of important issues in their music education. First, there is a shared perception that the traditional Western classical music pedagogical approach continues to prevail in the school classroom. When music technology was introduced in the classroom it was used mainly to support composition within the Western classical musical tradition, not the composition of popular electronic styles of music. Consequently, none of the musicians in this study experienced popular electronic styles of music during their (pre-higher education) school experiences. However, responses showed that different musical styles were included in the curriculum of formal education beyond the years of compulsory education (post-16 years of age). In addition, popular electronic musical styles were more likely to be included within music technology programmes than traditional music programmes. Including popular electronic styles of music earlier on in the music curriculum could not only benefit musical development of all students in the classroom, but could also help to remove the privilege and perceived importance of Western classical musical styles in music education.

Second, and in relation to the first point, a fundamental issue highlighted by the responses from the musicians was that more appropriate musicological and analytical methods could be used in the study of popular electronic music. This was highlighted specifically because the musicians in the study emphasized that Western Art musical frameworks that were introduced to them during formal education weren't necessarily applicable or effectively contextualized to support their current knowledge, understanding or musical practice. Despite the development of more contemporary forms of musical and sonic analysis,[19] Hodgson argues that musicologists still "remain largely fixated on musical details that can be notated (i.e. pitch relations, formal contour, metered rhythms, harmonic design, and so on)" (2011, n.p.). Introducing new approaches to popular music education that recognize the informal learning practices of electronic music has been proposed by other studies (Ruthmann et al., 2008; Tobias, 2014; Tobias & Barrett, 2009). Lauri Väkevä makes a salient point in suggesting that "music educators need to welcome a critical attitude towards existing musical practices" (2010, p. 66). In the case of hip-hop, Snell and Söderman state that "we need to approach teaching Hip-hop in ways that adhere to the principals of critical pedagogy and democratic theory" (2014, p. 198). This would reflect current thinking regarding HPME more generally (Hooper, chapter 13, this volume).

The findings from this study encourage us as educators to make the case for the inclusion of popular electronic styles of music earlier on in formal education, both practically and academically. Quinn suggests that employing music technology could provide a "way into music, specifically composition" (2010, p. 28). However, the present study indicates that teachers and educators should go beyond employing music technology within a Western classical context and use it within its specific musical contexts and related popular electronic musical style (such as dance music or hip-hop). Doing so may not only help to more usefully engage young people in music by including the musical styles that they identify with most (Partti, 2012; Snell & Söderman, 2014; Söderman & Sernhede, 2015; Wright, 2010), but also help students gain a more comprehensive insight into music-making more generally. Furthermore, there is a case to be made for the development and application of appropriate theoretical and pedagogical frameworks that allow educators to include popular electronic music in a substantial way at all levels of education. This may help to increase the visibility of popular electronic styles of music, and in turn, alter the perception felt by some musicians in this study that popular electronic styles of music are considered academically 'unworthy'.

Conclusion

Although small in scale, this study explored the experiences and reflections of a group of musicians who are often overlooked in music education research. It is clear that there is still much to be done, and this chapter has underlined findings from other research in this area (Ruthmann et al., 2008; Tobias, 2014; Tobias & Barrett, 2009), indicating that formal popular music programmes could benefit from more inclusive curricula that acknowledge popular electronic styles of music

---

19 See, for example, Butler (2006), Hawkins (2009), Snoman (2009) and Solberg (2014).

as commendable additions to the more established popular musical styles such as rock. The musicians in this study also highlighted how more appropriate musicological and analytical methods could be used in the study of popular electronic music, rather than traditional Western-Classical frameworks. Developing more appropriate analytical and musicological methods may also ease the integration of popular electronic music into all levels of music education, and help to improve the perceived academic status of popular electronic music as worthy of study. Although not necessarily indicative of a wider trend, some educational programmes have begun to address this lack of popular electronic music in HPME. Some examples include the BA in Commercial Music and BA in Commercial Music Performance at the University of Westminster, BA in Electronic Music Production at the Academy for Contemporary Music, and MA in Electronic Music Production and Sound Design at the Berklee College of Music, USA. This small-scale study is a useful starting point; however, additional research in this area is needed to further explore the issues raised by the musicians in this study in order to more reliably inform the development of popular music curricula at all levels of education.

References

Bennett, H.S. (1980). *On becoming a rock musician*. Amherst, MA: University of Massachusetts Press.

Berkaak, O.A. (1999). Entangled dreams and twisted memories: Order and disruption in local music making. *Young*, 7(2), 25–42.

Boekaerts, M. & Minnaert, A. (1999). Self-regulation with respect to informal learning. *International Journal of Educational Research*, 31(6), 533–544.

Burnard, P. (2013). *Developing creativities in higher music education: International perspectives and practices*. New York, NY: Routledge.

Butler, M.J. (2006). *Unlocking the groove: Rhythm, meter, and musical design in electronic dance music*. Bloomington, IN: Indiana University Press.

Campbell, P.S. (1991). *Lessons from the world: A cross-cultural guide to music teaching and learning*. New York, NY: Schirmer Books.

Cohen, S. (1991). *Rock culture in Liverpool: Popular music in the making*. New York, NY: Oxford University Press on Demand.

Cohen, S. (1993). Ethnography and popular music studies. *Popular Music*, 12(2), 123–138.

Finnegan, R.H. (1989). *The hidden musicians: Music-making in an English Town*. Cambridge: Cambridge University Press.

Folkestad, G. (2006). Formal and informal learning situations or practices vs formal and informal ways of learning. *British Journal of Music Education*, 23(2), 135–145.

Gaunt, H. & Papageorgi, I. (2010). Music in universities and conservatories. In S. Hallam & A. Creech (Eds.), *Music education in the 21st century in the United Kingdom: Achievements, analysis and aspirations* (pp. 260–278). London: Institute of Education.

Green, L. (2002). *How popular musicians earn: A way ahead for music education*. Farnham: Ashgate.

Green, L. (2009). *Music, informal learning and the school: A new classroom pedagogy*. Farnham: Ashgate.

Hawkins, S. (2009). Feel the beat come down: House music as rhetoric. In *Analyzing popular music* (pp. 80–102). Cambridge: Cambridge University Press.

Hodgson, J. (2011). Lateral dynamics processing in experimental hip hop: Flying Lotus, Madlib, Oh No, J-Dilla and Prefuse 73. *Journal on the Art of Record Production*, 5. Retrieved from:

http://arpjournal.com/lateral-dynamics-processing-in-experimental-hip-hop-flying-lotus-madlib-oh-no-j-dilla-and-prefuse-73/ [Accessed 15 August 2016].

Horn, K. (1984). Rock music-making as a work model in community music workshops. *British Journal of Music Education, 1*(2), 111–135.

Jones, C. & King, A. (2009). Peer learning in the music studio. *Journal of Music, Technology and Education, 2*(1), 55–70.

Lilliestam, L. (1996). On playing by ear. *Popular Music, 15*(2), 195–216.

Mantie, R. (2013). A comparison of "popular music pedagogy" discourses. *Journal of Research in Music Education, 61*(3), 334–352.

McQueen, H., & Hallam, S. (2010). Music in the secondary school. In S. Hallam & A. Creech (Eds.), *Music education in the 21st century in the United Kingdom: Achievements, analysis and aspirations* (pp. 228–244). London: Institute of Education.

Mok, O.N.A. (2011). Non-formal learning: Clarification of the concept and its application in music learning. *Australian Journal of Music Education, 1*, 11–15.

Papageorgi, I., Haddon, E., Creech, A., Morton, F., de Bezenac, C., Himonides, E., & Welch, G. (2010). Institutional culture and learning: Perceptions of the learning environment and musicians' attitudes to learning. *Music Education Research, 12*(2), 151–178.

Partti, H. (2012). *Learning from cosmopolitan digital musicians: Identity, musicianship, and changing values in (in)formal music communities.* Helsinki: Sibelius Academy.

Price, E.G. (2006). *Hip hop culture.* Oxford: ABC-CLIO.

Priest, S. H. (1996). *Doing media research: An introduction.* London: Sage.

Quinn, H. (2010). Perspectives from a new generation secondary school music teacher. In J. Finney & P. Burnard (Eds.), *Music education with digital technology* (pp. 21–29). London: Bloomsbury Publishing.

Rambarran, S. (in press). DJ hit that button: Amateur laptop musicians in contemporary music and society. In R. Mantie & G.D. Smith (Eds.) *The Oxford handbook of music making and leisure.* New York, NY: Oxford University Press.

Randles, C. (2013). Being an iPadist. *General Music Today, 27*(1), 48–51.

Rennie, F. & Mason, R. (2004). *E-Learning and social networking handbook: Resources for higher education.* London: Routledge.

Rogers, A. (2004). *Non-formal Education: Flexible Schooling or Participatory Education?* Hong Kong: Comparative Education Research Centre, the University of Hong Kong.

Ruthmann, A., Finney, J., Seddon, F., Dillon, S.C., Leong, S., Burnard, P., & Collins, D. (2008). Music education with digital technology: Changing identities, researching digital classrooms, and strategies for change. In *International Society of Music Education Conference: Symposium*, 17–25 July 2008, Bologna, Italy.

Smith, G.D. (2013). Pedagogy for employability in a foundation degree (Fd.A.) in creative musicianship: Introducing peer collaboration. In H. Gaunt & H. Westerlund (Eds.), *Collaboration in higher music education* (pp. 193–198). Farnham: Ashgate.

Snell, K. & Söderman, J. (2014). *Hip-hop within and without the academy.* London: Lexington Books.

Snoman, R. (2009). *Dance music manual: Tools, toys and techniques.* Abingdon: Taylor & Francis.

Söderman, J. & Folkestad, G. (2004). How hip-hop musicians learn: Strategies in informal creative music making. *Music Education Research, 6*(3), 313–326.

Söderman, J. & Sernhede, O. (2015). Hip-hop – What's in it for the academy? Self-understanding, pedagogy and aesthetical learning processes in everyday cultural Praxis. *Music Education Research, 17*(4), 1–14.

Solberg, R.T. (2014). "Waiting for the bass to drop": Correlations between intense emotional experiences and production techniques in build-up and drop sections of electronic dance music. *Dancecult: Journal of Electronic Dance Music Culture, 6*(1), 61–82.

Thompson, P. (2012). An empirical study into the learning practices and enculturation of DJs, turntablists, hip hop and dance music producers. *Journal of Music Technology and Education*, *5*(1), 43–58.

Tobias, E.S. (2014). From musical detectives to DJs expanding aural skills and analysis through engaging popular music and culture. *General Music Today*, 1048371314558293.

Tobias, E.S. & Barrett, J.R. (2009). Counterpoint or remix? A dialogue on popular music and popular culture in the music teacher education curriculum. In *Collaborative action for change: Selected proceedings from the 2007 symposium on music teacher education* (p. 35). Rowman & Littlefield Education.

Topping, K. (2005). Trends in peer learning. *Educational Psychology*, *25*(6), 631–645.

Väkevä, L. (2010). Garage band or GarageBand®? Remixing musical futures. *British Journal of Music Education*, *27*(1), 59–70.

Westerlund, P.H., & Gaunt, H. (Eds.) (2013). *Collaborative learning in higher music education*. Farnham: Ashgate.

Williams, D.A. (2014). Another perspective: The iPad is a REAL musical instrument. *Music Educators Journal*, *101*(1), 93–98.

Wright, R. (2010). Democracy, social exclusion and music education: Possibilities for change. In R. Wright (Ed.), *Sociology and music education* (pp. 263–282). Farnham: Ashgate.

18

Artists to teachers – teachers to artists

Providing a space for aesthetic experience at secondary schools through popular music

Axel Schwarz and David-Emil Wickström

"Has there been a person in your life who inspired you to become a musician?"

"What would your life look like, if you never had met that person who brought active music making into your life?"

These questions open the first lecture of the course "Band Training / Ensembleleitung".[1] This course provides an introduction to music education at the state-funded university *Popakademie Baden-Württemberg – University of Popular Music and Music Business* (Popakademie) in Mannheim, Germany. Each student at the Popakademie has met such a special person who inspired him or her to learn an instrument. The students also consider a life without active music-making as very undesirable. Unfortunately, not every child in the Mannheim region will meet such a person, and thus a lot of children lack the joy and benefits that active music-making can bring. Together with the chemical company BASF SE (primarily as a financial supporter), the Popakademie runs the annual project "Pop macht Schule" (PoMS) which introduces music-making to school pupils and enables university students to potentially be such a special person.[2]

---

1 The authors would like to thank Danijela Albrecht, Catherine Gaillou and Heiko Wandler as well as this book's editors for commenting on drafts of the chapter, and Mel E. Harris for proofreading it.
2 PoMS was initially called *School of Rock der Popakademie Baden-Württemberg*. In this article "students" refers to those studying at the Popakademie and "pupils" to children / teenagers at the secondary schools participating in PoMS.

217

PoMS is part of the aforementioned university course offered to second-year students within the bachelor's degree programme *Pop Music Design*.[3] It is also an on-site coaching project for secondary school pupils in the Rhein-Neckar region around Mannheim, for which the schools have to apply to take part.[4] The main concept behind the project is that artists[5] visit schools to teach their art by creating music in peer groups, and to perform these songs in different bands in front of an audience. Initiated in 2004, the project's aim is to provide students on the degree programme with basic skills in the field of music education as well as to bring popular music to schools and empower pupils – who otherwise have not had opportunities to engage in creative work, play an instrument or start songwriting – through one-day crash courses. In addition, the teachers from the participating schools (and others) are offered state-accredited workshops in popular music education at the Popakademie, enabling them to continue working on new songs at their schools (Schwarz, 2015).

Popular music is a living music tradition, constantly changing and evolving. This is a challenge when popular music is taught within a school context. One way to face the dilemma of staying up-to-date musically is to bring active artists into an educational context (Smith & Shafighian, 2013). Thus, besides providing an example of how to bring popular music education to schools, this chapter also discusses the concept of letting creative professionals teach their art/craft in schools – a core tenet in the Popakademie's pedagogical work. After a brief overview of the university's educational philosophy, this article will discuss PoMS's methodology before concluding with the project's impact.

Popakademie and popular music education

Popular music is often seen by musicians as a field where formal education is more of a hindrance than an asset (Green, 2002; Parkinson & Smith, 2015). Reviewing previous literature on formal and informal learning, Folkestad (2006, p. 142) argues that learning situations are not necessarily linked to institutional settings or musical genres. Learning is dependent on the individual's intentionality as well as whether the learning situation is formalized. While arguing that teaching is always formal, he points out that teachers can create learning situations that also draw on informal learning processes, identifying four ways in which learning can be used and defined: situation, learning style, ownership and intentionality (2006, 141). This is also the approach at the Popakademie, where a mixture of formalized learning situations alternates with informal learning processes. This is especially applied in the core of the degree programme, band work, where the students are free to

---

3 The idea behind the term *Pop Music Design* is that students will design their act during their study, including performance, staging, sound, image, marketing and music.
4 Each year between 40 and 50 schools apply to take part, from which 12 are selected.
5 The term *artists* refers both to "a professional performer in music" and "someone who [...] writes music" (Rundell, 2002, p. 66) – in this case the students studying at the Popakademie. The German equivalent is *Künstler*.

create music. Similar to Lebler's (2007) description of student-as-master on a popular music programme, band work at the Popakademie is primarily self-directed learning among peers with a band coach providing limited feedback.[6] By enabling informal learning situations, 24/7 access to rehearsal rooms and band coaches who act as facilitators, the students are free to express their creativity in their band work (for similar approach cf. Gullberg, 2010).

Innovation, originality and creativity are arguably essential to popular music; however, the professionalization of the musicians working within the field calls for highly skilled and versatile musicians to fulfil the market's requirements. While some (Jones, chapter 27, this volume; Lebler & Hodges, chapter 22, this volume; McLaughlin, chapter 10, this volume; Parkinson & Smith, 2015; Wong, chapter 9, this volume) focus on employment in higher popular music education in terms of entrepreneurship, economic utility and neoliberalism – also reflected in the Bologna process (European Higher Education Area, 2015) – it is important to remember that popular music not only consists of new and innovative acts, but also established groups and vocalists in need of musicians, songwriters and producers.

The Popakademie, founded in 2003, was the first institution of higher education in Germany to include a bachelor's degree programme dedicated to popular music. The Popakademie aims to provide conservatory-level training for musicians within the field of popular music.[7] While the students' instrumental skills and band work are core tenets in the education, the approach is also designed to give students a broad artistic background. Hence, the Popakademie's philosophy is not that of a master-apprentice approach, where the students follow the same main instrument teacher during the duration of their study (Gaunt & Papageorgi, 2010). Instead, the teachers usually change every year – the underlying philosophy being that the students gain different ideas and impulses from each teacher. This widens their artistic knowledge, gives them a broad technical and musical background, and thus provides material for the students to continue to work on their musicianship after graduating.

Another central tenet is the strong link between the degree programmes and the future professions of the students (Bennett, 2013; Hallam & Gaunt, 2012). While the Humboldt-concept of *Bildung*, which unites teaching and research and thus strives for a holistic approach to education, remains important, the educational philosophy at the Popakademie is primarily based on the concept of *Ausbildung*. This vocational approach means that a stronger emphasis is placed on giving the students the tools needed for their future careers than a *studium generale* approach. Besides music business courses and two mandatory internships (after the first and

---

6 The band coach has 3x90 minutes a term per band. The students have to create 40 minutes of new self-composed music each year, which they have to perform live with their band at the end of the summer term and which is assessed by a commission consisting of a teacher from each main instrument.
7 While there were precursors at other institutions (with overlapping personnel) these were either annual short-term workshops (*Eventim Popkurs* in Hamburg) or vocational training programmes (*Berufsfachschule für Musik* in Dinkelsbühl).

second years), this can also be seen in the programme's total duration of six terms (180 ECTS) – shorter than the traditional eight terms (240 ECTS) in a German music conservatoire.[8] This forces the students to think about and plan their career as freelance musicians (which in essence is a portfolio career) as soon as they enter the programme. The link between theory and practice also applies to the non-music / academic courses taught in the degree program, as well as the course "Band Training / Ensembleleitung", PoMS's formal course title.

In his article regarding the epistemology of success in popular music, Smith (2013) cautions against defining success in higher popular music education "in terms of fame or commercial success" (p. 31), embracing instead the fact that most musicians will pursue portfolio careers. Pursuing a goal of being famous is for most musicians utopian. As an institution of higher education the Popakademie's goal is to provide its graduates with the necessary tools to pursue long-term, sustainable careers as freelance musicians. This means that the degree programme not only focuses on core competencies in students' main instruments as well as band work, but also provides secondary competencies in areas such as music business and pedagogy, and thus the necessary tools to enable a portfolio career. As Wickström (2015) has shown, this approach has proven successful and the Popakademie's graduate incomes are based on various revenue streams predominantly within the field of popular music. These primarily consist of a mix of live music, studio work and teaching (Wickström, 2015, p. 364). Wickström also argues that in order to provide the students with the relevant skills, constant reviewing and updating of the curriculum is essential.

Popular music in German schools

During the last 15 years, popular music has made inroads in [music] teacher education in Germany due to society's growing acceptance of the music as well as a generational shift in educational institutions (Jank, 1996; Terhag, 2000). This is also due to a move towards action-centred (*handlungsbasiert*) music education as well as a focus on practice instead of reception within aesthetic education (*ästhetische Bildung*) – aesthetic education through aesthetic practice – in German primary and secondary schools (Rolle, 2010; Wallbaum, 2006, 2008). Jank observes that primary and secondary schools in Germany are the only "music schools" accessible to everybody, and the challenge in teaching is to get everybody to engage in music-making – including children from underprivileged backgrounds (2005, p. 19). This is one of the reasons the educational projects run by the Popakademie (both those that are part of the degree programmes and coaching in schools, etc.) are centred around popular music and popular culture; in our experience working within the education sector in the Mannheim region, popular music not only

---

8 For this reason, the degree awarded by the Popakademie is a Bachelor of Arts, as opposed to the usual conservatoire Bachelor of Music. ECTS is the European Credit Transfer and Accumulation System, used in higher education institutions across the continent.

plays an important role in the identity formation of pupils in schools, but it is also increasingly becoming the main musical idiom of the working population – and even retirees.

The Popakademie's courses and projects share the following overarching goals:

- Arts education (*Kulturelle Bildung*)
- Aesthetic education
- Artistic education
- Developing creativity
- Intercultural learning and integration of minorities
- Motivating children and (young) adults to make music and thus motivating the participants to becoming active consumers
- Improving musical, language and social ("soft") skills

These goals are combined with an action-centred approach aimed at achieving predefined goals at the end of an overarching unit (either per module if embedded within the curriculum or – for non-academic endeavours – per workshop or project). Participants should at each stage know why they are undertaking particular tasks and what the goal of their actions is, enabling them to experience the benefit of the knowledge they acquire. This is an important difference from how music has been taught at German secondary schools. In the past the focus has often been put on talking about music, instead of performing (and thus experiencing) music (see the above-mentioned shift from reception to production). This difference is due to both a broader lack in pupils' overall musical skills and a reduction in music lessons in the school curricula. While schools offer extracurricular activities in music (choir, orchestra, school bands), these are available to interested pupils, not mandatory. They also depend on enthusiastic teachers being willing to teach those courses and, to some extent, the pupils' previous experience in playing instruments. In order to engage pupils they need to *experience* music. Rolle (2010) argues that spaces of aesthetic experience can succeed if classes in musical production are realized through project-based work with the goal of performing the resulting musical product together. 'Musical production' can include composing, writing lyrics and recording a song together as well as arranging a contemporary cover of an older song.

This also touches upon the tenets of arts education, which has been promoted by UNESCO in recent years. Arts education was adopted by the parliament of the federal state of Baden-Württemberg (under whose jurisdiction the Popakademie falls) in its 10-year strategy, "Kultur 2020". This outlines the federal state's cultural policy until 2020 (Radolko et al., 2010), in which arts education is stressed as being essential in keeping the state prepared for the future. Within the realm of arts and culture, fantasy and creativity are seen as central in promoting cognitive, emotional and creative competencies in the personality development of citizens (Radolko et al., 2010, p. 39). The authors emphasize that arts education is primarily developed through participants' own artistic activities (p. 41). Thus their concept mirrors Rolle's (2010) call for an approach to popular music in schools where classes are seen as places for independent and experience-based learning. This also enables teachers to act as *facilitators* and thus help the pupils towards achieving the goal of experiencing the music – without teachers having to be up-to-date on current musical genres – by creating learning situations with informal/non-formal learning processes (D'Amore & Smith, 2016; Folkestad, 2006).

Another way to face the dilemma of staying up to date with popular music is by bringing artists into an educational context – which is PoMS's aim. The students who enter the bachelor's degree programme are all already highly skilled and active musicians.[9] Thus all the students in the degree programme can be considered artists in their own right. Here PoMS differs from regular music lessons in German public schools by using active musicians (the students) as teachers. Although not pedagogical professionals, they are successful in getting the pupils engaged with music, in part due to their being perceived by the pupils as 'authentic' artists. They have acquired the necessary skills to teach these one-day workshops through an intensive one-week seminar covering basics of music pedagogy, and the necessary tools for other workshops that are to follow. The students spend the following three weeks after the course on a teaching tour – teaching pupils at schools in and around Mannheim in five-hour workshops. During the workshops the students are evaluated by their peers and the Popakademie faculty, receiving feedback on their teaching skills. This practical part enables students to apply the theoretical component – pedagogical concepts – while still fresh in their memories. In this way PoMS turns artists into teachers.

The PoMS methodology

PoMS's underlying methodology was first developed at the Popakademie in 2004 by Axel Schwarz with input from vocal teacher Petra Scheeser (Singalong, Words & Raps), drum teacher (and the Popakademie's director) Udo Dahmen (Body Percussion) and bass and band coaching teacher Frank Itt (Bandcoaching). It draws on the aforementioned musicians' previous experiences within the field of popular music education, as well as their experience playing in bands. During PoMS's conception phase, the main features of the project were defined as:

- A modular and flexible workshop concept (referred to as "tools")
- Work with complete school classes
- Make it a part of the degree programme *Pop Music Design*
- Involvement of the school's teachers
- The necessary equipment for the PoMS tour is provided by the Popakademie
- Pupil concerts

The main pedagogical aim was to create a space for aesthetic experience (Rolle, 2010) through composing and performing popular music. Due to its seemingly

---

9 Each year about 450 applicants compete for 30 places in the bachelor's degree programme *Pop Music Design*. The competition, therefore, is fierce, and successful applicants enter the degree programme at a high musical and technical level.

simple structure, the basic form of many contemporary chart songs can be reduced to units that can be taught to novices. Riffs can be broken down for beginners to learn, while more advanced participants can focus on micro-time, sound design, perfecting solos, etc. The workshop participants thus experience musical creativity through their own actions.[10] In order to create this space for aesthetic experience, a flexible modular workshop system based on units called "tools" was developed. The main intention was to create a system that got each participating pupil involved in the creative process. At the same time, these tools enable the workshop's teachers to react to the possible school – and learning – situations encountered during the tour. This includes selecting, as well as adapting, the appropriate tools for each school and its pupils. Importantly, the tools' outcomes result in a final concert (staged as a small festival) where the pupils perform their musical creations to their fellow pupils, teachers and coaches.

An important factor for creating the modular tool system was the intention to work with complete school classes, not a selection of 'musically gifted' pupils, in line with Jank's (2005) call to engage everybody and thus make music-making accessible for everybody. This means working with groups that are heterogeneous in:

- Age
- Gender
- Social and cultural background
- Musical background and preferences

In addition, the students have to work with pupils from different types of secondary schools (*Gymnasium*, *Realschule*, *Werkrealschule* and *Förderschule*).[11]

In order to include all the pupils from a class, each tool (the smallest PoMS teaching unit) includes the following features:

- Each tool can be used as a stand-alone workshop;
- The combination of different tools creates new workshops;
- Within the pool of tools each pupil can find a suitable workshop;
- The methodology of one tool can be used in other tools;
- The tools are inter-linkable – parallel working tools can work towards a common goal;
- Tools are flexible and adjustable to the groups and the school situation; and
- Tools are adoptable to new trends within popular music as well as to new educational contexts.

---

10 This approach is similar to the Modern Band pedagogy of Little Kids Rock (Powell & Burstein, chapter 20, this volume), though Modern Band is primarily aimed at teachers rather than active musicians.
11 After primary school, pupils can choose (depending on their grades) if they want to pursue an academic or vocational path in secondary school. *Werkrealschule* (9 years) and *Realschule* (10 years) cater to pupils following a vocational path. Pupils who want to study at a university or other institution of higher education have to pass the 'Abitur', which is the final exam at the *Gymnasium* (12 years). *Förderschule* cater towards children with special needs or learning disabilities.

The following tools were developed for PoMS (see Schwarz, 2015, for more in-depth descriptions):

Body Percussion: A method to teach metric and rhythmic structures, activating the cognitive and motor skills through clapping, stamping and using 'vocussion' in a group. This tool is also used as an opening exercise for all PoMS participants due to its characteristics of a warm-up.

Singalong: A vocal tool used to introduce the pupils to singing and its main techniques, as well as creating and performing songs.

Words & Raps: A songwriting tool whose main purpose is to teach pupils how to write and structure their thoughts and emotions and how to create rap or song lyrics based on that.

Meet the Band: This tool teaches the pupils to play a simple riff or chord progression on bass, electric guitar, keyboards or drums, which they then perform within a (rock/pop) band context.

Band Coaching: For musically more advanced pupils, the tool Band Coaching offers a chance for existing school bands and individual musicians to compose new songs in a band context.

We Are Producers: This tool enables the pupils to become creative with computer and music software. Working as a producer group, they create a track by recording music and lyrics (see also Ojala, chapter 6, this volume).

Not only the process, but also the result is, as mentioned, an important element in creating a space for aesthetic experience: each tool's goal is to share the tool's artistic results at the end of the workshop in the form of a public concert.

These tools are used as building blocks during a PoMS visit to a school.[12] Drawing on the different tools, a typical day could be structured in the following way:

After meeting at the Popakademie, the students depart, with equipment, for the day's school. After unloading the vehicle and setting up the equipment in the rooms together with the pupils (getting them involved as soon as possible) the day starts with a small concert in the school's assembly hall, where the tool "Meet the Band" is taught. Two Popakademie bands play two songs to clearly mark the break from the daily school routine, which is followed by a body percussion session for all participating pupils. Besides functioning as an icebreaker, this tool lays the foundation for groove and rhythm apprehension – skills needed later in the day – and defines some of the key terms (for example *beat, measure, groove*) used in the tools throughout the morning.

Pupils are then introduced to the various tools and can choose those in which they wish to participate. In the following two hours each group works on its tool:

---

12 Before the PoMS tour begins, the schools are chosen in cooperation with BASF based on the schools' applications. What tools are offered depends on the school, its needs and its capacity. At the same time the schools have to prepare a certain amount of rooms depending on the tools used. Before PoMS starts, the students receive their tour schedule for each day, which includes the address of that day's school, the school type, amount of pupils and any special needs and requirements, as well as the tools taught and which students will be examined.

a group of students using the Meet the Band tool works with pupils to reproduce a song by a popular artist. At the same time a student leads the Singalong tool in another room, where the pupils learn the song's lyrics aided by the song's playback. A third group works on writing and performing new lyrics to the song in the Words & Raps tool. Towards the end of the morning the three groups meet and rehearse their versions of the song. The day ends with a mini-concert in which the pupils perform the song with the new lyrics, the other groups present their work (songs, raps, recorded tracks) and the coaches perform their songs with their bands. Afterwards, pupils help pack the equipment back into the vehicle. After the PoMS tour is over, the most interesting school acts are chosen for a final public concert in the *Alte Feuerwache Mannheim*, one of Mannheim's major concert venues; with a capacity of about 1000, it is normally reserved for known national and international groups. This two-hour mini-festival features student bands from the Popakademie and pupil bands performing their best songs in front of an audience consisting of their teachers, fellow pupils, family, friends and the general public.[13] In addition to this, the Popakademie offers workshops for teachers from the participating schools, explaining the PoMS methodology and providing them the necessary skills to continue the musical education of their pupils in their daily lives at school.

The pillars and benefits of PoMS

The four main 'pillars' of PoMS can be summed up as:

- A one-week intensive music-pedagogical degree programme course
- A tour with student-led workshops for school pupils
- A small festival at the end of the tour, bringing the most interesting pupil acts together
- A state-accredited workshop programme for the teachers' professional development, ensuring sustainable continuation of musical education at the schools

As mentioned, the second-year students comprising the PoMS educators are primarily artists, not trained music teachers. A prime motivator for the course is the notion that active musicians can ignite an interest in the subject in a way that regular teachers, for the most part, might be less able to do (notwithstanding the crude dichotomy assumed here). This is also the underlying tenet of the workshop-based approach: by breaking the daily school routine, pupils are more receptive to new input. The Popakademie bands performing for the pupils signal both that the day will be different and that the workshop leaders are musicians in their own right. An added bonus of using students is that they are closer in age to the pupils than other teachers, lending the students an added element of bonding and 'coolness'.

---

13 This final concert is organized by students in the bachelor's degree programme *Music Business*, and they are supervised by a coach from A.S.S. Concerts & Promotion GmbH, one of Germany's major tour promoters.

Having to create something also forces the pupils into a more active consumer role regarding music. This can lead to new paths of self-realization and open up new perspectives for them. An added benefit of using a collaborative music approach is that the participants work on their soft skills, such as teamwork. This has opened the methodology up for application in other areas as well (for example, coaching of business managers). Soft skills also come into play through presenting the results by performing in front of an audience. Here, the dynamics of a concert within a secure setting – preparation, being nervous before the concert, tension during and release after the concert – provide a new set of experiences and learning that can be applied to other areas of the participants' (professional) lives, such as, for example, (board room) presentations and sales pitches. At the same time, the performance enables participants to experience some elements of what it feels like to be an artist.

As the students are placed in the position of role models, they have to familiarize themselves with taking responsibility for themselves and "their" pupils. Teaching the PoMS units also makes the students reflect upon their approaches to music and learning. This is aided by the requirement that students, as a part of their assessment, reflect upon the tools they taught in an oral exam and a written assignment. The goal here is that the students learn through self-reflection on what they can improve upon for the future. The students – who, after graduating, go on to become freelance musicians – also profit from the teaching experience since teaching skills can provide a key income source. The Popakademie regularly conducts surveys of its graduates, and the numbers for 2013 showed that, in addition to working with their band projects, being studio musicians and working as producers, about 45% of the *Pop Music Design* graduates supplemented their income with teaching jobs (Wickström, 2015).

The teachers at the schools taking part in PoMS benefit from the project through the contact with the students, seeing how they approach music with, at times, unorthodox teaching methods, along with the workshops for school teachers from participating PoMS schools, organized by the Popakademie. Besides teaching the PoMS methodology, these workshops also help teachers 'rediscover' and reinvigorate their artistic personalities – turning them (back) into artists. This approach creates a 'win-win-win-situation': pupils benefit from working with active musicians to create music by themselves; teachers are provided with new methods and ideas for teaching popular music; and artists develop the necessary skills to work as music coaches.

Impact

Between 40 and 50 schools apply every year, from which an average of 12 schools with about 1000 pupils in total are chosen to take part in PoMS, making it a very successful endeavour in the Rhein-Neckar region.[14] More important, however, are

---

14 While the participating schools change every year, broadening the scope of pupils participating, the project's reach is limited both by the provided funding (and thus staff) and by the participating schools, since they have to actively apply to be considered.

the long-term effects of the coaching – especially keeping the pupils involved with music. Besides the teacher coaching, giving the teachers the necessary tools, some of the schools also hire Popakademie students as music teachers and band coaches.

A more in-depth coaching based on the PoMS methodology was made possible with "InPop", funded through a grant from the Federal Ministry of Education and Research (BMBF), the State Ministry of Education, Youth and Sports and the city of Mannheim. The goal of this was to use music as an integration tool at five schools in Mannheim over a three-year period, from 2009 until 2012. At the same time, the tools have been used in other educational projects run by the Popakademie. One such project is PASCH (*Schulen: Partner der Zukunft* – Schools: Partners for the Future), which is undertaken in cooperation with the Goethe-Institut;[15] the primary aim of this project is to teach German outside of Germany. This approach has also been adapted for company coaching aimed at managers in (large) companies.

The PoMS approach also influenced the conceptualization of the master's degree programme, *Popular Music*, introduced at the Popakademie in 2011. One of this programme's three areas of study – Educating Artists – is aimed at educational training. Similar to PoMS, the idea is to develop creative artists who also can teach. Besides being given a solid foundation in music education (drawing on PoMS and other relevant methodologies), the students have to conceptualize and implement an educational project at schools or other institutions, spanning everything from pre-school to extracurricular school activities and care homes.

PoMS has won several awards for its innovative methods. In 2009, the State Ministry of Science, Research and the Arts (MWK) in Baden-Württemberg awarded PoMS the state teaching prize (*Landeslehrpreis*). In 2010, the project was selected as an educational landmark in the "365 Landmarks in the Land of Ideas" and the project "Germany – Land of Ideas", initiated by the German federal government and the Federation of German Industries (Deutschland – Land der Ideen, 2010); this prize is awarded for innovative ideas shaping Germany's future. In 2012, BASF was awarded the AKS-Award for the project by the *Arbeitskreis Kultursponsoring* (AKS, Working Group for Arts Sponsorship, Federation of German Industries – Kulturkreis der deutschen Wirtschaft, 2012). As such, this project has received critical acclaim from both pedagogical peers (*Landeslehrpreis*, Land of Ideas) and industry, for the BASF's long-term commitment to arts sponsorship.

Summary

While no substitute for Germany's formal teacher education (nor intended as such),[16] PoMS and its pedagogy offer a workshop-based approach to popular

---

15 See http://www.pasch-net.de (accessed 23.04.2015) for more information regarding PASCH. The *Goethe-Institut* is a state-run institution whose task is to promote German language and culture abroad (similar to *Alliance française*).
16 While slowly changing, Germany's teacher's education policies for teachers at primary and secondary schools are highly regulated. Teachers have to study on a specific degree programme

music education that focuses on engaging pupils to create popular music. Through one-day workshops, PoMS and its student coaches give pupils an insight into the world of music-making. Based on feedback from the schools, PoMS leaves a lasting impression on pupils, inspiring some to learn an instrument, to form a band or to start singing, writing or producing music – and thus opening a creative outlet where they can express themselves and find their own identities through active engagement in making popular music. Anecdotally, teachers also tell us of how PoMS impacts on the children's personalities – pupils who had been extremely shy and excluded by their peer groups gained in confidence after their final PoMS concert. While the project's reach is admittedly limited due to various constraints, including funding, other projects like the aforementioned InPop and the master's degree programme have broadened the reach of Popakademie beyond secondary school to include youth centres, kindergartens and other areas of extracurricular activities.[17] The PoMS tools can also serve as 'teasers', which might be followed by other pedagogical approaches – such as Ojala's "Learning Through Producing" (chapter 6, this volume), Musical Futures (D'Amore & Smith, 2016) or Modern Band (Powell & Burstein, chapter 20, this volume).

PoMS also influences the ways that music teachers modify their teaching by introducing the PoMS methods into their work at school while remembering their own musical or artistic background and reinforcing it for their educational work. At the same time, the Popakademie students go through a maturing process – not only by thinking about their coaching tasks but also by reflecting on their own music education. These reflections improve both their musicianship – since they see certain musical processes in a different light – and their teaching skills, avoiding pitfalls into which their own teachers may have stumbled. While only an initial step, the space for aesthetic experience provided by PoMS helps to give the various participants – teachers, students, pupils – the agency to become and develop as future active musicians – even aspiring artists. As Tia DeNora (2000, p. 62) has pointed out, "music is a device . . . to which people turn in order to regulate themselves as aesthetic agents, as feeling, thinking and acting beings in their day-to-day lives". In line with Partti's aspirations, we view "the school (or college) as an institution that guides students towards increasingly agency" (2012, p. 88).

References

Bennett, D.E. (2013). The role of career creativities in developing identity and becoming expert selves. In P. Burnard (Ed.), *Developing creativities in higher music education: International perspectives and practices* (pp. 224–244). London: Routledge.

---

that includes two state licensing examinations (*Staatsexamen*) as well as a teaching training at a school before they can be employed as teachers and qualify to become civil servants. The degree programmes at the Popakademie do not qualify.

17 Due to the described limitations within Germany's teacher education, the master's degree programme students' educational projects usually take place at extracurricular, non-school institutions.

D'Amore, A. & Smith, G.D. (2016). Aspiring to music making as leisure through the musical futures classroom. In R. Mantie & G.D. Smith (Eds.), *The Oxford handbook of music making and leisure* (pp. 61–80). New York: Oxford University Press.

DeNora, T. (2000). *Music in everyday life*. Cambridge: Cambridge University Press.

Deutschland – Land der Ideen. (2010). School of rock – Schüler rocken die Region. Retrieved from: https://www.land-der-ideen.de/365-orte/preistraeger/school-rock [Accessed 6 November 2014].

European Higher Education Area (2015). How does the Bologna process work? Retrieved from: http://www.ehea.info/article-details.aspx?ArticleId=5 [Accessed 23 September 2015].

Folkestad, G. (2006). Formal and informal learning situations or practices vs formal and informal ways of learning. *British Journal of Music Education, 23*(2), 135–145.

Gaunt, H. & Papageorgi, I. (2010). Music in universities and conservatoires. In S. Hallam & A. Creech (Eds.), *Music education in the 21st century in the United Kingdom: Achievements, analysis and aspirations* (pp. 260–278). London: Institute of Education.

Green, L. 2002. *How popular musicians learn: A way ahead for music education*. Farnham: Ashgate.

Gullberg, A-K. (2010). Boomtown music education – An introduction. In C.F. Thorgersen & S. Karlsen (Eds.), *Music, innovation and education: Festschrift for Sture Brändström* (pp. 123–143). Piteå: Luleå University of Technology – Department of Music and Media.

Hallam, S. & Gaunt, H. (2012). *Preparing for success: A practical guide for young musicians*. London: Institute of Education.

Jank, W. (Ed.) (1996). *Schulmusik – ein Studium im Umbruch*. Mannheim: Palatium-Verlag.

Jank, W. (2005). Grundlagen und Bestandsaufnahmen. In W. Jank (Ed.), *Musik-Didaktik Praxishandbuch für die Sekundarstufe I und II* (pp. 9–68). Berlin: Cornelsen.

Kulturkreis der deutschen Wirtschaft. (2012). AKS-Award 2012. Retrieved from: http://www.kulturkreis.eu/index.php?option=com_content&task=blogcategory&id=430&Itemid=558 [Accessed 6 November 2014].

Lebler, D. (2007). Student-as-master? Reflections on a learning innovation in popular music pedagogy. *International Journal of Music Education, 25*(3), 205–221.

Parkinson, T. & Smith, G.D. (2015). Towards an epistemology of authenticity in higher popular music education. *Action, criticism, and theory for music education, 14*(1), 93–127.

Partti, H. (2012). *Learning from cosmopolitan digital musicians: Identity, musicianship, and changing values in (in)formal music communities*. Helsinki: Sibelius Academy.

Radolko, H.P., Schäffner, A., Limberg, A., & Dannecker, E. (Eds.) (2010). *Kultur 2020 – Kunstpolitik für Baden-Württemberg*. Stuttgart: Ministerium für Wissenschaft, Forschung und Kunst Baden-Württemberg.

Rolle, C. (2010). Über Didaktik Populärer Musik. Gedanken zur Un-Unterrichtbarkeit aus der perspektive ästhetischer Bildung. In J. Terhag & G. Maas (Eds.), *Zwischen Rockklassikern und Eintagsfliegen – 50 Jahre Populäre Musik in der Schule* (pp. 206–215). Oldershausen: Lugert Verlag.

Rundell, M. (Ed.) (2002). *Macmillan English dictionary for advanced learners*. Oxford: Macmillan Education.

Schwarz, A. (2015). *Pop macht Schule – Neue Wege zur Vermittlung von Popmusik*. Mainz: Schott.

Smith, G.D. (2013). Seeking "success" in popular music. *Music Education Research International, 6*, 26–37.

Smith, G.D. & Shafighian, A. (2013). Creative space and the "silent power of traditions" in popular music performance education. In P. Burnard (Ed.), *Developing creativities in higher music education: International perspectives and practices* (pp. 256–267). London: Routledge.

Terhag, J. (2000). Zwischen oraler Tradierung und medialen Lebenswelten. *Populäre Musik und Pädagogik, 3*, 8–20.

Wallbaum, C. (2006). Das Exemplarische in musikalisch-ästhetischer Bildung – Ästhetische Praxen, Urphänomene, Kulturen – Ein Versuch. *Polyästhetik im 21. Jahrhundert – 24. Polyaisthesis-Symposion*, 99–124.

Wallbaum, C. (2008). Zur ästhetisch-kulturellen Bildung mit Stimme. In A. Lehmann-Wermser & A. Niessen (Eds.), *Aspekte des Singens – Ein Studienbuch* (pp. 23–110). Augsburg: Wießner-Verlag.

Wickström, D.-E. (2015). Von Get Well Soon zu Hinterland – Strategien zur Reaktion auf Bedürfnisse von MusikerInnen und Märkten in der Curriculumsentwicklung künstlerischer Studiengänge. In M. Ahlers (Ed.), *Popmusik-Vermittlung – Zwischen Schule, Hochschule und Beruf* (pp. 335–370). Münster, Berlin: Lit.

19
Musical listening
Teaching studio production in an academic institution

Eirik Askerøi and André Viervoll

> In the studio, technical decisions are aesthetic, aesthetic decisions are technical, and all such decisions are musical.
> —(Frith & Zagorski-Thomas, 2012, p. 3)

Introduction

As indicated by Frith and Zagorski-Thomas, above, a producer/engineer must exceed basic expectations regarding technical competence. S/he needs to know how the equipment works and when to use what, including which microphones to set up, where to place them in relation to the given sound source, and what preamps may be the most suitable for a specific job. All of these choices (and a great many more), therefore, have implications for a range of aesthetic preferences, and the producer/engineer must remain vigilant in this regard, whatever the context. Studio production and engineering are not just about making the right technical decisions but also about remaining aware of their potential aesthetic consequences.

In much scholarly literature on record production practice, there seems to be an imbalance in focusing on technical knowhow. For example, a range of books (Eargle, 2001; Huber & Williams, 1999; Izhaki, 2012; Moylan, 2007; Owsinski, 2005) deal with microphone techniques, complex technicalities related to mixing and mastering and so on. Some work has also been done to align these technicalities with different kinds of listening. In *Audio Production and Critical Listening*, Jason Corey describes technical ear training as "a type of perceptual learning focused on timbral, dynamic and spatial attributes of sound as they relate to studio production" (Corey, 2010, p. 5). While this is a useful delineation of certain engineer attributes, ear training itself is a technical rather than an aesthetic aspect of the craft. There are studies within the field of popular musicology (Doyle, 2005; Lacasse, 2000; Moore, 2005; Wicke, 2009) that look at the complex relationship between recording technologies and their potential effects on musical output. There is, however, little existing literature connecting the practical side of production to these potential effects.

The aim of this chapter is to establish a case for teaching and learning what we refer to as *musical listening* as a potential inroad to bridge the gap between practical and analytical studies of popular music, and therefore to teaching music production. As suggested in the title, we draw on our experience in teaching studio production in academic institutions, where studio production classes are taught alongside popular music studies, popular musicology and pedagogy, providing students with an interdisciplinary grounding in popular music. Building on this interdisciplinarity, musical listening is about understanding music on (at least) two levels at the same time. On the one hand, a studio production context requires the ability to discern the technicalities required to produce a piece of music. On the other hand, producers are also expected to be sensitive to the potential effects of their choices. In short, then, and in line with Frith and Zagorski-Thomas's (2012) observation (above), we suggest musical listening as a means of coupling the technical with the aesthetic in order to help students focus *musically* on producing music.

Listening as a component of record production is mostly about the ability to make quick, qualified and aesthetically sound decisions. As Mike Howlett puts it, constant evaluation is a crucial part of the recording process – an evaluation that is necessarily based on emotional response:

> For the producer, trusting this emotional response is a quintessential function. The confidence to say, "I like this one", is at the heart of a producer's role. The same critical function is applied at virtually every stage of the recording process – from the decision that a particular backing track performance has the right feeling and energy, to the approval of a guitar solo, and, of course, the sound of the various instruments coming through the monitors, all come back to the producer, who must make that judgment.
>
> *(Howlett, 2007, p. 3)*

The ability to say "I like this one" is, however, based on a certain skill set, the skill set of the producer. We propose musical listening to be a crucial part of this skill set, and, as such, central to learning music production. As grounding for our further argument, we offer the following working definition of the term *musical listening* as it is used in this article:

> *Musical listening is the ability to listen to a recording and through that listening dissect a production into parts, both musically and technically, and at the same time maintain a focus on the aesthetics of the production as a whole.*

The engineering producer

What, then, is a producer? After all, even producers of renown seem unsure of the scope of activity and set of expectations involved in what they do. Brian Eno, for example, who is credited as producer for Robert Fripp, U2, Talking Heads, Coldplay and a vast array of others, states:

> Being a "producer" – my frequent job description – introduces a whole new set of complications. First of all, no one really knows what the job description means. Is it the guy who sits in the corner of the control room grinning encouragingly and chopping cocaine, or is it Phil Spector, who writes the music, hires the musicians, grooms the vocalists, invents the sound, designs the image and then marries the lead singer? Somewhere between these extremes is a vague cloud of activities that get credited on record covers "produced by . . ."
>
> *(Eno, 1996, p. 393ff)*

As Virgil Moorefield observes, the roles associated with the producer have expanded vastly since the role came into existence:

> The places one may expect to find the producer have become more and more inclusive, ranging from sitting at the back of the control room (the fifties), to moving up to the board (the sixties), to taking over the job of the composer (the seventies and eighties), to becoming the performer onstage (the nineties).
>
> *(Moorefield, 2005, p. 109)*

Moorefield's generalization reveals an important aspect of this position's development: rather than a linear change in roles, the producer has gradually taken on a range of added roles. This development has arisen partly as a result of the technical revolution in the industry, whereby 'anyone' now can afford decent recording equipment (Bell, 2015). But does this actually mean that anyone can also be a producer?

Sylvia Massy, who has worked with Johnny Cash, Tool, Prince, System of a Down and a host of others, outlines different types of producer:

> The broad definition of a Record Producer is someone responsible for making sure a project gets done within time and budget constraints. There are also 3 sub-types of Producers. The musician/producer, like the Neptunes or Rodney Jerkins, the engineer/producer like Jack Joseph Puig or Nigel Godrich, and the fan/producer, like Rick Rubin and Jimmy Iovine. The musician/producer usually creates all the music and often writes the songs, bringing in vocal talent to front the project. The engineer/producer will craft the sound of an existing project, often using equipment and technique to create the magic in the studio. The fan/producer may never actually touch the console,

but will help choose the songs and guide the project by bringing the right people together.

(Massy, 2014)

Massy's 'fan/producer' (and presumably Eno's 'cocaine chopper') would not appear to be expected to touch the console, but even this producer must boast a high degree of *musical knowledge* to be able to do the work. At the same time, given the current availability of music production tools and the vagaries of teaching music production, we must educate producers with both aesthetic and practical knowledge. Although the commercial music business and the available technology seem to be in constant development, the need for people who can use the available equipment creatively and not least musically seems to be constant. Recording technology is, after all, not merely a means to record music; it has in so many ways also become a musical instrument (Lacasse, 2000, p. 15). We therefore seek to educate the *engineering producer*, and, from here on, all references to 'producers' will indicate this particular profession/role.

Learning the 'tradition'

Historically, studio production and engineering have not been taught in academic institutions. Recently, the studio/academic environments have merged in unprecedented ways, such as with the initiative at Abbey Road Studios in London, which, since September 2015, has offered a year-long training programme leading to an "Advanced Diploma in Music Production and Sound Engineering" (Abbey Road Institute, 2015). Another example of studio/education hybrid is the UK's Academy of Music and Sound, where degree programmes are taught between college buildings and local professional recording facilities (Academy of Music and Sound, 2015). Traditionally, however, studio production and engineering have been learned in the studio itself, through master/apprentice relationships in which the student/assistant would typically start off as a so-called runner.

Nick Raskulinecz, who was hired as a runner at Sound City Studios (allegedly because he was good at making guacamole!), explains, "As a runner, you know, I would go in there and empty the ashtrays and dust the console and vacuum. And that's when I started to learn the board" (Raskulinecz in Grohl, 2013). On the one hand, the assistant would come to understand the technical equipment and its various applications through observation, and eventually attempting recordings during spare time. On the other hand, and of equal importance, he or she would also experience how the various producers and technicians responded to different situations that arose during production, musically, emotionally and practically.

In this way, producers will need a wide range of skills, most of which could be categorized as 'tacit' – that is, unspoken or experience-based – knowledge (Polanyi, 1967). While one of course could not be expected to acquire the level of depth of knowledge acquired over, say, 20 years of experience, during a single course of study, our track record with teaching studio production leads us to believe that by engaging with the historical as well as the practical tradition of studio production through musical listening, students are able to acquire a solid base for further artistic development as producers. Whereas a jazz performance student might learn the relevant tradition by transcribing and analyzing solos, because the phrasing of Charlie Parker represents a crucial conduit to the characteristics of be-bop, for the engineering producer there is a similar relationship between listening to recorded music and recording music, and we would argue that intense, focused listening competence is in fact a fundamental part of working in a recording studio. Moore argues:

> As listeners, although we must recognize and exteriorize our grounds for cognizing the text, this does not imply that we will all do it in the same way. How we do it will depend on the style to which we assign that text, and our competence within that style.
>
> *(2001, p. 17)*

In her seminal study of the learning processes of popular musicians, Green (2002) makes useful distinctions between *purposive*, *attentive* and *distracted* listening. While attentive and distracted listening cover most daily interactions with music, purposive is another matter altogether:

> [It is] the sort of listening that any musician would employ when, for example, learning to play an exact copy or cover of a song, making a mental or written note of the harmonies, the form or other properties of the song in order to be able to use them in another context, undertaking an analytic exercise and so on.
>
> *(Green, 2002, p. 24)*

While Green here concentrates on (performer, as opposed to producer) musicians, her point holds for producers as well – the more focused one's listening, the more one takes back to one's own practice. If one relies solely or mostly on the literature capturing technical knowhow, one likely misses out on the unspoken knowledge to be gained from the typical master/apprentice model, which involves, among other things, shared and purposive listening.

How the music sounds

Questions concerning how music sounds have been posed from various angles within the field of popular music studies for more than four decades, including the following: For whom does the music sound the way it does? How is this sound actually produced? To what extent are listeners affected by non-musical aspects when listening to the music in question? Or, as Philip Tagg puts it: "Why and how does who communicate what to whom and with what effect?" (1982, p. 3). These sorts of questions are highly relevant when one attempts to unpack music's potential meanings within its sociocultural contexts, and are also salient, if more sound-specific, in the arguably narrower context of the recording studio.

Producing vocals, for example, is a delicate affair at every level. What works for one singer may not (and probably will not) work for another. Flexibility and communication are key factors here, and as an engineering producer, one must acquire a repertoire of techniques that go beyond the strictly musical, including "emotional labour" (Ward and Watson, 2016) and a host of other skills and approaches. For instance, Sylvia Massy describes her approach:

> I have a whole bag of tricks to get what I want out of a vocalist. I'll often distract them in ridiculous ways to get their mind off of their throat. Tasks like "pretend you are swimming", or "jump up and down", or "run around the block three times and come back and sing". Once I had a singer dress up in a wedding dress to get her magic vocal performance. On the System of a Down record, I had Serge hang upside down and scream. His face turned bright red and his eyes started to pop out. Almost killed the guy . . . so I stopped doing that!
>
> *(Massy, 2014)*

For Massy, a good vocal performance seems to be closely connected to the singer's physical presence and condition in the recording situation. Beyond focusing on the voice as a sonic medium, Massy orchestrates calculated physical distractions to complement her highly developed technical skills in order to produce the best performance from the vocalist. This compensates for the rather unnatural circumstances of vocal recording while also acknowledging that the voice and vocal performance are closely connected to the body, and that a sense of bodily presence in the voice can act as an effective bearer of meaning for the listener (Barthes, 1977; Hawkins, 2009; Steinskog, 2010).

Another example of an extra-musical approach – although practical and reliant on a high degree of technical method of vocal production – is Mike Howlett's notion of a "familiar place" (2007, p. 1). Howlett describes a process of vocal recording that attempts to account for the rather constrained conditions of the studio setting. In most recording sessions, the vocals are often 'laid down' ('tracked' or recorded) as the last element in the process. In many cases, this puts an enormous pressure on the vocalist (2007)[1]. As an alternative approach to this, Howlett's method basically involves having already prepared for vocal recording (microphones, preamps, compressor and EQ settings) at the start of a given recording session:

> In this way the vocalist returns often to what becomes a familiar environment – the sound in the headphones, the position in the studio, and the relationship with the producer through the glass – through repetition all become

---

1 Howlett describes this pressure as ". . .the intimidating effect that pressing the record button might have – by the implied demand that now is the moment to produce the best that the artist can give" (Howlett, 2007, p. 1). Howlett explains that this is also widely known as "red light syndrome" (ibid).

a comfortable place. By removing the imperative to deliver a final take the artist feels less pressured and can feel able to test ideas and ways of treating the song.

(Howlett, 2007, p. 2)

Given that many listeners relate especially to the lyrics and the singer's delivery of them, the producer must be able to coax out (or even cajole) the best performance possible (Ward & Watson, 2016). Howlett's familiar place sets the stage for doing so.

Unnatural as it might seem to an outsider, performing in the studio is a situation that one adjusts to with time and experience. For how they play matters, despite the conveniences and possibilities of complex post-production editing using advanced editing tools such as Beat Detective and Melodyne,[2] and to a large degree it is the producer's job to make them perform well. In short, one should never underestimate the value of a good performance – that is where it all begins. At the same time, decent equipment and relevant acoustic surroundings also play a part. An example of an almost dogmatic relationship to recording equipment and musical instruments is Mark Ronson's recording of Amy Winehouse's single "Rehab" from *Back to Black* (2006) with the New York–based soul band The Dap Kings. This particular track features a 1960s funk and soul sensibility, subtly paired with certain more contemporary features of hip-hop and modern soul. Mixing engineer Tom Elmhirst recalls:

> They recorded drums, piano, guitar and bass all together in one room. The drums were recorded with one microphone, and there's lots of spill between the instruments, which was great. . . . It is definitely a nod to '60s soul wall-of-sound production. For me, the mix had to have a contemporary feel to it as well.
>
> *(Tingen, 2007, p. 2)*

Ronson's role as producer here is manifested around making clear aesthetic choices: the choice of musicians, how and where to record them and, most significantly, determining how these choices would construct a distinct sonic environment for Winehouse's *persona* (Moore, 2005). In mixing the track, then, Elmhirst was responsible for keeping the 1960s references from the recording session intact, while at the same time adding what he refers to as "a contemporary feel" (in Tingen, 2007).

The risk of creating a false musical binary between vocals and instrumentals is that we are wandering into one of what Hawkins calls the potential "quagmires" (2001, p. 13) of popular music research – that is, a focus on some musical details at the expense of the musical whole, to say nothing of the wider context within which the music is experienced. Hawkins, writing for an academic audience, argues that any interpretation incorporates a "balance between the autonomy

---

2 In short, Beat Detective allows musicians/producers to work with the rhythmic part of an audio track, while Melodyne is more focused on melodic and harmonic parts of an audio track.

of the detail and the discourse that describes the whole" (Hawkins, 2001, p. 4). We would argue that this is as true for engineering producers as it is for critics and scholars. We believe that the production student needs the ability to dissect music into its parts *without* losing sight of the big picture. A bass player would, for example, listen to recordings to understand how the bass can relate to the drums and other instrumentalists; a producer does the same, so as to work with the bass player and discuss such things as 'leaning back' or 'pushing forward' in a given passage of a song. The producer also needs to learn to listen so as to compare the frequency content of the bass drum signal to that of the bass guitar. In other words, the producer needs to relate the effect(s) of these choices to larger aspects of the music, in the context of the overall aesthetics of the production.

Teaching musical listening

As we have seen so far, becoming an engineering producer involves a complex set of skills. The producer must have a fundamental understanding of how to place a microphone, create a foldback mix[3] and so on. The producer must also understand styles of, aspects of and approaches to music at many levels; one has to know almost as much about songwriting as a songwriter, almost as much about arranging as an arranger and almost as much about instruments as the instrumentalists. At the same time, one has to keep an eye on – or, more accurately, have an ear for – the potential implications of effects processing, including, for example, gated reverb on a snare drum, the pronounced auto-tune effect now heard on a lot of modern recordings or the 'slap-back' echo of the 1950s rockabilly sound.

In guiding our students towards the ability to listen musically, we therefore suggest a process consisting of three main steps: 1. Re-production: learning the 'tradition' by reproducing existing recordings. 2. Re-flection: applying reference tracks as means for comparison and reflection upon choices made in the first step. 3. Re-contextualization: applying the knowledge and experience from the former two steps as a creative basis for their own recordings. It should be noted at this stage that these three steps are not intended as a linear path. Rather, they must be seen as components in what Jerome Bruner (1960) has conceptualized as a spiral curriculum wherein a main idea is repeated several times, but in an increasingly advanced form.

1. Re-production

The purpose of re-producing a piece of existing music is that the student should learn the craft and eventually acquire a sonic repertoire that derives specifically from a musical understanding of the interaction between technology and

---

3 The foldback system represents for a studio setting what is known as the monitor system in a live setting. A foldback mix is one or more separate mixes that are sent back to performers so that they can hear themselves in a studio recording situation.

performance. People without significant practical experience of working as a producer would not be able to describe or explain finer technical points of a recorded musical artefact. It would be unreasonable to expect an inexperienced individual to distinguish between, for instance, a Shure SM57 and a Neumann U47[4] if they had not heard those microphones being used in isolation in the studio. Testing the two microphones against each other in recording vocals, so-called A/B-testing, however, can give the student a clearer picture of the individual characteristics of the microphones, and hopefully also an idea of when to choose one over the other.

In the context of a spiral curriculum, the level of the re-productions should rise proportionally with a gradually increasing complexity of the recording session. A re-production at 'beginner's level' for example, could be restricted to programming the song in question in a MIDI-sequencer. On a more advanced level one starts including effects processing and audio recording. At the most advanced level, the reproduction could be undertaken by mic'ing up a full band in a recording studio. If necessary, this way of thinking would also allow for the teacher to test the student and decide on what level they should start off.

2. Re-flection

The second step in our suggested continuum is an analytical one. Reflecting upon one's own production in light of the original version opens for a range of possible inroads to the production. "What have I managed to reproduce? What have I missed or not been able to reproduce? Which elements provide the music with its characteristics?" When we encourage students to reflect critically on the choices made in their own re-productions, we allow them to gain confidence in making artistic choices. This confidence would normally take longer to develop as a runner in the traditional studio apprenticeship model, because one would not so easily be afforded the opportunity of hands-on experience with the equipment.

Returning to Amy Winehouse's "Rehab", this is an example where the borrowed sonic specificities gain a narrative purpose by combining the historical codification of vintage instruments, recording techniques and playing styles with more contemporary mixing techniques. Askerøi has conceptualized this mechanism *sonic markers* – "musical codes that have been historically grounded through a specific context, and that, through their appropriation, serve a range of narrative purposes in recorded music" (2013, p. 17). In other words, the sonic specificities of the music occupy a great deal of the producer's attention in the studio context.

3. Re-contextualization

In a recording session, one way to make sense of what is being recorded, and thus to strike a balance between the practical, technical details and the overall musical

---

4 Both the microphones mentioned here are widely used in recording contexts, but they have very different sonic footprints, and therefore also very different uses.

whole, is to borrow elements from existing recordings. Of course, the extent to which such borrowings take place will vary from session to session, and all music is in one way or another contingent on some form of borrowing in order to be recognized as music at all. At the same time, if one attempts to reproduce the sound of a previously recorded song, the goal should not be the reproduction itself but the possibility of thereby increasing or enhancing one's compositional or engineering repertoire. Using reference tracks when recording music, then, one must always remember that the *effect* of a piece of music depends on both who the performer is and how the music is performed. Constructing sonic markers through record production could thus be a process that can appear almost coincidentally. At the same time, we strongly believe that an awareness of the narrative potential of musical sound in a recording is a valuable compositional asset for the producer that can be learned and trained through musical listening.

When artists turn up in the studio with their pre-productions[5] and a more or less vague vision of where they want to take their music (as is not at all unusual), it is often up to the producer to point or guide them in a clear direction, and to do so quickly and responsively to the artists' wishes, needs and demands. The producer must be able to make qualified choices for the good of the project while at the same time preserving the artists' agency and confidence. In this way, the producer also needs a certain level of social competence in order to relate to another creative force in the studio, particularly when everyone seems to need something different to be at his or her best (Ward & Watson, 2016). The only way to develop this skill is to interact with other people, in the studio, working on music.

Teaching studio production, we have experienced that the social side of the producer's repertoire can be trained by focusing musically on the production process. The ability to make qualified choices for the song in question should, more often than not, be prioritized over stylistic or technological aspects as such. We have found that feedback on *how* one performs according to *what* one communicates within a musical whole is often easier to tackle than critique of the performance as such. The question of why a particular piece of music works the way it does is undoubtedly problematic and open-ended, in that it tends to produce a range of possible answers. The point, nevertheless, is to provoke students to look beyond the bounds of studio technicalities. By asking students to start an imaginary conversation with their potential listeners, we are constructing a bridge between practical and academic approaches to studio production. The primary goal of studio production is, after all, a musical, or aesthetic, one (Frith & Zagorski-Thomas, 2012, p. 3). And when one's goal is to teach music production to students, one must keep the practical, tangible outcome – the recording – foremost in one's mind.

---

5 The *Oxford English Dictionary* defines pre-production as "Work done on a product, especially film or broadcast programme, before full-scale production begins" (Oxford Dictionaries, 2015). In music, pre-production would refer to a home studio recording of the music, which would equal what was earlier referred to as a demo or demo tape. Pre-production is thus a healthy way of preparing for a studio recording.

Concluding remarks

In this chapter we have argued that, in order to become an engineering producer, a student needs not only a vast amount of technical knowledge and practical experience, but also a great depth of musical knowledge and understanding – as well as other emotional and social skills. In practice, musical listening of course overlaps with practical training and technical skills. Our argument, though, is that keeping these elements largely separated for teaching purposes offers teachers as well as students three inroads to a fuller understanding of music production: the technical, the aesthetic and the musical. If, as Frith and Zagorski-Thomas (2012) suggest, technical and aesthetic decisions in the studio are in fact musical *altogether*, then musical listening works well as a conceptual backdrop and practical approach for teaching and learning studio production. Therefore, by suggesting this perspective and approach, our intention is not to underestimate the high level of technical skills required to produce music, but rather to emphasize that these skills should not be the only, isolated goal of educating, developing and preparing aspiring producers. We therefore argue that technical and practical skills can be complemented by *listening musically* to recordings – pre-existing, and in progress, in real time.

References

Abbey Road Institute. (2015). *Homepage*. Retrieved from: https://abbeyroadinstitute.co.uk/en [Accessed 10 September 2015].
Academy of Music and Sound. (2015). Foundation degree in creative music production. Retrieved from: http://academyofmusic.ac.uk/courses/h-e-courses/full-time-foundation-degree-in-creative-music-production-2yrs/ [Accessed 10 September 2015].
Askerøi, E. (2013). *Reading pop production: Sonic markers and musical identity*. Kristiansand: University of Agder, Kristiansand.
Barthes, R. (1977). The grain of the Voice. In R. Barthes & S. Heath (Eds.), *Image, music, text*. New York, NY: Hill and Wang.
Bell, A.P. (2015). DAW democracy? The dearth of democracy in "playing the studio". *Journal of Music, Technology and Education, 8*(2), 129–146.
Bruner, J.S. (1960). *The process of education*. Cambridge: Harvard University Press.
Corey, J. (2010). *Audio production and critical listening: Technical ear training*. Burlington/Oxford: Focal Press.
Doyle, P. (2005). *Echo and reverb: Fabricating space in popular music recording, 1900–1960*. Middletown, CT: Wesleyan University Press.
Eargle, J. (2001). *The microphone book*. Woburn: Focal Press.
Eno, B. (1996). *A year with swollen appendices*. London: Faber and Faber.
Frith, S. & Zagorski-Thomas, S. (2012). *The art of record production: An introductory reader for a new academic field*. Farnham: Ashgate.
Green, L. (2002). *How popular musicians learn: A way ahead for music education*. Aldershot: Ashgate.
Grohl, D. (2013). *Sound city*. San Francisco: Roswell Films.
Hawkins, S. (2001). Musicological quagmires in popular music: Seeds of detailed conflict. *Popular Musicology Online, 1*.
Hawkins, S. (2009). *The British pop dandy: Masculinity, popular music and culture*. Farnham: Ashgate.

Howlett, M. (2007). Fixing the volatile: Studio vocal performance techniques. Paper read at the 3rd Art of Record Production Conference, 10–11 December 2007, at Queensland University of Technology, Brisbane. Retrieved from: http://eprints.qut.edu.au/33275/ [Accessed 4 August 2015].

Huber, D.M. & Williams, P. (1999). *Professional microphone techniques*. Vallejo: MixBooks.

Izhaki, R. (2012). *Mixing audio: Concepts, practices and tools*. Second ed. London: Focal Press.

Lacasse, S. (2000). *Listen to my voice: The evocative power of vocal staging in recorded rock music and other forms of vocal expression*. Liverpool: Liverpool University Press.

Massy, S. (2014). *Q&A with Sylvia Massy*. Retrieved from: https://www.gearslutz.com/board/q-sylvia-massy/ [Accessed 8 January 2015].

Moore, A.F. (2001). *Rock: The primary text: Developing a musicology of rock*. Second ed. Aldershot: Ashgate.

Moore, A.F. (2005). The persona-environment relation in recorded song. *Music Theory Online, 11*(4). Retrieved from: http://www.mtosmt.org/issues/mto.05.11.4/mto.05.11.4.moore.html [Accessed 10 September 2015].

Moylan, W. (2007). *Understanding and crafting the mix: The art of recording*. Second ed. Oxford: Focal Press.

Owsinski, B. (2005). *The recording engineer's handbook*. Boston: Thomson Course Technology.

Oxford Dictionaries. (2015). Pre-production. Oxford: Oxford University Press.

Polanyi, M. (1967). *The tacit dimension*. London: Routledge.

Steinskog, E. (2010). Queering Cohen: Cover versions and subversions of identity. In G. Plasketes (Ed.), *Play it again: Cover songs in popular music*. Farnham: Ashgate.

Tagg, P. (1982). Analysing popular music: Theory, method and practice. *Popular Music, 2*, 37–67.

Tingen, P. (2007). Secrets of the mixing engineers: Tom Elmhirst. *Sound on sound*. Retrieved from: http://www.soundonsound.com/sos/aug07/articles/insidetrack_0807.htm [Accessed 10 September 2015].

Ward, J. & Watson, A. (2016). FX, drugs and rock "n" roll: Engineering the emotional space of the recording studio. In R. Mantie & G.D. Smith (Eds.), *The Oxford handbook of music making and leisure* (pp. 451–468). New York, NY: Oxford University Press.

Wicke, P. (2009). The art of phonography: Sound, technology and music. In D.B. Scott (Ed.), *The Ashgate research companion to popular musicology*. Farnham: Ashgate.

20
Popular music and Modern Band principles

Bryan Powell and Scott Burstein

Introduction

The inclusion of popular music in United States (US) public school music education classrooms has become increasingly common in the 21st century. Recent literature has outlined the variety of popular music programs in the US in an attempt to position current efforts to include popular music education in the US among the history of this movement (Krikun, chapter 4, this volume; Powell et al., 2015). An increasing body of academic work promotes the need for inclusion of popular music pedagogies in the curriculum of universities training future music educators (Jones, 2008; Mantie, 2013; Wang & Humphreys, 2009; Williams & Randles, chapter 5, this volume). The National Core Arts Standards – a conceptual framework for arts learning, adopted by the National Association for Music Education in the US for K–12 schools (mandatory public education) (NCAS, 2014) – recommend music education based on creativity and improvisation, as well as a focus on iconic notation alongside standard notation. The College Music Society's Task Force on the Undergraduate Music Major (2014; a cadre of CMS members assembled to rethink music teacher education in higher education) also pointed to the need for an expansion of traditional music departments from classical and jazz performance-based ensembles to include classes that give students options in modern music career development, pointing often to the inclusion of popular music performance, composition, improvisation and cultural understanding (i.e. popular music studies; see Hooper, chapter 13, this volume) (CMS, 2014).

Despite the increased presence of popular music education at primary and secondary levels, American 'pre-service' music teacher education programmes face many roadblocks to establishing classes courses in popular music, in large part because those teaching future teachers were trained in school by educators inexperienced in popular music styles and pedagogy (Green, 2008; Price, 2006; Purves, 2002). Much of the mention of popular music classes in public schools refers to isolated case studies of standout programs around the country, many of which are not scalable or replicable due to instrument limitations and teacher expertise (Clements, 2010). There seems to be a tendency for much of the existing discourse about popular music education to lean heavily on the informal learning model (Jaffurs, 2004; Karlsen & Väkevä, 2012), which while rich in theory is difficult to utilize in the US model of music classrooms that contain large student numbers with an attendant logistical inability to have small groups each rehearsing in the same music room. Most of the current popular music education approaches in music teacher education lean heavily on teaching the important and necessary key concepts that distinguish facilitation of the learning of popular music from teaching traditionally included musics, instead of using a blended approach that can be utilized in a wide range of settings (Heuser, 2014). These concepts include learning music through recordings instead of staff notation, performing on traditional rock instruments, working with repertoire that students have a role in choosing and introducing technology through, for example, iPad ensembles (Davis & Blair, 2011; Williams, 2014). While these are great strides towards a fuller popular music strand of education, they do not address how to teach a large class of students to play popular music on modern instruments in order to create and improvise utilizing the styles of music that they enjoy and experience day-to-day in their own musical, cultural world(s).

Teachers in a typical music class face many barriers to teaching beyond just their own knowledge of the subject material. According to Green (personal communication, February 4, 2011) ideally teachers teaching popular music in the classroom would have access to small rooms comprising rock band set-ups as well as technology workstations complete with current recording, engineering and music-making software. These teachers would act not as instructors but as facilitators and advisors, wandering freely from room to room, checking in on the students learning informally in small groups and creating new music, free from fear of capricious administrators who may see this instruction as unstructured or unsupervised (D'Amore & Smith, 2016). These issues help illuminate the practicality of ensembles such as concert band, orchestra, marching band, choir and jazz band in the contemporary teaching environment; these classes are improved with an increased number of student participants and high student-to-teacher ratios in a system that constantly promotes larger class sizes. The larger class sizes, however, are not ideal for conventional popular music ensembles. It is for this reason that many of the larger school districts in the United States (including New York City and Los Angeles) now offer courses in Modern Band. This chapter outlines some of the core values of Modern Band as defined by Little Kids Rock (LKR). In so doing, the authors hope to explain the rationale behind LKR's approach to training teachers to incorporate Modern Band in their classrooms.

Modern Band

So what precisely is Modern Band? Modern Band is a stream of music education that has two simple guiding attributes: repertoire and instrumentation. The repertoire is what might typically be thought of as 'popular music' (the term *popular* being used to mean 'of the people' – in this case, 'of the students'). The term 'popular music' has been problematized in research literature (Gammond, 1991; Smith, 2014), and since popular music is always changing, we use the term to encompass a broad scope of music characterized by Bowman (2004) as having at least some of the following characteristics: "(a) breadth of intended appeal; (b) mass mediation and commodity character; (c) amateur engagement; (d) continuity with everyday concerns; (e) informality; (f) here and-now pragmatic use and utility; (g) appeal to embodied experience; and (h) emphasis upon process" (pp. 36–37). Modern Band encompasses broad genres of music (such as electric dance music) and more narrow genres such as djent, reggaeton, banda and shoegaze. Including these musics in the popular music category perhaps implies a level of commercial success that may not apply to all of the genres mentioned. Recent scholarship (Frith, 1998; Smith, 2014) debates whether 'popular music' presupposes or even has to include commercial viability or success. Therefore, the repertoire consideration of Modern Band is student-centred first and foremost, reflecting the music that students listen to on their own and with others.

Music classrooms incorporating Modern Band help to "bridge the gap" (Rodriguez, 2004) between the music that children experience in schools and the music they experience in their communities. Through focusing on music that is familiar to students, Modern Band allows students "to see themselves reflected in the curriculum. By validating and leveraging their cultural capital, (music educators) can forge stronger bonds between traditionally marginalized students and the schools that serve them" (Modern Band, 2014).

The second consideration in Modern Band is instrumentation. Just as orchestras and jazz bands have a typical instrumentation, so do Modern Bands: guitar, bass, keyboards, drums, vocals and technology. Much like orchestras allow for the addition and subtraction of certain instruments (e.g. adding an English horn or a harp), Modern Band allows for adding and subtracting instruments such as ukulele or traditional jazz or concert band instruments. Modern Band is thus arguably a unique ensemble concept that incorporates (indeed, presupposes) popular music and popular music instrumentation, but is not strictly defined by them.

Music as a second language and Modern Band

US music educators teaching Modern Band have become more prevalent in the last decade, particularly in larger urban school districts such as New York City and Los Angeles. The non-profit organization Little Kids Rock has trained over 2000 public school teachers in 31 cities and 127 school districts in the US, providing curriculum, pedagogy and instruments to schools in order to offer Modern Band courses. Little Kids Rock provides teacher training and a gift of popular music instruments (guitar, bass, drums, keyboards and technology) to be used in the classroom for those teachers who participate in the training.

The core pedagogical principle employed by LKR is "Music as a Second Language" (MSL). Developed by LKR founder Dave Wish, a former first-grade ESL (English as a Second Language) teacher, MSL focuses on learning music in the way second languages are sometimes learned. MSL is based on the principles of

Stephen Krashen's *Second Language Acquisition* (1982), and likens the development of music knowledge to that of the development of speech. While LKR uses the title "Music as a Second Language" when describing its approach to teaching music, this moniker is less about music as a communicative tool (language) and more about music learning. As such, Music *Learning* as Second Language *Learning* (MLSLL) could arguably be a more accurate description.

The MSL approach holds that when exploring how students are exposed to music education educators should look to how children first learn to speak. Between the ages of eight months and two years of age, children begin trying to imitate the sounds of the language that they hear all around them. Parents delight as their babies start to babble and to use 'baby talk'. This babbling is an approximation of true speech. What sounds like 'nonsensical' syllables are actually sounds derived from the language that the baby is trying to speak. As babies babble, adults babble back, completing the approximation of a conversation.

Music, like language, is best learned in conversation with others who have already achieved some level of fluency and in such a way as allows for uncorrected musicking. While some approaches to musical learning, like Suzuki, for instance, start with music-making, often (school) music education takes an opposite course. When students arrive at school, they usually have not had the opportunity to play with musical instruments. Instead of first teaching children to produce music on instruments through imitation and approximation, the concept of 'musicianship' in US music curricula is often closely tied to competency with notation and its implicit underlying analysis (Swanwick, 1994; Williams & Randles, chapter 5, this volume). This comparison has implications for how music can be taught. Insofar as it is possible, LKR advocates that music instruction should emulate language instruction. Speech is not best learned as a series of discrete skills mastered out of context, nor is it learned by mastering the alphabet and decoding words. Rather, it is acquired in a meaningful, context-rich environment and with the invaluable assistance of other 'speakers'. A key principle of LKR's approach to music pedagogy, song before sight (or playing music before reading it) is also championed by organizations such as Musical Futures and supported by observations from research into how popular musicians learn (Green, 2002).

Core values of Modern Band

The basic values of LKR's approach to Modern Band are: Comfort Zone, Approximation, Scaffolding, Composition and Improvisation (Modern Band, 2014). These core values are focused on developing musical skills through learning to play familiar music in a way where pupils can be immediately successful. The following sections explore these core values.

'Comfort zone' and the 'affective filter'

Music performance anxiety (MPA) is a widely acknowledged condition for music performers of all ages. It has been studied from physiological (Salmon, 1990), social psychological (Scanlan & Lewthwaite, 1984), developmental psychological (Richard, 1992) and gendered response perspectives (Kenny, 2013; Ryan, 2000, 2004), to name a few. While the phenomenon of MPA has been widely researched, it is rarely discussed in teacher education or the music classroom, leading to a situation in which "teachers observe their students experiencing MPA related to performances, examinations or auditions, but few have the prerequisite skills to manage the condition" (Patston, 2014, p. 85).

Recent studies have found MPA to be an issue for developing musicians as early as third grade (Boucher & Ryan, 2011). Since MPA often starts when a student is young and stays with individuals into their adult life, it is reasonable to conclude that music educators have a critical role in the developmental trajectory of musical anxiety in students. Indeed, Hendricks et al. (2014) demonstrated that teachers can foster emotionally safe learning environments and instil music students with a positive sense of self-belief, creative freedom and purpose. With this in mind, LKR has focused on training teachers to create 'comfort zones' in their music classrooms, which are safe spaces for students to learn, perform and express themselves. LKR's approach to developing safe spaces for learning is greatly influenced by Krashen's (1982) work, in which he develops the affective filter hypothesis postulated by Dulay and Burt (1977), which states that affective factors relate to the second language acquisition process. Krashen claims that learners with high motivation, self-confidence, a good self-image and a low level of anxiety are better equipped for success in second language acquisition. A student's debilitating anxiety, low motivation and low self-esteem can and often do combine to form a 'mental block' – the "affective filter" (Krashen, 1982, p. 13) – that prevents successful second language acquisition.

Applying the affective filter hypothesis to learning music, it is easy to see that music-learning practices that include competitive structures, critical, demeaning or fear-based attempts at motivation and elitist notions of what it means to be a musician can stymie the creation of a safe space for music learning (Hendricks et al., 2014). There are three basic ways in which to lower a student's affective filter and create a comfort zone: engaging their interests, providing a low-anxiety environment and bolstering their self-esteem. Utilizing student-centred music can not only engage students' interests but also show them that their own musical choices and values have merit. One of the best ways to create a low-anxiety environment is by performing in large groups – an easy task in the typically large class sizes found in US music classes. Students often feel more confident learning when surrounded by others, where mistakes can be masked or absorbed and worked on until mastery. Another factor is using 'input plus one', or taking what the student feels comfortable with and introducing only one new element to work on at a time (Krashen, 1982, p. 24). With popular music, this can be done easily, as many songs use very few harmonies and simple 'riffs', making it relatively straightforward for teachers and students to break down the learning of a song into small, comprehensible steps. Finally, a teacher can bolster students' self-esteem by noting the students' individual successes in a non-competitive environment. All of these factors are within reach when the concept of approximation is taken into account.

Approximation

Approximation theory is used in mathematics to understand how functions can best be approximated with simpler functions (De Boor, 1986). In behavioural theory, successive approximation is described as a process whereby a behavioural demonstration most similar to the behaviour to be learned is reinforced and the criteria for reinforcement are gradually increased in complexity to the point that only the desired or goal behaviour is reinforced (Greer & Lundquist, 1976). As it pertains to music education and LKR's pedagogical approach to teaching Modern Band, approximation is best understood as the process by which students create and replicate versions of songs that, while not without flaws, are close enough to the original piece to be both fulfilling and educational for the student. While students' cover versions of songs may not be note-for-note reproductions of the originals, the music educator as part of the learning process embraces the approximation because it allows for the learning of musical concepts, ensemble participation and student enjoyment.

Embracing approximation is closely linked to the previously mentioned practice of creating a safe space for music students. According to Bartel (2004), the observation and study of how children learn language shows that focusing on the positive attempt at speech and continually modelling the desired target is a particularly productive way of encouraging language learners, whereas pointing out incorrect attempts and scolding are not productive. Through the encouragement of approximation, the teacher creates an environment where musical amateurism is embraced. Bowman (2004) pointed out that the root of amateur means 'to love'; i.e. amateurs are individuals who do what they do for the love of it. Promoting a love of music for all children is a central component of teaching music, and creating an environment where approximation is embraced can help lead to a classroom full of musical amateurs (students who engage with music for the love of it). Regelski (2007) stated that "the stigma attached to amateurs, and the cultural pedigree behind [this stigma] are increasingly major problems for the health and well-being of music and music education in society today" (p. 26). However, a growing area of research (Mantie & Smith, 2016) supports the notion that amateurism in the sense intended by Modern Band is a wholly positive notion and practice.

Christopher Small (1998) offered the term *musicking* to encompass the active process that extends to all kinds of musical involvements, interests and actions in society, including and beyond performing music. Similarly, Regelski (2007) utilizes *amateuring*, based on the work of Booth (1999), who defined this as an active, committed, disciplined, enlivening and loving pursuit that is vigorous, demanding and compelling. LKR promotes *amateuring* through embracing approximation. This approach encourages enthusiasm on the part of all students. As Reglski stated, "Study without such enthusiasm – or studies in which such enthusiasm is thwarted by parental pressure or fear of teacher censure – will rarely if ever lead to dedicated amateuring" (2007, p. 30).

Whereas most concert-goers of classical music would be uninterested in attending a concert where the orchestra merely approximated Beethoven or Brahms, the basis of much popular music is re-working and approximating different versions of the same song in a variety of styles. It is for this reason that using approximation to lower the affective filter is so effective in Modern Band classrooms. Once songs are looked at as simple harmonic progressions, students can perform thousands of them after learning a few simple chords. Modifications can be made to simplify chart-toppers for a variety of levels and instrumental combinations, leading to the concept of scaffolding in order to guide students towards a path of progressive steps for a level of participation that is rewarding and educative for students.

Scaffolding – conversations with fluent speakers

Scaffolding is a form of socially mediated learning in which teacher and student constantly adapt their behaviour to one another's behaviour in order to reach a goal (Küpers et al., 2014). From a language acquisition standpoint, scaffolding is how new speakers learn through being surrounded by and conversing with fluent speakers. Language scaffolding is modelled by an infant beginning to learn their first language by hearing the phrases around them and starting to decode their meaning through conversation. This is apparent not only with the very young but also in the way fluent speakers change their vocabulary and tone based on audience; one would speak, for instance, to a group of peers differently than at a job interview or in an academic setting.

Through the lens of MSL, scaffolding is a way to create and/or modify lesson plans to be accessible at a variety of levels of experience, and for students at these levels all to interact at the same time. Therefore, it is not unusual to see a class at a variety of levels performing at once: guitarists who may be playing barre chords sitting next to others strumming open chords, pianists split two to a keyboard with one covering a simpler bass line while another plays inversions of chords, multiple percussionists playing everything from basic back-beats to more complex syncopated patterns. It is due to the approximation factor that scaffolding becomes applicable and desirable, giving beginning students models to aspire to while affording space for more advanced students to maintain their interest. This is something that once again can work fluidly in a Modern Band classroom but may not be advisable in the traditional US music classroom, where many ensembles are geared towards either beginners or advanced students, but clearly not to both.

Composition

Traditional approaches to music education in the US (concert band, marching band, jazz band, choir and orchestra) contain very little composition (Beckstead, 2001). Although composition is listed in the United States National Arts Standards, when students are taught solely to read notes off of a method book page the focus becomes reading and interpreting the compositions of others, not composing music of their own (Williams & Randles, chapter 5, this volume). Beckstead has argued that "historically, composition's most conspicuous attribute in music education is its absence, especially in the public school setting" (2001, p. 44).

Composition in public school music education is often stymied by the teacher's perception that students must first learn Western musical notation as well as have great facility in one or more instruments before they are able to communicate their ideas in a composition (Cerana, 1995).

With these barriers to composition in mind, the MSL approach instead focuses on encouraging students to compose from an early age, initially with the use of one or two chords. This approach stands in stark contrast to many traditional music programs, which teach that reading and writing music are prerequisites for composing music. LKR believes that a well-run Modern Band program teaches children to write their own music: "Modern Band integrates composition and improvisation at the beginning of children's education as a means of ensuring that they experience the confidence-building and self-esteem-raising benefits that come with authorship" (Modern Band, 2014).

In order better to understand composition in the classroom, it may be helpful to look at the question of how people who cannot read music can write it through an MSL approach. People acquire their first language before they can read or write it. Linguists who study second language learning have argued that this same sequence should be employed as people acquire a second language (Bartel, 2004; Krashen, 1982). When children begin speaking they use verbs, nouns, pronouns, adverbs, conjunctions, prepositional phrases and many more parts of speech long before they can name and explain them. Children can also learn to 'speak' music long before they can explain it in academic terms. LKR encourages teachers to facilitate a nurturing environment through which students' tastes and personalities illuminate abilities that make their lives more beautiful (Modern Band, 2014). This focus on composition encourages all students to be musical storytellers, and not simply the readers of others' musical stories. LKR advocates for the integration of improvisation as a means of ensuring that students experience the confidence-building and self-esteem-raising benefits that come with authorship through composition. Authorship is an area that is curiously absent in many music education programs in the United States, often only found in high-level jazz courses where students learn through rigorous study of music theory.

Improvisation

The importance of improvisation in a student's musical education is well documented (Aaron, 1980; Burnard, 2000). Despite its inclusion in the National Core Arts Standards (2014), and research demonstrating the benefits of the inclusion of improvisation in the music classroom (Allsup, 1997; Hargreaves, 1999), the majority of music education classes in the US include very little improvisation outside of some jazz music. This holds true even into higher education music classes (Song, 2013).

LKR (and it is not alone in this belief) holds that in a safe and supportive environment – one that fosters the idea that 'there are no wrong notes' – improvisation can come from the outset. In an effort to demystify the process of improvisation for students, LKR encourages teachers to have students solo initially using just two notes. This process opens up improvisation for all students, leading to success. Throughout the process, students are encouraged to bring their own musical ideas to the table as two-note solos progress into four-note solos, pentatonic solos and so on. In a Modern Band classroom, precise rhythms are unnecessary as students can experiment with different composing patterns (chords used to support solo or melodic lines) in order to create a rhythmic, musical tableau that works in conjunction with their peers. The successful inclusion of student improvisation includes composition, approximation, scaffolding and the creation of a safe space for student expression.

Conclusion

Outlined in this chapter is an explanation of the components of Modern Band as defined by Little Kids Rock. The authors have briefly outlined LKR's approach to Modern Band through the framework of Music as a Second Language. As mentioned in the introduction, it is not necessary to adopt the core values of LKR's pedagogy in order to identify a program as a Modern Band; however, the pedagogical foundations presented above (comfort zone, affective filter, composition, improvisation, approximation and scaffolding) provide context for how thousands of teachers in the US have been, and continue to be, trained to teach popular music in the classroom. It is also worth noting that multiple higher education institutions (including California State University, Long Beach; Eastern Washington University; University of South Florida and Montclair State University) have incorporated Modern Band and MSL into their music teacher education curriculum. This pedagogical foundation can help teachers who are hoping to reach more of their students but are unprepared in how to teach styles that are meaningful and relevant to their students (Abril, 2014).

This chapter has outlined an approach for implementing Modern Band in the music classroom. The authors are careful to point out that this is *an* approach, and not *the* approach, to teaching and learning Modern Band. As Modern Band's presence in the music classroom grows, it is imperative to recognize the diversity of experiences encompassed by the approach. Although there are many arguments for the inclusion of popular music in the US music classroom in order to reach the large percentage of students who are uninterested in traditional ensembles (Bowman, 2004; Fesmire, 2006; Tobias, 2010), just performing popular songs on traditional instruments or using the strict formal learning techniques often found in band and orchestra can fail to match the content with appropriate tools for learning (Green, 2002, 2008.) Utilizing a framework of Music as a Second Language in the Modern Band classroom is one solution to this inherent problem.

References

Aaron, T. (1980). Music improvisation and related arts. *Music Educators Journal, 66*(5), 78–83.
Abril, C.R. (2014). Invoking an innovative spirit in music teacher education. In M. Kaschub & J. Smith (Eds.), *Promising practices in 21st century music teacher education* (pp. 175–188). Oxford: Oxford University Press.

Allsup, R.E. (1997). Activating self-transformation through improvisation in instrumental music teaching. *Philosophy of Music Education Review*, *5*(2), 80–85.

Bartel, L. (2004). What is the music education paradigm? In L. Bartel (Ed.), *Questioning the music education paradigm*. Volume II of the Series "Research to Practice: A Biennial Series" (pp. xii–xvi). Toronto: Canadian Music Educators Association.

Beckstead, D. (2001). Will technology transform music education? *Music Educators Journal*, *87*(6), 44–49.

Booth, W.C. (1999). *For the love of it: Amateuring and its rivals*. Chicago: University of Chicago Press.

Boucher, H., & Ryan, C.A. (2011). Performance stress and the very young musician. *Journal of Research in Music Education*, *58*(4), 329–345.

Bowman, W.D. (2004). "Pop" goes . . . ? Taking popular music seriously. In C.X. Rodriguez (Ed.), *Bridging the gap: Popular music and music education* (pp. 29–49). Reston, VA: MENC.

Burnard, P. (2000). How children ascribe meaning to improvisation and composition: Rethinking pedagogy in music education. *Music Education Research*, *2*(1), 7–23.

Cerana, C. (1995). Touched by machine? Composition and performance in the digital age. *Computer Music Journal*, *19*(3), 13–17.

Clements, A.C. (2010). *Alternative approaches in music education*. Lanham, MD: MENC.

CMS. (2014). Transforming music study from its foundations: A manifesto for progressive change in the undergraduate preparation of music majors. Report of the task force on the undergraduate music major. Retrieved from: http://www.music.org/index.php?option=com_content&view=article&id=1859 [Accessed 1 December 2014].

D'Amore, A., & Smith, G.D. (2016). Aspiring to Music Making as Leisure through the musical futures classroom. In R. Mantie & G.D. Smith (Eds.), *The Oxford handbook of music making and leisure* (pp. 61–80). New York, NY: Oxford University Press.

Davis, S.G. & Blair, D.V. (2011). Popular music in American teacher education: A glimpse into a secondary methods course. *International Journal of Music Education*, *29*(2), 124–140.

De Boor, C. (1986). *Approximation theory*. Providence, RI: American Mathematical Society.

Dulay, H. & Burt, M. (1977). *Viewpoints on English as a second language*. New York, NY: Regents.

Fesmire, A. (2006). A survey of middle and senior high school guitar programs in Colorado: Understanding curricular design (Doctoral dissertation, University of Northern Colorado). Retrieved from: ProQuest Dissertations & Theses database. (UMI No. 3231306).

Frith, S. (1998). *Performing rites: On the value of popular music*. Cambridge, MA: Harvard University Press.

Gammond, P. (1991). *The Oxford companion to popular music*. Oxford: Oxford University Press.

Green, L. (2002). *How popular musicians learn: A way ahead for music education*. Aldershot: Ashgate.

Green, L. (2008). *Music, informal learning and the school: A new classroom pedagogy*. Farnham: Ashgate.

Greer, D.R. & Lundquist, R. (1976). The discrimination of musical form through "conceptual" and "non-conceptual" successive approximation strategies. *Bulletin of the Council for Research in Music Education*, *47*, 8–15.

Hargreaves, D.J. (1999). Developing musical creativity in a social world. *Bulletin of the Council for Research in Music Education*, *142*, 22–34.

Hendricks, K.S., Smith, T.D., & Stanuch, J. (2014). Creating safe spaces for music learning. *Music Educators Journal*, *101*(1), 35–40.

Heuser, F. (2014). Juxtapositional pedagogy as an organizing principle in university music education programs. In M. Kaschub & J. Smith (Eds.), *Promising practices in 21st century music teacher education* (pp. 107–124). Oxford: Oxford University Press.

Jaffurs, S.E. (2004). The impact of informal music learning practices in the classroom, or how I learned how to teach from a garage band. *International Journal of Music Education*, 22(3), 189–200.

Jones, P. (2008). Preparing music teachers for change: Broadening instrument class offerings to foster lifewide and lifelong musicing. *Visions of Research in Music Education*, 12, 1–15.

Karlsen, S. & Väkevä, L. (2012). *Future prospects for music education: Corroborating informal learning pedagogy*. Newcastle-upon-Tyne: Cambridge Scholars.

Kenny, D. (2013). Music performance anxiety: Origins, phenomenology, assessment and treatment. Retrieved from: https://corpoemusica.files.wordpress.com/2013/03/1-music-performance-anxiety-origins-phenomenology-assess.pdf [Accessed 3 January 2015].

Krashen, S. (1982). *Principles and practice in second language acquisition*. Retrieved from: http://www.sdkrashen.com/content/books/principles_and_practice.pdf [Accessed 4 January 2015].

Küpers, E., van Dijk, M., & van Geert, P. (2014). "Look closely at what I'm doing!" scaffolding in individual string lessons: Two case studies. *International Journal of Music Education*, 32(3), 375–391.

Mantie, R. (2013). A comparison of '"popular music pedagogy"' discourses. *Journal of Research in Music Education*, 61(3), 334–352.

Mantie, R. & Smith, G.D. (2016). Introduction: Grappling with the jellyfish of music making and leisure. In R. Mantie & G.D. Smith (Eds.) *The Oxford handbook of music making and leisure* (pp. 3–12). New York, NY: Oxford University Press.

Modern Band. (2014). Little Kids Rock website. Retrieved from: http://www.littlekidsrock.org/thehang/teacher-resources/ [Accessed 1 March 2015].

National Core Arts Standards. (2014). Retrieved from: http://www.nationalartsstandards.org [Accessed 1 March 2015].

Patston, T. (2014). Teaching stage fright? Implications for music educators. *British Journal of Music Education*, 31(1), 85–98.

Powell, B., Krikun, A., & Pignato, J. (2015). Something's happening here: Popular music education in the United States. *IASPM@Journal*, 5(1). ISSN 2079-3871 | DOI 10.5429/2079-3871(2015)v5i1.2en

Price, D. (2006). *Personalising music learning*. London: Paul Hamlyn Foundation.

Purves, R. (2002). Effective teaching in secondary school music: Developing identities in teachers and pupils. Retrieved from: www.leeds.ac.uk/educol/documents/00002229.pdf [Accessed 1 December 2012].

Regelski, T. (2007). Amateuring in music and its rivals. *Action, Criticism, and Theory for Music Education*, 6(3), 22–50.

Richard, J.J., Jr. (1992). The effects of Ericksonian resource retrieval on musical performance anxiety. *Dissertation Abstracts International: Section B: The Sciences & Engineering*, 55(2-B), 604.

Rodriguez, C.X. (2004). Popular music in music education: Toward a new conception of musicality. In C.X. Rodriguez (Ed.), *Bridging the gap: Popular music and music education* (pp. 13–28). Reston, VA: MENC – The National Association for Music Education.

Ryan, C. (2000). *A study of the differential responses of male and female children to musical performance anxiety*. Unpublished doctoral Dissertation, McGill University.

Ryan, C. (2004). Gender differences in children's experience of musical performance anxiety. *Psychology of Music*, 32(1), 89–103.

Salmon, P. (1990). A psychological perspective on musical performance anxiety: A review of the literature. *Medical Problems of Performing Artists, 5*, 2–11.

Scanlan, T.K., & Lewthwaite, R. (1984). Social psychological aspects of competition for male youth sport participants: I. Predictors of competitive stress. *Journal of Sport Psychology, 6*, 208–226.

Small, C. (1998). *Musicking: The meanings of performing and listening*. Hanover: University of Press New England.

Smith, G.D. (2014). Popular music in higher education. In G.F. Welch & I. Papageorgi (Eds.), *Advanced music performance: Investigations in higher education learning* (pp. 33–48). Farnham: Ashgate.

Song, A. (2013). Music improvisation in higher education. *Components: The Journal of the College Music Society, 53*. Retrieved from: http://symposium.music.org/index.php?option=com_k2&view=item&id=10308:music-improvisation-in-higher-education&Itemid=124

Swanwick, K. (1994). *Musical knowledge: Intuition, analysis and music education*. London: Routledge.

Task Force on the Undergraduate Music Maker (2014). Retrieved from: http://www.music.org/index.php?option=com_newsfeeds&view=newsfeed&id=2:events&catid=46&Itemid=203 [Accessed 2 March 2015].

Tobias, E. (2010). Crossfading and plugging in: Secondary students' engagement and learning in a songwriting and technology class. Unpublished doctoral dissertation, Northwestern University. Retrieved from: ProQuest Dissertations and Theses database. (UMI 3402496)

Wang, J.C. & Humphreys, J.T. (2009). Multicultural and popular music content in an American music teacher education program. *International Journal of Music Education, 27*(1), 19–36.

Williams, D.A. (2014). Another perspective: The iPad is a real musical instrument. *Music Educators Journal, 101*(3), 93–98.

Part IV
Careers, entrepreneurship and marketing

21

Professional songwriting

Creativity, the creative process and tensions between higher education songwriting and industry practice in the UK

Matt Gooderson and Jennie Henley

Introduction

Musical creativity has been scrutinized from a variety of perspectives (Burnard, 2012); however, research into the creation of songs remains limited (Bennett, 2013). This chapter presents research that explores the creative process of songwriting. Two contrasting perspectives are considered: a professional songwriting team and a student songwriting team, both working to the same 'real-world' brief. Key findings reveal that both teams worked in a similar way in terms of the procedure of songwriting, but that there were great differences in the way that each team searched for and selected ideas, and evaluated the emerging song. We question why these differences occurred, offering a discussion of the context and role of songwriting in the curriculum in relation to the growing trend placing entrepreneurialism and creativity at the centre of Higher Education (HE) agendas (Odena & Welch, 2013).

The context

Creativity forms a crucial element of modern economies (Hallam & Rogers, 2010). Employment in the creative industries in the UK rose 8.6% between 2011 and 2012, a higher rate than the UK economy as a whole, while Gross Value Added (GVA) and Exports of Service also rose between 2008 and 2012 (Creative Industries Economic Estimates, 2014). These rises suggest a dramatic shift away from an economy based on 'things' and towards an economy based on 'ideas' (Sawyer, 2012). As the UK transitioned from an industrial age to this new 'knowledge' or 'creative' economy (Powell & Snellman, 2004), government departments and advisory committees were established to explore and implement creativity in education (Odena & Welch, 2013). Creativity was also found to be one of the key attributes employers expected to find in university graduates (Pedagogy for Employability Group, 2004). In response to these findings, the European University Association issued the following statement:

> The complex questions of the future will not be solved "by the book", but by creative, forward-looking individuals and groups who are not afraid to question established ideas and are able to cope with the insecurity and uncertainty that this entails.
>
> *(2007, p. 6)*

Set against a backdrop of 21st-century economic and employment flux, a new learning initiative is in the process of being implemented at the university where this small-scale study was conducted. The philosophy of this new initiative is directed (in-part) towards fostering greater student attributes in the areas of entrepreneurialism and creativity.

The student songwriting team in this study were in their final year of a degree programme titled Commercial Music Performance. The programme is advertised to students as an "innovative course . . . for those entering the music industry as performers, songwriters, composers, musicologists and educators" (University of Westminster, 2014). Two terms are particularly relevant in the context of this chapter: the word *commercial* in the title of the programme, and the clear description that the programme is aimed at those *entering* the music industry. The emphasis on the word *commercial* reflects the fact that popular music as an art form is predominantly market-driven (Bennett, 2011). Unlike other art forms, such as ballet and opera, popular music in the UK is largely un-subsidized by government. Consequently, professional songwriters have to create original works that are 'validated' by the public by way of sales, online plays, clicks, downloads, radio plays, brand collaborations, synchronizations, merchandise and the sale of concert tickets (Sylvester & O'Reilly, chapter 24, this volume). Bennett (2011) describes the difference in this economic climate as representing "a paradox for the songwriter who is trying to create an original work in a highly evolved, market-driven and tightly constrained creative palette" (p. 2).

Creativity and social systems

Creativity is often regarded as a "puzzle, a paradox" or even a complete "mystery" (Boden, 1996, p. 519). One of the reasons for this "mystery" is that the music industry perpetuates the notion that inspiration – a core element of creativity – is synonymous with the moment when an artist is struck by a sudden revelatory vision. On examining songwriting practices, though, we encounter a different understanding of creativity. Bennett (2011) reveals that many contemporary artists use "back-room co-writers" (p. 3). This is suggestive of songwriting creativity being largely collaborative in nature (Burnard, 2012). Moreover, Negus (2008), speaking of Bob Dylan, says "Bob Dylan has been able to draw influence and find inspiration by closely following an existing tune, lyrical theme or chord sequence" (p. 72). This implies that the creative process draws influence from *existing* material rather than moments of 'divine' inspiration (although these may not be mutually exclusive).

In line with this view of songwriting creativity, we can draw a parallel with Csikszentmihalyi's Systems Model of Creativity (1988; see Figure 21.1). Csikszentmihalyi (1999) explains that "ideas do not exist in a vacuum"; they must "operate on a set of already existing objects, rules, representations, or notions" (p. 315). From this perspective, rather than ideas originating in the mind of the creator as a moment of divine inspiration, it can be argued that the idea itself existed before the creator thought of it, as if it were lying dormant within the culture. Consequently, Csikszentmihalyi clarifies creativity as any act, idea or product that changes an existing domain or that transforms an existing domain into a new one. His model consists of three components: a domain of knowledge, a field where the knowledge is understood and an individual who creates work in order to change the domain and culture. The process is cyclical in nature; if work is accepted into the culture, it then influences further individuals in their creations.

Perhaps a clearer way to comprehend the creative practices behind songwriting is to view songwriters as complex weavers of "multiple languages" (Toynbee,

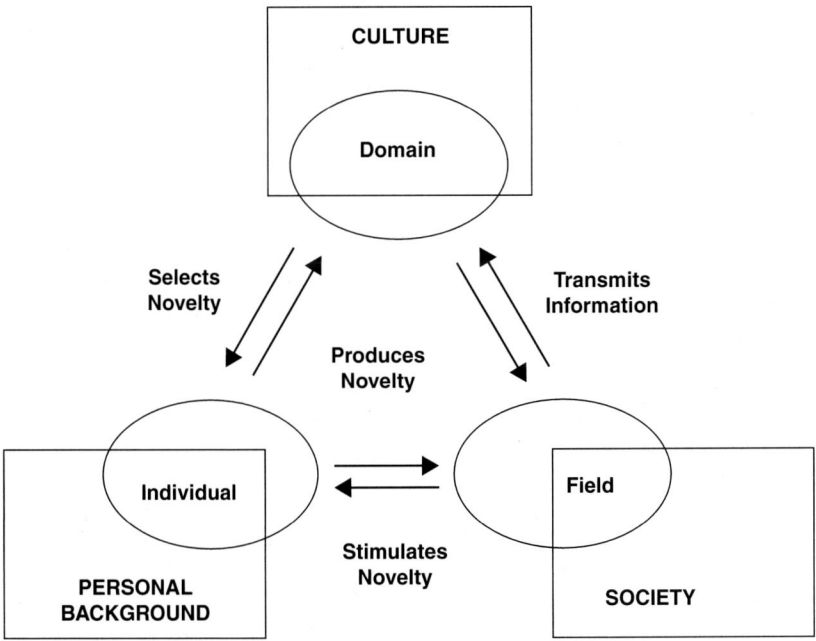

Figure 21.1 Csikszentmihalyi's systems view of creativity
Source: Csikszentmihalyi (1988, p. 315)

2000, p. 43). In this sense, songwriters resemble craftspeople, selecting and combining existing materials into new forms. It is in this way that the songwriter can be understood as an "editor and parodist" rather than a "transcendental spirit" (Bakhtin, 1981, pp. 314–315, cited in Toynbee, 2000), whose materials are "located in the field of the social" (Toynbee, 2000, p. xv) rather than divine.

Commensurate with Negus's (2008) understanding of Dylan's songwriting creativity, we can surmise that songwriters produce variation in the set of conventions, rules and ideas that exist in the structured knowledge of songs to which the songwriter has access (McIntyre, 2008). To be able to work well within the system, individuals must "internalise the rules of the domain and opinions of the field" (Csikszentmihalyi, 1999, p. 332). This allows informed decisions to be made about which ideas are 'good' and 'bad'. Therefore, if a person wants to become a 'good' songwriter, they must acquire the ways of thinking and being, and codes of knowledge, necessary to make informed decisions. In other words, they must acquire cultural capital – "a form of knowledge, an internalised code for cognitive acquisition which equips the social agent with empathy towards, appreciation or competence in deciphering cultural relation and cultural artefacts" (Bourdieu, 1993, p. 7). Turning our attention to the creative process of songwriting, Sawyer (2012) elaborates that the work is actually a product of smaller steps or phases:

> Instead of the mystical view of creativity that places a moment of insight in a wondrous moment of divine inspiration, creators experience small insights throughout a day's work, each of these insights is accompanied with micro evaluations and further perspiration. These mini-insights only gradually accumulate to result in a finished work, as a result of a process of hard work and intellectual labour of the creator.
>
> *(Sawyer, 2012, p. 139)*

The creative process

Wallas (1926) was one of the first thinkers to consider creativity as a process involving separate stages or steps, dividing creativity into four key stages:

Preparation – definition of issue, observation and study;
Incubation – laying the issue aside for a time;
Illumination – the moment when a new idea finally emerges;
Verification – testing it out.

While this model favours a view of creativity that moves from inception to completion via sequential stages, educationalist Petty (1997) perceives the creative process to involve a chain of interlinked phases. These phases are revisited any number of times and can occur in a variety of combinations and sequences:

Inspiration – uncritical search for new ideas;
Clarification – planning, discussing and agreeing aims;

Evaluation – critical analysis of the music, identifying strengths and weaknesses based on aims agreed during the clarification stage;
Distillation – sifting through the ideas generated in the inspiration phase;
Incubation – maturation of ideas;
Perspiration – working on a chosen part or idea.

Petty's model of the creative process offers a powerful analytical framework for us to examine the creative process of songwriting in a more detailed, or phase-by-phase, manner.

Researching songwriting teams

In order to gain an insight into how musical creativity occurs within songwriting teams, a small-scale qualitative study was carried out. Working to the same professional brief, two teams were asked to create a new piece of music for a TV commercial that was due for broadcast in August 2014. The purpose of this research was to attempt to reveal what actually happened during the creative process of songwriting. Participant observation made it possible to gain an insider's perspective, rather than the more mythologized perspective that tends to be perpetuated via press and media (Bennett, 2011). It was important to use participant observation as a way of looking at what *actually* happened alongside the songwriters' perceptions of events afterwards, giving the researcher experience both *within* and *of* the field (Henley, 2015; Labaree, 2002).

The songwriting teams

One professional team and one student team were selected for the study. The reason for choosing these particular teams was to provide an extreme instance case study. This would allow the work of the two teams to be contrasted (Denscombe, 2007), thus enabling an examination of the creative process through exploration of how the participants interacted as they composed, and what kinds of knowledge were key to their songwriting. The teams used computer cameras to video themselves during the processes of generating and developing music for the commercial, and were interviewed afterwards about their work.

Team A: The professional songwriters

Participants A1 and A2 are professional in the sense that the majority of their income stream is generated from writing songs. Participant A1 is an award-winning songwriter, singer, guitarist, pianist, drummer and top-line writer. She has toured internationally, written music for herself and other artists, adverts, computer games and corporate brands. Participant A2 is a founding member of a successful band and has worked as a songwriter, re-mixer and producer for Sony/ATV, Wall of Sound and P.I.A.S. He plays the electric guitar, piano and synthesizer. The pair have collaborated on a variety of projects since meeting on a commercial music degree in 1996.

Team B: The student songwriters

Participants B3 and B4 were both in their final term of a degree in Commercial Music Performance at the time of the study. They have collaborated often since 2011 as songwriters in their band and are highly competent producers able to finish songs to a very high standard. While B3 specializes in guitar and production, B4 sings and plays keyboards. They have performed live in London as part of their final year show but have not written music specifically to a brief before.

The brief

The brief, set by an agency, contained images and text detailing the brand, advertisement concept and story and, perhaps most importantly, provided two pre-existing musical works as 'reference tracks' – original works that, for a variety of reasons, the agency could not legally acquire. Despite the fact that the licenses, in this case, were unavailable, as is not uncommon, the client still *desired* to use the music in a reference track. It is also not uncommon for an agency's client to want music that closely resembles the reference track in a number of ways, such as instrumentation, tempo, melody, harmony, rhythm, dynamics and form. This could be considered, in Bennett's terms, as being required to produce original work using a "constrained creative palette" (Bennett, 2011, p. 2).

Validity

Representing a valid form of professional songwriting remained a crucial aspect of the research, so it was important to conduct the case study in a setting that was 'natural'. The study was designed so that the participants were pre-established songwriting teams and worked in their own chosen and familiar environments. Their computer cameras, rather than a stand-alone camera or camera held by a third person, were used to retain the naturalistic setting, and to eliminate observer effect as far as possible.

Data mapping

Attempting to map the data to the above models of the creative process presented a variety of challenges. Wallas's four-stage model did not enable us to view how the writers searched for new ideas or worked on improving ideas; it merely provided an overview of the sequence of events. Petty's model did not enable us to view processes that often occur outside of the studio environment (incubation). Nevertheless, this model did provide a useful framework for analysis, allowing us to compare the way the teams constructed the song. Interview questions were designed to investigate the cultural capital upon which participants drew upon in the studio.

Findings

Sequence of events

The procedure that both teams used when creating the song, viewed through Wallas's model (Figure 21.2), shows that each team sequenced their work in a similar way. Following the process of working out the piano riff from the reference track, both groups began to experiment, morphing it into their own version. In both cases, one member began jamming on the piano while the other listened; while

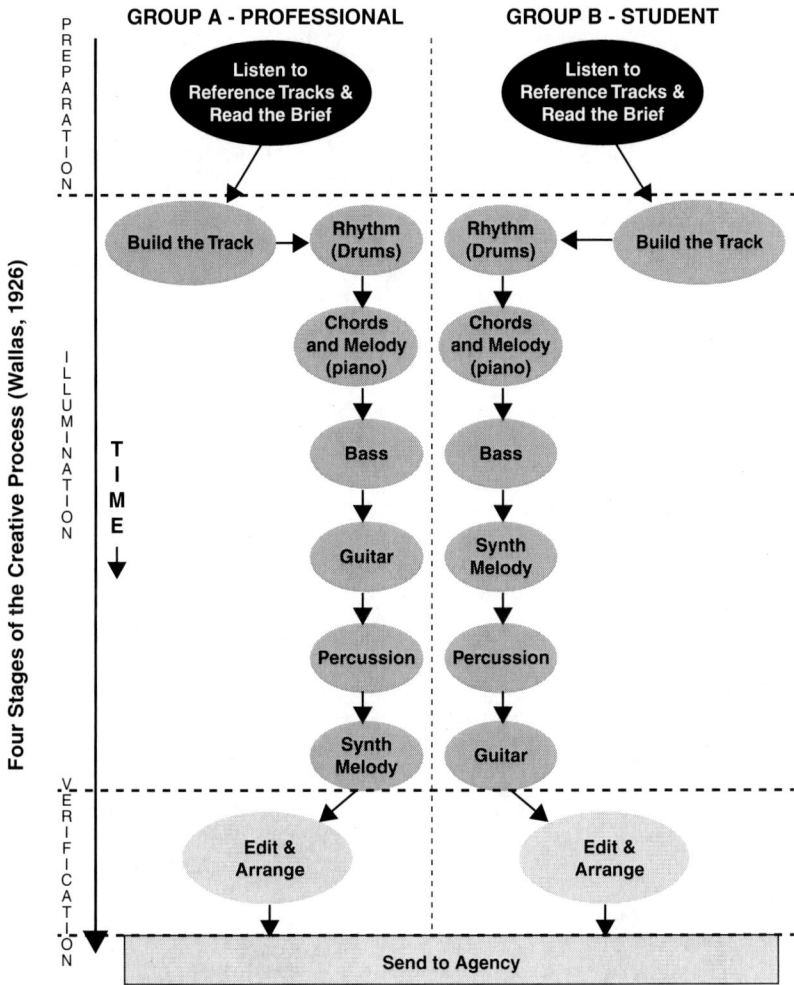

Figure 21.2 Sequence of events

one musician was acting as the creator, the other was appropriating the role of the audience (Hennion, 1983). Unlike classical composition, where it is reported that composers often 'hear' the music in their heads before writing it (Younker & Smith, 1996), the composition process undertaken was closer to Toynbee's (2000) description of popular musicians as re-arrangers of material already located in the social domain. Moreover, there is a similarity between the creative processes found in these cases and those of professional songwriters Stock, Aitken & Waterman and Xenomania (Higgins, 2012; Waterman, 2009). This would indicate that the student team worked in a way that reflected industry practice.

Phases of the creative process

The similarities between the two teams' procedures as viewed through Wallas's model are striking. However, viewing the actions of each team through Petty's model shows a different picture (Figure 21.3).

As phases do not occur in a linear fashion, and they interact with each other, each code was given a time allocation. This allowed a comparison of how much time each team spent in each phase. Although going through the same procedure, there were differences in how the two teams used their time. Team A distributed their time fairly evenly across the different phases, but Team B awarded radically different amounts of time to each phase. Mapping the different phases onto a timeline shows an intricate web of interactions, some phases only being entered momentarily before moving to a different phase, demonstrating the complex nature of how both teams worked. Even where there were equal amounts of time spent in a phase, there were clear differences in the way the teams were working, as highlighted by work in the inspiration and evaluation phases.

Petty (2009) suggests that "uncreative people will tend to latch on to the first idea that comes to them, and quickly and uncritically bring it to completion

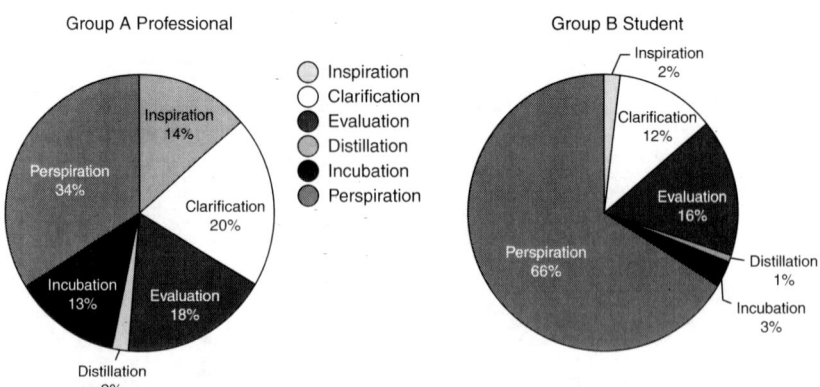

Figure 21.3 Time spent in phases of creation

without serious thought about what they are trying to achieve" (p. 326). Participant B3, upon reflection, also appeared to reach the same conclusion:

> (B3): We don't change the initial idea very often. I don't know why we don't do that, because I think it would actually be a good idea sometimes.
>
> *(interview transcript)*

Our analyses suggest that the professional team were more able to locate their work in the social domain, draw on cultural capital, evaluate their work in both a micro and macro way, and allow different phases to interact more easily (Gooderson, 2014). In other words, they applied more criticality to their work. The student team seemed to focus more on the task of completing the composition (working on ideas), whereas the professional team seemed to focus more on the transaction between the social domain (drawing ideas), the creative work and then back to the social domain (evaluating how these ideas might be received). These differences lead to an important question: Why did the students spend more time working on ideas but less time generating new ideas? In other words, (why) did the student team appear to be less *creative* than the professional team? In the context of Higher Education, this then raises the question of whether an understanding of the creative process could help students learn to be more creative and, consequently, to develop their critical, evaluative thinking.

Tensions between HE and professional practice

For ethical reasons, the research for this project was carried out after the students had just completed their degree programme, so it did not form part of an assessed module. However, a close inspection of the songwriting module offered by the university shows that it does not draw students' attention to their creative process, but rather focuses on identity, promotion and industry feedback. The purpose of this chapter is not to critique this existing module, as it offers extremely valid learning outcomes; moreover, it is important to note that these learning outcomes clearly fit within the qualifications framework within which the degree programme operates (QAA, 2014). However, if a clearer understanding of the creative process is central to success as a songwriter in the 'creative economy', and the degree programme specifically aims to prepare students for entry into the commercial music industry, then maybe greater provision should be made for this essential component in creative modules.

The constantly changing landscapes of our personal, social and economic worlds require creativity, and thus "education systems are faced with the challenge of equipping individuals with skills that will enable them to fulfil their potential in a world where change is rapid and relentless" (Hallam & Rogers, 2010, p. 105). Ultimately, "we are trying to prepare students for jobs that don't yet exist, using technologies that have not yet been invented, in order to solve problems that we don't know are problems yet" (Jackson, 2010, p. xi). Despite the growing realization that creativity is seen as a key ingredient in sustained personal and economic growth (Sawyer, 2006), educational establishments (schools, colleges and universities) are still teaching students how to answer, rather than how to think (Csikszentmihalyi, 2006, cited in Jackson, 2006). This claim is supported to some extent by the level description of a UK bachelor's degree with honours.

According to the UK Higher Education Qualifications Framework, bachelor's degree students should demonstrate:

> a systematic understanding of key aspects of their field of study, including acquisition of coherent and detailed knowledge, at least some of which is at, or informed by, the forefront of defined aspects of a discipline
>
> an ability to deploy accurately established techniques of analysis and enquiry within a discipline
>
> conceptual understanding that enables the student:
>
> - to devise and sustain arguments, and/or to solve problems, using ideas and techniques, some of which are at the forefront of a discipline
> - to describe and comment upon particular aspects of current research, or equivalent advanced scholarship, in the discipline with an appreciation of the uncertainty, ambiguity and limits of knowledge
> - the ability to manage their own learning, and to make use of scholarly reviews and primary sources (for example, refereed research articles and/or original materials appropriate to the discipline).
>
> *(QAA, 2014, p. 26)*

By comparison, master's degrees are awarded to students who have demonstrated:

> a systematic understanding of knowledge, and a critical awareness of current problems and/or new insights, much of which is at, or informed by, the forefront of their academic discipline, field of study or area of professional practice
>
> a comprehensive understanding of techniques applicable to their own research or advanced scholarship
>
> originality in the application of knowledge, together with a practical understanding of how established techniques of research and enquiry are used to create and interpret knowledge in the discipline
>
> conceptual understanding that enables the student:
>
> - to evaluate critically current research and advanced scholarship in the discipline
> - to evaluate methodologies and develop critiques of them and, where appropriate, to propose new hypotheses.
>
> *(QAA, 2014, p. 28)*

This strongly implies that the difference between a bachelors' degree with honours and a master's degree within the Government framework is criticality – master's students being required to demonstrate critical awareness and critical thinking. It is therefore significant that the differences between the professional and student teams in this study appeared to be related to the use of criticality. If criticality is key to engaging in the creative process, yet criticality is a feature of graduate rather than undergraduate degree programmes, what opportunities are there to foster creativity in undergraduate commercial music degree programmes?

In a report by the National College for School Leaders, eight key attributes of creativity were identified: connecting, risking, envisaging, analyzing, thinking, interacting, varying and elaborating (Burgess, 2007). Creativity in education also requires teachers to "judge carefully when to intervene and when to take a 'hands-off' approach and to balance planning with improvisation" (SEED, 2006). If creativity is about recognizing a problem, finding a fresh perspective, making unusual links and developing original solutions (Cropley & Cropley, 2008), then we can rule out a simple empirical division between 'right' and 'wrong' answers. Consequently, as teachers, we risk eliminating the 'divergent' thinking deemed necessary for creativity. However, if we do not scaffold learning we risk not developing students' "convergent thinking" – another necessary component of creativity. Here lies the problem – "creativity is mutually contradictory" (Cropley & Cropley, 2008, p. 355) and paradoxical in nature.

Assessment is also problematic. Higher education has rarely made creativity "an explicit objective of the learning and assessment process" (Jackson, 2006, p. 4). The reason for this is that the current education system revolves around the idea of the student meeting a learning outcome (a tangible product of the process). Creativity, on the other hand, can require a lack of structure and direction. In a musical context, Kleiman (2008, p. 213) describes this as "playing for the sake of playing". Tangible outcomes suit technical development; it is far easier to prove that a student has a greater technical grasp of a subject through performance testing (Garnett, 2013). Conversely, it is much tougher to assess whether creative capacity has increased as a direct result of study (McWilliam & Dawson, 2008). Fautley clarifies, observing: "Since creative thinking by definition goes beyond knowledge, there is explicitly or implicitly assumed to be a tension between knowledge and creativity" (Weisberg, 1999, p. 26, cited in Fautley, 2010). In music education, "this tension can be readily seen in assessment" (2010, p. 72).

This leads to a further tension concerning the knowledge that students are expected to demonstrate a systematic understanding of in their degree programme. In arguing that arts are simultaneously objective and subjective, Aspin (1990) describes art knowledge in terms of aesthetic meanings that can be underpinned by a benchmark of what is aesthetically acceptable. The argument he makes is based on the non-instrumental nature of art and, in a similar way to Hennion (1983), the role of the artist as spectator/audience is crucial. The creator needs to adopt the spectator role in order to take a critical stance in developing the work. Moreover, this stance must be underpinned by some benchmark of what is aesthetically acceptable, as, "Someone wishing to make such judgements of works of art will be one who has learned somehow to appreciate the different kinds of meaning in the world of aesthetics and the arts" (Aspin, 1990, p. 38).

A difficulty therefore arises when the nature of art itself requires the artist to take a critical, socially located stance, yet according to the curriculum documentation (QAA, 2014), demonstrations of critical awareness are not required features of undergraduate programmes. In reality, the development of critical awareness is considered a fundamental part of undergraduate study, but programmes could potentially be validated using the government criteria without this fundamental aspect of artistic development. Moreover, the criticality necessary to engage in artistic reflection at undergraduate level should ideally be developed throughout an artist's core learning prior to reaching that level of study, not as an adjunct as part of a higher education programme.

Learning through reflection

The notion of socially located aesthetic meanings suggests that the more aware songwriters are of the field and the domain of the creative work, the more successful they are likely to be. This was apparent from the data pertaining to the professional team; not only were the team able to reflect throughout the process, but they were also able to locate their work in the social domain through cultural reference points. Viewing this from the perspective of Csikszentmihalyi's (1988) Systems Model of Creativity would suggest that reflection both during and after the songwriting process is crucial to the cyclic nature of creativity. Therefore, time and space are needed for this reflection on the part of the learner.

Working without traditional lecturer feedback and assessment appeared to allow the students greater space to develop their own critical evaluation skills and facilitated an environment where they decided for themselves what worked in a given situation (Berkley, 2001). Perhaps the most interesting outcome of the study came from the students reflecting on their own creative process. In interview the students were able to reflect upon their work at a meta-level, and, with the help of the pie charts to demonstrate visually how their time was distributed across the different creative phases, this reflection continued long after the study had ended. Shortly after the study ended, Participant B4 sent the following reflection by email:

> (B4) I feel that doing that [songwriting] exercise was something where I actually learnt the most about MYSELF and how I work, creating music. The course does give you a good grounding in popular music culture and touches on necessary areas, but I believe not enough focus is really given to the students themselves, and how they work.

While the student believed that the course provided a "good grounding in popular music culture", he clearly felt that completing the songwriting task provided a greater emphasis on students' own working practices. So whereas educators might say that in the context of this task the student appeared to receive *less* focus, that is to say no formal teaching or feedback, the student felt that there was *more* focus on him (see Lebler & Hodges, chapter 22, this volume). Furthermore, the reflective process was still taking place some time after the study. Upon discovering a book on improving creativity published by music software manufacturers Ableton, 10 months after completing his degree, B4 sent an email relating his experience of the songwriting task to the book:

> (B4) [this book contains] a well designed article explaining the creative process for budding producers. Especially the blue section – reminded me of when [B3 & B4] were recording a project [for the authors] and [the authors] noticed that we spent 5% of our time generating the idea and 95% on polishing it.

Conclusion

The purpose of this research was to gain insights into the epistemology of the practice of songwriting, for us to develop "new understandings, new practices and new pedagogies" (Burnard, 2012, p. 237). Through volunteering to participate in this task, the students clearly created an opportunity to develop their own creativity (or creativities (Burnard, 2012)). Motivation drove the pair to complete a difficult task. They overcame setbacks and frustrations, and, in doing so, anecdotally participant B4 believed he learned more about himself and the way he works than he did in other areas of his studies.

It would be difficult to measure whether partaking in this small-scale research has helped foster greater entrepreneurialism in the participants. However, the (former) students involved in the study have asked to work on more songwriting briefs. This shows the authors that they have gained the confidence to try, and are learning through the experience of trying. These students are developing their confidence, knowledge and capabilities to be creative. In other words, we could say that they have developed the ability to see and fully understand the complexity of songwriting creativity, or that they have learned to *look* at achieving success as songwriters in a more entrepreneurial and creative way.

The findings of this research highlight that the differences in the way that the student team and professional team worked lay in engagement in critical reflection and locating their work in the social domain. Our findings also suggest that in the absence of any teacher feedback, the students developed their own self-reflective critical evaluation skills. Although based on just two cases, this study demonstrates the potential for songwriting processes to be analyzed and described. By allowing students to analyze and describe their own songwriting processes, teachers in higher education can develop pedagogy that enables students to gain a more developed sense of reflection and criticality, ultimately leading to clearer insight into how creative work is produced.

References

Aspin, D. (1990). The problem of aesthetic education. In K. Swanwick (Ed.), *The arts and education: Papers from the National Association for Education in the Arts 1983–1990* (pp. 31–47). Oakham, Leics: NAEA.

Bennett, J. (2011). Collaborative songwriting: The ontology of negotiated creativity in popular music studio practice. *Journal of the Art of Record Production, 5*, np.

Bennett, J. (2013). "You won't see me": In search of an epistemology of collaborative songwriting. *Journal of the Art of Record Production, 8*, np.

Berkley, R. (2001). Why is teaching composing so challenging? A survey of classroom observation and teachers' opinions. *British Journal of Music Education, 18*, 119–138.

Boden, M.A. (Ed.) (1996). *Dimensions of creativity.* Cambridge, MA: MIT Press.

Bourdieu, P. (1993). *The field of cultural production: Essays on art and literature.* New York: Columbia University Press.

Burgess, T. (2007). Lifting the lid on the creative curriculum: How leaders have realised creativity in their schools through curriculum ownership. National College for School Leadership. Retrieved from: http://dera.ioe.ac.uk/7340/1/download%3Fid%3D17281%26filename%3Dlifting-the-lid-on-the-creative-curriculum-full-report.pdf [Assessed 22 August 2014].

Burnard, P. (2012). *Musical creativities in practice.* New York: Oxford University Press.

Creative Industries Economic Estimates (2014). *January Report.* London: Department for Media and Sport. Retrieved from: https://www.gov.uk/government/uploads/system/uploads/attachment_data/file/271008/Creative_Industries_Economic_Estimates_-_January_2014.pdf [Assessed 22 August 2014].

Cropley, A. & Cropley, D. (2008). Resolving the paradoxes of creativity: An extended phase model. *Cambridge Journal of Education, 38*(3), 355–373.

Csikszentmihalyi, M. (1988). Society, culture and person: A systems view of creativity. In R. Sternberg (Ed.), *The nature of creativity: Contemporary psychological perspectives* (pp. 325–339). New York, NY: Cambridge University Press.

Csikszentmihalyi, M. (1999). Implications of a systems perspective for the study of creativity. In R.J. Sternberg & T. Lubart (Eds.), *The concept of creativity: Prospects and paradigms in handbook of creativity* (pp. 313–335). New York: Cambridge University Press.

Denscombe, M. (2007). *The good research guide.* Milton Keynes: Open University Press.

European University Association. (2007). *Creativity in higher education.* Brussels, Belgium: European University Association.

Fautley, M. (2010). *Assessment in music education.* Oxford: Oxford University Press.

Garnett, J. (2013). Beyond a constructivist curriculum: A critique of competing paradigms in music education. *British Journal of Music Education, 30*(2), 161–175. doi.org/10.1017/S0265051712000575.

Gooderson, M.C. (2014). *Learning to look the 'right' way: Towards an understanding of songwriting creativity.* Institute of Education, Unpublished MA Dissertation.

Hallam, S. & Rogers, L. (2010). Creativity. In S. Hallam & A. Creech (Eds.), *Music education in the 21st century in the United Kingdom: Achievement, analysis and aspirations* (pp. 105–122). London: Institute of Education.

Henley, J. (2015). Musical learning and desistance from crime: The case of a "Good Vibrations" Javanese gamelan project with young offenders. *Music Education Research, 17*(1), 103–120. doi.org/10.1080/14613808.2014.933791.

Hennion, A. (1983). The production of success: An anti-musicology of the pop song. *Popular Music, 3*, 159–193.

Higgins, B. (2012). *Songwriting with Mistajam and Brian Higgins.* BBC 1Xtra. Retrieved from: http://www.bbc.co.uk/programmes/p00ndwgm [Accessed 22 August 2014].

Jackson, N. (2006). Imagining a different world. In N. Jackson, M. Oliver, M. Shaw, & J. Wisdom (Eds.), *Developing Creativity in Higher Education: An imaginative curriculum* (p. xviii). London: Routledge.

Jackson, N. (2010). *Teaching creativity: Creativity in teaching* (Learning in Higher Education). Oxfordshire: Libri Publishing.

Kleiman, P. (2008). Towards transformation: Conceptions of creativity in higher education. *Innovations in Education and Teaching International, 45*(3), 209–217.

Labaree, R.V. (2002). The risk of "going observationalist": Negotiating the hidden dilemmas of being an insider participant observer. *Qualitative Research, 2*(1), 97–122.

Lubart, T.I. (2001). Models of the creative process: Past, present and future. *Creativity Research Journal, 13*(3–4), 295–308.

McIntyre, P. (2008). Creativity and cultural production: A study of contemporary Western popular music songwriting. *Creativity Research Journal, 20*(1), 40–52.

McWilliam, E. & Dawson, S. (2008). Teaching for creativity: Towards sustainable and replicable pedagogical practice. *Higher Education, 56*, 633–643.

Negus, K. (2008). *Bob Dylan*. London: Equinox Publishing Ltd.

Odena, O. & Welch, G. (2013). Teachers' perceptions of creativity in musical creativity. In O. Odena (Ed.), *Insights from music education research* (pp. 29–48). Farnham: Ashgate.

Pedagogy for Employability Group (2004). Pedagogy for employability. Higher Education Academy. Retrieved from: http://www.heacademy.ac.uk/assets/documents/employability/id383_pedagogy_for_employability_ 357.pdf [Assessed 22 August 2014].

Petty, G. (1997). *How to be better at creativity*. London: Kogan Page.

Petty, G. (2009). *Teaching today: A practical guide*. Cheltenham: Nelson Thornes.

Powell, W.W. & Snellman, K. (2004). The knowledge economy. *Annual Review of Sociology, 30*, 199–220.

QAA (2014). *UK quality code for higher education part A: Setting and maintaining academic standards: The frameworks for higher education qualifications of UK degree-awarding bodies*. Retrieved from: www.qaa.ac.uk/assuring-standards-and-quality/the-quality-code/qualifications [Accessed 23 August 2014].

Sawyer, R.K. (2006). The schools of the future. In R.K. Sawyer (Ed.), *Cambridge handbook of the learning sciences* (pp. 1–6). New York, NY: Cambridge University Press.

Sawyer, R.K. (2012). *Explaining creativity: The science of human innovation*. Oxford: Oxford University Press.

SEED. (2006.) *Promoting creativity in education: Overview of key national policy developments across the UK*. Retrieved from: www.educationscotland.gov.uk/Images/hmiepcie_tcm4-712760.pdf [Accessed 22 August 2014].

Toynbee, J. (2000). *Making popular music: Musicians, creativity and institutions*. London: Arnold.

University of Westminster. (2014). BMus honours commercial music performance. Retrieved from: http://www.westminster.ac.uk/courses/subjects/music/undergraduate-courses/full-time/u09fumup-bmus-honours-commercial-music-performance [Accessed 5 August 2015].

Wallas, G. (1926). *The art of thought*. London: Jonathan Cape.

Waterman, P. (2009). Classic tracks: Rick Astley "Never gonna give you up". *Sound on Sound*. Retrieved from: http://www.soundonsound.com/sos/feb09/articles/classictracks_0209.htm?print=yes [Accessed 21 August 2014].

Younker, B.A. & Smith, W.H. (1996). Comparing and modelling musical thought processes of expert and novice composers. *Bulletin of the Council for Research in Music Education, 128*, 25–36.

22
Popular music pedagogy
Dual perspectives on DIY musicianship

Don Lebler and Naomi Hodges

Introduction

The ways music is learned, created, disseminated and accessed are changing rapidly, partly as a consequence of technological advancements. Accessible recording and information technologies now enable the autonomous creation and marketing of music, independent of major record companies. Literature on current music industry trends notes the shift of control from corporations to musicians (Burrell, 2013), with an increased incidence of do-it-yourself (DIY) musicians, and the higher music education literature describes new pedagogical structures that prepare students for diverse outcomes. One of these structures can be found in the Bachelor of Popular Music (BPM) programme at the Queensland Conservatorium, Griffith University, Australia, which commenced in 1999 and was one of the first university degree programmes in Australia to focus exclusively on popular music. It remains one of very few programmes to declare its focus through being named a Bachelor of Popular Music, rather than the much more common bachelor of music or arts with a major in popular music.

This chapter incorporates the dual perspectives of an academic who was instrumental in the development of the innovative pedagogies described below, and one of its recent graduates who undertook a research study about her experiences of the programme. The academic has a background as a drummer and now identifies himself as an academic. The graduate has a background as a singer-songwriter and now identifies herself as a DIY musician. By including the student experience as well as the intentions of the developers of the programme, this chapter provides dual perspectives on the functions of participatory assessment and holistic pedagogical practices in higher music education, and recognizes the role of accessible recording technology as a source of instant feedback and as a creative tool that has reshaped the way music is produced.

Higher music education

Since the 18th century, conservatoires have been at the core of higher music education, educating world-class performers mainly through a master-student learning model (Jørgensen, 2009; Lebler, 2004). Heidi Westerlund (2006) describes the tradition as an apprenticeship model where a master is the initiator, verifier and controller of a student's learning process. A reliance on the master's teaching is cultivated, possibly at the expense of the development of autonomy (Carey & Lebler, 2008; Lebler, 2005). Such observations are not intended to challenge the master-student model, though some writers are more critical than others of the dominance of this mode of teaching in higher music education (see, for example, Gaunt, 2010; Smith, 2013), nor do the authors question the validity of higher music education; the intention, rather, is to identify an opportunity for the re-evaluation of educational practices to "prepare students more effectively for sustainable learning outcomes that are required for a portfolio career" (Carey & Lebler, 2008, p. 5). As Westerlund (2006) states,

> It can be argued that the traditional focus on performance and composition as the products of a conservatoire education may not be sufficient to prepare graduates for professional lives that are likely to include a wide range of musical and paramusical activities.
>
> *(p. 13)*

Partti and Karlsen (2010) assert the need for a "paradigm shift in education . . . to make formal education correspond more closely with the world our students are facing" (p. 377; see also Smith & Shafighian, 2013).

The ways in which music is produced and consumed are challenging traditional modes of music dissemination and the pedagogies used in educational institutions (Kusek et al., 2005; Lebler, 2007a). Lebler and Carey (2008) describe contemporary society as rich in information and growing in complexity; importance is placed on creativity, adaptability, reflexivity and innovative problem-solving skills (Lebler & Carey, 2008; Lebler & McWilliam, 2008). Kusek et al. (2005) identify a need to be creative and possess the ability to wear "several hats" (p. 21). Seeking creativity as an outcome is becoming more common in higher education institutions (Lebler & McWilliam, 2008), in order to prepare graduates for diverse portfolio careers, as acknowledged by Lebler et al. (2009), among others. Consequently, pedagogical researchers and conservatoires are reappraising traditional education frameworks, seeking new pedagogies and in some cases, adopting or adapting what has been referred to as "popular music pedagogy" (Lebler, 2007a, 2008; Mantie, 2013).

Popular music as content is no longer unusual; however, the processes by which it is learned in formal settings often still rely on the master-student model (Green, 2001, 2006; Lebler, 2008; Smith, 2013; Smith & Shafighian, 2013). When this occurs, the informal learning practices of a popular musician are frequently forsaken. Lebler and Carey (2008) describe understanding the nature of students' prior learning experience as a crucial element in the structuring of educational processes, and it is known through the work of researchers such as Lucy Green (2001, 2006, 2008) that popular musicians learn informally outside institutional environments (see also Lebler, 2004; Lebler & Carey, 2008; Lebler & McWilliam, 2008; Westerlund, 2006). Through her studies, Green demonstrates the applicability of informal learning in formal education (Green, 2001, 2010). The notions of community, collaboration and informal learning practices are explored by Westerlund (2006), who proposes:

> Expertise is more likely to flourish in communities where students support one another in knowledge construction and where, at the same time, they develop collective expertise . . . students are participants of musical practices instead of the end points of carefully planned instructional inputs on their way to a possible real-life expertise in the future.
>
> *(pp. 122–123)*

Likewise, Pitts (2010) found that musical communities are contexts within which learning is enhanced, so, by incorporating these characteristics, a 'real world' learning experience can be cultivated in formal educational settings.

Defining 'do-it-yourself' (DIY)

The term *indie* (independent musician) is commonly used to describe a musician who works independently of major record labels (Bianchi, 2009; Marrouat, 2011). Paul Oliver (2010) has replaced *indie* with *DIY* in his writing, "in an attempt to move away from misconception of how local artists are creatively active by not only being independent but also self-sustainable" (p. 1431).

DIY musicians are self-reliant and autonomous, writing, performing, recording and producing original music. This is not to say that they are working alone – indeed, collaboration and networking are important aspects of most DIY musical practice (Morrow et al., chapter 26, this volume; Smith & Gillett, 2015). They use recording as part of creative processes and are not confined to purely digital technologies. According to Dave Grohl, who is the former drummer of Nirvana and the founder and frontman of Foo Fighters, "Now, more than ever, independence as a musician has been blessed by the advance of technology" (2013, p. 5). Because this chapter includes descriptions of the creative processes of the graduate author who writes, performs and records original music, the *do-it-yourself musician* (DIY) is an appropriate term.

A graduate perspective

The graduate author continued in pursuit of a musical career after graduating from the Bachelor of Popular Music (BPM) programme in 2011. She met her duo partner during the programme and together they write, perform, record, produce and master their own music under the name of the Phoncurves. Upon reflection, she realized how well the degree has prepared her for this kind of music career and how the pedagogy is structured in a way that can develop a DIY approach. Indeed, the DIY approach is embedded in the curriculum and pedagogy of the BPM. The approach is by no means confined to the BPM, and nor is it the only outcome for graduates. Nonetheless, it could be argued that a DIY approach is essential for survival in the dynamic 21st-century music industry. Hallam and Gaunt (2012) advocate that music students should broaden their thinking and pay attention to a range of aspects of a career in music, and that they should play an active role in their learning and planning processes. Writing a reflective journal each semester was a requirement of the BPM programme, and the graduate author's journals have provided rich data that illustrate the development of her creative processes over her three years in the programme and her subsequent Honours year. Even after graduation, she has continued to reflect on her practice and her reflections are included to represent her perspectives on her development during her studies and subsequently as a DIY musician.

The Bachelor of Popular Music

In the mid-1990s, an opportunity for pedagogical change was recognized at the Queensland Conservatorium Griffith University, and the innovative BPM programme was introduced in 1999 (Lebler, 2004). The programme design was led by Garry Tamlyn, who wanted to bring the popular music industry into the Conservatorium (Lebler, 2007a). A wide range of skills is acquired during the three-year undergraduate programme, including those in the domains of audio production/engineering, musical theory, creative music technologies, music history and analysis and popular music production (Lebler, 2008, p. 4). Some students go on to complete a one-year Honours research programme. Further innovations in the pedagogy (particularly the assessment practices) were developed by Lebler (see 2004, 2005, 2006b, 2007a, 2007b, 2008, 2015, 2014). Lebler's research informed developments in the BPM process and drew on Green's (2001, 2006, 2008) informal learning practices; Biggs's (1999) 3P learning model (presage, process and product) and assessment *of, for* and *as* learning; McWilliam's (2004) *prod-user* model; Claxton's (1999, 2000, 2002) work on critical reflection and the relationship between knowledge and know-how; and Csikszentmihalyi's (1991) notion of 'flow' in learning.

The programme is designed to enhance the abilities of its students to make popular music, including the aspects of performance and songwriting, along with the development of skills in related audio and computer technologies and the academic study of popular music (i.e. contextual studies). Popular Music Production is a course undertaken in each of the six semesters of the programme, and it is referred to as the programme's major study. It requires the submission of recorded original songs among a number of other assessment tasks. In this course, students undertake self-assessment and peer assessment – collectively referred to as *participatory assessment* – which is one of the defining characteristics of the programme (Lebler, 2007b, 2008; Partti et al., 2015). The contention is that this kind of assessment process will enhance students' learning autonomy, enhance their abilities to objectively assess the quality of their own work while it is in progress and develop their abilities to provide constructive feedback to their colleagues. Significantly, many of the activities included in this formal assessment process can be found in the learning of popular music outside structured formal learning environments. The provision of feedback to colleagues is normal practice in informal learning contexts, making the institutional study of popular music an ideal context for the use of these processes. In this programme, not only are the artistic values of popular music adopted in terms of what constitutes quality in students' creative work, but also these valuable learning activities are included.

The BPM programme exemplifies a *community of practice* (Wenger, 1998), a "scaffolded, self-directed learning environment" (Lebler, 2008, p. 2). Students are chosen in the programme's application and audition process for their diverse abilities in popular music (Lebler, 2005) and are encouraged to collaborate across year levels (Lebler & McWilliam, 2008). The academic framework and processes acknowledge the value of students' know-how and the autonomous, self-assessed and intrinsically motivated nature of prior music learning activities. The formalized structure enables and enhances these processes, enriching the learning experience and nurturing creative development. This is achieved through a carefully crafted BPM community, including students and lecturers as co-producers of learning, and the recording studio/process as the central connector and a source of instant feedback (Lebler, 2007a).

In Popular Music Production, the major study in the programme, learning is self-directed, with students deciding what they will record and with whom they will collaborate, submitting a proposal early in the semester which describes what they are planning to achieve. There is no direction from teachers about the style of music to be submitted, so students engage in a broad range of popular musical styles, from folk to death metal. This aligns with both the students' prior learning experiences (Lebler & Carey, 2008) and the intended learning outcome of independence, as explained by Lebler (2013): "Because independence is an important intended outcome, the appropriate pedagogical approach is the provision of support, stimulation, exemplars of previous student work and facilities rather than the imposition of too much micro management of the process by teachers" (p. 119). The major study courses include assessment *of* learning, *for* learning and *as* learning, and written submissions that foster self-reflection and self-assessment. In addition, students assess other students' work and provide constructive feedback through the assessment panel process, which is designed to encourage objective assessment and enhance communication skills. Graduates of the BPM programme will have a wide range of musical knowledge and training as well as the skills of autonomy, critical reflection and adaptability, which are nurtured through the participatory assessment activities, preparing students for a portfolio career (Lebler, 2006b). Lebler and Carey (2008) point out that "graduates have an impressive rate of employment in the areas for which they have been trained, that is, the autonomous practice of popular music" (p. 5).

Recording and reflection

Recording is an important contributor to the autonomy of students' learning; they can perform intuitively and afterwards reflect on the process and product of their work, creating a *master-less studio* (Lebler, 2006a).[1] Lebler (2007a) presents the view of recording as a valuable learning tool, providing the opportunity for critical reflection through instant playback, enabling the separation of performance and evaluation. Students' engagement in critical reflection can develop skills to monitor their own development (McWilliam et al., 2007). It is imperative for participants to be able to reflect critically on their practices (Lebler, 2008; Lebler & Carey, 2008; McWilliam et al., 2007). In the words of the graduate author in her BPM Honours Thesis:

> By third year, I was accepting myself as an engineer and producer, through knowledge and practices learnt from the programme and working with others. As a result my confidence as a player, performer, and songwriter was heightened. My creative process had come from relying on the skills of others to develop my song ideas to self-producing, using the creativity I had unlocked in previous collaborative projects. Being able to record opened up possibilities of layering instrumentation myself.
>
> Recording has been key at every stage, even when I have an idea (it may be melodic, harmonic or both), I record it with my home recording set up (computer, mbox and microphone) or on my iPhone. It is possible for me then to listen back with fresh ears and to judge the quality. Also, recording is useful as my partner and I can send each other ideas, add to them and send them back. Our writing process heavily relies on recording to develop ideas into a produced song. We set up keys, guitar and a vocal microphone in the studio. It is a creative space to record guides and continue re-working songs. In this environment it is possible to be creating while also having the ability to critique through play back and continually transform the song through layering tracks.
>
> The [recording] studio became a large factor in the creation of music. The processes of songwriting and recording were becoming more unified, while I was doing one the other was in mind. Our writing process heavily relies on recording to develop ideas into a produced song. It is a creative space to record guides and continue re-working songs. In this environment it is possible to be creating while also having the ability to critique, alternating between these activities rather than trying to create and critique simultaneously.
>
> (Burrell[2], 2013)

---

1 In this context, "studio" refers to both the recording studios in which students record, and "studio" as in "teaching studio", referring to the location for one-to-one teaching in Australia and elsewhere.
2 Note: The graduate author has married since her honours thesis was completed, and now uses her married name of Hodges rather than her maiden name of Burrell.

Collaboration

It was always the intent of the designers of the programme that students would work collaboratively, not just with fellow students from their own year, but also with students from other years in the programme, and even with people from outside the programme. The contributions of others are acknowledged in the written components of the major study, and most submissions are prepared collaboratively, but submitted individually. For the graduate author, this was an important aspect of her development.

> In semester two of my second year, I collaborated with a folk singer-songwriter, who was in his third year of BPM. In this collaboration, I was a producer as well as an engineer and performer ... That semester I discovered many things about my creative process; the studio became a large factor in the creation of my music.
>
> In my final semester of the degree programme I joined forces with a dear friend, who was also a singer-songwriter in my year. We began learning each other's songs and writing new songs together, working as a partnership creating an EP, playing most of the instruments ourselves. Through working closely with another singer-songwriter and recording the songs ourselves, I have improved both my writing and performance skills.
>
> I feel confident as an artist to write, perform and record my original material and also to collaborate. Now having left the structure of the BPM, I am still continually learning from listening to music and working with others. I feel established as an artist, I am confident to share my ideas and continue to improve my creative process ... While directed by the curriculum and the structure while I was a student, I was in control of my artistic development, with the freedom to choose my musical direction and my collaborators.
>
> (Burrell, 2013)

Supporting courses

Students are required to submit audio recordings of their original material in each of the six semesters of the programme, providing an opportunity for them to assimilate "skills and applications of knowledge learnt in other courses" (Lebler & McWilliam, 2008, p. 4); these other courses include audio engineering and production, creative music technologies, the analysis and history of popular music, live performance and music business (Lebler, 2006b, 2007a; Lebler & Carey, 2008; Lebler & McWilliam, 2008). The graduate author's reflections indicate that learning in the supporting courses was a major contributor to her development as a creative artist:

> My creative process was continually enriched by the knowledge learnt in supporting subjects. By the beginning of second year I had settled in to a journey of artistic discovery and development. Listening and learning about

music history and analysis, audio engineering and production, creative music technology and music theory was opening me up to new creative possibilities. Without the musical history and analysis stream my musical style would not be the same. Through learning about the history of popular music, I have developed a more diverse and informed musical knowledge that inspires my creative process.

The way I listen to music has changed, reflecting on how it makes me feel and what it is communicating. A new skill set developed as a result of writing an abundance of popular music production explanations over the years, and through learning and practicing semiotic analysis. The music industry course was not my favorite aspect of the programme, however, when looking back, it is clear I have already used what I learnt in this course in many ways. The ability to pick sounds and find a way to recreate similar ones has given me greater control over my production, expanding my instrumentation and mixing options in my music. What I learnt in the audio production courses has greatly shaped the way I make music.

(Burrell, 2013)

The major study assessment process

The academic author's publications on this topic reveal how pedagogy is embedded in the assessment processes, which include the participatory forms of self- and peer assessment in addition to assessment by teachers (Lebler, 2005, 2006b, 2008; Lebler & Carey, 2008; Lebler in Gaunt & Westerlund, 2013; Lebler & McWilliam, 2008). Lebler and Carey (2008) note that the development of critical reflection skills enables students to monitor their own progress and exhibit professional judgement (see also Lebler, 2005, 2014). The courses provide a structure in which students produce original music in a self-directed manner and self-assessment is achieved through written documentation (a proposal, reflective journal, track reports and self-marking), providing insight into the creative and learning processes, and furthered by a peer-assessment process in which each student is involved in an assessment panel comprising peers and a teacher (Lebler, 2006b, p. 203; Lebler in Gaunt & Westerlund, 2013). Moreover, the availability of peer and staff feedback is enhanced through work-in-progress sessions, held in a class for all year levels, and through an online application known as the Bachelor of Popular Music Assessment Tool (BoPMAT)[3] (Lebler in Gaunt & Westerlund, 2013). These structures are akin to the self- and peer assessment of informal learning among popular musicians (Lebler in Gaunt & Westerlund, 2013).

The act of assessing oneself and one's peers is a valuable learning practice, as noted by Biggs (1999) and Lebler (in Gaunt & Westerlund, 2013), and is important in the development of professionalism in any field of endeavour (Lebler, 2014).

---

3 "online submission and feedback forum … designed … with a look and feel intended to resemble popular social media sites" (Lebler in Gaunt & Westerlund, 2013, p. 116).

In addition, Lebler describes the intended learning outcomes for these courses, in Gaunt and Westerlund (2013), as "the ability to manage all aspects of complex recording processes independently and the ability to make systematic judgments as to the quality of their own work and the work of others" (p. 121). Active engagement of students and critical reflection are developed through the BPM assessment structure. In the words of the graduate author:

> I entered the Bachelor of Popular Music as a timid, unsure musician, seeking to gain knowledge. However, what I learnt was extraordinarily deeper than I had expected. I found a creative voice within myself and left the programme with confidence. No longer was I focused exclusively on the end result; I had learnt to enjoy the journey, the process of creating, assessing, and learning. The assessment process in the BPM shaped this deeper learning.
>
> It was confronting to mark, not only yourself, but also your peers. I had to sit back and assess myself, forced to view my "creative baby" objectively, not downplaying successes, but also not sugar coating shortcomings. The more I could be honest with my success and failures, the more I began to refine my creativity and try new ideas, unlocking potential and developing self-assessing skills. In the same way, I had to learn how to give feedback to my peers. As a people-pleaser and non-confrontational person, I found it difficult to write feedback. The panels enabled my development of assessing others as I listened, participated, and gleaned knowledge from the community of peers and lecturers, my fellow panel members. While refining my feedback skills, I also honed my self-assessing skills and gained confidence in my creative voice.
>
> My first engagement in reading feedback given to me was tough. It was hard to read a collective assessment of the work you have put your heart into. This was a major turning point for me; I had to learn to read feedback through a different lens, objectively deciphering and implementing feedback to further my creative skills. I knew all too well, outside the four walls of the university, criticism is a reality. I began to realize, perhaps the assessment was nurturing the ability to receive and give feedback in the professional world. I had awakened to the notion that creativity can be subject to a wide variety of human responses. Thus, it is through this journey we become stronger as artists and find our voice. In essence, through the assessment processes I grew a "thicker skin" and developed my creative self, which has enabled me to be a DIY musician ... Feedback is an aspect of my creative process that I continue to seek and apply.
>
> *(Burrell, personal communication)*

Conclusions

From its inception in the late 1990s, the formalized structure of the BPM programme was intended to develop in its graduates the attributes of self-direction, self-monitoring, autonomy, intrinsic motivation, diverse skills and the capacity to continue learning. These are attributes that the graduate author has identified as characteristics of DIY musicians, a term that was not in common use at the time the programme was designed, but relevant for emerging independent musicians in the 21st century; this kind of musical activity is becoming more common as DIY musicians achieve commercial success, aided by the constantly improving quality and accessibility of computer-based recording platforms such as the free application *GarageBand* through to the professional standard ProTools (Bell, 2015).

From the perspectives of both authors, it is clear that participatory assessment and holistic pedagogical practices have enhanced the skills of students in this programme in ways that are appropriate and useful in the current popular music context. The programme is routinely reviewed and improved incrementally (Lebler & Weston, 2015), but none of the practices mentioned in this chapter have been modified significantly in more than a decade because they are performing as expected, to the satisfaction of the students, graduates, teachers and managers of the programme.

Considering the important roles played by students in the programme, it is fitting that the graduate author has the last word:

> My musical identity as a DIY musician has developed through engagement in BPM's community of practice, centered on recording as feedback, student autonomy and a supporting curriculum. It is hard to fathom the breadth of my learning in the short space of three years. While not always fun or seemingly helpful at the time, I have found that every subject and every collaboration has enriched my creative process in ways that would not have been possible otherwise. This degree has been key in my development as an artist, and perhaps more significantly, as a person who is ready and able to face future challenges with confidence in my own abilities.

To quote a fellow student:

> Eventually a wise teacher came his way, but instead of telling him how to do it he told him the answer was in the doing, so he began to try on his own. I believe that this process is being used with us, giving us the power to learn what we need to by teaching ourselves.
>
> *(Student quoted in Lebler, 2007a, p. 126)*

References

Bell, P. (2015). DAW democracy? The dearth of diversity in "playing the studio". *Journal of Music, Technology and Education, 8*(2), 129–146.

Bianchi, A. (2009, July 28). Indie music 101: How to define independent music [Web log post]. 11 April 2013, from http://www.examiner.com/article/indie-music-101-how-to-define- independent-music [Accessed 11 April 2013].

Biggs, J.B. (1999). *Teaching for quality learning at university: What the student does*. Philadelphia, PA: Society for Research into Higher Education/Open University Press.

Burrell, N. (2013). *The BPM and the DIY musician*. Bachelor of Popular Music Honours Thesis. Queensland Conservatorium Griffith University. Brisbane.

Carey, G. & Lebler, D. (2008, July 15–20). *Prior learning of conservatoire students: A classical music perspective*. Paper presented at the 17th International Seminar of the International Society for Music Education Commission for the Education of the Professional Musician Commission, Spilamberto, Italy.

Claxton, G. (1999). *Wise up: The challenge of lifelong learning*. London: Bloomsbury.

Claxton, G. (2000). *Hare brain, tortoise mind: Why intelligence increases when you think less*. New York, NY: Harper Perennial.

Claxton, G. (2002). *Building learning power*. Bristol: TLO.

Csikszentmihalyi, M. (1991). *Flow: The psychology of optimal experience* (Harper Perennial ed.). New York: Harper Collins.

Gaunt, H. (2010). One-to-one tuition in a conservatoire: The perceptions of instrumental and vocal students. *Psychology of Music, 38*(2), 178–208.

Gaunt, H. & Westerlund, H. (Eds.) (2013). *Collaborative learning in higher music education*. Burlington, VT: Ashgate.

Green, L. (2001). *How popular musicians learn: A way ahead for music education*. Burlington, VT: Ashgate.

Green, L. (2006). Popular music education in and for itself, and for 'other' music: Current research in the classroom. *International Journal of Music Education, 24*(2), 101–118. doi:10.1177/0255761406065471.

Green, L. (2008). *Music, informal learning and the school: A new classroom pedagogy*. Burlington, VT: Ashgate.

Green, L. (2010). Informal learning in the music classroom: A seven-stage program. In J. Ballantyne & B. Bartleet (Eds.), *Navigating music and sound education* (pp. 96–114). Newcastle Upon Tyne: Cambridge Scholars Publishing.

Grohl, D. (2013, March, 15). Dave Grohl's SXSW keynote speech: The complete text. *Rolling Stone*, 1–5. Retrieved from: http://www.rollingstone.com/music/news/dave-grohls-sxsw-keynote-speech-the-complete-text-20130315 [Accessed 25 April 2013].

Hallam, S. & Gaunt, H. (2012). *Preparing for success: A practical guide for young musicians*. London: Institute of Education.

Jørgensen, H. (2009). *Research into higher music education: An overview from a quality improvement perspective*. Oslo: Novus Press.

Kusek, D., Leonhard, G., & Lindsay, S.G. (2005). *The future of music: Manifesto for the digital music revolution*. Boston: Berklee Press.

Lebler, D. (2004, November 4–5). *"Get smarter" music: Making knowledge from know-how*. Paper presented at the Effective Teaching and Learning Conference, Brisbane.

Lebler, D. (2005). Learning and assessment through recording. In E. Mackinlay, D. Collins, & S. Owens (Eds.), *Aesthetics and Experience in Music Performance* (pp. 319–328). Newcastle: Cambridge Scholars Press.

Lebler, D. (2006a). The master-less studio: An autonomous education community. *Journal of Learning Design, 1*(3), 41–50. Retrieved from: http://webcache.googleusercontent.com/search?q=cache:5ARTfTuIbRwJ:https://www.jld.edu.au/article/download/31/23+Lebler,+D.+(2005).+The+master-less+studio:+a&cd=1&hl=en&ct=clnk&gl=au&client=safari [Accessed 16 March 2012].

Lebler, D. (2006b, July 10–14, proceedings published 2007). *3D assessment: Looking through a learning lens*. Paper presented at the new models for educating professional musicians in the twenty-first century: Proceedings of the 16th International Seminar of the Commission for the Education of the Professional Musician (CEPROM), Hanoi National Conservatory of Music.

Lebler, D. (2007a). *Getting smarter music: A role for reflection in music learning.* (Unpublished doctorate thesis) Queensland University of Technology, Brisbane.

Lebler, D. (2007b). Student-as-master? Reflections on a learning innovation in popular music pedagogy. *International Journal of Music Education, 25*(3), 205–221. doi:10.1177/0255761407083575.

Lebler, D. (2008). Popular music pedagogy: Peer-learning in practice. *Music Education Research, 10*(2), 193–213. doi:10.1080/14613800802079056.

Lebler, D. (2013). Using formal self- and peer-assessment as proactive tools in building collaborative learning environments: Theory into practice. In H. Gaunt & H. Westerlund (Eds.), *Collaborative learning in higher music education: Why, what and how?* (pp. 111–121). Burlington, VT: Ashgate.

Lebler, D. (2014, July 15–18). *Promoting professionalism: Developing self-assessment in a popular music program.* Paper presented at the Relevance and Reform in the Education of Professional Musicians, 20th International Seminar of the ISME Commission for the Education of the Professional Musician (CEPROM), Belo Horizonte, Brazil.

Lebler, D. (2015). The BoPMAT: Bachelor of music popular music program. In D. Lebler, G. Carey & S. Harrison (Eds.), *Assessment in music education: From policy to practice.* (pp. 221–236) London: Springer.

Lebler, D. & Carey, G. (2008, July 15–20). *Prior learning of conservatoire students: A popular music perspective.* Paper presented at the 17th International Seminar of the International Society for Music Education Commission for the Education of the Professional Musician Commission, Spilamberto, Italy.

Lebler, D. & McWilliam, E. (2008, June 25–27). *Aligning curriculum, pedagogy and assessment for building creative capacity in undergraduate students: A case study from the conservatorium.* Presented at the Creating Value: Between Commerce and Commons Conference, Brisbane.

Lebler, D., Perkins, R.B., & Carey, G. (2009). What the students bring: Examining the attributes of commencing conservatoire students. *International Society for Music Education: Research, 27*(3), 232–249. doi:10.1177/0255761409335950.

Lebler, D. & Weston, D. (2015). Staying in sync: Keeping popular music pedagogy relevant to an evolving music industry. *IASPM Journal, 5*(1), 124–138.

Mantie, R. (2013). A comparison of "popular music pedagogy" discourses. *Journal of Research in Music Education, 61*(3), 334–352.

Marrouat, C. (2011, November 15). What is an independent artist? [Web log post]. Retrieved from: http://www.creativeramblings.com/what-is-an-independent-artist/ [Accessed 9 April 2013].

McWilliam, E. (2004). W(h)ither practitioner research? *Australian Educational Researcher, 31*(2), 113–126. doi:10.1007/BF03249522.

McWilliam, E., Lebler, D., & Taylor, P.G. (2007, June 17–21). *From passive consumers to active prod-users: Students as co-teachers in a popular music program.* Paper presented at the 13th International Conference on Thinking, Norrkoping, Sweden.

Oliver, G.P. (2010). The DIY artist: Issues of sustainability within local music scenes, *Management Decision, 48*(9), pp. 1422–1432. doi:10.1108/00251741011082161.

Partti, H. & Karlsen, S. (2010). Reconceptualising musical learning: New media, identity and community in music education. *Music Education Research, 12*(4), 369–382. doi:10.1080/14613808.2010.519381.

Partti, H., Westerlund, H., & Lebler, D. (2015). Participatory assessment and the construction of professional identity in folk and popular music programmes in Finnish and Australian music universities. *International Journal of music education.* doi:10.1177/0255761415584299

Pitts, S.E. (2010). Musical education as a social act: Learning from and within musical communities. In J. Ballantyne & B. Bartleet (Eds.), *Navigating Sound and Music Education* (pp. 115–128). Newcastle-upon-Tyne: Cambridge Scholars Publishing.

Smith, G.D. (2013). Pedagogy for employability in a Foundation Degree (FdA) in Creative Musicianship: Introducing peer collaboration. In H. Gaunt & H. Westerlund (Eds.), *Collaborative learning in higher music education: Why what and how* (pp. 193–198). Farnham: Ashgate.

Smith, G.D. & Gillett, A. (2015). Creativities, innovation, and networks in garage punk rock: A case study of the Eruptörs. *Artivate: A Journal of Entrepreneurship in the Arts, 4*(1), 9–24.

Smith, G.D. & Shafighian, A. (2013). Creative space and the "silent power of traditions" in popular music performance programmes. In P. Burnard (Ed.), *Developing creativities in higher music education: International perspectives and practices* (pp. 256–267). Abingdon: Routledge.

Wenger, E. (1998). *Communities of practice. Learning, meaning, and identity*. Cambridge: Cambridge University Press.

Westerlund, H. (2006). Garage rock bands: A future model for developing musical expertise? *International Journal for Music Education, 24*(2), 119–125. doi:10.1177/0255761406065472.

23
Towards a framework for creativity in popular music degrees

Joe Bennett

Introduction: Music education and popular music education

Let us begin with semantics. The only reason we might use the term 'popular music degree' is to differentiate its content from that of a 'music degree' – not 'classical music degree', but 'music degree'. That is to say, the *default* semantic in higher music education is to assume that 'music' means 'classical music', despite the fact that the Western Art-music/classical canon represents only a tiny proportion of the music that global society consumes today, and an even smaller proportion of what has been produced historically. Specialized music education in the developed world is dominated by the Western classical music tradition, and in higher education this is historically characterized by the 'conservatoire'.[1] In the 17th century the primary function of the earliest French and Italian music schools developed out of the church's need for composers to write music, and singers to perform it. As the demand for secular instrumental music expanded, what we might call the 'Naples model' of selective conservatoires spread across Europe;[2] their primary *raison d'être* was to train instrumental and vocal performers to achieve sufficient expertise to play the music of the day (Nettl, 1995; Papageorgi et al., 2010; Parkinson, 2013; Stakelum, 2013).

I begin this chapter about popular music curricula by talking about classical conservatoires in order to demonstrate that the latter were called into existence with an employability[3] agenda – to provide people who could fulfil society's musi-

---

1 In Australia, 'conservatorium'; in the USA 'conservatory'.
2 For a historically specific description of this spread see Freeman (2014, Kindle loc. 641).
3 Not all of these societal needs related to professional musicians. Music-making was also considered a social activity, and the conservatoires had a partly social agenda. Robert Freeman (2014, Kindle

cal needs. The Enlightenment's music industry needed, in descending order of quantity, players to fill its orchestras, teachers to sustain itself and, occasionally, composers to provide content for the first two groups to play and teach. These were some of the drivers of conservatoire institutional admissions decisions and curriculum designs.

Much has been written about how instrumentalists learn, and some authors (Freeman, 2014; Gaunt & Westerlund, 2013; Hallam et al., 2012; Small, 1998) have begun to argue for a more holistic approach to conservatoire music education that adds more contextual listening, composing and entrepreneurial skills to the historically dominant instrument-based tradition. Learning to play an instrument requires 'interiorized' physical skills acquisition, as famously articulated in David Sudnow's autoethnographic account of learning to play jazz piano, *Ways of the Hand* (1993). As Dreyfus (in Sudnow, 1993, p. xi) notes, the iterative learning through repetition implicit in teaching our bodies to play an instrument is the opposite of the "cognitivist theory of skill acquisition":

> Rather than moving from specific cases to abstract principles, skill acquisition seems to move in the opposite direction, from principles followed until they are interiorized, to the possession of so many types of concrete cases that the types of responses that each situation leads fluidly to the next.

I shall call this approach 'instrumentalism'; learner and teacher alike are concerned with the internalization of sophisticated motor and audio/visual recognition skills required to play an instrument or to sing, with supporting activities such as aural acuity and harmonic literacy. These skills bring with them forms of cognition, but Sudnow's experience demonstrates that instrumental skills cannot be developed through cognition alone. Speaking as a musician, composer and musicologist, but as someone who cannot play the violin, I may understand the instrument cognitively; I have some knowledge of its range, construction, timbral qualities and its role in various ensembles and repertoire, and I might even be able to brief a violinist in a rehearsal. But this knowledge base does not go very far in helping me to create beautiful music when I pick up a violin.

To an experienced music teacher in higher education, most of the above discussion is self-evident, and pedagogies that acknowledge it have long been established. Although instrumental *learning* can and does take place in many contexts, including private practice and ensemble work, most instrumental *teaching* takes place in a one-to-one environment, and the lesson plan is paced

---

loc. 649) notes that the European conservatoires of the early 1800s were "anti-intellectual" with a "Protestant ethic", and that one of their functions was to develop music skills in young ladies "as a social grace and as a means of attracting a good husband". Freeman argues that during the 20th century, US conservatories shifted from primarily training musicians for music education and social cohesion towards an aspiration to "develop graduates who can fill the nation's very small number of professional positions in the performance of classical music".

according to the student's progression through pre-established learning outcomes. Both tutor and student have a common goal to *play the piece well*. In this regard, the conservatoire's aims are closely aligned with the goals of the society it serves. Society needs orchestras and other ensembles in the Art-music tradition,[4] and there is a threshold of technical competency that a musician must meet in order to participate in these. The iterative and linear journey towards this threshold is commonly undertaken in music schools, and is ingrained in pedagogical practice. Most conservatoires and many universities also teach music (teacher) education, ensuring that pedagogical traditions are passed on to the next generation.

Recent music pedagogy has begun to wrestle with the way popular musicians acquire their requisite skills. Lucy Green's influential book *How Popular Musicians Learn* (2002) acknowledges that popular musicians acquire musical skills differently from classical musicians, using the respective terms "haphazard" and "linear" (Green, 2002, pp. 207–209); Green is one of a small number of music education scholars who have discussed the role of songwriting in the curriculum.[5] Andrew Hugill (2012) categorizes musician types, and related curricular approaches, by music's raw elements of pitch, rhythm and timbre, and broadly aligns these three with classical, popular and digital musicians respectively. Although he acknowledges that such distinctions have necessary levels of overlap, his core argument is that higher music education concentrates disproportionately upon pitch-based music skills and disproportionately under-develops learners in the "rhythmic" (pop/rock) and "timbral" (digital) categories (Hugill, 2012, pp. 4–5).

What, then, should be the goals and aspirations of a popular music curriculum in higher education? To answer this question we might begin from the perspective of society's requirement for musically proficient people, and work our way backwards from the music to identify the individuals who create it. Popular music, as famously argued by Adorno (1941), is a mass-market, commoditized product, designed and manufactured to appeal to a large number of people and, at least during the sheet music and phonographic eras of the 20th century, built on a retail-based economic model, albeit with signs of erosion in the early 21st century due to the de-commoditization immanent in online digital distribution. Its market-driven, quasi-Darwinist existence requires neither subsidy nor preservation; it needs only an audience, without whom it cannot exist. Therefore, like the conservatoires before them, schools and departments of popular music need to teach skills that can supply the needs of the listeners their students intend to serve.

---

4 Some recent writers (Covach, 2015; Fitzpatrick, 2015; Freeman, 2014) have bemoaned the oversupply of classical music graduates to the professional orchestral workforce. I do not intend to dwell on this particular issue here, but the debate does have obvious implications for the future curricular balance between popular and classical musics in music schools generally. It also highlights the assumption that conservatoires' primary raison d'être is to train graduates for employment as performers, despite this oversupply being so widely acknowledged.

5 See also Bennett, 2015; Kratus, 2014; Randles, Clint, 2014.

Joe Bennett

Making popular music

Popular music's aural product manifests itself in one of two ways – as a sound recording, or as a performance. Each of these has, since the mid-20th century, been monetized differently for the consumer, respectively as a retail audio product (vinyl, cassette, CD) and as a live show. The sound recording can exist in a stand-alone format or can be combined with other media (e.g. film and TV or video games). Indeed, the world's collection societies (e.g. the Performing Right Society in the UK, or ASCAP/BMI in the USA) have built entire administrative systems around the distinction between the performance of a work and the sound recording of that work. Both of these aural products are manifestations of creative teamwork (Jones, chapter 27, this volume). A sound recording may represent the work of songwriters, arrangers, programmers, performers, producers, digital audio workstation operators and mixing/mastering engineers. A live show may include all of the above (due to the common reliance on technological augmentation through sample triggering, backing tracks or live production editing), and has the additional requirement that performers need to be able to play and sing consistently well for the duration of an evening's entertainment.

Allan Moore (2012, p. 15) classifies popular music's recorded artefact as a "track" which consists of two elements – the "song" and the "performance". His definition aligns broadly with most of the world's collection agencies, in that the composition and the recording are considered separate copyrights. In my "Track Imperatives" (Bennett, 2015, p. 45; see Figure 23.1), I have attempted to sub-categorize Moore's definition further in order to identify the core skills that recorded popular music production requires. These activities were identified through ethnographic work interviewing professional songwriters, 2005–2013 (Bennett, 2014). The attributes themselves could be further sub-categorized, and for each analogue and real-time manifestation of them there is a digital and/or non-linear equivalent (e.g. instrumental performance could be replaced by programming beats or notes).

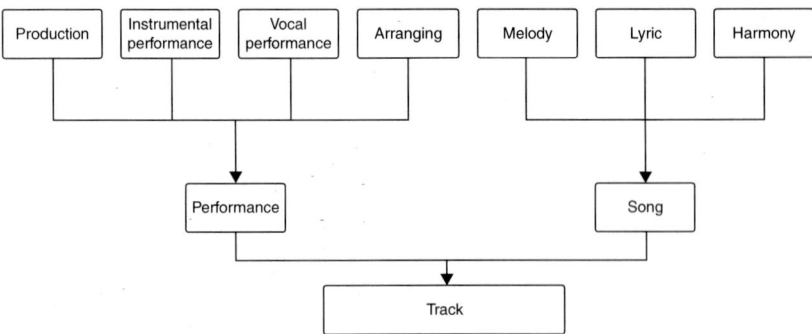

Figure 23.1 Track Imperatives
Source: Bennett (2015, p. 45)

Instrumental or vocal performance skills, then, represent only a small part of the popular music production chain. This has been the case throughout the phonographic era. Carole King (2012) identifies the contributors to her 1967 hit '(You Make Me Feel Like a) Natural Woman', citing (in addition to vocalist Aretha Franklin) a long list of arrangers, co-writers, session players, mix engineers and even the marketing department as the creative team behind the success of the work. Almost 50 years after King's recording was released, German pop producer and songwriter Marc Mozart (2009) identifies very similar teamwork requirements for 21st century Europeans. Interestingly, his list of requirements omits instrumental facility entirely:

> Few people if any excel in all areas. A hit song requires a lot of specialized knowledge: melodies; a lyrical concept (and of course lyrics); chords; arrangement; production/sound design; vocal arranging; vocals (singing); vocal editing; mixing. Form partnerships where . . . 2–4 people bring top quality in all these areas to the table.

It follows that a popular music education curriculum that focuses exclusively on the instrumentalist is unlikely to beget meaningful creative outcomes in terms of popular music's product. At best it would generate session musicians who could succeed in particular roles in music performance, e.g. theatre pit or cruise ship band performance (Cashman, 2014), studio session work, cover bands or touring bands for existing artists. Many music graduates go on to become successful music teachers, but I suggest that the requisite pedagogical skill set is acquired additionally to the core musical learning developed through instrumentalism.

What is the role of instrumental technique in popular music education? An orchestral musician may be required to play anything that the session/concert requires, and this requires a sophisticated level of technique. By contrast, many of the top pop performers – that is, mainstream bands/artists who work on original material – may not need an advanced level of instrumental skill. The recording process does not necessarily require this due to the ubiquity of multi-tracking, multiple takes, non-linear editing and 'comping' tools.[6] There are of course sub-genres of popular music that require advanced instrumental skills and harmonic knowledge (prog rock, some heavy metal and particularly jazz, which unsurprisingly was the first 'popular' genre to be embraced by conservatoires), but most popular music does not require virtuosity from its instrumentalists, although it almost always requires timbral or technical distinctiveness from the vocalist. At the

---

6 Compositing, or compiling. The term refers to the practice of performing multiple studio takes – most commonly of a vocal – and choosing the best parts of each to create a single superhuman performance with the best attributes selected. Comping has been common practice in recorded music since the common availability of multi-track recording from the 1960s, and computer-based digital audio recording makes it a simple matter to select any part of a performance and combine it with any other. For example, it is not uncommon to splice single syllables or even parts of syllables in a vocal take to achieve the desired result.

time of writing (January 2015), none of the top 10 most popular iTunes downloads feature what might be called technically demanding instrumental performances – not least because some do not feature live instruments at all. The most downloaded song in the UK is currently Mark Ronson's 'Uptown Funk' (2014), which is heavily based upon a Dm7-G two-chord disco groove. Although it does include some live or quasi-live instruments (notably, percussively strummed electric guitar and a repeating 4-bar brass riff), performing these parts as a live band would not require particularly advanced instrumental technique (at least, in the way the term 'technique' would be used in a conservatoire). This is not to denigrate Ronson's (or any other pop artist's) work, but rather to observe that in popular music, songwriting, arrangement and production are as important as the ability to play an instrument. To design a popular music curriculum exclusively around iterative instrumental learning, then, would be unlikely to produce meaningful creative work in itself.

Returning to my Track Imperatives (Bennett, 2015), it is clear that not only does popular music not always demand advanced instrumental technique, but its production also includes creative acts that do not require instrumental skills at all. How are these other 'Track Imperatives' learned? Can they be taught? I now consider a few of these creative contributions to popular music and discuss possible pedagogical approaches and challenges.

Songwriting

The traditional definition of a songwriter is someone who creates the melody, lyric and harmony in a song (McIntyre, 2001). Music industry administrative systems reward the songwriter separately from the performer, and copyright protects the song as a composition differently from the sound recording of the song, privileging melody above all other creative content (Demers, 2006). This pre-digital-age definition of the songwriting act is problematic for some contemporary popular music, given the other Track Imperatives, and considering that most popular music is at least partly created using a computer. However, it is clear that the traditional melodic, harmonic and literary skills associated with mid-20th century songwriting are alive and well in the 21st century pop mainstream; from the 1990s to the 2010s producer-created computer-based music has coexisted easily with the music of bands and singer-songwriters who play live instruments. One of the Beatles' many innovations was arguably to steer the industrial model of pop creation, at least for bands, towards writing one's own material. Before 1962 it was commonplace for music publishers to provide songs for bands to record – indeed, music publisher Dick James persuaded George Martin to arrange the newly signed Beatles to demo the Mitch Murray song "How Do You Do It", although both Martin and the band successfully stood by their preference for the self-written song "Please Please Me" (Davies, 2009, p. 258). The artist-as-songwriter model became, and remains, the music industry norm for 'authentic' bands and artists, and although present-day pop aimed at younger audiences often maintains the separate-songwriter production model, some artists whose songs are written by others may be incentivized to conceal this fact or find a way of ensuring a songwriting credit (Bennett, 2013).

Regardless of the extent of the overlap between songwriter and artist, arguments for including songwriting in a popular music curriculum may be as strong as the arguments for including instrumental lessons in a classical one, even though such inclusivity is still considered in many institutions to be subversive (Kratus, 2014). Of course, not all working popular musicians make their living writing songs, but a significant number of bands and artists co-write material. There is an obvious incentive for portfolio-career popular music graduates to have an awareness of music publishing, and to experience the creative and artistic rewards of writing original music.

Andrew Hugill argues that musicians who use digital tools are not necessarily digital musicians:

> "Digital musicians" are . . . not defined by their use of technology alone. A classical pianist giving a recital on a digital piano is not really a digital musician, nor is a composer using a notation software package to write a string quartet. These are musicians using digital tools to facilitate an outcome that is not conceived in digital terms.
>
> *(2012, p. 5)*

I agree with his assertion, and it is something of a truism; digital tools augment many aspects of our lives but are not always used to create an inherently digital product. However, in the case of popular music, the product itself is partly digital, not only in its means of distribution and consumption but also in its means of production. Most 21st-century popular music that we hear is impossible to produce without a computer. Even 'authentic' bands and artists who appear to market an uncontrived recorded product may benefit from an array of studio and production techniques. One of the paradoxes of rock music, for example, is that it is a recorded medium that purports, perhaps falsely, to document a performance medium authentically, and that bands therefore need producers in order to contrive this authenticity (Frith, 2012, pp. 207–208). It follows, equally paradoxically, that an authentic contemporary rock band will need at least one member of their creative team with a mastery of digital production techniques.

Should digital production skills be ring-fenced to specialist 'music production' programmes? I suggest not; 21st-century popular musicians have access to digital production tools that 20th-century phonographic-era creators could only dream of, and these tools are becoming ever more affordable and usable (Bennett, 2010). Musicians frequently self-demo their own work, and sometimes fully self-produce the finished recording. It is difficult to argue that a hypothetical popular music curriculum that eschews digital music production skills is not hindering its students' creative development.

Marketing and distribution

If the democratization of music production has allowed artists to self-produce to some extent, then the equivalent trend in marketing has created related autonomies in self-promotion. Since the early 2000s a band web presence has been a commercial necessity, and the rise of social media ensures that online communication with fans must be two-way (Dubber, 2012). An artist's 'creative team', whether corporate or home-grown, will include those who can manage social media, and learning this skill set could reasonably be argued to be an important part of a popular music curriculum. The distribution online of promotional materials invokes creative questions about the materials themselves: Should artists undertake their own photography, shoot their own videos and design their own logos? If so, perhaps a crash course in camera-work and an academic study of semiotics is the order of the day.

The popular music industry has changed in the 21st century, to the extent that the retail-based economic model of the phonographic years, whereby fans bought a physical recording or a single-file download, is declining faster than streaming-based funding models are rising (Degusta, 2011). The recorded product, whether video or audio, is now perhaps nothing more than a loss-leading calling card for live shows (and their attendant merchandizing). Consumers seem happy to pay ever-inflated concert ticket prices (Jones, 2010), while being disinclined to spend anything at all on a 'purchased' recording (Page, 2006). This does not mean that popular music students do not need to learn to make recordings, just that the recordings themselves – and the attendant royalties – may not be their primary source of income when they graduate. If live performance is so important, then, curriculum will need to include performance skills beyond those of simply playing an instrument; stagecraft will play a necessary part, because employable popular music graduates are likely to spend a significant amount of their work time performing live.

Popular music studies

If the conservatoires in the late 20th century initially responded to the societal rise of popular music with indifference (Covach, 2015), some universities took a different approach. This is often euphemistically referred to as 'Popular Music Studies' (PMS), and it has its roots in sociology and cultural studies. PMS holds that popular music can be studied as a social, cultural or economic phenomenon rather than an aural, creative or otherwise musicological one, and many current university popular music programmes and modules[7] in the UK include considerable PMS-related content. Tagg (2006, p. 47) describes the two approaches as 'conventional muso formalism (MUSIC AS MUSIC – the TEXT) and conventional social or cultural theory (EVERYTHING ABOUT MUSIC EXCEPT THE MUSIC – the CONTEXT)'. He notes a minority of musicians and musicologists ('musos') in PMS:

> ... conventional music studies deals a lot with the music as sonic text and only a little, if at all, with music as social practice and context; popular music

---

[7] Modules are sometimes called 'units' (UK) and 'courses' (US).

studies, on the other hand, tends to deal much less with THE MUSIC and a lot with its social, cultural, economic and political ramifications. This difference between the two traditions of studying music relates to the simple fact that their institutional habitats are also different: while musicians and musicologists (musos) dominate classical music studies, they are a minority in popular music studies which is dominated by scholars from the humanities and social sciences (cultural studies).

Many outstanding scholarly contributions have been made in both areas over the years, and the research community has often debated the tensions between the two approaches. Sociologists such as Frith and Toynbee are able to discuss popular music with barely a nod to musical or technical specifics; musicologists such as Moore, Everett and Tagg can provide sophisticated analyses of works and artists without the need to analyze their cultural environment. Tagg implies that the approaches have, in the past, been in opposition; recent research into popular music in higher education (Cloonan & Hulstedt, 2012; Parkinson & Smith, 2015) suggests that PMS has developed considerably and is moving away from (what Tagg argues to be) its exclusively cultural studies roots.

Returning to the idea of a creativity-focused popular music curriculum, I suggest that PMS may not necessarily be the first port of call in providing a scholarly context to underpin the learning of students who wish to *make* popular music. A classical conservatoire might see the benefit of a musicology module inasmuch as it would inform the study of particular techniques, works or composers, but it would not necessarily expect its students to be better players or singers as a direct result of studying musicology. I am not arguing here for an entirely practical curriculum (and certainly not for an anti-intellectual one), but rather for a more holistic approach to contextual study. Musicology is one of the areas of knowledge-based learning that might support a popular musician's creative skill set, but it is one among many. In addition to the aforementioned marketing and semiotics, improved musical creativity could be supported by study of acoustics (harmonic series, waveforms, dynamics, principles of synthesis, etc.) or poetry appreciation (imagery, rhythm, prosody, rhetoric, narrative).

Recalling Marc Mozart's perspective as a popular music practitioner, his analyses of bass mixing in Meghan Trainor's "All About That Bass" and Taylor Swift's "Shake It Off" (Mozart, 2014a, 2014b) discuss frequency curve, the significance of the 2nd harmonic, the application of high pass filters and the perceptual loudness of the mix. The musicological content of each song is described in a single sentence by identifying the simple three-chord/four-bar loop on which it is based. The dynamic and timbral content of these tracks is arguably as significant a part of the listener's experience as their pitch-based content. So a popular music student aiming to create a recorded object would benefit equally – or perhaps more – from interpreting the timbral characteristics of a mix as from undertaking pitch-based chord analysis. This might be taught through expansion of popular musicology into more production-based research (which in the 21st century is beginning to happen through organizations such as the Art of Record Production and the

Audio Engineering Society) or the inclusion of extra-musicological contextual learning in a popular music curriculum.

Transferable skills and employability

Implicit in classical conservatoires' curricula is an assumption that the curriculum's primary outcome is one of employment in music. Indeed, many such institutions (including my own, The Boston Conservatory in the USA) explicitly use the word 'training' to describe the student experience. Given the inescapable fact that many music graduates have successful careers outside music, and many of these speak proudly of the contribution their music degree made to their lives (National Association for Music in Higher Education, 2015), it is clear that a music-only employability focus should not be the sole consideration in designing a music curriculum.

Higher education, even in specialist music institutions, can and should go beyond skills training for a specialist career. The idea that the student learning experience should engender transferable skills and self-development is established in institutional cultures, specified in national curricular frameworks (QAA, 2008) and much discussed in pedagogical research (Bridges, 1993; Hallam et al., 2012). Contemporary US conservatories often include substantial liberal arts provision to support their core performer-training curricula, but this is less common in the UK. Transferable skills can include teamwork, problem-solving, critical thinking and the exercise of initiative and personal responsibility, and in recent decades these have inevitably placed increased focus on digital, online and information literacy.

Defensible as the inclusion of a focus on transferable skills may be, it raises a dilemma for curriculum design in training-based music curricula because a balance must be struck between depth and breadth. If music-making skills are not explored sufficiently, the graduate risks being under-skilled and therefore under-employable in music. But if transferable skills are under-taught, the risk to graduates' future career prospects may be even greater, because such skills are by definition applicable to a variety of future life or career paths. Clearly, popular music curriculum designers have a moral responsibility to find this balance, and to consider the manifold career paths that a graduate may take within and beyond music.

Why 'popular' music education?

I have argued for a 'reverse-engineered' approach to curriculum design, working back from the musical product to identify its creators and therefore the requisite learning. This is not to say that we need to define 'popular music' purely as recorded mainstream pop product. If one interprets the term more broadly to mean any music that large numbers of people might engage with, then 'popular music' would include music for TV and film, advertisements, games and apps and websites; supermarket 'muzak'; phone on-hold music; karaoke backing tracks; radio jingles; community choirs; folk clubs; music for dance and theatre (and musical theatre itself) and church music in all its forms. All of these are 'real-world' uses of music, and all are popular. Writing, recording and performing them requires advanced skills of artistic craft, and music graduates might find themselves commissioned to create any of them professionally, whether as a composer, performer, producer, MD, programmer or teacher.

When popular music is defined societally in this way – less by its musicological or aesthetic content than by its usage – the absurdity of any mono-cultural music curriculum, whether popular or classical, starts to become clear. Employable music graduates of the future may find themselves in any number of different, unpredictable musical (and extra-musical) situations in their professional lives. The broader their skill sets and the wider their personal listening canons, the better placed they will be to respond to whatever creative gigs might come their way. By this logic, perhaps what is needed is less a definition of popular music curricula in higher education than a more holistic approach to all music degrees.

References

Adorno, T.W. (1941). On popular music. *Studies in Philosophy and Social Science*, IX, 17–48.

Bennett, S. (2010). Revisiting the "Double Production Industry": Equipment manufacturing, consumption and the music technology press in the late 2000s. Presented at the Music, Law & Business – Biennial Conference of IASPM, Helsinki, Iceland. Retrieved from: http://www.academia.edu/1517580/Revisiting_the_Double_Production_Industry_Equipment_Manufacturing_Consumption_and_the_Music_Technology_Press_in_the_Late_2000s

Bennett, J. (2013). "You Won't See Me" – In search of an epistemology of collaborative songwriting. In *JARP Issue #8: 8th Art of Record Production Conference Proceedings (published Dec 2013)* (Vol. 8). Quebec, Canada: Art of Record Production.

Bennett, J. (2014). *Constraint, creativity, copyright and collaboration in popular songwriting teams*. Guildford, UK: Surrey.

Bennett, J. (2015). Creativities in popular songwriting curricula. In P. Burnard & E. Haddon (Eds.), *Activating diverse musical creativities: Teaching and learning in higher education* (pp. 37–55). London: Bloomsbury.

Bridges, D. (1993). Transferable skills: A philosophical perspective. *Studies in Higher Education*, *18*(1), 43–51. Retrieved from: http://doi.org/10.1080/03075079312331382448

Cashman, D. (2014). Corporately Imposed Music Cultures: An Ethnography of Cruise Ship Showbands. *Ethnomusicology Review*, *19*. Retrieved from: http://ethnomusicologyreview.ucla.edu/journal/volume/19/piece/797

Cloonan, M. & Hulstedt, L. (2012). *Taking notes: Mapping and teaching popular music in higher education*. Higher Education Academy. Retrieved from: https://www.heacademy.ac.uk/sites/default/files/Cloonan_2012.pdf

Covach, J. (2015, February 2). Rock Me, Maestro. *The Chronicle of Higher Education*. Retrieved from: http://chronicle.com/article/Rock-Me-Maestro/151423/?key=T211dAM6NSdMY3piMjxCYz5SaXNsNhgiYCNJPyx1bl1dFw==

Davies, H. (2009). *The Beatles* (Updated and rev. ed). London: Ebury Press.

Degusta, M. (2011, February 18). The REAL death of the music industry. *Business Insider*. Retrieved 1 December 2014, from http://www.businessinsider.com/these-charts-explain-the-real-death-of-the-music-industry-2011-2?IR=T

Demers, J. (2006). *Steal this music – How intellectual property law affects musical creativity*. Athens : University of Georgia Press.

Dubber, A. (2012). *Music in the digital age: Making sense of the commerce and culture of popular music*. Retrieved from: https://leanpub.com/dubber

Fitzpatrick, R. (2015, April 16). A vicious cycle exists in American Higher Music Education. Retrieved from: http://slippedisc.com/2015/04/robert-fitzpatrick-a-vicious-cycle-exists-in-american-musical-higher-education/?utm_source=feedburner&utm_medium=email&utm_campaign=Feed%3A+slippedisc%2FnICW+%28Slipped+Disc%29

Freeman, R. (2014). *The crisis of classical music in America: Lessons from a life in the education of musicians*. Lanham, MD: Rowman & Littlefield.

Frith, S. & Zagorski-Thomas, S. (Eds.) (2012). *The art of record production: An introductory reader for a new academic field*. Burlington, VT: Ashgate.

Gaunt, H. & Westerlund, H. (2013). *Collaborative learning in higher music education*. Retrieved from: http://www.dawsonera.com/depp/reader/protected/external/AbstractView/S9781409446835

Green, L. (2002). *How popular musicians learn: A way ahead for music education*. Aldershot, Hants; Burlington, VT: Ashgate.

Hallam, S., Creech, A., Adams, P., Conlon, J., Durrant, C., Ellison, J., . . . Welch, G. (2012). *Music education in the 21st century in the United Kingdom: Achievements, analysis and aspirations*. London: Institute of Education Press. Retrieved from: http://public.eblib.com/choice/publicfullrecord.aspx?p=1047876

Hugill, A. (2012). *The digital musician* (2nd ed.). New York; London: Routledge.

Jones, R. (2010, March 13). Ticket inflation – The new rock "n" roll. Retrieved 3 February 2015, from http://www.theguardian.com/money/2010/mar/13/ticket-price-inflation-rock-n-roll

King, C. (2012). *A natural woman: A memoir* (1st ed). New York: Grand Central Pub.

Kratus, J. (2014). The role of subversion in changing music education. In C. Randles (Ed.), *Music education: Navigating the future* (pp. 322–346). Routledge.

McIntyre, P. (2001). The domain of songwriters: Towards defining the term "Song." *Perfect Beat: The Pacific Journal of Research into Contemporary Music and Popular Culture*, 5(3), 100–111.

Moore, A.F. (2012). *Song means: Analysing and interpreting recorded popular song*. Farnham, Surrey; Burlington, VT: Ashgate.

Mozart, M. (2009, August). Mozart & friends blog – Three ground rules for pop songwriters. Retrieved from: http://www.mozartandfriends.com/news/2009_08_three_ground_rules_for_pop_songwriters_by_marc_mozart.htm

Mozart, M. (2014a, October). "All About That Bass", Tutorial, Mix by Kevin Kadish. Retrieved from: http://www.mixedbymarcmozart.com/2014/10/08/all-about-that-bass-shake-it-off-mixing-advice-mix-analysis/

Mozart, M. (2014b, October). Mixing low end: "Shake It Off" by Taylor Swift (Mix by Serban Ghenea). Retrieved from: http://www.mixedbymarcmozart.com/2014/10/15/mixing-low-end-shake/

National Association for Music in Higher Education. (2015). *The value of a music degree 1*. Retrieved from: https://vimeo.com/114657208 [Accessed 1 September 2015].

Nettl, B. (1995). *Heartland excursions: Ethnomusicological reflections on schools of music*. Urbana: University of Illinois Press.

Page, W. (2006, December 2). Is the price of recorded music heading towards zero? *PRS for Music "Transmission" Magazine*.

Papageorgi, I., Creech, A., Haddon, E., Morton, F., De Bezenac, C., Himonides, E., ... Welch, G. (2010). Perceptions and predictions of expertise in advanced musical learners. *Psychology of Music*, *38*(1), 31–66.

Parkinson, T. (2013). Canon (re)formation in Popular Music Pedagogy. In M. Stakelum (Ed.), *Developing the musician: Contemporary perspectives on teaching and learning* (pp. 155–170). Burlington, VT: Ashgate.

Parkinson, T. & Smith, G.D. (2015). Towards an epistemology of authenticity in higher music education. *Action, Criticism, & Theory for Music Education*, *14*(1), 92–127.

Perkins, R. (2013). Learning cultures and the conservatoire: An ethnographically-informed case study. *Music Education Research*, *15*(2), 196–213. Retrieved from: http://doi.org/10.1080/14613808.2012.759551

QAA. (2008). *The framework for higher education qualifications in England, Wales and Northern Ireland (FHEQ)*. Quality Assurance Agency for Higher Education, UK. Retrieved from: http://www.qaa.ac.uk/publications/informationandguidance/pages/the-framework-for-higher-education-qualifications-in-england-wales-and-northern-ireland.aspx

Randles, Clint. (2014). A theory of change in music education. In Randles, Clint (Ed.), *Music education: Navigating the future* (pp. 323–339). London: Routledge.

Ronson, M. (2014). *Uptown Funk* [Audio download] (Vol. Uptown Special). London: Sony/Columbia/RCA.

Small, C. (1998). *Musicking: The meanings of performing and listening*. Hanover: University Press of New England. Retrieved from: http://site.ebrary.com/id/10468483

Stakelum, M. (Ed.) (2013). *Developing the musician: Contemporary perspectives on teaching and learning*. Burlington, VT: Ashgate.

Sudnow, D. (1993). *Ways of the hand: The organization of improvised conduct* (1st MIT Press ed). Cambridge, MA: MIT Press.

Tagg, P. & Clarida, R. (2006). Ten little title tunes. Retrieved from: www.tagg.org.

24
Re-Mixing Popular Music Marketing Education

Ray Sylvester and Daragh O'Reilly

Introduction

This chapter aims to offer a new way of imagining popular music marketing education, based on a fusion of different perspectives. The first author has always integrated his music industry experience (practice) with his (academic) research interest in music marketing and brand management at teaching-orientated business management schools. So, as a popular music marketing 'pracademic' (Posner, 2009), he co-wrote the first music business degree in Europe in the mid-1990s. Currently he combines his music industry practice as a Music Manager with being an Associate Professor in Marketing and Personal Branding in the Falls School of Business at Anderson University, Indiana, USA. The second author is a commercial sales/marketer who became a full-time educator, completed a cultural studies PhD on a popular music topic, and works in a research-orientated UK management school teaching arts marketing and branding. In this chapter we suggest that popular music marketing, as taught in the classroom, needs to be set in a wider sociocultural context and to draw upon insights from other disciplines, including, for example, cultural studies, media studies, consumer culture and sociology of the arts – hence the notion of 're-mixing' in the chapter title. Teaching popular music marketing to students without adapting the subject to the wider context in which music-making and -marketing practices occur is unlikely to be of lasting benefit in the lives and careers of students (see also Hooper, chapter 13, this volume). We make this assertion based on our extensive experience as marketing practitioners and educators, and, in the case of the first author, as an artist manager.

Marketing and promotional practices have always been a fundamentally important aspect of the popular music business. They have helped to establish what we know as the global popular music market today. However, marketing has become increasingly heterogeneous, with each market existing in its own sociocultural context, which in turn shapes and impacts musicians, popular music creativity, classification (genre), the company or companies involved, marketing channels, pricing, communications and ultimately consumption, including consumer choice. The end of the 20th century and the beginning of the 21st century have marked a transition into a digital age, which has had a profound impact on the traditional supply chain for music and, subsequently, music marketing practices (Sylvester, 2012). These major changes, together with advances in marketing and consumption theory and empirical research (e.g. O'Reilly, Larsen, & Kubacki, 2013; Szmigin & Piacentini, 2014; Tadajewski & Brownlie, 2009), make it timely and necessary to review how popular music marketing education (PMME) is construed.

Contemporary PMME has, arguably, been generally slow to respond to developments and to provide new approaches that encompass changes in practice and insights from relevant theoretical disciplines. New or adapted conceptual models are continually needed to sensitize students to the dynamic complexities of music marketing practices. A key part of higher popular music education (HPME) should be developing an up-to-date knowledge and understanding of the role of marketing in 21st-century popular music culture. Students require a conceptual and theoretical base that is responsive, flexible and can accommodate changes in practice as well as making good use of strong insights from research and theory. In this regard, our focus is primarily on third-level education. We offer some suggested guidelines for PMME as well as a PMME Repertoire designed to act as an aide for the design of educational offerings.

Contemporary music marketing: The importance of the music brand

Music is a domain of human activity about which marketers feel they have something to say, insofar as music is exchanged between producing companies (or, increasingly, artists) and consumers, directly or via channel intermediaries. Marketing is seen as being part of the business of popular music, where the tactics of marketers can persuade and often manipulate consumer and artist behaviour (Frith, 2007). So, what is meant by popular music marketing? A marketing campaign might involve a supply chain including any of the following members: an artist performer or band, management, record label, A&R, product manager, promoter and agents. It might therefore include one, or a combination, of the following actions: a band or artist launches a new album, EP or mix-tape, and/or announces a tour; a television station screens a documentary about a record label; a major music festival takes place over several days, attended by tens of thousands of people; magazines, websites and newspapers discuss the performance and reception of music; music artists appear on talk shows or on the front page of the tabloids; fans search for musical work and music-oriented fan-groups with which they can become deeply engaged; YouTube and MTV and many other stations continually screen videos of musical artists; a student union entertainments officer tries to secure a band for her programme; a chain of radio stations decides its musical and advertising policies; session musicians are hired to work on a recording or a tour;

a musician writes his/her autobiography and does interviews about it in the press, on television and online; a rock band gives away their latest album or performs a free gig, in person or online, to fans.

The market is no longer only a propaganda-led one-way transaction environment (Hunt & Grunig, 1994), as it tended to be when the major labels had firmer control of the market and distribution channels. Today, popular music businesses have adopted a two-way relational approach to marketing (Hunt & Grunig, 1994). This in turn has created the music brand – a strategic combination of negotiated cultural messages that provide meaning, value and connection to an audience or community (Sylvester, 2012). A successful music brand will consistently communicate and address the expectations that customers have when interacting with the brand (Sylvester, 2012). The brand can include a music artist and all of the affiliate physical or digital product offerings; these will include, but need not be limited to radio, television, venues, festivals, webcasts, press and merchandise – these are all now part of a popular music marketing proposition. The 21st century's digital era has reduced the value of the traditional dominant singular income channel derived from physical recorded music product sales. Multiple copyright management now dominates the value of the cultural offering that is derived from numerous channels (Sylvester, 2012).

Today, many music consumption practices involve an intangible music product, such as MP3s (iTunes, for example) and streaming services (such as Spotify, Deezer, Tidal and Apple Music). Music products are much more than a physical representation of ownership. They are better read as music-centred brands, as they offer cultural meaning and association that can be mobilized for the creation of consumer identities. Self-identification, the creation of distinct and distinctive brand identities, has been a key marketing strategy in the phenomenal rise and success of popular music reality TV shows. For example, *The X-Factor*, the manufactured group One Direction, and music mogul and personality Simon Cowell, all represent success and an opportunity for fan involvement to which many consumers of such TV programmes aspire (*Huffington Post*, 2012).

A music brand holds the negotiated set of cultural meanings that determine the brand value. For example, Dr Dre has established a strong music brand identity. He was a member of the commercially successful group NWA. He then found commercial and critical success as a musical artist in his own right, winning a Grammy award in 1993 for best rap solo performance on "Let Me Ride", from his *Chronic* album. As well as producing the multiple-platinum-selling debut album of Snoop Dog in 1993, Dr Dre also set up his own record label, Aftermath Entertainment, and signed artists such as Eminem and 50 Cent. In 2008, Dre formed a company to produce Beats by Dre, which has become a global headphone sensation. In 2014, Apple purportedly offered around $3 billion to acquire the 'Beats' company, which now includes a music streaming business element (Solomon, 2014). This will reportedly make Dr Dre one of the most valuable music brands in the world today (see O'Malley Greenburg, 2014).

Music brands are monetized via a variety of income channels; e.g. Beyoncé is a singer, actress, writer, fashion designer, fragrance manufacturer, music producer, choreographer, wife and mother who derives income from many channels (Sylvester, 2013). Each music brand channel has its own music brand community. For example, the loyal fans of Lady Gaga are known as 'Little Monsters', while Justin Bieber has an 'army' of followers known as 'Beliebers'. To members of music brand communities (Sylvester, 2012), brands should share first, and then let their consumer-perceived value determine any subsequent sales exchange. Examples of this include Radiohead's *In Rainbows* (pay-what-you-want) album,[1] or the case of Ed Sheeran, who, after being rejected by traditional company labels (Hooper, 2013), found popularity via digital release of singles on SB.TV, an independent music media company founded by Jamal Edwards[2] in 2008 (Edwards, 2013). Roster and individual artist management present complex marketing management problems, which means that students of PMME need access to resources, ideas and learning experiences that enable them to understand, appreciate, analyze and manage that complexity.

Institutional positionality

At an institutional level, the positionality of PMME depends, for example, on the mission or purpose and values of the academic department or institution within which the marketing is being taught. For example, within a management or business school, marketing tends to be taught differently than in a media or communications school, or a music department. If marketing is being taught in a music department, the approach taken may depend on the extent to which provision is orientated towards, for instance, music and production or towards performance. The degree to which the relevant institution's programmes have been semesterized and modularized also has an influence on how marketing is taught. The teaching of PMM depends also on the level at which a programme is offered, e.g. bachelor or master's degree. Additionally, the teaching content will depend on the pedagogical approach, and on the means (e.g. face-to-face or online), and the mode of delivery (full-time, part-time or executive). It will also depend on whether the course/module is being taught in a linear or block form. Other factors to be considered are whether the course/module is a mandatory module or elective, and whether it is for a single programme or shared across programmes. The requirements for prospective students to have prior learning or professional experience, as well as the social, economic and cultural backgrounds from which they are drawn, also help to shape a programme or course/module. Pedagogically, the learning outcomes of the degree programme and its constituent modules, courses[3] or taught units are highly important. These in turn are influenced by factors such as programme accreditation by industry and professional partners as well as any academics in other

---

1 Radiohead invited fans to pay whatever they liked for the album, which at the time was a highly unusual pricing strategy (Basset, 2008; Ogden, Ogden, & Long, 2011).
2 Jamal Edwards is one of the youngest entrepreneurs to succeed in the digital era.
3 In the UK context, "modules" refer to course of study within a higher education programme, equivalent to "courses" in other contexts, such as the US.

institutions which act on validating committees or as external examiners.[4] These partners may help to shape the balance between research-led and employability-orientated teaching. Modules are usually focused at different levels of knowledge and understanding, critical analysis or creative implementation.

The delivery of a unit or module depends on the disciplinary perspective/s adopted by lecturers – e.g. sociology, psychology, anthropology or economics. It also depends on whether they use a managerial marketing approach or a hybrid perspective such as arts marketing, cultural marketing, cultural branding or creative and cultural industries management. The cultural space and time within which the institution is historically grounded and operates deeply affects the expectations and prospects of its students (Jones, chapter 27, this volume; Smith, 2015a). Increasingly, the business model of an institution and how it brands itself affect what is taught and researched, in terms of availability of resources to support educational provision, as well as the values which an institution or department seeks to inculcate in its students.

Professional positionality

The design and execution of any module or unit depends on the positionality of the educator herself or himself. Relevant factors include whether they are (or were) professionally engaged with the music industry – as, for example, record label executives, musicians, artist managers, product managers, pluggers or venue promoters; their formal educational attainments; their research interests; their academic disciplinary background; the thought directions of any affiliated learned society; their sense of priorities for student learning; their pedagogical imagination; the resources available for their professional development and the degree to which they are engaged in strong professional and academic networks. Also of importance to PMME educators' 'performance' are the ways in and degree to which they depend on their academic and professional background. Is the educator, for example, a musician who has become an educator and acquired knowledge of marketing to facilitate their teaching work within a music department? Or is s/he a commercial sales/marketing professional working in a business or management school who teaches on an arts management programme? Or is s/he a trained journalist who finds him/herself working in a media studies department that is running a course for music industry professionals or aspirants?

Because of the importance of empirical research and evolving theoretical insight into music marketing and consumption, we feel it is important to mention that there is currently a relative lack of academic popular music marketing (as distinct from music management) textbooks. Arts management or marketing textbooks do not have a single focus on music, and are not suited as core texts for a music marketing module. There are professional books on popular music

---

4 In the UK, external examiners are colleagues from other higher education institutions who provide quality assurance for the learning process and assessment outcomes.

marketing, each of which focuses on particular areas of marketing.[5] However, in the authors' view, there is no textbook that directly demonstrates a representative and multidisciplinary account of marketing theory or contemporary popular music marketing practice. This makes it difficult for PMME educators to do full justice to the subject, notwithstanding the aforementioned need to be responsive and up-to-date, against which need publication times and (reified) texts can tend to mitigate. Other important issues include the labour market conditions for PMM educators, including levels of pay, terms of employment and precarity of tenure. Labour politics have an important influence on these issues, and what PMM educators are in fact enabled or empowered to achieve in the classroom.

We advocate to PMM educators a reflexive consideration of their own positionality as well as that of their institutions and programmes. The fundamental issue, we suggest, is the conflict or balance between, on the one hand, how much freedom they have to teach what they believe really matters to them and to their students, and, on the other hand, how much other agents (institution, accreditation partners, industry actors) are 'telling' them what they should be teaching. This is a perennial issue across HPME, and not limited to PMME (Smith, 2015a, 2015b). Other considerations include issues around how much of the subject they can or should cover; what perceived fidelity to the discipline or field requires; what design of programme serves the subject well, etc. Somewhere in the middle is the learning experience for the students as well as the educators themselves. The struggle is for something that works, that results in a meaningful and fulfilling high-quality learning experience for all concerned.

Suggested guidelines for popular music marketing education

We suggest in the following guidelines that PMME should:

- Embrace and understand popular music as music, and not just as a commodity; this involves understanding different philosophical perspectives on what music 'is';
- Use an inter/multidisciplinary lens, gathering in light from different theoretical and disciplinary traditions to focus them on popular music marketing and consumption practices;
- Explicitly address symbolic and cultural (branding) aspects of music in its regulatory context, as well as its production, marketing and consumption;
- Always keep its finger on the pulse of contemporary music marketing practice, while remembering the lessons of popular music marketing history;
- View popular music marketing as an embodied, historical, artistic, commercial-economic, social, political, cultural and technical practice;

---

5 For example: Borg (2014), *Music Marketing for the DIY Musician: Creating and Executing a Plan of Attack on a Low Budget*, whose focus is clear from the title; or King (2009) *Music Marketing: Press, Promotion, Distribution, and Retail*, which focuses on communications and distribution.

- Maintain an international as well as a local orientation;
- Maintain an ethical orientation which is cognizant, respectful and inclusive of equality and diversity issues.

Re-mixing the subject

If one asks the question, "How might one teach popular music marketing successfully?", the answer is that *it depends* on all of the above issues. We offer, therefore, a broad framework that highlights the important issues of which, in our shared opinion, a PMM educator needs to be aware when designing programmes or modules. S/he can then select and mix these issues in line with their cultural context, and the positionality of their institution and their own professional practice in order best to provide for their students' learning needs, processes and outcomes.

The framework below, which we call the Popular Music Marketing Education Repertoire, combines insights from Sylvester (2012) and Baumgarth and O'Reilly's C-Framework for Arts and Culture Brands (2014), and adapts and develops them for popular music marketing education. The Repertoire lists the range of issues of which we suggest PMM educators should be aware of when designing a course. Any analysis of a popular music brand needs to take account of these issues, their relative importance and any overlaps. We suggest that educators should be able to help students to develop rich and holistic understandings and critical analyses of popular music brands and their marketing. The framework loosely groups the 36 issues into four categories: the environment, marketing mix, consumers and producers. PMM educators can use the repertoire to design an appropriate mix of issues for particular educational projects. Limitations of space mean that we have had to shorten the narrative in certain categories. We hope that readers will see this repertoire as a jumping-off point for deeper exploration.

The Popular Music Marketing Education Repertoire

Environment

Case

Music marketing practice varies considerably from case to case. The marketing responsibilities of a venue promoter differ from those of a record label executive, opera house general manager, artistic manager, festival organizer, frontman, radio presenter, public relations agent and so on. Similarly, the act, offering, brand or organization being marketed has a strong determining influence on how the marketing is done. Consequently, clarity on what precise type of case is under discussion is fundamental.

Context

This relates to whether the market being discussed is located within a business-to-consumer or business-to-business context, as well as to the historical situatedness in time and space of the relevant musical brand – politically, socially, culturally, materially, technologically and economically. This category also takes account of the fact that music that is produced in one cultural context may be exported to different international contexts, e.g. Cuban music being exported to Europe. Finally, context can be temporal: in the pre-millennial era (20th century) physical music product was predominantly marketed (vinyl, cassettes, CDs), whereas, in the 21st century, non-physical (intangible) music product is predominantly marketed (MP3s, streaming, the musical brand).

Control

The degree to which efforts are made by governments or other regulators to suppress, censor, regulate, license or otherwise control music, as well as issues to do with artistic control.

Popular music marketing re-mix
Classification (genre)

Popular music marketing identifies and uses various music classifications or genres. Subsequently, popular music is divided in to many different sectors. Examples include pop, rock, hip-hop, indie, grime, garage, RnB, metal, urban, dub-step, folk, house, etc. In terms of marketing, these can be simplified into five music meta-classifiers: the sound, image, beliefs, behavioural practices and consumption practices. One can think of these classifications as the particular musical and sociocultural codes that inform the production, regulation and consumption of the musical genre concerned.

Concept

The concept relates to what commercial marketers would call the positioning of the offering: not just musical, but also commercial, cultural, social and political.

Content

The ideas 'contained within' the music. 'Content' must be related to music brand identity (on the producer side) and brand image and communication (on the consumer side). It also relates to the ideology that informs the music and its use by different stakeholders.

Cultural Offering

The nature of the musical offering, the 'product' in a wide sense, whether it is, for example, a project, performance, person, programme, place, legal right, physical artefact, service, experience, event, recording, brand or many/all of these things in a specific configuration.

Copyright

A fundamental issue in any case is who owns the rights to the music. In the music industry they are now commonly shared among multiple authors or rights-holders, who each possess rights to exploit the creative work. The music industry labels and management have moved from largely singular rights to multiple rights management – 360-degree deals, where the creative shares their creative rights with other rights-holders. Rights-holders can exercise reproduction, market control, distribution, public performance and moral and licensing rights, thus impacting marketing.

Cost

This is what it costs the consumer to own or engage with the music product. This price could be free or have an economic value appended to it. It could be a one-off transaction or an ongoing relational subscription. This also relates to pricing strategies of music providers, as well as to the important notion of musical value, and the value chain reaching from producer to consumers.

Convenience

This relates to how a consumer gets access to a music product. It was traditionally related to the physical distribution of music products, such as vinyl and CDs through retail outlets. It now relates to a specific geographical location such as a festival, or a particular physical space, such as a specific position in a gig or festival. It also relates to virtual online access to MP3 music files via iTunes or digital streaming services such as Spotify, Tidal or Apple Music.

Communication

This relates to the multi-vocal construction of the music act or organization by relevant stakeholders, including the full range of signifiers and texts mobilized by all parties to any given marketing exchange or relationship. This includes commercial or marketing communications as well as communications which might be considered as part of the brand's cultural strategy.

Campaign

The deliberate sequence of marketing activities established to market a music product, service or business. A marketing campaign will include the promotion via differing coordinated marketing channels (television, radio, print, online, personal appearances and word of mouth).

Collaboration

This area can include any project or arrangement, which involves musical partnership, sponsorship, celebrity endorsement, product placement, co-branding and brand alliances.

Channel

The journey of a musical offering from its creative origin to its final destination: the end user.

Connection

This relates to the digital connectedness of markets, where customers are continually connected via social media networks both to music providers and to each other.

Consumers
Customers and customer needs

The consumer, consumer group or organization which purchases the musical offering. This relates to the nature and realm of what drives and motivates customers to engage with a particular popular music proposition. It may include the following:

- Physiological (practical elements involved in the delivery of a music product)
- Cognitive (the need to know and attain knowledge)
- Hedonic (the need to feel sensory pleasure)
- Experiential (the need to experience)
- Social (the need to share and be social)
- Symbolic (the need to possess and present articulations' of your popular music affiliations)

Customer choice

This relates to the portfolio or range of choices open to the customer. This includes the choice of music available to the consumer from the range of relevant providers.

Contract

The contract, covenant or brand promise in the exchange relationship, explicitly or implicitly.

Contact

This area relates to brand touch-points, i.e. occasions, spaces and places where the music brand comes into material, sensory or imaginal contact with the producer or consumer. It can also cover issues such as relationship and resonance.

Consumption

This area includes generic ideas from consumer studies such as decision-making, rituals, involvement, identity, needs, motivation, perception, attitude, preference, behaviour, etc. but also notions from other theoretical frames such as fandom, audiences and consumption cultures.

Community

Collective aspects of consumption, primarily, but also attempts to frame the production-consumption nexus (e.g. a 'community' or 'tribe').

Co-creation

This is an increasingly important aspect of music marketing today, engaging fans to the point that they provide explicit lyrics, composition and production ideas. Equally, 21st-century music marketing is about inculcating an iterative process that allows the customers to feel a sense of belonging to a music brand, and therefore be part of the music brand community.

Crowd-funding

A model for existing and new customers (fans) to provide monetary support, often achieved via online platforms, to enable a popular music brand to create, produce or perform (and receive something of value in exchange. This may overlap with Capital (see below).

Producers

Character

The identity of the musical act or organization. Here, brand identity, reputation or personality, as well as musical mission, vision, philosophy and values are taken into consideration. Like all of these areas, it can relate to any brand referent, such as an organization, a celebrity, an event, a musician or even a fictional character (e.g. in a film musical).

Celebrity

This relates to the identification of the role that the celebrity plays in the marketing management of music artists' and prominent music business professionals. It should acknowledge the emerging marketing area known as personal branding. It provides concepts, theories and case material linked to the marketing management of individuals who possess a potential or actual status that can attract attention, generating commercial returns and other benefits for being well-known.

Company

The supply-side organization of individuals who manage the production of the musical brand. It relates to the type and nature of the company. It could be a traditional major 'corporate' record label, such as one of the 'big three' (Warner, Sony, Universal), or a small, localized, independent (indie) label, a technology company such as Spotify or Google, a promotions company such as Live Nation or AEG, a publisher, an agent or management company, and could also mean an individual entrepreneurial musician.

Capital

The financial resources which are used to fund the business, where they come from, how they are raised, what the returns are and how they are spread among stakeholders. This can include, by analogy, the political, social, cultural and subcultural capital (value) which can be acquired around the regulation, production, intermediation and consumption of the music in question.

Configuration

The relationship in which the music brand stands to other brands within the same portfolio or family. Issues to do with brand architectures and extensions are considered, with particular reference to record label rosters or discographies.

Cause

Corporate social responsibility and cause-related marketing are important aspects of all businesses these days. Popular music artists and organizations have often allied themselves to specific causes. Analysts should be alert to the wider social dimension of music marketing.

Career

Analysts of popular music marketing should consider the track record or career of the organization or artist in focus. The marketing of an early career, mid-career or late-career artist will be quite different. Similarly, the marketing of an established organization will differ considerably from a start-up.

Creativity

The marketing management of creativity. This includes an appreciation of New Product Development (NPD) or Artist and Repertoire (A&R) process in popular music business. It covers the search for commercially viable popular music offerings within a differing range of environments and individuals involved in creativity and their respective practices.

Commerciality

The extent to which the musical offering is commercial, promoted by or associated with commercial interests.

Competence

It is important that any popular music offering possesses an appropriate level of expected competence. This applies also to organizational capabilities in the key processes of composition, rehearsal, recording, touring, performing and promotion.

Consideration

This relates to the considerateness (or not) of all the 'frontline' people or individuals involved in ensuring the successful delivery of music products and/or service experiences to consumers. It could include all customer-facing contacts, such as musicians, sound engineers, security, runners, box office staff, cloak room attendants, bar staff, festival toilet attendants, etc.

Consistency

As popular music products/services involve experience, the marketer must ensure that each customer encounter provides a consistent delivery of physical evidence. This can be in the form of brand names, logos, signage, buildings, programmes, posters, flyers or uniforms, etc.

Credibility

Popular music marketing success is largely determined by credibility and market reputation. This is the extent to which the product offering is associated with market attractiveness. Ultimately the knowledge, understanding and prediction of credibility will determine the acceptance of any particular music brand. The music business is predicated by finding 'the next big thing'.

We suggest that a thorough understanding of any musical act, organization or brand requires a systematic investigation of each of the issues listed above, and that any of these issues is potentially relevant to popular music marketing teaching and to students' subsequent careers.

Conclusion

In this chapter we have sought to make a contribution to the discussion of popular music marketing education by suggesting a 're-mix', in other words putting insights from cultural, musical, media, sociological and other studies in the pedagogical 'mix'. We have discussed developments in music industry practice, as well as the issues of the professional and institutional positionality of the popular music marketing educator. We have offered a suggested set of guidelines for PMME and a framework of issues from which we believe popular music marketing educators can usefully draw and mix to design the most appropriate pedagogical framework for their specific needs.

References

Bassett, J. (2008, October 15). Radiohead reveal how successful 'In Rainbows' download really was. *NME*. Retrieved from: http://www.nme.com/news/radiohead/40444 [Accessed 19 August 2015].

Baumgarth, C. & O'Reilly, D. (2014). Brands in the arts and culture sector. *Arts Marketing: An International Journal*, 4, 2–9.

Borg, B. (2014). *Music marketing for the DIY musician: Creating and executing a plan of attack on a low budget*. Milwaukee, WI: Hal Leonard Corporation.

Edwards, J. (2013). *Self belief: The vision: How to be a success on your own terms*. London: Virgin Books.

Foxall, G., Goldsmith, R.E. & Brown, S. (1998). *Consumer psychology for marketing* (2nd ed.). Andover: Cengage Learning EMEA.

Frith, S. (2007). *Taking popular music seriously: Selected essays (Ashgate contemporary thinkers on critical musicology)*. London: Routledge.

Hooper, R. (2013, July 2). Ed Sheeran: I was ginger and chubby and so struggled to get a record deal. *The Independent*. Retrieved from: http://www.independent.co.uk/arts-entertainment/music/news/ed-sheeran-i-was-ginger-and-chubby-and-so-struggled-to-get-a-record-deal-8682793.html [Accessed 8 April 2016].

Huffington Post. (2012). 'Take Me Home' review: Simon Cowell, 'X Factor' Judge, praises one direction's new album (WATCH). Retrieved from: http://www.huffington-post.com/2012/09/27/simon-cowell-on-one-direc_n_1920084.html? [Accessed 20 April 2015].

Hunt, T. & Grunig, J.E. (1994). *Public relations techniques*. Fort Worth, TX: Harcourt Brace.

King, M. (2009). *Music marketing: Press, promotion, distribution, and retail*. Boston, MA: Berklee Press Publications.

Ogden, J., Ogden, D. & Long, K. (2011). Music marketing: A history and landscape. *Journal of Retailing and Consumer Services*, 18(2), 120–125.

O'Malley Greenburg, Z. (2014, December 29). The world's highest-paid musicians of 2014. *Forbes Magazine* [Accessed 20 April 2015].

O'Reilly, D., Larsen, G. & Kubacki, K. (2013). *Music, markets and consumption*. Oxford: Goodfellows Publishers.

Posner, P. (2009). The pracademic: An agenda for re-engaging practitioners and academics. *Public Budgeting and Finance*, 29, 12–26.

Smith, G.D. (2015a). Neoliberalism and symbolic violence in higher music education. In L. DeLorenzo (Ed.), *Giving voice to democracy: Diversity and social justice in the music classroom*. New York: Routledge.

Smith, G.D. (2015b). Masculine domination and intersecting fields in private-sector popular music performance education in the UK. In P. Burnard, Y. Hofstander, & P. Dyndahl (Eds.), *Bourdieu and the sociology of music and music education*. Farnham: Ashgate.

Solomon, B. (2014, May 28). It's official: Apple adds Dr. Dre with $3 billion beats deal. *Forbes*. Retrieved from: http://www.forbes.com/sites/briansolomon/2014/05/28/apple-brings-dr-dre-on-board-with-official-3-billion-beats-deal/ [Accessed 19 August 2015].

Sylvester, R. (2012). Brand you. In C. Fitterman Radbill (Ed.), *An introduction to the music industry: An entrepreneurial approach*. New York: Routledge.

Sylvester, R. (2013). Beyoncé – how brand licensing influences popular music acts. In C. Fill (Ed.), *Marketing communications: Brands, experiences and participation* (6th ed.). Harlow: Pearson.

Szmigin, I. & Piacentini, M. (2014). *Consumer behaviour*. Oxford: Oxford University Press.

Tadajewski, M. & Brownlie, D. (2009). *Critical marketing: Issues in contemporary marketing*. Hoboken, NJ: John Wiley & Sons.

25
University music education in Colombia
The multidimensionality of teaching and training

Luz Dalila Rivas Caicedo

Introduction

The following arguments outline some dichotomies behind higher music education in Colombia, based on the curricular construction of training programmes for teachers. On the one hand, I consider society's educational needs; on the other I focus on the great diversity of actions and dynamics behind the music field. I am using the concept of 'field' as defined by Norbert Elías in figurative sociology (2006), for it allows an understanding of the social framework around individuals and collectivities, the correlational link between them and the different levels of social organization. It also allows us to place the individual by recognizing the 'other', and to understand individuals from a cultural perspective, where culture has an influence on the individual who, in turn, responds to the pressure exerted by culture (see also Barrett, 2011). Elías defines the term 'figuration' to designate the structure of interdependent people, whether as groups or as individuals. Figurations end up being constructions of intersubjectivity on both individual and collective levels, thus shaping the 'social' outcome. This framework reflects aspects of Colombian higher education in music, because most university music programmes educate music teachers; however, both teaching and music majors graduate and face the job market as performers, conductors, cultural entrepreneurs, arrangers and composers, among other profiles. Higher education in music and teacher training is therefore facing conceptual, theoretical, epistemological and methodological difficulties; the discussion in this chapter leads, below, to an analysis of new approaches and perspectives.

Luz Rivas Caicedo

Teachers, training and labour conditions

As the Research Committee Coordinator at my institution, my discussions with music colleagues and teachers have focused on the multiple concerns, fears and dissatisfactions that lead to frustration as musicians and teachers. This frustration oscillates between their own educational background as artists and creative individuals, and their self-consciousness as teachers in their working environment. This was evident during the National Colloquium: Music as a Profession, which took place in Bogotá in April 2015.[1] Researchers, teachers, producers and others involved with the music field gathered at this event to express their perceptions of an urgent necessity for new paths in higher music education in the country. Finding academic excellence, settling labour needs imposed by society and facing the local and international competitive market are all concerns that demand renovation and reformation of higher education, including in music (Casas, 2015; Niño, 2015; Rivas Caicedo, 2015). Bennett (2010) analyzes and reflects upon these issues in detail in an Australian context, but her work remains largely unknown in Colombia despite its relevance to the field. Transformations are required in the epistemic and academic structures of institutionalized university programmes – public or private, technical or technological.

Music and music education face difficulties *vis-à-vis* such transformation. According to Bennett (2010), success relies on the achievement of a sustainable career, in which the musician is able to apply several dimensions of music; in other words, an occupation that requires specialized knowledge, thus allowing a response to social needs with an economic return. This implies an understanding of music as an academic, scientific, inter- and trans-disciplinary area, whose study and reconfiguration can create and re-create labour conditions around its own professional paths.

The emergence of new ways to organize music production, education and work – where technological innovation play such an important role – is recognizable within the configuration of the job market, which also determines the restructuring of employment. This is of course related to current social and cultural conditions, and the search for educational and labour flexibility. Hiring requirements for young people in the current market for music employment illustrate the growing complexity of school-university-labour transitions.[2]

According to the Labour Observatory for Education from The National Ministry of Education in Colombia (MEN; Republic of Colombia, 2015), the arts only represent 1.9% of the active offering from higher education programmes. Of

---

1 Organized by the Ministry of Culture, the Centre for Music Documentation, the Social and Human Sciences Faculty from the Externado University of Colombia, the Arts Faculty from the District University 'Francisco José de Caldas' and the Colombian Association of Music Researchers (ACIMUS). The minutes and memoirs will be published in the 25th *A Contratiempo* review (July-December 2015), edited by the Centre for Music Documentation.
2 For related international perspectives, see Jones, chapter 27, this volume, McLaughlin, chapter 10, this volume; Morrow, chapter 26, this volume; Wong, chapter 9, this volume.

315 registered programmes in the arts, 101 are currently not active, and they are mostly offered in the three main cities of the country: Bogotá, Cali and Medellín. When it comes to music, programmes are offered in 23 higher education institutions, from which 3278 students graduated between 2001 and 2013. One-hundred seventy of them were trained in technical and technological programmes. As for students of music teaching, the total number of graduates between 2001 and 2013 was 2628. This number of graduates is important, keeping in mind that there is a strong proposal from the National Government to highlight the role of education as a contribution to reaching "justice, sustainability and solidarity in human development, in order to improve the life quality of Colombians and achieve peace, reconciliation and thus fight poverty and exclusion" (Decennial Plan of Education 2006–2016, p. 13).[3] It is necessary to recognize the diversity of the music field and its corresponding work venues, which cannot be ignored by higher music education.

On the other hand, concern regarding the challenges of reinforcing teacher training has been expressed by international organizations such as UNESCO, the Regional Platform for Music Education in Latin America (PREAL, 2004), the Organization of Ibero-American States for Education, Science and Culture (OEI, 2008), the Southern Common Market (MERCOSUR, 2010), the Organization of American States (OEA, 2012), the Regional Office of Education for Latin America and the Caribbean (OREALC) (2012), the Organization for Economic Cooperation and Development (OECD, 2011) and the World Bank, among others. This can be seen in reports from each of these organizations since 2001, where they agree with the idea that teacher training should seek to graduate professionals with wide disciplinary and pedagogical knowledge, who can be independent, responsible, thoughtful, critical, innovative, effective and socially involved (OREALC / UNESCO, 2012). Therefore, these organizations argue, those institutions offering this type of training must guarantee a high-quality introduction in how to perform professionally in diverse circumstances, and a clear outline of labour conditions under a living wage with dignifying opportunities for further training and professional development.

In response, the Colombian National Ministry of Education proposed a reformulation of the guidelines for teacher-training and related programmes in 2014 (Republic of Colombia, 2014b). One reason for this was the visible disarticulation between epistemological and disciplinary knowledge and the pedagogic/didactic nature of the discipline of music education (OECD for Colombia, 2012). In this context of change and transformation, it is complicated for higher music education to meet the labour needs of the music field, given that most graduates are music teachers and that non-teaching musicians have no clarity as to how to proceed professionally, apart from in music performance.[4]

---

3 Translation: Luis Gabriel Mesa Martínez.
4 See how related concerns are addressed in other contexts, in, for example, Jones (chapter 27, this volume), Lebler and Hodges (chapter 22, this volume), Morrow et al. (chapter 26, this volume) and Wong (chapter 9, this volume).

Luz Rivas Caicedo

Professional practice and the labour market for music teachers in Colombia

In Colombia, as mentioned previously, most higher music education programmes are based on teacher training. A great number of music performance and composition programmes, on the other hand, are offered in private institutions (Labour Observatory for Education from the National Ministry of Education, MEN / Colombian Association for Faculties of Arts [ACOFARTES] 2014). Additionally, the National Service of Learning (SENA) is the only public institution in the country with an exclusively technical/technological approach, which is known in Colombia as education for labour and human development. This latter institution is regulated by the Ministry of Labour, unlike universities and other higher education providers, which are supervised by the Ministry of Education. According to Law 1064 (2006) and Decree 4904 (Republic of Colombia, 2009):

Educational process in technical training for labor and expertise in arts and crafts seeks to prepare people in different areas of the productive sector, as well as developing specific work skills related the performance areas listed on the National Classification of Occupations,[5] which will allow them to work on productive activities as independent or dependent entrepreneurs.

Graduates of this institution earn occupational skill certificates. In 2006, SENA sought a normative definition of labour skills, and to categorize the labour market and the field of music, musicians, arts and culture in general, resulting in the definition of "Occupations whose main purpose relies on offering entertainment, relaxation and communication, which are related to art, culture, theatre arts, journalism, literature, creative design. The occupations in this area result from a creative talent requisite" (Ministry of Education, 2015). This led to the first offering of music in a technical/technological discipline by a public Colombian institution, together with a legitimate approval to award formal degrees and certificates that would be valid in the labour market (SENA, 2006). Nonetheless, teacher-training and music graduates are often perceived as performers, conductors, cultural entrepreneurs, arrangers, composers and researchers, regardless of their college-level specialization in music and music education (technical, technological or bachelor's).

The situation exposed by Bennett (2010) in an Australian context, is similar in Colombia: the cultural industries and the current job market have transformed the different spheres of action and the demand for music. In spite of this, educational institutions have not managed to respond to this environment, based on their own models of training. Likewise, Zapata Restrepo et al. (2005) explain the musical practices of students who are being educated in teacher-training programmes, including a range of music genres such as rock, jazz and salsa, and participating in local and foreign bands. The authors establish that there is no meaningful relationship between the students' music education training and their roles as musicians in

---

5 Translated by Luis Gabriel Mesa Martínez. Refer to the following link to read the National Classification of Occupations; http://observatorio.sena.edu.co/Comportamiento/CnoQueEs

different contexts, and also acknowledge the distance between academic training and musical practice more generally.

Furthermore, the *Occupational Characterization for the Field of Music* study conducted by historian Diego Felipe Giraldo Serna (SENA, 2006) for the National Service of Learning (SENA), shows the diversity of bands and music practices among itinerant musicians, unstable in the spheres of action where they would mainly work as performers and/or music teachers (Giraldo Serna/SENA, 2006, pp. 105–106); this music performance work is mostly related to the practice of popular and traditional musics. The study also points out that the general pattern for musicians – with no distinction between professional musicians and future music teachers – who seek music education usually corresponds to private lessons (25.5%), followed by those who seek university programmes (24.3%). Informal schools,[6] on the other hand, count up to 23.1%, whereas self-taught education is limited to 16.5%. Finally, conservatories were mentioned by 10.6% of respondents (2006, pp. 97–99). Along the same lines, Beatriz Goubert describes the characteristics of formal education programmes in their *State of the Art of Music in Bogotá*. The results imply that, although most programmes train their students in performance, conduction, composition and teaching, among other areas, there is a stronger focus on music performance (2009, p. 14).

The musicians' field of action within Colombia's cultural policies

It is necessary to transform the model of higher education in music in order to reinforce the future projection for different fields of action, as well as higher levels of creativity, training, employment and quality job offers inside Colombia, which can enhance competition in the labour market for music. In this regard, Colombia's Ministry of Culture has established the following fields of action to be considered in music training: creation, practice and performance, appreciation, research, documentation, instrument building and maintenance, production and academic development and cultural entrepreneurship (Arts Policy, 2006–2010). The Ministry of Culture – in agreement with the Ministry of Education – also states that different types of music training are required, regardless of the traditional/existing offerings from conservatories or universities.

Local music schools are thus part of an alliance with the governments in each region of the country; this leads to constant updating of procedures for music teachers and assistants, as well as educating of children and teenagers who would have an impact in their local communities, and therefore facilitate social opportunities, generating a strong sense of identity and diversity. The purpose of these schools is to educate about creative and entrepreneurial processes as a way to

---

6 According to the 43rd article (Chapter III) in Law 115 de 1994 from Colombia's National Congress, informal-education schools are those where free knowledge is 'spontaneously' or 'naturally' acquired, coming from people, organizations, mass media, press, traditions, customs, social behaviour and others (not necessarily part of a specific syllabus).

reinforce productive skills, as well as artistic and educational planning, by means of music production/services and community projects.[7] Other degrees are therefore established, ones different from those offered at the conservatory or the university. They should respond to the institutional normativity of the Colombian Ministry of Education (July 29, 2002), which regulates the public service of higher education at technical, technological and professional levels. This type of learning could include professionalization, technical level training, certification of labour skills and informal education (Arts Policy: 2006–2010, pp. 160–161):

1 *Professionalization* is aimed at musicians with several years of experience in practice, even if they did not pursue formal studies in music. This would give access to graduate school programmes. It is an option for them – and also for those who work in music teaching without a degree – to complete their professional training in approximately 20 months. Universities must offer this type of training.
2 Technical-level education comes from the necessity to fulfil the "elementary music training, as applied in the development of local music schools". That is to say, formal and informal learning of music, based on popular and traditional music (2006–2010, p. 101). These programmes intend to cover a wider number of schools in all regions of the country.
3 *Certification of labour skills* give a chance to experienced musicians to validate and qualify their labour capacity in a specific musical practice. These certificates are different from professionalization because they do not make teaching official, and they do not grant access to graduate studies.
4 *Informal education* focuses on music practice *per se*, preparing musicians for opportunities to access formal education in the future. It seeks to value musical practice without the need for professional degrees or certificates.

Feeding into this discussion, the policies of the National Ministry of Education describe the teacher as a social mediator, someone who guides the construction of specialized knowledge, a planner who provides educational contexts for teaching and learning, and not merely an operator of processes and procedures (Republic of Colombia, 2014a). Once teacher training became a part of university education[8] – as

---

7 For more detailed information about music schools and the Ministry of Culture's assessments, see: http://www.mincultura.gov.co/areas/artes/musica/escuelas-de-musica/Paginas/default.aspx.
8 This process was generalized in all areas of knowledge with the establishment of the National Pedagogic University in 1955. The Teaching Programme in Educational Sciences – with a particular emphasis on Music Pedagogy – was founded in 1976 (National Pedagogic University, 2009). A similar programme was created at the School of Arts and Crafts in San Juan de Pasto in 1938, and then transferred to the University of Nariño as a bachelor's Teaching Programme in Music in 1985. The Medellín Conservatory also approved a bachelor's Degree in Music Education in 1968, in agreement with the Education Faculty from the University of Antioquia. Along the same lines, the National Conservatory of Colombia – founded in 1882 – began to offer Music Pedagogy in 1965 (an option that gradually disappeared in the mid-1990s). These are a few examples of the configuration of music and music teacher training in Colombian higher education.

well as a part of *escuelas normalistas* (teaching-training schools) – it acquired a professional connotation that suited the context of higher education – research training, teaching, scientific spreading and courses related to disciplinary issues, pedagogy, culture, society, politics, ethics and preparation for the labour market.

Configuration of music in higher education in Colombia

In agreement with Law 30 (Republic of Colombia, 1992) and Law 749 (Republic of Colombia, 2002), higher education in Colombia is expected to divide undergraduate programmes into preparatory cycles. These provide a comprehensive education, where each cycle leads to an academic degree, which entitles people to work, according to their level of training. The titles also validate access to the next level.

The cycles are:

1. Technical Level: It trains professionals by reinforcing skills for job performance in specific areas, where somebody else's leadership and collaboration are required.
2. Technological Level: It is meant to develop skills related to applied and practical knowledge in more complex activities; the theory contributes to an understanding of the concepts behind the process so that the individual feels capable of an intervention.
3. University Professional (Bachelor) Level: It prepares students for an independent, autonomous performance in a specific area of knowledge (Republic of Colombia, 2007). These professionals are capable of proposing original solutions; they participate in innovative and autonomous creation projects, in addition to analyzing and running assessments of their own performance. This training requires theoretical and epistemological depth.

In Colombia, most private and some public universities have welcomed this type of structure in their undergraduate programmes, especially for specialties like engineering, economics, finance and management. However, there is no record of any academic programmes related to music or the arts being constructed along these lines (at least not that I could find for this study), including in relation to teacher training. Keeping in mind that this latter represents the highest coverage by and offering from universities, and that students and graduates perform diverse activities within the music field, music careers offering teacher training should consider changing their academic structures.

Multidimensionality of music educators

The following section is based on work undertaken for my doctoral dissertation (Rivas Caicedo, 2011). The study was designed in order to collect information from a population of students, teachers and graduates from three music teaching programmes in Colombia, all offered by public universities. The main purpose was to identify whether this population felt the need to include popular and traditional musics within their professional training, together with a critical and analytical position *vis-à-vis* the improvement of their teaching skills. Thus, the benefits of the study would not only apply to future teachers, but also to future students.

Methodology: Collection sample

A study was conducted by means of collecting different points of view, in order to address the research question, following McMillan and Schumacher's approach (2005). Three groups were selected as representative of the institutional agents, as such: students, graduates and teachers (professors) from the bachelor's programmes in Music Education. The sample included 200 student subjects, who were registered in teacher-training programmes in music. Ages ranged between 20 and 23 years. It is worth noting that observations throughout the research revealed that many students[9] tend sporadically to withdraw from these programmes. Thirty teachers aged 30–46 were part of this sample. Roughly 80% were male and 20% female. Of 120 graduate subjects aged 26–40, 78% were male and 22% were female. It is important to point out that the population was unbalanced, at least in part because of the difficulties in keeping contact with all of them, especially since the participating universities did not always keep updated records of their graduates.

Collection tool

Three surveys were designed, one for each group of the sample.

> *Students*: The following items were included: six questions referred to socio-demographic variables, 18 concerned early and continuous music training (with an emphasis on the teacher's performance and their teaching processes) and 11 were based on instrument performance.
> *Teachers*: The following items were included: five questions about socio-demographic data, 26 related to the musical teacher's activity and years of experience, and 15 in reference to the teaching training in music education.
> *Graduates*: The following items were included: five questions about socio-demographic variables, six about academic training, six about professional and teaching activity, 21 about teaching tools and 13 related to the teacher's training in music education.

Results and analysis

Results are based on the group of graduates, where it was demonstrated that both teaching and music graduates tend to work in different activities simultaneously:

---

9 According to this study, approximately 50% of students quit the programme, and 25% of this group eventually return and complete it.

Twenty-five per cent of the people who completed the surveys were independent musicians and teachers at the same time, while another 25% worked as teachers and belonged to music bands or projects simultaneously – music for children and symphonic bands were the most common. Fifty per cent claimed to be teachers, band members (rock, pop, traditional music), producers and composers. Graduates worked as teachers in different levels of education: 22% in pre-school, 12% in middle and high school, 33% in informal schools and the remaining 33%, sporadically, at a university level. Fourteen per cent of the survey respondents had less than one year of work experience; 28% had experience ranging between two and four years; 42% had been working between five to seven years and only 14% had above 10 years of professional activity. Findings suggest that the job market for graduates is relatively wide, but also limited and unstable, and that 71% have also taught at a university level; however, a majority (42%) of these experiences lasted less than a year. These numbers confirm the irregularities of labour activity, especially due to the different contexts in the country: armed conflict, social displacement and cultural diversity (Rivas Caicedo, 2011).

As for the question, "Do you think it is necessary for the music teacher to develop knowledge and fundamental skills in traditional Colombian music and/or popular music?", the general response was an affirmative 100%. The reasons given by respondents were that "it gives context to your job at every level", "it provides many alternatives to apply in your profession", "it enhances your appreciation of several types of music" and "it reinforces identity values" (Rivas Caicedo, 2011, pp. 155–157). The music field for teachers in Colombia is wide and diverse, which makes it necessary to consider the diversification of relevant training, according to the different profiles in music and work positions mentioned above. Future teachers must develop skills in order to know, execute, interpret and understand different music spheres, as to confront the job market with stability. Higher education must respond to this professional reality by offering alternatives for future teachers to take, always keeping their own interests in mind.

Teacher training in music programmes in Colombia

I refer here to music programmes at three public universities in Colombia: the University of Antioquia, the University of Valle and the National Pedagogic University.[10] These programmes are organized in five academic years, divided into 10 semesters. The three of them share common goals: to educate with high academic and artistic standards, thus promoting training activities for individuals and collectivities; these should contribute to the reinforcement of the artistic, cultural,

---

10 The academic syllabi are available via the following links: http://sikuani.udea.edu.co/programas UdeA/block/resource/MTIyNDgxODc1MA==/export_1430164358834.pdf, http://escuelade musica.univalle.edu.co/index.php/programas-academicos-2/licenciatura-en-musica/malla-pii-4/, http://www.pedagogica.edu.co/admin/UserFiles/PLAN%20DE%20ESTUDIOS%20LICEN CIATURA%20EN%20M%C3%9ASICA%202014-I.pdf.

educational and aesthetic development that the country requires (Rivas Caicedo, 2015, p. 7). Table 25.1 includes the common topics in the curricular programmes of the universities mentioned previously.

These programmes follow a two-cycle structure: a cycle for fundamental training, followed by a deepening cycle. They include three dimensions: music, pedagogy and research (see Table 25.2), from which the first two are taken as theoretical and practical subjects. The music dimension integrates subjects such as music theory (10 semesters), main instrument (eight to 10 semesters), supplementary instrument

Table 25.1 Professional training of current music teachers in Colombia

Training needs		
Development of the personal and the social being	*Professional training*	*Training for the development of basic skills*
• Free development of personality. • Education in values. • Sense of belonging: identity, culture and multiculturalism. • Sense of belonging: Historical and social reality. • Regional and national sustainable development. • Cultural development.	**KNOWLEDGE IN PEDAGOGY:** • History and epistemology of pedagogy. • Social trends. Ethical, cultural and political dimensions in the reality of education. • Methods and models of music education. **MUSIC KNOWLEDGE:** • Composition. • Performance. • Choir and band conduction.	• Training in communication skills. • Literacy. • Telecommunication networks and new technologies. • Foreign/second language. • Expressive and body language. • Education in research.

Source: Rivas Caicedo (2011, p. 103).

Table 25.2 Structure of teaching-training programmes of music in Colombia

Dimensions	Area	Subjects
Musical Training	• Musical Structure	• Music theory • History and aesthetics • Musical culture
	• Performance	• Instrument • Instrumental ensembles
Pedagogical Training	• Educational	• Fundamentals of education • Music didactics • Assessment and curriculum
	• Sociocultural	• Music, culture and society
Research Training	• Research component	• Capstone project workshop • Capstone project seminar

(four to six semesters), instrumental ensembles (four to six semesters) and musical culture (usually three semesters). The pedagogic dimension includes courses to introduce the epistemology of pedagogy, as well as the teaching and learning of music, academic curriculum and assessment. This dimension is developed throughout 10 semesters. The research dimension refers to those classes whose main purpose is to develop a capstone project, meaning that it takes place within the last two to three semesters.

The study showed that universities, technical/technological institutes and conservatories follow similar academic curricula; their structure and contents tend towards a high (possibly excessive) number of subjects and *in situ* study hours; they do not seem to be updated and do not respond to the current status of musical practice and education.[11] There is a very high number of subjects, hours and contents, whereas the academic purpose is based on the students' acquisition of knowledge, skills and capabilities. They emphasize learning over teaching. It is evident that specific areas of music, pedagogy and research are not articulated in a comprehensive manner in the academic curriculum, and therefore in the training process for future teachers. There is hardly a distinction between the different profiles and fields of action resulting from this training.

Organizing the curricular structure in preparatory cycles represents an alternative to reinforce multidimensional training for music teachers in Colombian programmes. These proposed cycles are:

1. A professional technical level that could be completed by the student during the last two years of high school to reinforce work skills in specific areas.
2. A professional technological level for the first two years of a university cycle, which would develop skills related to the application and rather complex performance of knowledge.
3. A professional university level, as the last cycle to complete a professional career. This would prepare the student for an autonomous and thorough performance in music education, being able to propose original solutions and therefore participate, analyze and assess innovative and creative processes. This training requires theoretical and conceptual depth. Those who conclude with this cycle must have completed the previous ones, either as independent preparatory cycles or as a thorough professional career (Rivas Caicedo, 2006, pp. 120–121).

Conclusions: Conceptual basis for the training of music teachers

It is necessary for Colombian institutions offering higher education in music to acknowledge the different professional roles and activities for music teachers in the country. These institutions are responsible for a diverse offering that will lead

---

11 The syllabi used for this study are being currently offered in the three universities mentioned above.

graduates closer to the variety of the music field. It is therefore essential for higher education to understand work possibilities and labour markets, and design sufficiently flexible academic curricula in response. In this regard, higher music education must be reconsidered from its epistemic and methodological structures. We can consider education in diverse types of musical thinking, based on expertise, reflection and music practice, in order to understand its different configurations. The learning process of the students who will eventually become music teachers must first acknowledge what they know and what they think. I recall Elías (2006) in support of what I hereby propose about the music field, which results from the interdependent (music) connections that individuals construct in their relation to others. It is possible to build the music field from this (music) network. I support the assumptions in Berger and Luckmann's approach (1967); they claim that individuals internalize daily reality by means of peer interaction, which confirms the individual's place and role in society, as well as her/his participation in social processes. This latter represents what Schütz calls "biographical situation", meaning that

> common-sense reality is given to us all in historical and cultural forms of universal validity, but the way in which these forms are translated in an individual life depends on the totality of the experience a person builds up in the course of this concrete existence.
>
> *(1995, p. 17)*

We can talk about a musical biographical situation if we relate this situation with what a student knows and thinks when beginning formal studies in music: their concepts, tastes, musical practices and job background, among other factors. The music field responds to the social/cultural context as well as to the local market, as mentioned above. It is related to the co-dependence and correlation of social groups that determine intersubjectivity constructions in the music field and the labour market. The music biographical situation helps us know and understand the needs of the labour situation – in other words, a world that represents the perspectives of individuals who want to become teachers but who might feel conditioned by the circumstances of their own biographical situation. The biographical situation helps students to confront the challenges of this in becoming music teachers. The value of this biographical situation leads to an exploration process to generate new knowledge, epistemologies and training methods for potential teachers in the academic field, specifically in education research. This is connected to the fact that academic programmes aim at the construction of knowledge through teaching and research for future graduates who will confront the labour market.

Teacher-training programmes must provide theoretical, conceptual and methodological elements in order to reinforce a critical and interdisciplinary approach. Likewise, as long as the specific conditions for each academic area are relevant to the professional domain of education, there will be room for critical thinking around the social validation and construction of educational practices. In agreement with Habermas (1982), individuals know what they are interested in knowing. It is thus possible to identify three categories of knowledge:

a   Technical knowledge: to know and to master nature. It can be accessed through empirical sciences (technical or analytical).
b   Practical knowledge: linked to the symbolic interaction that seeks to understand the sense of reality.
c   Emancipating knowledge: enabling and empowering to alter or shape reality and therefore society.

From this perspective, academic processes in teacher-training programmes are inclined towards different paradigms. Theoretical, methodological and educational elements are acquired in order to address all fields of action, teaching and learning. Knowledge must be linked with current practices in a constant cultural transit, which questions the validity of what we know and therefore enriches elaboration of the academic curriculum, in addition to people's participation according to their interests, needs and particular circumstances.

From all this, I suggest three perspectives for the training of teachers:

1   An education based on specialized research.
2   Teaching their own didactics for each area of knowledge.
3   A social and humanistic education that promotes awareness of the political, ideological and social situation of the country.

These perspectives emerge from the spheres of action mentioned above; they are comprehensive and mutually influential. If future professionals manage to learn more than mere curriculum 'content' and/or pre-established techniques, focusing on skills and strategies to understand the sociocultural context around their profession – and the labour market – they will know what to do, and how to face challenges, as a musician/teacher.

There are multiple issues that higher music education must resolve when training professionals. Introducing students to a diverse work market and dealing with national requirements of official authorities in order to be suitable for international standards forces and obliges the higher education establishment to offer the skills and tools to achieve. Higher music education in Colombia needs paradigmatic shifts in the institutions involved, keeping in mind the work market as well as the different types of training (as suggested by the Colombian education system). It faces conceptual, theoretical, epistemological and methodological uncertainties, and this is the problem underlying the curricular transformation debate; the great diversity of actions and dynamics within the music field means that new perspectives on the education requirements are required. The academic curriculum should contribute to the education of unified and integral individuals who will manage to face and address the range of challenges in their discipline and field. This will open up possibilities for finding suitable work in the field for music professionals.

References

Barrett, M.S. (Ed.) (2011). *A cultural psychology of music education*. Oxford: Oxford University Press.

Bennett, D.E. (2010) [2008]. *La música clásica como profesión. Pasado, presente y estrategias para el futuro*. Madrid: Graó.

Berger, P.L. & Luckmann, T. (1967). *The social construction of reality: A treatise in the sociology of knowledge*. New York: Anchor Books.

Casas, V. (2015). Música y educación superior en Colombia. Antecedentes y transformaciones en Santiago de Cali. Bogotá, D.C: En Revista A Contratiempo. ISSN 2145–1958. Retrieved from: http://www.territoriosonoro.org/CDM/acontratiempo/?ediciones/revista-25/artculos/educacin-superior-en-msica-y-formacin-docente.html [Accessed 21 June 2015].

Colombian Association for Faculties of Arts. (2014). Retrieved from: http://acofartes.org.co/ [Accessed 11 May 2015].

Elías, N. (2006). *Sociología fundamental*. Barcelona: Gedisa.

Giraldo, S.D.F. (2006). *Caracterización ocupacional sector de la música*. Medellín: Servicio Nacional de Aprendizaje – SENA.

Goubert, B. 2009. *Estado del arte del área de la música en Bogotá D.C*. Bogotá, DC: Ministerio de Cultura. Retrieved from: http://www.culturarecreacionydeporte.gov.co/observatorio/documentos/investigaciones/estadosArte/estadoArte_Musica_abr_23.pdf [Accessed 5 May 2015].

Habermas, J. (1982). *Conocimiento en interés*. Buenos Aires: Taurus.

McMillan, J.H. & Schumacher, S. (2005). *Investigación educativa* Trad. Pearson Educación. Madrid: Addison Wesley.

MERCOSUR (2010). VII Reunião do grupo de trabalho de formação docente. Salvador: Author.

Ministry of Education. (2015). Labor Observatory for Education. Available from:http://www.graduadoscolombia.edu.co/html/1732/w3-channel.html [Accessed 3 April 2015].

Niño, S. (2015). Interdisciplinariedad y economía creativa: Estrategias de sostenibilidad en el mercado laboral de las prácticas musicales. Bogotá, DC: *En Revista A Contratiempo*. ISSN 2145–1958. Retrieved from: http://www.territoriosonoro.org/CDM/acontratiempo/?ediciones/revista-25/artculos/educacin-superior-en-msica-y-forma-cin-docente.html [Accessed 21 June 2015].

OECD. (2011). *Building a high quality teaching profession. Lessons from around the World*. Paris: OECD.

OEA. (2012). Documentos oficiales del proceso de Cumbres de las Américas. Retrieved from: http://www.summit-americas.org/pubs/pos_ctg.pdf [Accessed 3 February 2015].

OEI. (2008). *Metas educativas 2021. La educación que queremos para la generación de los Bicentenarios*. España: OEI-Fundación Santillana.

PREAL. (2004). *Maestros en América Latina: Nuevas perspectivas sobre la formación y el desempeño*. Santiago: Editorial San Marino.

Republic of Colombia. (1992). *Law 30. council for higher education. Where the public service of higher education is established*. Bogotá, DC: National Ministry of Education/ National Council for Higher Education.

Republic of Colombia. (2002). *Law 749. Where the public service of higher education in technical, technological and professional levels is established*. Bogotá, DC: National Ministry of Education/ National Council for Higher Education.

Republic of Colombia. (2007). *Public policy on higher education in cycles and skills*. Bogotá, DC: National Ministry of Education.
Republic of Colombia. (2009). *Decree regulating the organization, supply and operation of the provision of educational services for work and human development*. Bogotá, D.C: National Ministry of Education/ National Council for Higher Education.
Republic of Colombia. (2014a). *Colombian system for teacher training and policy guidelines*. Bogotá, DC: National Ministry of Education.
Republic of Colombia. (2014b). *Quality guidelines for degrees in education*. Bogotá, DC: National Ministry of Education.
Republic of Colombia. (2015). Ministry of Education. Labor observatory for education. Retrieved from: http://www.graduadoscolombia.edu.co/html/1732/w3-channel.html [Accessed 3 April 2015].
Rivas Caicedo, L.D. (2006). *Ethnomusicology in the Bachelor's Music Education program. Colombia's case*. (Master Thesis in Pedagogy). México, DF: National Autonomous University of Mexico, 176.
Rivas Caicedo, L.D. (2011). *Ethnomusicology in the bachelor's program of music education from the University of Nariño in Colombia*. (Doctoral Thesis). National Autonomous University of Mexico México, DF: 276.
Rivas Caicedo, L.D. (2015). *Educación superior en música y formación docente*. Bogotá, DC: En revista a contratiempo. ISSN 2145–1958. Retrieved from: http://www.territoriosonoro.org/CDM/acontratiempo/?ediciones/revista-25/artculos/educacin-superior-en-msica-y-formacin-docente.html [Accessed 21 June 2015].
Schütz, A. (1995). *El problema de la realidad social*. Buenos Aires: Amorrortu.
UNESCO. (2012). *Antecedentes y criterios para la elaboración de políticas docentes en América Latina y el Caribe*. Santiago de Chile: OREALC.
Zapata Restrepo, G., Goubert, B.M., & Marldonado, J.F. (2005). *Universidad, músicas urbanas, pedagogía y cotidianidad*: *Una etnografía de los territorios musicales de los estudiantes de la Facultad de Bellas Artes de la Universidad Pedagógica Nacional*. Bogotá, DC: Colciencias/ Universidad Pedagogica Nacional.

26
Popular music entrepreneurship in higher education
Facilitating group creativity and spin-off formation through internship programmes

Guy Morrow, Emily Gilfillan, Iqbal Barkat and Phyllis Sakinofsky

Introduction

The purpose of this chapter is to investigate student team-based possibilities for expanding the range of delivery modes for internship programmes within a popular music degree. A case study of the collaborative approach used in an arts entrepreneurship and management internship programme at Macquarie University (MQ)[1] is provided, in addition to pre- and post-programme experience interview data featuring the perspectives of some of the students and staff involved. This exercise in self-reflection concerning the pedagogical approach we have taken at MQ explores the following research question: What is the nature of student team-based internships in terms of collaborative creativity? Through an engagement with the literature pertaining to higher popular music education (HPME), arts entrepreneurship curricula in higher education and group creativity, we examine our case study data in order to explore the possibilities for building teams of student interns in our popular music programme.

---

1 Macquarie University is a public research university based in Sydney, Australia, in the suburb of Macquarie Park. Founded in 1964 by the New South Wales Government, it was the third university to be established in the metropolitan area of Sydney. www.mq.edu.au

In addition, we suggest potential ways in which popular music-related internship programmes can further develop and progress in ways that support a deeper development of students' creativities (Burnard, 2012). Our findings relating to student group creativity have enabled us to evaluate the feasibility of shifting (or partly shifting) the focus of our internship programmes from a mindset that emphasizes placing students individually with pre-existing organizations, towards harnessing the potential of student team-level creativity, thereby enabling students to establish their own start-up organizations and pursue their own entrepreneurial curiosity (Jeraj & Antoncic, 2013; Smith, 2013).

Popular music entrepreneurship has received scant attention within the field of work-integrated learning (WIL). This case study demonstrates how popular music entrepreneurship can inform WIL models in order to enhance graduate employability, and, in particular, graduate self-employment. The establishment and maintenance of an internship typically involves primary interaction between three people: the intern, the mentor and the associated organization, as well as the field advisor and the university (Brindle, 2011, p. 207; Hanson, 1984, p. 56; Wong, 2011, p. 526). The argument in this chapter, however, is that we need to think more divergently about the possibilities for internships within the field of HPME. This is because arts entrepreneurship is unique (Bridgstock, 2012), and this uniqueness means that this field of study readily leads to the establishment of start-ups and to spin-off formation (Rasmussen & Borch, 2010) because self-employment/entrepreneurship is the default setting in this field. According to Bridgstock (2012), "In first world countries, visual, literary and performing artists are generally between three and five times more likely to be self-employed or working on a freelance basis than workers in other occupations" (Bureau of Labour Statistics, 2011 cited in Bridgstock, 2012, p. 122), while according to Throsby and Zednik (2010), four in five professional artists in Australia maintain their own businesses. The question of how we can better prepare students for this reality is the focus of this chapter.

Higher popular music education

It is important to note here that, while there are some commonalities, the field of HPME is different to that of arts entrepreneurship education generally for a number of reasons. These differences further complicate attempts to encourage student-artist entrepreneurship within HPME programmes. Parkinson and Smith (2015) posit that:

> Historically, popular music has developed outside of intellectual institutions, and the ideological currency of some subgenres of popular music has arguably resided in living and championing values that exist in counterpoint to institutionalized culture (Parkinson, 2013), and thus to the traditional practice of higher education institutions.
>
> *(p. 98)*

In addition to this counter-cultural baggage, Parkinson and Smith note that HPME bears a narrative of struggle for recognition alongside more established and historically 'academic' disciplines and fields (Parkinson, 2013); that the academic legitimacy of HPME is "inevitably tethered to perceptions of the academic legitimacy of its object of study – popular music" (Parkinson, 2013); and, unlike other sectors of the arts, popular music has traditionally been a 'non-academic' cultural form. Therefore, the pressure exerted on arts entrepreneurship programme teams to focus curricula explicitly towards the acquisition of professional skills by the current 'employability' agenda of many tertiary institutions is accompanied, in the case of HPME, by pressure to argue for the legitimacy of the very subject matter taught within the field. However, the fact that popular music is a cultural form that can readily be lent to mass production means that this field of study can more easily adhere to the employability agenda than other sectors of the arts. This is because profitable businesses that do not rely on taxpayers' money for existence can more easily be established around this art form.

Context: PACE

This study was funded by an MQ Professional and Community Engagement (PACE) development grant. The PACE initiative is an example of MQ's institutional creativity (Burnard, 2012; Smith & Shafighian, 2013). MQ's institutional creativities relating to this initiative are driven by a desire to use PACE to address issues relating to social disadvantage and social inclusion, as well as by employment/workplace imperatives. While at an institutional level such creativity is in part driven by a desire to achieve world-changing impact by generating more opportunities for 'privileged' university students to help disadvantaged members of society, the initiative is also advertised to students in the following way:

> [PACE] will take you out of the lecture theatre and place you in the heart of your chosen career well before you graduate. PACE broadens your university knowledge by embedding practical experience into your degree. You'll be able to apply your ideas in real settings locally, regionally or internationally, while gaining invaluable life experiences and adding credit to your course.
>
> *(Macquarie University, 2015a)*

In the context of this study, the issue for the field of HPME is this: if four in five professional artists in Australia maintain their own businesses, then the "real" (Macquarie University, 2015a) setting involves popular music entrepreneurship and a need for students to work towards setting up their own businesses "well before" (Macquarie University, 2015b) they graduate. In a study of similar issues in the UK, Smith (2013) notes that:

> a pedagogy for employability should aim to instil in students the skills for, and a sense of, collaborative entrepreneurialism, because it is widely agreed that

a key to achievement in the professional music environment of the future is likely to be an ability to work successfully in teams.

(Smith, 2013, p. 193)

This reality of practice for popular musicians exists regardless of whether universities become (even more) subservient to neoliberal market fundamentalism or not (Jones, chapter 27, this volume).

The goal of MQ's PACE initiative is, by 2016, for every student constituting the university's approximately 38,000 population to complete a PACE programme as part of their degree. This means that in any one semester, approximately 10,000 students will be completing PACE activities (Macquarie University, 2015b). Therefore, with rising student numbers in our PACE programmes, the internal departmental context for this study involves generating findings that will help us to ensure the ongoing sustainability of the PACE initiative within the context of the Media, Music, Communication and Cultural Studies (MMCCS) department. We are addressing the issue of the potential saturation of internship opportunities by researching student team-based possibilities for expanding the range of delivery modes for PACE programmes and activities offered by MMCCS.

In terms of our own individual creativities, we, the authors, are involved with a number of internship, or PACE, programmes of study at MQ. While the case study of Suburban Bootleg that is featured in this chapter is an example of a specific HPME-related project, it took place through a broader creative industries programme. The arts industries and management internship programme, within which this activity was located, sits alongside a popular music major within a bachelor of arts (BA) degree. This creative industries programme is available to students majoring in popular music.

Collectively, we, the authors, are also involved with internship programmes that fit within the broader fields of the creative industries and media. These include programmes titled Media Internship and Public Relations, as well as a programme that involves student team-based film production for community partners, run through a general PACE programme within the faculty in which our department is located. The latter programme is the closest example of what we are trying to achieve through PACE in terms of HPME.

Literature review

A number of scholars within higher music education have published studies examining aspects of the field such as collaboration, curricula, assessment and programme structure (Burnard, 2012, 2014; Carey & Lebler, 2012; Feichas, 2010; Gaunt & Westerlund, 2013; Lebler, 2007, 2008; Parkinson & Smith, 2015; Smith, 2013; Smith & Gillett, 2015; Smith & Shafighian, 2013). There is also a body of literature concerning arts entrepreneurship in higher education (Beckman, 2007; Bridgstock, 2012; Brindle, 2011; Daniel, 2010), and another body of work that relates to broader issues involved in experiential learning in entrepreneurship education (Smith, 2014; Chen, Zou and Wang, 2009; Cope, 2005; Dhliwayo, 2008; Rasmussen & Borch, 2010). One point that a number of authors have made is that entrepreneurship can be a significant source of confusion and even controversy among arts educators (Beckman, 2007; Bridgstock, 2012; Hong et al., 2012).

In his comprehensive study of arts entrepreneurship education in the US, Beckman (2007) notes that despite the fact that students in the creative arts are eager for both professional development and entrepreneurship education – with many questioning why the "arts academy took so long to 'get it'" (p. 95), and arguing that from the perspective of administrators involved, student outcome is a "moral imperative" (p. 93) – it remains in the minds of some academic staff solely a path towards monetary success at the expense of art because culture and commerce can only ever have an awkward alliance (e.g. McGuigan, 2009a, 2009b, 2010). Beckman (2007) contends that despite attempts to define entrepreneurship in an inclusive manner, the rhetoric relating to this topic needs to be presented within the context of disciplinary culture for it to be understood and accepted by faculty (p. 94). Likewise, regarding the extent to which arts entrepreneurship is unique, Bridgstock (2012) posits that:

> The act of being enterprising in the arts probably involves a somewhat different set of capabilities to being enterprising in business. Not only are the contextual patterns the Opportunity Recognizing Mind must identify likely to be quite idiosyncratic to the arts, the strategies the Designing and Effectuating Mind must employ to bring artistic enterprises to fruition are also likely to be unique.
>
> (p. 127)

In this chapter we therefore take the position that entrepreneurship within the context of popular music is unique, and thus it needs to be studied within the field of PME/HPME rather than in a separate business school. In terms of HPME, Bridgstock's argument is similar to Burnard's (2012, 2014) notion of multiple musical creativities. Burnard's (2014) work is of particular relevance to this chapter because it provides examples drawn from international sources based on original practices and various educators' experiences of the diversity of creativities. This chapter in turn also aims to make a contribution to understandings of how to foster multiple creativities at individual, group and institutional levels.

In terms of the employment/workplace imperatives that drive creativities at programme and institutional levels within HPME, in addition to the two streams of curricular thought among arts educators that Beckman (2007) identifies – entrepreneurship as "new venture creation" (involving start-ups and their management), and the "transitioning" approach, which corresponds broadly to career self-management and being employable – Bridgstock (2012) adds a third sense to arts entrepreneurship: "being enterprising", which she notes aligns with "Schumpeterian and Druckerian (Dees, 1998; Drucker, 1985; Schumpeter, 1934) notions of opportunity identification and adding value of some kind" (quoted in Bridgstock, 2012, p. 125). In this chapter we build on the work of these scholars by arguing that popular music educators who are convening internship programmes need to facilitate 'opportunity creation' by focusing on student peer-to-peer networks and clusters of students, rather than isolating students from one another by placing them individually with pre-existing organizations. There is a gap in the literature relating to the facilitation of on-campus and emergent student team creativity that will feed both new venture creation, as well as transitioning outcomes, through what we call 'collaborative-emergent opportunity creation'. The argument here is that in the context of internship programmes, opportunities cannot simply be 'identified' – they need to be *created*, because novelty is sometimes emergent and creativity is often distributed between members of a group (Sawyer & DeZutter, 2009).

Theoretical framework

The placement of individual interns with pre-existing organizations is arguably partly informed by the (now dated) view that creativity is purely the product of individual talents and traits. If the student is uniquely talented and well-trained, and possesses numerous other personality traits, then there is the hope that they will be recruited by the organization with which they are interning and the university will have helped to achieve a career outcome for the student upon graduation. However, recent trends in creativity research involve researchers from a number of disciplines examining the social environmental forces that can influence creativity (Amabile & Pillemer, 2012; Simonton, 1999; Taggar, 2002). Understanding the micro-level social psychology of creativity is key to the facilitation of internships within popular music education because, typically, musicians themselves have to build a team around them (Smith, 2013, p. 193), and self-employment/entrepreneurship is the default setting in this field (Hughes et al., 2013).

For the purposes of understanding how best to design an internship programme in a popular music major or degree, Amabile's (1983a, 1983b, 1996) componential theory of creativity is useful when it is considered in conjunction with Taggar's (2002) work, which has expanded upon parts of Amabile's model. Amabile's componential theory includes three intra-individual components and one external component (the social environment) that influence creativity. The intra-individual components are:

a   Domain-relevant skills (expertise, technical skill and innate talent in the relevant domain(s) of endeavour);
b   Creativity-relevant processes (flexible cognitive style, personality traits such as openness to experience, skill in using creative-thinking heuristics and persistent work style);
c   Intrinsic task motivation.(Amabile & Pillemer, 2012, p. 10)

Taggar (2002) has expanded this original model with his discovery of "team-level creativity-relevant processes" that have been added to "creativity-relevant processes" in the original theory (p. 315). Team creativity-relevant processes involve a group's ability to work together effectively and make the most of each member's skill set.

In terms of the theoretical framework for this chapter, it is useful to consider team creativity-relevant processes as part of the broader componential theory of creativity while also zooming in to consider the exact mechanisms whereby creative products emerge from groups. To this end, Sawyer and DeZutter's (2009) work is useful. Drawing on the work of cognitive scientists who have conducted a broad range of empirical studies of how various cognitive processes are distributed across groups, Sawyer and DeZutter use the term 'distributed creativity' to refer to instances of collaborating groups of individuals generating a shared creative product. In this chapter, our case study group was an improvisational one, so the terms 'distributed creativity' and 'collaborative emergence' are used when analyzing the data.

Case study

In order to address the research question that drove this study, the field research was conducted on two levels. First, we used a case study approach (Yin, 1989, p. 14) in order to examine one specific student group's productivity in our arts entrepreneurship and management PACE programme. This case study enabled us to examine how the students in this team-based internship worked together to create their own project relating to popular music. The field research therefore involved examining the team-level creativity-relevant processes of this student team. The aforementioned theories of group creativity were critically applied. Of particular importance are the notions of how group creativity emerges from, and is therefore a characteristic of, the group rather than the individuals involved, and of how team-based processes are considered to be intuitive, dynamical and non-linear as well as being contextually located and dependent (Sawyer & DeZutter, 2009). Second, semi-structured interviews were conducted with members of the university-wide collaborative network involved in our PACE initiative, and with other students enrolled in our PACE programmes, in order to assess broader participant perceptions of the process. Participants were female and male, between 18 and 50 years old. Eight participants were involved.

Suburban Bootleg

In a typical internship programme, the student's mentor at a pre-existing organization with which they are interning provides the student with an opportunity in line with such a mentor's understanding of the university's policies, and with the learning outcomes for the internship programme (Hanson, 1984, p. 58; Wong, 2011, p. 517). In the case of a group of students who were interested in completing internships relating to popular music, as convenors of internship programmes we decided – together with the students – to think more divergently about the possibilities for their internships than this. Three participants were involved. The convenor of the internship programme worked with the students in an attempt to collaboratively create an opportunity or opportunities for the group. We applied the idea that "when groups of individuals work together to generate a collective creative product, the interactions among group members often become a more substantial source of creativity than the inner mental processes of any one participating individual" (Sawyer & DeZutter, 2009, p. 83). Collaboratively, as a group (including the programme convenor), we purposely set out to think divergently about the possibilities for a group internship. The following ideas were generated:

a   We would set up a music agency website that would become a conduit for MQ student band and singer-songwriter performance opportunities, as well as providing opportunities for external artists to perform (in an effort to generate links with the broader live music industry that could be utilized by student bands).
b   We would set up a journalistic blog as part of the project website that would feature reviews of student musicians' recordings and performances in addition to featuring video interviews with artist managers and other industry practitioners.
c   A novel idea that emerged from our group discussion was that we could approach 10 different artist managers about providing half an hour of their time for a video interview concerning their work (a much easier sell than asking them to take on an intern for 100 hours). This way, the student group could garner more (albeit potentially less substantive) insights from more artist managers than they potentially would if they interned with the one manager for 100 hours, and then these video interviews would be made available on the website. A link to this content would then be sent to the artist managers involved, who would hopefully view the videos of their interviews, as well as the student musicians' work available on the site. Therefore their knowledge could also be shared with other students and student musicians by way of the embedded videos on the website.

With these ideas in place, the student group was then left to collectively decide upon their processes for developing this project. The URL for the resulting website for the project is: www.suburbanbootleg.com.

In line with Amabile's (1983a, 1983b, 1996) componential theory of creativity, intrinsic task motivation was needed across the group. Regarding their intrinsic motivation, or lack thereof, throughout the project, one of the students who participated in the group reported:

> I experienced highs and lows in motivation across the semester, but once I regained motivation, quick progress was made and I began to enjoy the experience and learn more. I got the opportunity to interview Dan Medland[2] . . . My experience made me understand the need for motivation and hard work in an internship as things would not just simply happen and I could not just sit down and take everything in as if I was in a lecture.

---

2   Daniel Medland is a British artist manager who is currently located in Sydney and who personally manages Ladyhawke and Passenger. He also represents IE:music artists' interests in Australia, New Zealand and in the Asian Pacific markets.

Another requirement for Amabile's (1983a, 1983b, 1996) componential theory of creativity involves domain-relevant skills. Regarding this factor, this particular group participant continued: "In my interview with Dan Medland, I was able to ask questions about his experiences because of my knowledge of the field of artist managers, because of this, my knowledge was then enhanced from the responses I got". In terms of this group internship, this student's domain-relevant skills (which were acquired from other undergraduate programmes) combined with his intrinsic task motivation, and then both of these factors fed into what Taggar (2002) refers to as "team-creativity relevant processes" (p. 315). Regarding the collaborative process of generating a name for the project, one of the students noted in relation to his interaction with another student:

> I felt that throughout I was on an equal level with him. We were talking over the phone for 10 or 15 minutes ... We were using a name generator, I was doing all the generating stuff, so that was kind of my job ... Then we'd collaborate and say "okay here's the word we want to use next". Then I think at the end of the day, we were pretty happy with the word "suburban"; we used to highlight the words we liked ... There were two words actually pulled from separate spots, so the generator had actually made "Suburban Bootleg" ... But in terms of power structure I felt on the way that we collaborated that it was fair.

The name for the initiative, "Suburban Bootleg", in addition to the three ideas that were generated for this initiative overall (outlined above), are examples of collaborative emergence. Sawyer and DeZutter (2009) note that collaborative emergence is more likely to be found as a group becomes more aligned with the following four characteristics:

- The activity has an unpredictable outcome, rather than a scripted, known end-point;
- There is moment-to-moment contingency: each person's action depends on the one just before;
- The interactional effect of any given action can be changed by the subsequent actions of other participants; and
- The process is collaborative, with each participant contributing equally.

(Sawyer & DeZutter, 2009, p. 82)

This on-campus and team-based internship led to collaborative emergence because the participants contributed equally, the interactional effect of any given action was able to be changed by the subsequent actions of the other participants and there was moment-to-moment contingency: each student's actions depended on the previous one. Overall, this particular type of team-based internship had an unpredictable outcome. While the goal for it was in line with Beckman's (2007) notion of "new venture creation" (involving enterprise start-up and management) within arts entrepreneurship education, what specifically emerged as the new venture was unpredictable and unscripted. This type of internship therefore differs from conventional internships, which have a predictable end-point (i.e. being placed with a pre-existing organization as an individual), and is an example of 'collaborative-emergent opportunity creation'. In addition, on-campus and team-based internships such as this potentially have an 'opportunity multiplying effect' on the internship programme from which they stem: Suburban Bootleg will provide opportunities for student musicians and bands, graphic designers, music video directors and music journalists, as well as for other ideas that we cannot yet envisage because they are yet to collaboratively emerge.

Supervision

On-campus team-based internships are potentially more resource-intensive for the university. Typically the responsibility for identifying opportunities for student interns consumes the programme convenor's time in a way that does not fit into the neat box of a lecture/tutorial or seminar format; such work is more email- and consultation-heavy, with some of the convenors we interviewed stating that they felt more like "internship agents" than lecturers. In contrast to this way of working, on-campus and team-based internships draw more widely on the university's resources. There is a need to provide collaborative learning spaces for students, studio time and potentially equipment such as cameras and microphones so that the students can produce the work.

In order to address this issue, we plan to learn from recent international research into it. Smith and Shafighian's (2013) work is significant here. Their case study of student-team collaboration with the band Snarky Puppy at the Institute of Contemporary Music Performance (ICMP) in London has provided insights into the interplay between a familiar 'place' (in their case, the ICMP was the institutional location) and the more dynamic and creative 'space' of a new recording studio at this institution in which the student team collaborated with members of the band Snarky Puppy. Their project indicates the value of the "institutionally creative act of building and curating a recording studio that can be utilized as a unique space for facilitating depth of learning, exploration and meaning-making, through the development of student and teacher creativities" (Smith & Shafighian, 2013, p. 263). Engaging with the work of Randles (2013), Smith and Shafighian (2013) observed that "while it is in the unexplored 'space' that creativities and musicalities may be most excitingly realized, the onus remains on educators and administrators to be creative at institutional and programme levels in creating and curating appropriately conducive 'place'" (p. 263). MQ has a number of new collaborative learning spaces and studios that can be used to this end.

Conclusion

This chapter is an exercise in self-reflection concerning the pedagogical approach we have taken at MQ – an approach that involves facilitating student team-based HPME internships. The prospect of enabling students to establish their own start-up organizations to pursue their entrepreneurial curiosity is an exciting one, although this topic is still a subject of debate within this field (Jones, chapter 27, this volume; Lebler & Hodges, chapter 22, this volume; Smith, 2015). The argument in this chapter, within the context of this debate, is that as educators we need to use our creativities to design programmes of study that are suited to the nature of the industries into which our students graduate. This is a moral imperative (Beckman, 2007, p. 93) if we are to offer specific vocationally oriented popular music degrees, or popular music majors within arts degrees. It is unethical not to consider these issues, because students often enrol in our programmes with expectations of employment due to the way in which we, or our institutions, market our offerings. The counterargument – that we should avoid an attempt to facilitate entrepreneurship within our student body, because doing so makes us subservient to a neoliberal agenda – is an ethical one only if we run (or are running) our popular music programmes as 'elective' offerings for students who are majoring in different, more vocational, subjects; or if we advertise our popular music degrees on the grounds that students study music with the goal of attaining individual well-being outcomes rather than career ones.

Because collaborative emergence results from interactions among participants, it must be analyzed as a discursive, distributed process, and therefore an area for future research would be to use interaction analysis as a method for studying students' work with each other and with objects in their environment (Sawyer & DeZutter, 2009, p. 83) during an on-campus, student team-based internship. In encounters such as the one outlined in our study, knowledge and action are often better viewed as social, rather than located in the heads of the students as individuals, and this has implications for the design of appropriate assessment tasks for collaborative internships. There are also a number of resourcing issues that need to be addressed. Distributed creativity within on-campus student teams also has certain fluidity to it. It can occur in single encounters, or across multiple ones, and so the design of the space(s) for the internship programme needs to allow for this.

This chapter has offered insights into how we can better align our internship programmes with the realities of practice students experience upon graduating into the creative industries. Both within the 'place' of a university and the 'spaces' of the industries, distributed creativity is the norm within performing arts such as popular music (Sawyer & DeZutter, 2009, p. 83). Situations when the same group comes together multiple times are common; for instance, musical groups rehearse many times in order to generate a collectively created performance. The argument in this chapter is that new venture creation through internship programmes involves a similar team creativity-relevant process.

References

Amabile, T. (1983a). The social psychology of creativity: A componential conceptualization. *Journal of Personality and Social Psychology*, 45(2), 357–376. doi:10.1037/0022-3514.45.2.357.
Amabile, T. (1983b). *The social psychology of creativity*. New York, NY: Springer-Verlag.
Amabile, T. (1996). *Creativity in context*. Boulder, CO: Westview Press.
Amabile, T. & Pillemer, J. (2012). Perspectives on the social psychology of creativity. *Journal of Creative Behavior*, 46(1), 3–15. doi:10.1002/jocb.001.

Beckman, G. (2007). "Adventuring" arts entrepreneurship curricula in higher education: An examination of present efforts, obstacles, and best practices. *The Journal of Arts Management, Law, and Society, 37*(2), 87–112. doi:10.3200/jaml.37.2.87–112.

Bridgstock, R. (2012). Not a dirty word: Arts entrepreneurship and higher education. *Arts and Humanities in Higher Education, 12*(2–3), 122–137. doi:10.1177/1474022212465725.

Brindle, M. (2011). Careers and internships in arts management. In M. Brindle & C. DeVereaux (Eds.), *The arts management handbook: New directions for students and practitioners* (pp. 185–216). New York: M.E. Sharpe.

Bureau of Labour Statistics. (2011). *Occupational outlook handbook, 2010–11 edition: Artists and related workers.* Retrieved from: http://www.bls.gov/oco/ocos092.htm [Accessed 5 December 2014].

Burnard, P. (2012). *Musical creativities in practice.* Oxford: Oxford University Press.

Burnard, P. (2014). *Developing creativities in higher music education* [Kindle for Mac version]. Retrieved from: Amazon.com.

Carey, G., & Lebler, D. (2012). Reforming a Bachelor of Music programme: A case study *International Journal of Music Education, 30*(4). doi:10.1177/0255761412459160.

Chen, X., Zou, H., & Wang, D. (2009). How do new ventures grow? Firm capabilities, growth strategies and performance. *International Journal Of Research In Marketing, 26*(4), 294–303. doi:10.1016/j.ijresmar.2009.08.004.

Cope, J. (2005). Toward a dynamic learning perspective of entrepreneurship. *Entrepreneurship Theory And Practice, 29*(4), 373–397. doi:10.1111/j.1540–6520.2005.00090.x

Daniel, R. (2010). Career development and creative arts students: An investigation into the effectiveness of career theory and WIL experiences on practice. *Australian Journal of Career Development, 19*(2), 14–22. doi:10.1177/103841621001900203.

Dees, J.G. (1998). *The meaning of social entrepreneurship.* Retrieved from: http://www.partnerships.org.au/library/the_meaning_of_social_entrepreneurship.htm [Accessed 31 August 2016].

Dhliwayo, S. (2008). Experiential learning in entrepreneurship education. *Education + Training, 50*(4), 329–340. doi:10.1108/00400910810880560.

Drucker, P.F. (1985). *Innovation and entrepreneurship.* New York: Harper and Row.

Feichas, H. (2010). Bridging the gap: Informal learning practices as a pedagogy of integration. *British Journal of Music Education, 27*(1), 47–58.

Gaunt, H. & Westerlund, H. (Eds.) (2013). *Collaboration in higher music education,* [Kindle for Mac version]. Retrieved from: Amazon.com.

Hanson, J. (1984). Internships and the individual: Suggestions for implementing (or improving) an internship program. *Communication Education, 33*(1), 53–61. doi:10.1080/03634528409384717.

Hong, C., Essig, L., & Bridgstock, R. (2012). The enterprising artist and the arts entrepreneur: Emergent pedagogies for new disciplinary habits of mind. In: N. Chick, A. Haynie, R. Gurung (Eds.), *Exploring more signature pedagogies: Approaches to teaching disciplinary habits of mind* (pp. 68–84). Sterling, VA: Stylus.

Hughes, D., Keith, S., Morrow, G., Evans, M., & Crowdy, D. (2013). What constitutes artist success in the Australian music industries. *International Journal of Music Business Research, 1*(4), 61–80.

Jeraj, M. & Antoncic, B. (2013). A Conceptualization of entrepreneurial curiosity and construct development: A multi-country empirical validation. *Creativity Research Journal, 25*(4), 426–435. doi:10.1080/10400419.2013.843350.

Lebler, D. (2007). Student as master? Reflections on a learning innovation in popular music pedagogy. *International Journal of Music Education, 25*(30), 205–221.

Lebler, D. (2008). Popular music pedagogy: Peer learning in practice. *Music Education Research*, *10*(2), 193–213.

Macquarie University. (2015a). Retrieved from: http://students.mq.edu.au/opportunities/professional_and_community_engagement/ [Accessed 1 December 2014].

Macquarie University. (2015b). Professional and community engagement. Retrieved from: http://mq.edu.au/about_us/offices_and_units/professional_and_community_engagement.[Accessed 1 December 2014].

McGuigan, J. (2009a). *Cool capitalism*. London: Pluto Press.

McGuigan, J. (2009b). Doing a Florida thing: The creative class thesis and cultural policy. *International Journal of Cultural Policy*, *15*(3), 291–300. doi:10.1080/10286630902763281.

McGuigan, J. (2010). Creative labour, cultural work and individualisation. *International Journal of Cultural Policy*, *16*(3), 323–335. doi:10.1080/10286630903029658.

Parkinson, T. (2013). Canon reformation in popular music pedagogy. In M. Stakelum (Ed.), *Developing the musician: Contemporary perspectives on teaching and learning* (pp. 155–171). Farnham, UK: Ashgate.

Parkinson, T. & Smith, G.D. (2015). Towards an epistemology of authenticity in higher popular music education. *Action, Criticism, and Theory for Music Education*, *14*(1), 93–127.

Randles, C. (2013). A theory of change in music education. *Music Education Research*, *15*(4), 471–485.

Rasmussen, E. & Borch, O. (2010). University capabilities in facilitating entrepreneurship: A longitudinal study of spin-off ventures at mid-range universities. *Research Policy*, *39*(5), 602–612. doi:10.1016/j.respol.2010.02.002.

Sawyer, R. & DeZutter, S. (2009). Distributed creativity: How collective creations emerge from collaboration. *Psychology of Aesthetics, Creativity, and the Arts*, *3*(2), 81–92. doi:10.1037/a0013282.

Schumpeter, J. (1934). *The theory of economic development*. Cambridge, MA: Harvard University Press.

Simonton, D. (1999). *Origins of genius*. New York, NY: Oxford University Press.

Smith, G.D. (2013). Pedagogy for employability in a foundation degree (FdA) in creative musicianship: Introducing peer collaboration. In H. Gaunt & H. Westerlund (Eds.), *Collaborative learning in higher music education* (pp. 193–198). Farnham: Ashgate.

Smith, G.D. (2014). Seeking "success" in popular music education. In C. Randles (Ed.), *Music education: Navigating the future* (pp. 183–200). New York, NY: Routledge.

Smith, G.D. (2015). Neoliberalism and symbolic violence in higher music education. In L. DeLorenzo (Ed.), *Giving voice to democracy: Diversity and social justice in the music classroom* (pp. 65–84). New York, NY: Routledge.

Smith, G.D. & Gillett, A. (2015). Creativities, innovation, and networks in garage punk rock: A case study of the Eruptörs. *Artivate: A Journal of Entrepreneurship in the Arts*, *4*(1), 9–24.

Smith, G.D. & Shafighian, A. (2013). Creative space and the "silent power of traditions" in popular music performance education. In P. Burnard (Ed.), *Developing creativities in higher music education: International perspectives and practices* (pp. 256–267). London: Routledge.

Taggar, S. (2002). Individual creativity and group ability to utilize individual creative resources: A multilevel model. *Academy of Management Journal*, *45*(2), 315–330. doi:10.2307/3069349.

Throsby, D. & Zednik, A. (2010). Do you really expect to get paid? An economic study of professional artists in Australia. Melbourne: Australia Council for the Arts.

Wong, A. (2011). How is the internship going anyways? An action research approach to understanding the triad relationship between interns, mentors, and field advisors. *Educational Action Research*, *19*(4), 517–529. doi:10.1080/09650792.2011.625704.

Yin, R.K. (1989). *Case study research: Design and methods*. Newbury Park, CA: SAGE.

27

Teaching music industry in challenging times

Addressing the neoliberal employability agenda in higher education at a time of music-industrial turbulence

Michael Jones

Introduction

I lead an MA programme in Music Industry Studies at a higher education (HE) institution in the UK. The title of the programme is intended to signal that I favour teaching about 'music industry' as a system and set of practices of creating, marketing and distributing music goods for profit, rather than as a representation of a 'place' called 'The Music Industry'. Clearly, there are different approaches to teaching and understanding 'The Music Industry'; for example, Cloonan and Williamson (2007) argue that the term is a misleading one, favouring instead "The Music Industries". Their alternative, pluralized label enjoys the great usefulness of distinguishing various sectors of the industry/ies from one another – i.e. live performance from recording or music publishing. However, it implies a conceptual separation of musicians from engagement in activities that different kinds of music companies undertake, ones which define them as 'industries'. In this way, while the separation helps in the organization of degree programmes – inviting modules that explore particular industrial sectors and, in so doing, reducing a preoccupation with major record companies – it works against discussing the 'joint-working' of musicians with music companies, where it is joint-working that brings industry to music and music to industry. 'Joint-working' refers to collaboration between musicians and representatives of music industry agencies in all their myriad forms.

My determination to understand music industry as an *activity* or *activities* in favour of conceptualizing it as a removed and self-sufficient *place* derives in part from my experience of joint-working with music companies. I have made records for major and independent labels over a 30-year period. As songwriter for the band Latin Quarter, I experienced being 'signed' by the short-lived UK independent record company, Rockin' Horse, which was quickly bought out by (larger) Arista Records. However, almost as soon as the band experienced the transference of its contract to Arista, that company was merged, by its owners Bertellsmans, with the recently acquired RCA Victor to form Bertellsmans Music Group (BMG) in 1986. Through the course of these upheavals, Latin Quarter released one album through Rockin' Horse, one through Arista and two through RCA. Upon later being 'dropped' by BMG, the band made further albums for German independent companies: one for Verabra, one for SPV and seven for Westpark. Additionally, Cherry Red Records re-released the first two Latin Quarter albums under license from BMG, and RCA released two 'Best of' compilations.

While Latin Quarter was only a limited commercial success and lacks any significant subcultural purchase, what counts from a research and teaching perspective is that a commercially and culturally unsuccessful band experiences exactly and identically all of the industrial processes experienced by better-known and more culturally credible musicians. As Kirschner (1998, p. 250) has, for instance, observed of rock music culture, there is

> a huge amateur and quasi-professional realm supported by a well developed production and distribution infrastructure . . . [e]ven though most popular music consumption revolves around major label star acts, there are far more bands, venues, record labels, support personnel, etc., that exist at the low end of the spectrum.
>
> *(1998, p. 250)*

My own experience suggests that the 'harder' and more attenuated the experience, arguably the more inescapable is the sense that musicians work neither alone nor on terms of their own choosing or creation when attempting to gain, maintain and extend the attention of paying audiences for their market offers. As I have noted elsewhere, popular music is a social practice; it is the product neither of the 'artist' working alone, nor of the 'standardizing' efforts of global media conglomerates. In order to understand what pop is, we need to be able to explore that practice as a whole; consequently, our method of analysis needs to be a holistic one. Ultimately, we should understand records in the dual sense of recordings and of diaries or logs – a record is the outcome of all the process interactions that led to its recording and release, and to its fate as a commodity (Jones, 1997). Such was the conclusion of my PhD thesis, which was driven by a single recognition: that the vast majority of solo musicians or bands signed by major record companies failed to recoup the costs of the record companies' outlay on them (Anderton et al., 2012, p. 6). In this way, the majority product of the recording industry was market failure, rather than market success – notwithstanding notions of success in popular music beyond or existing alongside commercial value (Smith, 2013).

Although the statistics were always difficult to verify, in the pre-digital days major record companies contracted with only a tiny percentage of all acts pursuing commercial success in any one period. They then had hit records with only one in 10, and made profit on only one in 20. One consequence of attempting to account for how this happens (and what it means for an understanding of music industry *that* it happens) is that it reinforced in me a deep distrust of claims for the expertise of music company personnel. It did so because, however unscientific the metrics, major record companies were wrong not 99 times out of 100, but nearer to 999 times out of 1,000, and they used the glow from the enormous success of a tiny handful of their signings to blind musicians and consumers to what amounted to a determinate practice of risk aversion; one that accommodated a > 90% market failure rate as a deliberate strategy for company prosperity. Essentially, it could be argued that the surplus of signed acts underwrote a destructive approach to producing recorded music goods. The approach was destructive because, at all stages of the production process, major record companies eliminated from the market all acts they believed would not achieve commercial success, and did so largely by stealth. Clearly, such a strategy could not but impact on their relationships with musicians; however, whatever level of conflict thus engendered in those relationships, the imperative remained to keep musicians 'on-side' until the final decision to withdraw company support from them was made.[1]

To accomplish all of this took forms of management that were both precise and blunt. The strategy pivoted on a record company's ability to accomplish, on a case-by-case basis, the operational re-positioning of musicians from business partnerships to positions of subordinacy within a mode of production that depended on the musicians' collective ability to absorb this re-positioning and to continue to function as contributors to the production process. This absorption came at considerable ontological expense, because individual musicians would need to exist in three simultaneous roles – as (effectively powerless) business partners, as creative labour and as a commodity. Further, to survive as people rather merely than as musicians, they needed to be able to deal with the repercussions of failing to become market successes, especially when all such failure would be attributed by record companies to the inadequacies of their music rather than the structured outcome of a largely invisible production process whose governing strategy was predicated on risk aversion and the rational production of failure.[2]

'Music industry', as I conceive, teach and organize my programme, is a detailed examination of the working methods employed by music company personnel in their dealings with musicians. Generally, within these encounters 'music' can be seen to be subject to 'industry' in all of the ways music company actions are

---

1 For example, Morrissey was dropped by Capitol Records' Harvest label three weeks after the release of his album in August 2014. His comment was that "the pop or rock industry can be as dedicated to perpetuating public deception as the world of politics itself" (Bychawski, 2014).
2 As one A&R executive told the Guardian newspaper "the second album by every single band I've ever signed has flopped miserably, and no one really understands why" (Fitzpatrick, 2011), In this (typical) example, the record company employee distances himself from any responsibility for the market failure of a product by mystifying a process to which he has consciously contributed (an example of un-theorized industry 'common sense' in action).

interpreted and reacted to by musicians, as a serial need to meet specific contingencies. Although taking place in vast numbers and always difficult to access, the conduct and consequences of such serial contingencies (e.g. changes of release dates or key personnel in production and marketing of a product) can be shown to be patterned. It is the dynamic total of such patterned specificities that Becker (1982) is alert to but does not theorize adequately, that Caves (2000) senses but does not pursue and which theorists associated with the 'production of culture' perspective have long hovered above but somehow never quite elucidated (Banks, 2007; DuGay, 1997; DuGay & Pryke, 2002; Hesmondhalgh, 1996, 2002, 2013; Negus, 1992, 1999; Peterson & Berger, 1975; and Ryan, 1985). As Cottle (2003, p. 4) explains, where cultural and media industries are concerned "there is a relatively unexplored and under-theorized 'middle ground' of organizational structures and workplace practices".

Three sea-changes

A first major sea-change has taken place across the music industries under the impact of digital technologies (Kusek & Loonard, 2005). The work of theorizing the experiences summarized above took place in the 1990s, under industry conditions very different from today. First, the 'music industry' I theorized (Jones, 1997, 2005, 2012) was a phenomenon associated with the market dominance of the major record companies. Under the pre-digital music-industrial order, the 'majors' largely dominated the proceedings of the other music industries: the live performance sector had become shaped by the majors' need to market albums (live agents signed major-label 'signings' and dutifully organized 'album tours') while music publishers were rendered comparatively passive; no longer the vibrant 'Tin Pan Alley' of old, they 'signed' the songwriters from (often) their partner record companies and sat back to collect the royalties (or not, as the case may be) (Jones, 2012, pp. 32–27). This model no longer applies (Cartwright et al., 2015), although what has replaced it is not at all clear (International Federation of Phonographic Industry, 2014), and major labels continue to be 'big players' in contemporary music industry despite the decline in sales of recordings on physical formats and the disappearance of BMG and EMI.

A second, personal, sea-change was that all of my theorizing took place before I accepted a position teaching music industry in HE. On appointment I encountered multiple issues: I needed to 'deliver' an MBA programme that had already passed through the University's accreditation process, so the moulds into which I poured my understanding were prefigured and this meant that I needed to fight for my particular analysis within a comparatively unsympathetic representation of it as a set of modules whose titles sent 'messages' I could not control. Further, an MBA is an expensive degree, and students come with career ambitions that I could not ignore. Further still, this was a cohort who, mostly, sought work in what they conceived to be the music industry, and also in roles that, from my perspective, relied on an essentially destructive, or at best negligent, attitude to musicians, premised as they were on the business model described above. Addressing this complex mixture of imperatives was a challenge. Finally, this was a programme which came under the jurisdiction of the forerunner of the university's Management School; in whatever ways I directed my half of the programme, it was never going to chime with the management studies perspectives and protocols, which left me to somehow finesse the difference because no clear framework for teaching music industry management existed in the academy.

Taken together, in the absence of consultation on programme design, authority within the governance structure and any form of teacher education, my own version of teaching music industry grew in an *ad hoc* way, through an application of self-generated theory together with interpretation of existing literature and of events as reported in the trade and business press, at a time when HE programmes in music industry were almost unheard of – with the consequence that there were limited sources of external reference, discussion and guidance. (Today, by contrast, there are in excess of 40 music industry education providers at degree level across FE and HE and beyond, into the private sector (UCAS, 2015)). Presumably, all programmes generate local responses to similar sets of challenges, and yet there has been, to my knowledge, no dedicated conference or publication on teaching music industry throughout the years of its expansion in HE, and no dedicated communication forum exists to raise and address concerns and questions.

The third sea-change took place within the broader HE sector in the UK. In November 2014, the Conservative government's Secretary of State for Education, Nicky Morgan, declared that, once upon a time:

> Arts and humanities were what you chose [to study at university]. Because they were useful for all kinds of jobs. Of course now we know that couldn't be further from the truth, that the subjects that keep young people's options open and unlock doors to all sorts of careers are the STEM subjects: science, technology, engineering and maths.
>
> *(GOV.uk)*

Morgan's inflammatory comment, carrying as it does the weight of Government authority, presents HE staff and faculty working in Arts and Humanities with a considerable challenge. Essentially, if the production of graduates ready for jobs is a university's primary function, then all programmes need to be able to argue that an incoming student's chances in the 'job market' will be enhanced definitively by the time they graduate. In this way, what must now be in the forefront of the minds of academics is the quotient of 'employability skills' they can argue to be present in and through their teaching (McLaughlin, chapter 10, this volume). In my own university, the employability skills we are meant to embed in our modules and programmes are those identified by the Confederation of British Industries as essential to the workplace. In this way, critical thinking *about* work is substituted for uncritical obedience to the needs of employers. As Parkinson and Smith (2015, p. 102) explain, "the field [of higher popular music education] has developed from an internal genesis within liberal disciplines (such as cultural studies), and has become more vocational as a result of epistemic drift in UK education policy". Morgan's unvarnished pronouncement is thus part of a continued determination to transform HE so that it responds solely to market forces (Giroux, 2007).

As Allsup pointedly observes, "market forces are rapidly reshaping relationships between teachers, students and their forms of study . . . Neoliberalism is flourishing as a structuring ideology, compressing time and space, consuming identities and standardising production" (2015, pp. 251–252). This project can be traced to its roots in the publication of a series of polemical works on the nature and future of education in the UK: the "Black Papers in Education" (Cox & Dyson, 1971). These were, according to Limond (2012),

> avowedly conservative polemics on educational matters . . . issued . . . initially under the auspices/imprint of the Critical Quarterly Society (CQS), an influential forum for literary debate, founded some years previously by the academics and critics C B Cox and A E Dyson.
>
> *(2012, p. 52)*

The publication of the Black Papers was inspired by the wave of student unrest then sweeping the USA/UK/Europe. The Papers' editors attributed 'student unrest' to what they considered to be the "hasty expansion of student numbers", which "had led to a dilution of intellectualism" (2012, p. 55). It is reasonable to argue that these publications put reform of the University system onto Conservative Party radar (if not yet its agenda) in subsequent years.

The turn to neoliberalism

The 'turn to neoliberalism' is the subject of an extensive literature. Yergin and Stanislaw (1999) offer an early, partisan and (thus) revealing account of its origins and distinctiveness as an aggressive ideological project (see especially pp. 74–91). The overarching vision of the ideology is to replace any form of national government policy that might embody or derive from collectivist ideals with ones that make all decisions on the raising and spending of tax income consonant with, and responsive to, 'market forces' (which are always naturalized and never opened to scrutiny). Where the UK is concerned, the prosecution of a neoliberal agenda began with the two general election defeats suffered by the Conservative Party in 1974. The replacement of Edward Heath by Margaret Thatcher as leader was the decisive turning point in that party's reformulation of its core politics (Thatcher had been Secretary of State for Education and Science during the years of the Black Paper–inspired debates). Thatcher's ascendancy saw the party turn away from a generalized compliance with the post-war settlement, which soubriquet can be summarized as the welfare state and a commitment to full-employment, towards the economic and political philosophy of Friedrich von Hayek and the Mont Pelerin Society (Harvey, 2007, p. 21). This revolved around the deregulation of 'markets', and opening to market forces government-funded enterprises such as nationalized industries and services including health, welfare and education. Following four successive general election defeats, the (UK) Labour Party regained power in 1997, but as a much-changed entity, under the leadership of Tony Blair and (informally) branded as 'New Labour'. In committing to a notional 'Third Way' (between social reformism and neoliberalism), this incarnation of the Labour Party, in fact, quickened many neoliberal policies, particularly in regard to the privatization of HE (signalled by the Conservative Further and Higher Education Act of 1992)[3] and the arts (Hewison, 2014).

'New Labour' introduced HE tuition fees under the Teaching and Higher Education Act of 1998, and the first decade and a half of the new century has witnessed five acts of Parliament, all extending the core logic of privatized HE driven by neoliberal ideology. This accumulation of legislation has introduced and entrenched two invidious couplings – (1) that to be 'value for money', degrees must produce graduate employment; and its corollary, (2) that to produce graduate employment, degree programmes must enhance student employability. Fanelli and Evans (2015), Giroux (2014), Brown and Carasso (2013) and McGettigan (2013) – among others – track HE's permeation by neoliberalism, where the ultimate goal of this relentless strategy is, as Giroux argues it, the extinguishing of the capacity for universities to be agencies of critical inquiry (Giroux 2014, p. 313). If "critical inquiry" (Giroux 2014, p. 313) can finally be excised from the academic body, then the chance that universities will ever again become, as the Black Papers had it, sites of "student unrest" (Swann, 1969, p. 147) is nullified. In this way, the current wave of HE reform is a political project with very deep, and deeply Conservative, roots. This seems to be at odds with popular music, which is so often seen as a source of articulating what might be considered to be broadly more collectivist – or certainly non-neoliberal – values (Smith, 2015). It is the vagueness at the heart of this tentative supposition that so exposed music industry education (and music education more generally – see Allsup (2015)) to an unremarked drift towards congruence with the neoliberal agenda.

Doing it for the kids

In the late 1980s and early '90s, several schemes and projects emerged in the UK in response to a perceived need to help and support young people in the UK. This need arose from the steep and rapid decline in primary and secondary industrial production (Harvey, 2011). In 1988, Creation Records released a compilation album, *Doing It for the Kids*, the proceeds from sales of which went to charities working with youth. To help address the combined disappearance of skilled apprenticeships and unskilled work opportunities, metropolitan counties, under governance of the Labour Party, began to use their own, and latterly European, funds to finance initiatives in training for post-industrial occupations (in the sense that, for example, jobs in coal mining would no longer be widely available). The opportunity to access such funds derived from the 1986 revision to the Treaty

---

3 That act transformed 35 polytechnics into universities and introduced a very strong element of competition into the HE sector (Parkinson & Smith, 2015).

of Rome, which sought to establish a single European market by 1992 (Laursen, 2012). For example, the South Yorkshire council's version of *Doing It for the Kids* was to create Red Tape Studios in Sheffield (Brown et al., 2000; Frith, 1993) as the first stage in the formation of a Cultural Industries Quarter. The studio complex consisted of one publicly owned and two privately owned studios. It was the publicly owned studio that was designed to offer skills training and career development for young people with newly limited job prospects.

Such schemes were launched with the barest academic groundwork and in the absence of the theorization of music as a workplace – a characteristic shared with various 'vocational' institutions being established around the same time in popular music performance (McLaughlin, chapter 10, this volume; Parkinson, 2014; Parkinson & Smith, 2015). In the years after the opening of Red Tape Studios, a slew of similar initiatives across the UK ushered in an era of ongoing expansion in para-academic education in music industry. Under the feel-good and vocationally focused rubric of 'training' and 'apprenticeship', initiatives such as Generator, in Newcastle (1991 onwards), and the Manchester *In the City* conference (1992–2011), created templates for learning about the music industry where the underpinning knowledge was, and remains, the testimony of 'industry insiders'. This formula survived the farrago that was the government's 'New Deal for Musicians' (Cloonan, 2002, 2003; Jones, 1999) and remains not just the key selling point for, but also the primary source of legitimation of an increasingly narrow vocational approach. For example, the BA in Media and Communication (Music Industries) at Birmingham City University attracted students with the strapline "Get real and rare insight from regular guest speakers".[4] Such advertising invites questions such as: "How insightful is this 'insight'?" and, second, "Is it robust enough to act as a form of knowledge in the academic interrogation of music industry, where the point is that merely 'reporting' back how industry functions is not equivalent to analysing those functions?"

As a way of illustrating this point, we might consider an example of a virtual 'guest speaker' – former CEO of Sony Music UK Nick Gatfield – offering his "Top Five Tips" for "How to Make it in the Music Industry" (Gatfield, 2013). The video was created by Dillon Khan, who hosts a website ('The Intern'), which is "dedicated to interns past, present and future" (Khan, 2015). The video forms one of a set of interviews with 'industry heads' and would be exactly the kind of presentation a music industry lecturer might organize for a class. Gatfield uses the term 'the music industry' freely throughout the video, implying that it is indeed a place and not an activity ("the great thing about the music industry is it's a very flat organisation") – a place to which he explains how access can be gained. In the presentation, the terms 'passion' and 'passionate' are used several times; passion, Gatfield alleges, being means of entry to the inaccessible place. Gatfield goes on to

---

4 The page containing this quote has been re-designed since first being accessed: BA (Hons) Media and Communication (Media Industries) Birmingham City University, but the reference can still be found at http://www.dreamfoundation.eu/ro_RS/courses/course/3568#.

describe the music industry as "a human business ... you are ... trying to sell an artist, and a human being". Even so, he does not go on to explain or examine, for example, how a human being becomes a commodity and what this might mean for that human being or for those who effect their transformation into a commodity (such as those on music industry programmes in HE). Gatfield's clearest piece of advice for would-be entrants to the music industry is to "start your business yourself; become a (sic) entrepreneur in the music space". While this guidance is in line with a good deal of contemporary thinking in the arts (Hewison, 2014) and music education (Lebler & Hodges, chapter 22, this volume; Morrow et al., chapter 26, this volume), spurred by the neoliberal mantra – the "myth of the transformation of all wage earners into dynamic small entrepreneurs" (Bourdieu, 2003, p. 30) – Gatfield's advice leaves us well short of understanding how the highly commercialized, major-label music industry that he inhabits proceeds as a joint-working, collaborative enterprise between musicians and music companies, where the needs of the latter exert their own logic and discipline – a logic and discipline in which he is (as a CEO) evidently steeped.

Gatfield's advice is, I contend, of little practical value, but it is worth further consideration. For example, his identification of a need for 'passion' is revealing, since it seems deliberately to mystify and obfuscate the rational, business-orientated process of signing musicians and keeping them under contract while company employees delay (or accelerate) market entry depending on their anticipation of its trends. The appeal to passion is cheap and lazy – after all, what young entrepreneur would wish to be seen as anything less than passionate about her or his work? The implication that heightened emotion is necessary and sufficient to work successfully to create market-ready popular music products, that this and a palette of skills are all that is required is to enter 'the industry', is misleading. It also reduces the value of vocationalism by not just resisting theory but also making a virtue of its repudiation.

More than anything, Gatfield's talk is evidence of the studied lack of self-reflexivity emblematic of music-industrial *realpolitik*. In this, it is not so much a rejection of academic learning in preference for learning at 'the School of Hard Knocks' and 'the University of Life' (although this macho-bravado is never far beneath the surface in music industry insider presentations); it is more a prostration before what are constructed as a set of 'natural' processes supposedly governing the everyday world. Here (to paraphrase Negus, 1992, pp. 54–55), music company personnel are 'nurturers' of music and musicians. As in a maternity unit, 'services' are implicitly necessary, constructive and non-intrusive; all that counts is the health of 'the child'. Consequently, we learn nothing of how joint goals pursued by unequally resourced partners are accomplished, and nothing of how decisions are arrived at, in whose interests and with what consequences – there is no sense that the process impacts on the product; music industry as an impactful process of commodity production remains veiled.

In responding to Gatfield's presentation in this way, I am not suggesting that it is – or that similar presentations on campus, in front of students, are – worthless; I argue that what guest speakers do is to construct discursively their experience of 'the industry' from available raw materials, tending to be commonsense formulations that routinely and habitually obscure the day-to-day industrial dimensions of music industry. In contradistinction, our work as academics is to analyze and evaluate what people say they do; it is this that is valuable to our students, not the uncritical endorsement of whatever it is our speakers tell us. Music industry guest speakers offer rationalizations of their activity for the reason that they are not in the business of producing theory; they work to create market-successful symbolic goods. In a 'numbers game', what counts are market successes, but as these flow from the same processes that produce an over-abundance of market failures the tendency is to off-set failures onto deficiencies beyond the actions of companies. These deficiencies lie, then, with the music made by the musicians, as if music alone decides its fate in the market. But if the total of all of the actions taken by music producers, music publishers, live agents and promoters, marketing and promotions people, and sundry other personnel have no bearing on market performance, then why study (and revere) these people as 'The Music Industry'? Rather than revere them, I would not disparage such people but urge evaluation of their claims against analyses of their (and their industry's) track record.

Conclusion

I have referred to 'narrow vocationalism' and implied that it works, hand-in-glove, with the inflexible neoliberal emphasis on teaching 'employability' in HE. Narrow vocationalism is best understood as the teaching of skills without locating (and evaluating) those skills in the historical and working contexts of their evolution. It seems practically and ethically impossible, to me, to teach vocationally without first analyzing work and the structure and organization of the workplace. If we do not analyze production, how can we specify production roles? If we do not specify production roles then how can we ask questions about authority and power? Rather than teaching skills in a way that encourages students to be compliant with what exists, HE would be more useful to them if we continued to fight for the right to be critical of social and economic relations and to refuse to take them at face value. Our role is to teach individuals to think critically so that they make better-informed choices in the music and employment market places (Lebler & Hodges, chapter 22, this volume; Morrow et al., chapter 26, this volume).

Neoliberal-driven change appears to be irresistible (Niknafs & Przybylski, chapter 32, this volume); and certainly the ongoing digital transformation of the music industries is equally irresistible and almost impossible to predict. Today it is moot whether new pop stars (such as Rita Ora, for example) are part of the music industry at all, so extensive are their television, filming and branding activities. Whether this heralds the emergence of an 'entertainment industry' model in lieu of a music industry is beyond the scope of this paper. However, industrial production resists, favouring the selectors over the selected in that global companies will always have more market power than individual musicians. If we are to prepare students for this reality, then an 'industry-compliant' education is no education at all, because it represents a historically contingent configuration of capital and labour as a natural configuration, and in doing so places it beyond reproach. As I indicated above, I would welcome much-needed discussion on the themes touched upon in this chapter, among other important, related, topics salient to teaching music industry in higher education. I hope that this short essay might help to provoke such a conversation. I conclude with Allsup's optimistic counter to increasingly normative neoliberal narratives. He writes:

> Humanity cannot be reduced to a market force, nor the person to a brand. We want to work collaboratively, fairly and intentionally within conditions that provide for our flourishing; we are also wondrously irrational actors, following ends that are outside the logic of personal gain or use value. And as musicians, we know intimately that the arts have values that are richer, more complex and more confusing, than those attributed to commerce or mere self-identity.
> *(2015, p. 259).*

References

Allsup, R.E. (2015). The eclipse of a higher education or problems preparing artists in a mercantile world. *Music Education Research, 17*(3), 251–261.

Anderton, C., Dubber, A., & James, M. (2012). *Understanding the music industries*. London: SAGE Publications.

Banks, M. (2007). *The politics of cultural work*. Basingstoke: Palgrave MacMillan.

Becker, H. (1982). *Art worlds*. Berkeley, CA: University of California Press.

Bourdieu, P. (2003). *Firing back: Against the tyranny of the market 2*. London: Verso.

Brown, A., O'Connor, J., & Cohen, S. (2000). Local music policies within a global music industry: Cultural quarters in Manchester and Sheffield. *Geoforum, 31*(4), 437–451.

Brown, R. & Carasso, H. (2013). *Everything for sale? The marketisation of UK higher education*. Abingdon: Routledge.

Bychawski, A. (2014). Morrissey reportedly dropped by record label. *NME*. Retrieved from: http://www.nme.com/news/morrissey/79087#KqE3jPRw7GdJ7U83.99 [Accessed 1 September 2015].

Cartwright, P.A., Gillett, A., & Smith, G.D. (2015). Valuing networks for emerging musicians. In V. Lejeune (Ed.), *Les Tendances technico-économiques de la Valeur* (pp. 129–160). Paris: 'l'Harmattan.

Caves, R.E. (2000). *Creative industries*. Cambridge, MA: Harvard University Press.

Cloonan, M. (2002). Hitting the right note? The new deal for musicians. *Journal for Vocational Education and Training, 54*(1), 51–66.

Cloonan, M. (2003). The new deal for musicians: Teaching young pups new tricks. *Music Education Research, 5*(1), 13–28.

Cloonan, M., and Williamson, J. (2007). Rethinking the music industry. *Popular Music*, 26 (2), pp. 305–32.

Cottle, S (ed) (2003). *Media Organization and Production*. Thousand Oaks, CA: Sage p. 24.

Cox, C.B. & Dyson, A.E. (1971). *The black papers on education*. London: Davies-Poynter Ltd.

Du Gay, P. (1997). *Production of culture/cultures of production*. Thousand Oaks, CA: SAGE.

Du Gay, P. & Pryke, M. (Eds.) (2002). *Cultural economy: Cultural analysis and commercial life*. Thousand Oaks, CA: SAGE.

Fanelli, C. & Evans, B. (2015). Neoliberalism and the degradation of education. *Alternate Routes: A Journal of Critical Social Research, 26*.

Fitzpatrick, R. (2011). When bands fall off cliffs. *The Guardian*. Retrieved from: http://www.theguardian.com/music/2011/oct/27/when-bands-fall-off-cliffs [Accessed 1 September 2015].

Frith, S. (1993). Popular music and the local state. In T. Bennett, S. Frith, L. Grossberg, J. Shepherd, & G. Turner (Eds.), *Rock and popular Music: Politics, policies, institutions* (pp. 14–24). London: Routledge.

Gatfield, N. (2013). How to make it: Music industry (Top 5 Tips – Nick Gatfield, Sony Music). Retrieved from: https://www.youtube.com/watch?v=rLw65evUfzI [Accessed 8 September 2015].

Giroux, H.A. (2007). Utopian thinking in dangerous times: Critical pedagogy and the project of educated hope. In M. Coté, R.J.P. Day & G. de Peuter (Eds.), *Utopian pedagogy: Radical Experiments Against Neoliberal Globalization* (pp. 25–43). London, ON: Toronto University Press.

Giroux, H A. (2014). *Neoliberalism's war on higher education*. Chicago, IL: Haymarket Books.

GOV.co.uk. Speech: Nicky Morgan speaks at Launch of Your Life campaign. Retrieved from: https://www.gov.uk/government/speeches/nicky-morgan-speaks-at-launch-of-your-life-campaign [Accessed 9 September 2015].

Harvey, D. (2007). *A brief history of neoliberalism*. Oxford: Oxford University Press.

Hesmondhalgh, D. (1996). Flexibility, post-Fordism and the music industries. *Media, Culture and Society*, 18, 469–488.

Hesmondhalgh, D. (2002). *The cultural industries*. Thousand Oaks, CA: SAGE.

Hesmondhalgh, D. (2013). *Why music matters*. Chichester: Wiley-Blackwell.

Hewison, R. (2014). *Cultural capital: The rise and fall of creative Britain*. London: Verso.

International Federation of Phonographic Industry. (2014). IFPI Digital music report: Lighting up new markets. Retrieved from: http://www.ifpi.org/downloads/Digital-Music-Report-2014.pdf [Accessed 1 March 2015].

Jones, M.L. (1997). Organising pop: Why so few pop acts make pop music. PhD diss., University of Liverpool.

Jones, M.L. (1999). Changing slides: Labour's music industry policy under the microscope, *Critical Quarterly*, *41*(1), 22–31.

Jones, M.L. (2005). Working for your supper: Creative work and the contexts of popular songwriting. In J. Williamson (Ed.), *Words and music* (pp. 219–249). Liverpool: Liverpool University Press.

Jones M.L. (2012). *The music industries: From conception to consumption*. Basingstoke: Palgrave Macmillan.

Khan, D. The Intern. Retrieved from: http://www.theintern.co.uk/ [Accessed 24 September 2015].

Kirschner, T. (1998). Studying rock: Toward a materialist ethnography. In T. Swiss, J.M Sloop & A. Herman (Eds.), *Mapping the beat: Popular music and contemporary theory* (pp. 247–268). Malden, MA: Blackwell.

Kusek, D. & Loonard, G. (2005). *The future of music: Manifesto for the digital music revolution*. London: Omnibus Press.

Laursen, F. (2012). *Designing the European Union: From Paris to Lisbon*. Basingstoke: Palgrave Macmillan.

Limond, D. (2012). Silencing the "other" Black Paper contributors. *History of Education Review*, *41*(1), 52–65.

McGettigan, A. (2013). *The great university gamble: Money, markets and the future of higher education*. London: Pluto Press.

Negus, K. (1992). *Producing pop culture and conflict in the popular music industry.* London: Edward Arnold.

Negus, K. (1999). *Music genres and corporate cultures.* Abingdon: Routledge.

Parkinson, T. (2014). Values in higher popular music education. PhD diss., University of Reading.

Parkinson, T. & Smith, G.D. (2015). Towards an epistemology of authenticity in higher popular music education. *Action, Criticism, and Theory for Music Education, 14*(1), 93–127.

Peterson, R.A. & Berger, D.G. (1975). Cycles in symbol production: The case of popular music. In S. Frith & A. Goodwin (Eds.), *On Record* (1990) (pp. 140–158). London: Routledge.

Ryan, J. (1985). *The production of culture in the music industry: The ASCAP-BMI controversy.* Lanham, MD: University Press of America.

Smith, G.D. (2013). Seeking "success" in popular music. *Music Education Research International, 6*, 26–37.

Smith, G.D. (2015). Neoliberalism and symbolic violence in higher music education. In L. DeLorenzo (Ed.), *Giving voice to democracy: Diversity and social justice in the music classroom* (pp. 65–84). New York, NY: Routledge.

Swann, M. (1969). Black paper two: The crisis in education. *Critical Survey, 4*(3), 147–149.

UCAS (2015). Music business. Retrieved from: http://search.ucas.com/search/providers?Feather=7&Vac=5&AvailableIn=2016&Query=Music%20Business&MaxResults=1000&page=2 [Accessed 15 August 2015].

Yergin, D. & Stanislaw, J. (1999). *The commanding heights: The battle for the world economy.* New York, NY: Simon and Schuster.

Part V
Social and critical issues

28
Popular music meta-pedagogy in music teacher education

Ian Axtell, Martin Fautley and Kelly Davey Nicklin

In this chapter we discuss issues surrounding the training of secondary school classroom music teachers in England and share some findings from a small-scale action research project. In order to prepare beginning music teachers to teach music lessons which have value and are meaningful to a broad range of young people, it is important to include pedagogies for popular music as part of initial teacher education. International modalities for initial teacher education differ significantly between jurisdictions, but however they are conceived, Shulman's (1986) notion of *pedagogic content knowledge* features as an important element. Pedagogical content knowledge for popular music is a relative newcomer to the toolkit of the classroom music teacher despite the importance of popular music to young people and the broader community outside schools. Popular music deserves separate consideration from other types of musical stylistic learning, in particular because it has no long history of pedagogy (Mantie, 2013), and expertise can be gained without formal musical tuition (Green, 2002, 2008).

Popular music in initial teacher education

We have known for some time now that beginning music teachers come into their teacher training from a variety of routes. There is a wide variety of music degree programmes, and within this variety there is also considerable variance in the depth and breadth of music curricular content. In some cases, students approaching initial teacher education may have experienced trajectories which have not included significant amounts of either academic study or professional practice with regards to popular music; neither, in many cases, will graduates of these programmes have undertaken significant study in composing or arranging in popular music styles and genres. As Hargreaves, Welch, Purves and Marshall (2005, p. 1) observe:

> Many secondary music specialist teachers have been trained within the Western Classical tradition, in which music-making is dominated by a "professional performance" career model based largely in conservatoires and university music departments, and this may be inappropriate for the demands of the secondary school classroom.

In their study of initial teacher education, Finney and Philpott invoke Bourdieu's notion of habitus, aligning this with the prioritizing of certain types of musical knowledge linked to a subversion of some popular styles and genres of music:

> Music graduates arrive for initial teacher education having acquired habitus where an awareness of the informal moment in musical learning can lie "buried", even for those who have learned as a stereotypical "informal" pop musician! Our system of music education (and wider education and culture) has the potential to subvert the informal, a consequence of which is that what counts as musical knowledge, learning and pedagogy for the musicians who embark on teacher education programmes can often be defined in terms of the formal moment.
>
> *(Finney & Philpott, 2010, p. 10)*

However, alongside such beginning music teachers, there are also a significant number who have undertaken study which has included, or been focused on, aspects of popular music. In her study of music initial teacher education, Kokotsaki (2010) found that 20% of students had *not* come from degree programmes which could be considered as being primarily based in a Western classical tradition: a small, but significant minority.

Whatever their background, the reality of the contemporary secondary school music classroom is that all beginning music teachers need to be able to function pedagogically with a secure understanding of popular music and associated music technology. A key question that underpins the work of university-based tutors in initial teacher education is posited by Russell and Loughran (2007, p. 14), namely: "How do you develop and enact your pedagogy of teacher education?" In teaching novice teachers how to teach, or 'enact their pedagogy', a key notion is that of *meta-pedagogy*, which we take to mean the process through which beginning music teachers learn about pedagogical content knowledge. This is the way in which Finney and Philpott (2010, p. 7) use the term when they talk of "the pedagogy for learning pedagogy".

As teacher educators we want to enable beginning music teachers to develop an understanding of how and what to teach so that they can function in a variety of school settings. The aim is not to restrict beginning music teachers' experiences to 'what works for us'. An issue here is how students recognize and develop their own perceptions of popular music pedagogy, particularly in terms of pedagogical content knowledge, "the ways of representing and formulating the subject to make it comprehensible to others" (Shulman, 1986, p. 9), as this is central to discussion of meta-pedagogy.

In most higher education-based teacher-training programmes in the United Kingdom, a period of learning away from schools is followed by a practicum, a teaching practice experience in the classroom. Once beginning music teachers begin to function as novice teachers, their main focus tends to be upon their own personal classroom performance, where they are concerned with reproducing the "idiosyncratic and contextual factors" (Bronkhorst, Meijer, Koster & Vermunt, 2011, p. 1122) of a school setting. At this stage beginning music teachers are apparently functioning as teachers; indeed, many see this as a sort of extended role play activity, but while operating at this functioning and reproductive stage many beginning music teachers are not yet able to recognize how their teaching impacts upon learning. Working away from schools enables beginning music teachers to explore in a secure environment many of the pedagogic issues they will encounter for real in the practicum. This means that they are able to experience what Vescio, Ross and Adams (2008, p. 83) define as an "authentic pedagogy" which "emphasises higher order thinking, in other words, the construction of meaning through conversation and the development of a depth of knowledge that has value beyond the classroom".

Popular music education or informal learning

Much of the recent work on popular music in education has focused on what is often termed *informal learning*. Indeed, an axiological approach including popular music in the context of informal learning has underpinned a significant amount of music education research and subsequent school approaches in England (Green, 2008) and elsewhere (Georgii-Hemming & Westvall, 2010) in the past decade. Based upon her investigations into how popular musicians learn (Green, 2002), Green has achieved significant impact on music education at Key Stage 3 (in the UK this covers the first three years of secondary school, for pupils aged 11 to 14). In the UK, Key Stage 3 is the principal concern of beginning music teachers studying Secondary Music Education since it will normally form the majority of their teaching in schools. Therefore, a meta-pedagogy for popular music needs to enable these students to develop their pedagogical content knowledge in the context of Key Stage 3 classroom music education, particularly in terms of how they "bring non-formal teaching and informal learning approaches into the more formal context of schools" (Musical Futures, 2014). The five key principles of informal learning that underpin the Musical Futures project (from Green, 2008) are:

1 Pupils work with music that they choose for themselves, often music that they like, enjoy and identify with;
2 Pupils primarily work aurally, by listening and copying;
3 Pupils work alongside friends, in groups that they choose for themselves;

4   Skills and knowledge tend to be assimilated haphazardly, starting with whole, real-world pieces of music;
5   There is an integration of listening, performing, improvising and composing throughout the learning process, with an emphasis on personal creativity.

These principles of informal learning are important and can form an initial framework for a meta-pedagogy that reflects what has been happening in schools:

- Students choose their learning groups (principle 3);
- Students share the music they listen to (principles 1 and 4);
- Students create their own arrangement of existing music chosen from the music they have shared (principle 2),
- These arrangements are created through performance-based listening and copying (principles 1, 2 and 4),
- From this initial arrangement students then choose a musical device that featured in their arrangement (such as a chord sequence, melodic fragment or bass riff) to initiate some composing (principle 5).

However, as Folkestad observes:

> Having established that learning, and the learning situation, can be both formal and informal, it is important to clarify that this is not the case with teaching: teaching can never be carried out using "informal teaching methods".
> (Folkestad, 2006, p. 142)

This is an important point, as there is not an automatic linkage between popular music and informal learning. Simply because some programmes of popular music learning employ informal learning strategies in schools does not mean that all popular music learning has to be this way. Hodkinson, Colley and Malcolm (2003) identify informal learning as an unstructured process lacking overt assessment, with no certification, no time constraints, no predetermined learning objectives, no specified curriculum with the focus on everyday practice and non-elite knowledge where learning is decided on and initiated by the learner. This can provide an initial stimulus for learning, but there is a danger that if there is little or no form of intervention, learning becomes unfocused, lacking appropriate challenge, and that the hegemonic valorization of certain types of music, including certain types of popular music, can be reinforced. This can result in students becoming disengaged, and some might even regard the process as meaningless, particularly if they feel they are outside that valorization process (Wright, 2008). Folkestad (2006, p. 143) identifies that:

> Formal–informal should not be regarded as a dichotomy, but rather as the two poles of a continuum, and that in most learning situations, both these aspects of learning are in various degrees present and interacting in the learning process.

Distributed and situated learning in communities

One approach to mitigate against learning that lacks challenge might be some form of intervention by a teacher. However, the motivation engendered by an active engagement in learning by pupils cannot be ignored. In effect, a balance between teaching and learning needs to be attained, especially between the formal moment where the content is decided by the teacher, and the informal moment where the content is chosen by the pupil. Professional judgements that teachers make with regard to this balancing act centre on their perceptions of pedagogy. Pedagogy and meta-pedagogy can be seen as forms of social discourse, where teachers and learners are part of learning communities, and where knowledge is actively co-constructed. Learning communities provide the capacity for taking risks, which are necessary to promote change (Vescio et al., 2008, p. 84).

Placing beginning music teachers in learning communities presents the possibility of challenging preconceived ideas about teaching based upon their own experiences in education. It is important that students share their reservoirs of experience in terms of personal musical enculturation, but if learning communities are created that include a balanced mix of musical experiences then there is the potential to challenge Bourdieu's notions of personal habitus, and simultaneously promote the potential for social equality. To address this, beginning music teachers can be placed as though along a continuum, both as novices and experts in different areas of music and musicianship, helping to encourage mutual learning readiness. Yang and Liu provide a clear summary of the importance of learning communities where student teachers can engage in discourse with teacher educators in a non-threatening manner. They help to develop "collegiality and cooperative problem solving, promoting the growth of reflective discourse" (2004, p. 735). Yang and Liu also observe that student teachers' "participation in a knowledge-building community has been envisaged to facilitate the development of subject matter and pedagogical content knowledge" (2004, p. 735).

If the beginning music teachers become part of a learning community their learning about pedagogical content knowledge can be conceptualized as being distributed. Distributed cognition (Salomon, 1993) takes into account how individuals interact with their environment and the objects or artefacts within their environments, how groups of individuals in learning communities interact and communicate in an organized way, and how the products of earlier cognitive processes change the nature of later cognitive tasks. Salomon characterizes distributed cognition in real-life problem-solving situations where people appear to think in conjunction or in partnership with others and with the help of culturally provided tools and implements: "the thinking of these individuals might be considered to entail not just solo cognitive activities but distributed ones" (Salomon, 1993, p. xiii). Distributed cognition is apparent when music is performed in a group, where musicians fulfil different musical roles.

Salomon (1993) warns against assuming that distributed cognition can replace individual cognition. He also identifies (along with Pea in the same publication) that cognitive "off-loading" can occur when people interact with "powerful tools" (such as a computer) or with others who are more competent, resulting in them unloading their "cognitive burden onto a tool or human partners" (Salomon, 1993, p. 132). This can result in blocking development or can "even de-skill" (Salomon, 1993, p. 135). Ideally, distributed cognition should "promote or scaffold, rather than limit, the cultivation of individual competences" (Salomon, 1993, p. 135). It is important, therefore, to encourage students to share their thinking about music, particularly their own performing and composing. Meta-pedagogy for popular music enables students to go beyond reflection-in-action and encourages a more reflexive response through reflection-on-action (Gaunt & Westerlund, 2013). Points of critical reflection to promote reflexivity occur before, during and after performing and composing through the use of a virtual learning environment.

By providing opportunities for students to explore domain-specific learning situations and then critically reflect upon them, meta-pedagogy for popular music is creating what Barab and Duffy would call "practice fields", a metaphor for meaningful situated learning where:

1   students should do domain-related activities, not just learn about them;
2   students need to take ownership of the inquiry;
3   coaching and modelling of thinking skills is needed;
4   students should be provided with explicit opportunity for reflection;
5   dilemmas are ill-structured and complex;
6   learners must be supported to engage with the authentic complexity of the task, rather than simplifying the dilemma with unrealistic problems;
7   students work in teams to address contextualised problems(Barab & Duffy, 2000, pp. 25–55).

Priorities for popular music meta-pedagogy

The meta-pedagogy described in this chapter for popular music challenges dominant discourses in music education (evidenced by the National Plan for Music Education in England: DfE/DCMS, 2011), which tend to centre on a performance modality with the associated skills of reading and playing music. Here, a perception of musical literacy that is built on Western classical stave notation is replaced by one outlined by Kwami (1998) which focuses on internalization and improvisation, meaning the priority for learning becomes sound, rather than notation, as dominant musical discourse. Internalization and improvisation support a range of practical music-making activities that are "authentic and educational" (Finney, 2007, p. 12).

Experimenting with and exploring new musical ideas through performance-based improvisations, where learners take ownership of their learning, underpins a powerful form of music education and reflects a process that is central to the creation of popular music. In a meta-pedagogy for popular music the creative potential of improvisation should be reinforced by encouraging students to recognize links between improvisation and internalization as part of a composing process. Progression from performing arising from improvisation to compositional internalization moves internalization away from being based upon remembering and recalling musical ideas created by other people, as part of a process of musical enculturation, to becoming the memorizing or capture of new musical ideas that have been improvised. This is a process identified by Burnard (2000, p. 21), who suggests viewing, improvising and composing being on an overlapping continuum, from separated to indistinguishable. Green alludes to this improvisation-to-composition process when she talks about "original . . . changeable" and "memorised" improvisations (Green, 2002, p. 42) in the context of popular music.

The process of improvisation to composition can be supported through the use of music technology where more complex improvisations can be captured instantly through the use of recording. A university setting can provide opportunities for students to explore different perceptions of music learning environments, including those that link to contemporary methods of performing and composing music through the use of music technology. This approach is particularly important in the context of popular music where music technology is an embedded feature. Music technology provides a bridge between traditional, given approaches towards instrumental technique, and a more open and creative approach towards how we use sound sources as part of a composing process. All beginning music teachers can explore how technology provides opportunities to enhance and extend the range of sounds available, beginning from their own instrumental expertise. Therefore, the need to record and manipulate live sounds using music technology is an important aspect of this meta-pedagogy, providing the potential to explore more complex ideas and dilemmas. It is important to acknowledge that support to engage with music technology exists within the student body, and it is a question of enabling access to that knowledge rather than university tutors modelling a limited perspective.

Through use of music technology in a studio setting (group rehearsal rooms in the university equipped with music technology), with opportunities for a group of musicians to use a variety of sound sources, musical learning is situated in an appropriate popular music context. Such situated learning provides the opportunity to bring together different types of musical knowledge and enables beginning music teachers to engage in authentic complexity of performing and composing popular music.

In this meta-pedagogy, performing and composing are supported by exploration of existing music to scaffold the creative process. Students are asked to analyze their own musical preferences prior to any composing in order to provide a cultural reference point and to define the musical framework that will then be used to underpin their composing. Through a managed process of analyzing existing music, which is then responded to through composing, students are encouraged to think in ways that are both unique to music and connected to the culturally rich and diverse world in which we live. Students sharing music they listen to can be engaging and motivating, but they need to explain why they have chosen a particular piece of music, in order to encourage musical analysis. Comments need to focus on encouraging students to think musically and use sophisticated musical vocabulary. This process of musical analysis can be enhanced when students are encouraged to take ownership of their music and create covers and even mash-ups that provide "pleasurable forms of critique, folding musical analysis into musical experience" (Marshall, 2011, p. 307). Meta-pedagogy for popular music values the rich sources of knowledge that can be mined from active engagement in re-arranging and combining existing music. These activities are enhanced because of their authenticity in the context of popular music (Ruthmann, 2012).

After creating covers and mash-ups, an initial composing task can reflect the early stages of Key Stage 3 music education based on establishing the "vernacular" (Swanwick & Tillman, 1986). However, in order to enable students to develop a sense of musical progression, a final composing stage is used to extend these initial musical ideas into a more significant and complex, but authentic, musical structure, such as composing a song. This enables students to engage with the "speculative" and even "idiomatic" (Swanwick & Tillman, 1986) stages of progression, associated with the latter stages of Key Stage 3 music education. By actively engaging (physically, emotionally and cognitively) with a range of musical knowledge, through the setting of a composing challenge, the aim is to promote a greater depth of musical understanding.

Challenge occurs through engaging with tasks but also through sharing and subsequent peer assessment. This sharing occurs when the final covers, mash-ups and composing are uploaded and commented upon through a virtual learning environment. However, this process also needs to be carefully managed in order to avoid the natural predisposition of students to offer phatic praise rather than engage in critical reflection and reflexivity. An example of how this can be managed is to encourage students to initially reflect on their own learning journeys and to identify the significant landmarks or "critical incidents" (Tripp, 1993) on those journeys. This autoethnographic approach can help students to become more empathetic towards their colleagues when providing feedback. Through the use of musical analysis that employs increasingly sophisticated musical language, rather than emotive language that seeks to valorize certain types of music, a community of learning where knowledge is actively co-constructed is enhanced.

Popular music meta-pedagogy in practice

Russell and Loughran (2007) assert that teacher education must go far beyond the transmission of information about teaching. Learning to teach is a complex and personal process. Beginning teachers need opportunities to reflect upon and critically evaluate their own experiences; they need to find their own teacher identities and reflect upon their own development as learners. Russell and Loughran identify personal and professional risks that are involved in reflecting upon one's own personal and professional practice, and stress the need for beginning teachers to articulate issues about their work under safe conditions and with trusted colleagues:

> in doing so, [beginning] teachers gain confidence and develop deeper understandings of what they do and why, which helps them to uncover assumptions about teaching and learning that then inform their practice.
>
> *(Russell & Loughran, 2007, p. 5)*

At Birmingham City University beginning music teachers' own meaningful active learning was enacted in order to promote their learning about popular music pedagogical content knowledge. Favourable environments, with mutually constituted spaces free from externally determined agendas of compliance or assessment, and independent of any particular school context, were provided so that beginning music teachers could take responsibility for their own learning in collaboration with their colleagues. Beginning music teachers were seen as learners, and at different times had opportunities to become teachers, experts and critical friends. University tutors took background roles, defining tasks and initiating the learning process but avoiding overt interventions so as not to be seen simply as the experts with all the answers.

The beginning music teachers' responses to meta-pedagogy reflect the ups and downs of engaging with a challenging learning process. Finney and Philpott (2010, p. 12) identify two possible outcomes for the beginning music teachers exposed to this form of meta-pedagogy:

1. those who find a 'dissonance' with the implications of this way of working and who do not break or morph their habitus;
2. those who work through a productive dissonance and adapt their habitus (on a continuum from epiphany to gradual change).

Some responses from beginning music teachers reflect the first outcome:

> I found it very frustrating and felt like I wanted a teacher to come and help us decide how to move forward. Most of the time I felt completely up against a brick wall and that I needed help.

However, the same beginning music teacher identified that this experience had helped her to learn about teaching:

> I think now I have learnt the importance of scaffolding and when I teach I'll try and be really observant to see if a group is struggling or a pupil in a group is struggling and try and help.

The majority of beginning music teachers worked through a productive dissonance, and adapted:

> There was a moment in each of the tasks where everything clicked: in the first task it was when we stumbled across exactly the right synth sound, the third was where the lyrics suddenly fell into place. There was one moment each week when this happened and that's the part I'll remember the most.

There were some notable changes in opinion which suggest the transformative nature of this type of meta-pedagogy:

> I will never look with the same eyes at the process of creating music. My group have inspired me to try new things out at school and use music technology more actively within music education.

> It made me realise that whatever you do with the pupils at school, you have to make sure that they are doing something musical, playing music is really important. Music is such a creative subject, there is no point in getting bogged down in the history or techniques of instruments, when actually the most important part of music is being creative with it.

A key theme that kept being emphasized was the importance of meaning-oriented learning in a community of practice:

> They made sense to do and were meaningful as personally I feel that some group members (including myself) may have been too "bogged down" in historical context of music through our degrees to actually sit back and play music. So it was meaningful to get back to actually being musical and composing (which is a skill I haven't really looked at in a long while).
>
> Each member of the group brought different skills and it was great learning how other people compose. I can see that they helped me learn and appreciate something new in a safe and comfortable setting.
>
> I think one of the qualities of being a good teacher is being able to work well in a team. These sessions helped develop our collaborative skills and brought the whole group closer together. This was a great experience, plenty of meaning.

Conclusion

The notion of meta-pedagogy is an important one when considering ways in which popular music education can be fostered in schools by the next generation of classroom music teachers. This chapter has examined ways in which new entrants to the teaching profession can be helped along their own pathways from novitiate to expert in terms of both their theoretical knowledge and their enacted pedagogies. We have explored how Shulman's notion of pedagogic content knowledge can be seen to be significant in this regard. We have also shone a light onto the ways in which the new teachers' own pedagogy can be developed by the pedagogies of those involved in training and educating them, hence *meta-pedagogy*.

We have discussed how key tenets of historical orthodoxy need re-engineering when considering this topic. The place of Western Art music and the role of Western classical stave notation are two central areas in this which serve, unwittingly, to delimit the ways in which some new entrants both conceptualize and, importantly, put into action their views of what counts as music for young people in schools. There will, inevitably, be those for whom this can be seen as 'selling out' to the demands of a consumer-driven popular culture which should not be the property of education. But this argument, a hegemonic one based on notions of cultural supremacy, does not recognize the importance of engaging with, and in the true sense *educating* the young people of today. The place of the music teacher as cultural gatekeeper is a problematic one to justify, and this chapter has explored several issues as to why that is the case.

A further argument, if one were needed, as to the importance of music education is to be found in the notion of education for progression. A key thrust of contemporary thinking about teaching and learning is that education is well-served by beginning at the point where the child or young person is, and then moving along to the nearly related, before venturing off the beaten track. This involves purposeful learning that is meant to be challenging but clearly delineated and achievable for the young people involved: "Give the pupils something to do, not something to learn; and the doing is of such a nature as to demand thinking" (Dewey, 1916, p. 181).

In this chapter, theoretical and situated philosophies for popular music education have been described alongside practical aspects of organization and operation. This has been done purposefully, as we are constantly working with the shifting sands of public opinion, and political interference (certainly in the UK!) with ways in which teachers are trained and prepared for their teaching careers in schools. Theoretical location therefore becomes as significant as the practical, as uninformed onlookers are always able to fall back on personal experiences, which are often generationally dated. Music education can become a political football in this regard, and so this chapter has endeavoured to locate and situate rationales for these meta-pedagogies.

Pedagogies and meta-pedagogies for popular music as described in this chapter are designed to open up, not restrict; they enable, not disable; and they facilitate learning the knowledge, skills and understanding required for thoughtful engagement with creative activity in the 21st century for all our young people.

References

Barab, S.A. & Duffy, T. (2000). From practice fields to communities of practice. In D. Joanssen & S. Land (Eds.), *Theoretical foundations of learning environments* (pp. 25–56). Mahwah, NJ: Lawrence Erlbaum Associates.

Bronkhorst, L., Meijer, P., Koster, B. & Vermunt, J. (2011). Fostering meaning-orientated learning and deliberate practice in teacher education. *Teacher and Teacher Education*, 27, 1120–1130.

Burnard, P. (2000). How children ascribe meaning to improvisation and composition: Rethinking pedagogy in music education. *Music Education Research*, 2(1), 7–23.

Dewey, J. (1916). *Democracy and education*. New York: MacMillan.

DfE/DCMS. (2011). *The importance of music: A national plan for music education*. London: Department for Education & Department for Culture, Media and Sport.

Finney, J. (2007). The place of music in the secondary school: Ideology – history – justification. In C. Philpott & G. Spruce (Eds.), *Learning to teach music in the secondary school: A companion to school experience* (2nd ed., pp. 4–15). London: Routledge.

Finney, J. & Philpott, C. (2010). Informal learning and meta-pedagogy in initial teacher education in England. *British Journal of Music Education*, 27(1), 7–19.

Folkestad, G. (2006). Formal and informal learning situations or practices vs formal and informal ways of learning. *British Journal of Music Education*, 23(2), 135–145.

Gaunt, H. & Westerlund, H. (Eds.). (2013). *Collaborative learning in higher music education*. Farnham: Ashgate.

Georgii-Hemming, E. & Westvall, M. (2010). Music education – a personal matter? Examining the current discourse of music education in Sweden. *British Journal of Music Education*, 27(1), 21–33.

Green, L. (2002). *How popular musicians learn: A way ahead for music education*. Aldershot: Ashgate.

Green, L. (2008). *Music, informal learning and the school: A new classroom pedagogy*. Farnham: Ashgate.

Hargreaves, D., Welch, G., Purves, R. & Marshall, N. (2005). *Effective teaching in secondary school music: Teacher and pupil identities, ESRC End of award report, Award R000223751. Executive summary*. Retrieved from http://www.imerc.org/papers/time/summary.pdf [Accessed 15 November 2014].

Hodkinson, P., Colley, H. & Malcolm, J. (2003). The interrelationship between informal and formal learning. *Journal of Workplace Learning*, 15(7/8), 313–318.

Kokotsaki, D. (2010). Musical involvement outside school: How important is it for student-teachers in secondary education? *British Journal of Music Education*, 27(2), 151–170.

Kwami, R. (1998). Non-Western musics in education: Problems and possibilities. *British Journal of Music Education*, 15(2), 161–170.

Mantie, R. (2013). A comparison of "popular music pedagogy" discourses *Journal of Research in Music Education*, 61(3), 334–352.

Marshall, W. (2011). Mashup poetics as pedagogical practice. In N. Biamonte (Ed.), *Popculture: Pedagogy in the music classroom* (pp. 307–316). Lanham, MD: Scarecrow Press.

Musical Futures. (2014). *Musical futures – about us*. Retrieved from: https://www.musicalfutures.org/about [Accessed 2 November 2014].

Russell, T. & Loughran, J. (Eds.). (2007). *Enacting a pedagogy of teacher education: values, relationships and practices*. Abingdon: Routledge.

Ruthmann, A. (2012). "Engaging Adolescents with Music and Technology" In S.L. Burton (Ed.), *Engaging musical practices: A sourcebook for middle school general music*. Lanham, MD: Rowman & Littlefield Education, pp. 177–192.

Salomon, G. (1993). *Distributed cognitions: Psychological and educational considerations (learning in doing: Social, cognitive and computational perspectives)*. Cambridge: Cambridge University Press.

Shulman, L.S. (1986). Those who understand: Knowledge growth in teaching. *Educational Researcher*, 15(2), 4–14.

Swanwick, K. & Tillman, J. (1986). The sequence of musical development: A study of children's composition. *British Journal of Music Education*, 3(3), 305–339.

Tripp, D. (1993). *Critical incidents in teaching: Developing professional judgement*. London: Routledge/Falmer.

Vescio, V., Ross, D. & Adams, A. (2008). A review of research on the impact of professional learning communities on teaching practice and student learning. *Teacher and Teacher Education*, 24, 80–91.

Wright, R. (2008). Kicking the habitus: Power, culture and pedagogy in the secondary school music curriculum. *Music Education Research*, 10(3), 389–402.

Yang, S.C., & Liu, S.F. (2004). Case study of online workshop for the professional development of teachers. *Computers in Human Behaviour*, 20, 733–761.

29
A place in the band
Negotiating barriers to inclusion in a rock band setting

Jesse Rathgeber[1]

John drums a solid rock groove. Alana punches out a loose eighth note root pattern on keys while Karen fills out the chords higher on the keyboard. Kelly counts Dylan in on bass, saying, "red, blue," while Adam and I play guitars. Tim steps up to the mic, hands in his pockets, and starts to sing as the Smooth Criminals begin their set.

In this chapter I discuss means of fostering inclusive music-making experiences as demonstrated in the practices of a music therapy rock band, the Smooth Criminals. The band uses many adaptive strategies to mitigate physical barriers to participation that may be useful in other music learning spaces. The band's practices provide means of identifying and negotiating social barriers deeply rooted within popular and informal learning practices.

Meet the band

The Smooth Criminals is a music therapy rock band made up of young adult band members and adult assistants. Young adult members include: Adam,[2] a practical joker; Alana, an award-winning athlete; Dylan, a dancer and ladies' man who loves Bruno Mars; John, a quiet Marvel superhero aficionado; and Tim, a cheerful Bronie[3] who likes the Beatles and Train.[4] Each young adult member is diagnosed with

---

1 With thanks to Ryan Bledsoe for critical and supportive feedback on drafts of this chapter.
2 Pseudonyms are used for all research participants.
3 A Bronie is an adult fan of the cartoon series *My Little Pony: Friendship is Magic*.
4 Train is a pop band from the United States famous for hits like "Drops of Jupiter" and "Hey Soul Sister".

either Down Syndrome (DS) or Autism Spectrum Disorders (ASD), developmental disabilities that manifest as differences in cognitive or physical patterns of receptive and expressive language, memory, learning, mobility and/or self-direction (Friend, 2014). Four adult assistants in the band include: Kelly and Karen, certified music therapists; Sam, a music therapy intern; and myself, a volunteer, music educator and researcher. The band gathers weekly at a music therapy clinic in the Southwest United States to socialize, develop communication skills and make music together.[5] Young adult members select, arrange and perform all repertoire, with assistants playing supporting roles in scaffolding the learning and performance of songs. Everyone participates and performs in weekly rehearsals and biannual concerts. The community model of music therapy informs the band's practices, emphasizing "how music can *build networks, provide symbolic means* for underprivileged individuals or use music to *empower subordinated groups* . . . a way to *heal and strengthen communities* as well as individuals" (Ruud, 2004, emphasis in original).

Data informing this chapter come from an ongoing case study of the Smooth Criminals. Data generation for the study included participant observation and audio-visual recording of practices and concerts over the span of 10 months, informal interviews with band members and family members/caregivers and researcher field notes and reflexive journaling. Data were analyzed using Green's (2008b) characteristics of informal learning as a heuristic for coding and putting these findings in dialogue with the theoretical framework.

Theoretical framework

Oliver (1983) identifies disability as a social construction, rather than a personal deficit, comprising oppressive barriers to participation faced by persons considered to have cognitive, physical or functional differences. Bell (2014) situates the social model within music education, urging music educators to focus on and remediate barriers to participation in learning spaces rather than inabilities of learners. Bell (2014) and Lubet (2011) note how physical layout of instruments as well as socially and historically accepted instrumental techniques may act as barriers to musical participation. Social barriers include interactions among disabled persons,[6] 'typical' peers and music learning facilitators (MLF),[7] as well as conceptualizations of disability. Social barriers are often difficult to observe and counteract; it is for this

---

5 The clinic offers individual music therapy as the Smooth Criminals and five other music therapy rock bands.
6 Within disability literature, there are different approaches to the construction of labels and terms of identity. Some literature uses a 'people first' construction (e.g. person with a disability). Disability studies literature often uses the construction 'disabled person'. I use both constructions intentionally in this chapter.
7 I use the term 'music learning facilitators' (MLF) to refer to anyone who leads music learning experiences. This term is more inclusive and less bounded by disciplinary or licensure issues. The term might be applied to music educators, music therapists, community music leaders, learners themselves and many others.

reason that I draw on Bourdieu's (1977, 1986) work to assist in uncovering these hidden barriers.

Bourdieu's (1977, 1986) notions of habitus and symbolic capital provide tools useful in identifying social barriers. Habitus is a learned "system of durable, transposable dispositions" (Bourdieu, 1977, p. 72) grounding one's actions, practices and conceptions of the world. Habitus inscribes one's practices and beliefs with social constructions taken as universal truths. One's beliefs about with whom (e.g. disabled musicians) and what (e.g. the genre or form of musicking) they are engaged inform the ways in which they interact with others. These beliefs and practices indicate the value of certain kinds of symbolic capital – ideas, objects, distinctions and relationships (Bourdieu, 1986). Within music learning spaces (MLS),[8] symbolic capital might include recognition of being able to play an instrument, personal ownership of said instrument, institutional certification of one's instrumental abilities and relationships one may have due to perceived abilities and other social characteristics. Possession of symbolic capital can empower and enable a participant within these spaces or, conversely, barriers to sites of its distribution can inhibit, disempower or *disable* a participant.

In this chapter, I highlight possible physical and social barriers to participation that might limit learners with developmental disabilities in a rock band MLS. I then offer approaches to musicking and learning that mediate such barriers. My intentions are to illuminate enabling approaches to musicking, with and through popular music, that guarantee a place in the band for all participants. I now turn my attention towards exploring how disability and inclusion are discussed, or not discussed, in related literature.

Review of literature

Green, though not specifically addressing musicking of persons with disabilities, speaks of disaffected pupils (2008a, 2008b), "pupils of low-ability" (2008b, p. 140), both self-differentiation (2008b) and "differentiation of outcome" (2008a, 2008b), and makes a passing reference to learners with "special educational needs" (2008b, pp. 147–148).[9] Two popular approaches informed by Green's work, Musical Futures and Little Kids Rock's Modern Band, provide suggestions for working with learners with learning differences (D'Amore, 2008) by means of flexible instruction (Powell & Burstein, chapter 20, this volume; Wish et al., 2015). However, there is a lack of specific discussion of physical or social barriers that limit the involvement of persons diagnosed with DS, ASD, or other developmental disabilities in this literature. As such, we look to music therapy,

---

8 I use the term 'music learning spaces' to refer to all social spaces where persons engage in musical learning.
9 I wish to acknowledge considerable contributions made in popular music pedagogy literature beyond those cited above. Due to the constraints of the chapter, I focus on the well-cited work of Green and those connected to her approach in order to draw out implicit discussion related to disability and inclusion as well as to note absence of explicit discussion of these issues.

community music and other music education literature for information related to disability and inclusion in MLS.

Music therapy

Music therapy literature concerning community music therapy regularly explores issues, outcomes and approaches to musicking with persons with developmental disabilities. Community music therapy works to help clients, but also to help the social systems within which clients live (Ruud, 2004) as a means of countering oppressive and marginalizing habitus in communities. This approach to therapy focuses of creating community (Stige et al., 2010) by using music as a tool to empower and make visible marginalized persons, while providing them access to the symbolic capital afforded by musicking (Ruud, 2004).

Community music

Community music research seeks to uncover how musical practices "enable and empower people to develop their cultures, artistry, creativity, identity, health and 'community'" through music (Veblen, 2008, p. 180). Higgins (2012) suggests that "the *community* in *community music* is best understood as *hospitality* . . . broadly understood as people, participation, places, equality of opportunity, and diversity" (p. 133, emphasis in original). Issues of inclusion, equity and shared symbolic capital are important in this literature. Examples of this literature include Kivijärvi's (2012) discussion of the approach of Resonaari Special Music Center to disability and inclusion, in which individually tailored adaptations assist learners with developmental differences to access the tools and spaces in which they develop high levels of popular musicking skills. McHale's (in press) exploration of Cork City, Ireland's SoundOUT inclusive music programme demonstrates how technology and a Universal Design-informed attitude to musicking minimizes restrictive barriers to community musical engagement. Hullick's (2013) work with "differently abled sound artists" (p. 219) demonstrates a dedication towards exploration that eschews existing musical practices and notions of technique in order to empower collective musical creation and community. From these examples, we might see how community music offers insights into the realization of inclusive, adaptive and equitable practices.

Music education

Music education literature related to disability tends to centre on special education-derived inclusive practices (e.g. Hammel & Hourigan, 2011, 2013; Jellison, 2012). In a different vein, Bell (2014), explores issues of disability and popular musicking within a social model framework. His work with a young man diagnosed with DS examines ways in which physical barriers might be mediated through instrumental adaptations. Bell discusses the importance of valuing learner choice/self-determination, style and personal approach, even if the outcomes counter the habitus-informed expectations of an MLF. The valuing of self-determination and personal approach grounds the practices of the Smooth Criminals, to whom we now turn our attention.

The musicking of the Smooth Criminals

The music-making practice of the Smooth Criminals demonstrates many connections to what Green (2008b, p. 10) identifies as five characteristics of informal learning: participant-selected repertoire; learning by-ear; working alone or in self-selected peer-groupings; a haphazard learning process; and the overlapping nature of listening, performing and creating music. The vignettes and interview excerpt below demonstrate how the band negotiates exciting and possible barriers related to each of these characteristics. Following each vignette or excerpt, I discuss the adaptive and inclusive practices and suggest how MLF might realize these practices in other MLS.

Participant-selected repertoire

The Smooth Criminals selected new 'popular' repertoire through band-member suggestion and whole-group discussion. This process can result in unanimous agreement or, as depicted in the vignette below, in uncovering conflicting habitus:

> *Dylan shouts out "'Billie Jean' or 'Treasure,'" as suggestions for a new song. These are standard pop fare and the kind of music that the group normally performs. Tim softly offers, "'Babs Seed.'"*
> "Like Nick Cave, those Bad Seeds?" Sam questions.
> "No, Apple Bloom on 'My Little Pony.'" *Tim smiles in response.*
> "Like, the 80's cartoon?" Kelly inquires.
> "No, Friendship is Magic!" *Tim explains.* "I'm a Bronie."
> *We find a recording of "Babs Seed" on YouTube and everyone begins dancing.*
> "This is good!" *Alana interjects mid-dance.*

Tim's identification as a 'Bronie' surprised us. In making sense of his suggestion, we drew upon our shared habitus (Bourdieu, 1977). This habitus defined popular music as works within a specific spectrum of music, one that did not include *My Little Pony*. Sam's guess of Nick Cave being the source made sense to the adults, as it fit well within our definitions of popular music and our expectations of what popular music might mean to a young adult male. Never before had we considered that 'popular music' for Tim might include music from a cartoon seemingly geared towards young female viewers.

It would be easy to read our confusion as unfamiliarity, yet it is an example of a possibly complex social barrier. The illusion of a shared and concise group definition of popular music came into question with Tim's musical offering. In that moment, the band confronted the diversity and fluidity of our small group's understanding of popular music. At issue here was not *that* Tim suggested a song from a cartoon but, rather, that his *conception* of popular music was apparently different from that of others in the group. The adult assistants should not have been surprised by the suggestion of a cartoon song; Tim and other band members spoke about cartoons and other popular media. These were the sources from which they found *their* music; these were the sources of *their* symbolic capital. Yet, the assistants' habitus-informed expectations of what might be popular to a young adult band member nearly caused a problematic barrier in how we valued the musical interests of band members, thus perhaps limiting the possible musical experiences available in the band.

The example above illustrates the need for a constantly fluid definition of 'popular music' in MLS. It is vital to uncover *what* popular music is to participants and *where* it comes from, rather than assuming that a unity of what 'popular music' means and entails exists between MLF and learners. By seeking to outline the habitus that informs learners' understandings of popular music, possible barriers to participation might be levelled early on in music-making experiences. MLF might do well to regularly consider how their understandings of what popular music is may cause unintentional barriers for learners. Those definitions may carry with them barrier-inducing expectations, with regards to technique and skills, that require inspection.

Learning by listening and copying

Green (2008b) situates ear-playing (p. 138) as a central skill for learning music in informal learning. Yet, the Smooth Criminals approach this skill, and the notion of the "authority of the [recording]" (p. 55), in a manner that may conflict with the expectations of some MLF:

> *"Okay, so it's 'Mr. Crowley,'" Kelly announces after counting band members' votes. "Pick an instrument and let's listen."*
>
> *Dylan practices singing along to the track – as he does at home with the game RockBand.*
>
> *Alana explores the drum set, trying out sounds with little attention to the track playing in the background. John grabs the bass and starts to eagerly pluck the E string in rhythm with the recording. I place some coloured stickers to indicate the pitches used in the song and tell John that the pattern starts on orange (D). Adam grabs a guitar and strums the open strings. Kelly places stickers on the frets of the two bass strings of Adam's guitar so he can play inverse power chords.[10] She plays along and says the colours aloud two beats before the chord changes to give Adam time to move to the next chord. Meanwhile, Sam points out keys on the keyboard for Tim to play as they figure out a rhythm that fits.*

---

10 An inverse power chord is a re-voicing of the common open fifth power chord. This inversion has the fifth of the chord in the bass with the root above it. These dyads are located on the same fret of two adjacent strings (for all but the third/second string combination), and are playable with one finger.

In this vignette, a recording of "Mr. Crowley" acts as a framework, rather than a blueprint, for collaborative music-making. Each band member creates their own part, informed by their own strengths and abilities. Adult assistants act as scaffolds for participation by transmitting just enough information from the aural example to band members for them to create their own parts. The focus of learning shifts from *copying* towards making group arrangements of songs filled with idiosyncratic material. The point is not to progressively fill in details from the recording with each successive listening but, rather, to get a 'gist' of the fundamental structure of the music and then to create something nearly brand new.

The reason for this approach derives from specific needs of the band members. The band members demonstrate a need for longer cognitive processing time and require structures to assist with difficulties in drawing from working and long-term memory, characteristics common among persons with developmental disabilities (Friend, 2014). In order to mitigate possible barriers to participation that might rise out of a need to listen, play along and continually refine one's part, the Smooth Criminals seek to develop workable part sketches during initial ear-playing. As the members work out these outlines alone and with adult assistants, coloured stickers are used to act as visual memory anchors, as depicted above. Adult assistants indicate changes in harmony, pattern and section, often beats ahead of time in order to help members process and/or remember their next moves in a song. While the young adult members develop the rhythmic, timbral and expressive aspects of their parts, the adult assistants fill in other details, helping to foster band unity in performance.

For the Smooth Criminals, possible difficulties in copying music by ear are mitigated by rejecting a focus on replication of a song in favour of co-developing idiosyncratic group arrangements. From this standpoint, abilities to self-differentiate or to create workable, though not duplicate, parts take on a central aspect to music learning over a more dominant habitus-informed conception of replicating a recording by ear. The point is to 'get into the music' as quickly as possible and to experience making music together, rather than to create an 'accurate' and technically proficient 'cover' of a musical work. The practices of the Smooth Criminals offer ways to foster inclusivity in MLS by affording learners the chance to collaborate in creating their own musical parts that value their physical and cognitive abilities, rather than replicating parts from a recording. Additionally, MLF might join learner groups to act as musical scaffolds. These strategies could foster inclusion in such groups, but the process of accessing a musical group might pose its own barriers to participation.

Working alone and in self-selected peer groups

Working together with one's peers is clearly important in MLS, but what happens when one has had limited interactions with peers to the point that one is nearly a stranger? The following interview excerpt demonstrates how a group forms when self-selection is not particularly an option:

> "The Smooth Criminals are a cobbled-together group", Kelly explains. "The music therapists try to match up like abilities and personalities as best as we can". Alana, the sole female band member, was provisionally placed in the Smooth Criminals until a space came open in a group with other females. "We asked her if she wanted to switch groups and she adamantly refused". When I asked Alana what she liked so much about the Smooth Criminals, she said it "makes [her] feel good". Like Tim and John, this band is the first time Alana has been included in a group musical activity. It is an extended family for her. It is a point of pride for her and even something of which typical peers are envious.

The Smooth Criminals marked the first time many band members had the chance to engage in a group music-making experience. As Tim's mother noted, "[He] has never had an opportunity to participate in any type of music [education or performance] program in the past". Tim, John and Alana's lack of prior social music experiences might question the inclusivity or access to MLS for learners with developmental disabilities. Though all three band members currently attend school or have in the past, they have somehow been excluded from social music-making experiences that might have allowed them to develop their musical abilities and foster peer relationships.

Green (2008b) asserts the importance of friendship groupings and common musical affinities as core elements of functional informal learning groups. These two conditions require an individual to possess multiple types of symbolic capital prior to joining a group. What happens if one lacks both valued symbolic capital and established friendships? What if no one else shares a member's musical affinities? In what group do such learners belong, as in the case of Tim the Bronie? The extracurricular and therapeutic setting of the Smooth Criminals is different from many other more integrated MLS, yet its practices suggest the need for MLF to consider carefully how to scaffold inclusion into group experiences when a learner might not possess the symbolic capital requisite to find and join peer groups. This is not to say learners in peer groups will be fully reluctant to include disabled learners but, as with any unfamiliar student, it is important to reflect on how we foster inclusion if MLF adopt practices of friendship groupings identified by Green (2008b).

Inclusion itself is a practice that relies on and generates symbolic capital in many forms. Admission into friendship groups based upon the prior accumulation of social capital – "the aggregate of actual or potential resources which are linked to possession of a durable network . . . of relationships" (Bourdieu, 1986, p. 151) – suggests either prior engagement with peers that developed this capital or the possession of cultural capital, like musical taste, valued by the group. These types of symbolic capital are prerequisites for group admission; group engagements also act as sites of symbolic capitals' creation and dispersal. Inclusion in friendship groupings might not only lead to one's ability to access music learning experiences, but also allow for the fostering of friendships and the possible alteration of group and individual conceptions of disability, as community music therapy seeks to do. Yet this type of inclusion and change of mind does not simply occur; it requires scaffolding. Stige et al. (2010) discuss such scaffolding, proposing large-group musical experiences where all learners are able to develop musical skills, interpersonal bonds and different means of communication. These experiences allow for equitable generation and collection of symbolic capital. Such experiences might also be used to foster empathy, care and hospitality (Higgins, 2012; Stige et al., 2010) among the community. Out of this community, friendship-based groupings and shared musical interests might be equitably accessible for all members and afford access for all to engage in the haphazard work of making music.

A haphazard process

The approach to music learning demonstrated by the Smooth Criminals embodies the haphazardness of informal learning. The following vignette illustrates how even adaptive strategies might develop in such a haphazard process:

> *Adam holds his guitar flat on his lap and strums all six strings. Sam notes, "Adam, you look like you want to do some strumming. Let's try something different". He retunes the guitar to open D and shows Adam how to barre across the strings by pushing down on a slide. Sam then holds counting fingers to denote the chord changes (two fingers for second fret/E, zero fingers for open strings/D). Tim pounds away on the keyboard, playing a single note with his left pointer finger. Then, he takes his right pointer finger and plays the same rhythm on another key. Karen adds another green sticker to B and says, "green". Tim plays both G and B. Karen adds colour-matched stickers to the keys corresponding to the major third of each chord. At the drum set, Dylan is frustrated with trying to play a kick/bass, snare pattern; he can't seem to get the timing down between his arm on snare and his leg on kick/bass. He grabs another stick, experiments with different sounds to replace the kick/bass and lands on playing a low tom, snare pattern using both arms and no legs. Kelly sings with Alana while she plays a simple bass line on her guitar. John begins playing Kelly's rhythm on the bass, using his thumb to fret each note, and figures out a similar part. Kelly tries to put stickers on his fret board, but Jon turns away and keeps playing.*

This vignette articulates "differentiation of outcome" (Green, 2008b, p. 138) and the haphazardness of learning within informal music learning settings. Each band member has a different spectrum of abilities and each works to develop different skills within the same learning space. From the above vignette, it is clear that the band members' musicking is supported by many responsive adaptive practices, which enable the band members to access musical experiences via instrumental, communicative and arrangement adaptations.

Instruments can present physical barriers to participation (Bell, 2014). Some instruments or techniques can be changed or adapted to suit a musician's needs;

however, habitus informing correct technique often obscures these possibilities. In the vignette above, numbers and colours were used to replace the common musical vocabulary of chord names. This represents a different and differently accessible symbolic notation system. For Adam, a colour-coded system was not always useful; through experimentation, Sam and Adam discovered the number and finger system to be a better fit for them. The assistants in the room scaffold the young adults' playing by identifying chord changes, but not rhythms, communicating musical information using the symbolic system favoured by each band member.

What is important here is not *that* adaptations are provided, but that the band members have the *freedom* to use, or not to use, adaptations provided to them as well as the power to adapt their parts and approaches as they deem fit. These practices rely upon self-determination, which Jellison (2012) identifies as vital in supporting the musicking of persons with developmental disabilities in learning spaces. Alana demonstrates self-determination by asking Kelly to sing along to bolster her own confidence. Tim decides to play a second pitch. John chooses to ear-learn his part and to disregard Kelly's proffered assistance. Adam's desire to strum the guitar is honoured by adapting the instrument around his technique. Dylan changes his pattern in order to negotiate barriers hidden within how traditional rock drum patterns are played when one has different cognitive and physical processing. Band-member agency is highly valued within this setting, hence proposed adaptations come secondary to their choices. The Smooth Criminals show little reverence for traditional or accepted instrumental techniques, preferring the kind of self-accommodation identified by Hullick (2013), where physical, cognitive and agentic needs are met in the choices one makes when freely engaging in music-making.

MLF might do well by contemplating the extent to which they afford learners self-determination in MLS. Green (2008b) discusses the importance of self-differentiation of musical parts, and MLF ought perhaps to consider whether self-differentiation extends to using instruments in non-traditional ways, as did Bell's (2014) research participant. If MLF were to put aside their intuition regarding the 'right' ways to play instruments, perhaps they might be better able to enter learners' musical worlds, as Wright (2008) advises, in order to learn their personal musical styles and abilities. MLF must identify the adaptive strategies they possess and constantly seek new strategies to create inclusive MLS. Additionally, if music is, to an extent, a 'second language', as Wish et al. (2015) propose, MLF will need to learn the 'dialects' of performance and understanding of the learners with whom they work. Perhaps idiosyncratic playing styles and adaptations will help learners develop and experience the "feel" many find so important in musicking (e.g. Green, 2008b; Keil & Feld, 1994; Smith, 2013).

Integrated performing, improvising, composing and listening

As demonstrated in previous vignettes, making music in the Smooth Criminals relies upon an approach to performing that relies upon improvisational flexibility

A place in the band

and a multifaceted approach to listening – to both musical examples as well as the desires and needs of each member. The following vignette demonstrates this flexibility and approach to listening in action:

> Tim's kick/bass always lands just after beat one; his snare hit on two is solid. His pattern subtly morphs into something reggae-like. Adam's guitar playing shifts to fit Tim's pattern. Alana's syncopated, single-note keyboard playing falls into place, acting like a ska horn part. "Yeah!" Dylan exclaims as he plays the bass. When the song is over, Kelly says, "Well, that's a new version. What did you think?" "Liked it", Alana responds. "Maybe that's what we've been looking for the whole time", Sam remarks. Kelly suggests, "Let's run it again". This time around, Alana's driving pattern pushes the group toward a hard-rock style version of the song.

In this example, each play-through is a mix of performing previously developed parts and improvising new ones over a group-arranged rendition of a pre-composed song. The fluid conceptualization of musical performance acts as an important enabling structure for the Smooth Criminals. Following the authority of the recording, or replicating parts learned in prior rehearsals, could present disabling barriers for band members, preventing them from accessing these musical experiences. A replication approach might be more orderly in structure, yet it can lead towards a pedagogy fetishizing technique and hyperability/talent, which can further disable learners (Lubet, 2011). An inclusive approach values the haphazard and idiosyncratic nature by which popular musicians learn (Green, 2008b), empowering a flexibility of habitus towards genre, technique and 'correctness' of performance. Such an inclusive approach, as demonstrated by the Smooth Criminals, might embolden learners in these spaces to develop complex musicking and social engagement, leading to increasingly barrier-free musical environments and communities for all.

Conclusion: Ensuring a place in the band

Throughout this chapter I have described possible physical and social barriers that might disable learners in MLS in popular and/or informal MLS. Popular music pedagogy literature notes a need to embrace flexibility, fluidity and adaptability towards issues of repertoire, learning and music-making. The practices employed by the Smooth Criminals display these values, illuminate some adaptive strategies and suggest how more deep-rooted barriers to inclusion might be removed. Strategies like the use of visual/communicative aids (coloured stickers and numbers) and adaptive instrumental technique (e.g. re-voicing of chords, retuning of instruments and non-traditional uses of instruments/tools) are useful means of confronting possible physical barriers to participation. However, social barriers are more deeply rooted in MLS. Navigating social barriers requires changes of mind and practice, necessitating group negotiation and confrontation of habitus. For the Smooth Criminals, this meant critically examining what MLF and learners consider to be popular music, reconceptualizing skills like ear-playing and notions of 'appropriate' musical technique, fostering an inclusive, hospitable environment where each learner collaboratively generates and accumulates symbolic capital, embracing a haphazard approach to learning and adaptation and valuing the overlapping nature of performing, creating and listening. Applications of the adaptive and habitus-confronting practices of the Smooth Criminals into other types of MLS may offer avenues for fostering more inclusive music-making experiences and, in doing so, might ensure all learners a place in the band.

References

Bell, A.P. (2014). Guitars have disabilities: Explore guitar adaptations for an adolescent with Down syndrome. *British Journal of Music Education*, *31*(3), 343–357.

Bourdieu, P. (1977). *Outline of a theory of practice*. Cambridge: Cambridge University Press.

Bourdieu, P. (1986). The forms of capital. In J.G. Richardson (Ed.), *Handbook of therapy and research for the sociology of education* (pp. 241–258). New York, NY: Greenwood.

D'Amore, A. (Ed.) (2008). *Musical futures: An approach to teaching and learning. Resource pack* (2nd ed.). London: Paul Hamlyn Foundation.

Friend, M. (2014). *Special education: Contemporary perspectives for school professionals* (4th ed.). Upper Saddle, NJ: Pearson HE Inc.

Green, L. (2008a). Group cooperation, inclusion and disaffected pupils: some responses to informal learning in the music classroom. Presented at the RIME Conference 2007, Exeter, UK. *Music Education Research*, *10*(2), 177–192.

Green, L. (2008b). *Music, informal learning and the school: A new classroom pedagogy*. Farnham: Ashgate.

Hammel, A.M. & Hourigan, R. M. (2011). *Teaching music to students with special needs: A label-free approach*. New York, NY: Oxford University Press.

Hammel, A.M. & Hourigan, R.M. (2013). *Teaching music to students with autism*. New York, NY: Oxford University Press.

Higgins, L. (2012). *Community music: In theory and in practice*. Oxford: Oxford University Press.

Hullick, J. (2013). The rise of the amplified elephants. *International Journal of Community Music*, *6*(2), 219–233.

Jellison, J.A. (2012). Inclusive music classrooms and programmes. In G. McPherson & G. Welch (Eds.), *The Oxford handbook of music education*, Vol. 2 (pp. 65–80). New York, NY: Oxford University Press.

Keil, C. & Feld, S. (1994). *Music grooves*. Chicago, IL: University of Chicago Press.

Kivijärvi, S. (2012). Project disabled people as musicians: A systemic approach. *Procedia-Social and Behavioral Sciences*, *45*, 416–427.

Lubet, A. (2011). *Music, disability, and society*. Philadelphia, PA: Temple University Press.

McHale, G. (In press). SoundOUT: Examining the role of accessible interactive music technologies within inclusive music ensembles in Cork City, Ireland. In D. Blair & K. McCord (Eds.), *Exceptional music pedagogy for children with exceptionalities: International perspectives*. New York, NY: Oxford University Press.

Oliver, M. (1983). *Social work with disabled people*. Basingstoke: Macmillan Press Inc.

Ruud, E. (2004). Foreword. In M. Pavlicevic & G. Ansdell (Eds.), *Community music therapy* (pp. 11–14). London: Jessica Kingsley Publishers.

Smith, G.D. (2013). *I drum, therefore I am: Being and becoming a drummer*. Farnham: Ashgate.

Stige, B., Ansdell, G., Elefant, C., & Pavlicevic, M. (2010). *Where music helps: Community music therapy in action and reflection*. Farnham: Ashgate.

Veblen, K.K. (2008). The many ways of community music. *International Journal of Community Music, 1*(1), 5–21.

Wish, D., Speicher, C., Zellner, R., & Hejna, K. (Eds.) (2015). *Music as a second language & the modern band* movement. Verona, NJ: Little Kids Rock.

Wright, R. (2008). Kicking the habitus: Power, culture and pedagogy in the secondary school music curriculum. *Music Education Research, 10*(3), 389–402.

30

Teaching the devil's music

Some intersections of popular music, education and morality in a faith-school setting

Tom Parkinson

Introduction

Prior to working in higher education, I worked as a peripatetic music teacher in schools around southeast England. This experience was invaluable in helping me to develop a clear sense of my aims and values regarding music education through reflective practice (Parkinson, 2014). One of the schools in which I taught was run by the Church of England, and overseen by the local diocese. Although the student body included children of Sikh, Muslim and Jewish backgrounds, the majority of pupils were baptized Christians whose parents regularly attended church (or who at least had professed to do so when applying for their children to attend the school). Christianity was thoroughly embedded into the physical landscape of the school; crosses were present in all classrooms, and in the music department where I worked Biblical or otherwise-religious quotations and images were displayed on the walls. This traditional religious backdrop seemed to sit in juxtaposition with other aspects of the music classroom, such as students' homework posters featuring images of artists such as One Direction, Nicki Minaj and Rihanna. One corner of the room was occupied by a full set of drums, amplifiers and electric guitars on stands.

In the cupboards of the music classroom were multiple copies of Rutter and Willcocks' *100 Carols for Choirs* (1988), and large numbers of brass, woodwind and string instruments with a look of not having been played for decades. This was to the regret of my colleagues John, a brass and drum teacher and Salvation Army captain, and Alf, a woodwind teacher and former Grenadier Guardsman, who had taught at the school long enough to remember an active orchestra and a healthy take-up in music lessons for these instruments. Now only a handful of students played them; John spent most of his time teaching drums, while Alf had to play lead saxophone for the school's woodwind group himself because of a shortage of musicians. Somewhat embarrassingly for me, demand for guitar lessons was huge, and I was unable to give lessons to all those who wanted them.

This typifies a shift in music education, in the United Kingdom (and elsewhere), away from a traditional Western Art focus and towards broader curricula and pedagogies incorporating popular music (Smith et al., chapter 2, this volume), yet it also points to tensions that have arisen from this shift, which in some settings have seen Western Art music's extracurricular presence diminish to the point where it is almost entirely usurped – in practice, culture and physical space – by popular music. The Christian elements of the description above lead to consideration of the confluence of religious moral purview and popular music education, which although inevitable in faith schools (accounting for at least a third of the UK's secondary schools), has hitherto been largely overlooked in music education literature.

In this chapter I continue with a summary of faith-based education in the UK, and review some of the literature and other responses to the intersection of religion and education. The following section considers the relationships between music education, religion and morality, and how these relationships have been understood historically. I then consider societal responses to popular music in terms of morality, and the implications that this has for co-opting popular music as an object and mode of study in education. Following this, I examine popular music education in a faith school setting through three semi-fictional vignettes (Roberts, 2002). In doing so, I draw out and consider dilemmas that popular music educators might encounter, and which require the negotiation of a complex and ambiguous moral and musical terrain, and an awareness of potentially conflicting responsibilities to a number of stakeholders.

Faith schools in the UK

Schools with a religious ethos and affiliation have existed for centuries in the UK. Since 1997 there have been Jewish, Muslim and Hindu schools, and the term 'faith school' has emerged in official discourse to refer to any school with religious oversight, accounting for around a third of all schools. The vast majority of faith schools, however, are Christian, 68% being Anglican and overseen by the Church of England and 30% Roman Catholic, overseen by the Catholic Education service. Since the emergence of academies (schools permitted to devise their own curriculum) following the 2010 Academy Act, many faith schools have converted to academies and have become known collectively as 'faith academies'.

The reasons for parents' choice to send their children to faith schools are various (King, 2010), and their right to make such a choice is enshrined in Article 2 of The Human Rights Act of 1998 (p. 26). Critics of faith schools have suggested that faith-based education is tantamount to indoctrination and precludes the development of individual autonomy in children (Lawton & Cairns, 2005; Paton, 2008; Pring, 2005; Romain, 2013; Short, 2003). King (2010), however, argues that

> autonomy as an educational aim can only be achieved through critical analysis of different beliefs [which] requires a full investigation into personal faith traditions, practices, theology, and evolvement . . . before engaging in discussion of, and reflection on, different belief systems.
>
> *(p. 291)*

Other criticisms of faith schools include the assertion that nurturing faith and morality is inappropriate within formal education, which should seek to develop faculties of rationality and reason (Pring, 2005, p. 55), and that such schools are divisive and segregationist (British Humanist Association, 2015; Cantle, 2013).

Despite faith schools accounting for a significant proportion of compulsory education provision in the UK, King (2010) suggests that "matters of faith are rarely considered by government and civic authorities in terms of educational delivery" and that "educational guidance from the state is anything but clear, particularly within the latter's 'social inclusion' agenda" (p. 296). Consequently, difficulties arise in seeking to "reconcile religious and secular notions of cultural, spiritual, and moral truth" (p. 296). In particular, King (2010) suggests that the demands of citizenship education (CE) and religious education (RE), which appear primarily to promote a secular agenda of pluralism and communitarianism within a multi-faith society, can potentially be at odds with the specific values of religious denominations, and thus with the missions of faith schools to nurture them. Beyond this, aspects of curricula and pedagogy across the range of subject areas might feasibly conflict with the faith-based mission and ethos of a school.

Music education, morality and religion

The value of music education has been rationalized in moral terms since antiquity. Plato declared "education in music [to be] most sovereign, because more than anything else rhythm and harmony find their way into the innermost soul and take strongest hold upon it, bringing with them and imparting grace" (1969, p. 401). This was not an encomium for music *per se*, however; Plato maintained the proviso that "one [be] *rightly* trained" (p. 401, emphasis added), lest the effects prove deleterious. Thus, for Plato, music education was a precarious thing, having the potential both for moral good and harm.

Among modern critics, Scruton's moral analyses of popular music rest heavily on Plato's reasoning, focusing not so much on the explicit lyrical content of pop songs as on their rhythmic construction. For Scruton (2010), the use of repetition, particularly that which involves computers, demands submission to a beat or pulse (which he distinguishes from rhythm), atomizing the individual and causing them to dance "at", as opposed to "with", other people, which, he suggests, tips inevitably into "lewdness" (p. 45). The resulting effect is, according to Scruton, the denial of social communion. As such, Scruton concurs with Plato that musical embodiment, as learning, can have "virtuous and vicious forms" (p. 45), and that, accordingly, educators have a moral duty to promote some forms of musicking over others.

Willis (2009) suggests that 16th-century translations of classical texts gave rise to "a sophisticated awareness of the pedagogical utility of music" (p. 296) in Elizabethan England, with curricula premised on the arguments of Aristotle and Plato and the latter's accounts of Socrates. Willis reports that during this period, something of a consensus emerged regarding the virtuous nature of music. However, in contrast to classical treatises, music's moral potential was largely understood to lie not in its intrinsic properties but in its devotional facility as a carrier of Christian text. Thus, across classical and Elizabethan writings (e.g. Jewel, 1560; Lupton, 1582; both cited in Willis, 2009) around music and morality, two preoccupations emerge – one that focuses on the intrinsic properties of music and their relationship to the soul and the body, and another that focuses on the pairing of lyrics to music. These preoccupations continue to endure.

Cox (1997) describes the visions of music education of Victorian and Edwardian education reformers in the UK, beginning with the first government inspector for music, John Hullah (1812–1884), who, inspired by Victorian Christian Socialists, held to a conviction that music was a moral force that could promote "patience, temperance, power of attention, presence of mind, self-denial, obedience and punctuality" (Hullah, 1854, p. 15). His successor, John Stainer, and Stainer's assistant W.G. McNaught, focused on producing "intelligent hearers" (Stainer, 1892, pp. 57–58), believing this to be more in the nation's interest than performers or composers. Both men were cautious in extolling music's moral capacities. At the beginning of the 20th century, Stainer's successor, Arthur Somervell, held an altogether more idealistic and esoteric vision, grounded in Platonic notions of goodness and beauty, and the Hellenic ideal of rhythm as a divine property that would reconcile human existence with nature and promote social harmony (Cox, 1997).

Cox (1997) suggested that the concern among these Victorian and Edwardian educationalists to relate music education to positive extrinsic social and moral impacts endured in contemporary discussions and could be identified in contemporary education policy. Arguments for the extra-musical social and developmental benefits of music education are still in evidence 20 years later (e.g. DfE, 2011), and are arguably even more emphatic in the current climate, where music's – and other arts subjects' – place in education is being reappraised and the primacy of STEM subjects is frequently hailed by government (e.g. Ritchins, 2015). Yet the moral aspect of these arguments is muted, and in the vast majority of cases pertains to what Annette (2005, p. 191) terms "secular communitarianism" rather than religious moral codes. Similarly, most late 20th- and early 21st-century policies relating to music education make little explicit reference to religion. In practice, however, morality, religion and music inevitably intersect in at least a third of all state-funded UK schools, and these interactions warrant attention.

Tom Parkinson

Popular music and morality

In recent decades, school music across a number of international contexts has moved away from its traditional focus on Western Art music to incorporate musics of other global cultures, in recognition of increasingly multicultural school populations, and has been accompanied by research attesting to music's facility in promoting values of inclusion and communitarianism within this context (e.g. Ilari et al., 2012). However, alongside this acknowledgement of the need to represent children's filial cultures in curricula, there have also been moves to incorporate their a-ffiliative cultural experiences in the form of popular music. The impact of pedagogical innovations issuing from Green's work (2001, 2008), or from the climate surrounding it, is evident not only in curricula and pedagogy but also in the culture and physical space of school music departments. Furthermore, they have accompanied, and are consistent with, a more general turn in education towards learner-centredness and "cultural responsiveness to learners' rights" (Allsup & Westerlund, 2012, p. 126).

Given the moral panic that has historically surrounded popular music (discussed below), it is perhaps surprising that concerns surrounding popular music in music education have not tended to focus on its moral implications. Those that have done so have often intersected with discussions surrounding the sexualization of children. McKenry (2011), for example, considers this issue in relation to the singing syllabi of the Australian Music Examinations Board and Australian and New Zealand Cultural Arts Association, which in the last decade have broadened to mitigate against "the historical marginalization of . . . popular music" (p. 11), and conducts a content analysis of lyrics from their repertoires. McKenry notes that even seemingly innocuous lyrics relating to adult love can seem "increasingly incongruous when sung by younger children" (p. 9), and that sexualized content tends to provoke moral concern when the children exposed to it are under the age of 12. McKenry is critical of both organizations' deferral of responsibility regarding lyrical content to the teacher and student, noting that in offering exams they have "created a cultural space that is significantly occupied by children" (p. 8), and recommends that "in embracing contemporary repertoire, [organizations] should also embrace contemporary standards regarding the ethical provision of syllabi" (p. 11). Elsewhere the need to protect children from sexualized media, including popular music, has been asserted (e.g. APA, 2010), although as a generalization this has tended to focus more on visual images and the physical appearance of pop stars.

The increased presence of popular music in music education has not been without detractors, but the lack of criticism voiced on explicitly moral grounds is surprising, given the historical anxiety surrounding popular music's moral influence on young people, particularly since the advent of youth culture and rock 'n' roll in the 1950s. Outside of music education, Buckingham (1993) notes that "the spectre of young people narcotized by . . . the overt sexual nature of popular music, their intellect and imagination destroyed by the mindless products of the culture industry, is one that is routinely invoked in debates about education" (p. 3). Lyrics extolling rebellion and the rejection of authority, coupled with the use of insistent rhythms designed to accompany dancing, have often been presented as symptoms of moral decline among the youth, and have prompted calls for, and actual instances of, censorship. In the Anglo-American context, tolerance in relation to such content has, with notable exceptions, increased iteratively and incrementally across the era of popular culture in line with a changing normative moral landscape. Examples of music or performances that once provoked outrage, such as Elvis Presley's hip gyrating in 1956, can seem tame and naive. Yet, to read across the media hysteria that surrounded Presley's early work is to remind ourselves that at the heart of the moral panic surrounding popular music is a sense of pastoral responsibility towards the next generation that persists among adults (Buckingham, 1993). In the UK, similar concerns surrounding groups such as the Beatles and the Rolling Stones in the 1960s were voiced by the National Viewers' and Listeners' Association (NVLA), led by Mary Whitehouse. The NVLA's social conservatism was explicitly rooted in a Christian moral framework, yet was strikingly Platonic in its linking the creative and cultural pursuits of society and its polity (Buckingham, 1993; Jeffries, 2012). With regard to sexualization and child pornography, her campaigns have been deemed "prophetic" (Kenny, 2010).

The two genres that have, arguably, provoked the highest levels of moral panic are heavy metal and hip-hop. In the former case, critics have focused variously on lyrical content, the volume and aggression of the music and the associated imagery and behaviour. Addressing a US Senate Hearing in 1985, musicologist Dr Joe Stuessy of the University of Texas suggested that heavy metal was "categorically different from previous forms of popular music, [and its] principal themes are . . . extreme violence, extreme rebellion, substance abuse, sexual promiscuity and perversion, and Satanism" (Stuessy, 1985, quoted in Weinstein, 2009, p. 2). In her analysis of that Senate Hearing, Binder (1993) suggested that the concerns raised corresponded to frames of "(moral) corruption", "danger to society", "threat to authority" and "generation gap" (p. 759). Opposition to heavy metal in the UK has been muted by comparison, but some protests nonetheless received media attention in the 1990s, notably the picketing of 'satanic' heavy metal star Marilyn Manson's 1997 concert tour by Scottish Presbyterian groups.

In the case of hip-hop, moral panic has focused primarily on explicit lyrical reference to sex, drugs and violence. However, Richardson and Scott (2002) note that the heterogeneity of rap music is glossed over, and that criticisms of rap lyrics frequently fail to situate them within a wider context of structural inequality, and thus to acknowledge hip-hop as a "cultural response from the working and lower income youth segment of the African American community to perceptions of their economic and social stigmatization" (p. 177). As such, a moral agency relating to civil rights in (some) rap music is infrequently acknowledged, and calls for the censorship of rap music display as racial bias (Binder, 1993; Richardson & Scott, 2002), as similar lyrical content that escapes such opposition is to be found in other genres.

Popular musics have also been seen as a moral force, with revolutionary and prophetic potential (Hebdige, 1988; Richardson & Scott, 2002; Strachan, 2003). This complexity inheres in popular music – in its lyrics, its rhythms and its aesthetics. In the bringing of popular music into formal education settings, the moral anxieties surrounding it are drawn into engagement with those surrounding the moral functions of music education and of education more generally. Within a faith school setting, this moral aspect is further complicated by the dual and potentially conflicting missions of sustaining and promoting a specific religious moral ethos and adhering to national frameworks that enshrine secular moral principles.

Vignette 1: The sacred and the profane

In the after-school live music club that I ran, I would arrange the children into performing groups based largely on mixing their abilities. For the weaker groups I would provide songs for them to play – typically 'standards' within the Anglo-American rock band repertoire with simple chord structures and riffs, or more contemporary songs that I selected on the same bases. I would gradually increase the level of technical complexity as the groups progressed. I allowed the more advanced groups to choose their own repertoire based on their own developing tastes and interests, much as I would in my guitar lessons, in the manner of the Musical Futures approach (D'Amore & Smith, 2016). For the most part, this increased the level of intrinsic motivation and provided valuable opportunities for students to problem-solve without supporting materials, and to develop their aural skills and musical understanding.

> *Jason, Alex, Evan and Nisha, all 15, are waiting outside the music room when I arrive. All have been attending since year 7 and have progressed well in their ensemble playing, as well as on their chosen instruments. I open the door and the pupils head straight for the equipment cupboard and begin to set up. Heather, the band's singer, is absent today as she was last week, and Alex is centre-stage at the microphone. I recognize the chords, but not quickly enough, and can only watch as Alex sings: "Rape Me! Rape Me, my Friend".*[1] *I rush to the mixing desk and slam the sliders down.*
>
> *"Stop, stop", I say. "No way. You're not playing that."*
> *"But sir, we've practised it. It's a well good song."*
> *"You're not doing it. You're not singing that song at the school concert in front of parents and the governors, and the bishop."*
> *Alex's eyes light up. "Of course not sir. Just at our gig. Mrs Henson says we can put on our own gig in the chapel if we practice enough."*

---

1 From Kurt Cobain's "Rape Me" (1993).

"Not there either, I'm afraid."

"But sir, you told us to listen to Nirvana. You taught us 'Smells Like Teen Spirit'."

"Play that one then. That sounded great."

"It's boring, sir."

At this point the school chaplain arrives. *"Hello Tom. Hello Everyone. How is it all going? It was sounding great last week."*

"Good, thank you, Reverend Nicky. Guys, why don't you play the White Stripes? That's one you're going to play at the concert, isn't it?"

The band begins to play – a tight, charismatic rendition, attesting to the hard work they've put into it. I glance nervously at Reverend Nicky, who is watching with a smile. As Alex hurtles through the lyrics, the word "cigarette", hitherto unnoticed, jumps out at me. So does "hounds of hell", sung with crisp enunciation and menace. By *"I'm bleeding, and I'm bleeding, and I'm bleeding right before the lord"*, I am unexpectedly concerned by Reverend Nicky's unchanged facial expression. Eventually, she smiles warmly, gives a thumbs-up to the band, and leaves.

Vignette 2: Highway to Hell?

Alex has been having guitar lessons with me for three years. He has progressed well and is motivated by technical challenges. In the last year he has developed an interest in heavy metal, and we have worked together on learning some advanced solos by ear. I have monitored the development of Alex's listening tastes by the badges and patches affixed to his school bag; he has moved from Jimi Hendrix and Led Zeppelin, through Green Day and Blink 182, to Avenged Sevenfold.

Today, the first lesson of Autumn Term, Alex is his usual polite and friendly self, but his hair is dyed black. He has been practising over the summer and is keen to show me what he wants to work on over the next term, during which he will have to undertake an assessed performance for GCSE[2] music. He reaches into his bag and pulls out

---

2 General Certificate of Secondary Education – the qualification level attained at the end of compulsory schooling in England.

a collection of CDs by death metal bands. He doesn't show me the cases, but I am familiar with them – the cover art is alarmingly gruesome, depicting sexualized self-harm, violence, subverted Christian iconography and a flagrantly anti-Christian aesthetic in general. His school bag is now adorned with a patch bearing the name of the band Cradle of Filth, dripping in blood.

We listen to a song. The music is relentless, aggressive and technically impressive; the words are shouted in a deep, demonic tone, such that they are hard to discern. Alex professes not to know what the singer is singing, and in any case has never been into lyrics. For a performance, he wants to play a medley of two solos, one played low on the neck of the guitar, and the other high. I have promised to accompany him as I have all of my pupils. We work on the solos for the remainder of the session, and set targets for next week.

Vignette 3: Amazing grace?

Jane has been taking guitar lessons for three years. She has progressed fairly well, gradually building her knowledge of open chords and strumming. We began by following my syllabus, which combines focus on chord work alongside simple melodic pieces using standard notation resources (such as The Guitarist's Way *(Nuttall & Whitworth, 2000) and the* Trinity Guildhall syllabus *(Trinity Guildhall Examinations, 2010)), but lately, at the request of Jane's father, we have been working on songs that their church's band performs. These songs are composed for a 'worship band' ensemble of bass guitar, keyboards, acoustic guitar and drums, and feature simple chord structures playable on the acoustic guitar with the use of a capo. Jane is not yet in the church band, but is due to join in the next couple of years.*

Jane arrives five minutes late to her lesson and has forgotten her sheet music. I tell her not to worry, as I have a copy of the song her father wanted us to learn. She seems disappointed, but we run through the song and she strums the chords. She seems distracted, looking out of the practice room window onto the main music classroom where her classmates are having their music lesson and are playing on the electronic keyboards. We change activities and work on some melodic pieces. It is clear that Jane has not practised and is struggling to remember the parts and to read fluently. As I am writing in Jane's book at the end of the lesson, she plays "Seven Nation Army" by the White Stripes on her guitar. She has clearly taught herself, as we have not covered this in our lessons, as I have with one of her classmates.

Discussion

Buckingham (1993) suggests that the same themes of moral anxiety surrounding popular culture have emerged across different geographical, ideological and historical contexts, and to some extent the issues alluded to in the vignettes above are not limited to a Christian faith-school setting. As educators, however, our responses to these themes are determined by our responsibilities, such as within a faith-school setting where a religious moral lens is prescribed for our appraisal of that which we encounter in teaching. In the first vignette the presence of the school chaplain – the embodiment of the school's religious ethos – provoked me to appraise the pupils' repertoire through (my version of) this lens. In my anxiety I presumed that the chaplain's Christian appraisal would be conservative and that she would disapprove of the potentially blasphemous lyrics. In the event, neither appeared to be the case.

This can perhaps first be read as a reminder that most people alive today have lived their entire lives in the era of commercialized popular culture, and are thus familiar with, and perhaps likely to be inured to, provocative lyrical content – rock music in particular has for decades played with religious and anti-religious aesthetics. Second, popular music-making commonly plays a significant role in the extracurricular life of schools, providing opportunities for young people to collaborate, problem-solve and express themselves (Green, 2001), and, given the chaplain's reaction, we might assume that these were her priority. Nonetheless, my role as a teacher required me to consider the potentially conflicting aims of maintaining the moral ethos of the school and promoting learner autonomy (King, 2010), which manifested in the challenge of mediating performance repertoire in terms of its appropriateness according to various measures, while also allowing and encouraging students to pursue their own musical interests and identities.

The issue of learner autonomy also arises in the second vignette, where a student was developing an affiliation with a subculture in the aesthetic of which the desecration of Christian themes and imagery is a central aspect, and which has given rise to moral outrage. In this instance, the pupil was older and a greater degree of autonomy could be sanctioned, yet it still provoked anxiety as the music is, *prima facie*, starkly at odds with the school's moral framework. In the third vignette, the issue of learner autonomy arises again; the student's parents had exercised their right – enshrined in human rights legislation – to choose a faith-based education for their child, and as such their expectation that she learn to perform

Christian repertoire was arguably entirely reasonable. Nonetheless I was troubled by the fact that her enthusiasm for learning an instrument was being undermined by worship repertoire in which she appears to have little interest. She was younger than pupil in the second vignette, and as such a smaller degree of autonomy in choosing repertoire was arguably appropriate, but I was conscious that I had, in a sense, discriminated against her in not teaching her a song I had taught some of her peers on the basis of an assumption that her parents might disapprove of its 'un-Christian' content (despite the pupil's clear enthusiasm for the song).

Conclusions

Throughout this chapter my own position is characterized by an anxiety around the collision of popular culture and Judeo-Christian morality, and my relative responsibilities to pupils, the school and parents. I should note here that when such situations arose, my response was always informed by discussion with colleagues, a reflective approach to practice and direct consultation with parents where I felt it necessary. With regard to pupils' experience, however, a crucial point becomes apparent: outside of the bounds of the vignettes, all of the pupils have engaged independently with popular music, as listeners and musicians, regardless of whether I, the school or their parents have included it in our teaching or sought to discourage them.

Within the confines of formal education, it is doubtless our duty as educators to protect young people from invidious and harmful elements of popular culture, yet the manner in which we ought to do so is not straightforward. We might consider points of analogy here with sex education, where evidence-based pragmatism has in most Western countries superseded the promotion of extra-marital abstinence (UNFPA, 2015). Evidence suggests that openness and frankness promote an informed approach to decisions regarding sex among young people, reducing adverse personal and societal consequences (UNFPA, 2015). A similarly pragmatic approach to popular music might be the best way to ensure that young people are adequately equipped to encounter it from an informed position. Green (2001) suggests that incorporating popular music-making in curricula can help us to better "protect [children] against delusion from the machinations of mass media . . . from uncritically embracing mechanical commercialism" (p. 201). Yet to understand popular music's ideological multivalency and moral complexity, arguably more attention and time should be given to *listening to* and *critical appreciation of* popular music alongside its performance (Scruton, 2010)

Critical listening could be supported through Socratic dialogue; Allsup and Westerlund (2012) suggest that in the case of students being drawn to sexualized lyrical content, the teacher has an ethical responsibility to initiate discussion surrounding the consequences of (for example) sexual promiscuity, for while "motivation, having fun, student ownership, and 'celebration' . . . are deeply admirable [ends], a teacher must be more than a witness to student freedom" (p. 134). The same approach might be taken in relation to other content to develop young people's capacity to understand the music they listen to. In so doing, we might safely and meaningfully scaffold their ascent to autonomy, engaging their affiliative cultural experiences in ways that need not contradict moral frameworks set out by schools and chosen by parents.

References

Allsup, R.E. & Westerlund, H. (2012). Methods and situational ethics in music education. *Action, Criticism, and Theory for Music Education, 11*(1), 124–148.

American Psychological Association, Task Force on the Sexualization of Girls. (2010). *Report of the APA task force on the sexualization of girls*. Retrieved from: http://www.apa.org/pi/women/programs/girls/report-full.pdf.

Annette, J. (2005). Faith schools and communities: Communitarianism, social capital and citizenship. In R. Gardner, J. Cairns & D. Lawton (Eds.), *Faith schools: Consensus or conflict?* (pp. 191–201). London: Routledge.

Binder, A. (1993). Constructing racial rhetoric: Media depictions of harm in heavy metal and rap music. *American Sociological Review, 58*(6), 753–767.

British Humanist Association. (2015). "Faith" Schools. Retrieved from: *https://humanism.org.uk/campaigns/schools-and-education/faith-schools/* [Accessed 1 June 2015].

Buckingham, D. (1993). Introduction. In D. Buckingham (Ed.), Reading audiences. *Young people and the media*. Manchester: Manchester University Press.

Cantle, T. (2013, December 3). Faith schools are creating more and more boundaries between pupils. *Guardian*. Retrieved from: www.theguardian.com [Accessed 3 December 2013].

Cobain, K. (1993). Rape Me [Recorded by Nirvana]. On All Apologies. Rape Me. [Single]. Seattle: DGC.

Cox, G. (1997). "A great civilising and humanising force": Some aspects of a debate about music in English schools, 1872–1928. *Bulletin of the Council for Research in Music Education, 127*, 35–39.

D'Amore, A. & Smith, G.D. (2016). Aspiring to music making as leisure through the musical futures classroom. In R. Mantie & G.D. Smith (Eds.), *The Oxford handbook of music making and leisure* (pp. 61–80). New York, NY: Oxford University Press.

Department for Education. (2011). *The importance of music: A national plan for music education*. London: Department for Education.

Green, L. (2001). *How popular musicians learn: A way ahead for music education*. Aldershot: Ashgate.

Green, L. (2008). *Music, informal learning and the school: A new classroom pedagogy*. Farnham: Ashgate.

Hebdige, D. (1988). *Hiding in the light: On images and things*. London: Routledge.

Hullah, J. (1854). *Music as an element of education: Being one of a series of lectures delivered at St Martin's Hall, in connexion with the Educational Exhibition of the Society of Arts, July 24, 1854*. London: John W. Parker.

Human Rights Act. (1998). Article 2, Protocol 1. Retrieved from: http://www.legislation.gov.uk/ukpga/1998/42/data.pdf [Accessed 3 June 2015].

Ilari, B., Chen-Hafteck, L., & Crawford, L. (2012). Singing and cultural understanding: A music education perspective. *International Journal of Music Education, 31*(2), 202–216.

Jeffries, S. (2012, October 12). Ban this filth!: Letters from the Mary Whitehouse archive by Ben Thompson – Review. *Guardian*. Retrieved from: www.theguardian.com [Accessed 4 September 2015].

Kenny, M. (2010, June 10). In defence of Mary Whitehouse. *Spectator*. Retrieved from: www.spectator.co.uk [Accessed 3 September 2015].

King, C. (2010). Faith schools in pluralistic Britain: Debate, discussion, and considerations. *Journal of Contemporary Religion, 25*(2), 281–299.

Lawton, D., and Cairns, J. (2005). Faith schools: Some political issues and an agenda for research. In R. Gardner, J. Cairns, & D. Lawton (Eds.), *Faith schools: Consensus or conflict?* (pp. 224–256). London: Routledge.

McKenry, T. (2011). Fever when you kiss me: An examination of the ethical issues surrounding the inclusion of sexualised music repertoire in Australian contemporary singing syllabi. *Victorian Journal of Music Education, 1,* 3–12.

Nuttall, P. & Whitworth, J. (2000). *The guitarist's way: Book 1* (9th ed.) Bournemouth: Holley Music.

Parkinson, T. (2014). Mastery, enjoyment, tradition and innovation: A reflective practice model for instrumental and vocal teachers. *International Journal of Music Education* (via OnlineFirst).

Paton, G. (2008, September 19). Faith schools may "indoctrinate" children, says leading headmaster. *Telegraph*, September. Retrieved from: www.telegraph.co.uk [Accessed 2 September 2015].

Plato (1969). *Republic in 12 volumes*. London: William Heinemann.

Pring, R. (2005). Faith schools: Can they be justified?' In R. Gardner, J. Cairns, & D. Lawton (Eds.), *Faith schools: Consensus or conflict?* (pp. 51–60). London: Routledge.

Richardson, J.W. & Scott, K.A. (2002). Rap music and its violent progeny: America's culture of violence in context. *The Journal of Negro Education, 71*(3), 175–192.

Ritchins, F. (2015, July 17). Nicky Morgan defends her attitude to arts education. *Arts Professional*, July. Retrieved from: http://www.artsprofessional.co.uk/news/nicky-morgan-defends-her-attitude-arts-education [Accessed 17 July 2015].

Roberts, B. (2002). *Biographical research*. Buckingham: Open University Press.

Romain, J. (2013, October 11). Schools should be a place to educate, not indoctrinate. Should faith schools be allowed to ghettoise children in the first place? *Independent*. Retrieved from: www.independent.co.uk [Accessed 4 September 2015].

Rutter, J. & Willcocks, D. (Eds.) (1988). *100 carols for choirs*. Oxford, Oxford University Press.

Scruton, R. (2010). Music and morality. Plato remains our greatest rock critic. *American Spectator*, 42–45.

Short, G. (2003). Faith schools and indoctrination. A response to Michael Hand. *Theory and Research in Education, 1*(3), 331–341.

Stainer, J. (1892). *Music in its relation to the intellect and the emotions*. London: Novello.

Strachan, R. (2003). Moral panic. J. Shepherd, D. Horn & D. Laing (Eds.), *The Continuum encyclopedia of popular music of the world: Volume I: Media, industry and society* (pp. 279–281). London: Continuum.

Trinity Guildhall Examinations. (2010). *Guitar grade 1: Pieces and exercises for Trinity Guildhall Examinations 2010–2015*. London: Trinity College London.

United Nations Population Fund. (2015). *The evaluation of comprehensive sexuality education programmes: A focus on the gender and empowerment outcomes*. New York, NY: United Nations Population Fund. Retrieved from: http://www.unfpa.org/sites/default/files/pub-pdf/UNFPAEvaluationWEB4.pdf [Accessed 1 December 2014].

Weinstein, D. (2009). *Heavy metal: The music and its culture*. Boston, MA: Da Capo.

Willis, J. (2009). "By these means the sacred discourses sink more deeply into the minds of men": Music and education in Elizabethan England. *History, 94*(315), 294–309.

31
Social justice and popular music education
Building a generation of artists impacting social change

Sheila C. Woodward

Introduction

Popular music is increasingly achieving a respected position in school and community music education programmes in many countries across the globe. While this is also true of the USA where this has been openly promoted since the benchmark 1967 Tanglewood Symposium (Volk, 1993), it may be happening at a slower pace there, which is ironic considering the massive development of popular music within its borders (Powell & Burstein, chapter 20, this volume; Williams & Randles, chapter 5, this volume). Regions such as Scandinavia have long-established histories of popular music education in school and music teacher education (Dyndahl & Nielsen, 2013; Georgii-Hemming & Westvall, 2010). The increasing presence of popular music in education across the world has brought with it an inherently democratic vehicle for the expression of young people's voices (Christophersen & Gullberg, chapter 33, this volume; Niknafs & Przybylski, chapter 32, this volume). Music carries their feelings, ideas, comments and vision to a potentially global audience that crosses cultural and national borders, made possible by the explosion of social media now at the fingertips of our youth.

With the underlying philosophy that music is more than a mirror of society – it is also a force for change – I explore in this chapter an internationally and culturally diverse range of popular music teaching and learning practices in which children are empowered to take an active role in offering a critical narrative of society and promoting social change. The investigation addresses relevant philosophical values in teaching and administration as well as pedagogies of inclusion, collaborative learning environments and fostering critical thinking. Finally, it touches briefly on the role of music teacher preparation in preparing teachers for applying principles of social justice in the classroom.

Sheila C. Woodward

In addressing issues of popular music education and social justice, it is imperative first to acknowledge the multiple and diverse meanings of the terms 'popular music' and 'social justice' that exist across the globe and have been considered in the music education literature (Hamm, 1982; Campbell, 1995; Petersen, 1997; Bowman, 2007; Elliott, 2007; Silverman, 2009). To avoid diverting into lengthy discussion of these terms, 'popular music' in this chapter refers to diverse genres not typically falling under categories of 'art' or 'traditional' music, and 'popular music education' encompasses education in the multiple facets inherent in the creation, performance, recording, production and dissemination of such music (Bowman, 2004). Admittedly, 'social justice' holds multiple meanings for educators across the world, with situational, contextual, individual and cultural factors impacting perceptions of what it might represent at any given moment. While recognizing those realities, in this chapter I broadly refer to 'social justice' as encompassing principles of respect, equity and dignity for all (Bell, Joshi & Zuniga, 2007). Furthermore, there is an underlying understanding that any perception of social justice is impacted by individual and social identities.

Exploring philosophical values

Teaching

The historical legacy of popular music being a widely accessible vehicle for exposing realities, voicing ideas, prophesying futures and being an agent of change (Byerly, 2008) lends the discipline of popular music education the ability to exist naturally as a home for the promotion of social justice. However, it is conceivable that not all school administrators and teachers would be open to including a platform in the classroom that might question authority structures and defy standard codes of behaviour within a formal educational institution. In the mid-1990s, there was some question as to whether popular music (or specifically rock music) might be out of context in a school institution, considering how it "has historically contained within it an element of rebellion" (Campbell, 1995, p. 19; Kallio, 2015; Parkinson, chapter 30, this volume). Across the world, we see examples of youth seizing the opportunity to explore and discover their identity through their own musical cultures (Green, 2011) and motivating for social change. When South African schools burned in the 1970s, I experienced the youth fighting their struggle through their own hybrids of ethnic, church, jazz and popular musical cultures on the streets, chanting for freedom of the people from an oppressive Apartheid government (Woodward, 2015). The late '60s social consciousness of young British rock musicians was followed by the progressive rock bands of the '70s, which offered a "utopian model" by merging elements of musical cultures from across the globe and "a sense of depth, both sonic and cultural, to a popular music that had been trivialized and desacralized under the deadening weight of corporatism" (Magan, 2013, p. 127). Following on from the explosion of socially conscious popular music in the 1960s, youth in the '70s were bold in their criticism of society and brazenly outspoken against the "coercive and manipulative" controls of media by government and commerce (Magan, 2013, p. 139). The songs captured youth contempt for "blind conformity; rejection of militarism; . . . the automization and commoditization of society; and above all, scorn of philistinism and materialism" (Magan, 2013, p. 139). In the *Nueva Canción* (New Chilean Song) movement of the '60s and '70s, young musicians embraced urban public folk music in voicing their hopes for liberty and a just society, partly as a rejection of European and Anglo-American commercial music influences (Boyle & Cánepa, 1987). In the face of violent oppression of the artist voice, the New Chilean Song movement called on the Chilean people to use peaceful means in defending justice (Gutierrez, 1998). While recognizing that all forms of culture can be used by youth to promote social activism, Ginwright and Cammarota (2002) acknowledge the politicizing function that hip-hop culture in the USA has played in educating youth about critical social issues. They highlight hip-hop's role in developing self-identity and social awareness, while inspiring action towards social change. In Australia, indigenous Aboriginal youth offered unprecedented self-determination and expression through their lamenting personal "narratives of dispossession and injustice" that wailed between lively celebrations (Gibson, 1998, p. 177).

Perhaps the most striking difference between today and the period of the '60s and '70s, when popular music rose rapidly as a powerful mass medium for youth protest, is that we now see formal institutions and community-based programmes directly supporting youth empowerment and the expression of youth protest through popular music. For example, I recently encountered the Head of Popular Music Studies at Auckland University, Stephen Matthews, connecting students in meaningful ways with their cultural heritage and developing an empowering awareness of their identity. Students research and compose songs that comment on topics or issues they personally see as relevant and important. Many of these compositions are protest songs that are performed publicly in order to activate awareness of their role as social commentators and advocators for social justice. At Northern Beaches Christian School in Sydney, Australia, music teacher Brad Fuller has installed innovative designs of comfortable sofa-style furnishings and soundproof glass partitions that foster collaborative student research, small group rehearsal, stage performance and audio engineering, all in one classroom. He and music colleague Peter Orenstein achieve an impressive level of inclusion and student engagement. Songwriting is at the core of the programme, with students encouraged to tell their stories through music as a tool for personal reflection and social change. Helen McVey, head of the degree programme at the Royal Conservatoire of Scotland and working on the *Coorie Doon* project with *Enterprise Music Scotland*, is guiding young mothers on composing their own lullabies for their unborn babies. One mother in the project proudly reported that "when young Calvin comes into the world he's going to have his very own little hard rock soundtrack" (Pickering, 2015). In her visits to remote regions of Brazil, Ilari (2009) found severely disadvantaged children engaged in collaborative music learning. A father described the activities as "pushing them away from all the bad influences that modern life brought to the neighborhood" (p. 126). Ilari determined several associations with music learning: "Development of musical competence through shared activities; Mood and affect regulation; Cultural appropriateness and empowerment; Identity construction; Sense of self-worth and belonging" (pp. 132–133). In her reflections on the New York community *Hip Hop Project*, Silverman (2009) reports the outreach programme for homeless and at-risk youth as exemplifying what author bell hooks (2000, as cited in Silverman, 2009, p. 188) refers to as "pre-requisites for social justice: care, commitment, trust, responsibility, respect, acceptance and self-efficacy". Silverman sees these as values as appropriate for both community and school music programmes on both a human and an educational level. She promotes the view that "all forms of music teaching and learning should consider people's humanity first and foremost" (p. 189).

The harsh reality is that, while we can find such exemplary models of popular music education impacting social justice in community and school music programmes across the world, it is unrealistic to assume that all popular music teachers might be concerned with social justice issues. Allsup and Shieh (2012), who self-identify as gay music educators, both admit to being bullied and the one to being beaten. They declare, "At the heart of teaching others is the moral imperative to care. It is the imperative to perceive and act, and not look away" (p. 48). They challenge us to explore why some students might be withdrawn in music classes or avoid them altogether and why some parents don't show up at school meetings.

Frierson-Campbell (2007) suggests that music teaching takes place in a paradigm of social consciousness that involves modelling equity and social justice in the unique daily situations of the classroom. Jorgensen (2007) promotes similar sentiments, recognizing that justice in music education is connected with ethics and morals, and the regulations that seek to support them. She reminds us that focusing on social justice in the classroom is an inescapable outcome of Dewey's proposal that music links to all of life (Dewey, [1934] 1980 cited in Jorgensen, 2007). Endorsing social justice in music education, Gould (2007) suggests that an underlying system of ethics should lead to affirmation and evaluation rather than judgment. Wilingham (2009) sees the music learning world as existing in a framework of "the public greater good", citing "the failure of science to morally advance the species" and the teacher's role in impacting curriculum and practically applying principles of "ecological accountability, equity, and reconciliation" (p. 52).

Popular music programmes, by their nature, might possibly offer more flexibility than traditional programmes for opening doors to diverse student populations. However, a pioneering teacher wanting to implement popular music into a school curriculum might face opposition from colleagues and administrators who do not share the same values of cultural inclusion. The issues of multiculturalism must necessarily be addressed in any discussion on popular music, recognizing not only its distinction from musical cultures traditionally taught in many schools, but also the multiple subcultures and styles represented by the term. As Peterson (1997) declares, "Popular culture is plural" (p. 55). He points out that the vast differences within each subculture are so many that they even render "the standard categories such as rock and country ... virtually meaningless" (p. 55). One approach for curricular selection might be for teachers to first integrate the musical cultures most familiar to their students before expanding further.

Spradley (2010) approaches the subject of achieving social justice through the lens of multiculturalism. She quotes the (USA) National Association of Multicultural Education's (2010) definition: "Multicultural Education is a philosophical concept built on the ideals of freedom, justice, equality, equity, and human dignity"

(p. 4). Supporting popular music education programmes in schools and communities provides opportunities for opening discussion with students on the inherent value of including, respecting and celebrating music from diverse cultures in the curriculum. Karlsen and Westerlund (2010) set democracy issues firmly beside those of immigration, highlighting "music's capacity as a means for human growth and enhancement of agency" (p. 237). Teachers apply a foundational philosophy of multiculturalism in practice through their attitudes and decisions in daily teaching (Spradley, 2010). With popular music historically being a powerful vehicle for exposing injustice and calling for change, Bradley (2011) suggests that facilitating student exploration of new musical genres provides them not only with opportunities for diversifying their musical understanding but also with ways to manipulate music to articulate "oppressions and resistance" (p. 93). Ethics of caring (Noddings, 1994), associated with critical reflection and valuing of self and all others appear to underlie the above key philosophies concerned with aspiring to and achieving social justice in the classroom.

Administration

Frierson-Campbell (2007) recognizes the additional challenge these teachers may face if they are operating within a community that does not share the same concerns. While acknowledging that school teachers may well be committed to "ethics of care, commitment, respect and love", Silverman (2009) expresses concerns that constraints from policy-makers and administrators may negatively impact school teachers' perceptions of the broader value of their efforts (p. 189). Echoing those sentiments, Bradley (2011) states:

> The call I hear, and to which I respond, obliges me to teach for social justice in education. When I compare this perceived ethical obligation to the state's expectations for my job as articulated in the guidelines, I feel caught between two radically different phrase universes that bump against each other at every turn.
>
> *(p. 93)*

Administrators serve as agents of change when they "step outside their comfort zones and challenge the beliefs that make up their individual core dispositions about equity" (Reed & Johnson, 2010 p. 402). Reed and Johnson further refer to the constant need for administrators to be re-evaluating whether they are thinking and acting based on student need. The philosophical values, critical curricular design and reflective pedagogies that enable social justice in the popular music education programmes benefit from a context of strong administrative support.

Pedagogies of inclusion

As discussed above, much popular music was created and exists as a medium that challenges power structures (while, arguably, necessarily operating within them in order to become 'popular' at all – see Hebert et al., chapter 35, this volume). Perhaps one of the reasons why it works so well in addressing inequities both in and outside of school/community music programmes is that it portrays and enacts these issues. It is heartening to see the self-reflection that is taking place among music educators who want to promote social justice in the world and in their own classrooms. At the 2008 *Engagements and Exclusions* conference in Toronto, delegates grappled with questions of "the portrayal of women in popular music", "the silence surrounding students who identify as queer" and "the exclusion of students with disabilities" (Allsup & Shieh, 2012, p. 49).

In a review of general music in USA schools, Frierson-Campbell (2007) discusses questions of equity and social justice, challenging inequities in resource distribution and questions of cultural relevance in the curriculum. She points out that, as secondary level music instruction in the USA often encompasses specialized, elective programmes, equity and social justice are more especially dependent on resources and teaching approaches. She further highlights inequities pertaining to instruction time, number of courses, teacher qualifications and teaching space:

> the equitable distribution of a socially just music education for all students is in question. This is especially true for those schools that serve our nation's neediest students, where overburdened teachers and administrators strive to keep up with the latest political demands, and at the same time provide services to an ever more diverse student body.
>
> *(p. 264)*

A possible place to start nurturing student critical thinking is in reflection on the music classroom itself, with teachers and students considering how we might inadvertently be proponents of injustice and what we might do to be more inclusive. In pondering issues of inclusivity and social justice for special needs students, I recall a severely dyslexic middle school student lamenting over the humiliation she faced in her music class. While all the music teacher did was roll his eyes in response to her issues, this small facial gesture in front of her peers added a considerable emotional burden to what was already a daily struggle. Gerrity, Hourigan and Horton (2013) support teachers being especially mindful of their interactions with special needs students. They advocate "repetition, student choice, and increased response time" as well as "providing clear directions and expectations, implementing a behavior plan, and fostering a positive learning environment that is mostly free of distractions" (p. 156).

In my own experience of teaching visually impaired students in South Africa, I encountered a boy suffering from an extreme hyperactivity disorder. He was unsuccessful on each instrument he tried to learn, being unable to contain his energy. Finally, of his own accord, he picked up a shaker and the problem was solved. Due to his excellent rhythmic sense, he was permitted to play at his own will throughout the performances. The lack of musical restrictions allowed him to expend all the energy he desired. Despite his visual impairment, he managed to steal the show at each performance by mischievously jiving his way over to join whichever artists were at the musical forefront at any given moment. The humour and vibrant personality he contributed to the overall musical performance would have been lost, had the programme been less inclusive.[1]

An action inquiry into arts programmes in schools in Nottingham, UK (Griffiths, Berry, Holt, Naylor & Weekes, 2006) found evidence that the arts provide an avenue for engaging otherwise disadvantaged or disaffected children and give them the tools that enable them to express their voice and be agents of change. The authors advocate for resource redistribution and recognition of all individuals. They demonstrate the potential of arts-based programmes to provide an accessible activity to children with profound learning disabilities, social interaction difficulties and behavioural challenges. They stress that "education for social justice – for democracy – can reach all the children, not just the confident and articulate ones" (p. 369).

Scrutinizing accessibility to popular music education for students with special needs in Britain, Challis (2009, citing Zahradnicky, Lorencz and Musil, 2008) highlights that industry standard programme ProTools is especially inaccessible to the visually impaired. He further notes that the very nature of the recording studio (both in physical dimension and the lengthy time it takes to learn the discipline) puts restrictions on class size, thus reducing accessibility for large numbers of students. Challis discusses the changes in the industry, where previously popular music tended to be transmitted through recordings and later transcribed. He points out that popular music education programmes tend to demand notation skills (taking into account the complexities and inadequacies of Braille music), and that this presents another challenge for visually impaired students.[2]

Another area for self-reflection is gender bias in our classrooms (see Hebert et al., chapter 35, this volume). Alexander's (2011) article laments, "Where are the girls?" in school jazz programmes (p. 16). Similarly, masculine domination of popular music performance and music production makes the demand for gender equity in the popular music classroom all the more challenging. Smith's recent (2015) study of private-sector popular music performance education in the UK confirms his earlier findings on gender and drumming in popular music (2013), as well as the previous work of authors Abramo (2011a, 2011b) and Green (1997).

Investigating how administrators address the needs of LGBT students, Reed and Johnson (2010) advocate making definite decisions in order to ensure a safe environment for thriving. They promote the Gay, Lesbian and Straight Education Network (GLSEN) guidelines for school leaders in serving as LGBT allies, including "learning the language kids use to self-identify, supporting students who come out, addressing bullying in school, and creating inclusive curricula" (p. 402). In the

---

1 See also David Aldridge's *Tourette Syndrome and music: Discovering peace through rhythm and tone* for a personal account of how inclusive music teaching helped him to realize his identity as a musician and thus as a person.
2 See Fleet (chapter 14, this volume) for a discussion around inclusion of notation in popular music programmes in higher education, and see Bell (2012) for a discussion of digital audio workstations and democracy.

music world, we need to be aware of how our programmes may be marginalizing LGBT students who may not identify with the gender stereotypes with which they are associated.

A look at an Australian alternative school by Cleaver and Riddle (2014) revealed that its popular music education programmes provided an engaging educational milieu for students not engaging with the mainstream. An important element in the effectiveness of the programme was reported to be the matching student/teacher identities: not only do students identify themselves as popular musicians but their teachers are also gigging musicians and recording artists. The teachers foster a student lifestyle of engagement in popular musical culture outside the classroom, preparing them for the music industry and music-rich lives through activity-based approaches. My music diversion programme for juvenile offenders in South Africa (Woodward, Sloth-Ngielson, & Mathiti, 2008) may offer some inspiration for the potential social impact that might be achieved through the skills and attitudes students learn in our music classrooms. The project aimed to provide a healthy diversion from crime through musical skill development, while also aiming to socially reintegrate offenders. Returning to the area some years later, I found several past students earning financial income through performing for tourists, a factor that may conceivably have directly prevented them from returning to a life of crime motivated by extreme poverty.

Spradley (2010) questions whether teachers are purposefully implementing strategies to engage students from diverse backgrounds and whether curricular materials represent diverse cultures while avoiding stereotypes and assumptions. Music educators are encouraged to "collectively engage with matters of justice and injustice that go beyond music classrooms and deal with wider societal issues of religious, familial, political, and economic injustices" (Jorgensen, 2007, p. 182). The challenge is not only addressing inequities within their own classrooms, but actively seeking students usually marginalized from local school or community opportunities and providing them with access to music learning.

Pedagogies of facilitating collaborative learning environments

Pedagogies for learning and applying principles of social justice in popular music education are likely as diverse as the field of popular music. In exploring ideas in this area, Spradley (2010) believes that "the most valid and credible development of socially-just teaching occurs when teacher expectations are conceptualized within the context of a richly diverse teaching and learning environment" (p. 6). The snowballing of digital devices, apps and social media presents educators with ever-expanding platforms for student learning environments.

If students value and make music outside of the classroom in a "do-it-yourself" kind of way (likely using technology tools of all kinds), then we owe it to them to value this music-making and the strategies inherent in it (Bell, 2012; Green, 2002, 2008b, 2014). It might be argued that the peer-learning environments typical of many popular music education classrooms provide more opportunity to practise inclusion and cooperative learning activities than might traditional teacher-directed environments. The informal learning practices of popular musicians that Green (2002) advocates be implemented in music classrooms provide rich opportunities for students to listen to and integrate the perspectives of their peers. Green (2008a) observed that students participating in her study of several popular music education classrooms were remarkably responsible and cooperative when given new liberties through informal learning within their more traditional school learning environments. A suggested reason is that students felt "less intimidated by and alienated from each other's knowledge and expertise" (p. 183). Furthermore, it was noticed that group learning, peer-directed learning and leadership are more evident and effective than teachers previously observed. Moreover, teachers noticed students who generally appear disaffected in school being enthusiastically integrated into peer activities. However, it would be naïve to imagine that informal learning practices will inherently always involve exclusively healthy social practice, and teachers may well encounter students discriminating against one another. This leads to the importance of the role teachers play in developing critical and self-reflective thinking in students.

Pedagogies of fostering critical thinking

The fostering of critical thinking is a key strategy through which a social justice paradigm might be explored in the popular music classroom. While students who are or who have been victims of racial, gender or any number of other prejudices might more naturally resonate with concern for social justice issues, those students who have had little personal experience of social injustice might less readily buy into the agenda. I have found that analysis of popular music songs, sharing of personal stories in the classroom, and discussion of social issues to be as successful approaches for empathy-building. Another effective tool I have used at the collegiate level is having students view and reflect on video interviews of survivors and witnesses to genocides (USC Shoah Foundation, 2016). Elliott and Silverman (2015) express their belief that "critically reflective thinking can and should aim to enable and empower people, including music teachers and learners, to interrogate unexamined systems of belief and action that cause and sustain unjust power structures within societies" (p. 29; see also Niknafs & Przybylski, chapter 32, this volume; Barnett, 2010). Mantie (2008) proposed that "by emphasizing diversity, individuality, collaboration, and nontraditional views of 'musical literacy'", teachers can facilitate student development of a "sense of dignity, self-worth and empowerment" (p. 473).

Ginwright and Cammarota (2002) advocate that, in order to develop critical consciousness among young people, teachers might lead them specifically through the praxis of "critical consciousness and social action" (p. 88). They recommend a three-stage process. The first is the development of "self-awareness", which celebrates their diversity in all its forms, but also analyzes any threats of "power, privilege, and oppression" to their identities and self-determination (p. 80). They see the common use of music "to express pain, anger, and the frustration of oppression" (p. 91) as part of the process of developing self-awareness. The second stage is "social awareness", where teachers encourage critical thinking on social issues (p. 89). The authors provide examples of hip-hop culture being used "to organize, inform, and politicize at the community level" (p. 91). They acknowledge that the key to avoiding despair when exposing social ills is to emphasize the politicizing aspect, which provides a sense of hope and healing through engaging in action towards change. They describe the process of healing and holistic well-being that can be promoted through enabling a social environment for growing through interacting, sharing and listening. In a music class, one could engage students in dialogue around the issues raised in songs they perform and/or write (Bennett, chapter 23, this volume; Hooper, chapter 13, this volume). Ginwright and Cammarota further suggest that such dialogue facilitates a "sense of optimism, emotional stability, intellectual stimulation, positive self-regard, and general resilience when facing personal, family or community challenges" (p. 92). They see healing as the most essential component of practising critical consciousness and social action, impacting meaning and purpose in students' lives. The third, and final, stage is referred to as "global awareness", which they describe as encouraging youth to "practice critical reflection in order to empathize with the struggles of oppressed people throughout the world" (p. 90). They propose that students not only become familiar with oppression through history and systemic causes of suffering but also actively engage in the practice of connecting with others, empathizing with suffering and resisting oppression. The critical pedagogies explored above include common threads of facilitating critical reflection, listening, connecting, expressing, collaborating and advocating.

A word of caution is shared by Berman (2015), who suggests we be aware that dealing with some topics in the music classroom might cause a backlash from some students and/or parents. A music colleague of mine in Florida, for example, was temporarily suspended from an elementary school as a result of allowing students to express their responses to the 9/11 attack in New York in drawings. Some parents objected when they saw pictures drawn by their children of people jumping out of burning buildings.

What we find in both school and community popular music education programmes (see later in this paragraph) are practices that line up remarkably well with Spradley's (2010) summative reflections suggesting that social justice can be achieved in the music classroom by:

> (1) making relevant connections between the cultural experiences of the student and content matter; (2) discovering ways to meet students where they are and utilizing students' prior knowledge as a point of reference for expanding their learning; (3) demonstratively viewing each student with unending potential by increasing the levels of expectations for all students and (4) developing a forum in which to critically analyze and reflect upon the thinking process before, during and after the teaching moment.
>
> (p. 7)

Examples of these ideas succeeding in practice include Allsup and Shieh's (2012) account of the Metropolitan Expeditionary Learning School students who dedicated a musical performance to a New York City community devastated by an oil spill. In rewriting the lyrics of the song "Where is the love?" they confronted economic issues through music. After the devastating 2004 Indian Ocean tsunami, I was shown a DVD recording of a Burnside High School, Christchurch, production where students produced the music, script and choreography in a powerful expression that challenged the world not to forget those victims of the tsunami who were still suffering. The students reflected on how they felt empowered that their voice might have an impact on those attending the show. It should be remembered, however, that while students may be encouraged to think critically, not all might find it easy to articulate their ideas. The role of teachers may be crucial in helping students to develop skills to express their individual or collective voices successfully through music and lyrics.

Pedagogies of nurturing the student voice

The first step in nurturing student voice is paying attention to that voice. Stedman's (2008) review of Lucy Green's (2008b) *Music, informal learning and the school: A new classroom pedagogy* highlights how Green urges us "to listen to young people's voices and, as music educators, to take their values and culture seriously" (p. 61). Silverman (2009) explains that, through artistic communities, youth experience a sense of belonging, expression and creative engagement in tackling problems. She observes students being "enabled and empowered . . . to rap about issues they (feel) uncomfortable discussing and to express their feelings creatively, in order to work through their pain" (p. 185). Silverman reports that the teens are able to express "their personal narratives", by "moving away from the misogynistic attitudes that commercial rap can deliver and toward topics they dealt with in their own lives, such as abortion, violence, drugs, death and absent fathers" (p. 185).

Griffiths et al. (2006) explain how it is not enough to provide a public space for expressing student voice. (They stress that the term *space* is not limited to a physical domain.) They insist we cannot assume that simply because such a space exists, that all students will use it: some will need to learn how to exist in a public arts space before they will be ready to decide on participation. Furthermore, they explain that some children may never believe they have the capacity to exercise voice and agency unless they've had opportunities to practise doing so. They refer to an earlier model (Griffiths, 2003) that includes the essential elements of "five mutually reinforcing essentials for improving social justice in education . . . self-esteem, partnership, action, collective action and empowerment through voice" (p. 358). They discuss how student participation in a socially focused programme can be their means of impacting society.

Of course, in nurturing expression of student voice, teachers are helping students balance the intricate relationship between that expression and musical structure. As Eyerman and Jamison (1998) point out that, while songs need to be both musically and lyrically sound, there also needs to be that intangible human element that connects these elements into a meaningful whole. Helping students achieve this woven fabric of lyrics and music, in which both elements need to be successful in their own right, is no easy task. This leads us to the question of whether teachers in schools and community settings are receiving the kinds of teacher training needed to meet these demands.

The need to address music teacher preparation

It would be interesting to know if the expansion of popular music programmes in schools and community settings is being matched in teacher education programmes. Allsup and Shieh (2012) ask "why do we [in the USA] sometimes still feel apologetic about the place and purpose of popular music in teacher preparation programs?" (p. 49). Bradley (2011) suggests that integrating popular and cultural diversity into music-teacher education might spark preservice teacher awareness "that cultural capital may be resistant capital" (p. 93). She quotes Yasso's (2006) definition of 'resistant' as "knowledge and skills fostered through oppositional behavior that challenges inequity" (p. 179). However, it is not only the impacting of attitudes that is important in teacher preparation.

Spradley (2010) offers numerous suggestions in support of the role of teacher preparation in impacting social justice through:

> (1) improving teacher quality by adequately preparing *all* teachers to teach in culturally diverse environments (2) developing and providing a broader cultural scope of pedagogical content knowledge; (3) developing innovative ways to provide opportunities for pre-service teachers to work in diverse settings; (4) orchestrating opportunities for pre-service teachers to critically discuss their experiences and critically analyze and reflect on their beliefs, attitudes and expectations while working in culturally diverse learning environments, and (5) developing a stronger knowledge base of methods, instructional strategies and resources that reflect culturally responsive pedagogy.
>
> (p. 7)

Teacher-training programmes should offer opportunities for students to acquire skills in facilitating informal music learning practices typical of popular music pedagogies (Davis & Blair, 2011; Dunbar-Hall & Wemyss, 2000). Students need to learn approaches that are not prevalent in traditional programmes but are developing their skills in "other types of music literacy and musicianship" (Giddings, 2008, p. 34). Lebler (2008) found students to be very at home with peer learning environments, as these students reported having experience of that prior to higher education.

While music teacher preparation programmes likely include some preparation in working with students with special needs, music students would benefit from music-specific applications to their learning in this area. Gerrity, Hourigan and Horton's (2013) research indicates that music teachers desire more professional guidance on teaching special needs students (p. 157). Similar findings by McCord and Watts (2010) revealed tendencies to report low self-esteem in the field. These research participants stressed the limitations of their knowledge base for the informed and creative development of curricular design for teaching students with special needs. Nevertheless, they describe music educator ability to recognize value in assistive technology despite a lack of training in the field.

Internationally, academics are highlighting the need for teacher training programs to include philosophical and sociological components that would provide a basis for addressing social concerns in the classroom. For example, recognizing the ever-increasing diversity in student populations within the USA, Kindall-Smith (2012) emphasizes the importance of not only preparing teachers for multicultural education but also helping them to understand what contributes to prejudice. A campaign of the Chinese government to introduce popular music into schools was apparently achieved through promoting socialist and Confucian ideas (Ho & Law, 2012), placing possible expectations on teachers with regards to philosophical frameworks. Whyte (2009), writing about a Canadian context, laments her sense that teacher education seems to lack relevance and appear arbitrary when the world is in crisis. She is "enraged" by the "narrow and archaic vision for music education" that is "seemingly concerned with efficacy and mere musical objectives" without "addressing the needs of students and of our world" (p. 317). She sees music education playing a leading role "as the heart of a core curriculum, as an opportunity for students and teachers to develop their compassion, tolerance, mindfulness, and empowerment" (p. 324). Bradley (2011) points out that the language of State Teacher Education guidelines in Wisconsin, USA, is so tightly tied to an aesthetic view of music education that it effectively leaves socially concerned university professors "between a rock and a hard place" (p. 80). Teacher-training programmes that present barriers to accepting popular musicians into their student population may need to consider developing alternative requirements for admission. For example, if auditions require the performance of Western classical music, institutions may struggle to attract applications from practising popular musicians. Or, if tertiary music education programmes require participation in traditional ensembles such as Western classical choirs, orchestras and bands (and furthermore require that students learn skills to teach those ensembles), they may fail to attract popular musicians. Music teacher education would do well to embrace these popular music specialists while also offering diverse options for more traditional students to develop skills in popular music (Williams & Randles, chapter 5, this volume) and to explore the philosophies, approaches and pedagogies for promoting social justice.

Conclusion

Teachers play a vital role in creating awareness of principles of democratic practice in the popular music classroom, in affirming and reinforcing inclusion, in promoting listening and cooperative learning experiences, and in providing opportunities for voicing opinions and collaborative decision-making in impacting change. These times call for music educators to re-examine the limits of our curriculum and our outreach to all students in schools and communities. Students live in an era of astounding global crisis. Pounding on the doors of our classrooms are gargantuan issues including global health, armed conflict, international terrorism, mass migration of refugee populations, rapid climate change, economic catastrophe, prejudice, discrimination, oppression, violence, slavery, dwindling energy sources, poverty, hunger, water shortages and species extinction. While some students appear unaffected by these issues, others carry these burdens through the doors of our classrooms, often in the weighty form of their own of poverty, abuse or discrimination. Music teachers aim to create collaborative learning environments (see Blom, 2011) with safe places of opportunity for students to address their own struggles with these issues, and they have the benefit of doing so through a field of music that is already engaged in addressing such issues and lends itself naturally to collaborative and joyful learning environments. Music teachers and music teacher educators strive towards inclusion through addressing bias and prejudice in our own classrooms (sometimes despite unsupportive environments) and recognize our roles in helping students to find and express their voices through the spaces and musicking opportunities we create. Our courage is all the more rewarded by the healing and empowerment our students can achieve.

> As a social, political, and pedagogical practice, transformative social justice learning will take place when people reach a deeper, richer, and more textured and nuanced understanding of themselves and their world.
>
> *(Torres, 2007 p. 244)*

References

Abramo, J.M. (2011a). Gender differences of popular music production in secondary schools. *Journal of Research in Music Education, 59*, 21–43.

Abramo, J.M. (2011b). Gender differences in the popular music compositions of high school students. *Music Education Research International, 5*, 1–11.

Alexander, A. (2011). Where are the girls? *JAZZed, 6*, 16–20.

Aldridge, D. (2014). *Tourette syndrome and music: Discovering peace through rhythm and tone.* Los Angeles, CA: Rollinson.

Allsup, R.E. & Shieh, E. (2012). Social justice and music education: The call for public pedagogy. *Music Educators Journal, 98*(4), 47–51.

Barnett, A.C. (2010). *Critical voice and social justice in the urban music classroom.* (Doctoral Dissertation).

Bell, A. (2012). *Homemade records: A multiple case study of the role of recording technology in the music-making processes of informally trained musicians.* (Unpublished dissertation). New York: New York University.

Bell, L.A., Joshi, K.Y., & Zuniga, X. (2007). Racism, immigration, and globalization curriculum design. In M. Adams, L.A. Bell, & P. Griffin (Eds.), *Teaching for diversity and social justice* (pp. 145–166). New York: Routledge.

Berman, A. (2015). Teaching social justice in the music classroom. *Teaching Music, 22*(4), 38–41.

Blom, D. (2011). Inside the collaborative inter-arts improvisatory process: Tertiary music students' perspectives. *Psychology of Music, 40*(6), 720–737.

Bowman, W. (2004). Pop goes . . . ? Taking popular music seriously. In C. X. Rodriguez (Ed.), *Bridging the gap: Popular music and music education* (pp. 29–49). Reston, VA: National Association for Music Education.

Bowman, W. (2007) Who's asking? (who's answering?) Theorizing social justice in music education. *Action, Criticism, and Theory for Music Education*, 6(4), 1–20.

Boyle, C., & Cánepa, G. (1987). Violeta Parra and Los Jaivas: Unequal discourse or successful integration? *Popular Music*, 6(2), 235–240.

Bradley, D. (2011). In the space between the rock and the hard place: State teacher certification guidelines and music education for social justice. *Journal of Aesthetic Education*, 45(4), 79–96.

Byerly, I. B. (2008). Decomposing apartheid: Things come together. In G. Olwage (Ed.), *Composing apartheid: Music for and against apartheid*. Johannesburg: Wits University Press.

Campbell, P. (1995). Of garage bands and song-getting: The musical development of young rock musicians. *Research Studies in Music Education*, 4, 12–20.

Challis, B. (2009). Technology, accessibility and creativity in popular music education. *Popular Music*, 28(3), 425–431.

Cleaver, D. & Riddle, S. (2014). Music as engaging, educational matrix: Exploring the case of marginalized students attending an "alternative" music industry school. *Research Studies in Music Education*, 36(2), 245–256.

Davis, S. & Blair, D. (2011). Popular music in American teacher education: A glimpse into a secondary methods course. *IJME*, 29(2), 124–140.

Dewey, J. (1980). *Art as experience*. New York, NY: G. P. Putnam's Sons. (Original work published 1934).

Dunbar-Hall, P. & Wemyss, K. (2000). The effects of the study of popular music on music education. *IJME*, 36, 23–34.

Dyndahl, P. & Nielsen, S. G. (2013). Shifting authenticities in Scandinavian music education. *Music Education Research*, 16(1), 105–118.

Elliott D. J. (2007). Socializing music education. *Action, Criticism and Theory for Music Education*, 6(4), 60–95.

Elliott D. J. and Silverman, M. (2015) *Music matters: A philosophy of music education*. 2nd Ed. New York, NY: Oxford University Press.

Eyerman, R. & Jamison, A. (1998). *Music and social movements: Mobilizing traditions in the twentieth century*. Cambridge, UK: Cambridge University Press.

Frierson-Campbell, C. (2007). Without the "ism": Thoughts about equity and social justice in music education. *Music Education Research*, 9(2), 255–265.

Georgii-Hemming, E. & Westvall, M. (2010). Music education – a personal matter? Examining the current discourses of music education in Sweden. *BJME*, 27(1), 21–33.

Gerrity, K. W., Hourigan, R. M. & Horton, P. W. (2013). Conditions that facilitate music learning among students with special needs: A mixed methods inquiry. *Journal of Research in Music Education*, 61(2), 144–159.

Gibson, C. (1998). "We sing our home, we dance our land": Indigenous self-determination and contemporary geopolitics in Australian popular music. *Environment and Planning*, 16(2), 163–184.

Giddings, S. (2008). Popular music education: A different type of musicianship. *The Canadian Music Educator*, 49(3), 31–35.

Ginwright, S. & Cammarota, J. (2002). New terrain in youth development: The promise of social justice approach. *Social Justice*, 29(4), 82–95.

Gould, E. (2007). Social justice in music education: the problematic of democracy. *Music Education Research*, 9(2), 229–240.

Green, L. (1997). *Music, gender, education*. Cambridge: Cambridge University Press.

Green, L. (2002). *How popular musicians learn: A way ahead for music education.* London: Ashgate.
Green, L. (2008a). Group cooperation, inclusion and disaffected pupils: some responses to informal learning in the music classroom. Presented at the RIME Conference 2007, Exeter, UK. *Music Education Research, 10*(2), 177–192.
Green, L. (2008b). *Music, informal learning and the school: A new classroom pedagogy.* London: Ashgate.
Green, L. (2011). *Learning, teaching and musical identity: Voices across cultures.* Bloomington: Indiana University Press.
Green, L. (2014). *Hear, listen, play! How to free your students' aural, improvisation, and performance skills.* New York: Oxford University Press.
Griffiths, M. (2003). *Action for social justice in music education: Fairly different.* Buckingham: Open University Press.
Griffiths, M., Berry, J., Holt, A., Naylor, J. & Weekes, P. (2006). Learning to be in public spaces: In from the margins with dancers, sculptors, painters and musicians. *British Journal of Educational Studies, 54*(3), 352–371.
Gutierrez, A. (1998). Peace profile: Victor Jara. *Peace Review, 10*(3), 485–491.
Hamm, C. (1982). Some thoughts on the measurement of popularity in music. In D. Horn & P. Tagg (Eds.), *Popular music perspectives* (pp. 3–15). Goteborg: Wheaton.
Ho, W. & Law, W. (2012). The cultural politics of introducing popular music into China's music education. *Popular Music and Society, 35*(3), 399–425.
hooks, b. (2000). *All about love: New visions.* New York, NY: William Morrow.
Ilari, B. (2009). Music learning and the invisible: Cultural appropriation, equity, and identity of underprivileged Brazilian children and adolescents. In E. Gould, J. Countryman, C. Morton, & L.S. Rose (Eds.), *Exploring social justice: How music education might matter* (pp. 121–138). Toronto, Ontario: Canadian Music Educators' Association.
Jorgensen, E. (2007). Concerning justice and music education. *Music Education Research, 9*(2), 169–189.
Kallio, A.A. (2015). Drawing a line in water: Constructing the school censorship frame in popular music education. *International Journal of Music Education, 33*(2), 195–209.
Karlsen, S. & Westerlund, H. (2010). Immigrant students' development of musical agency: Exploring democracy in music education. *British Journal of Music Education, 27*(3), 225–239.
Kindall-Smith, M. (2012). What a difference in 3 years! Risking social justice content in required undergraduate music education curricula. *Journal of Music Teacher Education, 22*(2), 34–50.
Lebler, D. (2008). Popular music pedagogy: Peer learning in practice. *Music Education Research, 10*(2), 193–213.
Magan, E. (2013). The music's not all that matters, after all: British progressive rock as social criticism. In J.C. Friedman (Ed.), *The Routledge history of social protest in popular music* (pp. 123–141). New York: Routledge.
Mantie, R. (2008). Getting unstuck: The One World Youth Arts Project, the music education paradigm, and youth without advantage. *Music Education Research, 10*(4), 473–483.
McCord, K.A. & Watts, E.H. (2010). Music educator's involvement in the individual education program process and their knowledge of assistive technology. *Application of Research in Music Education, 28*(2), 79–85.
Peterson, R.A. (1997). Popular music is plural. *Popular Music and Society, 21*(1), 53–58.
Pickering, D. (2015). Coorie Doon at North Edinburgh Arts. *North Edinburgh News.* Retrieved from: http://nen.press/2015/08/06/coorie-doon-at-north-edinburgh-arts/. [Accessed 30 October 2015].

Reed, L. & Johnson, L.T. (2010). Serving LGBT students: Examining the spiritual, religious, and social justice implications for an African American school administrator. *The Journal of Negro Education* [The role of spirituality, religion and African American church on educational outcomes], *79*(3), 390–404.

Silverman, M. (2009). Sites of social justice: Community music in New York City. *Research Studies in Music Education, 31*(2), 178–192.

Smith, G.D. (2013). *I Drum, Therefore I Am: Being and becoming a drummer*. Farnham: Ashgate.

Smith, G.D. (2015). Masculine domination and intersecting fields in private-sector popular music performance education in the UK. In P. Burnard, Y. Hofstander, & J. Söderman (Eds.), *Bourdieu and the sociology of music and music education*. Farnham: Ashgate.

Spradley, M.V. (2010). Achieving social justice in the music classroom. *Connections, 25*(1), 4–7.

Stedman, P. (2008, autumn term). Products [Review of the book *Music, informal learning and the school: A new classroom pedagogy* by L. Green]. Classroom Music, 1, p. 61.

Torres, C.A. (2007). Transformative social justice learning: The legacy of Paolo Freire. In M. Coté, R.J.P. Day, & G. de Peuter (Eds.), *Utopian pedagogy: Radical experiments against neo-liberal globalization* (pp. 242–247). Toronto, Ontario: University of Toronto Press.

USC Shoah Foundation. (2016). *Full Length Testimonies*. Los Angeles, CA. Retrieved from: https://sfi.usc.edu/full-length-testimonies [Accessed 30 October 2015].

Volk, T. (1993). A history and development of multicultural music education as evidenced in the Music Educators Journal. *Journal of Research in Music Education, 41*(2), 137–155.

Whyte, B. (2009). The Heart of the Matter: A pre-service teacher's narrative on coming to a social justice oriented vision for music education. In E. Gould, J. Countryman, C. Morton, & L.S. Rose (Eds.), *Exploring social justice: How music education might matter* (pp. 317–324). Toronto, Ontario: Canadian Music Educators' Association.

Wilingham, L. (2009). Educating for the greater good: Music's flame of hope. In E. Gould, J. Countryman, C. Morton, & L.S. Rose (Eds.), *Exploring social justice: How music education might matter* (pp. 52–69). Toronto, Ontario: Canadian Music Educators' Association.

Woodward, S.C. (2015). Music: An alternative education in the South African freedom struggle. In C. Benedict, P. Schmidt, G. Spruce, & P. Woodford (Eds.), *The Oxford handbook of social justice in music education* (pp. 614–630). New York: Oxford University Press.

Woodward, S.C., Sloth-Nielson, J. & Mathiti, V. (2008). South Africa, the arts, and youth in conflict with the law. *International Journal of Community Music, 1*(1), 69–88.

Yasso, T.J. (2006). Whose culture has capital? A critical race theory discussion of community cultural wealth. In A.D. Dixson & C.K. Rousseau (Eds.), *Critical race theory in education: All God's children got a song* (pp. 31–56). New York: Routledge.

Zahradnicky, T., Lorencz, R., and Musil, P. (2008). Making ProTools accessible for the visually impaired. In Proceedings from *11th International Conference on Computers Helping People with Special Needs*. Heidelberg: Springer-Verlag.

32
Popular music and (r)evolution of the classroom space
Occupy Wall Street in the music school

Nasim Niknafs and Liz Przybylski

"Space makes a difference"[1]

> In a music department computer lab, two students use a Digital Audio Workstation to mix the sound of police sirens and aerosol cans over synth pop beats. From a dorm room, a student writes about punk's potential to provide anti-capitalist commentary to the masses. Away from the music school, students craft their radio show to play popular music alongside commentary about the situations that songs critique. In a university classroom, a group of students in a music course listens to an indie musician who has made new music for Occupy Wall Street (OWS).[2] And at a local dance club, an engineering student DJs for a crowd thirsty to sweat off their daily routines and access an extraordinary experience.

Each activity, motivated by a course on popular music incorporating the music of OWS, happened in a different kind of space; each activity had a unique relationship to the institutionalization of both OWS and the music classroom. Acknowledging shifting peripheries of institutional space in academia, this chapter examines a co-taught university course on popular music.

---

1 McGregor, 2004, p. 2
2 Occupy Wall Street began as a response to global economic crises in 2011. It involved demonstrations in public areas, notably encampments in financial districts, and online action.

Introduction

The course under discussion attracted students with majors outside of music. The authors taught the course in two consecutive terms at a university in the United States. Typically, students in a class like this would learn about elements of music through listening, reading, lectures and in-class activities; the material mainly would focus on Western Art Music. While this new course maintained the goal of teaching musical vocabulary and developing critical listening skills, it expanded to focus on a new kind of musical practice: popular music. Further, it required students to compose their own popular-style songs. Based in a music department, this course ran contemporaneously with OWS.

Using the OWS movement in the classroom both as a contentious case that questioned power relations and as a metaphor describing the course, we critically examine the interplay between concept and practice of learning and teaching popular music in- and outside of institutional spaces. This chapter provides a contextualized definition of 'space' and its uses based on Lefebvre's (1974/1991) concept of space as a produced condition and on Lim et al.'s (2012) categorization of classroom space. Connecting these concepts to the spatial and temporal origins of OWS, we discuss a popular music course incorporating OWS and its spatial parameters, and how bringing popular music into the classroom as both content and pedagogy blurs the lines between institutional and non-institutional spaces. Labelling OWS as non-institutional and the classroom as institutional risks presenting a simplistic and at times inaccurate binary. Rather, students' experiences in this course and community suggest an opening of dialogical space at the time in which popular music-making enters the institutional sphere. Mirroring the ways that popular musicians teach and learn (Green, 2001), the popular music pedagogy in this course incorporated cooperative, informal and bottom-up elements. Further, improvisatory and participatory characteristics reflected ways in which OWS functioned.

Re-defining the classroom space

If we consider the classroom a social space where teachers and students interact with one another through verbalization of subject matter as well as through body language and power relations, we can apply Lefebvre's conceptual triad to discuss students' learning experiences and meaning-making. In *Production of Space*, Lefebvre (1974/1991) challenged how social space is observed, offering a nuanced understanding of humans' lived experiences with surrounding space. Lefebvre proposed three interlocking notions that productively conceptualize active use of space: spatial practice, representations of space and representational space (Lefebvre, 1974/1991, p. 33). The first – spatial practice – refers to everyday movements and day-to-day routines; it can also be referred to as physical space. The second – representations of space – signifies the abstraction of relations from the perceived space; this area encompasses conception and theorization of the space. Representations of space, as Lefebvre noted, "Tend . . . towards a system of verbal (and therefore intellectually worked out) signs" (1974/1991, p. 39), which take physical arrangements such as guidelines, road maps, charts, structural designs and curriculum; this space can be understood as mental space. Third, representational space suggests an embodiment of the space by its dwellers where the space is acknowledged through living in it. As Lefebvre remarked, this space is "directly *lived* through its associated images and symbols, and hence the space of its 'inhabitants' and 'users'" (1974/1991, p. 39).

Lefebvre re-focuses critical attention on how space structures experience and how experience in turn structures space. This allows teachers to focus on the social space that is created by all class participants, including themselves. In the classroom, spatial practice can translate to following a routine to 'ground' students at the start of the class, building on a shared musical or academic experience. Representation of space is manifested as curriculum, which establishes goals and objectives; it also sets out smaller steps to reach goals, creating a representation that structures the learning processes. Representational space translates to how teachers set up a space to facilitate learning in order to produce knowledge as students interact in the space.

By analyzing physical signs of this course, encapsulated in our curriculum, we centre on the movements, daily routines and ways in which students' and teachers' lived experiences contribute to learning. Curriculum thus symbolizes students' mental processes and a springboard for knowledge creation. It is only through living socially in this space that our classroom space can be actualized. As Lefebvre stated, "If space is a product, our knowledge of it must be expected to reproduce and expound the process of production. The 'object' of interest must be expected to shift from *things in space* to the actual *production of space*" (p. 37). In this way, the space can be asserted by students and teachers centred on the values and conceptual principles that they enact.

The course design

We designed a course on popular music that used contemporary political issues to facilitate a space where students could become engaged with their own learning, not only through music-making, but also by actively engaging with the surrounding community. Incorporating political cases, including OWS,[3] helped students examine how public spaces are used by people in their daily routines. In this movement, participants re-drew the ways in which individuals and groups moved through space in daily life. The activities of the protesters, particularly the music made in public spaces – such as jamming, drumming and singing – remapped spatial practice in urban centres.[4] One course goal was developing analytical thinking

---

3 Other cases included underground music scenes in Iran and issues related to punk music in the UK and US, as together we had first-hand experiences of these musical environments. All of these cases allowed us to discuss the physical use of public spaces and the manners in which actors move through space in daily life.
4 Both teachers leveraged their knowledge from participation in various political grassroots movements, one of which was OWS. In this respect, OWS was also used as a metaphor to encourage students to think beyond the coursework in the official space of learning of the classroom.

about musical events outside the classroom space. To this end, the professors transcended classroom walls by moving to a differently configured space – the music composition lab. Equally important to this reconfiguration of the classroom space, the professors incorporated creative assignments that drew on students' intrinsic motivation, such as composing music related to a political event (detailed below). Additionally, the professors invited community music experts from outside the university into the classroom. In these ways, the professors co-created an organic space where students felt at ease to collaborate, create music and provide feedback to one another. Using some of the bottom-up organizational principles active in OWS, discussed later in the chapter, students participated in creative musical activity and decision-making. The physical and mental classroom space became a movement within itself; professors encouraged students' outside activities in unofficial spaces,[5] and together brought these into the classroom. The lines of learning spaces thus blurred. Producing a space that facilitated student learning through more than listening and reading, the space invited active participation in music creation and performance.

Assessment

Students completed three major assignments during the term in order to develop and demonstrate their critical thinking and musicianship: an autobiographical essay, a musical project and a written case study. First, students critically examined their musical background and relationship with music they considered significant. These essays also provided us (the professors) a space to start knowing our students through their musical preferences and behaviours, which gave us an opportunity to refine our syllabus towards their needs. Reciprocally, students made a space to think deeply about their past musical journeys and share their music with us and one another in an environment designed to be open to their ideas. Through this approach, the curriculum that was designed by the professors became a blueprint for the students to actively create meaning; the representation of space became a representational space. Second, the students created a musical project based on political issues that resonated with them. Together as a class, we began by analyzing participatory music in the Civil Rights movement in the United States.[6] Students subsequently chose contemporary examples of a social or political issue that incorporated music-making. After participating in a class workshop introducing students to a digital audio workstation (DAW), students worked alone or in groups to make their own songs, corresponding to their chosen topic.[7] The DAW served as a virtual space in which students could be musically creative. Because we welcomed

---

5 In spaces outside of the official classroom, students engaged in activities such as DJing and radio broadcasting.
6 The civil rights movement advanced equal rights for African-Americans in the United States (see Turino, 2008).
7 Students were encouraged to use the DAW GarageBand if they were new to music technology, or Logic if they were more advanced.

students without musical training, those who did not play acoustic instruments or were not confident singing could learn basic techniques on the DAW, thus enabling them to create music at an introductory level. This process helped even beginners to feel ownership of the music they were creating. As one student noted,

> When I hear remakes of the original song, all I can think about is my song, [the course], . . . and about my last spring semester at [the university]. Most importantly, I pause for reflection at the intellectual and emotional development that I underwent that semester . . . [The course] ended up being meaningful and memorable in ways that I simply had never imagined.

In the last assignment, students wrote a case study that related to a current political issue, which encapsulated both their learning in the classroom space and their musical engagements outside of class.

The role of space

Space played an important role in students' learning and musical projects. Lefebvre's concept of *representations of space*, where the "mode of production" (1974/1991, p. 39) is imposed by the dominating relation (in this case students' learning in class), morphed into *representational space*, where students created their own scenarios within and through space and inhabited it with their own aspirations. The course invited students to adapt the learning environment to their needs. They worked in multiple spaces when creating their popular musical projects – first, the flexible space of the music computer lab, not typically used for this course, afforded an adaptable working environment; unlike a lecture hall, in which movement is discouraged and space is highly regulated, the lab offered a place for learners to move around the room, ask questions of one another and receive feedback from their fellow students and the professors. In communicating via the internet and using online material, students were able to access another space for making their music.

A group of two students created a musical project about OWS. They compiled audio clips from various sources, including news broadcasts and protesters' speeches and chants, and spliced and edited these together over a musical backdrop. Another student composed a song about the Red Power Movement.[8] To address Native American organizing in the 1960s, the student used samples of the song "Going In for the Kill"[9] by La Roux and mixed it with recordings of Red Power Movement leaders, specifically from an activist group's occupation of Alcatraz.[10]

---

8 The Red Power Movement involved political organizing for civil rights led by Native Americans in the United States, notably in the 1960s (Cobb & Fowler, 2007; Smith & Warrior, 1996).
9 Song "In for the Kill" [FN] by La Roux (2009).
10 Native activists occupied Alcatraz, an island on Ohlone territory in the San Francisco Bay which housed a federal prison until 1963. Protesters did so in 1964 and again in 1969, at which time activists claimed the space as "Indian land" and set up homes, a school and a clinic in the space where the prison had previously operated. See Strange and Loo, 2001.

The student described the process of using "a popular song with an incredibly catchy and hypnotic chorus. That song had been used to create the foundation for an upbeat pop song, a bass-bumping dance song, and also a hip-hop song". Reflecting on the composition experience, the student described, "to this day, I can remember thinking about how neat it was to have the chorus of [the song] mixed with the repetition of a San Francisco reporter saying 'nobody wants to leave' in reference to the activists' occupation".[11]

An additional space that students used was the physical classroom space whence the entire project stemmed, which is described in the following section. Other utilized spaces were students' dorm rooms and personal spaces, where they could make their music without an authoritative gaze. Sometimes universities use lecture-style teaching; a lecture hall full of students at desks affords a minimal amount of movement. When possible, we created room for students to move within the physical classroom space. Movement in space paralleled decision-making about their music and political case studies and allowed them to provide feedback for one another. We fostered discussions on qualitative elements of the music they were creating and the political discourse around their chosen topics. Additionally, the course created opportunities for connections outside of the classroom. Instead of using only one type of space, students were able to use multiple kinds of spaces.

Any space, including classrooms, can have multiple functions and various attendant meanings. Framing their conceptual structure on Hall's *distance-set* hypothesis, Lim et al. (2012, p. 237) proposed that, based on the proximity of the teacher and students and their physical movements, four different sets of classroom space exist: (1) Authoritative Space, (2) Personal Space, (3) Supervisory Space and (4) Interactional Space.[12] Authoritative space refers to the greatest physical space between the teacher and students in a formal relationship, whereas personal space signifies an informal physical and mental space between the teachers and students. Supervisory Space indicates a space in which "extreme control [is] exerted implicitly through a sense of 'invisible' monitoring" (p. 238). In Supervisory Space, the teacher's position is established through surveillance practices where the students are constantly visible. In Interactional Space, leaning towards a more Personal Space, the teacher stands among the students rather than standing behind them (as in Supervisory Space), or directly in front of them (as in Authoritative Space). Generally, Interactional Space occurs when students are involved with a task in groups or individually: "The closer proximity between the teacher and the student(s) facilitates interaction and reduces interpersonal distance. The interaction usually takes the form of personal consultation where the teacher offers guidance on the task set or clarification on an earlier instruction" (p. 238). Most of the activities that occurred during this course were within the Interactional Space, where the movements, conversations and feedback took place in a consultative manner.

---

11 All quotations from students are excerpts from their written feedback on the course, used with permission.
12 See also Smith and Shafighian (2013).

Synthesizing Lefebvre's concept of lived space and Lim et al.'s conceptual framework of classroom space, we propose that bringing OWS in to an official educational institution through popular music education afforded teachers and students the interactive capacity and (relatively) unrestricted physical and mental movement that allowed navigation of power hierarchies within an official/authoritative space. As one student reflected, "I contextualized OWS with the struggles of other political and social activists in the distant and near past, drew inspiration from another topic . . . and focused in on music-creation software to create my own form of musical activism". Together with the students, we re-defined classroom space, moving from an institutionalized and authoritative space with set boundaries to a space where music and discussion emerged in a grassroots and bottom-up manner.

OWS: Reclaiming contested space

OWS provided a fertile external context for students to discuss and participate in music-making inside and outside the classroom. It demonstrated a complex relationship to space that parallels the authors' exploration of space in the classroom. Furthermore, the participatory elements used music performance in ways that engaged students' imaginations. OWS manifested in different locations across the United States and online, and participants rallied around various and often apparently unrelated aims. Even the genesis of OWS is diffuse.[13] Many accounts recall that *Adbusters* magazine called for people to occupy space in lower Manhattan on 17 September, 2011. Described as a "shift in revolutionary tactics", the call cited protests in Spain and Egypt and invited "various physical gatherings and virtual people's assemblies" in order to make demands against Wall Street (*Adbusters*, 2011). Activities in response to rising social inequality had already started in other areas, including among a group of artists, theorists and activists who had been meeting even before the *Adbusters* call and were prepared for gathering in a public space by the time the call was issued in September (Rosler, 2012). But what were the goals of these constituencies?

Loosely, the OWS protests arose as a response to growing economic inequality in the United States following the financial crash of 2008. The first street-based protest occurred in September of 2011. This was precipitated by the influential "Arab Spring" events, in which groups of citizens organized in public to argue for social and political change (Fusco, 2012). Images of protests in Europe, broadcast around the world, brought discussions around economic justice to the fore. Concerns around economic access, democracy and freedom from police control were expressed in these movements (Calhoun, 2013, p. 28). As protests developed, they enlarged to included participants of diverse ideologies and goals.[14]

---

13 For example, some sources credit the *Adbusters* call as the movement's spark, while others reference organizing that pre-dated this (see Rosler, 2012; Fusco, 2012; *Adbusters*, 2011).

14 While many groups sprang up without official leaders, OWS came to have specific sources and voices associated with it. The website Occupywallstreet.org offers one history of the movement,

Claiming space on Wall Street was a way for participants to call attention to unequal economic systems and argue for change. In OWS, as in the Arab Spring and European protests, young adults were central. Many of these individuals revealed their struggles to find a place as adults in precarious economic and political conditions (Beard, 2012). These young people sought to enact major reforms: "The generation that is driving the movement has redefined politics and called into question core social values and economic injustices. Their proposal is not to simply right wrongs, but to transform" (Sgambati, 2012, p. 7). Physical encampments emerged across the US in the autumn of 2011, spreading from New York. Participants shared information about events, news and conversation online and through physical events including the Global Occupy Day and Global Day of Action.[15]

OWS caught students' attention immediately. Events from across the country were in the news, and a local OWS presence had grown in our city.[16] Members organized marches, played drums and shared signs in the streets and maintained a physical presence in the downtown financial district.[17] The professors invited a musician who composed music for and about OWS as a guest speaker. This musician described to students how he negotiated the multiple spaces he was involved with as a musician within the movement. As a singer-songwriter, he composed songs based on the movement and shared them online. At the same time, he was involved with the movement by physically participating in demonstrations at physical OWS sites, sharing knowledge at open learning events called teach-ins and collaborating on other musical projects with OWS musicians.[18]

As OWS was inspired by larger global movements to claim space in public, it demonstrated groups struggling to become manifestations of publics and to speak to social inequalities. Occupy has been praised for creating a "new relationship to the political" (Deutsche, 2012, p. 42). As OWS participant Yotam Marom remarked, "something has been opened up, a kind of space nobody knew existed" (Gitlin, 2012, p. 4). In the OWS camps, spaces emerged for sharing food, for making music and for discussions. On Wall Street, "hundreds stayed every night for two months and created an encampment in the park, a model that was adopted by people all over the country as the movement spread to well over 500 cities" (#Occupytogether). Describing the OWS spaces, a New Yorker says that there are "'mic checks'

---

saying that it "has spread to over 100 cities in the United States and actions in over 1,500 cities globally" (OccupyWallStreet, 2014). #Occupytogether focuses on the start of OWS in lower Manhattan, the wide geographic spread afterwards and the centrality of economic concerns to the movement. Its website states, "Organized in over 100 cities in the United States, #occupy aims to fight back against the system that has allowed the rich to get richer and the poor to get poorer" (#Occupytogether).

15 These were held 15 October 2011 and 17 November 2011, respectively.
16 Occupy Chicago began in September 2011.
17 https://www.facebook.com/OccupyChicago.
18 These participatory events are an organizing strategy in which participants learn and share information about a topic related to the political issue at hand. While they vary in structure, the focus is on learning together in an open and non-judgmental fashion.

where one person talks and everyone repeats, and then everyone behind everyone repeats, so everyone can hear. It's pretty powerful" (Albu, 2011).

While protesters rallied with cries including "Whose streets? Our streets!" the ownership of space was actively being contested. In Chicago, officials and citizens debated whether or not protesters could congregate in Grant Park. Located in downtown Chicago, Grant Park is city-owned, so some citizens claimed the space as their own. Yet protesters who stayed in the park overnight were arrested, as police claimed this "public" space was not actually "theirs" (Huffington Post, 2011). In New York, the status of Zucotti Park was similarly under discussion. One participant remarked that the park "belongs to the owner of One Liberty Plaza (the 1%!) but he made a deal with the city to open it up for 'public use' if they could build the buildings up to a certain height". Rights of access to public spaces were "a very grey area" (Albu, 2011). OWS protestors occupied a park that was managed by a private company "to reflect the ongoing intentions of the movement as reclaiming – not merely protesting – unequal economic structure" (Schmidt & Babits, 2014, p. 85). Protesters proudly transformed space for communal meals and conversations, teach-ins and political organizing. The space used bottom-up organizing practices, like general assemblies, to try out dialogue that could be "exemplars of substantive democratic voice and interaction" (p. 85). Crucially, OWS occurred when official public spaces had been diminished in size and number and were being increasingly monitored (Calhoun, 2013, p. 29). Unlike previous protests, in which marchers arrived with signs and drums, chanted in streets and then left after making their statements, OWS produced long-term encampments; "Claiming a common space in violation of the rule of property" was "in no way secondary to the exigencies of protest" (Mansoor et al., 2012, p. 49). Rather than protesting and then returning home, taking over space was a primary goal.

Physical presence in city centres helped OWS participants interact with space differently than previous movements and demonstrate a new relationship with performance. These manifestations played a role as public art: "When #OWS seized the park for an active use – critical speech – it not only contested an existing public space but also produced a public space, in the sense of a democratic public sphere" (Deutsche, 2012, p. 43). Unlike some previous movements, there was something strange and original about OWS (Gitlin, 2012, p. xiv) – puppets, dance, costumes, drums and a human microphone were central to it. People sang, played fiddles and drums, shouted and engaged in performance art in large-scale events. A variety of performance techniques made OWS physical presences "like 1960s street theatre" (Calhoun, 2013, p. 37).

As sound, movement and creativity played out in OWS gatherings, students of popular music found them to be fascinating spaces in which to learn and improvise. In our course, when moving from the classroom into the composition lab, students improvised and created their own musical pieces with a sense of play similar to that of OWS. For example, one student used a speech made by an OWS participant. She explained that "like many political speeches, I think being present in the actual movement adds to the power of the speech". Creating a collage of different voices, she also cited another participant, who suggested that "love is the key to fixing the problem". The student used diverse audio samples and musical contrast. Reflecting on the process, she explains that this "highlights how much variety in opinion" is present among OWS participants. She combined a personal musical voice with the voices of ordinary people, thus creating music that conveyed multiple perspectives of those "who the movement is supposed to represent".

De-institutionalizing space through popular music

Acknowledging the complexities of bringing an anti-establishment movement into an establishment setting created an opportunity for challenging dominant discourses of power and space, recalling Lefebvre's (1974/1991, p. 33) third concept of representational space, where students create their own meaning and understanding of music and politics. In this course, the concept and practice of popular music worked hand-in-hand with OWS, where the students moved in and out of the academic setting, each type and location of experience enhancing the others. Academic spaces became active parts of a dialogue that integrated institutional and non-institutional domains and encouraged students to create multiple narratives.

Learners actively claimed the space. Interacting with OWS and its musical practices, students took ownership of their musical activities inside and outside of the classroom space. For example, one student noted that this learning experience continued be an influence after graduation:

> Post-graduation I moved to New York to write about music, DIY music in particular, which has always been intrinsically linked to protest and politics. From anti-consumerist punk revivalists to bedroom electronic production, I'm surrounded by a very politically active circle of friends, many of whom were involved in Occupy Wall Street and continue to participate in very similar events.

Echoing Lefebvre's spatial triad, the classroom space in this respect is a representational space where the space is perceived "as directly *lived* through its associated images and symbols" (Lefebvre, 1974/1991, p. 39). It transforms into a spatial practice through which dialectical and dialogical communication are generated "slowly and surely as it masters and appropriates" and decrypts the space (p. 38). The aforementioned student, a journalism major without prior musical education, subsequent to graduation moved to New York City as a freelance journalist to encourage the younger generation to be more involved in their community through popular music-making. By implementing how popular musicians learn (Green, 2001) through collaborative and DIY approaches, students took responsibility for their own learning and created spaces that, as Rosler (2012) discusses regarding OWS activists, could enable them to take their futures into their own hands. Reflecting on the impact of composing a piece of music for class, a student noted:

> I feel like it gave me a lot of insight into the process of sonic creation and how it's so easy today to make something on GarageBand, upload it to YouTube

and see it go viral. I guess I just found the egalitarian nature of this all really interesting, which is probably why I actually write about DIY electronic production now.

In ways similar to occupiers in OWS, the students in our course changed a uniform abstract space into one that was lived through and contextualized towards each student. This participatory action shifted away from authoritative space in which professors would maintain power over all classroom activities. In this new space the students became agents of their own learning through the use of various kinds of space. For example, a student who used OWS during the musical project became engaged in political activism through technology and alternative spaces, reflecting,

> I've found it interesting that technology has been in revitalizing these kinds of movements, especially since there's such a problem of apathy among many of my peers. It's incredible how much access technology affords us and how that was a really important component of this class.

Learning about OWS through making popular music and learning about the music that was part of the movement, students were encouraged to explore various spaces and use sounds gathered in them. For example, two of the students in the course decided to collaboratively create music on OWS. They used a speech by an OWS protester made while the crowd was chanting, "We are the 99%". Further, they note:

The final sound of the aerosol can indexes the infamous pepper spraying of protesters at UC Davis.[19] This sound effect also silences the chants and, along with the sirens used in the piece, represents the brutal actions of oppressive authoritative police forces. Pepper spray, tear gas, rubber bullets – these are all examples of unacceptable violence in reaction to civil disobedience.

The course also provided room for students to work in a participatory manner, discussing and refining their music organically in an interactional space, similar to OWS activists. Called a leaderless (but leader-full) movement (OccupyWallStreet, 2014), students worked in similar fashion. One student recalled:

> I feel like I definitely got a better grasp on how powerful creative dissemination can actually be. Or how much easier it is to relay a message when it's presented in a way people can understand and adhere to a concept in a broader, more universal sense. After all, music is the great unifier and a wonderful way to spread a message.

By making their own pieces of music, students improvised, played with sound and created songs that spoke to issues that were important to them.

---

19 At a non-violent protest at the University of California, Davis, on November, 18, 2011, campus police used pepper spray against student protesters. This event attracted significant media attention, particularly an image of a uniformed officer spraying students seated on the ground.

Implications for teaching in the academy

Synthesizing how students became involved with ideas from OWS inside and outside of the classroom, it is possible to interpolate the possibilities and limitations of academia's prospective role in both popular music-making scenes and political events. By incorporating a composition assignment in a music class for non-majors, this course taught music fundamentals in context. Connecting to social events in which students were already interested – the OWS movement – helped students learn about the improvisatory and collaborative nature of popular music-making. Learners further explored creative tactics OWS participants used outside of the classroom space. Students of diverse backgrounds, whether specializing in music or not, could benefit from being invited to listen critically to music they already enjoy and to make their own songs.

Popular music helped re-define the learning space through references to OWS. Students took ownership of their learning, made their own musical choices and political decisions in multiple learning spaces and collaborated when creating music. This provided opportunities to go beyond the traditional university classroom space and bring in constructive aspects of bottom-up approaches that occur in unofficial spaces. Outcomes of this course extend beyond it;[20] as one student reflected, "The class resonated most with me because of [the professors'] urging that we continue to explore other manifestations of music and politics interacting, specifically with respect to significant historical and current events".

We took care to access both materials and spaces outside of the official classroom and geared them towards our students' learning goals. Professors can employ flexible methods like popular music composition and re-examining students' learning habits in order to create multiple spaces for learners to connect activities outside class with those inside the classroom space. Power hierarchies can blur when students go in and out of various sonic spaces, creating potential for personal and social transformation (Lynch, Crean & Moran, 2010). Popular music courses can offer tools to help students grow beyond the confines of the classroom and make their own meanings and sense of space; one student who had been DJing only in a dorm room felt confident to bring this music out of personal space and into nightclub space after taking the course. Another student took this course as an inspiration to think differently about future career options in the realm of finance, "as many of the job opportunities [the student] was pursuing involved dabbling in the financial products specifically cited as catalysts for systemic failure and macroeconomic depression in the US and abroad".

Responding to different ways of using space, teachers can create interactional space (Lim et al., 2012) based on dialogue and fluidity, so that students easily move in and out of official space while taking charge of their own learning. The physical classroom space, though significant in many ways, is not the sole space where learners communicate with one another and learn about course-related topics. Students outside of the official learning environs, as Lefebvre explains, actively

---

20 These include ongoing engagement with community music.

produce their own learning spaces and have control and ownership of their activities. Incorporating multiple learning spaces in popular music education can thus allow professors and students to co-facilitate learning in and outside the classroom, preparing them to engage critically with music they enjoy long after the class ends.

References

Adbusters. (2011). The joyous freedom of possibility. Retrieved from: https://www.adbusters.org/campaigns/occupywallstreet [Accessed 5 October 2014].
Albu, R. (2011). Personal communication with author. 24 October.
Beard, T. (2012). Occupy response. *October, 142*, 35–36.
Calhoun, C. (2013). Occupy Wall Street in perspective. *The British Journal of Sociology, 64*(1), 26–38.
Cobb, D. & L. Fowler. (2007). *Beyond Red Power: American Indian politics and activism since 1900*. Santa Fe: School for Advanced Research Press.
Deutsche, R. (2012). Occupy response. *October, 142*, 42–43.
Fusco, C. (2012). Occupy response. *October, 142*, 46–47.
Gitlin, T. (2012). *Occupy nation, the roots: The spirit and the promise of Occupy Wall Street*. New York, NY: Harper Collins Publishers.
Green, L. (2001). *How popular musicians learn: A way ahead for music education*. Aldershot, UK: Ashgate.
Huffington Post. (2011). 175 Occupy Chicago protestors arrested in Grant Park Campout. NBC Chicago, Retrieved from: http://www.huffingtonpost.com/2011/10/16/175-occupy-chicago-protes_n_1014046.html [Accessed 8 September 2014].
La Roux. (2009). In for the kill. On *In for the kill* [Digital Download]. London, UK: Polydor.
Lefebvre, H. (1974/1991). *The production of space*. Oxford: Blackwell Publishing.
Lim, F.V., O'Halloran, K.L., & Podlasov, A. (2012). Spatial pedagogy: Mapping meanings in the use of classroom space. *Cambridge Journal of Education, 42*(2), 235–251.
Lynch, K., Crean, M., & Moran, M. (Eds.) (2010). Equality and social justice: The university as a site of struggle. In M.W. Apple, S.J. Ball & L.A. Gandin (Eds.), *The Routledge international handbook of the sociology of education* (296–305). New York, NY: Routledge.
Mansoor, J., Marcus, D., & Spaulding, D. (2012). Occupy response. *October, 142*, 48–50.
McGregor, J. (2004). Editorial. *Forum, 46*(1), 2–5.
OccupyWallStreet. (2014). About. Retrieved from: http://occupywallst.org/about/ [Accessed 4 September 2014].
Rosler, M. (2012). Occupy response. *October, 142*, 59–61.
Schmidt, S. J, & Babits, C. (2014). Occupy Wall Street as a curriculum of space. *The Journal of Social Studies Research, 38*, 79–89.
Sgambati, A. (2012). A photo essay of Occupy Wall Street, New York City, 2011. *Dialectical Anthropology, 36*(1/2), 7–20.
Smith, G.D. & Shafighian, A. (2013). Creative space and the "silent power of traditions" in popular music performance programmes. In P. Burnard (Ed.), *Developing creativities in higher music education: International perspectives and practices*. Oxford: Oxford University Press.
Smith, P.C. & Warrior, R.A. (1996). *Like a hurricane: The Indian movement from Alcatraz to Wounded Knee*. New York, NY: The New Press.
Strange, C. & Loo, T. (2001). Holding the rock: The 'Indianization' of Alcatraz Island, 1969–1999. *The Public Historian, 23*(1), 55–74.
Turino, T. (2008). *Music as social life: The politics of participation*. Chicago: University of Chicago Press.

33
Popular music education, participation and democracy
Some Nordic perspectives

Catharina Christophersen and Anna-Karin Gullberg

Introduction

Popular music has a relatively long history and a strong position in Nordic music education. It has been a part of Nordic music education practices for decades (Karlsen & Väkevä, 2012), and some consider the Nordic region[1] as the most advanced in the field of popular music pedagogy (Hebert, 2011). Popular music is integrated in Nordic compulsory school curricula, as well as in higher music education, and could be said to enjoy a privileged position in music education. Lucy Green's work (2002, 2009, 2014) has been seminal in the academic debate of popular music education, but it is worth noting that Nordic scholars have also published frequently in this area (e.g. Björck, 2011; Christophersen, 2009; Folkestad, 2006; Gullberg, 2010, 2002; Johansson, 2002; Lindgren & Ericsson, 2010; Onsrud, 2013; Partti, 2012; Snell & Söderman, 2014; Tønsberg, 2007; Väkevä, 2010, 2006; Westerlund, 2006). Popular music's position in Nordic music education provides a solid basis for a critical perspective on popular music education practices.

Reasons for inclusion of popular music in education are often based on more or less explicitly articulated ideals of cultural and educational democracy. Assuming a connection between popular music education and democracy raises questions. For example, much academic literature seems to conflate popular music with informal music-making practices like the garage band, and thereby overlooks more

---

1 The Nordic region consists of Norway, Sweden, Denmark, Iceland and Finland, as well as several autonomous areas. 'Scandinavian' is often used interchangeably with 'Nordic' in international contexts; however, the Scandinavian countries consist of only Norway, Sweden and Denmark. These three countries have mutually intelligible languages, while Finnish and Icelandic are different from the Scandinavian languages. Communication in Nordic contexts is therefore most often carried out in English.

contemporary popular music genres and other ways of popular music-making. One could then ask what 'popular music' refers to and what notions of democracy are invoked in debates on popular music education: Are all kinds of popular music included, or are some musics more 'suitable' than others, and who decides? Some Nordic higher education institutions accommodate students' learning in a way that is heavily influenced by popular musicianship, but does that necessarily mean that classes or the education itself are 'democratic'?

Against a background of such questions, we discuss popular music education in relation to ideas of cultural and educational democracy. Drawing upon Gert Biesta's (2006) notion of democratic education, we will focus on issues of diversity in repertoire and musical genres and on popular music's alleged inherent potential for democratic learning. The starting point is a brief overview of the historical, cultural and ideological foundations of the inclusion of popular music in Nordic educational practices; these foundations are closely related to Nordic ideals of equality, participation and democracy.

Popular music, popular culture, democracy and education

'Popular music'[2] and its relation to education and democracy will vary depending on how these concepts are interpreted. The inclusion of popular music in education is closely linked to ideals of cultural democracy: music education should include various musical styles, and thus mirror the cultural and musical diversity in society. Popular music is encompassed by the broader notion of popular culture. Certain questions have been raised when popular cultural expressions encounter the educational system, and debates about popular culture are in many cases almost invariably related to criteria for 'good' and 'worthy' artistic expressions, and thus to issues of cultural taste and social class (Dolby, 2003, p. 260). While some consider popular culture problematic in relation to education, others recognize popular culture as an important site for discussions and negotiations of meaning, and therefore also as an important pedagogical site, especially for young people. Popular culture could be perceived as especially significant because of its potential contribution to social change and democratization, not only in the form of justice and equality, but also in the form of agency and citizenship, as a site "where youth are invested, where things happen, where identities and democratic possibilities are worked out, performed, and negotiated" (Dolby, 2003, p. 276).

Within popular music pedagogy, similar arguments have been made regarding the creation of meaning for young people (Powell et al., in press). Popular music is, then, considered as more or less synonymous with music that students consider to be relevant and 'theirs'. For example, Green writes, "the school classroom is a notorious site for the entanglement of musical meanings, values and experiences.

---

2 In the Nordic countries, 'Afro-American music' and 'rhythmic music' are sometimes used interchangeably with 'popular music', and denote different kinds of groove-based music (Danielsen, 2002).

Perhaps this is particularly so in relation to pupils 'own' music – the popular field" (Green, 2006, p. 101). These claims are based on Green's research on rock musicians (2002), thus not taking into account more contemporary forms of popular music and musicianship, such as hip-hop, electronica, digital musicianship and production. Still, Green has been an eager advocate for the inclusion of popular music in schools, claiming that popular music provides experiences that are more relevant to young people's lives than classical music and that it can be a springboard to an expansion of their musical repertoire and engagement with music-making (Green, 2006, p. 115). A related point is the perception of popular music as being closely linked to democratic visions of music education. The traditional 'garage band' has regularly been referred to as a promising point of departure for a development towards a more open, collaborative and non-hierarchical pedagogical situation. Randall Allsup (2011), for example, regards classroom 'garage' bands as holding democratic potential because they "must work across differences and conflicts, learning from the talents and shortcomings of those who make up one's group, teaching what one does well to others, sharing leadership and followership, and composing music that reflects the makeup of one's group" (p. 31). Issues of democracy and participation in relation to popular music education could, as we have argued above, be linked to fundamental ideals of musical and cultural diversity, participation and democratic learning. These ideals correspond with Nordic cultural and educational ideals of equality, participation and democracy.

Culture and education for all

Although there are five independent Nordic countries with their own cultures and histories, there are marked similarities between them, and there has been considerable political and cultural collaboration. Scholars have argued that there are, in fact, such things as a "Nordic education model" (Frimansson, 2006) and a "Nordic cultural policy" (Duelund, 2008). Both models are closely connected to the development of Nordic welfare states following World War II, in which states assumed responsibility for their citizens' cultural lives and education (Blossing, Imsen & Moos, 2014).

The Nordic education model is based on an egalitarian philosophy and the state's perceived duty to provide equal opportunities for all citizens. Education for all was important when modern Nordic democracies took shape after the fall of political elites in the 19th century. The new democracies' strength was considered to be dependent upon the participation of "the people" and an idea of a "common culture" (Korsgaard & Wiborg, 2006, p. 362), which included education and enlightenment, and thus also empowerment, of the working class. These ideas gave rise to vernacular educational movements aiming at education for all, often executed within alternative arenas such as the "folk high school" or adult study circles (Larsson, 2007; Tøsse, 2004). According to Snell and Söderman (2014, p. 154), these educational ideas were "regarded as crucial to every human being's liberation, regardless of tradition, class and place in society". These Nordic democratic traditions have influenced music education. For example, in Denmark, popular music study circles were originally funded as adult education study circles, which helped establish popular music as a cultural political category in need of funding, and this led to the establishment of educational institutions (Brinck, 2014; Christophersen, 2009).

The inclusion of popular music in cultural and educational policies was connected to a cultural turn. After World War II, Nordic cultural policies[3] were developed to fight against "the damaging consequences of the commercial cultural industries" (Duelund, 2008, p. 14). Therefore, both arts in general and individual artists were supported. Fine arts and cultural expressions were made accessible to 'the people' through touring companies and itinerant exhibitions. From the 1970s onward, the state support of fine arts in Nordic cultural policies was maintained, but a broader concept of culture was adopted, one "which included amateur activities, a new focus on local initiatives and ideas of participation" (Duelund, 2008, pp. 15–16). This was a strategy to increase *cultural democracy*, and a wide variety of cultural expressions were recognized as valuable and worthy of funding (Mangset, Kangas, Skot-Hansen, & Vestheim, 2008). The political and financial support for diverse cultural expressions also benefited popular music. In this period popular music also started to appear in education and in national curricula in the Nordic countries (Georgii-Hemming & Westvall, 2012; Väkevä, 2006; Olsson, 1993).

Nordic educational values are, generally speaking, those of democracy, equality, progressiveness and pragmatism (Antikainen, 2006). These values acknowledge children as participants in a democratic society, and thus imply a progressive, student-centred approach to education in general, as well as to music education (Heimonen, 2006). As Sidsel Karlsen (2012) writes, students' experiences of music and music education are considered as points of departure to "provide meaningful and student-centred music education" (p. 132) in the Nordic countries. Add to this the previously mentioned frequent perception of popular music as students' 'own' music, the inclusion of popular music in Nordic music curricula is both logical and inevitable.

Popular music in Nordic music education

Strong democratic ideals appear to have contributed to the widespread acceptance and inclusion of popular music in the Nordic educational systems. According to Väkevä (2006), popular music was included in Finnish education without much reflection on pedagogical implications: "Its inclusion was based more on the pragmatic and democratic ideas of contemporary educational theory, recognizing the need to utilize students' own musical habitats as the point of departure" (p. 127). This is probably an accurate description of the rationale of much Nordic popular music education. There are some exceptions, such as the so-called rhythmic

---

3 The Nordic countries' historical backgrounds are different, and thus the national cultural policies were developed along different paths. Nonetheless, the development of cultural policies followed more or less the same direction after World War II (Duelund, 2008).

music education in Denmark, which is an oral approach to music education based on rhythm, movement, improvisation and interaction (Christophersen, 2009). The origins of rhythmic music teaching can be traced back to a cultural leftist movement in the 1930s (Michelsen, 2001), whose ideals of free, authentic, creative and playful human beings inspired a music education based on children's play and on jazz music of that time. Similar 'rhythmic' approaches to teaching have been increasingly important in Norwegian schools and teacher education.

The national music curricula throughout the Nordic region are wide-ranging, and music genres are generally not specified for activities in schools. Popular music is mentioned specifically only once in the Norwegian curriculum: one of four goals included under the heading "playing music" for grades 8–10 (ages 14–16) states that students should "rehearse and perform a repertoire of music and dance from different genres, with an emphasis on rhythmic music" (The Norwegian Directorate for Education and Training, 2006). In fact, Nordic curricula seldom specify genres, and if they do a variety are mentioned; for example, the Swedish curriculum specifies that 4th–6th graders (ages 11–13) have to learn about "art music, folk music and popular music from different cultures and their musical characteristics" (National Agency for Education, 2011).

Despite the fact that popular music is seldom mentioned in the curricula, the so-called garage band model seems to dominate in Nordic music education. According to Lindgren and Ericsson (2010, p. 36), "Swedish music education is dominated today by singing and playing in pop and rock bands, while Western classical music, jazz, folk music, and music from other cultures are only marginally represented". Westerlund (2006) describes a similar situation in Finland, where "microphones, drums, electric bass and guitars are the most common types of instruments in music classes" (p. 119). This emphasis on popular music predominates in all Nordic countries, with the exception of Iceland, where popular music is taught in schools but is not as dominant. This may be attributed to the fact that music is mostly taught in lower grades in Iceland, whereas other Nordic countries emphasize music education in teenage years (Gudmundsdottir, 2013).

The integration of popular music in Nordic higher music education has been slower than in compulsory education (Karlsen & Väkevä, 2012). Nevertheless, popular music programmes and courses are offered at most conservatories and universities. Indeed, the institutionalization of popular music in conservatories and the academization of popular music have meant that classical music has lost its hegemony in higher education, including teacher education (Dyndahl & Nielsen, 2014, p. 106). For example, a basic proficiency in playing electric and digital instruments, as well as in using music technology, is a common requirement in much of Nordic teacher education.

Discussing democracy and participation in popular music education

The inclusion of popular music in education could generally be seen as deriving from democratic ideals. According to Biesta, "Any discussion about democracy raises questions about its definition" (2006, p. 121). He challenges the understanding of democratic education as "'the production' of the democratic person" (p. 120). Instead, education should provide a space for subjects to act in relation to other subjects. A democratic education must, accordingly, allow for plurality and differences. Biesta therefore also indirectly challenges a consensual notion of democracy, which emphasizes sameness and agreement. Inspired by this notion of democracy, the guiding questions for our further discussion of popular music education, democracy and participation are related to how popular music education can make allowances for plurality, difference and (inter)action. This discussion will be structured around the themes of diversity in repertoire and popular music's alleged inherent potential for democratic learning.

Diversity in repertoire

Music's relevance for students' everyday lives is often emphasized when including popular music in education, and selecting students' 'own' music as educational content can thus be seen as twofold: contributing to both cultural democracy and educational democracy by increasing students' influence over their own education. This argument is based on assumptions about popular music, and about children's and adolescents' musical preferences and identities, which call for discussion (Powell et al., 2016).

First, this argument does not take into account the cultural lag of educational institutions. Contemporary cultural expressions are fluid, and students only spend a limited amount of time within educational institutions. If institutions should include students' own music in the curriculum, this logically implies a state of constant institutional flux, a frequent change of musical repertoire and/or more focus on creative processes and digital music production. However, educational institutions are slow by nature; it is unlikely that they would be able to keep up with rapid cultural changes, so teacher competence, curricula and equipment will thus inevitably lag. In other words, the fluid nature of popular music represents a problem for music education (Smith, 2014, p. 37), and this is evident in Nordic schools: "Although many of the school music programs in these countries [Sweden, Finland, Norway] focus on teaching popular music, most concentrate on more out-dated subgenres like rock and roll or classic rock" (Snell & Söderman, 2014, p. 166). Thus, the popular music most frequently used in schools is probably closer to being the teachers' music than the students' 'own' music. Second, the lengthy Nordic experiences with popular music in education suggest that the assumed musical diversity does not necessarily occur, even if popular music is included in education (Dyndahl & Nielsen, 2014), and that certain popular music styles have more or less displaced other musical expressions, such as Western classical music, folk music, world music, etc. (Georgii-Hemming & Westvall, 2012).

Third, although popular music is common in Nordic education, not all popular music styles are represented. There could be several reasons for this. One is that some types of music are easier to play and sing than others, and therefore better suited for students with limited technical skills. Another reason is that some types of music may be censored from educational contexts (Kallio, 2014; Parkinson, chapter 30, this volume) by teachers due to, for example, fear of parental reactions to offensive language, discriminatory texts, references to alternative lifestyles and life choices or strong political views. Some musics may be altered, toned down or softened, in an effort to make the musical expression more 'appropriate' or 'acceptable', which again could signal a lack of tradition or competence when it comes to articulating and discussing aesthetic issues in popular music education (Gullberg, 2002). Other types of popular music could be excluded on the basis of established taste hierarchies; while cultural political struggles may have contributed to a greater degree of equality between classical and popular music, there are still taste hierarchies within the popular music genres in education. For example, according to Dyndahl et al. (2014, p. 55), "genres such as heavy metal and country music (also) appear as relatively reviled". The basis for exclusion of music styles is not just musical, and, according to Wayne Bowman, "our exclusions, then, are always exclusions of people" (2007, p. 118). As a result, exclusions affect individuals' space for action, in this case musical action, which, according to Biesta (2006), is a requirement for democratic learning. Consequently, seemingly simple questions about preference are potentially linked to larger political issues of equity and justice, and hence to issues of democracy.

Music can serve diverse purposes in individuals' lives: passing time, self-care, emotional self-regulation, bonding with peers, etc. (Bonde, Ruud, Skånland & Trondalen, 2013). Contemporary technology gives access to a wide array of musical styles, and mobile music devices enable individual listening experiences. Thus, equating popular music with students' 'own' music, especially if it conflates popular music with the somewhat hackneyed concept of the garage band, is problematic. Not only does this conceptualization of 'own music' perhaps fail to take into account that adolescent individuals are different, it also overlooks contextual dimensions like gender and socio-economic status that would probably be taken into account in a discussion of adults' music preferences. Studies of popular music education suggest that popular music preferences and practices are gendered, and that scholars frequently overlook this gendering (Abramo, 2011; Björck, 2011). It is important, therefore, to ask whether repertoires of formal music education are sometimes shaped by clichés regarding youth culture and music preferences and, further, whether these contribute to limiting rather than expanding possible repertoires.

Popular music and democratic learning

Discussions of popular music's democratic potential in education must include considerations of popular music *pedagogy*. According to Green (2006), popular music's inherent, that is inter-sonic, meaning[4] must influence the way it is learned

---

4 For a more detailed discussion about popular music's inherent musical and aesthetic qualities, see for example Danielsen (2002) or Frith (2007).

and taught, and her research on rock musicians' learning processes (2002, 2009, 2014) implies that popular music pedagogy is linked to informal learning styles. The characteristics of such learning processes are, as exemplified in the garage band, aural, collaborative and self-directed within peer groups. Participants decide what they want to play, and how they would like to work in order to learn the music of their choice. Consequently, teachers must step back and leave a great deal of the responsibility to students. Due to the absence of a pedagogical adapted progression, informal learning will inevitably be more personal and haphazard than in more formal settings (Green, 2006).

Of particular interest here is the Swedish BoomTown Music Education (BTME) community, which represents a practical realization of the informal learning ideals outlined above. BTME is an undergraduate, self-governed, process-oriented popular music education project within a music business context, which welcomes existing bands as well as single musicians as students. The programme's scholarly roots are research studies which noted that the aural and informal learning processes of successful rock and pop musicians were not recognized and utilized by higher music education (Gullberg, 2002; Johansson, 2002). Diversity and plurality in music genres, along with learning strategies and artistic intents, are at core of BTME, and student musicians are encouraged to formulate, negotiate and assess their personal and collective musical goals. This way of organizing education can, however, be demanding for teachers who tend to conform to traditional educational concepts and principles (Gullberg, 2010, p. 8).

Returning to the issue of popular music learning as a possible site for democratic learning, according to Biesta, the most important question regarding democracy in education is whether it is possible for students to be democratic persons in schools (2006, p. 138), or, in this context: Is it possible for students to be democratic individuals in institutional popular music education settings? Could students bring their initiatives into such musical learning processes and still make room for other students' ideas? Drawing on Lee Higgins' (2012) concept of hospitality in music, one could rephrase the question: Are students *welcome* to participate and contribute musically?

There is undoubtedly potential for student exposure to difference and plurality through popular music informal learning practices; the awareness of different interpretational perspectives could very well develop in informal musical interaction with others, along with the insight that one's own views are open to negotiation and reformulation. Informal educational practices also require a retracted teacher role, decentring of expert authority and potential empowerment of students regarding their own learning (Folkestad, 2006). Informal learning practices could thus have potential for democratic learning, according to Biesta.

We would, however, point out a tendency to emphasize dialogue and consensus in discourses on informal learning, thereby ignoring tensions and conflicts. Consensus is important and necessary in collaborative environments, such as in BTME when band members have to agree on major goals for an activity, but an emphasis on consensus may obscure or even repress tension and conflicts in negotiation processes. Conflicting perceptions may thus not be considered as serious alternatives or sources of potential development, but rather as difficulties to be smoothed over. If plurality and diversity are indeed preconditions for democratic learning, as Biesta (2006) suggests, it would be essential to actively seek out disagreement and conflicting standpoints. One could, however, ask how much diversity it is realistic to expect in popular music education settings in schools. Nordic ideals of education for all imply an inherent diversity in educational settings. Even so, students are required to participate in educational forms like the study group, the lecture or the garage band, all of which require certain modes of participation. These educational forms imply a cultural formation in which students' practical sense (Bourdieu, 1990), the sense of what is considered right, important and appropriate, is shaped in order to ensure 'correct' participation. It could, for example, be considered inappropriate to insist on using sheet music in a 'proper' garage band. Herein lies the cunning of pedagogic reason: "It manages to extort what is essential while seeming to demand the insignificant" (Bourdieu, 1990, p. 69). Such aspects of "pedagogic authority" (Bourdieu & Passeron, 1977) will actively work against pluralism and diversity by promoting 'proper' participatory behaviour and repressing 'wrong' behaviour, thereby reducing tensions and resistance.

Mechanisms for promoting homogenous behaviour are obvious in higher music education. Conservatories and schools of music could in some ways be considered the opposite of pluralistic, considering that their purpose is actually *not* to promote musical diversity. Rather, such institutions are intended to support, even conserve (as implied by the word 'conservatory'), particular genres, instruments or methods (Allsup, 2012; Johansson, 2002; Kingsbury, 1998). Such institutions will probably attract students and staff with dispositions towards the particular music(s) offered in particular institutions, thereby sustaining homogenous musical and educational cultures (Christophersen, 2009). Issues of democratic learning, interpreted through concepts of plurality and diversity, are therefore also connected to recruitment of music teachers and educators: "How diverse and pluralistic music education is, or can be, is a direct function of the diversity and pluralism of our membership, our musical practices, and their attendant curricula" (Bowman, 2007, p. 119). Educators thus play a crucial role in implementing popular music practices that allow for pluralism, diversity and democratic learning.

Reflections on future developments

Popular music is often linked to ideals of democracy and participation, and this chapter has provided a discussion of such ideals from a Nordic perspective. Popular music is well integrated in Nordic music education, but there are still ongoing debates concerning popular music education's legitimization in other parts of the world, such as Brazil (Feichas, 2010), the USA (Hebert, 2011; Mantie, 2013), and China (Ho, 2014). The Nordic countries' long history of and experience with popular music education provides a privileged position, not only for critical discussion, but also for informed speculation about future developments.

The notion of 'popular music' may become redundant in the foreseeable future. Labelling music by genre may be educationally helpful, but it can also be perceived as limiting when it comes to creativity and musical expression (Smith & Shafighian, 2013). The 'popular music' genre notion seems to serve cultural politicians and music education scholars better than musicians and students, who generally appear quite comfortable with floating demarcations, not only between musical sub-styles, but also between artistic expressions and modes. Alternatively, the 'popular' could be connected to musical processes rather than styles. A concept of *popular musicking* ('popular' meaning vernacular or common) could be fruitful, connecting music to issues of everyday life and agency (O'Flynn, 2006), and thereby also increasing the potential for democratic learning. While having provided useful insights for music education, the formal-informal nexus appears somewhat hackneyed. A renewed vocabulary could serve the scholarly debate on popular music and education well.

The discussion of popular music, democracy and participation connects to a larger debate about one of the great democratic divides of our time – the access to digital tools, including the financial resources to acquire them and the competence to use them (Bell, 2015). History has shown that when musical instruments change, music and music education practices also change. Therefore, there is reason to believe that future developments in popular music education practices will be related to music technology: to the transition from analogue to digital musicianship or, as Väkevä (2010) writes, from the garage band to *GarageBand*. Given the availability of tools and the ability to use them, it is possible to create and play music without having undergone years of musical training. Digital tools represent democratic potential because they enable musicianship and creativity (Partti, 2012) that, more than before, are not dependent on socio-economic status and background. On the other hand, recognition of digital musicianship could signal a more individualistic approach to music education that does not necessarily allow for the confrontation and negotiation that will inevitably appear in other popular music education settings. It still remains to be seen whether digital technology in music education will actually allow for more plurality and diversity, or if it will represent another inverted hegemony.

References

Abramo, J.M. (2011). Gender differences of popular music production in secondary schools. *Journal of Research in Music Education*, 59(1), 21–43.

Allsup, R.E. (2011, March 23). Popular music and classical musicians: Strategies and perspectives. *Music Educators Journal*, 97(3) 30–34.

Allsup, R.E. (2012). Music education and human flourishing: A meditation on democratic origins. *British Journal of Music Education*, 29(2), 171–179.

Antikainen, A. (2006). In search of the Nordic model in Education. *Scandinavian Journal of Educational Research*, 50(3), 229–243.

Bell, A.P. (2015). DAW democracy? The dearth of diversity in "playing the studio". *Journal of Music, Technology and Eduacation*, 8(2), 129–146.

Biesta, G. (2006). *Beyond learning: Democratic education for a human future*. Boulder: Paradigm Publishers.

Björck, C. (2011). *Claiming space: Discourses on gender, popular music, and social change*. Gothenburg: Gothenburg University, Faculty of Fine, Applied and Performing Arts.

Blossing, U., Imsen, G., & Moos, L. (2014). *The Nordic education model: "A school for all" Encounters Neo-Liberal Policy*. Dordrecht: Springer.

Bonde, L.O., Ruud, E., Skånland, M.S., & Trondalen, G. (2013). *Musical life stories: Narratives on health musicking Norwegian academy of music*. Oslo: Center for Music and Health, Norwegian Academy of Music.

Bourdieu, P. (1990). *The logic of practice*. Oxford: Polity Press.

Bourdieu, P. & Passeron, J.C. (1977). *Reproduction in education, society and culture*. Beverly Hills, CA: Sage.

Bowman, W. (2007). Who is the "we"? Rethinking professionalism in music education. *Action, Criticism, and Theory for Music Education, 6*(4), 109–131.

Brinck, L. (2014). *Ways of the jam: Collective and improvisational perspectives on learning*. Aalborg: Dept. of Communication and Psychology, Doctoral Shool of the Humanities, Aalborg University.

Christophersen, C. (2009). *Rytmisk musikkundervisning som estetisk praksis. En casestudie*. Oslo: Norges musikkhøgskole.

Danielsen, A. (2002). Estetiske perspektiver på populærmusikk. In J. Gripsrud (Ed.), *Populærmusikken i kulturpolitikken* (pp. 129–155). Oslo: Norsk Kulturråd.

Dolby, N. (2003). Popular culture and democratic practice. *Harvard Educational Review, 73*(3), 258–284.

Duelund, P. (2008). Nordic cultural policies: A critical view. *International Journal of Cultural Policy, 14*(1), 7–24.

Dyndahl, P., Karlsen, S., Skårberg, O., & Nielsen, S.G. (2014). Cultural omnivorousness and musical gentrification: An outline of a sociological framework and its applications for music education research. *Action, Criticism, and Theory for Music Education, 13*(1), 40–69.

Dyndahl, P. & Nielsen, S.G. (2014). Shifting authenticities in Scandinavian music education. *Music Education Research, 16*(1), 105–118.

Feichas, H. (2010). Bridging the gap: Informal learning practices as a pedagogy of integration. *British Journal of Music Education, 27*(1), 47–58.

Folkestad, G. (2006). Formal and informal learning situations or practices vs formal and informal ways of learning. *British Journal of Music Education, 23*(2), 135–145.

Frimansson, G.H. (2006). Introduction: Is there a Nordic model in education? *Scandinavian Journal of Educational Research, 50*(3), 223–228.

Frith, S. (2007). *Taking popular music seriously: Selected essays*. Farnham: Ashgate.

Georgii-Hemming, E. & Westvall, M. (2012). Music education: A personal matter? Examining the current discourses of music education in Sweden. In S. Karlsen & L. Väkevä (Eds.), *Future prospects for music education* (pp. 97–116). Newcastle: Cambridge Scholars Publishing.

Green, L. (2002). *How popular musicians learn: A way ahead for music education*. Aldershot: Ashgate.

Green, L. (2014). *Hear, listen, play! How to free your students' aural, improvisation and performance skills*. Oxford: Oxford University Press.

Green, L. (2006). Popular music education in and for itself, and for "other" music: Current research in the classroom. *International Journal of Music Education, 24*(2), 101–118.

Green, L. (2009). *Music, informal learning and the school: A new classroom pedagogy*. Aldershot: Ashgate.

Gudmundsdottir, H.R. (2013). Tónmenntakennsla í íslenskum. *Uppeldi og Menntun / Icelandic Journal of Education, 22*(2), 37–54.

Gullberg, A.-K. (2002). *Skolvägen eller garagevägen. Studier av musikalisk socialisation*. Luleå: Luleå University of Technology.

Gullberg, A.-K. (2010). Music, education and innovation. In C. Ferm Thorgersen & S. Karlsen, *Music, education and innovation. Festschrift for Sture Brändström* (pp. 121–143). Luleå: Luleå University of Technology.

Hebert, D. (2011). Originality and institutionalization: Factors engendering resistance to popluar music pedagogy in the U.S.A. *Music Education Research International, 5*, 12–21.

Heimonen, M. (2006). Justifying the right to music education. *Philosophy of Music Education Review, 14*(2), 119–141.

Higgins, L. (2012). *Community music: In theory and in practice.* Oxford: Oxford University Press.

Ho, W.-C. (2014). Music education curriculum and social change: A study of popular music in secondary schools in Beijing, China. *Music Education Research, 16*(3), 267–289.

Johansson, K. (2002). *Can you hear what they're playing? A study in strategies among ear players in rock music.* Luleå University of Technology.

Kallio, A. (2014). Drawing a line in water: Constructing the school censorship frame in popular music eduation. *International Journal of Music Education.* DOI: 10.1177/0255761413515814.

Karlsen, S. (2012). Multiple repertoires of ways of being and acting in music: Immigrant students' musical agency as an impetus for democracy. *Music Education Research, 14*(2), 131–148.

Karlsen, S. & Väkevä, L. (2012). *Future prospects for music education: Corroborating informal learning pedagogy.* Newcastle upon Tyne: Cambridge Scholars Press.

Kingsbury, H. (1998). *Music, talent and performance: A conservatory cultural system.* Philadelphia, PA: Temple University Press.

Korsgaard, O. & Wiborg, S. (2006). Grundtvig – The key to Danish Eduation? *Scandinavian Journal of Educational Research, 50*(3), 361–382.

Larsson, A. (2007). *Musik, bildning, utbildning: Ideal och pracktik i folkbildninens musikpedagogiske utbildningar 1930–1978.* Göteborg/Stockholm: Makadam förlag.

Lindgren, M. & Ericsson, C. (2010). The rock band context as discursive governance in music education in Swedish schools. *Action, Criticism, & Theory for Music Education, 9*(3), 35–54.

Mangset, P., Kangas, A., Skot-Hansen, D., & Vestheim, G. (2008). Nordic cultural policy. *International Journal of Cultural Policy, 14*(1), 1–5.

Mantie, R. (2013). A comparison of "popular music pedagogy" discourses. *Journal of Research in Music Education, 6*(3), 334–352.

Michelsen, M. (2001). "Rytmisk musik" mellem høj og lav. *Musik og forskning 2001, 26,* 61–81.

National Agency for Education. (2011). *Curriculum for the compulsory school, preschool class and the recreation centre.* Stockholm: National Agency for Education.

The Norwegian Directorate for Education and Training. (2006). *Music Subject Curriculum.* Hentet fra The Knowledge Promotion – The national curriculum for primary and secondary education [Kunnskapsløftet: Læreplan for grunnskolen og videregående opplæring]. Retrieved from: http://www.udir.no/Stottemeny/English/Curriculum-in-English/Curricula-in-English/

O'Flynn, J. (2006). Vernacular music-making and education. *International Journal of Music Education, 24*(2), 140–147.

Olsson, B. (1993). *SÅMUS: En musikutbildning i kulturpolitikens tjänst? En studie om en musikutbildning på 1970-talet.* Göteborg: Göteborgs Universitet.

Onsrud, S.V. (2013). *Kjønn på spill, kjønn i spill: En studie av ungdomsskoleelevers musisering.* Bergen: Universitetet i Bergen.

Partti, H. (2012). *Learning from cosmopolitan digitial musicians.* Espoo: Sibelius Academy.

Powell, B., Smith, G.D., & D'Amore, A. (in press). Challenging symbolic violence and hegemony in music education through contemporary pedagogical approaches. *Education 3–13*.

Smith, G.D. (2014). Popular music in higher education. In I. Papageorgi & G. Welch (Eds.), *Advanced musical performance: Investigations in higher education learning* (pp. 33–37). Farnham: Ashgate.

Smith, G.D. & Shafighian, A. (2013). Creative space and the "silent power of traditions" in popular music performance programmes. In P. Burnard (Ed.), *Developing creativities in higher music education: International perspectives and practices* (pp. 256–267). New York NY: Routledge.

Snell, K. & Söderman, J. (2014). *Hip-hop within and without the academy*. Lanham, MD: Lexington Books.

Tønsberg, K. (2007). *Institusjonalisering av de rytmiske musikkutdanningene ved Høgskolen i Agder*. Oslo: Norges musikkhøgskole.

Tøsse, S. (2004). *Frå folkeopplysning til vaksenopplæring*. Trondheim: Fakultet for Samfunnsvitenskap og Teknologiledelse. Pedagogisk Institutt. Norges Teknisk-Naturvitenskapelige Universitet.

Väkevä, L. (2006). Teaching popular music in Finland: What' up, what's ahead?. *International Journal of Music Education,b24*(2), 126–131.

Väkevä, L. (2010). Garage band or Garageband? Remixing digital futures. *British Journal of Music Education, 27*(1), 59–70.

Westerlund, H. (2006). Garage rock bands: A future model for developing musical expertise? *International Journal of Music Education, 24*(2), 119–125.

34

Feral Pop

The participatory power of improvised popular music

Charlie Bramley and Gareth Dylan Smith

Introduction

In this chapter the authors discuss supplementation of existing PME models with an approach to free-form, improvised music-making. We argue that informal learning models – characteristic of much institutional and non-institutional popular music education (D'Amore & Smith, 2016; Green, 2002, 2008a; Lebler & Hodges, chapter 22, this volume) – provide a platform to support such development. We discuss 'Afrological' improvisation (Lewis, 1996, p. 93), which permits improvisers to embrace established musical styles, through a review of literature and in vignettes recalling a freely improvised musicking practice (Small, 1998) that we call *Feral Pop*. Free-form improvisation has been historically distanced from popular music because of a preoccupation in mainstream music education with what Lewis (1996, p. 93) has termed a "Eurological approach" to improvisation that explicitly seeks freedom from so much of what popular music is based upon: repetitive rhythms and structures, etc. An Afrological approach would embrace these characteristics.

One of the key figures of Afrological free-form improvisation since the 1970s, legendary double bass player William Parker, describes an Afrological approach to "free music": "The definition of free music is that you are free to choose whatever style you wanted to play ... It's not no-structure, it's free to use any structure that you want to use" (Parker, 2005, p. 2). We propose incorporating practices based on Afrologically influenced free-form approaches to popular music, drawing on notions such as Charles Keil's "participatory discrepancies" (1987, p. 275) and Nathaniel Mackey's "discrepant engagement" (1994, p. 368). Feral Pop opens up popular music structures to exploratory, wild, free-form improvisation and emphasizes performer agency. Thus it presents a powerful potential way to embed what Keil has termed the "flesh and blood of music-making" into PME, and, through doing so, to increase the "participatory power" (Keil, 1987, p. 279) of music education experiences: "Participation gives us the best answers to the oldest questions about the meaning of life" (Keil, 2002, p. 40).

Product, process and learning modes in PME

Christopher Small critiques traditional, formal approaches in music education, observing, "It is not surprising that education in music takes on the nature of both Western music and Western education . . . The concept of the product is dominant . . . the concern for the product, as usual, means that little attention is given to the process" (1977, p. 193). Small, and others in PME (Lebler, 2007; Niknafs & Przybylski, chapter 32, this volume; Smith & Shafighian, 2013), as well as music education more broadly (Elliott, 1995; Elliott & Silverman, 2014; Mantie, 2016; Randles, 2012), advocate for greater emphasis on process. By focusing less on product or (short-term) outcomes, music education becomes more about experiences that guide people towards agency (Partti, 2012; Wright, 2010) and identity realization (Smith, 2013a; Wenger, 1998).

PME (especially in higher education) is frequently geared towards a finished product (Lebler & Hodges, chapter 22, this volume; Morrow et al., chapter 26, this volume; Sylvester & O'Reilly, chapter 24, this volume). People engaging with popular music *processes* in the classroom can experience immense external pressure from a ravenous entertainment industry that places increasing demand on their creativities and musicalities. As hip-hop scholar Tricia Rose states:

> Young people are beginning to see their own creativity through a marketing logic: how can I promote what I do, how can I sell what I do, rather than imagining what they do as a creative force that should be nurtured and expanded. They're figuring out how to fit into already existing marketing categories . . . And that is stifling not only creativity, but it's turning . . . cultural spaces into product spaces.
>
> *(Rose, 2014)*

We contend that PME could do more to nurture the creative, in-the-moment, process-orientated potentialities inherent in popular music-making, rather than defaulting to nurturing the ubiquitous neoliberal ideology that pervades popular music, PME and (music) education more broadly (Allsup, 2015; Giroux, 2014; Jones, chapter 27, this volume; McLaughlin, chapter 10, this volume; Smith, 2015).

Informal and non-formal learning

PME in educational institutions frequently includes models of learning that are based on real-world music-learning experiences of popular musicians, integrating informal and non-formal learning processes[1] (Green, 2008a; Lebler, 2007; Lebler &

---

1 For exceptions, see for example, Smith (2014) and Smith & Shafighian (2013).

Hodges, chapter 22, this volume; Powell & Burstein, chapter 20, this volume). Musical Futures (D'Amore & Smith, 2016) is one such model, which has been central to the adoption and use of popular music in many curricula, and is described as "a radical approach offering new and imaginative ways of engaging young people in musical activities" (Finney, 2011, p. 178). Musical Futures is, "At its heart . . . a set of pedagogies that bring non-formal teaching and informal learning approaches into more formal contexts, in an attempt to provide engaging, sustainable and relevant music making activities for all young people" (Musical Futures, 2015a).

Lucy Green has been pivotal in developing the theoretical framework of informal learning at the core of Musical Futures' approaches. Informal learners choose music to learn themselves rather than being instructed by a teacher; they copy this music by ear rather than through written instructions; learning tends to take place in collaborative group work as opposed to individuals following 'expert' instruction from teachers; skills and knowledge are acquired through fairly haphazard methods, as opposed to the more linear progression with the syllabuses, exams, etc. associated with formal learning (Eraut, 2000; Jorgensen, 1997); informal learning integrates listening, performing, improvising and composing rather than these aspects being separated; there is an emphasis on creation, as opposed to the formal realm where the emphasis is on reproduction (Green, 2006, p. 106). Informal learning is combined with various 'non-formal' teaching methods designed so that music can be "caught", not "taught" (Musical Futures, 2015b); "The focus here is on learning by doing. Learning from fellow students/participants is as important as learning from the teacher or mentor" (Mak, 2012, p. 3).

PME represents a collective movement to attempt to work beyond more transmission-based modes of learning that are typical of much school-based music education (Green, 2002; Kratus, 2007; Powell et al., 2015; Williams & Randles, chapter 5, this volume). Green argues that informal learning approaches in the classroom practically enact a challenge to the orthodox "notion of education as a stable body of knowledge and skills which are unquestionably possessed by teachers, and which should be imparted to pupils" (Green, 2008a, pp. 2–3). Informal learning methods thus facilitate co-operative, unguided learning by allowing children to devise their own curriculum objectives. However, since in practice these methods are frequently used within the framework of specific guided objectives established in national curricula (e.g. in the UK) – while, to an extent, they challenge the notion of musical knowledge and skills as possessed unquestionably by teachers – it is arguably the case that they, and the values systemically ascribed to them, remain epistemologically reified. Thus it may be helpful to consider learning as taking place in various "hybridized" ways (Smith, 2013a, p. 34), or at points along a "continuum" of modes, as suggested by Folkestad (2006, p. 135), in seeking a fitting epistemology for PME pedagogy (Mantie, 2013).

Improvisation and music education

Within PME research, creativity and experimentation are often discussed in relation to songwriting (e.g. Bennett, 2012; Collinson Scott, chapter 16, this volume;

Gooderson & Henley, chapter 21, this volume) and other collaborative practices (e.g. Lebler, 2007; Ojala, chapter 6, this volume; Smith, 2013b) that ultimately lead to fixed compositions. The role of improvisation in PME models is typically that of a means-to-an-end process towards completed artefacts, or structures that can be reproduced; there appear to be few opportunities for learners to recognize the value of improvisation in and of itself. Part of the reason for this may be a negative association with the 1970s Creative Music Education (CME) movement, which sought to introduce improvisation and other avant-garde strategies into music classrooms.

The CME movement strongly emphasized a Eurological approach to improvisation (Lewis, 1996, p. 93), by means of a clearly delineated influence from high culture of the Euro-American avant-garde, in particular figures such as John Cage, Karlheinz Stockhausen and Edgard Varèse. Kanellopoulous suggests that the avant-garde's interest in children's music education was synonymous with a European Modernist ideology of the genius as "an otherworldly creature in search of divine naïveté" (2010, p. 125), going on to argue that "children's musical exploration was seen as analogous to that of the experimental composers; that is, as a search for the unknown" (2010, p. 127). There was thus a conscious attempt to align improvisation explicitly with the avant-garde, reflecting the tendency of that movement to reject established musical styles and create new music out of thin air. Eurological approaches to improvisation are, arguably, systematically opposed to popular music in their pursuit of improvisation that "excludes history or memory" and eliminates reference to known styles (Lewis, 1996, p. 147) – although there are many examples of performers 'crossing over' between Eurological and Afrological approaches ([George] Lewis himself being a notable example).

R. Murray Schafer, one of the pioneers of CME, expressed his opposition to popular music in education, arguing, "The introduction of pop music in the classroom is an example of . . . slovenliness" because it is a "social rather than a musical phenomenon and is therefore unsuitable as an abstract study, which music must always be if it is to remain an art and a science in its own right" (Schafer, 1969, p. 239–240). The legacy of this view is clear to see, with popular music still struggling for adoption in contexts such as the US (Powell & Burstein, chapter 20, this volume; Williams & Randles, chapter 5, this volume). In other places, meanwhile, PME has its feet firmly under the table, such as in the UK, Scandinavia, Finland and Australia (Christophersen & Gullberg, chapter 33, this volume; Till, chapter 3, this volume), where sociocultural benefits are often emphasized over 'purely' musical ones (Green, 2002; Partti, 2012; Wright, 2010), highlighting a tenuous yet tenacious bifurcation convincingly contested by Green in her discussion of ideology in music education (2008b).

Towards an Afrological approach

The Afrological principle of engaging with the memory, history and traditions of musical styles (Lewis, 1996) reflects much PME practice – especially at initial stages of learning in informal ways – based on learning from a notional canon of established songs or works (Green, 2002; Powell & Burstein, chapter 20, this volume;), beginning as the informal learning approach does with music familiar to learners (Green, 2008a). An Afrological approach to improvisation shares further congruencies with popular music and PME – perhaps most notably in its emphasis on personal narrative and performer agency, and its celebration of idiosyncratic styles (Bennett, chapter 23, this volume; Frith & Zagorski-Thomas, 2012; Moir & Medbøe, 2015; Parkinson, chapter 30, this volume): "One central aspect of Afrological improvisation is the notion of the importance of personal narrative, of 'telling your own story' . . . part of telling your own story is developing your own 'sound'" (Lewis, 1996, p. 156).

Lewis is keen to underline that the concept of Afrological is "historically emergent rather than ethnically essential, thereby accounting for the reality of transcultural and transracial communication" (1996, p. 133). As such, it is possible to read the influence of an Afrological conception in, for instance, Backstrom's comments on popular bands such as the Grateful Dead, who improvised free-rock live on stage for their entire career to unprecedented success – not to mention that free jazz legend Ornette Coleman once joined the band on stage during an improvisation (Trager, 1997, p, 68). Backstrom argues that "despite the critiques of the value of improvisation to, and indeed its actuality in, popular music (Frith; Adorno), its importance to the Grateful Dead would be difficult to overstate" (Backstrom, 2010, p. 1). Furthermore, as David Malvinni writes of the Grateful Dead:

> They owe much to the achievements of the jazz artists of their time . . . the African notion of spirit . . . According to Samuel A. Floyd Jr . . . the goal of jazz improvisation since bebop was for the spirit to "ride" the musician, similar to African trance rituals . . . with a rhythmic propulsion (auditory driving) that makes what follows appear as inevitable.
>
> *(2013, p. 9)*

Participation and discrepancy

Keil (1987, p. 281) argues that we can study music at its best "at its very point of creation, if we attend very closely to the discrepancies that enhance participation and the contexts that generate these discrepancies". These "participatory discrepancies" can also be described by terms such as "inflection", "creative tensions", "relaxed dynamisms" and a slight "out of syncness" (Keil, 1987, p. 275) – these elements of music invite performers and listeners to participate in a music that is not sterile, perfect and rigidly in time and in tune, but that has certain discrepancies displaying the 'lived-in' quality of music-making – Keil's "flesh and blood" of musicking (1987, p. 279). It is this that ultimately increases the participatory power to convey valuable personal meaning through (making) the music. "It is the little discrepancies within a jazz drummer's beat, between bass and drums, between rhythm section and soloists, that create 'swing' and invite us to participate" (1987, p. 277). Smith (2013a, p. 117), in his study of drummers, suggests that 'swing' is akin to 'groove' – "the magic ride" (Hart, 1990, p. 230) that musicians seek to create together, recalling the aforementioned notion of 'spirit' that 'rides' the musician, flow (Csikszentmihalyi, 1991) and notions of play (Bennett, 1980; Gadamer, 2004; Huizinga, 1976). This also invites comparisons with Jones and Baraka's (1963, pp. 212–213) contention that the discrepancies of swing enact a verb-like quality that is constantly in danger of becoming stifled into a static noun.[2]

Discussing Keil and Feld's notions of "groove" and/as "vital drive" (1994, p. 66), Heble explains that these are "not some essence of all music that we can simply take for granted, but must be figured out each time between players" and argues that the discrepancies resulting from such collaborative 'figurings' are what make music so compelling (Heble, 2000, p. 101). Being discrepant makes music "a peculiarly powerful vehicle for participatory consciousness and action" (Keil, 1987, p. 277). Keil quotes from Owen Barfield, arguing, "Participation begins by being an activity, and essentially a communal or social activity" (Barfield in Keil, 1987, p. 276). Keil goes on to assert, "The best music must be full of discrepancies, both "out of time" and "out of tune"' (1987, p. 279). Feral Pop – an approach to popular music fraught with contingency and risk – offers a potent means of generating participatory discrepancies, increasing the participatory power of musicking. We concur with Keil that the 'flesh and blood' of music-making are too often hindered and obscured by mediating devices applied to music-making in educational contexts (McLaughlin, chapter 10, this volume). As Mantie (2016, p. 635.) suggests, Keil's "'groovology' model of participation . . . should be part of every curriculum involving music and dance".

Feral Pop

Feral Pop is an emerging concept and practice being developed by the first author with improviser Will Edmondes. As a Lecturer on, and former Director of the BA in, Popular and Contemporary Music at Newcastle University (UK), Edmondes has forged connections between improvisation, experimentalism and mainstream approaches to popular music performance, based on the underlying, interconnecting theoretical framework of Afrological improvisation. What began as an idea – that of playing improvised music within and across recognizable popular styles – quickly became a reality through the music scene in Newcastle. Feral Pop is a type of improvised practice that runs counter to ideas of improvised music as a genre in itself (Lewis, 1996), showcasing the radical potential of improvisation as an *approach* that can cut across popular music styles while embracing elements of them. Due to the unpredictability of improvisation in practice, such a cutting across is arguably a kind of a *feralizing* of popular music – an opening up of rigid, 'domesticated', institutionalized popular music structures to the un-tamed nature of free-form improvisation, musicking beyond and in response to industrial conditions that produce marketable products.

Feral Pop consists of attempts to improvise freely around a popular music idiom. Rather than being a rigid dictate of what the music will be structurally, Feral Pop

---

2 Amiri Baraka was formerly known as LeRoi Jones, but is cited by Mackey here as Amiri Baraka.

understands the idiom to imply a *manner of doing things*, allowing performers to improvise freely across popular styles, with an unapologetic embrace of repetition. This resonates with Keil's theorizing of 'groove', in which he articulates the "slightly out of phase" characteristic of groove-based playing and celebrates "what a powerful feeling it is when that careful play of an agreed-upon group sound is enhanced with allowances for the give-and-take of personal expression" (Keil, 2010, p. 4). Feral Pop exemplifies and intensifies this powerful, participatory feeling by engaging in consistent groove-based playing that constantly allows for the give-and-take of improvised personal expression.

Questions that have emerged from and thence guided this emerging, ongoing practice-as-research include:

- Is Feral Pop successful in producing popular music through improvisation?
- Is it perceived to be a genuine attempt to engage in popular music culture, or as an inauthentic foray of an avant-garde concept *into* popular music culture?
- Is the music enjoyable for, or at least engaging to, an audience, and if so, is that a different audience than typically exists in avant-garde scenes?

The following section represents an initial attempt to address these questions. Data collection methods have consisted of observational diaries and recording informal conversations with audience members after performances. What follows are autoethnographic vignettes recalling creative music projects in which the first author was engaged from 2013 to 2015, serving as examples of how Feral Pop looks, sounds and feels.

Vignette 1

The following recounts a conversation between an audience member and the first author after a performance in 2014 by a trio playing in the vague style of synth pop utilizing hardware synthesizers and vocoder-effected vocals. These conversations were inadvertently captured on the audio recording of the performances, so the quotes remain anonymous:

> Audience member: Hey, that was really great! It reminded me a lot of bit-pop.
> Charlie: Oh, thanks so much, I'm pleased you enjoyed it. I haven't actually heard of bit-pop before, what's that?
> Audience member: it's like this really lo-fi synth pop thing, a bit like Electroclash, that kind of stuff – you should check it out?

> Charlie: I will yeah, so is that improvised is it?
> Audience member: Erm, no I don't think so, why?
> Charlie: Oh, just because what we were doing there was improvised.
> Audience member: Really – oh I had no idea, what, so like you guys didn't know what you were going to do at all?
> Charlie: No, nothing. We played together for the first time earlier in the week, and we knew we wanted to do something beat-based, but other than that we didn't put anything in place to make sure we were playing to a tempo or anything like that.

Vignette 2

Before Feral Pop, the first author improvised in a more 'Eurological' manner, in which audience members found very little to relate to in terms of established musical styles. The following are a range of comments taken from personal diaries at a monthly performance event titled Blue Rinse. Accounts from 2011–2012 refer to a pre-Feral Pop approach, and accounts from 2013–2015 are from when Feral Pop became more common at Blue Rinse events. All names have been replaced to retain anonymity, and we have retained the original informal language style:

> 28 March, 2011: Alice, John and Lisa all made some nice comments after the set, which made me feel a bit better, because audience applause was a bit muted, and numbers looked low.
>
> 23 May, 2012: Good audience numbers tonight and a decent applause. Some seemingly genuine positive comments. Might have been helped because of popular student band playing, so lots of initiated audience in room?
>
> 26 February, 2013: Very relieved to get such a good response tonight. I was really nervous about playing in this duo, playing pretty much straight-up techno made up on the spot. Felt really exposed, but sounded really good, audience applause felt bigger than usual, and lots of really positive comments afterwards, and even one or two from people I haven't met before, asking about equipment and what exactly we were doing.

> 25 January, 2014: Incredible response tonight. This trio felt amazing to play in, and the comments afterwards were like nothing I've experienced. Alice said it 'blew her mind'; loads of new faces came up to say how much they enjoyed it. Could totally feel the genuine vibe of how they said it as well – and that applause was huge.

The combination of these responses and audience feedback prompted some preliminary observations: Feral Pop provokes blurring of improvisation and composition that extends to audience perception; audience members instinctively make connections with other forms of popular music, suggesting that Feral Pop is valid as popular music/king (and not 'just' an improvised form); audiences become more engaged in response to the Afrological-motivated Feral Pop, as opposed to Eurological approaches to improvisation.

Making sense of Feral Pop

If Feral Pop is successful in producing engaging popular music, and if it merges improvisation and composition, what is the point in improvising? Why not just write and perform pop songs? The Feral Pop approach maximizes performer/creator agency, as performer-improvisers create music in the moment. Music is co-created with and by audience members who are, to varying degrees, familiar with and enculturated into popular and improvised idioms. Feral Pop produces (popular) music that is engaging and enjoyable for participants and audiences. Public performances notwithstanding, the activity is not industrialized, focused on commodity or narrow understandings of successful products (artefacts or students) (Smith, 2013b); instead it is about reclaiming the *process* of pop music via the relentless pursuit of immediate sonic pleasure – what Voegelin (2010, p. 64) has termed "An expansion of experience in timespace" – that is both individually empowering and socially meaningful. It thus embodies elements of a revolutionary politics that challenges constraints faced by popular musicians in the entertainment industry (Jones, chapter 27, this volume), as mentioned previously (Rose, 2014).

Emphasizing the importance of participation – of process over product – in music-making traditions (arguably largely lost in PME), Turino notes,

> What is important to understand is that for certain social groups throughout the world, participatory music, dance, sports and festivals are not merely the informal side lines to the "real" event – professional athletics, music and entertainment – but rather they are the center of social life.
>
> *(2008, p. 35)*

Richter further underscores the importance of recognizing the *making* of making music, arguing, "Music does not primarily crave public success. It invites human participation. It leads an autonomous existence of creative possibility and freedom" (2010). Feral Pop may offer an essentially human mode of musicking that is lacking in more mainstream PME practices. Given appropriate facilities, Feral Pop suggests an exciting, relevant and intense way to make, and to learn about making, music.

Conclusions

In popular music, with its informal and hybridized learning approaches, participation is not so much diminished, but dependent – predicated even – on adherence to a certain set of disciplines and dispositions that are to be learned in order to participate meaningfully. Through these methods, we have the musical 'flesh' (structures, forms, familiar styles), but it may be harder to get to the 'blood' (discrepancies, swing, groove). Much of PME – perhaps especially in higher education – remains mediated by the goal-orientated objective of learning a particular kind of music with certain fixed, fundamental principles. The *Feral Pop* model of free-form improvisation embraces Keil's concept of participatory discrepancy to open the doors to a different kind of musicking experience – offering access through the established familiarity of popular music culture while granting increased agency to performers through far greater freedom of sonic exploration. As such, Feral Pop also ties in well with the informal learning approach of Musical Futures, much of whose work has been conducted in the less goal-orientated early years of secondary education in the UK; it is perhaps thus that Musical Futures is able to aspire to and to encourage in young musicians an attitude "that deeply values people creating and making music, first and foremost *for the sake of making music*" (D'Amore & Smith, 2016, emphasis in original).

Nathaniel Mackey has long recognized potential connections and intersections between Afrological improvisation and popular music. He suggests that Afrological improvisation can enact a "discrepant engagement", which, drawing on Keil's (1987) understanding of "discrepant", means an engagement that *rattles* and *creaks* the entity with which it engages (Mackey, 1994, p. 19). Mackey refers to the ability of Afrological improvisation to disturb the fixity of standard musical organization, to distance itself from pre-composed, pre-conceptualized strategies and instead celebrate the instability of spontaneous musical organization. As Mackey writes,

> Improvisation, the pursuit of new expressivity . . . is an operation best characterized by the prefix "para", an activity supplemental to more firmly established disciplines and dispositions, an activity that hinges on a near but divergent identity with given disciplines and dispositions.
>
> *(2004, p. 371)*

Feral Pop therefore enacts a 'discrepant engagement' with popular music by rattling and creaking the fixed structures of popular music, creating a divergent and distinctive musical identity realized by performers at the time of performance.

A discrepant engagement then provides the ideal balance between engaging performers (and audiences) with the familiarity of popular music styles, while providing space to explore and widen their musical horizons.

The possibilities of collaboratively figuring out popular music styles spontaneously are fraught with risk, and, simultaneously, incredibly rewarding and exciting; as Heble (2000) argues, this combination is what ultimately makes participatory music-making so compelling. It is the discrepant life in the music, the lived-in 'flesh and blood' quality, that makes music human and allows listeners to connect to it and performers to participate more meaningfully in its performance. To enact this quality through an Afrologically influenced Feral Pop music that nurtures personality and performer agency is to create the potential for a distinctive, hyper-compelling form of music-making, as yet perhaps largely untapped in educational contexts.

References

Allsup, R.E. (2015). The eclipse of a higher education or problems preparing artists in a mercantile world. *Music Education Research, 17*(3), 251–261.

Backstrom, M. (2010). Review of the book, 'The Grateful Dead in Concert: Essays in Live Improvisation', Tuedio, J. & Spector, S. *Critical Studies in Improvisation, 6*(2). Retrieved from: http://www.criticalimprov.com/article/view/1332/1921 [Accessed 1 October 2015].

Bennett, H.S. (1980). *On becoming a rock musician*. Amherst, MA: University of Massachusetts Press.

Bennett, J. (2012). Constraint, collaboration and creativity in popular songwriting teams. In D. Collins (Ed.), *The act of musical composition: Studies in the creative process* (pp. 139–169). Farnham: Ashgate.

Csikszentmihalyi, M. (1991). *Flow: The psychology of optimal experience*. New York: HarperPerennial.

D'Amore, A. & Smith, G.D. (2016). Aspiring to music making as leisure through the musical futures classroom. In R. Mantie & G.D. Smith (Eds.), *The Oxford handbook of music making and leisure* (pp. 61–80). New York: Oxford University Press.

Elliott, D.J. (1995). *Music matters: A new philosophy of music education*. New York: Oxford University Press.

Elliott, D.J. & Silverman, M. (2014). *Music matters: A philosophy of music education*. New York: Oxford University Press.

Eraut, M. (2000). Non-formal learning and tacit knowledge in professional work. *British Journal of Educational Psychology, 70*(1), 113–136.

Finney, J. (2011). *Music Education in England 1950–2010: The child-centred progressive tradition*. Ashburton: Ashgate Publishing.

Folkestad, G. (2006). Formal and informal learning situations or practices *vs* formal and informal ways of learning', *British Journal of Music Education, 23*(2), 135–145.

Frith, S. & Zagorski-Thomas, S. (Eds.) (2012). *The art of record production: An introductory reader for a new academic field*. Burlington, VT: Ashgate.

Gadamer, H.-G. (2004). *Truth and method*. London: Bloomsbury.

Giroux, H.A. (2014). *Neoliberalism's war on higher education*. Chicago, IL: Haymarket.

Green, L. (2002). *How popular musicians learn: A way ahead for music education*. Aldershot: Ashgate Publishing.

Green, L. (2006). Popular music education in and for itself, and for "other" music: Current research in the classroom. *International Journal of Music Education, 24*(2), 101–118.

Green, L. (2008a). *Music, informal learning and the school: A new classroom pedagogy.* Farnham: Ashgate.

Green, L. (2008b). *Music on deaf ears: Musical meaning, ideology, education.* Manchester: Manchester University Press.

Hart, M. with Stevens, J. (1990). *Drumming at the edge of magic: A journey into the spirit of percussion.* New York, NY: Harper.

Heble, A. (2000). *Landing on the wrong note: Jazz, dissonance and critical practice.* London: Routledge.

Huizinga, J. (1976). Nature and significance of play as a cultural phenomenon. In R. Schechner & M. Schuman (Eds.), *Ritual, play, and performance: Readings in the social sciences/theatre.* New York, NY: Seabury Press, pp. 46–66.

Jones, L. & Baraka, I.A. (1963). *Blues people: Negro music in white America.* New York, NY: Harper Collins.

Jorgensen, E.R. (1997). *In search of music education.* Chicago, IL: University of Illinois Press.

Kanellopoulous, P.A. (2010). Towards a sociological perspective on researching children's creative music-making practices: An exercise in self-consciousness. In R. Wright (Ed.), *Sociology and music education* (pp. 15–138). Farnham: Ashgate.

Keil, C. (1987). Participatory discrepancies and the power of music. *Cultural Anthropology, 2*(3), 275–283.

Keil, C. (2002). They want the Music but they don't want the people. *City & Society, 14*(1), 37–57.

Keil, C. (2010). Defining groove. *PopScriptum 11 – The groove issue.* Retrieved from: http://www2.hu-berlin.de/fpm/popscrip/themen/pst11/pst11_keil02.html [Accessed 1 August 2015].

Keil, C. & Feld, S. (1994). *Music grooves.* Chicago, IL: University of Chicago Press.

Kratus, J. (2007). Centennial series: Music education at the tipping point. *Music Educators Journal, 94*(2), 42–48.

Lebler, D. (2007). Student as master? Reflections on a learning innovation in popular music pedagogy. *International Journal of Music Education, 25*(30), 205–221.

Lewis, G.E. (1996). Improvised music after 1950: Afrological and Eurological perspectives. *Black Music Research Journal*, 91–122.

Mackey, N. (1994). *Discrepant engagement: Dissonance, cross-culturality, and experimental writing.* Cambridge: Cambridge University Press.

Mackey, N. (2004). Paracritical hinge. In A. Heble (Ed.), *The other side of nowhere.* Middletown, CT: Wesleyan University Press.

Mak, P. (2012). Learning music in formal, non-formal and informal contexts. *Pedagog Stud 01/2012.* Retrieved from: http://www.emc-imc.org/fileadmin/EFMET/article_Mak.pdf

Malvinni, D. (2013). *Grateful Dead and the art of rock improvisation.* Lanham, MD: Scarecrow Press.

Mantie, R. (2013). A comparison of "popular music pedagogy" discourses. *Journal of Research in Music Education, 61*(3), 334–352.

Mantie, R. (2016). An open letter to Charles Keil. In R. Mantie & G.D. Smith (Eds.) *The Oxford Handbook of Music Making and Leisure.* New York: Oxford University Press, pp. 621–640.

Moir, Z. & Medbøe, H. (2015). Reframing popular music composition as performance-centred practice. *Journal of Music, Technology & Education, 8*(2), 147–161.

Musical Futures. (2015a). Work with us. Retrieved from: https://legacy.musicalfutures.org/resource/28109/title/musicalfuturesworkwithus [Accessed 5 September 2015].

Musical Futures. (2015b). Non-formal teaching. Retrieved from: Musical Futures, https://legacy.musicalfutures.org/resources/c/nonformalteaching [Accessed 5 September 2015].

Parker, W. (2005). Everything is valid. Retrieved from: http://www.allaboutjazz.com/william-parker-everything-is-valid-william-parker-by-eyal-hareuveni.php [Accessed 4 May 2015].

Partti, H. (2012). *Learning from cosmopolitan digital musicians: Identity, musicianship, and changing values in (in)formal music communities*. Helsinki: Sibelius Academy.

Powell, B., Krikun, A. & Pignato, P. (2015). Something's happening here!: Popular music education in the United States. *IASPM@Journal, 5*(1), pp. 4–22.

Randles, C. (2012). Music teacher as writer and producer. *The Journal of Aesthetic Education, 46*(3), 36–52.

Richter, G. (2010). "Music and Leisure": Thinking about music: Sounding out silence. University of Sydney. Retrieved from: http://blogs.usyd.edu.au/thinkmusic/2010/03/music_and_leisure.html [Accessed 1 June 2015].

Rose, T. (2014). Hip hop images: Women and exploitation. Retrieved from: https://www.youtube.com/watch?v=JhVOi8XQ7P8 [Accessed 2 June 2015].

Schafer, M.R. (1969). *The thinking ear: Complete writings on music education*. Toronto, Bernadol Music.

Small, C. (1977). *Music, society, education*. Hanover: Wesleyan University Press.

Small, C. (1998). *Musicking: The meanings of performing and listening*. Middletown, CT: Wesleyan Press.

Smith, G.D. (2013a). *I drum, therefore I am: Being and becoming a drummer*. Farnham: Ashgate.

Smith, G.D. (2013b). Pedagogy for employability in a foundation degree (Fd.A.) in creative musicianship: Introducing peer collaboration. In H. Gaunt & H. Westerlund (Eds.), *Collaboration in higher music education* (pp. 193–198). Farnham: Ashgate.

Smith, G.D. (2015). Neoliberalism and symbolic violence in higher music education. In L. DeLorenzo (Ed.), *Giving voice to democracy: Diversity and social justice in the music classroom*. New York: Routledge.

Smith, G.D. & Shafighian, A. (2013). Creative space and the "silent power of traditions" in popular music performance education. In P. Burnard (Ed.), *Developing creativities in higher music education: International perspectives and practices* (pp. 256–267). London: Routledge.

Trager, O. (1997). *The American book of the dead: The definitive Grateful Dead encyclopedia*. Hemel Hempstead: Prentice Hall.

Turino, T. (2008). *Music as social life: The politics of participation*. Chicago University of Illinois Press.

Voegelin, S. (2010). *Listening to noise and silence: Towards a philosophy of sound art*. New York: Continuum.

Wenger, E. (1998). *Communities of practice: Learning, meaning, and identity*. New York: Cambridge University Press.

Wright, R. (2010). Democracy, social exclusion and music education: Possibilities for change. In R. Wright (Ed.), *Sociology and music education* (pp. 263–282). Farnham: Ashgate.

35
Epistemological and sociological issues in popular music education

David G. Hebert, Joseph Abramo and Gareth Dylan Smith

Introduction

This chapter is intended largely as a response to the book, for which it serves as a conclusion. The response is twofold. First, the authors attempt to fill in some gaps by addressing what we perceive to be pertinent issues in popular music education that have been under-explored in other chapters. This is not to suggest that our colleagues' work is inadequate or unfinished, or that our thoughts should be taken as in any way superior to those of our esteemed fellow contributors. Rather, we view this chapter as a humble acknowledgement that any *Research Companion* necessarily excludes at least as much relevant and valuable scholarship as it manages to accommodate within its pages. While we cannot reasonably attempt to signpost every last item of scholarship pertinent to this volume, we hope nonetheless to shed light on what we see as pervasive, salient issues and perspectives at the heart of popular music education.

Due to the newness of the field of popular music education, its most central concerns are arguably – perhaps indeed inevitably – short, to date, on critical interrogation and theorized, reflective scholarship. This is not surprising, nor should this observation be taken as a criticism of extant writing, much of which is to a greater degree descriptive and explanatory rather than analytical (with a few notable exceptions). As a field, popular music education is still finding its feet and defining its parameters. One of the editors' hopes in curating this volume was to gather chapters that might begin to indicate *what popular music education is*. As the book has developed, so has a sense of what the emerging themes in PME might be. The second, and overlapping, aspect of our response to the book, then, is to suggest some ways in which cogent critique of and within the field might be constructed. This chapter is offered in humility, by authors aware of its concision. We hope, however, that, despite its shortcomings, the chapter serves to provoke and fruitfully challenge readers and, in turn, to help advance thinking and practice in the field.

'Success' as educational quality

One way to critique popular music education would be to ask what good or successful PME might look like. A successful education may, for instance, lead to agency, understanding, respect, compassion and self-empowerment (e.g. Dewey, 1938; Freire, 2000; Partti, 2012; Wright, 2010). Alternatively, it may lead to compliance; factual, tacit or embodied knowledge; and transferable and domain-specific skill sets, to name but a few possibilities. Perhaps a desirable end of a successful route through popular music education in compulsory schooling would lead to further study of popular music, in higher education, or at least would create strong opportunities for its learners to pursue such a trajectory. In this respect, though, one might also ask how desirable forms of *popular* music education might differ from *any* music education, or precisely what makes this field distinctive. Ojala, Powell and Burstein, Rathgeber, and Woodward (all this volume, chapters 6, 20, 29 and 31, respectively) suggest various aims and applications of PME in schools that are more democratic than personal or individual in orientation, which is arguably one of these distinctive features.

PME in higher education could – as numerous authors in this volume have demonstrated and discussed – have myriad objectives, deepening Parkinson and Smith's (2015) description of competing narratives, imperatives, agendas, traditions and authenticities, identifying higher popular music education (HPME) as a rich and complex arena for negotiating values, experiences and outcomes. While it may be desirable for graduates of popular music programmes to be able performers, composers, songwriters, producers and/or competent thinkers and theorists, there is also widespread acceptance of an imperative to balance (and thus, arguably, to compromise) technical-musical skills and critical-theoretical abilities with entrepreneurial business *savoir-faire*. Such career creativities (Bennett, 2013; Burnard, 2012; Hallam & Gaunt, 2012) are increasingly among the explicit aims of higher music education programmes around the world (Lebler & Hodges, chapter 22, this volume; McLaughlin, chapter 10, this volume; Morrow et al., chapter 26, this volume; Sylvester & O'Reilly, chapter 24, this volume; Wong, chapter 9, this volume), but these aspirations arguably run counter to what are generally perceived as the 'proper' aims of higher education. For Angus, the contemporary consensus in higher education creates "a public-private or corporate-state joint economic institution that produces training and credentials recognized in the global corporate economy or the national bureaucracy" (2007, p. 64). However, notable critical pedagogues, such as Giroux, caution that "increasingly, universities are losing their power . . . to offer the type of education that enables them to refute the neoliberal utopian notion that paradise amounts to a world of voracity and avarice without restrictions" in a capitalist, neoliberal scramble to (ethical) self-defeat (Giroux, 2014, p. 13).

Epistemological and sociological issues

Would we expect successful graduates of popular music education programmes to become successful in popular music? Such an end would not seem unreasonable to many in this field, but is fraught with difficulties – logistical, moral, ethical, economic, pedagogical and epistemological (Smith, 2013a). Success is a multivariate, contextual, highly subjective and ideologically loaded construct (Smith, 2016). Negotiating the highly problematic notion of, for instance, musical value (Green, 2008), and balancing or reconciling this aim with commercial, personal, financial, family, moral, eudaimonic, emotional or spiritual success can be extremely complicated (Jones, chapter 27, this volume; Smith, 2014, 2015a, 2016). Adding to this mix a less myopic and introverted, non-mainstream version of success would necessarily take into account, for example, success in terms of sustainability for the local and global environment and population. However, even the idea of a socially conscious, carbon-neutral, commercially successful popular music is at present practically unthinkable, in a global-industrial society predicated on producing and endorsing vast and soaring quantities of music that is played, recorded, stored, marketed, distributed and performed in ways that require assaulting the planet – not to mention the opportunities and lives of those born to less economic wealth than the privileged minority in the global North – in ways unconscionable to anyone with even peripheral awareness of some of the issues facing the world around us (Woodward, chapter 31, this volume).

Neoliberalism and the commercial dimensions of popular music

Popular music education does not always aim to meet instrumental ends. It is perhaps possible for education in and through popular music to serve its own ends. Bramley and Smith (chapter 34, this volume) advocate for "Feral Pop – an approach to popular music . . . [that] offers a potent means of . . . increasing the participatory power of musicking", although they do not offer suggestions for how to incorporate such a paradigm or approach into educational settings. D'Amore and Smith (2016, p. 65) explain that Musical Futures, employed in schools in several countries around the world, "is a learning system that deeply values people creating and making music, first and foremost *for the sake of making music*", a system that sees young people "aspiring to, and learning from, music making as leisure". Although Mantie observes (in a US context) that "leisure and recreation do not currently register as the proper concerns of music educators" (2015, p. 170), efforts have been made to integrate music-making into education founded on leisure ideals. This occurred notably in the US around the middle of the 20th century, often associated with the work of sociologist and musician Max Kaplan, whose innovative proposals appear to have been underappreciated during his lifetime (Krikun, 2016; McCarthy, 2016).

In higher education, it is arguably much more difficult to avoid adherence to a vocational-instrumentalist agenda than may be the case in compulsory schooling, since governmental, business and other imperatives increasingly compel institutions and educators to prepare students to survive and maintain careers. In some traditional universities, the notion of 'academic freedom' is to some extent preserved, enabling a bit of protection against such forces, yet such ideals are rapidly decaying as even the most traditional universities face new forms of management. As Parkinson and Smith explain, in the UK context higher education institutions are each required by government mandate to produce an

> "employability statement", detailing the professional opportunities that graduates of a program may expect to encounter. This was supplemented in 2012 by the further requirement of a "Key Information Set", a summary of hard statistical data relating to graduate employment and salaries.
>
> *(2015, p. 105)*

The imperative to produce employable graduates is global (e.g. Morrow et al., chapter 26, this volume; Rivas Caicedo, chapter 25, this volume; Sylvester & O'Reilly, chapter 24, this volume; Wong, chapter 9, this volume). At the institution where author Gareth Dylan Smith teaches, language around 'customer service' has recently become increasingly common in reference to what he prefers to think of as teaching, learning and assessment, rather than as a market transaction. Governmental rhetoric – and responses by institutions, educators and students – continue to shift, however, as the financial cost to students of higher education soars in some countries, while other nations manage to sustain education paid for by taxation. Is it, then, desirable, sufficient or even *moral* to aspire, as Mantie (2016, p. 636) suggests, to "all education as leisure education"? Maybe such a position is idealistic to the point of unrealistic, yet aspects of this vision remain attractive.

Bourdieu explained how we are all subjected to an "economic regime that is inseparable from a political regime, a mode of production that entails a mode of domination based on the institution of insecurity, [and] domination through precariousness", embodying an "instantaneist, individualistic, ultrasubjectivist philosophy" (2003, pp. 29–30). Perhaps the notion of the cultural creative, in today's environment where everyone is an 'entrepreneur' (Hewison, 2014), coupled with the expensive, mythologized past (and current 'hangover'), derived from a putatively meritocratic music-industrial machine gives musicians a sense of entitlement to a career earning money from their music. If only life were so simple!

As Gareth was writing the above passage, a frustrated musician colleague (with a full-time job in an assistant secretarial position) posted on her Facebook wall the following question: "Muso's [sic] . . . how the hell does anyone make a living when so much shit is unpaid?! Please tell me the magic answer!!!" This led to a lengthy and well-rehearsed discussion around how musicians should "never work for free", and how we should be respected for our art, with participants animatedly urging their co-complainants to keep hobbyists out of "their business". Blogger Daniel Brockman (2014) finds us experiencing today the breakdown of

> the essential unspoken concept behind music culture in the modern era, that important artists sing important songs that are important enough to the

general populace to make bajillionaires out of what used to be the travelling minstrels in a sane society.

As Gareth has noted elsewhere, "Rather than democratizing the creative sector or popular music culture, this brave new world has consistently driven more money into the hands of even fewer individuals, contributing to the capitalist consummation" (Smith, 2015a, p. 73). There are tensions, then, around a contemporary capitalist obsession with individuals following their dreams, and little or no overt consideration of how such a selfish, eudaimonic and anti-social paradigm might lead to and perpetuate more division, violence and harm than the happiness such a ubiquitous ideology leads millions of somnambulant adherents to presume (Norton, 1976; Smith, 2016).

Gareth has pointed out elsewhere (Smith, 2013a, 2016) that most 'popular music' is actually, by most measures, *unpopular* music (Bell, 2016; Kirschner, 1998), in terms of the relative amount of public attention paid to the total amount of music being made. With the closure of small venues all across the UK (Parkinson et al., 2015) and internationally, and challenges to the popular, idealistic notion of abundance for all artists and consumers in the 'long tail' thesis (Anderson, 2006; Cartwright & Smith, 2013), the 'people's music' (Middleton, 1990; Tagg, 1983) is becoming increasingly unpopular in terms of its sustainability as a career, or even as a leisure pursuit, for many musicians. In arenas beyond performance, meanwhile, popular music and popular music learning and education are burgeoning, including in such forms as online learning and participation (Trobia & Lo Verde, 2016), engagement with digital audio workstations (DAWs) (Bell, 2015) and gaming (O'Leary & Tobias, 2016; Tobias & O'Leary, in press).

Ideologies can be very powerful, and the societies to which they give rise shape the conditions in which people live their lives. Ideologies structure, and to an extent determine, how people think, speak and behave. The next section is devoted briefly to the work of one theorist (among a great many) whose influential work has helped scholars to grapple with and understand intersections between the framework/s of society and the roles and lives of individuals therein.

Bourdieu and popular music education

Gareth put the finishing touches to this essay on the eve of the publication of another book, *Bourdieu and the Sociology of Music and Music Education* (Burnard et al., 2015). The fact that such a book has been compiled speaks volumes about the influence of Bourdieu's thinking and his status as a key figure in the sociology of (music) education. It has become somewhat fashionable of late to 'look through a Bourdieusian lens' at any given issue in (music) education; however, it would, nonetheless, be remiss to avoid including here some consideration of how Bourdieu's ideas may shed light on aspects of PME. Burnard et al. (2015) present a richer, more complete and more nuanced discussion of Bourdieu's theories and tools than we could presume to do here (or, indeed, anywhere). We hope, however, that this necessarily concise essay might point readers in the direction of further examination of Bourdieu's work. Writing on sociology and music education, Wright notes that "Bourdieu's work develops three important concepts: habitus, capital and social field" (2010, p. 13). 'Capital' refers to the skills and (social) power held by individuals and social groups, while the spaces in which socio-historically constructed and construed practices are constituted are 'fields' (Bourdieu, 1984). We return to 'habitus' below. Consideration of Bourdieu is especially relevant here because of the salience of his ideas in music as well as education. As Prior has noted, Bourdieu's concepts of "cultural capital, field and habitus in particular, have been central to the formation of a critical paradigm in music sociology that demonstrates how the social penetrates, produces or contextualizes music" (Prior, 2015, p. 349).

Identity and masculine domination

Two recurring themes across various chapters in this book are (1) structure, and (2) agency. Authors share concerns around empowering students (encouraging and providing individuals with agency), and simultaneously preparing students to function within systems and structures (the education system, the music industry/ies, the creative cultural sector, society more generally). Citing Nash (1999) and Lévis Strauss (1978), Wright (2010, pp. 12–14) explains how Bourdieu's notion of habitus can serve as a 'missing link' between understandings of structure and agency. As such, habitus can assist in discussing the intersecting "fields of popular music performance, entrepreneurship and music education" (Smith, 2015b, p. 61). Bourdieu describes his bridging concept of 'habitus' as follows:

> Insofar as he or she is endowed with a habitus, the social agent is a collective individual or a collective individuated by the fact of embodying objective structures. The individual, the subjective, is social and collective. The habitus is socialised subjectivity, a historical transcendental, whose schemes of perceptions and appreciation (systems of appreciation, tastes, etc.) are the product of collective and individual history. Reason (or rationality) is "bounded" not only ... because the human mind is generically bounded ... but because it is socially structured and determined, and, as a consequence, limited.
> *(Bourdieu, 2005, p. 211)*

Wright also explains some of the shortcomings of the habitus concept, inasmuch as it emerges in and is defined as an understanding of "culture as a dominant and exclusive ideology imposed by ruling groups and incapable of admitting alternatives" (2010, p. 14). She recommends the work of Bernstein (1971, 1973, 1975, 1990) for providing a more nuanced and descriptive account of the workings of social structures and individual agency in and through education.

Agency and structure point to a third theme pervading this book – identity. Gareth has proposed elsewhere the model of "identity realization" (Smith, 2013b, p. 18), which takes account of the symbiosis of identity and learning, developed from Green (2002), Wenger (1998) and Barrett (2011). Identity realization describes two processual phenomena: (1) "a person's active identity realization ... is the *doing of things we do* that make us who we are as individuals", and (2) "a person's passive identity realization is a person's notion of *who they are*" (Smith, 2013b, p. 18, emphasis in original). Habitus can help to explain how identity realization works in particular contexts. One arena in which it may be especially enlightening to consider the intersection of habitus and identity realization is that of gender.

In his work on "masculine domination" Bourdieu describes how passive and active gendered identity realization are impacted through the construct of "female habitus" (2001, p. 63), in which masculine dominates feminine. In Western patriarchal societies (Green, 1997), we behave in ways that are organized according to "the pervasive, androcentric worldview, 'not linked to a biological or psychological nature', but, rather, a socio-historical construction, 'a historical unconscious' (Bourdieu, 2001, p. 54)" (Smith, 2015b, p. 63). Bourdieu explains that masculine domination is:

> Instituted through the adherence that the dominated cannot fail to grant to the dominant (and therefore to the domination) when, to shape her thought of him, and herself, or, rather, her thought of her relationship with him, she has only cognitive instruments that she shares with him and which, being no more than the embodied form of the relation of domination, cause that relation to appear as natural.
>
> *(Bourdieu, 2001, p. 35)*

It is, thus, socially 'unnatural' for men and women to act outside the expectations of a masculine-dominated societal system. Bourdieu sees masculine domination as a fundamental aspect of social structure wherein

> we have embodied the historical structures of the masculine order in the form of unconscious schemes of perception and appreciation. When we try to understand masculine domination we are therefore likely to resort to modes of thought that are the product of domination.
>
> *(2001, p. 5)*

It is, therefore, difficult to "kick the habitus" (Wright, 2008), for we cannot easily see how we think and behave, or the societal assumptions upon which our thoughts and actions are founded. The power of the "symbolic violence" (Bourdieu, 2001, p. 35) exerted by pervasive masculine domination is especially potent when considered in the context of the simplistic and often misleading bifurcation of 'gender' into masculine and feminine (Baron-Cohen, 2003; Butler, 2004).

Masculine domination leads to particular, narrow presentations and representations of women in popular music:

> The objectification of women in popular music is prevalent across genres and sub-genres, but is perhaps nowhere more obvious than in the globally popular musical style and culture of (Gangsta) rap and hip-hop (with the exception,

perhaps, of country music, whose lyrics and culture typically perpetuate the same aggressive gendering, but in a manner, ironically and possibly deliberately, altogether softer, subtler and more feminine, appearing on the surface to celebrate women, but doing so in ways that only strengthen the dominance of masculinity).

(Smith, 2015b, p. 64)

Against a background of such masculine domination, masquerading as false gender equality – dubbed "enlightened sexism" (Douglas, 2010), even sexual liberation of women and femininity serves to reinforce narrow normative expectations:

If the so-called liberation is done in accordance with socially-dictated feminine performances that appeal to the male audience, and the liberation thus becomes directed to and by the male gaze, it ceases to be about "liberating" the individual and is more concerned with appeasing collective masculine domination and reinforcing gender norms and inequalities.

(Pravodelov, 2014, p. 13)

Masculine domination exerts and reinforces its power and normativity in PME through institutionalized processes, curricula, repertoire (canon) and other music industry norms (Smith, 2014, 2015a, 2015b), including the gendering of musical instruments (Abovitz, 2014; Green, 1997; Smith, 2013b). Indeed, PME scholars have argued that "to be authentically gendered in popular music is to be masculine" (Parkinson & Smith, 2015, p. 110). In institutions of higher popular music education (HPME), masculine domination is "visible and invisible . . . in at least five places: (1) Disciplines [instrument or voice], (2) Teaching faculty and staff, (3) Curriculum, (4) Executive function and power structure and (5) Pedagogic models", with a more equitable situation being apparent on songwriting programmes (Smith, 2015b, p. 71). Given the increasing, governmentally mandated focus in HPME on preparing students for careers in industry (Jones, chapter 27, this volume; McLaughlin, chapter 10, this volume; Morrow et al., chapter 26, this volume; Parkinson & Smith, 2015), there are clear tensions and ethical challenges confronting educators and institutions who may be working towards equitable ends in and through music education and seeking simultaneously to effectively prepare students for an industry that endorses and perpetuates sexism and even misogyny (Smith, 2015a). Furthermore, the focus in contemporary capitalist societies, and thus in education, on entrepreneurship (Hallam & Gaunt, 2012; Hewison, 2014; Jones, chapter 27, this volume; McLaughlin, chapter 10, this volume) is further evidence that "masculine domination (arguably at the root of the neoliberal agenda) has stacked the cards against women in entrepreneurship and the wider employment marketplace" (Smith, 2015b, p. 67).

In light of gendered inequities, Bourdieu issues a call to action for educators:

If it is true that the principle of the perpetuation of this relationship of dominations [resides] . . . in agencies such as the school or the state . . . then a vast

Epistemological and sociological issues

field of action is opened up for feminist struggles, which are thus called upon to take a distinctive and decisive place within political struggles against all forms of domination.

(Bourdieu, 2001, p. 4)

Following Bourdieu, Gareth has argued (Smith, 2015b, pp. 77–78) that, "while dealing with the necessary and urgent work of tacking masculine domination, educators must see this in the wider context of fighting for democracy and social justice on all possible fronts" and suggests adoption and implementation of a "feminist pedagogy" in schools and in higher education (Coeyman, 1996), which would address equality and focus on the necessity of taking action.

Bourdieu's ideas, while illuminating, are not comprehensive or infallible (McNay, 1999). Limitations to the effective application of Bourdieu's models or tools can stem from, for instance, the origin of his theories from (largely, but not entirely) ethnographic work undertaken in France and other European locations in the mid-20th century. As such, Bourdieu's observations should not be over-generalized or presumed to be effective in wholesale transfer to sites and situations in other contexts (times, spaces and places). For instance, Butler's (1999) theory of performativity – discussed in the following section of this chapter by Joseph Abramo – challenges some of Bourdieu's assertions about how societies, and thus individuals, are structured and behave. As Prior points out, it may be especially important to consider "what is at stake in the 'post-Bourdieu' moment when a position once considered progressive and critical now acts as the foil against which new work is being conducted" (2015, p. 349). While Bourdieu's ideas offer no cure for any perceived ills of PME, they are valuable means for critiquing – and therefore, potentially affecting change – in the structures and systems of and around PME.

Several other chapters in this book have made brief reference to gender issues in the context of popular music education (see Hooper, chapter 13, this volume; Hughes, chapter 15, this volume; Schwarz, chapter 18, this volume; Rathgeber, chapter 29, this volume; Christophersen & Gullberg, chapter 33, this volume). This is a theme that we consider to be particularly important, meriting even deeper theoretical discussion for the purpose of illustrating constructive ways that the diverse manifestations of gender can be explored in popular music education.

Gender performativity in theory

The American philosopher, linguist and gender theorist Judith Butler's theory of *performativity* may situate performance and composition in popular music within a critical framework. Performativity offers a view of everyday actions, and music-making being one of them, in relation to social roles and norms. Looking at how these everyday actions are influenced, and in turn influence music-making, provides a way to see how music education is both bounded and restricted by these social norms and how it may be an avenue to question and challenge these roles when they become restrictive.

Butler's argument is the critique of an inner or inherent identity that gives rise to actions. The commonly held belief is that we are born as, say, a man, and because of that identity given at birth, men act in particular ways. In its extreme form, it is the belief that by being male, men and boys are more likely to be aggressive, or predisposed towards math or sports. Butler's argument of performativity is to reverse this view. It is not that identity gives rise to repeated actions, but that actions, when repeated, give the semblance of a fixed, natural identity one is born with. Butler (1999) states that "there need not be a 'doer behind the deed,' but that the 'doer' is variably constructed in and through the deed" (p. 181). For a subject to become intelligible and known, it must be mediated through the action. Even doing 'nothing' is understood here as an act. Through repetition of acts, beings appear as consistent and taking on a fixed identity.

Performativity suggests that gendered identities are constituted through acts. For Butler, "[t]here is no gender identity behind the expressions of gender; that identity is performatively constituted by the very 'expressions' that are said to be its results" (p. 33). Gender is a series of acts that are not determined by the biology of the person. Instead, through repeated acts, the semblance of a fixed gendered identity emerges.

These performative enactments are, however, not conscious or intentional, but are 'urged-on' by the discourse of gender difference and gender hierarchy. Performativity, then, will have direct bearing on the materiality of the body as well as how one perceives the sex of an individual's body. The discourse on gender urges subjects to act in accordance with either side of the gender binary, shape their bodies into these binaries of the male and female sex and gender, and also conceive of sex and gender as a binary. In lieu of creating 'hard' categories of male and female, it may be more accurate to view gender as multiple or on a continuum between two extremes of male and female. Performativity construes even biological sex not as something fixed, untouched by society, but as a social construct created by discourses and everyday interactions between people.

Because performativity is not intentional, performance and performativity are related but not synonymous. As Butler (1993) notes, "performativity [is] not [understood] as the act by which a subject brings into being what she/he names, but, rather as that reiterative power of discourse to produce the phenomena that it regulates and constrains" (p. 2). A performance implies intentionality; a musician shapes a performance by creating musical gestures with the explicit intent of generating a work of art or entertaining an audience. *Performativity*, however, is not as intentional as *performance*. When individuals performatively enact gender, they draw upon gender norms both consciously and unconsciously, and intentionally and unintentionally. Instead, "performativity", Butler (1993) writes, "must be understood not as a singular or deliberate 'act,' but, rather, as the reiterative and citational practice by which discourse produces the effects that it names" (p. 2). In other words, gendered identity is not a performance one wilfully enacts like a musical performer, but a set of expectations and norms that, when repeated by many individuals in many different contexts, create and justify themselves.

Epistemological and sociological issues

Performativity provides a fruitful way of understanding gender's relation to music, and particularly popular music where visual aspects – like an artist's image and music videos – lyrics and fashion are integral. Performativity might suggest how hegemonic gendered identities become reinscribed and reinforced through popular music. Musical gestures that performatively police and define gender are ubiquitous in contemporary popular music. Popular musicians readily call upon gendered and racial performative gestures to enact musical performances, and the audience uses discourses on gender and race to understand and interpret images and music. For example, when writing this chapter, the number one song on the Top 40 charts in the United States was pop star Taylor Swift's "Bad Blood", which also features the rapper Kendrick Lamar. The song putatively describes a romantic relationship that has "gone" bad. The opening of the video shows Taylor Swift, or more accurately a character played by Taylor Swift, engaging in hand-to-hand combat with men in an office building. As she deftly bests her opponents, her body is marked as feminine through certain corporal gestures. She wears a corset, miniskirt and stockings, displaying her, ostensibly, for the gratification and consumption of the heterosexual male gaze. She also applies makeup and continually fixes her hair. Similarly, Swift is accompanied by a fellow female fighter, who keeps tabs on Swift's whereabouts by viewing her in a compact mirror used to apply cosmetics. Later in the video, gendered performativity is apparent as other female characters test James Bond-like weapons that are made from women's accessories, such as a handbag that turns into *nun-chucks* and a compact mirror that shoots *shurikens*.

While the visual imagery of the video points to obvious gendering and objectification of the female body, the performativity influences the music as well. Since the 19th century, music theorists and the general public have associated lyricism with femininity and rhythm with masculinity. As musicologist Susan McClary (1991) has pointed out, in the 19th century, the rhythmic first themes of symphonies were described by musicologists as masculine themes, while the secondary, lyrical themes – often more chromatic in character – were called feminine themes. This dichotomy is shared between Taylor Swift and Kendrick Lamar. Swift sings a lyrical, albeit repetitive, hook, while Lamar raps rhythmic interludes. Racial performativity is also at play. In Western cultures, and in particular the US, white audience members have associated rhythms with black culture, like jazz and hip-hop, and black bodies, while harmony and melody have been associated with whiteness (Born, 2000; Radano, 2000). Swift and Lamar fulfil commonly held associations about white and black performers. One might argue that the roles that Swift and Lamar take are obvious because of their performing identities; quite simply Swift is a singer-songwriter and Lamar is a rapper. But their roles become intelligible, perhaps even popular and appealing to a large audience, because they fulfil their gendered and racial identities through music.

Key to this argument is not to assume that these roles are immutable and essential to their identities. Swift's singer-songwriter identity is not predetermined by her gender and race, due to biology or even strictly due to cultural norms, and similarly Lamar is not naturally rhythmic because he is male and black. Instead, according to the theory of performativity, it is the other way around. Their gendered and racial identities are in part understood through musical gestures.

As I have so far portrayed performativity, it appears as a restrictive hold that polices gender and people's gendered actions. But Swift and Lamar, or anyone else for that matter, are not necessarily to be understood here as inescapably determined by performativity. Rather, by becoming aware of the discourses that inform performativity, agents can begin to reform and challenge these discourses and norms. There are examples of gendered performativity in music that challenge and shift gendered norms and the related but different phenomenon of sexuality. Frank Ocean's album *Agent Orange*, for example, famously included songs about gay desire in the largely heteronormative genre of R&B. The 1970s and 1980s pop music scene was replete with gendered performativity that shifted hegemonic representations of gender through fashion, including androgynous use of make-up and 'feminine' clothes and gestures by Boy George, David Bowie's Ziggy Stardust and 'hair metal bands' such as Poison, Mötley Crüe and Twisted Sister (Walser, 1993). These performative acts, however, did not run deep; while these men wore cosmetics, they sang about sexual escapades and objectification of women. Perhaps more disruptive, the riot grrrls of the 1990s used punk music and fashion to challenge narrow conceptions of femininity (Feigenbaum, 2007).

The usefulness of the performativity concept should now be recognizable in relation to popular music generally, and in the next section we will demonstrate specific applications to educational contexts. But before moving on, we should also briefly acknowledge that while Butler's ideas have gained considerable attention across the humanities – particularly interdisciplinary fields such as cultural studies and queer studies – they are not as widely accepted by philosophers or scholars in the biological and social sciences. For instance, renowned philosopher Martha Nussbaum, author of *Sex and Social Justice* (1999), issued an especially cogent critique that charges Butler with offering nihilistic arguments in arcane postmodernist rhetoric which fail to acknowledge the influence of earlier feminists, such as Catherine MacKinnon, ultimately reaching the conclusion that "Feminism demands more and women deserve better" (Nussbaum, 1999). Biologists and social scientists have noted that with the rare exception of intersex/hermaphrodites, 99.9% of the population worldwide is effortlessly identified at birth (and at death by legally accountable coroners) as biologically male or female irrespective of 'performative' behaviours (such as clothing), so this 'binary' is universally recognized as an empirically functioning truism, not merely a social construct limited to specific cultures that force binary thinking onto what is naturally a continuum between male and female, as Butler has argued. Butler also appears to have not acknowledged sex differences among non-human mammals, preferring to limit her discussion to a view of 'culture' that is divorced from empirical sciences such as biology, which also support a binary view despite the occurrence of intersex/hermaphroditism and homosexual behaviours among other mammals. Our discussion of 'performativity' should not be taken as an assertion that Butler's theory is without notable flaws (for surely every theory has certain inadequacies). Still, we argue that performativity can function as an easily understandable and useful conceptual tool for practical discussions among students of popular music education.

Performativity in popular music practice

What are some ways that the performativity concept has been productively applied in educational settings? Some music educators have suggested that performativity in mainstream popular music and culture influences students learning to perform and compose popular music in formal educational settings. Abramo (2011a) has documented the different rehearsal processes employed by girls and boys. Boys used musical gestures – or playing of licks that overlapped with verbal communication – as outlined in the research in informal and popular music processes (Allsup, 2003; Green, 2002). Conversely, the girls used a cycle of discussion then playing that separated vocal communication and playing. As a result, the girls used more verbal language than the boys. When boys and girls rehearsed together there were moments of miscommunication when they boys did not value the girls' rehearsal techniques. Abramo (2011b) found similar differences in the compositions of the same boys and girls. He found that the musical forms, timbres and arrangements differed between the genders. Their lyrics also presented a different sense of agency; they boys projected a universalized sense of agency where they would topple world powers, where the girls wrote of helplessness and small acts of agency, usually within romantic relationships. In these studies, then, students largely conformed to their gendered identities; popular music in school became a space where their musical identities were influenced by discourses on gender and, conversely, they performatively constituted their gendered identity through music performance and composition.

Tobias (2014) extended and complicated gendered performativity in the classroom. In the study of an elective songwriting and technology course in a Southwestern US high school, Tobias found similar performativity of gender, but also moments when participants challenged the discourses that give rise to performativity. In particular, the participant 'Esmeralda' weaved in and out of differing performative discourses of gender. As a singer-songwriter, she wrote songs about love and strummed an acoustic guitar, similar to Abramo's (2011b) participants. But, as a heavy metal drummer, she challenged these gendered roles.

These studies, as well as the example of "Bad Blood", suggest that gender performativity and musical genre are linked. 'Male-dominated' genres, like heavy metal and rap, contrast with the female-dominated pop genres. As a result, musical gestures regularly employed with each of these genres often are associated with genders. This is not determinist; there is room for musicians to play with, challenge and change how these musical gestures relate to gendered identity.

Performativity provides one of many avenues towards critical popular music education. Music education through performance and composition is the gathering of musical gestures as well as the ability to generate new gestures. Students learn the licks by transcribing solos and other recordings; they understand, perform and create common chord progressions and melodic and rhythmic structures. They also gain the ability to create new licks, chord progressions, melodies and rhythms, all while staying with stylistic norms of the genre of music they learn, and at times, combining and altering these practices. In this way, students begin to form a musician identity. Performativity as a theory may be a way for students and educators to understand this as a citational process. These licks are not the creation of an individual actor, or a radically new product. Instead, they gesture to the past, citing past practices in ways that are similar to Barthes' (1977) ideas, particularly that of "the death of the author". But through repeated acts, the student, if studying for professional musicianship, starts to develop a performatively constituted musician identity. An understanding of this process enables students to make valuable insights into how they may best develop their musicianship.

But this must not be seen as merely an *inter-sonic* process, or limited to creative manipulation of sounds. Rather, musical gestures may be understood as influenced by gendered norms as well as norms around other identities, like race and class. Because genres and specific musical roles are often associated with particular identities, the musical gestures and roles available to students and how audiences will read them are influenced by gender. For example, because the drum set in popular music is perceived as a male-dominated instrument, when women play drums they must understand that the ways they perform on the instrument can be influenced by these discourses. But such awareness is not merely limiting; a female drummer might also use this to her musical advantage, as well as a means of making a political statement by challenging gendered norms. Whether they see performativity as a limiting parameter or a chance for agency, students can understand popular music and performance as a process intertwined with non-musical influences like gender and race.

Performativity also enables educators to ask, in what ways do my classroom and instruction reinforce and challenge gendered norms and provide a welcoming space for gender non-conforming students and those interested in playing with gender performativity? But this question is not guaranteed by the theory of performativity. Currently, in popular culture, there may be a shifting of gendered norms. Transgender celebrities such as athlete Caitlyn Jenner and actor Laverne Cox have shifted conversation in the mainstream to be more – but not completely – accepting of gender non-conforming persons. Within music education, Nichols (2013) has documented the narrative of one transgendered student who found acceptance and agency in a school band and choir. Regardless of these changes, some have critiqued how performativity may adequately address transgendered persons' experiences and desires. Transgender persons – who change gender and sex because they 'feel like they are in the wrong body' – wilfully and consciously construct their identity within gendered binaries because they identify as 'woman' or 'man'. Conversely, gender-queer people do not identify as a gender but fluctuate between genders or create categories of gender that are neither male nor female. Schep (2011) argues that performativity would privilege the gender-queer identity because they performatively play with identity, whereas a transgendered person "is a victim of essentialist delusions, unable to unmask the categories that underlie her experience as performatively established" (p. 868).

Even when performativity is actualized as a liberatory theory aimed at undoing restrictive and proscriptive gendered practices, it may still marginalize or at least fail to explain some non-gender conforming persons. Educators who want to create a more inclusive space, even with the best of intentions, might carefully attend to how they construe and justify difference.

Institutionalization of popular music education

Paradigms and precedents

In the introduction to the present book, Thomas Kuhn's notion of scientific "paradigms" was mentioned as one way of conceptualizing the emergence and development of academic fields. Here it is productive to also consider Stephen Toulmin's arguments against Kuhn as we assess whether it is fully accurate to claim that popular music education has indeed come into its own as a distinct field (Nickels, 2012). Philosophers Toulmin and Goodfield argued, contrary to Kuhn, that "thorough-going revolutions are just about out of the question" in the historical development of scientific knowledge (Toulmin & Goodfield, 1961, p. 164). According to Toulmin's perspective, "Kuhn's overly rigid conception of normal science requires him to make an overly sharp, revolutionary break between an instance of normal science and its historical successor" (Nickels, 2012, p. 113). This suggests that the bar may be unnecessarily high if we rely on Kuhn's conceptualization as a basis for determining the legitimacy of popular music education as a movement or field. Indeed, one might legitimately claim that several new music subfields have emerged across recent years, even if their emergence might not fully qualify as a scientific 'revolution'.

But is it necessarily an exaggeration to suggest that some form of revolution has occurred in this case? In the decades immediately before and after the turn of the 21st century, an array of competing arguments could be identified concerning the possible value and relevance of popular music education. As recently as 2004, in a resource called *The Popular Music Teaching Handbook*, Cooper declared that "Because few teachers consider rock to be 'serious music' – let alone 'serious history' – few classes have explored the sociopolitical imagery contained in songs" (Cooper & Condon, 2004, p. 2), and this was while prominent scholars continued to argue that even the most respected songwriters and bands in popular music genres lacked any artistic merit (Scruton, 1997), and deserved no place in education (Walker, 2007). A few philosophers were beginning to consider the opposite position, taking a courageous risk with their suggestion that rock music (Gracyk, 2007) and even hip-hop may have 'aesthetic' value (Shusterman, 2000). Forward-thinking musicologists also increasingly added pressure on those with more conservative views by studying various popular music styles under the presupposition that they had artistic value (Moore, 2001). By 2000, the UK had already experienced substantial growth in popular music studies, but in the US only a small number of music teacher educators were publicly arguing in favour of popular music, with such unambiguous statements as "progress in this area may take on many forms, ranging from hiring a popular music specialist to taking on new course offerings" (Hebert & Campbell, 2000, p. 19). The first scholarly book concerning issues in the teaching of popular music in the US was published in 2004, some decades after notable books in this field had been produced by Vulliamy, Swanwick and others in the UK (Rodriguez, 2004). Since 2010, several articles have celebrated signs of the emergence of 'popular music education' (Hebert, 2011a; Mantie, 2013; Powell et al., 2015; Smith, 2013a), but the present book appears to be the first major resource to formally define this as an established academic field of both research and practice. As recently as 2013, Roger Mantie had described a "lack of coherence and codification in the research and scholarship of popular music pedagogy" as "perhaps not surprising given its relative nascency" (Mantie, 2013, p. 335). It follows that the authors of the present book have sought to identify major themes and concepts, as well as prominent issues that largely serve to unify this young field. To some extent, such projects may inevitably be viewed as political acts, and some will surely question whether there is yet sufficient evidence to support the idea that popular music education is anything more than a minor subfield, perhaps merely a pedagogical approach that is likely to 'blur' with other approaches as it is inevitably accepted into mainstream music education (Bowman, 2014, p. 9), or a pedagogically oriented subfield within the broader field of popular music studies (Scott, 2009). But would that be a fair and accurate assessment of the status quo, or give reliable indications of what popular music education is actually becoming?

It stands to reason that one might also gain insights by comparing popular music education with other similarly young music fields, such as community music, which already has been productively theorized (Higgins, 2012; Veblen et al., 2013). Some universities have developed community music degree programmes, but they appear thus far to be relatively few, and in only a small number of countries, compared to other music fields with a longer history. However, community music is young, and it is difficult to predict whether this field might in time become extremely popular. Jazz studies, which gradually, across more than five decades, came to be accepted in many higher education programmes around the world, shares many features in common with rock music, and these two broad genres comprising diverse sub-styles can even be taught using some similar techniques (Hebert, 2011b). It remains to be seen how jazz studies will respond to the emergence of popular music education, and whether the two fields might merge to some extent, or remain distinct.

One aim of this research companion is to demonstrate that popular music education has indeed become established, as both a field of teaching practice and one of academic research. This requires careful consideration of what may be legitimately taken as reliable indications that a field has become fully 'institutionalized'. What could reasonably be taken as confirmatory evidence of the extent to which popular music has (or has not) managed to come into its own as an established academic field of study, practice and research? We acknowledge that thus far, few if any of the elite universities and conservatoires have established degree programs in popular music education, although we have witnessed a recent proliferation of bachelor's degrees in popular music performance as well as music education

Epistemological and sociological issues

degrees that unofficially emphasize the teaching of popular music styles. What evidence from various chapters of this book may legitimately be interpreted as supporting a compelling claim for its establishment as a distinct field? Conversely, what might be interpreted as evidence refuting this position, and how might we anticipate future developments?

Institutionalization theory

In order to address such questions systematically, it is useful to consider how institutionalization is conceived by sociologists, particularly in terms of social, artistic and academic legitimation. In an influential early discussion of the notion of institutionalization that has resonated across more than 50 years, Peter Berger and Thomas Luckmann argue that reality, as pragmatically understood within human relationships, is socially constructed via institutions that promote particular ideologies (Berger & Luckmann, 1967). According to this view, institutionalization ascribes "collective meaning and value to particular entities and activities" in a social context (Meyer et al., 1987, p. 13). In other words, as a social practice is institutionalized, it becomes associated with particular rules and norms of behaviour. Another theoretical approach that expands in a similar direction is semiotician Theo van Leeuwen's (2007) model of social legitimation in discourse (see discussion in Hebert & McCollum, 2014, pp. 110–111). Both Berger and van Leeuwen's conceptualizations enable assessment of how a practice becomes institutionalized in discourse via *general social legitimation*. This question can also be considered in relation to the more specific theme of *artistic legitimation*, for adoption into academic contexts may be taken as offering some reliable indication that an artistic movement has been fully accepted by society at large. Sociologist Shyon Baumann developed a theory of artistic legitimation (2007) featuring three essential components: (1) political opportunity structures, (2) resource mobilization and (3) frames of discourse. Baumann argues in this theory that the institutionalization of any new art form – including popular music – is profoundly affected by how the genre is perceived in terms of identity politics, financial backing and the ways in which its meaning and social function are interpreted. In relation to the aforementioned theme of educational 'success', it is also notable here that Bauman has argued that "social movement success and art world success are kindred legitimation processes" (Baumann, 2007, p. 61).

Finally, this question may be considered in relation to the theme of *academic legitimation*. When it comes to the specific issue of the institutionalization of academic fields, Tony Becher and Paul Trowler have produced what are probably the most notable contributions (Becher & Trowler, 2001; Trowler et al., 2012). Their delineation of academia into 'tribes' and 'territories' demonstrates how the dynamics of personal politics and group loyalties often plays a major role in the success of interdisciplinary projects and openness towards new fields of study. Through this book, we have demonstrated evidence of what may arguably be understood as a new field: *popular music education*. But we do so in the recognition that some academic 'tribes', with 'territories' already claimed as their own, may respond with enthusiasm, or ambivalence, or even reject this argument altogether. In our view, we have presented ample evidence to support our position. However, there are also some indications of valid claims to the contrary, which we regard to be rapidly fading. For instance, signs of the field's relative lack of maturity include a tendency for scholars of popular music education to work in theoretical silos with little awareness or recognition of each other's work. Specifically, some PME scholars tend to write about their own projects as if they alone are doing work in this field, and only rarely cite others where relevant or responsibly acknowledge the history of ideas and developments in the field. Others appear to intentionally misrepresent the positions of prominent scholars through exaggeration in order to make their own approach seem relatively stronger. We suggest that the present book may serve as a unique resource that to some extent helps alleviate this problem by clearly identifying some of the field's major issues and lineage of relevant scholarly work, which we have attempted to convey without fear or favour.

Commercialization, democracy and the Nordic model

One particularly complicated aspect of this field is the fact that 'popular music', according to its very definition, consists of what to some extent qualify as commercialized genres. Commercialization is a social force that, for good reason, is generally regarded with suspicion in both academic and artistic contexts (Ivey, 2010). However, we must also acknowledge that all forms of music, from campfire folk songs to professional opera, have been commercialized in the contemporary world, in which all aspects of human life are – sometimes quite regrettably – viewed in terms of commodities with exchange value as 'intellectual property'. The difference here may be merely one of degree, intention or public image. This point becomes especially clear when one considers that popular music education has become especially supported in nations known for socialistic (rather than corporate-capitalistic) policies, including the Nordic welfare states.

Several authors have suggested that the Nordic region is particularly advanced in the field of popular music education (Christophersen, 2013, and chapter 33, this volume), but this may also reflect more general trends across society at large (Holt & Kärjä, 2016). Indeed, across recent decades popular music has become intimately connected to the most high-profile public rituals in the Nordic countries (Hebert et al., 2012), and it has become firmly rooted in schools, at all levels of education (Brinck, 2014; Georgii-Hemming & Westvall, 2010; Kallio, 2015; Tønsberg, 2014). Still, we must also responsibly consider a widespread concern that in some Nordic countries this movement might have already been taken "too far" (Tønsberg, 2013). Many Nordic symphony orchestras and opera companies now hire numerous foreigners partly due to a widespread perception that, across recent decades, due to the explosive growth of popular music education in schools, few 'locals' are graduating with sufficient skills in art music, such as sight-reading ability and mastery of 'common practice' vocal and instrumental skills. While Nordic countries may now claim to have a disproportionately high amount of successful performers in popular music styles, the same could no longer be convincingly

Epistemological and sociological issues

said of European art music were it not for the practice of hiring foreign nationals for membership in professional Nordic ensembles. Is this the kind of issue that may legitimately cause concern among educators and cultural policy-makers, and should those in popular music education be wary of this development? With the previous discussion of educational 'success' in mind, should we consider whether it is possible in such cases to become victims of our own success?

And what of 'democracy', an ideology embraced in the Nordic countries as much as elsewhere in the contemporary world (Hebert & Heimonen, 2013; Heimonen & Hebert, 2010), as well as common claims that popular music education is inherently more democratic relative to other approaches to music teaching and learning? In some innovative approaches, "students are called upon to provide and replenish the cache of popular music source material used in the classroom" (Rosenberg, 2011, p. 48). Such practices enable popular music content to be continuously updated, without the teacher necessarily withdrawing to the point of becoming merely a 'facilitator' or encouraging observer of student learning. However, critics have claimed that in some approaches to popular music in schools the teacher is no longer expected to actively teach. If that were the case – and, in fact, it may actually be a misinterpretation – what impact would such an expectation ultimately have on the health of the music teaching profession? Should music teachers be expected to have expertise, irrespective of what genre they are teaching, and can an admirable openness to inclusion of diverse genres in schools be legitimately used as a long-term excuse for ultimately failing to develop relevant expertise? Critical interpretations of some approaches to popular music education have suggested there is some acceptance of this idea, yet we doubt whether that is truly what any major scholar in our field would actually advocate.

Conclusions and future directions

Research and social forces

In this concluding chapter we have discussed some general themes for the purpose of drawing together ideas from across the entire book. In one part of this chapter we chose to highlight performativity, a specific gender theory that has gained currency across recent decades. In another section, we discussed the relevance of Bourdieu's theories, including habitus, and his vision of structure and agency, and male domination. What are some alternative approaches also worth consideration? In addition to other gender theories is an array of social constructs linked to various themes associated with a social justice agenda (Benedict et al., 2015; Regelski & Gates, 2009), particularly social economic status (Doyle, 2014) and ethnicity (Hebert, 2010). Intertwined with such constructs are critical questions such as "how and why poverty and education are jointly linked and implicated in maintaining disadvantages and underachievement" (Raffo et al., 2010, p. 8), which may in both music and education be interpreted in relation to examination of an array of powerful social forces, including global 'free market' corporatization (Prest, 2013), nationalism (Hebert & Kertz-Welzel, 2012), postcolonialism (Hess, 2015), even militarism (Hebert, 2015) and a gargantuan global mass surveillance apparatus that increasingly makes democracy vulnerable to the whims of unrestrained governments and unregulated corporations that confiscate and analyze all digital communications without accountability (Schneier, 2015). Further studies in such directions promise to demonstrate the actual 'terms and conditions' of musical life in the contemporary world, potentially revealing ways that artistic freedom can be collectively nurtured despite the growing threats that it faces worldwide.

Popular music education could also arguably benefit from increased application of concepts and discoveries from the broader field of popular music studies (Scott, 2009). For instance, the finding that the general harmonic features of hit pop songs tend to evolve in predictable patterns across decades (Jensen & Hebert, 2015) supports the idea that musical trends can reasonably be projected using techniques similar to those for which economists and financial advisors command high salaries. Songwriters and musicians concerned about commercial viability might consciously choose to either follow or reject such predictions as they develop popular music to suit particular purposes. We recognize here that some styles are clearly situated in an aesthetic that is unlikely to ever appeal to the majority tastes – alternative sensibilities that are not confused with common 'pop' music – and this is fully understood by performers. Still, even the development of discrete subgenres could be studied using techniques based on meta-analyses of sound files that trace various musical parameters across historical time, which could inform the work of teachers and students in these genres.

How to proceed?

How might we view the bigger picture in terms of the potential impact of popular music education in broader society? And how are we to proceed? We should note here that the interconnected fields of popular music and popular music education may be understood as caught in a power struggle between the competing, contradictory and, paradoxically, *symbiotic* forces of capitalist market pressures, individual entitlement and agency, mutual dependency and social democratic aspirations. Allsup explains this complicated situation as "a great contradiction . . . a global world that is contracted and closed; the conflation of difference with market opportunity; a wondrous multiplicity of voices, along with their silencing; 'democracies' run by unaccountable experts and unaccountable elites" (2015, p. 251).

There are, then, for popular music educators – and for scholars and students (and their parents) in PME – difficult challenges around the ethics of encouraging, celebrating and perpetuating highly problematic practices and attitudes. To extend Woodward's argument from her chapter, perhaps popular music education is or *should be* in more ways a battleground for the ethical, musical, educational and fundamentally *human* struggles of our time. If, as Woodward states, in popular music we have a chance to make a difference in and through PME, to whose standards, attitudes or beliefs would we wish to be held accountable?

The issues facing popular music education are wide-ranging, interconnected and impossible to avoid. They can appear insurmountable. All the more reason, then, to discuss, debate and directly deal with them. The field would find itself in a bizarre situation were we to educate ourselves, and our students, out of making popular music altogether. It is, however, equally apparent that to continue to endorse socio-musical practices predicated on the perpetuation of brutal and oppressive symbolic and fiscal, social violence on a global scale would require a collective, complicit blindness and amnesia in which participation is not an ethical option. With popular music and education both being at the core of many of the most formative and transformative experiences of so many people, we are ethically and morally obliged as a profession to act. We are certain it is possible to achieve and sustain (through rethinking and re-creating) a popular music education that takes full account of its context as well as its consequences.

As teachers in higher education, it is both our privilege and responsibility to write for the purpose of producing and sharing new knowledge. Given the ideological and economic power structures that surround academic publishing, this volume will reach a tiny audience, whose individual and collective interests oblige it to contribute to, perpetuate, critique and *change* the systems that we sustain and, perhaps, sometimes, disdain. It is, nonetheless, our purpose, our calling and our obligation to act (Lynch et al., 2010). As for those studying in HPME, Giroux reminds us that:

> higher education may be one of the few sites left where students can learn about the limits of commercial values, address what it means to learn the skills of social citizenship, and work to deepen and expand the possibilities of collective agency and democratic life.
>
> *(cited in Bourdieu, 2003, p. 102)*

We state once more Allsup's affirming observations, cited earlier in this volume by Jones:

> neoliberalism is the true counter-narrative. We are inherently public people, not private; humanity cannot be reduced to a market force, nor the person to a brand. We want to work collaboratively, fairly and intentionally within conditions that provide for our flourishing; we are also wondrously irrational actors, following ends that are outside the logic of personal gain or use value. And as musicians, we know intimately that the arts have values that are richer, more complex and more confusing, than those attributed to commerce or mere self-identity.
>
> *(2015, p. 259)*

So to return to where the book began: this is a new moment. It may or may not represent a fresh paradigm *per se*, but at the very least this volume is the first of its kind, drawing together a wide range of perspectives and insights on popular music education that, together, elucidate, illuminate, complicate, challenge, provoke and invite discussion. The work of scholarship is never done; educational moments are different every day; and popular music does not stand still. This *Research Companion* is part of a continuing conversation – or, perhaps more accurately, contains threads of numerous conversations. We are delighted and honoured to take part in the debate, and we invite you to engage.

References

Abovitz, M. (2014). Letter from the editor. *Tom Tom Magazine: A Magazine About Female Drummers, 16*(3), 3.

Abramo, J.M. (2011a). Gender differences of popular music production in secondary schools. *Journal of Research in Music Education, 59*, 21–43. doi:10.1177/0022429410396095

Abramo, J.M. (2011b). Gender differences in the popular music compositions of high school students. *Music Education Research International, 5*, 1–11.

Allsup, R.E. (2003). Mutual learning and democratic action in instrumental music education. *Journal of Research in Music Education, 51*, 24–37. doi:10.2307/3345646

Allsup, R.E. (2015). The eclipse of a higher education or problems preparing artists in a mercantile world. *Music Education Research, 17*(3), 251–261.

Anderson, C. (2006). *The long tail: Why the future of business is selling less of more.* New York, NY: Hyperion.

Angus, I. (2007). Academic freedom in the corporate university. In M. Coté, R.J.P. Day & G. de Peuter (Eds.), *Utopian pedagogy: Radical experiments against neoliberal globalization* (pp. 64–75). London, ON: Toronto University Press.

Barrett, M.S. (Ed.) (2011). *A cultural psychology of music education.* New York, NY: Oxford University Press.

Baron-Cohen, S. (2003). *The essential difference: The truth about the male and female brain.* New York, NY: Basic Books.

Barthes, R. (1977). Death of the author. In S. Heath (Trans.) *Image-music-text* (pp. 142–148). New York, NY: Macmillan.

Baumann, S. (2007). A general theory of artistic legitimation: How art worlds are like social movements. *Poetics: Journal of Empirical Research on Literature, Media and the Arts, 35*(1), 47–65.

Becher, T. & Trowler, P.R. (2001). *Academic tribes and territories: Intellectual enquiry and the culture of disciplines* (2nd ed.). Buckingham: The Society for Research into Higher Education & Open University Press.

Bell, A.P. (2015). DAW democracy? The dearth of diversity in "playing the studio". *Journal of Music, Technology and Education, 8*(2), 129–146.

Bell, A.P. (2016). DIY recreational recording as music making. In R. Mantie & G.D. Smith (Eds.), *The Oxford handbook of music making and leisure.* New York, NY: Oxford University Press.

Benedict, C., Schmidt, P., Spruce, G., & Woodford, P. (Eds.) (2015). *Oxford Handbook of Social Justice in Music Education.* Oxford: Oxford University Press.

Bennett, D.E. (2013). The role of career creativities in developing identity and becoming expert selves. In P. Burnard (Ed.), *Developing creativities in higher music education: Practices and perspectives* (pp. 224–244). London: Routledge.

Berger, P.L., & Luckmann, T. (1967). *The social construction of reality: A treatise in the sociology of knowledge.* New York: Anchor Books.

Bernstein, B. (1971). *Class, codes and control, vol. 1: Theoretical studies towards a sociology of language.* London: Routledge and Kegan Paul.

Bernstein, B. (1973). *Class, codes and control, vol. 2: Applied studies towards a sociology of language*. London: Routledge and Kegan Paul.

Bernstein, B. (1975). *Class, codes and control, vol. 3: Towards a theory of educational transmissions*. London: Routledge.

Bernstein, B. (1990). *Class, codes and control, vol. 4: The structuring of pedagogic discourse*. London: Routledge and Kegan Paul.

Born, G. (2000). Music and the representation/articulation of sociocultural identities. In G. Born & D. Hesmondhalgh (Eds.), *Western music and its others: Difference, representation, and appropriation in music* (pp. 31–36). Berkeley, CA: University of California Press.

Bourdieu, P. (1984). *Distinction: A social critique of the judgement of taste*. Cambridge, MA: Harvard University Press.

Bourdieu, P. (2001). *Masculine domination*. Cambridge: Polity Press.

Bourdieu, P. (2003). *Firing back: Against the tyranny of the market 2*. London: Verso.

Bourdieu, P. (2005). *The social structures of the economy*. Cambridge: Polity Press.

Bowman, J. (2014). *Online learning in music: Foundations, frameworks, and practices*. Oxford: Oxford University Press.

Brinck, L. (2014). *Ways of the Jam: Collective and Improvisational Perspectives on Learning*. PhD dissertation, Aalborg University.

Brockman, D. (2014). The state of pop music 2014: Your average person doesn't give a shit about music, so why is it still popular? Retrieved from: http://www.vanyaland.com/2014/12/18/state-pop-2014-average-person-doesnt-give-shit-music-still-popular/ [Accessed 23 October 2015].

Burnard, P. (2012). *Musical creativities in practice*. New York, NY: Oxford University Press.

Burnard, P., Hofstander, Y., & Söderman, J. (Eds.) (2015). *Bourdieu and the sociology of music education*. Farnham: Ashgate.

Butler, J. (1993). *Bodies that matter*. New York, NY: Routledge.

Butler, J. (1999). *Gender trouble: Feminism and the subversion of identity* (10th anniversary ed.). New York, NY: Routledge.

Butler, J. (2004). *Undoing gender*. Abingdon: Routledge.

Cartwright, P.A. & Smith, G.D. (2013). Innovation and value in networks for emerging musicians. In N. Pfeffermann, T. Marshall & L. Mortara (Eds.), *Strategies and communications for innovations: An integrative management view for companies and networks*. New York, NY: Springer.

Christophersen, C. (2013). Future prospects for music education: Corroborating informal learning pedagogy: A review essay. *International Journal of Education & the Arts, 14* (Review 3). Retrieved from: http://www.ijea.org/v14r3/.

Coeyman, B. (1996). Applications of feminist pedagogy to the college music major curriculum: An introduction to the issues. *College Music Symposium, 36*, 73–90.

Cooper, B.L. & Condon, R.A. (2004). *The popular music teaching handbook: An educator's guide to music-related print resources*. Santa Barbara, CA: Libraries Unlimited.

D'Amore, A. & Smith, G.D. (2016). Aspiring to music making as leisure through the Musical Futures classroom. In R. Mantie & G.D. Smith (Eds.), *The Oxford handbook of music making and leisure* (pp. 61–80). New York, NY: Oxford University Press.

Dewey, J. (1938). *Education and experience*. New York, NY: Simon and Schuster.

Douglas, S. (2010). *Enlightened sexism: The seductive message that feminism's work is done*. New York, NY: Times Books.

Doyle, J.L. (2014). Cultural relevance in urban music education: A synthesis of the literature. *Update: Applications of Research in Music Education, 32*(2), 44–51.

Feigenbaum, A. (2007). *Remapping the resonances of riot Grrrl: Feminisms, postfeminisms, and "processes" of punk* (pp. 132–153). Durham, NC: Duke University Press.

Freire, P. (2000). *Pedagogy of the oppressed*. London: Bloomsbury.

Georgii-Hemming, E. & Westvall, M. (2010). Music education – A personal matter?: Examining the current discourses of music education in Sweden. *British Journal of Music Education, 27*(1), 21–33.

Giroux, H.A. (2014). *Neoliberalism's war on higher education*. Chicago, IL: Haymarket.

Gracyk, T. (2007). *Listening to popular music: Or, how I learned to stop worrying and love Led Zeppelin*. Ann Arbor, MI: University of Michigan Press.

Green, L. (1997). *Music, gender, education*. Cambridge: Cambridge University Press.

Green, L. (2002). *How popular musicians learn: A way ahead for music education*. Aldershot: Ashgate.

Green, L. (2008). *Music on deaf ears: Musical meaning, ideology, education*. Manchester: Manchester University Press.

Hallam, S. & Gaunt, H. (2012). *Preparing for success: A practical guide for young musicians*. London: Institute of Education.

Hebert, D.G. (2010). Ethnicity and music education: Sociological dimensions. In R. Wright (Ed.), *Sociology and Music Education* (pp. 93–114). Aldershot: Ashgate Press.

Hebert, D.G. (2011a). Originality and institutionalization: Factors engendering resistance to popular music pedagogy in the U.S.A. *Music Education Research International, 5*, 12–21.

Hebert, D.G. (2011b). Jazz and rock music. In W.M. Anderson & P.S. Campbell (Eds.), *Multicultural perspectives in music education*, Vol. 1 (3rd ed.) (pp. 112–127). Lanham, MD: Rowman-Littlefield Publishers.

Hebert, D.G. (2015). Another perspective: Militarism in music education. *Music Educators Journal, 101*(3), 77–84.

Hebert, D.G. & Campbell, P.S. (2000). Rock music in American schools: Positions and practices since the 1960s. *International Journal of Music Education, 36*(1), 14–22.

Hebert, D.G. & Heimonen, M. (2013). Public policy and music education in Norway and Finland. *Arts Education Policy Review, 114*(3), 135–148.

Hebert, D.G., Kallio, A.A., & Odendaal, A. (2012). Not *so* silent night: Tradition, transformation, and cultural understandings of Christmas music events in Helsinki, Finland. *Ethnomusicology Forum, 21*(3), 402–423.

Hebert, D.G. & Kertz-Welzel, A. (Eds.) (2012). *Patriotism and nationalism in music education*. Aldershot: Ashgate.

Hebert, D.G. & McCollum, J. (2014). Philosophy of history and theory in historical ethnomusicology. In J. McCollum & D.G. Hebert (Eds.), *Theory and method in historical ethnomusicology* (pp. 85–147). Lanham, MD: Lexington Books.

Heimonen, M. & Hebert, D.G. (2010). Pluralism and minority rights in music education: Implications of the legal and social philosophical dimensions. *Visions of Research in Music Education*, 15.

Hess, J. (2015). Decolonizing music education: Moving beyond tokenism. *International Journal of Music Education*. DOI: 10.1177/0255761415581283.

Hewison, R. (2014). *Cultural capital: The rise and fall of Creative Britain*. London: Verso.

Higgins, L. (2012). *Community music: In theory and in practice*. Oxford: Oxford University Press.

Holt, F. & Kärjä, A. (Eds.) (2016). *Oxford handbook of popular music in the Nordic countries*. Oxford: Oxford University Press.

Ivey, B. (2010). *Arts, Inc.: How greed and neglect have destroyed our cultural rights*. Berkeley, CA: University of California Press.

Jensen, K. & Hebert, D.G. (2015). Predictability of harmonic complexity across 75 years of popular music hits. In E. Miranda, J. Eaton & D. Williams (Eds.), Proceedings of the 11th *International Symposium on Computer Music Multidisciplinary Research*. (pp. 198–212). Retrieved from: http://cmr.soc.plymouth.ac.uk/cmmr2015/proceedings.pdf

Kallio, A.A. (2015). Drawing a line in water: Constructing the school censorship frame in popular music education. *International Journal of Music Education*, *33*(2) 195–209.

Kirschner, T. (1998). Studying rock: Toward a materialist ethnography. In T. Swiss, J.M. Sloop & A. Herman (Eds.), *Mapping the beat: Popular music and contemporary theory* (pp. 247–268). Malden, MA: Blackwell.

Krikun, A. (2016). "Perilous blessing of leisure": Music and leisure in the United States, 1890–1945. In R. Mantie & G.D. Smith (Eds.), *The Oxford handbook of music making and leisure* (pp. 241–260). New York, NY: Oxford University Press.

Lévis Strauss, C. (1978). *Structural anthropology, vols. 1 & 2*. Harmondsworth: Penguin.

Lynch, K., Crean, M. & Moran, M. (2010). Equality and social justice: The university as a site of struggle. In M.W. Apple, S.J. Ball & L.A. Gandin (Eds.), *The Routledge International Handbook of the Sociology of Education* (pp. 296–305). Oxford: Routledge.

Mantie, R. (2013). A comparison of "popular music pedagogy" discourses. *Journal of Research in Music Education*, *61*(3), 334–352.

Mantie, R. (2015). Liminal or lifelong: Leisure, recreation, and the future of music education. In C. Randles (Ed.), *Music education: Navigating the future* (pp. 168–182). New York, NY: Routledge.

Mantie, R. (2016). An open letter to Charles Keil. In R. Mantie & G.D. Smith (Eds.), *The Oxford handbook of music making and leisure* (pp. 612–640). New York, NY: Oxford University Press.

McCarthy, M. (2016). Creating a framework for music making and leisure: Max Kaplan leads the way. In R. Mantie & G.D. Smith (Eds.), *The Oxford handbook of music making and leisure*. New York, NY: Oxford University Press.

McClary, S. (1991). *Feminine endings: Music, gender and sexuality*. Minneapolis, MN: University of Minnesota Press.

McNay, L. (1999). Subject, psyche and agency: The work of Judith Butler. *Theory, Culture & Society*, *16*(2), 175–193.

Meyer, J.W., Boli, J., & Thomas, G. M. (1987). Ontology and rationalization in the western cultural account. *Institutional structure: Constituting state, society, and the individual*, 12–37.

Middleton, R. (1990). *Studying popular music*. Milton Keynes: Open University Press.

Moore, A.F. (2001). *Rock: The primary text – Developing a musicology of rock* (2nd ed.). Aldershot: Ashgate.

Nash, R. (1999). Bourdieu, "habitus", and educational research: Is it all worth the candle? *British Journal of Sociology of Education*, *20*(2), 175–188.

Nichols, J. (2013). Rie's story, Ryan's journey: Music in the life of a transgender student. *Journal of Research in Music Education*, *61*, 262–279. doi: 10.1177/0022429413498259.

Nickels, T. (2012). Some puzzles about Kuhn's exemplars. In V. Kindi & T. Arabatzis (Eds.), *Kuhn's the structure of scientific revolutions revisited* (pp. 112–132). New York: Routledge.

Norton, D.L. (1976). *Personal destinies: A philosophy of ethical individualism*. Princeton: Princeton University Press.

Nussbaum, M. (1999). Professor of parody. *The New Republic*. Retrieved from: http://faculty.georgetown.edu/irvinem/theory/Nussbaum-Butler-Critique-NR-2-99.pdf

Nussbaum, M. (2000). *Sex and social justice*. Oxford: Oxford University Press.

O'Leary, J. & Tobias, E.S. (2016). Sonic participatory cultures within, through, and around video games. In R. Mantie & G.D. Smith (Eds.), *The Oxford handbook of music making and leisure* (pp. 453–466). New York, NY: Oxford University Press.

Parkinson, T., Hunter, M., Campanello, K., Dines, M. & Smith, G.D. (2015). *Understanding small music venues: A report by the Music Venues Trust*. London: Music Venues Trust.

Parkinson, T. & Smith, G.D. (2015). Towards an epistemology of authenticity in higher popular music education. *Action, Criticism, and Theory for Music Education, 14*(1), 93–127.

Partti, H. (2012). *Learning from cosmopolitan digital musicians: Identity, musicianship, and changing values in (in)formal music communities*. Helsinki: Sibelius Academy.

Powell, B., Krikun, A., & Pignato, J.M. (2015). "Something's happening here!": Popular music education in the United States. *IASPM Journal, 5*(1), 4–22.

Pravodelov, V. (2014). *Changing the subject to object: The pendulum swing between feminism and objectification in popular music, and implications for female music artists*. Master Thesis, Institute of Contemporary Music Performance, London.

Prest, A. (2013). The corporatization of schooling and its effects on the state of music education: A critical Deweyan perspective. *Action, Criticism, and Theory for Music Education, 12*(3), 31–44. Retrieved from: http://act.maydaygroup.org/ articles/Prest12_3.pdf

Prior, N. (2015). Bourdieu and beyond. In J. Shepherd & K. Devine (Eds.), *The Routledge reader on the sociology of music* (pp. 349–358). New York, NY: Routledge.

Radano, R.M. (2000). Hot fantasies: American modernism and the idea of black rhythm. In R.M. Radano & P.V. Bohlman (Eds.), *Music and the racial imagination* (pp. 259–482). Chicago, IL: University of Chicago Press.

Raffo, C., Dyson, A., Gunter, H., Hall, D., Jones, L., & Kalambouka, A. (Eds.) (2010). *Education and poverty in affluent countries*. London: Routledge.

Regelski, T. & Gates, J.T. (Eds.) (2009). *Music education for changing times: Guiding visions for practice*. Dordrecht: Springer.

Rodriguez, C.X. (Ed.) (2004). *Bridging the gap: Popular music and music education*. Reston, VA: MENC.

Rosenberg, N. (2011). Popular music in the college music theory class: Rhythm and meter. In N. Biamonte (Ed.), *Pop-culture pedagogy in the music classroom* (pp. 47–71). Lanham: Scarecrow Press.

Schep, D. (2011). The limits of performativity: A critique of hegemony in gender theory. *Hypatia, 27*, 864–880.

Schneier, D. (2015). *Data and Goliath: The hidden battles to collect your data and control your world*. New York: W.W. Norton.

Scott, D.B. (Ed.) (2009). *Ashgate research companion to popular musicology*. Aldershot: Ashgate.

Scruton, R. (1997). *The aesthetics of music*. Oxford: Oxford University Press.

Shusterman, R. (2000). *Performing live: Aesthetic alternatives for the end of art*. Ithaca: Cornell University Press.

Smith, G.D. (2013a). Seeking "success" in popular music. *Music Education Research International, 6*, 26–37.

Smith, G.D. (2013b). *I drum, therefore I am: Being and becoming a drummer*. Farnham: Ashgate.

Smith, G.D. (2014). Popular music in higher education. In G. Welch & I. Papageorgi (Eds.), *Advanced musical performance: Investigations in higher education learning* (pp. 33–48). Farnham: Ashgate.

Smith, G.D. (2015a). Neoliberalism and symbolic violence in higher music education. In L. DeLorenzo (Ed.), *Giving voice to democracy: Diversity and social justice in the music classroom* (pp. 65–84). New York, NY: Routledge.

Smith, G.D. (2015b). Masculine domination and intersecting fields in private-sector popular music performance education in the UK. In P. Burnard, Y. Hofstander & J. Söderman (Eds.), *Bourdieu and the sociology of music and music education* (pp. 61–78). Farnham: Ashgate.

Smith, G.D. (2016). (Un)popular music making and eudaimonia. In R. Mantie & G.D. Smith (Eds.), *The Oxford handbook of music making and leisure* (pp. 151–170). New York: Oxford University Press.

Tagg, P. (1983). *Philip Tagg | Why IASPM? Which tasks? (Reggio Emilia 1983). Tagg.org.* Retrieved from: http://www.tagg.org/articles/iasptask83.html [Accessed 24 July 2015].

Tobias, E.S. (2014). Solo, multitrack, mute?: Producing and performing (gender) in a popular music classroom. *Visions of Research in Music Education, 25.* Retrieved from: http://www.rider.edu/~vrme

Tobias, E.S. & O'Leary, J. (in press). Video games. In A. King, E. Himonides, & S.A. Ruthmann (Eds.), *Routledge companion to music, technology & education.* New York: Routledge.

Tønsberg, K. (2013). Value changes in Norwegian music education: From increased acceptance of rock to a reduced status for classical music? *Nordic Yearbook for Research in Music Education, 14,* 145–166.

Tønsberg, K. (2014). Critical events in the development of popular music education at a Norwegian music conservatory: A schismogenic analysis based on certain conflict-and-power-theoretical perspectives. *Finnish Journal of Music Education, 17,* 19–34.

Toulmin, S. & Goodfield, J. (1961). *The fabric of the heavens: The development of astronomy and dynamics.* New York: Harper.

Trobia, A. & Lo Verde, F.M. (2016). Italian amateur pop-rock musicians on Facebook: Mixed methods and new findings in music making research. In R. Mantie & G.D. Smith (Eds.), *The Oxford handbook of music making and leisure* (pp. 491–520). New York, NY: Oxford University Press.

Trowler, P., Saunders, M., & Bamber, V. (Eds.) (2012). *Tribes and territories in the twenty-first century: Rethinking the significance of disciplines in higher education.* London: Routledge.

van Leeuwen, T. (2007). Legitimation in discourse and communication. *Discourse & Communication, 1,* 91–112.

Veblen, K., Messenger, S.J., Silverman, M., & Elliott, D. (Eds.) (2013). *Community music today.* Lanham, MD: Rowman & Littlefield Education.

Walser, R. (1993). *Running with the devil: Power, gender, and madness in heavy metal music.* Middletown, CT: Wesleyan University Press.

Walker, R. (2007). *Music education: Cultural values, social change and innovation.* Springfield, IL: Charles C. Thomas Publishers.

Wenger, E. (1998). *Communities of practice: Learning, meaning, and identity.* New York, NY: Cambridge University Press.

Wright, R. (2008). Kicking the habitus: Power, culture and pedagogy in the secondary school music curriculum. *Music Education Research, 10*(3), 389–402.

Wright, R. (2010). Sociology and music education. In R. Wright (Ed.), *Sociology and music education* (pp. 1–20). Farnham: Ashgate.

Index

Note: Page indicators in bold denote a table on the corresponding page; page indicators in italic denote a figure on the corresponding page.

Abbey Road Studios 234
Aboriginal musical cultures 16
Academy of Contemporary Music (ACM) 121, 155, 214
accreditation of prior experiential learning (APEL) 168
action-centred (*handlungsbasiert*) music education 220
Adbusters magazine 418
aesthetic experience at secondary schools: impact of 226–7; introduction 217–18; pillars and benefits of 225–6; Pop macht Schule (PoMS) methodology 217–18, 222–5; popular music education and 218–20; popular music in 220–2; summary 227–8
affective filter hypothesis 247
African-American music community 37
Afrological improvisation 438, 441–2
Ahlers, Michael 19–20
Allsup, R.E. 471
Amabile, T. 333, 335–6
amateuring, defined 248
amplification technology 178
Anglo-American popular music 90
Anhui Institute of Education in Hefei 80
Apple's Logic Pro 22
approximation approach to modern band 248–9
Arab Spring 418–19
arriviste pursuits as popular music studies 132
Artist and Repertoire (A&R) process 309
artist-as-songwriter model 290–1
artistic development and presence 184–5
artistic legitimation 467

artistic singing 178–9, **179**
art music *vs.* popular music 131–4
Ashgate Research Companion to Popular Musicology, The (Scott) 5
assessment approaches 147–8, 267, 279–80
Associated Board of the Royal Schools of Music (ABRSM) 168, 170–1
Association for Popular Music Education (APME) 6, 20, 42, 48
Astor, Pete 133
Audio Production and Critical Listening (Corey) 231–2
Australian and New Zealand Cultural Arts Association 386
Australian Music Examinations Board 386
Australian National University (ANU) 139, 143–7
Australian Office of Learning and Teaching 177
authentic pedagogy, defined 359
authoritative space 417
Autism Spectrum Disorders (ASD) 370
autonomy in public music education 88–9, 91, 123

Bachelor of Arts (BA) programmes 140
Bachelor of Music (BMus) programmes 140
Bachelor of Music Technology (BMuTech) programme 142
Bachelor of Popular Music Assessment Tool (BoPMAT) 279–80
Bachelor of Popular Music (BPM) programme 272, 274–80
back-room co-writers 258
Backstreet Boys 162

479

Index

band coaching tool 224
Barfield, Owen 443
Baron School of Music (BSM) 100, 106–11, **111**
Barthes, Roland 153, 154
base-building stage 61, *61*, 67–9
Baumann, Shyon 467
Becher, Tony 467
Beiber, Justin 301
Beidelman, Fred 38
Beijing Normal University 82
Berger, Peter 467
Bertellsmans Music Group (BMG) 342
Biesta, Gert 426, 429–30
Bildung concept 219
Birmingham Centre for Contemporary Cultural Studies 128
Birmingham City University 364
Björnberg, Alf 167
"Black Papers in Education" (Cox, Dyson) 346, 347
Boden, Margaret 191
body percussion tool 224
Bohlman, Philip 154
BoomTown Music Education (BTME) 432
Bourdieu, P. 371, 454, 455–9
Bourdieu and the Sociology of Music and Music Education (Burnard) 455
Bowman, Wayne 431
Bridging the Gap: Popular Music and Music Education (Rodriguez) 14, 42
British and Irish Modern Music Institute (BIMM) 121
Brockman, Daniel 454–6
Browne, Samuel 37
Bruner, Jerome 49
BTEC Higher National studies 168
Business and Technical Education Council (BTEC) 121–2
Butler, Judith 459–62
Byrn, Clarence 37
by-the-book learning 34–5

campaign in marketing 306
Campbell, Patricia Shehan 40
Cantonese popular songs (Cantopop) 75, 100, 101, 109
capital by producers 309
career concerns 309
Carlson, Ingegerd 197
Carter, Bill 34
CASH Song Writers Quest 110
celebrity of producers 308
Center for Music Education Research 48

Central Admission Services (UCAS) Student Guide 155
C-Framework for Arts and Culture Brands 304
channel in marketing 307
character of producers 308
Cherry Red Records 342
China Central Television (CCTV) 82
China's Ministry of Education (MoE) 77
Chinese University of Hong Kong (CUHK) 102
Ching Kiu Chan 103
Christensen School of Popular Music 36
Chun Hung Ng 103
Chun Tung Mak 110
citizenship education (CE) 384
Civil Rights movement 415
clarification in the creative process 260
classical musicology 155–6
classification (genre) in marketing 305
classroom space, re-defined 413–16
Cloonan, Martin 135
co-creation with customers 308
codes of behaviour 120
cognitive autonomy 89
cognitive psychology 49
Coleman, Ornette 442
collaboration in marketing 306
collaborative learning environments 402–3
College Music Society's Task Force on the Undergraduate Music Major 243
Collins, John 19
Colombian Association for Faculties of Arts (ACOFARTE) 316
Colombian National Ministry of Education 315
comfort zone approach to modern band 246–7
commerciality of production 310
commercialization and popular music education (PME) 468–9
Commercial Music in Popular Music Performance degree programme 258
Commercial Music program at South Plains College 41
common culture 427
communication in marketing 306
Communist Party of China (CPC) 75
community college programs 39
community music 372
community of customers 308
community of practice 276
company of producers 308
competence of production 310

Index

componential theory of creativity 333–6
Composers and Authors Society of Hong Kong Ltd (CASH) 110
composition approach to modern band 249–50
composition/songwriting classes 17
concept in marketing 305
conceptual definition of creativity 191
configuration by producers 309
Confucian ideas 407
connection in marketing 307
consideration of production 310
consistency of production 310
constitutive rules 120, 123
constructivist learning theories 49
consumers in PMME 307–9
contact with customers 307
Contemporary and Popular Music BA Honours programme 122
contemporary commercial music (CCM) 180
content in marketing 305
contested space, reclaiming 418–21
Continuing Education Fund (CEF) 100, 105–6
contract with customers 307
convenience in marketing 306
Coorie Doon project 397
copying in music learning 374–5
copyright in marketing 306
Corey, Jason 231–2
corporate social responsibility (CSR) 309
cost in marketing 306
Cox, Laverne 464
Crawford, Richard 34
Creation Records 347
creative block *see* songwriting and creative block
Creative Music Education (CME) movement 441
creative performance 52–4, **53–4**
Creative Performance Chamber Ensemble (CPCE) 52–4, **53–4**, *55*
creative processes: do-it-yourself (DIY) musicians 278–9; in education 267; overview 260–1; in PMME 309; in popular music 190–1; social systems and 258–60, *259*; thinking with music 57; *see also* songwriting and creative block
creativity in popular music degrees: componential theory of creativity 333–6; introduction 285–7; making popular music *288*, 288–90; marketing and distribution 291–2; popular music studies 292–4; reasons for 294–5; songwriting 290–1; transferable skills and employability 294
creativity-relevant processes 333–4
credibility of production 310
critical listening 393
Critical Quarterly Society (CQS) 346
critical studies *vs.* practical activity 130–1
critical thinking pedagogies 403–5
crowd-funding by customers 308
Csikszentmihalyi, M. 259, *259*, 268
cultural democracy 428
Cultural Industries Quarter 348
cultural offering in marketing 305
cultural politics and popular songs 75–9
Cultural Revolution (CR) in China 78
cultural theory in popular music programmes: conclusion 162–3; impact on students 157–60; introduction 153–4; modern differences 160–1; traditional *vs.* popular 155–7; uniqueness as art form 154–5
curricular components of vocal pedagogy 181–7, **182**
Curriculum Standards for Primary Education and Junior Secondary Education reform 81
Cyrus, Miley 160, 161

dance band curriculum 38–9
Davis, Bob 130
de-institutionalizing space through popular music 421–2
Del Rey, Lana 160
democracy: cultural democracy 428; Nordic music education 426–7, 429–33, 468–9; popular music and 426–7; popular music education 468–9
Deng Xiaoping 79
Denmark, popular music education 427–9
design-based research (DBR) 60, 63–7
Dewey, John 49
differentiation management 172
differentiation of outcome 377–8
digital audio workstation (DAW) 415–16, 455
digital Dictaphone 207
digital musicians 291
discrepancies in music making 442–3, 447
distance-set hypothesis 417
distillation in the creative process 261
distributed learning in communities 361–2
diversity in repertoire 430–1

481

Index

do-it-yourself (DIY) musicians: BPM programme 272, 274–80; collaboration 278; conclusions 280–1; defined 274; graduate perspective 274–5; higher music education 273–4; introduction 272; major study assessment practices 279–80; recording and reflection 277; supporting courses 278–9
domain-relevant skills 333
Down Syndrome (DS) 370
Duffett, Mark 135
Dylan, Bob 259, 260

economic bodies 120
Edexcel Anthology of Music (Winterson) 19
Edinburgh Napier University 121–2
editing practice with creative block 198–9
Edmondes, Will 443
educational bodies 120
education reform in China 79–80
egalitarian philosophy 427
electronic dance music (EDM) 23
electronic musicians in UK higher institutions: conclusion 213–14; contextual framework 204–5; discussion 212–13; introduction 203–5; methodology 205–7; previous experience 207–9; programmes of study 209–11
Elías, Norbert 313
Elmhirst, Tom 237
emic perspective 22–3
empathy-building approaches 403
Emperor Entertainment Group (EEG) 105
employability pedagogy 330–1, 454
employment/workplace imperatives 332
enculturation process 180
engineering producer 233–4
Enterprise Music Scotland 397
entertainers *versus* singers 188
entrepreneurship in higher education: case study 334; conclusion 337–8; internship programme 334–7; introduction 57, 328–9; literature review 331–3; overview 328, 329–30; PACE context 330–1; supervision 337; theoretical framework 333–4
environment in PMME 304–5
ethnomusicological study 16
Eurocentric education 101
Eurological approach to improvisation 438, 441
evaluation in the creative process 261

ex-musician identity students 65, 66, 68–9, 70
experiencing music pedagogy 221
Exports of Service 257
extra-musical approach 236

faculty member expertise 146
faith-based music education: conclusion 392–3; discussion 391–2; example vignettes 388–91; introduction 382–4; morality and popular music 386–8; morality and religion 384–5; overview of schools in UK 383–4
Federal Ministry of Education and Research (BMBF) 227
Feral Pop music 438–9, 443–7
Finland, popular music education 428
Finnish general upper secondary schools 63
flow experiences in pedagogic practices 88–9, 275
formal learning 439–40
formally trained musician identity students 65, 67, 69, 70
formal music instruction 88
for-profit music schools 41, 103–5, **104**
Foundations of Music Education course 52
free music, defined 438
Fripp, Robert 233
Further Education (FE) role 114, 114n1, 119

GarageBand app 281, 434
Gary, Charles 39–40
Gatfield, Nick 348–9
Gay, Lesbian and Straight Education Network (GLSEN) guidelines 401–2
gender bias in classrooms 401
gender performativity theory 459–63
General Music syllabus 89
general social legitimation 467
Geo. C. Dobson's World's Banjo Guide (White Smith) 34–5
Germany, popular music education 20
Ghana, popular music education 19
Giroux, Henry 161, 471
global awareness 404
Global Day of Action 419
Global Occupy Day 419
Goubert, Beatriz 317
government-funded education 101–3
graduates, professional prospects 148
Grateful Dead (band) 442
Great Depression 36

Index

Green, Lucy 24, 42, 49, 190, 235, 274, 405, 426–7
Greene, Harry P. 178–9, **179**, 187–8
Griffiths, Dai 132–3
Griffith University's Queensland Conservatorium 16
Grohl, Dave 274
Gross Value Added (GVA) 257
Grove Music Online (Kennedy) 33
guru-shishya tradition of North Indian classical music 167

habitus notion 371, 457
Hank Thompson School of Country Music 41
haphazard process of music learning 377–8
Harris, Charles K. 34, 35
Hartin, John 41
Harvard University 143
Hayeck, Friedrich von 346
Heath, Edward 346
Hebert, David 40
Higgins, Lee 432
Highbrow/Lowbrow (Levine) 35
Higher Education (HE): role of 114, 118–19, 257; teaching music in 344–5; tensions with professional practice 265–8; tuition fees 347
Higher Education Academy (HEA) 17, 158
higher education institutions (HEIs) 14, 23, 168, 171–2; *see also* electronic musicians in UK higher institutions
Higher Education Qualifications Framework (UK) 266
Higher Popular Music Education (HPME) 18, 128, 211, 303, 328–30, 452, 458
hip-hop culture/music 206, 387, 397, 404
Hip Hop Project (Silverman) 397–8
Holiday, Billie 158
home music-making 34
Hong Kong Academy of Performing Arts 102
Hong Kong Baptist University (HKBU) 102
Hong Kong Diploma of Secondary Education (HKDSE) 102–3
Hong Kong Institute of Education (HKIEd) 102
Howlett, Mike 232, 236
How Popular Musicians Learn (Green) 42, 190, 287
Hugill, Andrew 291
Hui, Sam 102
Hullah, John 385
Humphreys, Jere 33

IASPM Journal 14
identity in popular music education 456–9
illumination in the creative process 260
Imperial Qing Dynasty 75
improvisational flexibility in music learning 378–9
improvisation approach to modern band 250–1
improvisation-to-composition process 363
improvised popular music: Afrological improvisation 438, 441–2; conclusions 447–8; Feral Pop music 438–9, 443–7; formal/informal learning 439–40; introduction 438–9; overview 57–8; participatory discrepancies 442–3, 447; popular music education and 440–3
incubation in the creative process 260, 261
indie (independent) musicians *see* do-it-yourself (DIY) musicians
individual instrument study 121
individuality in vocal pedagogy 183–4
industry practices in vocal pedagogy 186–7
informal learning 24, 57, 88, 204, 359–60, 439–40
informally trained musician identity students 65, 66, 69, 70
inspiration in the creative process 260
Institute of Contemporary Music Performance (ICMP) 6, 108, 121, 131, 155, 337
institutional autonomy 123
institutionalization of popular music education 465–9
institutional positionality 301–2
institutional transitions and competition 145–6
institutions in post-compulsory music education 120–3
instrumental learning 286–7
integrated models concept 140–1
intellectualism 346
intellectual property 468
intentionality of informal learning 88
interactional space 417
intermediary action idea 115
International Association for the Study of Popular Music (IASPM) 14, 128
International College of Music in Kuala Lumpur 17
internship programmes 328–9, 334–7
Interpretation in Song (Greene) 178–9, **179**, 187–8

483

Index

inter-sonic process 464
intrinsic task motivation 333
iPad learning 63, 244
Irish Modern Music Institute 155
Isherwood, Martin 190

James, Dick 290
jazz education 33, 466
Jenner, Caitlyn 464
'joint-working' of musicians 341
Joplin, Scott 36
Journal of Music Technology and Education 14
Journal of Popular Music Studies 14, 20, 43
juvenile offenders music programmes 402

Kaplan, Max 38, 453
Karlsen, Sidsel 428
Keil, Charles 438
Khan, Dillon 348
King, Carole 289
Kit Wai Ma 103
Koo, Joseph 102
Krashen, Stephen 246
Krueger, Simone 133
Kuhn, Thomas S. 5, 465

Labour Observatory for Education 314
Labour Party (UK) 346–7
labour skills, certification 318
Lady Gaga (singer) 158, 160, 301
Lamar, Kendrick 461
Latin Quarter (band) 342
Learning Through Producing (LTP): conclusion 71–2; design-based research 60, 63–7; e-learning and *61*, 61–2, *62*; introduction 60; student learning in base-building stage 67–9; student learning in producing stage 69–71
Lebler, Don 198–9
Leeds University BAs 127
Lefebvre, H. 413–14, 420–1, 423
Levine, Lawrence 35
Lewis, Ryan 160
Liang Qichao 76
Liberal-Conservative coalition 123
Li Jinhui 78
Li Shutong 76
listening in music learning 374–5
Little Kids Rock (LKR) 42, 56, 103, 245–51
lived space concept 418
live performance courses **53**
Liverpool's Institute for Popular Music 128, 155

London College of Music Exams (LCM) 170
low-anxiety learning environment 247
Luckmann, Thomas 467
Lui, Patrick 106
Luova musiikin tuottaminen (Creative Music Producing) 62

McClary, Susan 461
MacKey, Nathaniel 438
MacKinnon, Catherine 462
Macklemore (singer) 160
McNaught, W.G. 385
Macquarie University (MQ) 328
McVey, Helen 397
Madden, Joel 179
major study assessment practices 279–80
male gaze 461
Malvinni, David 442
Mandarin popular songs 75
Mantie, Roger 466
Maori musical cultures 16
Mao Zedong 78–9
Mark, Michael 39–40
marketing re-mix in PMME 305–7
Marom, Yotam 419
Martin, George 290
Martin, Ricky 179
Marxist argument 118
masculine domination in popular music education 456–9
Massy, Sylvia 233–4, 236
master-less studio 277
matriculation examination statistics 63
Matthews, Stephen 397
May 4th Movement *see* New Culture Movement
Media, Music, Communication and Cultural Studies (MMCCS) 331
Media Internship programme 331
mediation-as-transmission idea 115–16
Meet the Band tool 224, 225
Merwe, Peter van der 36
meta-pedagogy in teacher education: conclusion 366–7; distributed and situated learning 361–2; informal learning and 359–60; introduction 357; popular music in 357–9, 364–6; priorities for 362–4
microphone technology 178
Miller, Sue 135
modern band principles: approximation approach 248–9; comfort zone approach 246–7; composition approach

249–50; conclusion 251; core values 246–51; improvisation approach 250–1; introduction 243–4; music as a second language 245–51; overview 56, 244–5; scaffolding approach 249
modern jazz and dance band 38–9
modular tool system 223
Mont Pelerin Society 346
Moore, Allan F. 134–5, 288
Moorefield, Virgil 233
moral analyses of popular music 384–5
Morgan, Nicky 345
Mozart, Mark 289, 293
MTV (Music Television) 159–60
MTV Video Music Awards 160
multidimensionality of music educators 319–21
Music, informal learning and the school: A new classroom pedagogy (Green) 405
musical creativities 182–3
Musical Futures project (UK) 49, 57, 359, 388, 440, 453
musicality in vocal pedagogy 185
musical listening (studio production teaching): concluding remarks 241; engineering producer 233–4; how music sounds 235–8; introduction 231–2; learning the tradition of 234–5; re-contextualization 239–40; re-flection 239; re-production 238–9; teaching of 238–40
musical notation 49
música popular in Buenos Aires, Argentina 21
music as a second language (MSL) 245–51
Music (Popular) BA (Hons) programme 121–2
Music Business (Cloonan, Hulstedt) 119
Music Department of the Education Department (Hong Kong) 101
Music Educators National Conference (MENC) 37, 38, 48
music industry teaching: conclusion 350–1; introduction 341–4; neoliberal music education 346–7; sea-change in 344–6; support for youths 347–50
musicking concept 248, 434
Music Learning as Second Language Learning (MLSLL) 246
music learning facilitators (MLF) 370–1, 376, 378
music learning spaces (MLS) 371, 376, 378

music notation studies: future for 174–5; introduction 166–8; provision of notion investigations 168–74, *169*
music performance anxiety (MPA) 246–7
music practice approaches 147–8
Music Supervisors National Conference 37
music teacher education: course offerings 52–4, **53–4**; curricular change in US 48; faculty positions 51–2; future changes 57–8; introduction 46–8; Little Kids Rock and modern band movement 56; performance curriculum 54–5, *55*; recording curriculum 55–6, *56*; University of South Florida (USF) music education 49–51
music teacher preparedness 406–7
Music Television (MTV) 116
"Music Theory Aural Transcription" module 172
music therapy rock band: community music 372; conclusion 379–80; haphazard process of music learning 377–8; improvisational flexibility 378–9; introduction 369; learning by listening and copying 374–5; literature review 371–3; music therapy overview 372; overview 369–70; participant-selected repertoire 373–4; theoretical framework 370–1; working together in peer groups 375–7

National Arts Standards (US) 249
National Association for Music Education (NAfME) 37, 243, 398
National Association of Schools of Music (NASM) 51
National College for School Leaders 267
National Colloquium 314
National Core Arts Standards 243, 250
National Ministry of Education in Colombia (MEN) 314, 316
National Music Content Standards 47
National Pedagogic University 321
National Service of Learning (SENA) 316, 317
National Standards for K–12 music classes 40, 51
National Viewers' and Listeners' Association (NVLA) 387
Neo-Adornian argument 118
neoliberal music education 110, 338, 346–7, 453–5
Newcastle University 122, 443
New Culture Movement 76

Index

new musician identity students 65, 67, 69, 70–1
Newport Folk Festival 160
New Product Development (NPD) 309
Ng, Ronald 106, 107, 109
Nie Er 77
non-formal music education 204
non-instrumental nature of art 267
non-musician identity students 65, 66, 68, 70
Nordic music education: culture and 427–8; democracy and 426–7, 429–33; diversity in repertoire 430–1; future developments 433; introduction 425–6; popular music education 468–9; popular music in 428–9
Nueva Canción (New Chilean Song) movement 396–7
Nussbaum, Martha 462

objectification of women in popular music 457–8
Occupy Wall Street musical project: academia's prospective role 424–5; assessment 415–16; classroom space, re-defined 413–16; contested space, reclaiming 418–21; course design 414–15; de-institutionalizing space 421–2; introduction 413; role of space 416–18
Ocean, Frank 462
October Revolution (Russia) 76
Office of Qualifications and Examinations Regulation (Ofqual) 170
Open Door Policy 83
operational definition of creativity 191, 193–5
Opportunity Recognizing Mind 332
oral-aural processes 88
Orenstein, Peter 397
Organization for Economic Cooperation and Development (OECD) 315
Organization of American States (OEA) 315
Organization of Ibero-American States for Education, Science and Culture (OEI) 315
Orr, Susan 192
Osborne, Richard 133, 135

parallel approach to pedagogy 140–1
Parker, Charlie 235
Parker, John 39
Parker, William 438

participant-selected repertoire 373–4
participatory assessment 275–6
participatory music-making 57, 442–3, 446, 447
PASCH (*Schulen: Partner der Zukunft* – Schools: Partners for the Future) 227
Pearson PLC 121
pedagogical theory 25
pedagogic content knowledge 357
pedagogic practices in Singapore: autonomy 88–9, 91; community of learners 93–5; conclusion 96–7; context of 89–91; discussion 95–6; facilitation of 92–4, 95–6; flow experiences 88–9; formal and informal approaches 88; group work 92–3; introduction 87; notions and definitions 88–9; orientation 88; reflections on 91–5
pedagogies of inclusion 399–402
peer-assessment with creative block 198–9
peer-learning in music education 375–7, 403
peer-to-peer student networks 333
performance curriculum 54–5, *55*
performativity in popular music 463–5
personal space 417
perspiration in the creative process 261
Pfleiderer, Martin 19
philosophical values of social justice 396–9
Piaget, Jean 49
political bodies 120
Popakademie Baden-Württemberg – University of Popular Music and Music Business (Popakademie) 217–19
Pop macht Schule (PoMS) methodology 217–18, 222–5
popular culture musics (PCM) 180–1
popular music: art music *vs.* 131–4; cultural politics 75–9; defined 153; de-institutionalizing space through 421–2; democracy and 426–7; diversification of 79–80; Feral Pop music 438–9, 443–7; in German schools 220–2; into globalized school music education 80–1; hip-hop culture/music 206, 387, 397, 404; making of *288*, 288–90; meta-pedagogy for 357–9, 364–6; morality and 386–8; Nordic music education 428–9; objectification of women in 457–8; patriotism and nationalism 81–2; performativity in 463–5; rock music 39–41; scope of 245; teacher education

Index

357–9; traditional music *vs.* 155–7; *see also* do-it-yourself (DIY) musicians
popular music education (PME): autonomy in 88–9, 91, 123; commercialization, democracy, and Nordic model 468–9; conclusions 24–6, 469–72; emic perspective 22–3; formal learning 439–40; for-profit music schools 41, 103–5, **104**; future of 470–2; gender performativity theory 459–63; global representations 15–22; Hong Kong 101–5, **104**; identity and masculine domination 456–9; improvised popular music 440–3; influence of Bourdieu 371, 454, 455–9; informal learning 24, 57, 88, 204, 359–60, 439–40; institutionalization of 465–9; introduction 5–7, 14–15, 451–2; music therapy and 372–3; neoliberal music education 110, 338, 346–7, 453–5; product, process and learning modes in 439–40; research and social forces 469–70; success as educational quality 452–3; *see also* creativity in popular music degrees; cultural theory in popular music programmes; electronic musicians in UK higher institutions; faith-based music education; Nordic music education; pedagogic practices in Singapore; tertiary models of popular music education; university music education in Colombia
popular music education (PME), current and future trajectory: art music *vs.* popular music 131–4; conclusions 136–7; findings and analysis 130–5; introduction 127–9; method 129–30; practical activity *vs.* critical studies 130–1; private *vs.* public provision 135–6; vocationalism 117–19, 134–5
popular music education (PME), historical foundations: by-the-book learning 34–5; introduction 33; modern jazz and dance band 38–9; rock music 39–41; Tin Pan Alley through Swing era 35–8; in 21st century 41–3
popular music education (PME), in Hong Kong: Baron School of Music 100, 106–11, **111**; conclusion 111–12; Continuing Education Fund 105–6; government-funded education 101–3; introduction 100; music education in Hong Kong 101–5, **104**; private (for-profit) music schools 103–5, **104**
popular music education (PME), Mainland China: conclusion 83–4; cultural politics and popular songs 75–9; diversification and education reform 79–80; globalized school music education 80–1; introduction 74–5; patriotism and nationalism 81–2; propaganda songs 78–9; protest songs 75–7; values and global harmony in 82–3
Popular Music Education Special Interest Group 6
popular musicking concept 248, 434
popular music marketing education (PMME): conclusion 310–11; consumers 307–8; environment 304–5; importance of music brand 299–301; institutional positionality 301–2; introduction 298–9; marketing re-mix 305–7; Popular Music Marketing Education Repertoire 304–5; producers 308–9; professional positionality 302–3; re-mixing the subject 304; suggested guidelines for 303–4
Popular Music Marketing Education Repertoire 304–5
popular music studies (PMS) 5, 15, 273–4, 292–4
Popular Music Teaching Handbook, The (Cooper) 465
post-compulsory music education in Scotland: conclusion 123–4; institutions 120–3; introduction 114–15; mediation process 115–17; vocationalism 117–19
practical activity *vs.* critical studies 130–1
pre-digital music-industrial order 344
preparation in the creative process 260
'pre-service' music teacher education programmes 243
Presley, Elvis 387
private (for-profit) music schools 103–5, **104**
private *vs.* public provision 135–6
producers in PMME 308–9
producing stage 61, 69–71
Production of Space (Lefebvre) 413
Professional and Community Engagement (PACE) development grant 330–1
professionalization in learning 318
professional positionality 302–3
professional prospects of graduates 148
professional songwriting: the brief 262; conclusion 269; creative process 260–1; creativity and social systems 258–60, *259*; creativity in popular music degrees 290–1; data mapping 262; HE tensions

487

Index

with 265–8; introduction 257–8; learning through reflection 268–9; master's degrees 192; overview 69–71; phases of *264*, 264–5; professionals 261; sequence of events *263*, 263–4; songwriting teams 261–2; students 262; validity 262
Progressive Methods (PM) course 52–4, **53–4**
propaganda songs 78–9
protest songs 75–7
ProTools programme 401
Public Relations programme 331

Qualifications Framework (QF) 105
Quality Assurance Agency for Higher Education Benchmark for Music (QAA) 173, 174
Queensland Conservatorium, Griffith University (QCGU) 139, 142, 145, 147, 272
Queensland University of Technology (QUT) 139, 142–3, 145, 147
Qu Qiubai 76

radically integrated approach to pedagogy 141
radio broadcasting 116
Rag Time Instructor (Harney & Northrup) 36
Raskulinecz, Nick 234
RCA Victor 342
real-life problem-solving situations 361
recording curriculum 55–6, *56*
recording technology 178
Red Tape Studios 348
reflection, as key in learning 184
Regional Office of Education for Latin America and the Caribbean (OREALC) 315
regulatory rules 120, 124
religious education (RE) 384
representational space 416
Research in Popular Music Education symposium 6
Rietveld, Hillegonda 134
ritualized/improvised performance classes **54**
rock music 39–41
Rock School television programme 120
Rodriguez, Carlos Xavier 42
Ronson, Mark 237, 290
Russia's October Revolution 76

scaffolding approach to modern band 249
Schafer, R. Murray 441
School of Ragtime (Joplin) 36
Schweizer, Kristen 161
Scott, Derek B. 132
Scottish folk/traditional music *see* post-compulsory music education in Scotland
Scruton, R. 384–5
Secondary Music Education 359
Second Language Acquisition (Krashen) 246
Second Sino-Japanese War 82
self-assessment with creative block 198–9
Self-Determination Theory 88–9
self-employment after graduation 329
self-monitoring/reflecting notion 93
Sex and Social Justice (Nussbaum) 462
Shen Xingong 76
singalong tool 224
Singapore Teachers' Academy of the aRts (STAR) 90–1, 90n3
Sino-British War 75
situated learning in communities 361–2
Small, Christopher 175, 248, 439
Smith-Hughes Act (1917) 36
Smooth Criminals (band) 369–70, 373–9
Snarky Puppy (band) 337
social bodies 120
social justice: in administration 399; collaborative learning environments 402–3; conclusion 407–8; critical thinking pedagogies 403–5; introduction 395–6; music teacher preparedness 406–7; pedagogies of inclusion 399–402; philosophical values 396–9; student voice and 405–6; in teaching 396–9
songwriting and creative block: conclusions 200; inappropriate criteria/editing 197; introduction 190–2; lack of space 196; lack of stimulus 195–6; lack of strategies against frustration/pain 198; methods 192–3; moving beyond 198–200; operational definition of creativity 191, 193–5; understandings of 195–8
sound carriers idea 115–16
Sound City Studios 234
Sound Effects: Youth, Leisure and the Politics of Rock 'n' Roll (Tagg) 128
Sounding Out Songwriting (Isherwood) 190
Southern Common Market (MERCOSUR) 315
Specifications of Competency Standards (SCSs) 105
Spector, Phil 233

Index

Stainer, John 385
Starr, Larry 158
State Teacher Education guidelines in Wisconsin, US 407
STEM subjects 385
stereotypical notions of singing pedagogy 177
stream structure of pedagogy 139, 142–3
student-as-master 219
"student-centric" education 87, 245
Student Financial Assistance Agency (Hong Kong) 105
student learning experiences 69–71
student voice and social justice 405–6
Studio Audio Art (Turino) 55
studio production teaching *see* musical listening
studium generale approach 219
Stuessy, Joe 387
Success in Music Charity Foundation 109
Sudnow, David 286
Suncoast Music Education Research Symposium (SMERS) 6, 42–3, 48
supervisory space 417
Sweden, popular music education 429, 432
Swift, Taylor 461
Swing era 35–8
Systems Model of Creativity 259, *259*, 268

Tabletkoulu ('Tablet school') 62, 63
Tagg, Philip 14, 128, 235, 293
Tanglewood Declaration 40
Tanglewood Symposium 40
teacher-centred performing ensembles 46
teacher education 88, 321–3, **322**; *see also* meta-pedagogy in teacher education
team-level creativity-relevant processes 333, 336
technical level education 318
technique, perfected *vs.* effective 188
technologies in vocal pedagogy 186
Television Broadcasts Limited (TVB) 110
tertiary models of popular music education: approaches to 147–8; faculty member expertise 146; identifying issues with 145–8; institutional transitions and competition 145–6; introduction 139–40; overview 140–1; professional prospects of graduates 148; stream structure of pedagogy 139, 142–3; summary 148–9
Thatcher, Margaret 346
Thicke, Robin 159

Thompson, Dick 40
Till, Rupert 132
Tin Pan Alley 35–8, 344
Track Imperatives example 288, *288*, 290
track production 69–71
traditional instrumentation 205
traditional *vs.* popular music 155–7
transgender persons 464
transition management 172
Trowler, Paul 467

UNESCO 315
Universities and Colleges Admissions Service (UCAS) 169
university music education in Colombia: collection tool 320; conclusions 323–5; introduction 313; methodology 320; multidimensionality of music educators 319–21; music configuration in higher education 319; musicians' field of action 317–19; professional practice 316–17; results and analysis 320–1; teachers, training, and labour conditions 314–15; teacher training 321–3, **322**
University of Antioquia 321
University of Hong Kong (HKU) 102
University of Newcastle (UoN) 139, 144–5, 147
University of South Florida (USF) music education 49–51
University of Valle 321

valorization process 360
verification in the creative process 260
video production 69–71
visually impaired students 400–1
vocal creativities 182–3
vocal pedagogy, contemporary approach: artistic development and presence 184–5; artistic singing 178–9, **179**; conclusions 187–8, **188**; contemporary vocal practices 179–80; curricular components 181–7, **182**; individuality in 183–4; industry practices 186–7; introduction 177–8; musicality 185; in PCM 180–1; technologies in 186; vocal and musical creativities 182–3
vocationalism 117–19, 134–5
Voice, The, Australia (TV show) 179, 183

Ways of the Hand (Sudnow) 286
We Are Producers tool 224
Westerlund, Heidi 273

489

Index

Western classical music 46, 209, 212, 285
Western European Art Music (WEAM) 15, 16, 130, 140, 167, 213
Western imperialism 76
Whitehouse, Mary 387
Whiteley, Sheila 130–1
White Smith Music Publishing Company 34
Winehouse, Amy 237
Wiseman-Trowse, Nathan 133
Wish, David 42, 56, 245
Wong, James 82

Words & Raps tool 224, 225
work-integrated learning (WIL) 329
World Bank 315

Xian Xinghai 77

Yiu Wai Chu 103
YouTube 159

Zagorski-Thomas, Simon 131, 132
Zeng Zhimin 76
Zhao Yuanren 77